CHRISTIAN SCIENCE

"ITS CLEAR CORRECT TEACHING"

AND

COMPLETE WRITINGS

By
HERBERT W. EUSTACE, C.S.B.

LEDERER, STREET & ZEUS CO.
(INCORPORATED)
Printers and Publishers
2121 ALLSTON WAY
BERKELEY, CALIFORNIA
U. S. A.

TABLE OF CONTENTS

★

CHRISTIAN SCIENCE,
"ITS CLEAR, CORRECT TEACHING"

★

"WHOSO READETH LET HIM
UNDERSTAND"

★

THE LINE OF LIGHT.
WHY AM I A CHRISTIAN SCIENTIST?
PLAGIARISM

★

YOUR POWER AND DOMINION.
DO YOU SAY, "THERE IS NO GOD?"
A LETTER

★

"SCIENCE UNDERSTOOD TRANSLATES
MATTER ('the Beast' of Revelation)
INTO MIND"

★

TRANSLATION OF
"the False Prophet" of Revelation
INTO MIND, ENDING ALL WARFARE

★

A LETTER, MARCH 22nd, 1947

★

THE EVIL AND ABSURDITY OF THINKING
MAN IS GOD OR EVER COULD BECOME GOD

★

GEMS OF ELUCIDATION ATTRIBUTED TO
MARY BAKER EDDY

PREFACE

Since this volume comprises all of my writings, it should be again clearly stated and thoroughly understood that there is not a single original idea in any of the books contained in this volume. Every statement presented finds its origin in the pure divine metaphysics, given by Mary Baker Eddy, the one Revelator of Christian Science, in SCIENCE AND HEALTH WITH KEY TO THE SCRIPTURES, the textbook of Christian Science and in her other writings.

God does not need two revelators of one spiritual fact. One is sufficient. Indeed there could not be two, for more than one would simply be repetition not revelation.

These books tell their readers nothing new whatever, but they have proved useful in reminding each reader of what he already knows and has learned from all that Mrs. Eddy demonstrated in her unselfish labours for mankind since 1866 and from her numerous writings. In reminding the reader of what he already knows, they have given an impulse to his thought, have encouraged him to use what he knows and have blessed him accordingly.

This Preface would not be complete unless I added the further statement that all my writings are the result of the devoted and tireless cooperation, these many years, of my dear wife, Bessie Moore Eustace, C.S.B. To her I owe my endless gratitude for having made it possible, under God's ever-guiding direction, to produce them.

Herbert W. Eustace

Los Angeles, 1953

It might properly be stated that in this single volume comprising my previously published books, there appear some 30,000 words of text which have not heretofore been put into book form.

Included is the 22,000 word report of meetings held recently in London, New York, Los Angeles, and Berkeley — under the caption "Translation of 'the false prophet' of Revelation into Mind," the Ascension, or Christian Science Era. — H.W.E.

CHRISTIAN SCIENCE:
ITS
"CLEAR, CORRECT TEACHING"

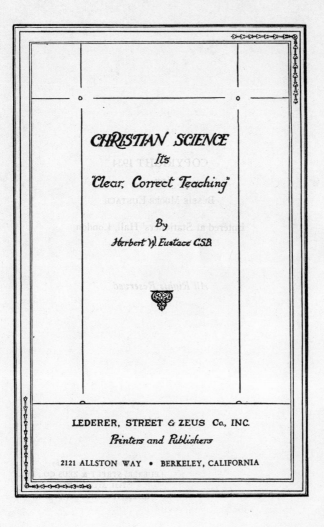

CHRISTIAN SCIENCE
Its
"Clear, Correct Teaching"

By
Herbert W. Eustace C.S.B.

LEDERER, STREET & ZEUS Co., INC.
Printers and Publishers

2121 ALLSTON WAY • BERKELEY, CALIFORNIA

COPYRIGHT 1934

BY

BESSIE MOORE EUSTACE

Entered at Stationers' Hall, London

Printed and Bound by
LEDERER, STREET & ZEUS CO., INC.
2121 ALLSTON WAY
BERKELEY, CALIFORNIA, U. S. A.

FOREWORD

The multiplication of books has no justification unless something new can be added to the subject-matter under discussion.

Nothing can be added to the completeness of Mrs. Eddy's statement of Christian Science, Science and Health, the textbook of Christian Science, for it is all-sufficient, needing no amplification or elucidation.

What, then, it may properly be asked, is the reason for this book?

The answer must rest upon the effectiveness with which it helps the reader to understand Christian Science and so proves *"useful"*[1] in compelling him to *think* Science and Health, instead of merely reading its words.

During the thirty-two years that I have been holding Christian Science classes, approximately twenty-seven hundred people have attended them and, inevitably, countless questions have arisen.

[1] S. & H. Pref. x :9.

Since 1923 there has been no restriction placed upon the taking of notes in the classes, as it has been my conviction that each one has the right to acquire an understanding of Christian Science in his own way. As a consequence, there are in circulation a great many notes taken by various persons and passed about among friends.

When these were brought to me, as sometimes happened, with the request that I correct or revise them, I invariably refrained from doing so because notes convey to the one who originally took them vastly more than appears on the surface. Were another to attempt to revise them, their meaning to the recorder might be endangered.

But with this large accumulation of notes in a wide diversity of phrasing already circulating freely, it is, I feel, not only expedient but honest that I should state clearly—by going completely through a class—the fundamentals of the pure metaphysical reasoning of *"clear, correct teaching"*[1] as it has unfolded in the various classes.

A class in Christian Science is spontaneous communion with Mind. Questions and answers arise naturally in the course of its unfoldment, for "Come now, and let us reason together, saith the Lord"[2], is the invitation of Mind always.

[1]My. 297:18   [2]Isa. 1:18.

Each class is individual in character and progresses from its own starting point as though it were evolving for the first time.

A Christian Science class is not a lecture course. It has nothing about it that is stereotyped. It is purely spontaneous from beginning to end, full of *"wit, humour, and enduring vivacity"*.[1]

However, there is the general foundation upon which all classes must be laid, and it is the purpose of this book to present such a foundation.

A record of what has taken place in the discussion of a subject is not at all the same thing as an effort to reformulate the subject. A book, for instance, may record facts deduced from mathematics without reformulating the basic principles of mathematics. It is impossible, in fact, to reformulate a subject that has once been revealed as exact scientific truth. As such, it is unchangeable, and thereafter it is only possible to draw conclusions from it that are applicable to human advancement. Hence this book will be a presentation of facts deduced and the fundamentals from which they are deduced, not an attempt to reformulate the subject.

It is, of course, impossible to go into the minutiæ of class discussion because every class takes its own trend according to the demand of

[1]**Mis.** 117 :11.

those in the class. It is my purpose to cover the general ground of what the metaphysical reasoning and the application of such reasoning in Christian Science actually means, and, in doing so, to show how it is in consonance with all that Mrs. Eddy has written on this subject.

For the unselfish assistance of a number of scholarly, consecrated Christian Scientists in the preparation of this book, I am deeply grateful.

If the book proves profitable to the reader, I know his appreciation of their work will be added to mine.

CONTENTS

CHAPTER V

CHAPTER VI

CHAPTER VII

CHAPTER X

ANSWERING SOME QUESTIONS ARISING IN CLASS 263

CONTENTS xv

APPENDIX

TO THE READER

A reader is entitled to ask what qualifications the writer of a book has to warrant a demand for attention. A short account, therefore, of my experience in Christian Science and my past relationship to that which is called the Christian Science movement, will throw light upon this question.

Looking back over the events which account for the present freedom of thought and action, personality fades out of importance and God's meaning becomes apparent. Events are found to have unconsciously interpreted the divine purpose far beyond the most earnest hope of unfoldment.

Christian Science was first brought to my attention when I was quite a young man and I was immediately interested, although not from the need for physical healing. I had always been in excellent health. Nor was I dissatisfied with my religion. My father being a clergyman in the Church of England, as had been each of my grandfathers, by natural inclination I adhered to that church. In fact, I was thoroughly satisfied with life as I found it.

But when a friend asked me to read Science and Health I discovered that one does not always know what is taking place in thought and that what I had accepted as satisfaction was really complacency rather than true satisfaction.

At that time, 1893, I was living on my ranch in California and had the long evenings for reading and studying. These I spent with Science and Health. During the day, while at work, I continually pondered the wonders and profound import of this new view of life, and, by the time I had finished reading the book, its teachings had become my own deep conviction.

From that time Christian Science has filled my life with a greater and more eventful happiness than I could have deemed possible. It has truly proved to be the "one pearl of great price", which, when the seeker had found, he "went and sold all that he had, and bought it."[1]

At the beginning of my study of Christian Science, I discovered that human opinion has not the slightest value in the understanding of this Science and that the author of Science and Health, Mary Baker Eddy, was the only one who was not swayed and influenced by human opinion, but, in her consecrated communion with Mind, stated the truth fearlessly and uncom-

[1]Matt. 13:46

promisingly, never deserting the goal of her vision.

I therefore determined at once to obtain all Mrs. Eddy's writings, which at that time were not published in book form but had appeared in pamphlets or magazine articles.

I was successful in securing much that she had written, and these writings, together with Science and Health, were to me invaluable.

Later, pursuing what then seemed the natural course, I joined The First Church of Christ, Scientist, in Boston, Massachusetts, in 1894, when the membership of that church was less than three thousand.

Afterward a branch church organization was formed in San Jose, California, and I had the experience of filling, through a period of fifteen years, nearly every office in that church.

In 1902, I had one of the most joyous and enlightening experiences that has come to me—two weeks spent in Boston attending, with Mrs. Eustace, the college class conducted by Edward A. Kimball.

Those who knew Mr. Kimball know what a profound and analytical thinker he was. In that class truths that were dimly stirring in the depths of my own aroused thought were elucidated—truths which with their logical sequences meant genuine Christian Science, truths that meant the *"clear, correct teaching of Christian Science"*,[1] rather than faith and belief in it.

A certificate of the Massachusetts Metaphysical College, conferring the degree of C.S.B., signed by Mrs. Eddy and Mr. Kimball, was given to each member of that class, together with the further designation of Normal Course Graduate, which meant that the holder was entitled to teach Christian Science.

After returning to San Jose, I soon began holding classes and have continued to do so ever since, each succeeding class being a larger unfoldment of Mind in its infinity of variety.

In July, 1909, I was asked to go to Boston to talk over the advisability of changing my residence to New York to teach there. After careful consideration, however, this plan was abandoned.

It was during this visit to Boston that some forty or fifty visiting Christian Scientists were invited to Mrs. Eddy's home at Chestnut Hill. Mrs. Eddy graciously said she wished to see us. It gave us the opportunity to refute the foolish story then prevalent that she was dead and that another was masquerading in her place.

It was on this occasion that Mrs. Eddy gave her followers that imperative admonition not to look for their leader in her personality, but only in her books and in her great love for all man-

[1]My. 297:18.

kind. It was during the following December, 1910, that Mrs. Eddy passed away.

In September, 1912, I received a letter from the board of trustees of The Christian Science Publishing Society, asking whether I would accept an appointment as a member of that board and requesting me to come to Boston to talk it over. There was nothing attractive to me in occupying an official position. It did not seem that it could in any way help toward demonstrating Christian Science, nor did leaving my home in California appeal to me.

I shall always look back with the deepest interest to the tremendous struggle of those few days in Boston, while considering the question of accepting the trusteeship. It seemed impossible to bring myself to the point of saying I would accept it. I could not have felt a greater reluctance had I known the subsequent necessities of this unfoldment. Finally I promised to give my answer on the following afternoon.

That night, as I debated all the arguments for and against the acceptance, I was forcibly reminded of Jacob's struggle which lasted "until the breaking of the day",[1] and which appeared as wrestling with the angel of the Lord all night.

I did not find, however, that with the dawn I had won a victory or that I had approached a solution of the question. Even when I started for

[1] Gen. 32:24.

the meeting in the afternoon, I was apparently as far from being ready to accept as I had been in the beginning. But, when I went into the meeting, without the slightest hesitation I said, "I will accept the trusteeship."

On September 23rd, 1912, I was elected a member of the board of trustees. I made the proviso, however, that before there was any public announcement I should be informed by telegram, on my return to California, whether or not every member of the board of directors of the Church was in hearty accord with my election. (It is to be remembered that I was appointed to the trusteeship of the Publishing Society by the board of trustees of that body, which under the terms of the Trust Deed, elect their own successors to office.)

In their personal capacity the individual directors of the Church had already expressed to me the friendly hope that I would accept the appointment, but I wanted a united statement assuring me of their support. Instinctively I felt that opposition between these two boards would be fraught with grave consequences. I seemed dimly to discern this storm center about which the oncoming battle would be waged,—the struggle to free Christian Science from the materiality of organization and loose it for its higher destiny of pure metaphysics *"uncontaminated and un-*

fettered by human hypotheses, and divinely authorized."[1]

When I received by telegram, September 28th, the assurance of the "unanimous and cordial" support of the directors, I wrote them a letter in which I used the expression, "I shall not falter or fail in any work He may give me to do." Before writing this sentence I hesitated and earnestly asked myself the question, "What is this 'I' that will not falter or fail?" I answered, "It is God, the one Mind." Later I was to learn the full significance of this statement and the great importance with which it was destined to be charged.

Immediately after my election, I received a copy of the Deed of Trust of 1898, constituting the board of trustees, and with it the following letter:

> "Herewith please find a copy of the Deed of Trust which the Trustees asked me to forward to you for your confidential consideration.
>
> It occurs to the Trustees that it may be an advantage to you to be able to familiarize yourself with the details of this Deed pending your residence in Boston."

During the next few weeks, before arriving in Boston, I carefully studied the Deed of Trust and learned something of its character, purpose and deep importance. Especially was I impressed with paragraphs 3, 6, and 8.

[1] C. S. Quar. 2.

No. 3.—Said trustees shall energetically and judiciously manage the business of the Publishing Society on a strictly Christian basis, and upon their own responsibility, and without consulting me about details, subject only to my supervision if I shall at any time elect to advise or direct them.

No. 6.—Said Trustees shall employ all the help necessary to the proper conduct of said business, and shall discharge the same in their discretion or according to the needs of the business, excepting that the business manager may call in at times of necessity such temporary help as will facilitate the business.

No. 8.—Said Trustees shall have direction and supervision of the publication of said Quarterly, and also of all pamphlets, tracts, and other literature pertaining to said business, using their best judgment as to the means of preparing and issuing the same, so as to promote the best interests of the Cause, reserving the right to make such changes as I may think important.

Mrs. Eustace and I moved to Boston in November, 1912. The years from that date until February, 1922, when we returned to California, were a period of increasing interest and joy. It was a time of spiritual opportunity.

I had not long been a member of the board of trustees before I began to feel an indefinable element at work with the directors of the Church, an apparent attempt to dictate to the trustees on matters wholly within the province of the trustees' duties as set forth in the Deed of Trust. I soon realized that it was the age-old demand of ecclesiasticism to rule, to allow nothing to inter-

fere with its thirst for power and authority. I
saw clearly, also, that while it might appear as
persons trying to acquire power and prestige, it
was not primarily person at all, but evil appearing as ecclesiastic despotism in an effort to substitute itself for the demands of Principle.

On examining the past relationships of the two
boards, I found that from the beginning of the
Trust (which I learned Mrs. Eddy had formed
without consulting either the church directors or
those whom she appointed to be the first trustees
under her Deed) there had been an antagonism
on the part of the directors against the Trust and
the trustees.

While Mrs. Eddy was present, there could
be no open friction and no overt act against
the trusteeship, but afterward there gradually
cropped up efforts on the part of the directors to
override the provisions of the Trust Deed.

It is significant that Mrs. Eddy did not make
it a requirement that a trustee of the Publishing
Society should be a member of The Mother
Church. He was, however, to be a good Christian Scientist. In this Mrs. Eddy gave more
than an intimation that Christian Science and
the church organization were not at all one and
the same.

It is evident that Mrs. Eddy's purpose in creating the 1898 Deed of Trust was, if possible,
to check this inevitable greed of ecclesiasticism

which she foresaw would seize everything in the line of power and authority. Mrs. Eddy determined to stem this tide by putting the entire authority for all Christian Science literature (apart from her own writings) under the trustees through her Deed of Trust, leaving only the authority for the church with the directors.

By this act Mrs. Eddy undoubtedly hoped to thwart the intent of evil to bury Christian Science in ecclesiasticism and materialism as it had previously buried Christianity. It was another evidence of her distrust in church organization as a possible channel for metaphysics.

The *"spiritual foresight"* that saw the *"nations' drama"*[1] unquestionably foresaw the inevitable conflict that would arise between her Deed of Trust and the vested church authority.

Was it any wonder, then, that Mrs. Eddy, in the clarity of her vision, sent to the newly appointed trustees the following three rules for their guidance and support? These rules were in her own handwriting and came by special messenger from Concord, New Hampshire, addressed, "For the Board of Trustees."

1. When mother foils a demon scheme, do not mar her success. The hardest battle is the *last* one.

2. Never act on first thoughts unless they be of Good, God, but watch and separate the tares from the wheat. Learn by experience and careful com-

[1] My. 281 :1.

parison to know *whence* cometh your conclusions. "Try the spirits" before acting, look over the purposes that the enemy might be trying to accomplish and so avoid the snare.

3. Have the bird in your hand before disturbing the bush that he hangs upon.

In these words, so graphically significant, one can hear the cry of Mrs. Eddy's heart yearning to save her *"young child"*[1] from the Herod of ecclesiasticism which was seeking its destruction. She saw the deadly conflict that would be waged in the final battle, and she asked her trustees not to "mar her success" but to "Follow the Deed of Trust",[2] that the "demon scheme" she foiled in establishing the Trust might not succeed.

No one can doubt that Mrs. Eddy foresaw and endeavored to foil the evil of ecclesiastical despotism. But this despotism was to grow and increase until it finally attempted to nullify the Deed of Trust, by making a demand in 1916 on the trustees to acknowledge the directors as the supreme governing power of the Christian Science movement, including the periodicals, thus endeavouring to destroy Mrs. Eddy's carefully thought out purpose. This was ecclesiasticism in its full measure of arrogance.

But the trustees in 1916, were not only under oath but equally under Mrs. Eddy's express admonition to follow the Deed of Trust.

[1] Matt. 2:13. [2] Proc. in Equity 113 Col. 3.

Finally when its provisions, as interpreted by its sworn executors, the trustees, were challenged, there was but one course to pursue. The Trust, itself, must take care of the situation. It was a legal instrument drawn by Mrs. Eddy in conformity with the laws of Massachusetts. Its interpretation, as with all legal instruments, lay with the courts. In making it a legal instrument and not a set of rules for the personal conduct of church members, as in the case of the Church Manual, Mrs. Eddy gave it the status of a civil contract under the jurisdiction of the laws of the land.

The trustees had only one course to pursue, namely, to "Follow the Deed of Trust" and let the Trust take care of the whole situation.

A letter written on September 30th, 1918, defined for the directors the trustees' understanding of the true democracy of Christian Science. This letter was published in full in The Christian Science Monitor of June 12th, 1919,[1] and should prove enlightening to every Christian Scientist. It was written with the deepest desire to work from the foundation of Principle and stated plainly and simply the position of the trustees.

That they might be sure they were making no mistake at this difficult moment and that they understood the meaning of the Trust which Mrs. Eddy had so carefully drawn up in accordance with law and given to them for their guidance,

[1] See APPENDIX, page 316.

the trustees decided to consult the best legal authority obtainable.

Seldom has the world seen such distinguished counsel collaborating on a case. The Senior Counsel was the Honorable Charles Evans Hughes, who is today, after a career of great honor to himself and his country, Chief Justice of the Supreme Court of the United States of America. Associated with Justice Hughes were Sherman L. Whipple, one of the most noted and talented members of the Bar of New England, and Silas H. Strawn, a leading member of the Bar of Illinois, and at one time President of the Bar Association of the United States. With these there was also associated as Junior Counsel, Lothrop Withington, a brilliant young member of the Massachusetts Bar.

The trustees have always felt that these gentlemen so generously contributed their services, refusing compensation beyond what virtually amounted to expenses, because they instinctively realized the great import of the conflict.

Under the advice of their Counsel, the trustees, while upholding their Deed of Trust, did everything in their power to prevent open conflict with the directors. But there was, of course, no possibility of preventing the inevitable clash between ecclesiasticism and Principle.

On March 17th, 1919, ecclesiasticism, appearing in the guise of the board of directors, decided to bring its authority to a test. It voted to remove one of the trustees from his office, and demanded that the remaining trustees appoint his successor.

This promptly brought the whole question of the Deed of Trust and the authority delegated under it to the front. Because it was a Deed of Trust under the Commonwealth of Massachusetts, there was only one tribunal that could give an authoritative interpretation of the duties of the trustees under the Deed, and that was the Supreme Court of Massachusetts. A Bill in Equity was therefore filed by the trustees on March 25th, 1919.

The case was referred by the Court to a Master, and Judge Frederic Dodge, who had just retired after twenty-eight years of service on the Federal Bench, was appointed Master to hear the case.

The entire proceedings in court were published in The Christian Science Monitor from June 4th, 1919, to the final end of the case January 31st, 1922, so that the world might become familiar with every phase of it.

On March 6th, 1920, Judge Dodge handed down his final report, finding for the trustees in all the essential facts and making his rulings of law in conformity with those facts. Lawyers recognize Judge Dodge's report in this case as one of the most masterly reports ever made in any case. The thoroughness and clarity of the decision could not be surpassed.

An appeal was taken by the directors to the full bench; and, after many months, a new decision was handed down November 23rd, 1921. The Master's findings of fact were undisputed—they were based upon testimony taken in the original hearings and were final—but the Supreme Court of Massachusetts reversed the rulings of law as handed down by Judge Dodge.

It could not have happened otherwise because, sooner or later, ecclesiasticism must be found by every Christian Scientist to have no relationship whatever to Christian Science. Without the despotic control of ecclesiasticism (masquerading as the Christian Science organization and demanding that it be allowed to govern every thought and action of the Christian Scientist) having been expressed we might have remained apathetic for many years, perhaps centuries, before turning to divine Principle as All-in-all.

When the Supreme Court handed down its decision reversing the Master's findings of law, the trustees were glad to resign their offices and elect new trustees in subordination to the directors, and to turn over to them, immediately, the business of the Publishing Society. In accordance with this intent, the trustees published the following statement:

WE LAY DOWN OUR TRUST.

During the period of each of our terms of office as a Trustee of The Christian Science Publishing Society, we have striven to uphold what we believed to be Mrs. Eddy's design for the welfare and maintenance of the Society. With the decision of the Court we cannot pretend to agree. It reverses what we believe to be the intention of the sacred trust we received from our Leader, and which we have pledged ourselves to defend. Nevertheless we are able to abide by the decision unhesitatingly since it is the finding of the Court which, as good citizens, we are bound to obey. And we have no difficulty in doing this, but only a deep sense of peace, because we know that Truth cannot perish from the world, so that, if we are right, our course must ultimately be vindicated, for Principle will overturn, overturn, and overturn, until He whose right it is shall reign.

To all of those who have supported us in the joyful work of carrying on our Leader's publications, we would offer our sincere thanks, for we realize that their support was given to us out of an understanding of Principle which never faltered, and could not be shaken. The knowledge of this will prove to them a reward which cannot be dimmed nor taken away.

Our Trust itself we are able to hand over in a perfectly sound condition. It owes no man anything. Its property is entirely intact. Whatever damage it may seem temporarily to have sustained has been wrought by Christian Scientists themselves, and can be repaired, for the outside public has never failed to support, but has rather grown in its support of, Mrs. Eddy's demonstration.

To be obedient to the teaching of Christian Science, every Christian Scientist must learn to be a law unto himself. He must follow the Christ as he sees the Christ. "Be sure," Mrs. Eddy says, on page 117 of "Miscellaneous Writings," "that God *directs* your way; then, hasten to follow under every circumstance."

HERBERT W. EUSTACE,
LAMONT ROWLANDS,
PAUL HARVEY.

The trustees found, however, that while the directors were most eager to have them resign and elect their successors in office, there was no intention of accepting their accounts before their retirement, although the books of the Society had been completely audited and found in perfect condition by public accountants.

Naturally the trustees could not allow this, much as they desired to be relieved from further responsibility. The months of controversy had engendered such bitterness in the ranks of church members that there were, among the former employees of the Publishing Society, a few whose blind partisanship on the side of the directors could be expected to drive them, when reemployed, as seemed likely to happen, to the depths of manipulating the books in order to discredit the trustees. In fact, some of the employees, on leaving the employ of the Publishing Society during the case, had even mutilated the books they were in charge of to show their allegiance to the directors.

If this statement seems extravagant, one needs only to point to the wave of religious fanaticism which swept through the ranks of the church members at that time and which resulted in the wholesale persecution of all who refused to declare themselves supporters of the directors while the case was still pending in the courts. A chronicler of the events of this period in the history of the Christian Science movement would unfold a tale in all essentials paralleling the Inquisition of the Middle Ages, the method of "discipline" being, of course, brought up to date.

In view of this emotional tenseness in certain quarters, and in order to adhere to strictly legal procedure, Counsel for the trustees prepared a bill presenting the resignation of the trustees to the Supreme Court of Massachusetts, to be accepted after the Court had passed upon the accounts.

The bill was duly heard by the Court, and, after the accounts had been examined and finally accepted by the Court, the resignations of the trustees were accepted and a final decree was entered January 30th, 1922, releasing them from all further responsibility under their Trust. The Court then appointed a new board of trustees.

No greater difference could possibly exist between two contentions than existed between the contentions of the ecclesiastical board and those of the board of trustees. This will finally be understood when the case is read in its entirety, as originally published in The Christian Science Monitor and later put into book form.

The trustees were standing for the absolute democracy of Christian Science, the right of the individual Christian Scientist to perform whatever duty is entrusted to him, in obedience to his own understanding of divine Principle, to live his

life as a Christian Scientist in accordance with
that understanding, and without interference
from any so-called supreme human authority.
The very opposite is the contention of ecclesiasticism and was the stand taken by the directors.

When this case is so read, the final argument
of Justice Charles Evans Hughes for the trustees' case, before the full bench of the Supreme
Court of Massachusetts, will also be so read and
its marvelous clarity of vision will be grasped and
appreciated.

Ecclesiasticism, now feeling itself more firmly
entrenched, promptly invoked its traditional
weapon of excommunication. Early in October,
1922, I received the following communication:

THE FIRST CHURCH OF CHRIST SCIENTIST
IN BOSTON, MASSACHUSETTS
Office of
THE CHRISTIAN SCIENCE BOARD OF DIRECTORS
September 29, 1922.

Mr. Herbert W. Eustace,
San Jose, Calif.

Dear Mr. Eustace:

The Christian Science Board of Directors instructs me to
inform you that formal complaints have been presented to the
Board which, if sustained, would affect your standing as a member of The Mother Church and as a teacher of Christian Science,
and to write you as follows:

It is alleged that you have violated Article XI, Section 7, of
the Manual of The Mother Church by reason of the following
particulars:

(1) That on or about September 11, 1918, and continuously
thereafter for over three years, you attempted to change the character of the office of trustee of The Christian Science Publishing
Society from the character given it by Mrs. Eddy in her trust

deed of January 25, 1898, and in her Church Manual, so that a trustee could not be removed and his position would not be subject to supervision by the Directors of The Mother Church;

(2) That you, during this time, attempted to change the relation of the Publishing Society to The Mother Church, from the relation established by Mrs. Eddy, to that of a separate institution to be conducted independently, whose trustees would not be subject to removal or supervision by the Directors of The Mother Church;

(3) That you, during this time, attempted to prevent the Directors of The Mother Church from exercising the powers relating to the Publishing Society which Mrs. Eddy conferred upon said Directors, and thus sought to deprive The Mother Church and the Cause of Christian Science of the advantages which would result from the exercise of those powers;

(4) That in March, 1919, you joined in a false and misleading Bill in Equity by which an ad interim injunction was obtained from the Supreme Judicial Court of Massachusetts, and attempted to obtain a final decree commanding the Directors of The Mother Church not to interfere with the conduct of the trustees of the Publishing Society and never to exercise the powers relating to the Publishing Society which Mrs. Eddy conferred upon the Directors for the benefit of The Mother Church and the Cause of Christian Science;

(5) That you joined in a petition based on the above false and misleading Bill in Equity by which a ruling was obtained from the Supreme Judicial Court of Massachusetts whereby the Directors of The Mother Church were commanded contrary to the plan of Mrs. Eddy in her Church Manual, not to elect editors for the Publishing Society;

(6) That from time to time during the prosecution of said Bill in Equity you falsely and dishonestly represented to branches and members of The Mother Church that the Publishing Society was being conducted in accordance with Mrs. Eddy's directions, whereas you were co-operating in conducting the Publishing Society in violation of Mrs. Eddy's directions and were preventing the Directors from complying with Mrs. Eddy's directions in relation to the Publishing Society;

(7) That after the Supreme Judicial Court of Massachusetts filed an opinion for the dismissal of the Bill in Equity, you persisted in working against the interests of the loyal members of The Mother Church and against the interests of Mary Baker Eddy and the accomplishment of what she understood to be advantageous to The Mother Church and to the Cause of Christian Science by refusing to elect a trustee to fill the vacancy caused by the dismissal of a former trustee, as was your duty under Mrs. Eddy's trust deed of January 25, 1898, and the Manual of The

Mother Church,—by holding your position as trustee contrary to the provisions of said trust deed and Manual,—and by publishing and circulating a certain statement headed "We Lay Down Our Trust" calculated to nullify the effect of the decision of the Supreme Judicial Court of Massachusetts sustaining Mrs. Eddy's plan of church government.

The complaints will be heard at a meeting of The Christian Science Board of Directors to be held Tuesday, October 24, at 11:30 a. m., in the Directors' room of The Mother Church. Any statement and evidence which you desire to submit will be carefully considered if the same is received before the date of the hearing.

The Directors regret the necessity of taking up these complaints with you but this is their duty under the By-Laws of The Mother Church.

Sincerely yours,

LUCIA C. WARREN,

Assistant Corresponding Secretary for

The Christian Science Board of Directors.

My reply was:

SAN JOSE, CALIFORNIA

October 17th, 1922.

Christian Science Board of Directors,
  The First Church of Christ, Scientist,
    Boston, Massachusetts.

Gentlemen :—

I have your letter of September the 29th, containing certain charges made against me upon which you inform me the Directors will hold a hearing on Tuesday, October 24th.

While you state that any evidence which I may desire to submit will be carefully considered, of course, it is apparent to any one having even a superficial knowledge of the recent controversy that a consideration of the evidence by your Board would be a mere formality.

Of course the very nature and wording of the charges show that they are sponsored. if not actually drafted, by your Board. Furthermore, it is ridiculous to believe, particularly in view of the Board's repeatedly announced attitude, that the matter has not in fact already been discussed and a decision reached.

As to the specific charges, all of them arise out of the fact that as a Trustee of The Christian Science Publishing Society I deigned to entertain theories as to my duties as a Trustee which were not in accord with the views of your Board. My entire stand with regard to these charges has been fully and completely stated by me in the various conferences between your Board and the Board of Trustees, in the various letters passing between these two Boards, and in my testimony on the stand and the position asserted by me in the court proceedings, all of which are virtually on record in printed form. I stand unreservedly on that record which I think, if it discloses anything, shows that I undertook to conscientiously carry out what I understood to be the duty imposed upon me by Mrs. Eddy's Deed of Trust.

As to my having joined in a false and misleading bill in equity I beg to call your attention to the fact that Judge Frederic Dodge found the allegations of the bill to be true in every substantial if not in every respect, and these findings of fact were fully sustained by the Full Bench of the Supreme Judicial Court of Massachusetts in its final decision, although in its interpretation of the law its decision was adverse to our contention.

A careful analysis of the complaints show the real charge to be that having disagreed with your Board in the interpretation of my duties as Trustee under a Deed of Trust, I appealed to the highest tribunal in the Commonwealth of Massachusetts to get from them an authoritative interpretation of those duties. It was, at the beginning of the controversy, and still is my conception of my duty as a Trustee in case of question or doubt as to the interpretation of a Deed of Trust to seek instructions from the only authoritative source available.

More and more I am reassured in my original belief that in the end my action in this controversy will prove of the greatest benefit to the unfoldment of Christian Science to the world.

The remaining charge that I calculated to nullify the effects of the decision of the Supreme Judicial Court of Massachusetts by publishing and circulating the statement "We Lay Down Our Trust" is best met by an honest reading of that document. I should be proud to submit to the Chief Justice of that Court the statement of which you complain and take his finding as to whether it does not in truth show a profound allegiance to Christian Science and an absolute willingness to obediently accept the interpretation of Mrs. Eddy's Trust as laid down by that Court.

Apparently those drafting the complaint have neither a full comprehension of the decision of the Court nor an ability to appreciate the sincerity of the statement in question.

Clearly the contemplated action against me is only the first step in a scheme to do everything within your power to attempt to injure and discredit each of the individuals who dared to raise their voice to question your individual interpretation of Mrs. Eddy's purpose.

I should not be true to what I understand of Christian Science if I did not add, that I believe your interpretation in regard to Mrs. Eddy's purpose for the Christian Science movement and what you term her plan of Church government is based upon fundamental error.

Christian Science demonstrates Principle, not person, and the fundamental basis of Christian Science is man's oneness with Principle. Nothing can substitute this as Christian Science. Apparently your concept of Christian Science and the entire effort of your Board has been to substitute the rule of persons for Principle and attempt to force this upon all Christian Scientists under the guise of calling it Mrs. Eddy's purpose and plan of Church government.

I believe the day will come when your Board may see this for each one of us must inevitably sooner or later face the judgment of our every thought and act by Principle. In such a judgment the unimportance of personal rule or interpretation will appear.

Very sincerely yours,

HERBERT W. EUSTACE.

Then followed the official excommunication:

THE FIRST CHURCH OF CHRIST SCIENTIST
IN BOSTON, MASSACHUSETTS
Office of
THE CHRISTIAN SCIENCE BOARD OF DIRECTORS

October 26, 1922.

Mr. Herbert W. Eustace,
   San Jose, California.

Dear Mr. Eustace:

The Christian Science Board of Directors instructs me to make the following reply to your letter of October 16 which was received by the Board on October 23. The following resolution was passed unanimously by the Board of Directors at its meeting of October 24:

WHEREAS, members of The Mother Church who are in good standing and were acting from Christian motives have voluntarily and independently filed complaints with this Board that Herbert W. Eustace, another member of this Church, has persisted in working against the interests of its loyal members and against the interests of Mary Baker Eddy "and the accomplishment of what she understands is advantageous to this Church and to the Cause of Christian Science," and that he has influenced other members of this Church thus to act, and

WHEREAS, a meeting of this Board was duly called for the examination of said complaints on October 24, 1922, and notice thereof was duly given to Mr. Eustace by a registered letter dated September 29, 1922, and

WHEREAS, instead of confessing and forsaking his errors, he has sent to this Board a letter which amounts to a defiant persistence in the errors specified in the complaints,

NOW, THEREFORE, on October 24, 1922, after having duly examined said complaints in accordance with the Manual of The Mother Church, The Christian Science Board of Directors, the Board of Directors of The First Church of Christ, Scientist, in Boston, Massachusetts, doth unanimously act upon the complaints and exercise the discipline of this Church as follows:

FIRST:—Pursuant to Section 7 of Article XI of The Mother Church Manual, the name of Herbert W. Eustace be and hereby is dropped from the roll of membership of this Church.

SECOND:—Pursuant to Section 1 of Article XII and Section 8 of Article XXX of the Church Manual, the authority of Herbert W. Eustace to act as a teacher of Christian Science be and hereby is revoked and terminated, because he has so strayed as not to be fit for that work and now ceases to be a member of this Church.   *   *   *   *   *

Sincerely yours,

Lucia C. Warren,
Assistant Corresponding Secretary for
The Christian Science Board of Directors.

Mrs. Eddy defines Church as *"The structure of Truth and Love; whatever rests upon and proceeds from divine Principle."*[1] To me, therefore, this so-called excommunication was simply a gesture of ecclesiasticism, because excommunication can be brought about only by one's own departure from Principle. The right to teach and to practise Christian Science is based upon one's own state and stage of consciousness. Therefore,

[1] S. & H. 583:12.

as a Christian Scientist, I could not do otherwise
than continue to practise and hold classes.

Particularly pertinent, in this connection, is
Mrs. Eddy's reference to *"our far Western students, the Christian Scientists,"*[1] in her letter to
the San Jose church, published at her request in
the Sentinel of December 23rd, 1905, and republished in 1913 with changes, in The First Church
of Christ, Scientist, and Miscellany.

Self-evidently Mrs. Eddy meant by her expression *"our far Western students, the Christian
Scientists,"*[1] those students throughout the world
who express and represent that for which the
West, and especially the far West, has always so
preëminently stood, namely: freedom, unbiased
by tradition; the determination to think and act
for one's self in line with right; the determination
to accord to all the same privilege, thereby typifying true individualism, namely, man's eternal
right to think and act in accord with Principle.

This attitude of mind and what it must and
does accomplish, is surely what Mrs. Eddy knew
would entitle one to be called a Christian Scientist. Without this attitude of mental freedom,
no real progress could be made, hence her further
statement in that letter, *"Comparing such students with those whose words are but the substitutes for works, we learn that the translucent atmosphere of the former must illumine the mid-*

[1] My. 197 :13.

night of the latter, else Christian Science will disappear from among mortals."[1] In other words, if the clear atmosphere of thought, the freedom of action represented by the *"far Western students"*, is to give place to ecclesiastical control, then *"Christian Science will disappear from among mortals."*

The directors' letter of October 26th, 1922, was followed a month later by a statement to the Boston Post on November 25th, 1922, by Clifford P. Smith, their committee on publication, saying that "Mr. Eustace is excommunicated forever."

Since that time I have been busier and more active in the work of Christian Science than ever before. In being released from every form of ecclesiastical organization, I was freed from such trammels, so that my work became to that extent unhampered by human belief and regulation. I have held numerous classes in various parts of the United States. The demand for *"clear, correct teaching"*[2] is becoming greater all the time, and will so continue, for it has no personality or human control attached to it, and it is this very freedom for which the mortal is striving. He is learning, at last, no longer to put his faith in person or organization, but to trust in his own effort to understand divine Principle.

[1]My. 197:15.   [2]My. 297:18.

It has been said that my experience in Christian Science has been slight, that I am not an "authorized" teacher, hence cannot teach correctly.

But I was an "authorized" teacher for twenty years during which the correctness of my teaching was not questioned. It is the same teaching today. For twenty-eight years I was an active member of the Christian Science Church, holding many offices in that Church. From 1912 to 1922 I was a member of the board of trustees that was in full charge of the publication of all the Christian Science organization literature, which included for several years the publication of Mrs. Eddy's works. The board of trustees also passed on all advertised professional cards, and appointed the Bible Lesson committee.

The first question ever raised about the authoritativeness of my teaching was after I had differed with the directors upon the interpretation of a legal document.

The intensity of disagreement was solely over the fact that as trustees we resolutely stood out against the demands of the directors to destroy the functions of the Deed of Trust.

However, the purpose of this book is not to deal with personality nor with human records but to deal with absolute Christian Science.

My experiences in Christian Science I consider a great privilege. Through them I have been able to understand more clearly the fallacy of ecclesiastical organization.

The especial privilege of being "excommunicated" has been tremendously enlightening. I understand it was not a person but that which was being upheld — *"clear, correct teaching"*, individual oneness and responsibility to divine Principle, true democracy, that was excommunicated (released) from ecclesiastical bondage.

Invariably "You may know when first Truth leads by the fewness and faithfulness of its followers. Thus it is that the march of time bears onward freedom's banner. The powers of this world will fight, and will command their sentinels not to let truth pass the guard until it subscribes to their systems; but Science, heeding not the pointed bayonet, marches on. There is always some tumult, but there is a rallying to truth's standard."[1]

This book must be its own evidence that it presents the *"clear, correct teaching of Christian Science"* that Mrs. Eddy referred to, and which she also declared *"has been and is an inspiration to the whole field"*, thus holding aloft "truth's standard."

H. W. E.

---

[1]S. & H. **225:5.**

ABBREVIATIONS

Works by Mary Baker Eddy

S. & H.—"Science and Health with Key to the Scriptures."

Mis.—"Miscellaneous Writings."

Ret.—"Retrospection and Introspection."

Un.—"Unity of Good."

Pul.—"Pulpit and Press."

Rud.—"Rudimental Divine Science."

No.—"No and Yes."

'00—"Message to The Mother Church, June 1900."

'01—"Message to The Mother Church, June 1901."

Hea.—"Christian Healing."

Peo.—"The People's Idea of God."

My.—"The First Church of Christ, Scientist, and Miscellany."

"There is no expedient to which man will not resort to avoid the real labor of thinking."

(Sir) Joshua Reynolds.

"Materialism, once a scientific theory, is now the fatalistic creed of thousands, but materialism is nothing better than a superstition on the same level as a belief in witches and devils."

John Scott Haldane.

"Some day people will learn that material things will not bring happiness and are of little use in making men and women creative and powerful. Then the scientists of the world will turn their laboratories to the study of God and Prayer, and the spiritual forces which as yet have hardly been scratched. When this day comes, the world will see more advancement in one generation than it has seen in the past four."

Charles P. Steinmetz.

CHRISTIAN SCIENCE:
ITS
"CLEAR, CORRECT
TEACHING".

CHAPTER I

EXPLANATIONS INTRODUCTORY TO CLASS

Solomon said, "there is no new thing under the sun".[1] This statement is metaphysical and therefore true. In the language of to-day it means, that no one can be told one thing that he does not already know. Because infinite intelligence is omnipresent, it is the intelligence of all, therefore one and all know all. Then what seems like the learning of something new is but the focusing attention on what one already knows even though he may seem completely unaware of knowing it.

Before beginning the routine of the class, a number of points should be carefully weighed and settled.

What is the purpose of any class?

Is it not self-evidently, enlightenment?

[1] Ecc. 1:9.

Then the purpose of a Christian Science class is to gain an understanding of what Christian Science really means and is, thus establishing a working basis for thinking.

This is the motive for your being in the class. The well-springs of that motive must be sincerity and honesty, without which little progress can be made.

In order that this understanding may be available for your use, it must be orderly and natural, with no "skipping of hurdles" and no lapse in the continuity of your argument.

Each step must be taken understandingly. This can be done only if each step is based logically and inevitably on the step previously taken.

A FOUNDATION STONE NECESSARY

First there must be the certain knowledge of some basic fact on which to start the structure: something so self-evident that it cannot be impugned, and so obviously true that it carries instant conviction.

Such knowing is the rock, and the only rock upon which to lay the foundation.

Then follows the orderly laying of one "stone",[1] one established fact, upon another, each one true to the "plumbline",[2] until the structure of reasoning is complete and available for use.

[1]Isa. 28:16.   [2]Amos 7:8.

Because the whole of Christian Science is correct thinking, in other words, communion with intelligence, it is understanding. Thus all laborious effort to remember is unnecessary.

Memory, as human belief conceives of it, consists of impressions, or grooves made on the brain as on a phonograph record, to be later reproduced.

Christian Science, being understanding, not a brain record, is thinking seen as action, not brain-grooves which can so easily fade.

Infinite Mind is infinite memory. It embraces within itself all knowing, which includes all memory, but this is Mind-action, not brain-action.

As in mathematics, the knowing that two times two is four obviates the necessity for remembering it. So is it with all understanding.

Knowing is understanding and includes within itself all memory.

ALONE WITH YOUR OWN UNDERSTANDING

This class, being understanding, is your understanding. In it you are alone with Mind. "Come now, and let us reason together, saith the Lord: though your sins be as scarlet, they shall be as white as snow."[1]

You must be willing to accept any statement of Truth that is your own logical deduction, and unwilling to accept anything equivocal, or not

[1] Isa. 1:18.

clear to you, no matter from what authority it may be said to have come.

You must be convinced by your own reasoning, for you can use nothing about which you are uncertain. *"Be thoroughly persuaded in your own mind concerning the truth which you think or speak, and you will be the victor."*[1]

Conversely, you must be just as determined to keep an open mind, remembering Paul's statement, "If any man think that he knoweth any thing, he knoweth nothing yet as he ought to know."[2]

When a truth, based on your accepted premise and correctly deduced, is established, even if the conclusion disagrees with your preconceived ideas, accept it gladly and do not allow prejudice to blind you.

Conceit is fatal to progress, and as Mrs. Eddy says, *"Conceit cannot avert the effects of deceit."*[3]

Self-opinion, except when based on reality, is valueless. On the other hand, *"Willingness to become as a little child and to leave the old for the new, renders thought receptive of the advanced idea. Gladness to leave the false landmarks and joy to see them disappear,—this disposition helps to precipitate the ultimate harmony."*[4]

Human opinion weighs not one iota in the scale of infinite intelligence.

[1] S. & H. 412:7.   [2] 1 Cor. 8:2.   [3] No. 2:24.   [4] S. & H. 323:32.

Then until you have made Christian Science your own through understanding and demonstration, it is folly to discuss what you believe it to be. Furthermore Jesus said, "neither cast ye your pearls before swine."[1]

In "thy closet"[2] alone with Mind, you find your strength.

There, "in the secret place of the most High",[3] your conclusions are your own. They are the truth to you because you have deduced them logically, not because the Bible or Science and Health has stated them.

Nothing is true merely because some one has said it or because it is in a book.

All that constitutes the truth is its own inherent truthfulness.

Then the truth of Christian Science must be established independently of what Mrs. Eddy or the Bible has said. It must be discovered as fundamentally true.

As this is done, it will be found that the statements in the Bible and in Science and Health are true, not because they are in these books but because they are true in themselves.

Because they are true, they are in these books. These books are a record of the truth, and are therefore to be earnestly studied.

[1] Matt. 7:6. [2] Matt. 6:6. [3] Ps. 91:1.

THE IMPORTANCE OF WORDS

Another fact to be understood is that no word, no combination of letters has any meaning to you unless it conveys something to your thought.

Only as a word gives impulse to your thought does it have any value for you.

Therefore, in using words, it is far better to find your own word, one that does definitely define something to you, than to adopt another's word that does not give impulse to your own thought.

Jesus said, "When ye pray, use not vain repetitions, as the heathen do: for they think that they shall be heard for their much speaking."[1]

Nothing is gained by the mere language you use.

Jesus also declared, "I say unto you, That every idle word that men shall speak, they shall give account thereof in the day of judgment. For by thy words thou shalt be justified, and by thy words thou shalt be condemned."[2]

Use, then, only the words which you understand. That gives account of them and justifies them. In turn, they give the right impulse to thought and you speak as one having authority and not as the Scribes and Pharisees. You think with authority also.

[1]Matt. 6:7. [2]Matt. 12:36, 37.

Avoid giving theological meanings to words, which may lead only to ecstasy of thought.

Simplicity in words makes them more forceful.

Jesus' words were simple and direct, and always powerful.

Lincoln's Gettysburg Address lives and is quoted because it is simple, direct, and sincere.

To be direct and sincere one must have definite conviction. *"Sincerity is more successful than genius or talent".*[1]

An honest Christian Scientist cannot remain a belief Scientist nor a faith Scientist: he must be an understanding Scientist, knowing what he knows.

WHAT DOES THE TERM CHRISTIAN SCIENCE SIGNIFY?

Christian means pertaining to the Christ. Jesus declared of the Christ, "I am the way, the truth, and the life: no man cometh unto the Father, but by me".[2]

Then the Christ is the truth, and therefore, the term Christian must mean "pertaining to the truth".

Science means exact knowledge. The word is derived from the Latin *scio*, I know.

Hence Christian Science means exact knowledge of the truth; in other words, right knowing.

[1]'00 9:18.   [2]Jno. 14:6.

Right knowing is what is meant by the word intelligence, another name for Mind. This we shall prove is synonymous with the word God. Thus we shall find Christian Science to mean God.

Speculation no more enters into the study of Christian Science than into the study of mathematics.

Understanding alone counts: therefore, "With all thy getting get understanding".[1]

"Reason is the most active human faculty."[2] Reason establishes every step in Christian Science.

Reasoning brings forth all opposing arguments and meets them with the true arguments, exactly as right mathematical reasoning meets every mathematical problem.

CERTAIN STATEMENTS EXAMINED

Let us now examine certain of Mrs. Eddy's statements and see if we can accept them through our own reason, wholly apart from the fact that it was Mrs. Eddy who made them. She says,

> "That glory only is imperishable which is fixed in one's own moral make-up."[3]

"Moral" means pertaining to action with reference to right and wrong, and refers always to the mental rather than to the physical.

[1]Prov. 4:7.   [2]S. & H. 327:29.   [3]My. 122:5.

Sin is considered a wilful mental act, a moral offense under the control of the individual, as contrasted to sickness, which is commonly, though erroneously thought of as physical, hence outside of mental control.

However, is it not a fact that that which you understand is alone truth to you — in other words, that which is mental or moral, and so fundamentally right, "imperishable"?

Nothing physical is "imperishable".

Mrs. Eddy's statement, then, means that the only glory that is imperishable is that glory which is established as understanding and is one's very own and so constitutes "one's own moral make-up".

Again she says,

> "The infinite will not be buried in the finite; the true thought escapes from the inward to the outward, and this is the only right activity, that whereby we reach our higher nature."[1]

The only thought that has permanency with you is the one that begins in yourself and is understood by you.

You may recall, as an act of memory, things which you have been told; but until you understand them, you do not actually know them. They cannot unfold into further understanding unless they begin in yourself, in what you comprehend.

[1]My. 159:14.

Beginning in your own comprehension, they escape from the finite, the inward, the lesser, to the outward, the greater, even as two times two escapes from its first limited sense of being just four, to the larger sense of two times two billions being four billions and so on to infinity.

So it is with all thinking, and particularly with that thinking which deals with man's relation to his divine Principle.

That which constitutes the "I" or consciousness of the individual—in other words, the "inward", can never rest in the finite or limited sense, but must ever reach out to oneness with the infinite, the "outward" or unlimited. Thus is the higher nature reached.

> "We must resign with good grace what we are denied, and press on with what we are, for we cannot do more than we are nor understand what is not ripening in us."[1]

In mathematics, the only thing one is denied is the point he does not grasp. He is denied nothing he understands. But he can utilize no fact he does not master.

It is exactly the same in the Science of being. You can use only what you understand; therefore, you are spontaneously denied what you do not understand.

What constitutes your being?

[1]My. 195:13.

Certainly you would not say it is your body.

So it must be your understanding. Therefore, it is your understanding that constitutes your real entity; in other words, what you are.

You can press on with what you are, with what you understand, because that constantly unfolds to you. Its basis is Mind, infinity. Therefore, it keeps "ripening" within you.

You gladly "resign" the rest, that which you do not understand, and therefore cannot utilize.

"We understand best that which begins in ourselves and by education brightens into birth."[1]

This statement again brings home the fact that understanding is not something that is told you, but something that is based upon and developed from that which you know and which by application "brightens into birth."

It is permanently yours, dependent upon nothing outside yourself, outside your consciously being, your communion with Mind.

However small the beginning, its growth will be *"sturdy, and its maturity undecaying."*[2]

"The burden of proof that Christian Science is Science rests on Christian Scientists."[3]

Again using mathematics as a basis of comparison, the burden of the proof of mathematics rests with the mathematician. He shows forth

[1]My. 253:26.   [2]S. & H. 463:16.   [3]My. 158:17.

mathematics. Without him, it would be unknown.

Without the Christian Scientist to prove it, Christian Science would be unknown.

But this point must be emphasized: it is the "proof" and not the fact of Christian Science that rests with the Christian Scientist.

The fact stands irrefutable, regardless of any so-called proof; but without the Christian Scientist to show it forth, the fact would not be known.

The "burden of proof" implies the necessity of being a consistent Christian Scientist so that the truth of Christian Science may be seen and known. That "burden" consists of merely *being* man.

> "Again I repeat, person is not in the question of Christian Science. Principle, instead of person, is next to our hearts, on our lips, and in our lives."[1]

Person does not enter into the consideration of any question in Christian Science.

But this does not mean that Christian Science, as Mind, does not appear as person. That is to say, we interpret it as person in the same way that we interpret music as notes. But we must *see through* this appearance, or interpretation, to the Principle underlying the outward expression or interpretation appearing as person.

[1]Mis. 135:2.

The entertaining of a finite or personal sense separates one spontaneously from Principle, the infinity that is Mind.

"Remember, it is personality, and the sense of personality in God or in man, that limits man."[1]

If you personalize two times two is four, and think of it as a thing instead of as idea, does not that instantly limit your use of it?

The value of mathematics to you is its ever-presence with you, occupying no space, and yet always available for your use in the way most suited to the need of the moment.

Personalizing, in other words, outlining, limiting, or forming a finite sense of either God or man, has the same effect in the Science of being that it has in the science of numbers. It finitizes your sense of it and makes its use impossible.

"To impersonalize scientifically the material sense of existence—rather than cling to personality—is the lesson of to-day."[2]

The one need for the thinker today is to impersonalize his sense of person, to dematerialize his sense of things. Only in doing this is he released from the finite sense of being with its picture of sin, disease and death.

In every new invention, thought breaks through the fetters of limitation, and invariably

[1]Mis. 282:4. [2]Mis. 310:7.

less and less matter accompanies the improvement.

Thought cannot be unfettered until it finds Mind as All-in-all.

A material or finite sense of existence must be exchanged for the spiritual or Mind-sense.

"To live so as to keep human consciousness in constant relation with the divine, the spiritual, and the eternal, is to individualize infinite power; and this is Christian Science."[1]

In the realm of music, the musician keeps his ear in constant accord with the correct tone. A true musician is never off the key.

This individualizes for him the power of music.

In like manner the true Christian Scientist finds the one Mind as the All-mind, as his Mind, as his "key" that individualizes for him the infinite power of Mind and maintains him "in constant relation with the divine, the spiritual, and the eternal."

This constitutes the Christian Scientist.

"Christian Science is absolute; it is neither behind the point of perfection nor advancing towards it; it is at this point and must be practised therefrom."[2]

Just as mathematics is the same yesterday, today, and forever, never behind the point of perfection nor advancing towards it but always de-

[1]My. 160:5. [2]My. 242:5.

claring two times two to be the same four, so the Science of being is intact and whole.

There is no advancing towards wholeness. It is already a fact; and just as mathematics is applied from the standpoint of absoluteness, so must Christian Science be applied from the same standpoint.

It does not bow down to human desire or weakness. Every thought must be brought into obedience to the truth of being.

Christian Science yields to nothing. It never changes. It stands as the perfection of all being, now and always. It reveals perpetual wholeness.

"Entirely separate from the belief and dream of material living, is the Life divine, revealing spiritual understanding and the consciousness of man's dominion over the whole earth."[1]

No human concept enters into your consideration of mathematics; neither can it enter into your understanding of Christian Science.

Human belief has to take off its shoes before entering the holy place of spiritual understanding. Materiality must give place to *"the spiritual fact of whatever the material senses behold"*[2] before the portals of Christian Science are entered.

Unwillingness to do this defeats progress, for "whoso builds on less than an immortal basis, hath built on sand".[3]

[1]S. & H. 14:25.   [2]S. & H. 585:11.   [3]Hea. 1:8.

"Every step of progress is a step more spiritual. The great element of reform is not born of human wisdom; it draws not its life from human organizations; rather is it the crumbling away of material elements from reason, the translation of law back to its original language, —Mind, and the final unity between man and God."[1]

"The Christian Scientist is alone with his own being and with the reality of things."[2]

You must be willing to abide alone with Mind, with all that Mind includes and is, just as you must abide alone with the principle of numbers if you are to progress in mathematics.

Into this aloneness that is isness, nothing can enter. It is the solitude of Mind embracing all. It is not emptiness, but the satisfaction of allness.

You are always alone with consciousness— with your own consciousness, and with all that consciousness is.

WHAT DO THESE STATEMENTS MEAN?

Summed up, what do all these statements mean?

They emphasize the fact that you are required to be materially selfless, to accept only what you know, what you understand. You are to disregard what you have merely believed or had

[1]Peo. 1:2.   [2]'01 20:8.

faith in because you accepted its source as humanly authoritative.

You can apply all that you understand; and what you understand constitutes what you really "are".

Into this understanding no personal or finite sense enters.

As the High Priest, the true sense of being, alone entered the Holy of Holies, so you are always alone in the Holy of Holies with your own consciousness, with what you admit consciousness to be.

With this foundation upon which to stand, one can go forward and establish what Christian Science is and what it teaches.

STEPS OF PROCEDURE IN CLASS

The natural order followed by a class in Christian Science is: first, it establishes the true; second, it defines and analyzes the false; and lastly, it shows how the true is the positive and the false is the negative aspect of the same truth which, when reversed, leaves *"nothing that can sin, suffer, be punished or destroyed"*.[1]

Under the first, or true sense of being, is found what is termed God and what God is God to; in other words, God and His man and all that this includes.

[1] S. & H. 340:29.

Under the second or false sense of being, we deal with the negative or suppositional opposite of God, called evil and its man.

The final step shows that the negative or opposite must have that which it negatives or is opposed to. Therefore the negation exists only as a negative definition or proof of the positive which is true.

When this is understood, thought turns spontaneously to the true and abandons the false sense that would have two realms, one good and one evil, one to be attained at some future time, the other to be combated as a reality now.

This is the true sense replacing the false sense of the negative, leaving the clear understanding that *"the reverse of error is true"*.[1] This is the quickening spirit that abandons the "first man Adam",[2] leaving only perfection, with its "last Adam".[2]

This constitutes Christian Science and its practice and follows the order of the Bible.

In the first chapter of Genesis, there is given the true picture of creation, God and His perfect man.

The second chapter portrays another picture, that of the so-called Lord God, and his man formed of the dust of the ground—the exact opposite of the first account of creation, wherein

[1] S. & H. 442:18.   [2] 1 Cor. 15:45.

man is portrayed as the image and likeness of Spirit.

The remainder of the Bible is devoted to showing how this suppositional creation, with all its false beliefs, is scientifically replaced by the understanding of the true creation as the only reality.

The Bible ends with the book of Revelation, in which is forecast the destruction of all evil through the "little book",[1] which is to rule "with a rod of iron".[2]

This "little book", Science and Health with Key to the Scriptures, by Mary Baker Eddy, is showing to the world that the false sense of being, and all that it includes, inevitably disappears with the realization that the real and true is All-in-all.

[1]Rev. 10:2.   [2]Rev. 12:5.

CHAPTER II

How Do You Know There Is a God?

Before defining what God is, it is essential to establish how one may know that there is a God.

Surely it would be a waste of time to talk about what God is, unless it were first understood that there is God. After having settled that question, it is in order to establish what God is, and why He is all that He is.

BLIND ACCEPTANCE INADEQUATE

The average mortal, Christian or pagan, acknowledges in his own way, that there is a supreme something which he calls God.

The Christian, if asked, would probably answer at once, "Of course there is a God".

In times of stress, however, when the opposite of that which he means by God, good, presents itself as real, he has no means of combating the apparent reality of evil, because he does not understand *why God is:* hence he falters, and too often falls a victim to evil in one of its various forms, whether it be limitation, sickness, sin or death.

A mere sense of or belief in God is really of no permanent help or value. When most needed, it does not stand the test.

A blind acceptance of God will never complete-ly satisfy. Reason must be satisfied in order to bring the certain knowledge that there is God.

Because mathematicians have proved the laws governing numbers, this does not prove them for you. It does, however, beckon you on to prove them for yourself.

The mathematician's understanding is not yours, until you yourself understand mathe-matics.

Thus, in like manner, you must also settle each point in Christian Science for yourself.

You must arrive at the point where it would make no difference to you if there were not an-other Christian Scientist in the world. You must so understand Christian Science, and its truth must be so vital to you that you would be satisfied to be the only Christian Scientist, if that were necessary.

It is useless to attempt to find a conclusive an-swer to any question outside of what constitutes yourself, and especially is this true of the pro-found subject: how you know there is God.

SENSE TESTIMONY CONTRADICTORY

To affirm that there is God because the testi-mony of the material senses declares the beauty and loveliness expressed by what you call nature —beautiful flowers, gorgeous sunsets, and count-less other expressions—cannot bring conviction to you because the same mind and its senses that declare this loveliness, just as positively declare the opposite—the flowers fading, the sunset dreary, and so forth.

A fountain cannot "send forth at the same place sweet water and bitter".[1]

Yet, if you accept the testimony as true in one instance, can you avoid consenting to it in another?

One appearance may be beautiful and harmonious, the other ugly, discordant and wretched.

You are compelled, then, to lay aside what comes to you as nature in establishing that there is God.

Then you ask, if nature cannot help me to understand, do I not still see on all sides love and kindness, and all the excellent qualities of that which I feel God must be?

Am I not justified in declaring that these attributes of good could not appear to me unless there were God whence they emanated?

But is it not true that just as you are aware of these qualities so you are equally aware of the countless activities of evil, expressed as anger, envy, hatred, and so forth?

Can such contradictory testimony safely lead one anywhere? Again, can the same fountain send forth both sweet and bitter water?

[1] Jas. 3:11.

In whatever direction you look, you find this apparent irreconcilable testimony of good and evil, life and death, presented side by side.

The unreliability of the testimony of the material senses is self-evident.

In the matter of sight, for instance, there is no reliability. A straight stick extending partly out of clear water will appear bent.

The law of optics explains this, but the explanation in no way changes the fact that your eyes have, nevertheless, deceived you.

Two parallel rail-lines appear to come together in the distance. Your eyes declare what your reason denies.

So it is with all the five senses. None of them can be trusted.

Hypnotism has shown how unreliable the senses are, how they will declare as true whatever the mind of the hypnotist suggests to his victim, regardless of its absurdity.

Does not the victim of the hypnotist seem to agonize over a pain that is pure illusion? The senses respond to whatever the hypnotized mind affirms. And so on through an inexhaustible range of phenomena.

The testimony of two reputable witnesses in court is at times contradictory, especially in the case of a sudden accident or dramatic occurrence.

The courts recognize that the witnesses are not intentionally unreliable or deliberately misstating facts, but that the minds of different people react differently under sudden emotion and that the senses testify in accordance with the mind and not of themselves.

But however explained, the fact remains that the testimony itself is utterly unreliable.

Of what value, then, is sense testimony in aiding you to establish the fact that there is God?

If once proven false, can the senses ever be trusted?

Obviously not.

In their testimony is no assurance, no peace, no proof that there actually is God.

Because of reliance on material sense testimony with its contradictions, many are faltering and even saying foolishly that there is no God.

You, too, may be tempted to say there is no God unless you understand *why* God is.

Being convinced of the hopelessness of attempting to satisfy yourself on this question through anything that the material senses declare, you turn forever away from such testimony.

HOW TO FIND THE ANSWER

Now ask yourself, what is there that I actually know of myself, that I am absolutely sure of, that is not dependent upon any thing to bear witness to it, that requires no justification, no verification, that just *is*?

There is one answer, and one only, to this question, and its conclusion is inescapable; one self-evident fact that defies refutation, before which all arguments are silenced forever, because there is nothing to argue against it.

It is, in Bible language, "The true Light, which lighteth every man that cometh into the world."[1]

This light belongs to every man; it belongs to you. It has no relationship to the so-called senses.

Ask yourself thoughtfully, "What is it?"

You will answer with absolute conviction: It is the fact that I exist; that I consciously am; it is my consciously being.

This, I know of myself. It is not dependent upon anything apart from me. I am conscious of being. Of this I am sure.

When I say that I consciously am, I am not referring, even remotely, to anything that I might seem to be conscious of through the physical senses. It is in no way a reaction. I mean simply that I consciously exist, and that that existence requires no testimony or witness of any kind.

It is a self-evident fact to me.

It is purity itself, for in it is not a single element contrary to itself.

Like an axiom of Euclid, it requires no demonstration because it is obvious.

[1] Jno. 1:9.

This fact of my consciously being is the one and only fact that, as a so-called mortal, I know of myself, wholly apart from any external evidence.

Of this one fact I am absolutely sure.

It is a certainty that begins and ends in myself. I have the verification of it at all times and every moment.

It is the rock of Truth upon which I must begin to build.

Dependence upon anything else would mean dependence upon something external to myself that did my thinking for me.

As you have already seen, you cannot be sure of that which testifies to anything outside yourself. Such testimony is often deceptive and may disappear: but you cannot lose yourself and disappear to yourself.

You are positive of your own being, of your consciously being.

Everything must start from this certainty of your own consciously being. It is the one and only thing of which you *are* sure.

You must think from this standpoint.

Does not your very being consist of just thinking?

Thinking must be based on *knowing*. Knowing must be built up from the consciousness of your own existence.

It does not include any external evidence.

It is "the true Light"[1] guiding every man.

It is the truth that is ever-present, and that always stands as the reality, even as in mathematics, two times two remains four, regardless of anything and everything that ignorance may say about it.

THE CAMEL AND THE NEEDLE'S EYE

When speaking of the difficulty to be experienced by those possessing riches in entering the kingdom of heaven, Jesus said, "Verily I say unto you, That a rich man shall hardly enter into the kingdom of heaven".[2] Of course he was not referring to the possession of money or material things as such, but to a trust in the material sense of things, rather than in the Mind-sense.

He further said that it was "easier for a camel to go through the eye of a needle, than for [such] a rich man to enter into the kingdom of God."[3]

Observe, he did not say it was *impossible*. He said the other was *easier*.

In using the word "easier", he certainly meant to imply that there was a way whereby the "rich man" might enter.

His illustration of the camel going "through the eye of a needle" explained how this entrance into the kingdom of heaven must be accomplished.

[1]Jno. 1:9.   [2]Matt. 19:23.   [3]Matt. 19:24.

The old walled cities of the East had large entrance gates that were closed at sundown, but by the side of each was a small gate called the "needle gate", through which belated travelers with their beasts of burden could enter after nightfall.

However, this could be accomplished only by stripping the camel of its burden, thus enabling it to crawl through the gate to safety.

This comparison indicates how a so-called mortal, in order to start on the true solution of being, must first strip himself of every vestige of dependence upon material evidence, and base his understanding of being wholly on his own conscious existence, as the one foundation from which to begin.

Doing this, he lays "aside every weight, and the sin which doth so easily beset"[1] him and runs "with patience the race that is set before"[1] him.

Like the camel, the mortal can retain no material possession, no mortal evidence, to help him; he must lay aside every testimony of the senses, and turn to the only fact he is sure of, his own consciously being.

By so doing, he finds himself on firm ground, the ground of his only reality, his only true immortality, the ground that is immutable and eternal.

[1]Heb. 12:1.

No single fact about the mortal is eternal, except his consciously being. This, of course, is not mortal, but immortal.

It is this rock alone upon which he can start to build. It is the Christ, the truth of being. No other foundation can endure.

THE IMMUTABLE STARTING POINT

With this consciously being as the basic fact, what is the inevitable deduction? Or, more accurately, what is the inevitable induction, for in this reasoning, we take one step from effect to cause, an inductive step, to wit:

I could not consciously be, unless consciousness were a fact.

Then my consciously being is the irrefutable proof that consciousness *is*.

Consciousness, to be consciousness, must be conscious *of* something. That of which it is conscious is essential to it, else it could not remain consciousness.

Consciousness, then, is the necessary cause or basis of my being; and since my being is a fact, it is equally self-evident that consciousness also is a fact.

You have now established consciousness as that which *is*. In other words, you have discovered and established for yourself that consciousness *is*.

You are as certain of this as you are of your own existence.

You know that one cannot be without the other, that each is essential to the other and that, given one, the other spontaneously *is*.

This eternal truth is yours because it begins with what you know yourself, and *"brightens"*[1] into the inevitable induction that consciousness *is* or you could not consciously be.

In Christian Science there is but one inductive step. Starting with the fact of your own consciously being, you (effect) induce consciousness as *is* (cause).

From this point on, only deductive reasoning is used—deducing the nature of effect from the nature of cause. Effect is of no further value for reasoning purposes.

To again repeat, reason must be as satisfied in Christian Science as it is in mathematics. No one is asked to accept any statement without complete conviction.

No faith, no mere belief, as such terms are commonly used, enters into the reasoning.

That is why it is incredible that, in this enlightened age, Christian Science is not universally accepted.

Were Christian Science in the realm of religious belief, people could be excused for not accepting it; but since it is the revelation of the

[1]My. 253:27.

Science of being, it would seem that all are "without excuse",[1] as Paul expressed it, in not accepting it.

Remember, however, you can make no progress in your understanding of Christian Science if you do not insist, at every step, upon having your reason thoroughly satisfied.

This reasoning from the fact of consciously being, to consciousness, is not new in one sense of the word. As long ago as 1670, John Locke logically established, for himself, the existence of a supreme being, but he could go no further. It was not until Mrs. Eddy discovered Christian Science that all deductions from this point could be correctly made and carried through to their ultimate conclusion.

In Science and Health Mrs. Eddy unfolds the reasoning so simply and logically that one who follows it cannot fail to be convinced.

[1] Rom. 1:20.

CHAPTER III

WHAT GOD IS

Having established that consciousness is, the next step is to prove that consciousness is all that is meant by the word God.

If it can be shown that whatever consciousness is, that also is what God is, then we have identified consciousness as synonymous with God and can proceed from that basis.

A Christian Science class is for the sole purpose of establishing the truth of Christian Science from one's own understanding.

Each one must draw his own conclusions spontaneously without the aid of any outside source.

THE REAL PURPOSE OF A TEXTBOOK

One is not made a Christian Scientist by the Bible or by Science and Health.

These books can no more make a Christian Scientist than a treatise on mathematics can make a mathematician.

The purpose of any textbook is to take the student to the source from which it came itself. In communion with that source, the student discovers for himself what the textbook on the subject declares to be true.

In exactly the same way, the Bible and Science and Health have one purpose as textbooks: to take the reader to Truth as the source from which these books came.

Thus the Bible and Science and Health become to him the records of Truth. They are the charts, so to speak, which the wise traveller frequently consults in checking his course of thinking, to see whether or not he is on the right path, just as the navigator checks the position of his ship, by constant comparison with his chart.

No wise Christian Scientist would imagine that he could dispense with his charts: the Bible, and Science and Health.

This does not mean that the Christian Scientist relies upon them for his understanding. He does not, because his understanding is based on that which he knows, through his communion with the infinite knower, with that which is Mind.

DEFINITION OF GOD

If you were asked to define exactly what you mean by the combination of letters, G-O-D, I believe you would unhesitatingly answer by using the very terms Mrs. Eddy has used to define the word in the best possible way: *"God is incorporeal, divine, supreme, infinite Mind, Spirit, Soul, Principle, Life, Truth, Love."*[1]

[1] S. & H. 465:9.

Taken together, these words express, in large measure, what is generally meant by the word God. So, if it can be satisfactorily proved that consciousness, which you have already established as *is*, means all that these words mean, then it follows that consciousness is God.

The little word *is* may properly be called the most powerful word in the English language.

When a fact or truth is established as *is*, it is in its final form. It is impossible to go beyond that.

When you have arrived at the *is* of anything, you have arrived at the truth of it, and there is nothing further to be attained.

Knowing this, you declare with absolute assurance that that which *is*, is therefore all that *is*.

There is nothing, and can be nothing outside of that which *is*.

Anything outside of *is* becomes *is not*.

Therefore that which *is*, is all there is.

It is well here to repeat that before using a word, you must define to yourself its exact meaning.

If a word has not a clearly defined meaning, that word is inert, and your thought can receive no impulse from it.

To employ words that are vague in meaning to you is futile. Such a practice is based on the erroneous belief rebuked by Jesus when he said, "for they think that they shall be heard for their much speaking. Be not ye therefore like unto them."[1]

Shakespeare discerned this futility of mere words when he said, "Words without thoughts never to heaven go."

It is not the word, but the thought back of it that counts.

Children wonderfully illustrate this truth. Often they use words that sound ludicrous to adults; but the power of deeds is in their meaning. Isaiah said, "A little child shall lead them."[2]

Analyze every word carefully, for only to the degree that it defines God to you does a word have value.

As previously stated you will find that the simplest words give the most direct and forceful impulse to thought.

Endeavor to think in the simplest language; then the words you use will instantaneously convey to you their full import.

Thus, your words may be few, but they will be to the point, and your understanding will be correspondingly enhanced.

In analyzing words in Christian Science, it is imperative to bear in mind that you have begun your structure without a single element of materiality—with just your own consciously being.

[1]Matt. 6:7, 8. [2]Isa. 11:6.

From that you have proved by induction that consciousness *is*. In that consciousness there is no element of materiality, even as there is none in pure mathematics.

Mathematics is the supreme term in the science of numbers, including within itself all that relates to numbers.

In like manner, consciousness is the supreme term in metaphysics, including within itself all that relates to being.

On this basis, let us analyze the following words from Mrs. Eddy's definition of God:

INCORPOREAL. Incorporeal means without a material body.

The dictionary defines it as "without matter".

Both terms mean without limitation or finiteness. In this sense it is immediately obvious that that which *is*, is incorporeal, because incorporeal means without limitation, boundless, hence can have nothing outside itself.

That which *is*, being all that is, having nothing outside itself, is necessarily incorporeal.

Therefore consciousness, being that which *is*, is incorporeal.

DIVINE. Divine means holy, pure. Holy implies completeness, holiness, or wholeness, without blemish; in other words, nothing apart from itself.

There can be no holy-ness without whole-ness.

One is synonymous with the other, since both mean wholeness, and therefore isness, or that which *is*.

Consciousness, being that which *is,* is therefore divine.

Considering "divine" from the standpoint of "pure", there is no purity, no pureness with the slightest extraneous element present.

Pure means absolute oneness, absolute alone-ness,—and because that which *is,* is all that is, it necessarily is one, alone, and must be purity itself; hence it is divine.

Therefore, again, consciousness, being that which *is,* is divine.

SUPREME. Supreme is an all-embracing term.

It is not to be limited to the sense of possessing more power or authority than something else.

It is a term that admits of no comparison, for there is nothing apart from it with which to compare it.

It implies greatest, in the sense of being all-inclusive; the final authority over all, the author of all, from which all proceeds.

Does not that which is head, over all, include within itself all, and is not that all, that which *is*?

Consciousness being that which *is,* is therefore supreme.

INFINITE. Obviously infinite must mean without boundary, finiteness, or end; without limitation of any kind. The very word at once conveys the concept *"without beginning and without end"*.[1]

What is it that alone is without beginning and without end?

Is it not that which you have found to be *isness,* or *is* embracing within itself all?

Hence consciousness being *is,* must be infinite.

MIND. Mind is that which thinks: the subject of all conscious state or consciousness.

That which thinks is that which knows. To know is to possess the truth or fact; in other words, to know is to have that which *is.*

Therefore, consciousness being that which *is,* is Mind.

There can be no thinking without knowing, for thinking ceases at once to be thinking unless it is based on knowing, based on that which is fact.

Admittedly, much is called thinking that is not based on fact, and only passes for thinking because of ignorance. In certain well-defined cases, however, where it is seen to be based upon palpable absurdity, it is called no thinking, in other words, insanity.

[1] Un. 40:23.

The time is not far distant when nothing will be called thinking that is not based on reality, Mind, that which *is*. When that time comes, all the foolish beliefs of materiality, based on human hypotheses, will be seen as insane beliefs and not as real thinking.

Mrs. Eddy foresaw this when she wrote: *"No human hypotheses, whether in philosophy, medicine, or religion, can survive the wreck of time; but whatever is of God, hath life abiding in it, and ultimately will be known as self-evident truth, as demonstrable as mathematics."*[1]

SPIRIT. Spirit is a word readily understood, for even in its commonest use it means essence.

In speaking of the spirit of a thing, do you not mean the very pith of it, the very essence or *is* of it?

By spirits of camphor or spirits of ammonia, you mean pure camphor or pure ammonia, the essence.

In other words, your use of the word spirit always means essence, isness, that which *is*.

Essence is derived from the Latin, *esse*, to be; being and essence are one and the same thing.

Consciousness is Spirit, because consciousness is that which *is*, is essence, isness, all that is. This completeness is its oneness. It follows that all

[1]Mis. 25:32.

that is synonymous with *is*, is one. Therefore, Spirit is one.

SOUL. The word Soul implies spirituality in contradistinction to corporeality; immateriality opposed to materiality.

Carrying it still further it means the vital Principle, the essence, the heart, the substance, as in the phrase, "soul of honor", meaning the very essence or substance of honor, honorableness itself.

In short, Soul signifies the spiritual nature, the innermost being, the very isness.

Consciousness, the innermost being, the isness, is Soul.

PRINCIPLE. The word Principle is derived from the Latin *principium,* a beginning.

Principle means law, basis, origin, foundation, fundamental truth or source, the animating governing influence.

Law means right, right means fact, that which *is.*

Law is the basic animation of being. Therefore all action is the action of law, the emanation of Principle, harmonious and perfect.

Basis means isness, that which *is.*

Origin means source, derivation, with nothing prior to it, which in turn means *is,* all that is, nothing beside it, the one Principle.

Foundation, that on which all rests, must be isness, being. All that *is,* is the one foundation, the one basis.

In Christian Science there must be a strict differentiation between the words principal and Principle.

Principal means chief or head in authority; whereas Principle is the fundamental basis of being, that which governs, not as a head or chieftain governing others, but as self-contained power including all within itself—the essence, the basic isness.

Principle is a word that must be used in its exact sense in order to carry thought instantly back to *is,* where it is found synonymous with consciousness. Consciousness is Principle.

LIFE. Life means self-existent being, which in turn means existence or that which *is.*

Consciousness, being that which *is,* is Life.

TRUTH. Truth is reality. Truth is just what *is.* To establish the truth of anything, you find the fact about it—you discover the *is* of it.

There is nothing further to find beyond that which *is,* for that which *is* must always be the fact.

Is not this the *is* that is consciousness?

Therefore consciousness is Truth.

LOVE. Love is a word that people delight to use.

Volumes have been written about it. But have not all these writings been based on the human concept of love rather than on John's concept "God is love",[1] meaning thereby that Spirit is Love?

Love, to be Love, must always be the same, having "no variableness, neither shadow of turning",[2] no personality in the sense of limitation attached to it. If these qualities are not present when the word is used, it is not Love.

Love is consummation, completeness. It implies beauty, order, perfection and rightness. With a single element or quality missing, the loveliness would be marred and incomplete.

There is but one word that expresses all that is implied by the word Love, and that word is *is*.

You have already proved *is* to be synonymous with incorporeality, divinity, supremacy, infinity, Mind, Spirit, Soul, Principle, Life and Truth. Do not these mean Love?

No human sense of love, because of its finiteness, enters the precincts of Love.

Human sense too often demands exclusive possession, exaltation of what is one's own to the elimination of others. Frequently it is the *"butcher fattening the lamb to slay it"*.[3]

The butcher tenderly guards his lamb, allowing nothing to harm it. For what end? To slay it for the purpose of enriching himself.

[1] Jno. 4:8. [2] Jas. 1:17. [3] Mis. 250:7.

Is this consideration for the lamb, this tenderness, love; or is it a parody on love?

When you declare that God is Love, you are not thinking in terms of your own enrichment. You mean that He is Love because that infinite *is* that is God, embraces all that is. In that enfoldment is the eternal care and protection of all.

If love is not, as it were, the two times two that remains always four, it is not Love, but human belief. This so-called love is a *"butcher fattening the lamb to slay it."*[1]

Human belief and opinion enter not the domain of Love.

The metaphysician uses Love as the all-inclusive word wherewith to sum up his various definitions for that which *is.*

"Love is the generic term for God."[2]

Reason reveals God to you as Life, Truth, all-inclusive good. But only as this revelation triumphs in experience, do you understand God as Love.

Mind, wisdom, intelligence, bestowing itself upon its idea, is Love.

In the last analysis, experience alone defines Love. It is beyond the reach of words.

When Jesus drove the money-changers out of the temple, was he not giving one of the clearest examples of what God as Love really means and is?

[1]Mis. 250:7.   [2]My. 185:14.

He showed that greed, selfishness and the gathering to oneself of materiality had no place in his Father's house, in real being.

Then did not Jesus, in what he did, illustrate the real action of God as Love?

Love never condones evil.

It is the law of extermination to all unlike itself.

Jesus again illustrated the same thought when he said to Peter, "Get thee behind me, Satan: thou art an offence unto me: for thou savourest not the things that be of God, but those that be of men."[1]

Peter's "offence" was his human sense of love attempting to dissuade Jesus from suffering the experience of the crucifixion.

The human sense is never the true sense. The human sense of love and finiteness is frequently the farthest from the divine.

Mrs. Eddy says, *"The divine significance of Love is distorted into human qualities, which in their human abandon become jealousy and hate."*[2]

In the foregoing analyses, you have proved that the words which Mrs. Eddy used to define God are all synonymous with the word consciousness because they all signify that which *is*.

Therefore the inevitable conclusion must be that consciousness is God.

[1]Matt. 16:23.   [2]Mis. 250:10.

Countless other words can be, and are, used to mean God.

In fact, every word must finally be brought to Truth and so found one with that which *is*.

The true meaning of every word is essential to metaphysical thinking. "As he which hath called you is holy [whole], so be ye holy in all manner of conversation".[1]

Continuing a further analysis of words:

SUBSTANCE. By substance is meant reality. It is derived from the Latin, *sub,* under, *sto,* I stand; that which stands under, supports, maintains; in other words, isness, or that which *is*.

That which *is* being consciousness, consciousness is substance.

INTELLIGENCE. Intelligence is knowing. You mean by it what you mean by the word Mind.

If there is no knowing, you say that there is no intelligence, no Mind.

Mind you have already found means consciousness. Therefore consciousness is intelligence.

LAW. Law means established fact, that which is right, the ever changeless, the fundamental basis, Principle, without which nothing can proceed or operate.

That which *is*, or consciousness, is the fundamental basis of reality, that from which all proceeds.

[1] 1 Peter 1:15.

Therefore law is a synonym for consciousness.

FATHER. Father means originator, that from which something is derived.

Hence the expression, "the wish is father to the thought", the father of it.

Thus father means the essence or origin.

Hence Father and consciousness are synonymous.

Furthermore, consciousness is the only Father, the infinite Father, the one *is,* precluding any lesser sense of Father. "Call no man your father upon the earth: for one is your Father, which is in heaven."[1]

MOTHER. No word implies a deeper sense of love and tenderness than the word mother.

Mother means that which enfolds and cherishes.

To enfold is to shut in or embrace.

That which *is,* shuts in or embraces all, since there is nothing outside of *is.*

It bestows its own qualities, cherishing and comforting by imparting its own insistent goodness and tenderness. "As one whom his mother comforteth, so will I comfort you".[2]

No word more completely expresses isness, or that from which all derives, than this word, mother.

[1]Matt. 23:9.   [2]Isa. 66:13.

"Necessity is the mother of invention" illustrates this. Here it means origin, or impulsion, that which *is*.

Consciousness, as that which *is*, is the infinite Mother.

BROTHER. This word indicates a sense of nearness, relationship, comradeship. Is not comradeship unity of purpose, oneness with Truth, identification with that which *is*? "For whosoever shall do the will of my Father which is in heaven, the same is my brother, and sister, and mother".[1]

SISTER. Sister means one of the same quality or condition; it is the quality which never forsakes, is always present alongside.

Is not that which *is*, being all that is, always present at one's side, the one and only sister?

HUSBAND. Husband means that which completes, protects, shelters, is faithful.

That which *is*, being all that is, includes all, and so is the one completeness, precluding all unlike itself, and so protecting and sheltering its own integrity.

Husband is always present, unchanging and ever faithful. "And I will betroth thee unto me forever".[2]

[1] Matt. 12:50.   [2] Hosea 2:19.

Husband provides, because that which *is*, being all that is, is the one infinite provider.

The Bible says, "For thy Maker is thine husband; the Lord of hosts is his name".[1]

WIFE. Wife indicates companionship, understanding, comfort.

That which *is*, being all that is, is infinite companionship, the one companion, the one understanding, the one comfort, and therefore the one wife.

Wife also denotes pure and true devotion. Again returning to that which *is*, is it not pure, knowing nothing outside of itself, absorbed in its own isness—the supreme devotion?

That which *is* is always identical with itself, always singly true to itself, true to one.

The Bible repeatedly uses the term "harlot" meaning an adulterous wife, to characterize the children of Israel when they became disobedient to Principle. It is used to describe the type of thinking that departs from the oneness of Truth, from *isness*.

The true wife is portrayed thus, "Come hither, I will shew thee the bride, the Lamb's wife. And he carried me away in the spirit to a great and high mountain, and shewed me that great city, the holy Jerusalem, descending out of heaven from God ... And I saw no temple therein: for

[1] Isa. 54:5.

the Lord God Almighty and the Lamb are the temple of it . . . And there shall in no wise enter into it any thing that defileth, neither whatsoever worketh abomination, or maketh a lie: but they which are written in the Lamb's book of life."[1]

CHILD. By child is meant innocence, simplicity, spiritual receptivity.

That which *is,* being one, is innocent of anything outside itself.

In short, it is that which *is,* consciousness, the one innocence, the one simplicity, the one receptivity, hence all the child there is. "Of such is the kingdom of heaven."[2]

NEIGHBOR. Neighbor is that which is close to one, a friend. "Love thy neighbor as thyself".[3]

The Bible speaks of "A friend that sticketh closer than a brother."[4] A friend seeks not his own but another's good.

That which *is,* being and having all, seeks nothing for itself, but holds to itself all that *is,* hence "Sticketh closer than a brother."

Consciousness, therefore, is the one neighbor, the one friend.

MARRIAGE. Marriage is union, a joining together, oneness.

"Marriage should signify a union of hearts."[5]

[1]Rev. 21:9, 10, 22, 27. [2]Matt. 19:14. [3]Matt. 19:19. [4]Prov. 18:24.
[5]S. & H. 64:17.

That which *is,* being all that is, joins and holds together all that is real in the perpetual oneness of its infinity.

Then marriage is the everpresence of the one Mind, the complete oneness of Principle and idea, consciousness and what it is conscious of. This one marriage appears, as God always appears, in the language each one can best understand, whether called single blessedness or as two "walking hand in hand." Regardless of the appearance of God He is all to every appearance and must be so acknowledged.

"What therefore God hath joined together, let not man put asunder."[1]

And again, "They shall ask the way to Zion with their faces thitherward, saying, Come, and let us join ourselves to the Lord in a perpetual covenant that shall not be forgotten."[2]

Consciousness, as all that *is,* is true marriage.

DIVORCE. Separation.

That which *is* spontaneously excludes, separates from itself, all unlike itself.

That which *is,* therefore, acts as the law of divorcement to everything unlike good, and thus meets every necessity for happiness and harmony. "Thou puttest away all the wicked of the earth like dross".[3]

[1] Matt. 19:6. [2] Jer. 50:5. [3] Ps. 119:119.

The living of this truth would establish the joy, fullness and permanency of every marriage.

RELATIVE. The terms usually classified under this heading need to be understood.

The consciousness that *is,* being all, must be the only relationship there is. How else could it be All-in-all?

Hence it is all the relative there is. Thus *"God is our Father and our Mother, our Minister and the great Physician: He is man's only real relative on earth and in heaven."*[1]

All these words, which you have analyzed and shown to be what consciousness is, lead to but one conclusion, namely, that consciousness is God.

Therefore you have the witness within yourself that God *is,* because you know consciousness *is* or you could not consciously be, and you now know what God is.

Knowing is understanding and interpreting *is.*

This knowing cannot be an impression received from outside, but is rather a conviction from within. "A double minded man is unstable in all his ways."[2]

You alone can say what a word means to you.

You must derive every word from that which you know Mind is, and keep every word in per-

[1]Mis. 151:13.   [2]Jas. 1:8.

petual oneness with the basis of your conscious being.

"Every human thought must turn instinctively to the divine Mind as its sole centre and intelligence."[1]

Every word must be taken back to *is,* where it is found to be one with consciousness, Mind, Truth.

This analysis of words is the very structure of consistent thinking.

Knowing can be arrived at in no other way.

It is the basis of everything. It is absolute consistency, self-contained and self-perpetuated.

It never deviates from itself. It expresses no quality opposed to itself.

Its purity, its confidence and its might, are the purity, confidence and might of your thinking. "Hast thou faith? have it to thyself before God. Happy is he that condemneth not himself in that thing which he alloweth."[2]

Having established that God is All-in-all, the infinite One, you have proved Him to be that which is, and all that *is;* thus you have left nothing but God with whom to deal.

Let us here consider three words often used with reference to God,—Omnipotence, Omniscience, and Omnipresence,—because these all-inclusive terms express the thought contained in numerous Biblical passages.

[1]Mis. 307:30. [2]Rom. 14:22.

OMNIPOTENCE. Unlimited power, all the power there is; "the Almighty".[1]

Consciousness, being all the *is* there is, leaves nothing apart from itself to dispute its power and authority. It is, therefore, all the power there is.

Consciousness is God, hence God is all the power there is, the one omnipotence, the Almighty.

OMNISCIENCE. All-knowing, all-wisdom, all-intelligence.

That which *is*, being all the *is* there is, is all the knowing, all the wisdom, all the intelligence there is, hence the one omniscience.

OMNIPRESENCE. *Is*, by its very nature, is the all-presence, filling immensity.

There is no conceivable place where it is not.

Then God, the one consciousness, the one *is*, is the one omnipresence.

Caution is necessary in the use of the noun omnipotence as distinguished from the adjective omnipotent.

The adjective form suggests a comparison; omnipotent might be thought of as the most powerful of lesser powers.

The noun gives the more spontaneous metaphysical sense of the allness of Mind, God, with-

[1] Job 37:23.

out any suggestion of something apart from Him.

The same differentiation should be made, of course, in respect to the words omnipresence and omnipresent, omniscience and omniscient.

In the final analysis, every term means exactly what every other term means. So while the terms we have been considering are called the synonyms for God, there is no actual difference between them and what are called the attributive qualities of God.

It is, however, in the attributive qualities that we gain an even larger sense of God.

The metaphysician must learn that every word shows forth the All-in-all of God.

This proof must be so convincing that not a doubt or question remains.

There can be no secret closet in thought where some word can hide from the light of understanding and escape its rightful classification as being one with the common denominator. When correctly analyzed, there is no word that can imply the existence of something apart from *is*, that can imply evil, lack of intelligence, or materiality.

Let us examine some of the words used as attributes of God.

First we will consider words that we are in the habit of associating with God. Then we will take up some that, at first thought, we might hesitate to apply to Him, but which, in the light of what we have just been proving, will be seen to be, none the less, the very essence of His infinite nature.

JUSTICE is easily recognized as a quality of God.

Justice means exact rightness; impartiality; that which *is; just is*.

Just is is not a play upon words because that which *is*, being all that is, is just isness all the time, and therefore an attributive quality of God.

In the Bible we read, "Thou art a God ready to PARDON, GRACIOUS and MERCIFUL".[1]

Does God pardon sin?

Can perfection countenance a defect?

Can Truth tolerate a falsehood?

Truth makes the lie tolerable only by declaring the fact, the *is* about it.

By reversing the negation, nothing of the lie remains.

This is the true pardon, not *a* pardon, but the universal law of divine pardon, the destruction of evil.

"When we understand that God is what the Scriptures have declared,—namely, Life, Truth, and Love,—we shall learn to reach heaven through Principle instead of a pardon; and this will make us honest and laborious, knowing that we shall receive only what we have earned".[2]

[1]Neh. 9:17.   [2]Hea. 8:19.

That which *is,* Mind, God, is ever itself, infinite goodness, ever ready to impart itself, and so is *gracious;* even as the sun imparts its own warmth and light.

The *mercy* of God lies in keeping that which *is* inviolate.

There is no mercy in the passing over of a mistake and leaving it uncorrected.

As long as five, as the product of two times two, appears in a problem, it is not merciful to ignore it.

The mercy consists in correcting the error, by showing forth the truth of which the error is the negation.

Principle never forgives in the sense of "overlooking".

The mercy of Mind is the utter annihilation of everything unlike good.

GOODNESS is another word readily attributed to God.

Goodness means everything exactly right and true, that which *is.*

That which *is,* being all that is, must be consciousness itself, God, the true goodness.

Unless words are correctly defined, the Bible will not be understood.

Furthermore, if there were any word that could not be found to be one with God in its true meaning, then God would be dethroned and would not be All-in-all.

The fact must be faced honestly and fearlessly that there is no word that cannot be satisfactorily carried back to Mind and there found to exemplify what Jesus meant when he said, "Let your communication be, Yea, yea; Nay, nay".[1] By this he did not mean Yes, Yes, and No, No, as though having no mind of one's own. He meant to understand right as right and wrong as wrong; to emphasize the necessity of standing always on the side of right, and of refuting the wrong. Such standing verifies Paul's assertion that "our conversation is in heaven".[2]

Let us now analyze a few of the Biblical terms used as attributes of God, but which in common usage are likely to denote the reverse of *godliness*.

JEALOUSY. "I the Lord thy God am a jealous God".[3]

Could this God that we have established as absolutely all there is, be jealous?

Jealousy, in its ultimate meaning, is that which tolerates no rival, no presence aside from its own.

Is not this the definition of *is*?

Is, by its very nature of being all that is, holds within itself all that is and becomes a law of an-

[1]Matt. 5:37. [2]Phil. 3:20. [3]Ex. 20:5.

nihilation to everything apart from itself. There could be no greater jealousy than this.

For example, the business man, jealous of his neighbor's business, would, if possible, annihilate or appropriate that business and keep his own business as the only one.

The nature of jealousy is ever the same, excluding from its presence all but itself.

The true sense of jealousy, as the law of exclusion to everything unlike good, is the spontaneous destroyer of that false jealousy which thinks in terms of something apart from itself— something "over there" to be jealous of or about.

The jealousy that is the presence of God, can have no jealousy of something apart from itself. It is jealous only of its own infinite *isness,* and maintains that oneness inviolate.

On the contrary, the human sense of jealousy envisages something apart from itself, something to be jealous of.

The understanding of God as the one jealous God, that *isness,* that is all that *is,* annihilates the human concept of jealousy by supplying its own perfect completeness.

The word LUST is one that in ordinary usage has many meanings.

There is every sort of lust, including the lust for money, the lust for position, the lust of the flesh, and so forth.

Lust signifies a reaching out for completeness.

In its rightful signification, it is the law of Mind, the consciousness that that which *is,* being all, holds all to itself, hence is completely satisfied. "The desire of our soul is to thy name, and to the remembrance of thee."[1]

Lusting after righteousness is true lusting. It is the consciousness of *having all*.

All lust, whether for money, power, position, or of the flesh, is the belief of incompleteness, which spontaneously vanishes before the realization that that which *is,* is all, has all, and is omnipresent.

Christian Science, by translating all terms into their rightful meanings, never leaves a lack, or a vacuum; it never leaves anything outside the kingdom of heaven.

Christian Science takes away only the false sense, leaving that which *is* as all that is.

Another expression familiar to readers of the Bible is, "The ANGER of the Lord".[2]

Anger annihilates, whenever possible, that with which it is angry. "So that in the day of the Lord's anger none escaped nor remained".[3]

Anger is never directed against that which is like itself, but at that which is unlike or contrary to itself.

[1] Isa. 26:8. [2] Isa. 5:25. [3] Lam. 2:22.

Even the human concept of anger, if given free rein, would utterly destroy that with which it is angry.

Anger analyzed to its ultimate is the destruction of all unlike itself.

There can not be a little anger or a little jealousy. It is the one anger, the one jealousy, and that one, infinite, knowing nothing but its own isness, utterly annihilating everything unlike itself.

That which *is,* being all that is, is the law of annihilation to everything unlike itself. This is the anger of the Lord.

This true sense of anger destroys the false sense. "The hand of the Lord was against them, to destroy them from among the host, until they were consumed."[1]

It is vitally important for the metaphysician to analyze every word to its final signification. Then only does the limited and mistaken human sense disappear and the true sense reveal itself.

The Bible repeatedly refers to God as a God of destruction.

To destroy is to kill, to wipe out, to MURDER.

Therefore, it follows that God must be a murderous God.

Because of the usual meaning attached to the word murder, it may, on first thought, sound

[1] Deu. 2:15.

sacrilegious to speak of God as a murderous God; but the sacrilegious sense disappears when it is seen that God could not remain God unless He were the exterminator of everything unlike Himself.

This is the most perfect form of murder conceivable. *"Truth, Life, and Love are a law of annihilation to everything unlike themselves, because they declare nothing except God."*[1]

Only as this one true murderer is seen as omnipresent will everything that is unlike good vanish. Not only will the desire to murder disappear, but even the ability to destroy in a harmful sense will disappear.

There remains but the consciousness that knows only itself and the things of itself, the consciousness that alone can and does so exalt thought that it is conscious only of the presence of good.

There is no word, no matter how objectionable the human sense of it may be, that when carried to its ultimate, into the "kingdom of heaven", does not signify the presence of God.

Remember "That every idle word that men shall speak, they shall give account thereof in the day of judgment. For by thy words thou shalt be justified, and by thy words thou shalt be condemned."[2]

[1] S. & H. 243:27. [2] Matt. 12:36, 37.

Jesus undoubtedly meant by this that every word must be found as belonging to God, as of Him, and therefore as one with Him. Only as this understanding of words obtains, will you be justified and your words be not "idle."

Failure to do this will leave you holding to something outside of that allness that constitutes *isness,* God; and so will you be condemned.

What does the word "HELL" mean?

Utter confusion, distress, disaster. It is synonymous with devil or evil.

You must take even this word into the kingdom of heaven or you will harbor something as consciousness that is apart from Mind and which would destroy Mind as All-in-all.

Hell, devil, evil, carried to their final meaning, denote utter chaos.

Is, being all that is, is the law of utter chaos, the total annihilator of anything apart from itself, even as mathematics is chaos, utter elimination, to everything unmathematical.

This true sense of hell immediately releases the bondage of finity, with all its burden of misery and unhappiness called hell, devil, evil.

These words in their true sense are found as the very essence of Mind, and when present in that sense, as your Mind, they spontaneously destroy all that is unlike good.

Do not be afraid to look dispassionately at any word. Instead of stamping it as evil and so implying something that is not wholly good which can come as your consciousness, carry the meaning through to its ultimate sense, and find it as communion with Mind. "Lo, I am with you alway, even unto the end of the world",[1] unto the final discernment of the rightness of all things which includes the right definition of words.

Such words as BANDIT, and ROBBER, are words in common vogue. But are these words thought of in their true sense, so that every atom of fear in connection with them is wiped out?

A robber or a bandit is one who appropriates unto himself what seems to belong to another.

Multiply this process of appropriation to infinity and it is seen that God appropriates to Himself everything.

Is, being all, appropriates all to itself, not by taking something from another, but by the supreme consciousness of its own allness.

Because it is all, it has all.

Would not the so-called finite sense, referred to as a bandit or robber, disappear instantly under this realization, "Son . . . all that I have is thine"?[2]

Finding himself in possession of all, what would there be left to steal?

[1]Matt. 28:20. [2]Luke 15:31.

Having the multiplication table, who would try to steal his neighbor's, or even imagine that he could?

FAILURE. Is it impossible to find failure as one with Mind?

Two times two being four, spells utter failure to the ignorance that accepts two times two as five. It causes the ignorance to vanish.

Infinite good as All-in-all is complete failure or annihilation to everything apart from itself.

IGNORANCE. Is that which knows not.

Infinite intelligence is infinitely ignorant of evil. Knowing only good its ignorance of evil is absolute.

Not knowing evil, it is the law of destruction to evil, destruction to the ignorance of good.

Oneness with infinite intelligence as the only Mind destroys the human sense of ignorance by becoming ignorant to ignorance—not knowing ignorance.

In thus analyzing terms, it is imperative to remind ourselves constantly how *"Entirely separate from the belief and dream of material living, is the Life divine,"*[1] in other words, how entirely separate from the belief of the material concept of any word is the divine reality of it.

[1] S. & H. 14:25.

No word, as you have seen, is too insignificant or too hateful to be taken into the kingdom of heaven.

Because it is a word coming to you as consciousness, giving impulse to your thought, you must find it one with consciousness, one with God as All-in-all.

You cannot escape the responsibility of establishing for yourself that which *is* as all that is.

It is the self-evident induction from your own consciously being.

You are compelled to follow through. As Isaiah said, "Go through, go through the gates; . . . . lift up a standard for the people."[1]

This standard is the standard of understanding, which must be lifted up at every point of experience, whether that experience seems to come as a word, a person, a place or a thing, or whether it is termed a thought.

No matter how presented, every concept must be taken into the kingdom of heaven. "*Science, understood, translates matter into Mind, rejects all other theories of causation, restores the spiritual and original meaning of the Scriptures . . . . It is religion's 'new tongue' . . . . It gives God's infinite meaning to mankind, healing the sick, casting out evil, and raising the spiritually dead.*"[2]

[1] Isa. 62:10.   [2] Mis. 25:12.

Everything unlike good thus spontaneously disappears. *It is not.*

Each step taken by the Christian Scientist in his search for truth becomes a fact that he will under no circumstances give up, for he knows that to do so, would undermine the integrity of his reasoning and nullify his conclusions. "If therefore thine eye be single, thy whole body shall be full of light."[1]

So in giving definitions of words, do it with such a scientific sincerity of purpose that the true replaces the false as your conscious conviction; then spontaneously your thinking will be based upon Truth.

" *'The new tongue' is the spiritual meaning as opposed to the material. It is the language of Soul instead of the senses; it translates matter into its original language, which is Mind, and gives the spiritual instead of the material signification.*"[2]

The spiritualization of word and thought is of paramount importance in metaphysics. Without it, vital right thinking is impossible.

It is the essence of *"Christian Science, with which can be discerned the spiritual fact of whatever the material senses behold; the basis of immortality."*[3]

Thought must turn from theology to Christian Science. Otherwise your study of the Bible will

[1]Matt. 6:22.   [2]Hea. 7:6.   [3]S. & H. 585:10.

engender a sentimental hypocrisy which attributes both a true and a false quality to the same object; in other words "good God and good devil". "Doth a fountain send forth at the same place sweet water and bitter?"[1]

This sort of sentimental thinking in mathematics would declare at one time that two times two is four and at another that it is five, without being disturbed by the discrepancy.

But a genuinely scientific mathematician would bring to bear what in Bible language would be termed the fury of the Lord and would utterly destroy the false, not with any morbid human emotion, but with the irresistible logic of pure reason.

The foregoing analysis of words indicates the work that lies before the metaphysician. He must constantly be "bringing into captivity every thought to the obedience of Christ".[2] And he must also drive home continuously and with renewed conviction the truth that *"The only logical conclusion is that all is Mind and its manifestation, from the rolling of worlds, in the most subtle ether, to a potato-patch."*[3]

[1]Jas. 3:11.   [2]2Cor. 10:5.   [3]Mis. 26:5.

CHAPTER IV

What God Is God to

Thus far, you not only have established the fact that there is God, but in defining these various terms for God, you have also determined what God is.

You have discovered that all of these terms, with countless others are synonyms for God, because in their ultimate meaning, they find their basis in that which *is*.

In that isness is infinity.

SYNONYMS FOR GOD INTERCHANGEABLE

You have found these synonyms also to be interchangeable because each word includes within itself all that every other word means.

Things which are equal to the same thing are equal to one another.

You have carried every word that you have used for God back to its basis or foundation, to that which *is*.

You have found that the word Life, for example, which means existence, that which *is*, must mean exactly what Truth means since you have established Truth as that which *is*.

Thus having found both Life and Truth as that which *is*, all that Truth means, Life likewise means.

In like manner you have established intelligence and have found it to be synonymous with Life and Truth.

The same rule applied to the attributive qualities of God, just as it did to every word you have used for God. You took them all back to *is,* the one common denominator to which "every knee shall bow, every tongue shall swear."[1]

Without this one *is,* this one common denominator from which all proceeds and to which all returns, there could be no oneness, no allness.

"In the beginning was the Word, and the Word was with God, and the Word was God . . . All things were made by him; and without him was not any thing made that was made."[2]

"From the infinitesimal to the infinite",[3] all is included in this "Word", this *is.*

Understanding this, you do not depart from this foundation. You know that the attributes and synonyms meaning God, as you have established them, are all one.

This one God you have found to be all the power there is, all the presence there is, all the Life there is, all the Truth there is, therefore all the "all" there is.

Could there be a God more absolute, more all-inclusive, than this God you have found to be your God? Not a God of theory but a God you know is God because of your own conscious ex-

[1]Isa. 45:23.　[2]Jno. 1:1, 3.　[3]S. & H. 336:7.

istence and the inevitable conclusion derived from that fact.

This God completely satisfies you because He includes within Himself all that is and leaves nothing apart from Himself.

CAUSE PRESUPPOSES AND DEMANDS EFFECT

Having established that there is God, the question immediately arises: Could God be and not be God to something?

In other words, could consciousness be, unless it were conscious of something? Would consciousness not spontaneously cease if it were not conscious *of* something?

Self-evidently, that *of which* consciousness is conscious is essential to the existence, or being, of consciousness.

The declaration of Mind, "Let there be light",[1] is the eternal necessity that Mind, to be Mind, shall be expressed.

God, consciousness, then, in order to be God, must have that which He is God *to*.

What words can we use to express this that is essential for God's being?

Of the words generally used to express this that is essential to God's being, the two most often employed are—man and idea.

[1]Gen. 1:3.

What does the word *man* mean when used in the sense of effect, or consequence of that which is primary?

What do we know about man as the effect of God?

Did God create man in the sense of God having been first in point of time? Or is this man of God forever one with God?

Obviously, man must be eternally one with God, for without him, God would not be God.

There could never have been a time when God was, and that which He is God to, namely man, was not.

God could not be, without that which He is God to.

THE NATURE OF THE MAN OF GOD

Hence it must follow that the man of God is all that God is.

The man of God possesses every quality of God, or God also would cease to possess these qualities.

"Spiritual man and his spiritual senses are drinking in the nature and essence of the individual infinite."[1]

At no time could God be and man not be.

The infinite wisdom, intelligence, Truth and Life that is God, is the infinite wisdom, intelligence, Truth and Life that constitutes man.

[1]No. 19:18.

This man of God is infinitely intelligent, infinitely wise, infinitely living, infinitely truthful, because this is his very being.

Man eternally does what God is.

Is it any wonder that the Psalmist should have declared, "What is man, that thou art mindful of him? and the son of man, that thou visitest him? . . . . Thou madest him to have dominion over the works of thy hands; thou hast put all *things* under his feet."[1]

Man is that which shows forth God.

Man shows forth God by his conscious agreement with God at every point. "I delight to do thy will, O my God: yea, thy law *is* within my heart."[2]

Man shows forth God's power and dominion, and there is no power and dominion apart from the power and dominion shown forth by the man of God. The Psalmist could well exclaim, "What is man, that thou art mindful of him?" God is mindful of man because man is the essential expression of God.

Man is the achievement of what God is, for how could God achieve except as expression?

One cannot be without the other, each being essential to the other, therefore one never is the other.

The elimination of one would be the elimination of the other.

[1] Ps. 8:4, 6.   [2] Ps. 40:8.

The one is always cause, the other always effect.

In the sense that cause is always primary, and in that sense only, is God greater than man.

In Christian Science, the term greater, as meaning greater than something else, should never be used without explanation.

It is the essential oneness of God and man, God as the cause and man as the effect, that Jesus referred to when he said, "My Father is greater than I";[1] "I and my Father are one."[2]

God is noumenon and phenomenon because the very term God must include within itself that which it implies, that which it is God to, that which enables God to be God.

Jesus exemplified this man of God as the man of power, authority, dominion.

Since there is only one God, one *isness*, there can be only one man. You have already proved that there cannot be more than one *is*.

With one God, how could there be more than one man, when this man is the infinite presence of God?

How much life has this man? How much good? How much intelligence? There is but one answer—infinite life, infinite good, infinite intelligence.

[1] Jno. 14:28.   [2] Jno. 10:30.

Nothing you can say about this man of God is too wondrous, for all that God is, this man of God must be.

Where is this man?

Is he "over there", outside of your consciousness?

Is there any "over there" or is "here" all the place there is? There is no "over there" to Mind.

Because your thinking is right here where you are, all that you call "over there" is "here". Therefore, this man of God is here.

When you say "here", you mean your own conscious being, your own identity, for that is "here" to you.

There is, then, one man and one man only; and you, inevitably, find yourself to be this man, and the Mind of this man is your Mind.

This is the man Mrs. Eddy refers to in Unity of Good, where she says, *"The scientific man and his Maker are here; and you would be none other than this man, if you would subordinate the fleshly perceptions to the spiritual sense and source of being".*[1]

You subordinate the fleshly perceptions, in other words, the material concept of all things, when, from the basis of your own being, you establish God and His one man as All-in-all.

Hence you are this "scientific man" here and now.

[1]Un. 46:9.

THE IDEA OF PRINCIPLE

Let us next consider the term *idea*.

Instantly arises the question: idea of what?

Can there be idea without its being the idea of something? And must not that something be the Principle to the idea?

In establishing Principle as a synonym of God, you found that all that God means and is, Principle also means and is. It is equally true that whatever the man of God is, the idea of Principle is also. The man of God is the *"conscious, constant capacity to understand God"*.[1]

Then the idea of Principle being synonymous with man must also be the "conscious, constant capacity to understand God".

You as this man of God, this idea, this effect of God are concerned only with God. David saw this when he declared, "My soul, wait thou only upon God; for my expectation is from him."[2]

There is one Principle and one only. Being God, that which *is* and therefore all that is, Principle must be one. Because it is infinite, there is nothing outside it.

Because Principle could not be Principle unless it was Principle to idea, the omnipresence of Principle must be accompanied spontaneously by the omnipresence of idea.

"Lo, I am with you alway,"[3] means infinite Principle made manifest as infinite idea. There

[1]S. & H. 209:31.   [2]Ps. 62:5.   [3]Matt. 28:20.

can be nothing held back from you, nothing un-expressed by you.

With one Principle, can there be more than one idea?

No, because this idea is infinite, and being the idea of infinite Principle, it is everywhere present; there is no place where the idea is not.

Is Principle limited by virtue of having but one idea?

Does it limit mathematics to have but one unit? There seem to be countless expressions of mathematics in what are called problems; but, as a matter of fact, the whole of mathematics is simply the addition, subtraction, multiplication, division and other operations performed on the unit.

The one idea of Principle never becomes ideas, but always remains idea—singular, not plural.

It is as impossible to have ideas as it is impossible to have Principles. Principle, being infinite, must always appear as infinity of variety and perfection, but it remains always one.

The oneness of idea must be thoroughly understood.

You are satisfied that there is and can be but one Principle. You must be equally positive that there is and can be but one idea, one man of God.

It follows self-evidently that you are this idea.

If there could be ideas, there would have to be Principles, because there cannot be idea without that of which it is the idea.

In other words, without its Principle the idea spontaneously ceases to be.

The Principle being infinite, the idea likewise is infinite; then, where is there room for ideas?

If you think in terms of ideas, you will inevitably think in terms of Principles or Gods—which is unthinkable.

It might be well to explain here why Science and Health uses the word "ideas", just as it uses many other words in the plural.

Science and Health does this as a concession to ignorance and the limitation of the human sense of language. It must meet every condition of thought, from the most simple to the most profound, from that of the beginner to that of the farthest advanced. To enlighten this wide range of human belief, called person, Science and Health necessarily has to be expressed in language suited to each condition of thought, otherwise it would be unable to lead thought forward.

If Mrs. Eddy, in writing the Christian Science textbook, Science and Health, had used only the singular form for the words "man" and "idea", the limited, finite mind (in other words, the mortal) might have become confused and might have had an even more finite, limited sense of God than it had before.

To say that man is the complete expression or reflection of God and then to think of man as a finite mortal, is a parody on what Christian Science means by the word "man".

To avoid this mistake, Mrs. Eddy endeavored to express in human language the fact that all men, all ideas, go into the making of man, in the generic sense, into man, the idea of God. Hence her statement, *"God is indivisible. A portion of God could not enter man; neither could God's fullness be reflected by a single man, else God would be manifestly finite, lose the deific character, and become less than God. Allness is the measure of the infinite, and nothing less can express God."*[1]

And again, *"Generically man is one, and specifically man means all men."*[2]

But Mrs. Eddy's necessity in the choosing of words is not yours. Science and Health is the textbook for every condition of thought, however ignorant. Its mission is to lift thought from where it finds it. Mrs. Eddy had *"to await the logic of events"*[3] and the unfolding of understanding.

But you are concerned only with your own understanding; so you use the language best adapted to establish the truth of being.

That language is in the singular, never in the plural form.

Science and Health can state things in the plural while thinking in the singular, and so do

[1]S. & H. 336:19.   [2]S. & H. 267:6.   [3]S. & H. 66:22.

only good. You might, at first, find this difficult, since your words give impulse to your thought.

Therefore, think and talk in the singular and you will avoid confusion.

Even Science and Health, when stating an absolutely metaphysical thought, uses the singular, as, for instance, in the scientific statement of being. *"All is infinite Mind and its infinite manifestation* [not manifestations], *for God is All-in-all."*[1]

You cannot be a metaphysician, a Christian Scientist, if you *think* in the plural.

"I and my Father are one."[2] *"Principle and its idea is one".*[3]

You must be absolutely convinced of this fact; otherwise you will discover that you are continually confronted with the temptation to think in terms of the plural, in terms of three or more.

If you are assuming something outside of God and man, something "over there", your whole structure of Christian Science will fall, for you are admitting something apart from Principle and that which Principle is Principle to—you, its idea.

There is but one Principle and one idea, and this idea is the spirit or likeness, in minutest detail, of its Principle. "God created man in his own image".[4] The very existence of God creates the necessity for His mental image, or idea, man.

[1]S. & H. 468:10.   [2]Jno. 10:30.   [3]S. & H. 465:17.   [4]Gen. 1:27.

THE BODY OF SOUL

The next word for consideration is *body*.

Should body be classified as cause or effect?

Every word falls into one or the other of these two categories.

What is body? Does it mean something formed or created?

Or do you mean by body that which is the embodiment of what it represents or shows forth?

Is not body, in that sense, a showing forth of that which you have established as Spirit, Soul?

Could Soul or Spirit *be,* without body to represent it, to make it known?

You have established man's essentiality to God, as that which makes God known, shows Him forth, performs what God *is;* then is not man, who embodies all that God is, the body of God?

The body of Spirit or Soul is the man of God. All that man is, as the embodiment of God, body is, also.

The one Spirit, being omnipotent, all-acting, is the action of its own body, man.

It is infinite action, harmonious action, eternal action; and this action is the law of being, consciously obedient to its Soul, its God.

Body shows forth Life in living. It is the eternal manifestation of Life. It proves what Life is.

There is only one body, because there is only one Spirit, one Soul; and this body of Spirit is all that Spirit is and means.

Its continuity is infinite; for Spirit, which is infinite, would instantly cease without its embodiment or manifestation.

Its purity and perfection is its oneness. There is nothing outside of its own being to contaminate it.

What is God's own can be His only as it is shown forth as idea, as man, as body.

Science and Health declares body to be *"the idea of Life, substance, and intelligence; the superstructure of Truth; the shrine of Love"*.[1]

BUILD ON A SURE FOUNDATION

Each one, as he erects the structure of Christian Science, must take every step logically, so that there may be an orderly sequence to his entire building. His must be the house of the wise man who, as Jesus said, "built his house upon a rock", understanding, so that it "fell not". The foolish man "built his house upon the sand", changing beliefs, and "great was the fall of it."[2]

Jesus did not say that the man who built upon the sand did not build a house, but that when the storm came, the house built upon sand fell and great was its fall.

[1]S. & H. 595:7.   [2]Matt. 7:24, 27.

How important it is then, to build our house on the rock of understanding, which *"begins in ourselves and by education brightens into birth"*.[1]

The rock is your consciously being, which inseparably unites you with the consciousness that *is*.

Your house is a "house not made with hands, eternal in the heavens";[2] and the stones are laid truly only as they are laid upon what you yourself *know*.

Of a surety, then, no storm that arises can destroy it.

Thus, not only have you established God, but you have established also that God must be God to something, and this something you have identified as your own conscious being, as the man of God, the idea of Principle, the body of Soul.

In other words, you are the demonstration of that which Principle is.

You have seen that each of these terms includes and means all that the other terms mean and include.

You recognize that whatever term you use for God must mean exactly what every other term used for God means in its fullest sense.

In the same way, every term you use to designate the effect of God includes all that any other term means that is used as a synonym of effect.

[1]My. 253:26.   [2]Cor. 5:1.

THE ORDERLY USE OF WORDS

While building your structure of reasoning in this class, you stand apart, as it were, and analyze God and what He is God to. You classify certain words which mean God to you and which you propose uniformly to use thus. You place these words in one column, so to speak, and in another you place the words you propose to use as synonyms of the idea of God.

However, you do this only to keep your thought uniform and free from confusion, because you recognize that there is no combination of letters that cannot be used to signify either cause or effect.

As an illustration, take the word Truth with a capital T. You place it in the column meaning God. Now take the same word with a small t, and you will place it in the effect column because you mean the truth of Truth.

In the same way you can say, the life of Life, or the love of Love.

In fact any word can be used interchangeably; but in accurate thinking, it is advantageous to have an orderly use of words and not to interchange them.

The three words that we have been analyzing and classifying, man, idea, body, are commonly used in the language of Christian Science to express the product, or effect of God.

However, one naturally thinks in his own particular language. That is why, in Christian Science, there is no formula, whether in the statement of what God is, why He is, or what the practice of Christian Science is.

Right practice is evolved from individual reasoning in strict adherence to Truth.

No one can formulate thought for another. Thought must always be spontaneous with the individual, or it will not be thought. Your Mind alone can think for you.

Anything cast in the mold of a formula instantly takes on the elements of materiality, because using a formula of necessity outlines, limits, and consequently materializes.

In Christian Science, therefore, there is no formulating by one individual for another.

Each puts into his own language what he understands being to be.

Any attempt on the part of another to do this for him results in no thinking on his part and destroys all impulse to his own thought.

Consecrated obedience to Truth alone is thinking.

THE EFFECT OF CAUSE

Let us consider some other terms not so commonly used as the three just analyzed, but which may be equally important in giving freedom to thought.

You have established cause as synonymous with God.

By cause you mean foundation, basis, origin —in other words, that which *is*.

That which *is*, being all that is, must be the basis, the foundation, the origin, the cause of all that is.

Paralleling the word cause, and always accompanying it, is the word *effect*.

Effect instantly implies that it is the effect *of* something that is primary to it.

For cause to be, it must have the effect that it is cause to, or there could be no cause. Then all that cause is, effect must be.

So you find that since cause is what you mean by the term God, effect is what you mean by the term product of God.

Effect expresses all the intelligence, all the Life, all the action, all the everything that God, as cause, means, and is.

There is one effect because there is one cause, one *is*.

Effect is synonymous with man, idea, body.

You are the effect of the one cause, God.

Effect is conscious identification with cause. "As the hart panteth after the water brooks, so panteth my soul after thee, O God."[1]

As the effect of God, you can never lack anything, for you understand that you are the con-

[1] Ps. 42:1.

scious and obedient functioning of what cause, God, is.

Man, as the effect of the one Mind, has infinite capability, boundless opportunity.

The infinite Mind can operate only as man—effect.

THE UNIVERSE OF MIND

How would you classify the word *universe* and what does it mean to you?

The usual answer to this question is: The universe is that in which I live. But is this a satisfying answer?

Universe must be classified under the heading of either cause or effect. Where will you place it?

Accepting what you have established: one infinite Mind and that Mind all the *isness* there is, it follows that this Mind must include within itself all.

From this premise you are forced to the conclusion that all in which you, the idea of God, are included, or live, or with which you can be concerned, is God the one Mind.

But is this what you mean when you say that the universe is something in which you live?

In saying that you live *in* the universe, are you not thinking of universe merely as a larger effect, in which you, a smaller effect, live?

Such a sense of universe immediately implies two effects, two ideas, one larger than the other in which the lesser dwells.

Admitting two ideas immediately dethrones the infinity of Principle. You have established that you cannot have Principle without its idea, and that idea is co-existent with Principle.

Two ideas would necessitate two principles. But you have proved that there is one Principle and its idea, one infinity.

Assuming, for the sake of argument, the possibility of two ideas, there would of necessity be a dividing line of space, however infinitesimally small, separating these ideas and, therefore, a point where Principle was unexpressed as idea. Consequently infinite Principle would be dethroned as All-in-all.

This being so, what you call universe cannot be another idea, a place in which you live. It must be merely another word for that which means the effect of God; hence it must be synonymous with every other word that is used to define that which God is God to.

So we have one universe, and this universe as infinite as the Mind of which it is the universe.

All that this Mind is, universe must be.

THE REFLECTION OF GOD

Mrs. Eddy tells us, *"Few persons comprehend what Christian Science means by the word reflec-*

tion."[1] In which column will you classify reflection?

Reflection means to give back, implying that it expresses something that *is*.

Then reflection must be another word for effect or man.

Does reflection imply three?

If, as an illustration, you are thinking of reflection as the image in the mirror which reflects the object in front of it, you at once introduce a third and dethrone the oneness of Principle and idea.

God, in His infinite allness, is a "jealous God"[2] and allows no third, no power, presence nor authority aside from Himself and His idea.

Principle and its idea is one—not two. Two is implied only in the sense that Principle is never idea and idea is never Principle. They are inseparably one in that one can never be without the other, but nothing apart from this Principle and idea can enter into that oneness.

If you concede a third something, you have entity apart from the one Mind and that to which it is Mind.

That, of course, destroys your heaven, for heaven means harmony, and harmony means isness; oneness; consciousness and that of which consciousness is conscious; God and His idea.

[1]S. & H. 301:5.   [2]Ex. 20:5.

The sun and its ray best illustrate what is meant by the word reflection. The ray of sunlight expresses, or reflects, every quality and characteristic of the sun. The sun and the ray are inseparably one, in the sense that there is nothing intervening.

The illustration of the mirror and the object before it does not accurately express the metaphysical meaning of the word reflection, because the mirror appears to be a third. There is no mirror in which the idea of God can be reflected.

The man of God, the reflection of God, is the eternal presence of God, and is that whereby God is known. *"Whatever is possible to God, is possible to man as God's reflection."*[1]

The only way in which you can safely use the illustration of the mirror, is to do as Mrs. Eddy does and call *"the mirror divine Science"*.[2] This avoids the "third".

You cannot afford to allow a thought to operate as your mind which implies, in the slightest degree, anything apart from Principle.

Be constantly on guard against a "third" in your thinking.

You cannot be too exact in satisfying your own thought.

No matter what the seeming appearance, there can no more be two ideas, (metaphysically, and

[1]Mis. 183:13.   [2]S. & H. 515:29.

therefore, absolutely) than there can be two gods.

"Spirit is the only creator, and man, including the universe, is His spiritual concept".[1]

THE USE OF "IN" AND "OF"

As man, you do not live *in* the universe or *in* anything. You exist as the idea *of* God.

Let us digress a moment to consider the two words "of" and "in".

"Of" means product of, that which is derived *from*.

"In" means contained within, that which is completely enveloped.

Accepting this definition of "in", it is obvious that God, who is All-in-all, cannot be *in* anything. If He were, He would be less than that which He is in and therefore, not all that is.

Because of this self-evident fact, the word *in*, as used in Christian Science is, as Mrs. Eddy says, *"A term obsolete in Science if used with reference to Spirit, or Deity"*.[2]

God is not, and cannot be, *in* anything.

The true interpretation of Paul's statement should read, Let that same Mind be Mind *to* you that was Mind *to* Christ Jesus, not, Let that same "mind be *in* you".[3]

Since God, Mind, cannot be in anything, neither can man, the idea of God, be *in* anything.

[1]Un. 32:6.   [2]S. & H. 588:22.   [3]Phil. 2:5.

You as man, are aware of consciously being. You do not find yourself *in* anything — you simply are.

If you could find yourself *in*, you would have to presuppose an outside from which you were looking *in* in order to find yourself—a manifest absurdity.

Metaphysically, the word "in" is as obsolete with reference to man as it is to God, except in the one sense that Mind, being infinite, embraces within itself all that it is Mind to.

You exist as the idea *of* God.

Therefore, never think of yourself as *in* anything.

You do not find yourself *in* God, because you are the idea *of* God. In communion with Him you discover all that appears to you as consciousness, whether appearing as person, place or thing.

THE LANGUAGE OF MIND

How do you define the word "language"?

Is it not that which Mind is Mind to, namely, the idea expressed? Mind outlining itself in expression is language.

Language then, in its broadest sense is the complete, all-inclusive symbol or image of Mind.

It is the idea of Mind, the mental or spiritual image, expressed; the ideal or model of Mind.

It declares in spiritual outline what Mind is; performs what Mind is.

Language draws its existence from Mind and so is the effect of Mind. Since it is the effect of Mind, it is one, and is synonymous with all words meaning effect.

You, then, are the language of God and carry out and express all that God is.

You are the idea of God, spiritually expressed, the language of Mind that maintains and enforces what Mind is.

Jesus declared, "The Son can do nothing of himself, but what he seeth the Father do: for what things soever he doeth, these also doeth the Son likewise."[1]

In Isaiah we read, "When the enemy shall come in like a flood, the Spirit of the Lord shall lift up a standard against him."[2]

What is this standard of God's power and authority? It is the language of Mind, the man of God, the conscious expression of what Mind is.

"THE DIVINE MANIFESTATION OF GOD"[3]

The next word to define is *Christ*.

Should Christ be classified as cause or effect?

The theological concept is that Christ is another name for God. If by "Christ" you mean that which appears *like* God, then it is not another name for God, but another name for the effect of God, for that whereby God is known.

[1]Jno. 5:19.   [2]Isa. 59:19.   [3]S. & H. 583:10.

Jesus said of the Christ, "I am the way, the truth, and the life".[1]

Then, he must have meant by "the Christ" the truth or the true way.

The name Christ Jesus means the true Jesus, which, in turn, means the man Jesus, demonstrating the reality of the true man of God.

It is in this sense of effect, or man of God, that the word Christ is used in Christian Science, rather than as a synonym for God.

Science and Health, however, in a number of instances, uses the word as synonymous with Life and Truth, and rightly understood it can be used in that sense as well as in the sense of reflection.

But the definition of Christ, as given in the glossary of Science and Health, indicates the best way in which to think of Christ. *"The divine manifestation of God, which comes to the flesh to destroy incarnate error."*[2]

Thus Christ means the manifestation or revelation of God; in other words, the man of God. That man of God is the man whereby God reveals or shows forth Himself.

Can there be more than one Christ?

No, that is impossible, because there is but one God.

Is there any place where Christ is not?

No. Christ is the one and only man there is.

[1] Jno. 14:6.   [2] S. & H. 583:10.

It is this Christ that is your reality, the verity of your conscious being, your very self.

Christ is forever one with Messiah, for Messiah means Saviour.

What is it that saves?

For example, what saves or corrects the error "two times two is five." Is it not the truth about two times two, that it is four?

Is not that what you mean by the Christ, the Messiah, the Saviour, the very presence of Principle, the truth, everpresent, now?

Christ, then, is the Messiah, and this Messiah is all the Saviour there ever is or can be.

God, divine Principle, cannot operate of Himself without expression.

He can operate only *as* His own idea or Christ.

The Saviour is not Principle; the Saviour is the presence of Principle, called Christ or man.

This is why Science and Health declares, *"God will heal the sick through man, whenever man is governed by God."*[1]

Think always of this Christ, this Messiah as the saving man, then, finding yourself as this man, you will cease looking for him to come.

With two times two as five confronting you in a mathematical problem, you would not ask the principle of numbers to correct it for you. In your communion with that principle, you would

[1] S. & H. 495:1.

find oneness with two times two as four, and the mistake would automatically disappear.

The same method corrects problems that seem to arise in the study of the Science of being.

Except for the word "Christ", you will find that Mrs. Eddy generally uses words in the sense in which she has classified them, and does not use them first as meaning God and then as meaning the idea of God.

This double use of the word "Christ", as a concession to popular Christian usage, is an endeavor to cause no offense, and so to be, as Paul puts it, "all things to all men".[1]

What Mrs. Eddy could do with perfect wisdom and understanding, you may not at once be able to do; hence you will find it wiser not to interchange words in your vocabulary but to use them uniformly in the sense in which you classify them metaphysically.

By so doing you will avoid confusion and be surer of the words you use. They will give impulse to your thought and spontaneously your understanding will respond.

This, however, does not mean that one has not the right to use a word in any sense he cares to give to it. You must, in fact, do so or you will not speak with authority.

To paraphrase the Scripture concerning the Sabbath one might say, "man was not made for

[1] 1 Cor. 9:22.

words but words were made for man." Therefore, any word is for you to use in the sense that
gives the best impulse to your thought and which
carries you most directly to the impersonal
Truth.

The point to be guarded against, however, is
the use of the same word to mean both cause and
effect. That might cause confusion and give a
wrong impulse to thought. Apart from this, there
is no inflexible meaning for words.

THE UNDERSTANDING OF GOD

Let us now establish what is meant by *understanding*.

This word, like the word Christ, is frequently
used as meaning both God and His idea.

God would cease to be God unless He were
known and understood, in other words, expressed
or shown forth.

In this sense of the word, man is the understanding of God, just as man is the body of God.

Man shows forth that which God is; hence
man must be the understanding of God.

But if you use the word understanding to imply that which supports or maintains, then it becomes synonymous with God.

Because God is Mind, and this Mind could not
be Mind without being understood or expressed,
is it not simpler to call man the understanding of
God?

In that case, understanding is synonymous with effect rather than with cause.

This is also the sense in which you accept *thought*.

Mind must have thought in order to be Mind, for thought is the product or effect of Mind.

So, understanding is the product or intelligent effect of intelligence, but it is not intelligence itself.

That which you have established as true understanding, the man of God, the forever showing forth what God is, immediately brings to light the folly of praying in the sense of asking God to grant a request.

True prayer is communion with God, the realizing one's eternal oneness with Him and so being like Him. "All things that the Father hath are mine."[1]

It would be impossible to define the true sense of prayer more clearly than Mrs. Eddy has done in No and Yes: *"Prayer is the utilization of the love wherewith He loves us . . . . It makes new and scientific discoveries of God, of His goodness and power. It shows us more clearly than we saw before, what we already have and are; and most of all, it shows us what God is."*[2]

[1] Jno. 16:15.   [2] No. 39:18.

CHAPTER V

The Holy Ghost: Man's Communion With God

In establishing your structure of Christian Science, you have accepted the word God to mean cause or Father, and man to mean effect or son.

In other words, you have established consciousness and that of which consciousness is conscious. You have seen that this constitutes the whole of being, namely, Principle and its idea, God and man, Mind and thought, Soul and body, your-Self and you.

But to establish full completeness there is one more point to settle.

It is to define the eternal relationship existing between consciousness and conscious being, the communion between God and man.

THE TRINITY DEFINED

These three elements—God, man, and the communion between them—constitute a trinity. This leads us to a consideration of the word Trinity, which means three-in-one.

In the old theological sense, it is called the Holy Trinity, meaning the three persons of the Godhead. It is defined as the three-fold personality of God the Father, God the Son, and God the Holy Ghost. But no theologian has ever explained this combination of three persons in one.

In Christian Science it is readily understood as God the Father and man the son, with the Holy Ghost as the communion between Father and son, their mutual awareness of each other, but never as one being the other.

You have found that Father and son are the first "two persons" of the Trinity, and that they are two-in-one, as it were, being Mind and its expression.

Could these intelligently know each other without communion?

This communion is the Holy Ghost.

By Holy Ghost you mean holy Spirit, or pure Spirit, isness, true being, true activity, conscious understanding, the activity that is ever present between Mind and thought, consciousness and conscious being—God directing His own idea.

Have you ever stopped to think what you yourself are doing every moment?

Are you not constantly meditating—thinking?

Does not this mean communing with something you call your mind? Paul expressed it, "Their conscience also bearing witness, and their thoughts the mean while accusing or else excusing one another".[1]

Where is the "accusing or else excusing" going on?

[1] Rom. 2:15.

Humanly speaking, are you not communing constantly with your own mind—a purely mental operation?

In the realm of pure Mind, the eternal communion between God and man, cause and effect, is the Holy Ghost, the necessary completion of Father and son.

This constitutes the Trinity.

Mrs. Eddy defines it perfectly in Science and Health: *"God the Father-Mother; Christ the spiritual idea of sonship; divine Science or the Holy Comforter. These three express in divine Science the threefold, essential nature of the infinite. They also indicate . . . the intelligent relation of God to man and the universe."*[1]

Can there be any oneness, any intelligent relationship, any understanding between Father and son unless there is communion between them?

Of course not. Mind and thought must commune with each other.

HOW COMMUNION APPEARS TO YOU

When you began to build your argument in this class, you started with your own consciously being as the one pure fact that needs no outward evidence to prove its reality—that is true to you because it is self-evident, wholly apart from sense testimony.

It is your own knowing.

[1] S. & H. 331:30.

From this you induced that consciousness is, otherwise you could not consciously be.

So you found consciousness as that which *is* and that which *is,* as all that *is.*

In this All that *is,* is included all entity or existence. Nothing can be added to it nor anything taken from it.

That "All" you named God, meaning by this term all *isness.*

Next you deduced idea or effect as necessary to God. For God to be God, to make Himself known, He must express Himself as man.

As you found God to be infinite, hence one, so you found man to be one man, not two; and you found yourself to be that man.

Does not that forever settle the question of man, in so far as your consideration of man is concerned?

He is accounted for as yourself.

But you cannot deal with yourself. All that you can deal with is God, the Self of you.

Effect does not turn to effect, to itself, but to cause.

In dealing or communing with God, how does the communing appear? *"The Soul-inspired patriarchs heard the voice of Truth, and talked with God as consciously as man talks with man."*[1]

It is self-evident that God's language, His manner of being known, which is your com-

[1] S. & H. 308:14.

munion with Him, appears as idea and all that you have established idea to be.

This communion is God talking to you in His own language because whatever God is, His language must be.

He appears to you as person, place, or thing. So your consciousness of being seems to be made up of men, animals, minerals, vegetables, mountains, rivers, worlds upon worlds throughout infinity.

This one infinite language is like its cause, from the infinitesimal to the infinite. *"The only logical conclusion is that all is Mind and its manifestation, from the rolling of worlds, in the most subtle ether, to a potato-patch."*[1]

Does not everything come as consciousness to you and mean simply your communion with God, your consciousness, appearing in the language that you can most clearly understand, and that will best meet your need for progress and unfoldment?

Language does not imply merely words. It implies any mode or method whereby understanding is conveyed.

In communion, the eternal oneness of man with his Maker, the oneness of the idea with its Principle appears always as language, as person, place, or thing—whatever will best convey the sense of the omnipresence of good.

[1]Mis. 26:5.

This is the language of God to man; in other words, this is the Holy Ghost.

Notwithstanding this self-evident truth, the constant temptation arises to imagine that you are dealing with persons, places, or things, as such, instead of knowing that you are communing with Mind in the language of Mind and so finding Mind to be all that you are concerned with.

This temptation to stop short of Mind will, if yielded to, destroy your structure of Christian Science and lead into the morass of human beliefs, which brings the fatal "three" into the argument.

Remember Jesus' warning, "What I say unto you I say unto all, Watch."[1]

CHRISTIAN SCIENCE AN EXACT SCIENCE

Christian Science is based upon one Principle and one idea, no matter what name you give to the Principle or to the idea. You may call it God and man, Soul and body, Principle and idea; but whatever name is used, it is always one, one cause and one effect.

Departure from this fundamental fact is fatal to understanding and therefore to all metaphysical demonstration of Christian Science. "*Whoever affirms that there is more than one Principle and method of demonstrating Christian Science*

[1] Mark 13:37.

*greatly errs, ignorantly or intentionally, and sep-
arates himself from the true conception of Chris-
tion Science healing and from its possible demonstration."*[1] Again, *"Principle and its idea is
one".*[2] *"To infinite Spirit there is no matter,—
all is Spirit, divine Principle and its idea."*[3]

When Jesus said, "I and my Father are one,"[4]
he was referring to this fundamental truth, this
eternal communion of Father and son, without a
third, this communion that is essential to your
understanding.

Because the language of God always appears
as idea; so, in your communion with God, God
appears to you as the infinity of variety called
persons, places and things.

But it is always God, with whom you are actually communing, and never what appears to be
persons, places or things.

Mrs. Eddy says, *"The Christian Scientist is
alone with his own being and with the reality of
things."*[5] God is the reality and isness of all
things, hence the Christian Scientist is alone with
God, his own being.

This must be clearly understood because no
other deduction can be drawn from the premise
that God is that which *is* and man is that which
God is God to.

[1]S. & H. 456:10.   [2]S. & H. 465:17.   [3]S. & H. 475:3.   [4]Jno. 10:30.
[5]'01 20:8.

You are dealing, then, with what God, consciousness, is to you—in other words, with your own Mind, with what you are acknowledging your God to be.

The Apostle John put it thus, "If a man say, I love God, and hateth his brother, he is a liar".[1] How could you love your God while hating that which is your interpretation of your God appearing to you? You interpret Him in your own language, in the only way you can understand Him.

If your God were to appear to you in language you could not understand, you would not know Him; therefore, He must of necessity appear to you in the language of your own acceptance.

This does not change the fact, however, that your God always appears to you in His own perfect language, as idea. But if you negatively interpret this appearing, He will seem to appear negatively, in other words, materially.

Are you tempted to murmur, as did the children of Israel in the wilderness, at the manner of His appearance, and to ask the reason for such an appearance?

You have your answer.

What are you acknowledging as consciousness, as God?

Is it Mind; or is it the negation, unreversed, of Mind, appearing as matter?

[1] Jno. 4:20.

If it is the latter, how can your God appear to you as anything but materiality? If you are accepting the negation of Mind as your God, He will appear in the language of ignorance, of finiteness, as death, in one form or another, for is not matter the negation of infinity, of Life?

Mrs. Eddy clearly states this: *"Christian Science shows that matter, evil, sin, sickness, and death are but negations of Spirit, Truth, and Life, which are positives that cannot be gainsaid. The subjective states of evil, called mortal mind or matter, are negatives destitute of time and space; for there is none beside God or Spirit and the idea of Spirit."*[1]

Your Holy Ghost, your communion with what *is,* determines the appearance of all things to you. You are always dealing with your own Mind, your own being; you are alone with your *"own being and with the reality of things."*[2]

The ever-active communion between Father and son, the reality of things, appears as the infinity of persons, places, and things. It includes all that means family, position, money, friends, neighbors, country, world, universe, body. It includes all the terms you use to mean God and that which God is God to.

"Many, O Lord my God, are thy wonderful works which thou hast done, and thy thoughts which are to us-ward: they cannot be reckoned

[1]No. 16:9.   [2]'01 20:9.

up in order unto thee: if I would declare and
speak of them, they are more than can be numbered."[1] Science and Health expresses the same
idea thus: *"There is but one creator and one
creation. This creation consists of the unfolding
of spiritual ideas and their identities, which are
embraced in the infinite Mind and forever reflected. These ideas range from the infinitesimal
to infinity . . . . Hence the eternal wonder,—that
infinite space is peopled with God's ideas, reflecting Him in countless spiritual forms."*[2]

SOME WORDS ANALYZED

What is meant by the word *person*?

The dictionary gives its origin as *per*, through,
and *sonare*, to sound, hence, to sound through,
show forth, identify.

Does not idea do that?

Idea shows forth Principle, hence person is
another word for idea, language.

God embraces all within Himself, all that
means, and is, person.

Hence God is the one and only Person. He is
that which is shown forth as Person, and person
is that which shows Him forth.

What is *place*?

Place means position, location, site of something.

[1]Ps. 40:5.   [2]S. & H. 502:29.

God being all the something that is, place means, where God is. However, since God is known only as idea, place is merely another name for idea, man, the language of Mind, that which declares the presence of God.

Thus there is but one place and that one infinite, the presence of God, the "here" of conscious being.

The word *thing* is analyzed in the same way.

Thing means entity, the product of, the idea of that which is shown forth.

God, being that which is shown forth, and being one, there is one *thing* only, one entity that fills all space.

Thus, person, place and thing, in their infinity of variety, show forth the infinity we call God.

Therefore, God includes within Himself all person, all place, all thing.

In your communion with God, the language of God appears always as person, place and thing,—as that which makes Him known.

But, regardless of what appears to you, your thought does not rest until it reaches Mind, the one source of conscious being, the source of all that comes to you as consciousness.

Universe means the aggregate of all existing things; the whole creation, the cosmos.

This universe comes to you as consciousness, otherwise there would be no universe to you. You could not cognize it.

Universe shows forth the infinity of Mind.

What you know about God as Mind is what you know about universe. There is but one infinite universe, because there is one infinite Mind.

This one universe is a living, intelligent universe because the Mind of which it is the idea, the language, is Life and intelligence.

It is a truthful universe because it is the presence of Truth.

The universe is obedient to law, for divine Principle is infinite law. It is therefore harmonious.

How will you interpret *body*?

It, too, comes to you as consciousness and is, therefore, your communion with God. It is consciousness, Mind, defining itself to you.

How old is body?

There is but one answer. Body is eternal. It is infinite in its every quality and attribute.

There never was a time when body began, any more than there was a time when Spirit, that which *is*, began.

Consequently there is no time when this body of Soul ceases to be. How could Mind ever cease defining itself to you? *"The so-called appearing, disappearing, and reappearing of ever-presence, ... is the false human sense of that light which shineth in darkness, and the darkness comprehendeth it not".*[1]

[1]Un. 63:7.

Body is the spiritual outline of being, of Soul, and defines the beauty, harmony, and perfection of being. *"The beauty of holiness* [wholeness], *the perfection of being, imperishable glory,—all are Mine, for I am God."*[1] Its loveliness is the loveliness of perfection.

Nothing short of eternity can show forth the beauty and loveliness and joyousness of body, since it is the language of Mind to you.

Like the unfolding of a beautiful flower, this body of God, this language of God, perpetually unfolds the beauty of holiness, completeness.

This body is one, and is, therefore, all the body you have.

Ask yourself, then, Do I love this body or do I wish to get rid of it?

Do I, as Paul says, present it "a living sacrifice, holy, acceptable unto God"?[2]

It is because of this truth about body that woman, the more spiritual sense of the so-called mortal, has ever endeavored to perfect her sense of body and make it more beautiful. In doing this, even though not understanding the reason, she has shown forth the innate spirituality of being. Materiality has laughed at her, calling it vanity, but she has persisted and won.

Body, then, is your conscious communion with Mind, that which declares Mind to you.

[1] S. & H. 253:2.   [2] Rom. 12:1.

Willingness to be "absent from the body, and to be present with the Lord"[1] means that body, as the language of Mind, must carry you through to Mind.

You relinquish it for Mind.

But if your thought deals with body as something in and of itself, you will find yourself, as Paul says, "at home in the body, ... absent from the Lord".[2]

This is true not only of body, but of every thought, word and deed. It is true of all that comes to you as your communion with God.

YOUR COMMUNION IS WITH GOD

You relinquish what appears for the substance of its appearing.

If you are concerned with anything apart from Mind, if your communion stops short of its goal—the finding of God alone as the reality of what appears—thought will perish in the darkness of ignorance and limitation, for there is no light there.

This is the whole of the anguish called sin, sickness and death.

Jesus exemplified man's communion with God and proved his identity with Christ.

He said, "He that hath seen me hath seen the Father",[3] and "No man cometh unto the Father, but by me."[4] Here the expression "cometh unto

[1] 2 Cor. 5:8.   [2] 2 Cor. 5:6.   [3] Jno. 14:9.   [4] Jno. 14:6.

the Father" means simply to know or understand the Father.

Peter declared, "There is none other name under heaven given among men, whereby we must be saved."[1]

Is not Christ the truth about all that *is*, from the infinitesimal to the infinite? This Christ, this truth about everything is the "Lo, I am with you alway."[2]

When you say "the truth about everything", remember that "everything" includes all, as in Mrs. Eddy's statement: *"from the rolling of worlds, in the most subtle ether, to a potato-patch."*[3]

This Christ is the truth or true idea unto which "Every knee shall bow . . . and every tongue shall confess".[4]

"The real Christ was unconscious of matter, of sin, disease, and death, and was conscious only of God, of good, of eternal Life, and harmony. Hence the human Jesus had a resort to his higher self and relation to the Father, and there could find rest from unreal trials in the conscious reality and royalty of his being,—holding the mortal as unreal, and the divine as real. It was this retreat from the material to spiritual selfhood which recuperated him for triumph over sin, sickness, and death."[5]

[1]Acts 4:12. [2]Matt. 28:20. [3]Mis. 26:6. [4]Rom. 14:11. [5]No. 36:12.

INSTANCES OF DIVINE PROTECTION

To Shadrach, Meshach, and Abed-nego, "the burning fiery furnace"[1] was not something to be feared.

Having faith in good, in reality, in Life, in Mind—their God, they knew that, if they remained true to the right interpretation of being, He could not appear in any language contrary to Himself.

So the fire became their protection and appeared as the destruction of all that threatened to harm them. "Therefore because the king's commandment was urgent, and the furnace exceeding hot, the flame of the fire slew those men that took up Shadrach, Meshach, and Abed-nego."[2]

Daniel faced the lions fearlessly because he knew that his God, being omnipresent good, could appear to him only in the language of good.

With this understanding, the language of God appeared as harmless, God-like lions. *"All that is, God created."*[3]

Since he realized that communion with God was all there could be to lions, it was easy to see God also as the only King and to declare from his heart "O king, live for ever."[4]

[1]Dan. 3:17.   [2]Dan. 3:22.   [3]Un. 64:1.   [4]Dan. 6:21.

This was no subserviency to a so-called human power or king, but the acknowledgment of God as All-in-all, regardless of the appearance.

Elijah beheld his communion with God in the language of fire, consuming the sacrifice. "Then the fire of the Lord fell, and consumed the burnt sacrifice, and the wood, and the stones, and the dust, and licked up the water that was in the trench. And when all the people saw it, they fell on their faces: and they said, The Lord, he is the God".[1]

Elisha saw his communion with God as a continuous supply of oil for the widow. "And it came to pass, when the vessels were full, that she said unto her son, Bring me yet a vessel. And he said unto her, There is not a vessel more. And the oil stayed."[2]

Note that the flow of the oil did not cease until the widow herself said that she did not have room for more.

Moses, under the government of fear, "fled from before"[3] the rod he had used for years as a shepherd's staff, when he saw it turn into a serpent. But when intelligence destroyed his fear, his old, familiar rod reappeared.

His realization that matter, under any name or in any form, animate or inanimate, is but a state of consciousness, became a staff upon which he could lean.

[1] 1 Kings 18:38, 39.   [2] 2 Kings 4:6.   [3] Ex. 4:3.

It was the understanding of this truth that enabled him to perform such wonders as the leading of the children of Israel out of Egypt in the face of what seemed to be insurmountable difficulties.

Your communion with God is constantly appearing to you as all that you are conscious of. You determine for yourself, by what you are beholding, whether or not you are acknowledging God as All-in-all.

The same sea in which the disciples caught nothing, after toiling all night, yielded fish in abundance when they entertained a different concept of Mind. This was spoken of as casting "the net on the right side."[1]

The Bible is full of instances which prove that what is seen takes outward form in accordance with what is acknowledged as consciousness. *"Mortal mind sees what it believes as certainly as it believes what it sees."*[2]

This proves that man's communion with his God determines the appearance of all that he is conscious of.

This constitutes man's power and freedom, and fulfills the promise, "as he thinketh in his heart, so is he."[3]

What a man thinks constitutes his communion, whether with reality or unreality, Life or death, good or evil, abundance or limitation.

[1]Jno. 21:6.   [2]S. & H. 86:29.   [3]Prov. 23:7.

Communion with reality is the Holy Ghost. Communion with unreality is hypnotism.

"Believing a lie veils the truth from our vision; even as in mathematics, in summing up positive and negative quantities, the negative quantity offsets an equal positive quantity, making the aggregate positive, or true quantity, by that much, less available."[1]

God appears or is known only in one way—as idea. "Thou canst not see my face: for there shall no man see me, and live."[2]

If man could see God other than as idea, man would be God; and, if man were God, there would be no man for God to be God to; consequently there would be no God.

Therefore, "no man shall see me, and live."

God sees Himself, God, as man or idea; but man does not see God. He sees God expressed in the language of his own understanding.

Completeness means Father, Son, and Holy Ghost; God, man, and the Comforter, which is the communion between them.

The three are one, and that one, God.

Paul sums it up, "Then cometh the end, when he shall have delivered up the kingdom to God, even the Father; . . And when all things shall be subdued unto him, then shall the Son also himself be subject unto him that put all things under him, that God may be all in all."[3]

---

[1]Mis. 62:9.   [2]Ex. 33:20.   [3]1 Cor. 15:24, 28.

CHAPTER VI

THE NEGATION OR SUPPOSITITIOUS OPPOSITE

Up to this point in our reasoning, we have established the positive facts: first, that there is God; second, what God is; third, what God is God to; and fourth, man's communion with God.

In establishing that there is God, you begin with that of which you are absolutely sure, that about which you can have no doubt: your own conscious existence or being.

Unless you are first conscious of being, you realize that you cannot even contemplate the question: whether or not there is God.

Simultaneously you discover that consciousness *is* or you could not be conscious.

Further, you prove that this consciousness that *is* includes within itself every term that expresses the meaning of the word *God,* whether used as a synonym or as an attribute.

Self-evidently, God could not be, without that to which He is God, that which you call expression, man, body, Christ.

You have identified this expression as the reality of your own being.

You have found this effect of God just as complete, perfect, infinite and pure as the cause of which it is the effect.

'S. & H., 450:27.

As the final step in this oneness, you have discovered and analyzed the conscious relationship between God and man, or the communion between Principle and its idea.

This completes the full measure of Being and that which Being is Being to.

Why, then, should not the analysis of the understanding of Christian Science end here, with the perfection of God and His idea, and the perpetual communion between them?

THE SUPPOSITITIOUS OPPOSITE

The answer is: Because in what you call your daily experience there appears, as your consciousness, as reality to you, the exact opposite.

Mrs. Eddy pertinently asks, *"Who, that has felt the perilous beliefs in life, substance, and intelligence separated from God, can say that there is no error of belief?"*[1]

It is essential that what seems to you to be the presence, power and being of evil should be dissected by the same analytical process used in finding God and His man as All-in-all.

You are confronted on all sides with a sense of limitation, finiteness, sin, sickness, death.

You can understand what it all means by facing it frankly and "Casting down imaginations, and every high thing that exalteth itself against

[1] S. & H. 450:27.

the knowledge of God, and bringing into captivity every thought to the obedience of Christ".[1]

There can be no permanent peace and happiness until this present finite sense of consciousness is transformed.

This can be done only by the transformation of the mind through understanding.

Let us then face the question: What is this that seems to confront us on all sides—this sense or consciousness of limitation, finiteness, and materiality, with all that it involves? What is its origin? What is its ultimate end?

With the appearance of any truth, there instantly arises, *by implication,* the suppositional opposite of it, just as with the presence of any intelligent statement, there arises, *by implication,* the ignorance with regard to that statement.

You have established the allness of God and His idea; therefore nothing unlike God and His idea actually arises.

When you use the word "arises" you mean that it does so suppositionally just as you think of ignorance arising as the suppositional opposite of intelligence.

Ignorance has no substantiality. It is merely the suppositional opposite of the intelligence that is present. Without the presence of intelligence the ignorance about it could not appear even suppositionally.

[1] 2 Cor. 10:5.

Ignorance is the false, in contradistinction to the true; the lie in contradistinction to the fact.

A lie is not anything of itself. It is merely the negation of the truth.

In order that a supposable condition may exist, no mind is required to suppose it.

It exists as the law of opposites, standing as the negative which always accompanies the positive—as darkness is the negation or opposite of light.

Truth, to be truth, must have the power to support itself.

It holds within itself the power to render null and void anything which could, even by implication, oppose it.

Truth exerts this dominion over the false by knowing nothing about it. "Thou art of purer eyes than to behold evil".[1]

The positive is reality and power; the negative, having no independent existence, is unreality and powerlessness.

The negation only masquerades as reality, disappearing simultaneously with the acknowledged presence of the positive.

Darkness immediately vanishes in the presence of light, leaving not a vestige of its recent apparent reality.

Darkness never puts out light because it exists only as a negation or the absence of light.

[1] Hab. 1:13.

Ignorance never destroys intelligence because ignorance is only the implied absence of intelligence.

You can exchange two times two as five, for two times two as four; but knowing that two times two is four, you cannot exchange it for two times two is five.

One is true, the other false.

The false always surrenders to the true, because it is only a *suppositional* opposite of the true, never a bona fide opposite.

Why suppositional?

A supposition is dependent for its entity upon the fact or truth about which it is the supposition.

Truth has its own entity, existing wholly apart from anything except itself.

Two times two stands as four in spite of any ignorance. This is equally true of all truths, from the infinitesimal to the infinite.

Truth is wholly self-contained and self-sustained. The exact opposite is the case, concerning the supposition or lie.

THE LAW OF OPPOSITES

But, you ask, How can God be All-in-all, if there be any one to suppose an opposite or to accept such a supposition?

It is not necessary for there to be any one to accept or suppose the suppositional opposite.

This is the age-old question—the origin of evil—the question that no ancient or modern philosopher has answered.

This is the problem that has heretofore always defied solution, except as solved by Jesus through demonstration. Now it is solved through Mrs. Eddy's discovery of the Science of being.

Until Mrs. Eddy's discovery, it was never understood that all finiteness, all evil of every name and nature, suppositionally exists and always has so existed as the opposite of Mind, by virtue of the law that every truth includes, within itself, by implication the concept of its own opposite.

This is the law of opposites. To illustrate: Obviously *is,* being is, because its "seed is in itself,"[1] alone determines itself, and so implies that anything outside itself, outside that which *is* must be *is not.*

Thus every truth by virtue of its own *isness,* hence allness, carries within itself the contradiction of the lie about itself.

Basic *isness,* Mind, carries with it its suppositional opposite, mindlessness, which appears as an implication contrary to Truth.

Ancient and modern philosophies—with the exception of Christian metaphysics—have always attempted to deal with the intricacies of this simulation of Truth, of reality, and have always ended in confusion.

[1]Gen. 1:11.

THE NATURE OF THE SUPPOSITIONAL OPPOSITE

Through the light of Christian Science, as we have established it, let us examine this suppositional opposite, and see what its claim is.

First, we will give it a name.

Being purely a supposition, it must be mental.

So we will call it mind, with a small *m,* to distinguish it from the Mind that is God.

Because the nature of the Mind that is God is infinite Life, the nature of the suppositional opposite would be infinite lifelessness——in other words, it would be death in its infinite form.

The term that best expresses death is maliciousness.

The term "malignant" disease means a malicious or deadly disease. The word malicious always means something viciously destructive, something which kills because killing is its nature.

The word malicious, then, expresses what Christian Science means by the suppositional opposite of Life——namely, death and more abundant death——and so expresses the suppositional opposite of the divine Mind.

Malicious mind, then, is the name we use for that negation, the implied mind which is not divine Mind.

What do we know about this malicious mind?

Being the suppositional opposite of the one infinite Mind, it is that supposition in all its minutiæ, and yet without the faintest real existence.

Since divine Mind is infinite, without beginning and without end, malicious mind, the suppositional opposite, must be infinitely finite, without beginning and without end—in other words, nothing.

Its finity has no stopping point, any more than has the minus sign in mathematics.

Infinite good, divine Mind, is suppositionally opposed by infinite evil.

Infinite intelligence is suppositionally opposed by infinite ignorance.

Infinite power by infinite powerlessness.

Infinite presence by infinite absence, no presence at all.

Everything that the one Mind is, in all its infinity of perfection, the suppositional opposite must simulate in exact opposition.

The suppositional opposite has no ability independently to declare itself, but by its very nature it automatically falls in line as the negation of that which *is*.

As such negation, its entire suppositional presence, thought and action are borrowed from that which *is*, even as any lie depends for its existence on the presence of the truth about which it is the lie.

Jesus said, "When he speaketh a lie, he speaketh of his own: for he is a liar, and the father of it".[1]

Divine Mind being one, malicious mind is suppositionally also one, or rather, to use the mathematical term, minus one.

The unlimited and unoutlined quality of infinite Mind, or substance, is suppositionally opposed by limitation, finiteness, outline in that which appears as the illusion and is called matter, a reverse sense of substance.

Mrs. Eddy defines matter as *"the opposite of Truth; the opposite of Spirit; the opposite of God;.. that which mortal mind sees, feels, hears, tastes, and smells only in belief."*[2]

Thus we find that while the language of divine Mind invariably appears as spiritual manifestation, or *generic man*, the language of the suppositional opposite always appears as matter, or mortal, material man.

The suppositional mind embraces within itself the infinity of evil, by whatever name it may be designated.

Like Truth, evil is always one. It is never two.

There are no varying degrees of evil, just as there are no degrees of error in mathematical mistakes. "Two times two equals three and three quarters" is just as fatal a mistake as "two times two equals three."

[1]Jno. 8:44. [2]S. & H. 591:12.

It is a question of being either right or wrong. There is no possibility of a compromise.

The Science of being does not differ from the science of numbers. It has no degrees of right or wrong. It admits of no "human mind" that is an improvement over mortal or malicious mind.

The Science of being insists unequivocally that if a thing is not right, it is wrong.

"All Science is divine. Human thought never projected the least portion of true being. Human belief has sought and interpreted in its own way the echo of Spirit, and so seems to have reversed it and repeated it materially; but the human mind never produced a real tone nor sent forth a positive sound."[1]

Little progress can be made in the understanding of Christian Science until it is recognized that no vesture of righteousness can cover any phase of malicious mind. Malicious mind cannot be reformed and emerge as an improved belief. It remains forever the suppositional opposite of good—wholly evil, incapable of being regenerated in any way.

That is why Mrs. Eddy declares: *"Christian Science is absolute; it is neither behind the point of perfection nor advancing towards it; it is at this point and must be practised therefrom."*[2]

[1] S. & H. 126:8.   [2] My. 242:5.

EVIL AS A NEGATIVE STATEMENT

We shall now consider this suppositional opposite from another angle. While this view of it does not change its nature as the embodiment of all evil, it does elucidate the true concept of the absolute oneness and allness of God.

In Unity of Good, Mrs. Eddy says, *"The use of a lie is that it unwittingly confirms Truth, when handled by Christian Science, which reverses false testimony and gains a knowledge of God from opposite facts, or phenomena."*[1]

This exactly defines the nature of evil as the negative of Mind, which reversed, declares the truth of Mind.

A dictionary definition of negation is, "Statement of what a thing is not or has not, from which may be inferred what it has and is."

Every negative by reversal declares the positive and every positive implies the negative.

Being the negative or negation of good, evil rightly understood, serves, when reversed, the purpose of good, as effectively as does positive good.

In mathematics the method of reasoning called *reductio ad absurdum* is the same method as reversing the negative in a metaphysical problem. In mathematics, the solving of a proposition may be arrived at by showing the absurdity of its contradictory opposite.

[1] Un. 36:6.

You start with a false statement, a negative, and by proving it an absurdity—which is but another way of saying that you reverse it—the statement of Truth is confirmed *"from opposite facts, or phenomena."*[1]

The mathematician recognizes the negative for what it is, and he attributes to it no inherent power or intelligence. He sees it clearly as the automatic contradiction of the true, its use being to identify as absurd any assumption of reality outside of the positive statement of truth.

The mathematician, in facing his innumerable problems, never thinks of the word *problem* as implying the presence of error, but rather accepts the word as meaning opportunity to commune with the principle of numbers in a practical and enlightening way.

The metaphysician faces the Science of being from the same confident and intelligent viewpoint. He does not deal with error as error but sees it as the negative interpretation of the positive truth. His activity is in the realm of the real. His problems are not difficulties, but rather opportunities to see Truth, face to face—the beholding of "the brightness of his glory".[2]

If a negative statement of Truth appears on his horizon, he is "not forgetful to entertain strangers", as Paul admonishes; for when he has entertained this stranger for what it actually

[1]Un. 36:6.   [2]Heb. 1:3.

is, and thereby has reversed it, he finds that he has "entertained angels unawares."[1] He has, in short, gained a fuller knowledge of God.

It is for this reason that you can never ignore or turn your back upon a lie—a negative statement. You must face it.

You cannot say: "There is no truth to it, it is nothing"; for a lie is always a lie about the truth, and, by reversal, declares the truth. All the presence it has is the very truth about which it is the negative statement. *"By reversal, errors serve as waymarks to the one Mind, in which all error disappears in celestial Truth."*[2]

When this is understood, evil is no longer feared as something in and of itself. It is seen as simply the negation of good, or the negative way of stating Truth.

Many readers of Science and Health have been puzzled by Mrs. Eddy's answer to the following question in the chapter, "Recapitulation": *"Is materiality the concomitant of spirituality, and is material sense a necessary preliminary to the understanding and expression of Spirit?"*[3] to which she replies, in part: *"If error is necessary to define or to reveal Truth, the answer is yes; but not otherwise."*[4]

The foregoing means that whenever the negation will best enforce the recognition of the presence of Truth, it will appear, claiming to be the

[1] Heb. 13:2. [2] S. & H. 267:24. [3] S. & H. 484:28. [4] S. & H. 485:1.

reality, for frequently the mortal understands the truth of being better when the negative form appears to him than when the positive form appears, because it arouses him to the necessity of reversing it.

The negative statement carries with it more discipline than the positive statement of Truth.

It challenges the human sense of good, and causes the mortal to move more quickly to the final triumph of Spirit over matter.

Regardless of the way in which Truth may appear — whether negatively or positively — remember that it is the same Truth. The only difference is that the negative appearance has to be *reversed,* in order to arrive at the positive Truth.

Truth is All-in-all, and into this All, nothing extraneous can enter.

Viewed from this standpoint, evil no longer has power to torment with the belief that it actually is an entity which can dethrone good as All-in-all.

The analysis of evil from the negative standpoint, reduces evil to its least importance and meaning in the process of its final disappearance.

Do not leave evil as a negative statement unreversed, but push on until thought relinquishes even that hold on error and acknowledges nothing but the absolute allness of good.

With this enlightenment, you are through with the negative. The negative has served its purpose.

"*In Christian Science the midnight hour will always be the bridal hour, until 'no night is there'*".[1] This means that the negative, which by its very nature must be reversed, is found to be "the bridal hour", Truth itself.

You never give the negative definition of the multiplication table a second thought. It does not exist for you, since "no night is there".

The recognition of the "negative" is only a quick way of reaching the conclusion that "*evil has no claims and was never a claimant*".[2]

Truth cannot exist both positively and negatively. "*The Science of Mind excludes opposites, and rests on unity.*"[3]

Mrs. Eddy is said to have written to a friend the following quotation, which is so true and applicable that it may well be supposed to have come from her pen: "*Whenever there seems to be a lack or need in your experience, that simply indicates the scientific fact that the seeming void is already supplied by God's gracious abundance. Then give thanks with your whole heart, because you have learned in Christian Science that God's supply is ever at hand.*"

[1]Mis. 276:15.   [2]No. 24:21.   [3]Ret. 75:18.

There could be no seeming lack unless the truth, the abundance that the "lack" is a lie about was actually present.

HOW TO HANDLE THE NEGATIVE

Because of this fact, the activities of malicious mind are discovered to be merely the negation of the activity of divine Mind; and when these are reversed, you find the very presence and power of good, and good only, for *"the reverse of error is true."*[1]

It is most important to understand this, or you will find yourself confronted, in spite of every argument to the contrary, with the subtle suggestion that evil, as evil, actually exists, and that good, therefore, is not All-in-all.

If you accept the negation as a reality, your power to reverse evil disappears. The suggestion of evil will become as truth itself to you, instead of being merely a negative interpretation of Truth, which needs only to be reversed to be seen as Truth.

Mrs. Eddy illustrates this in her statement: *"When examined in the light of divine Science, mortals present more than is detected upon the surface, since inverted thoughts and erroneous beliefs must be counterfeits of Truth. Thought is borrowed from a higher source than matter, and by reversal, errors serve as waymarks to the*

[1] S. & H. 442:18.

one Mind, in which all error disappears in celestial Truth."[1]

In photography, the lens inverts all objects in front of the camera, making them appear on the negative upside down; but the trained photographer, who never thinks in the language of the negative, sees the picture unreversed, in other words, positively.

This process is true also of the best instruments in surveying, but the engineer is never deceived.

The compositor reading type is another example of seeing correctly in spite of the appearances.

In like manner, *"Jesus beheld in Science the perfect man, who appeared to him where sinning mortal man appears to mortals. In this perfect man the Saviour saw God's own likeness, and this correct view of man healed the sick."*[2]

The only world Jesus accepted was the world of reality, of good. The only man, woman and child he saw was the presence of good.

This acceptance of the reality and the rejection of the lie appeared as the correcting or healing of the negative.

Jesus was the true photographer of Mind.

He saw being as it is, not as it appears in the camera of negation, the suppositional opposite. To him, the presence of God was the only presence.

[1] S. & H. 267:19.   [2] S. & H. 476:32.

When Pilate warned Jesus that he had power
to release him or to crucify him, Jesus, acknowledging God as All-power, replied, "Thou could-
est have no power at all . . . except it were given
thee from above".[1]

This was interpreting the suppositional opposite, the negation, positively. Jesus reversed
the false testimony and gained a greater *"knowledge of God from opposite facts, or phenomena."*[2]

This also enabled Jesus to come forth from
the tomb, demonstrating a knowledge of God far
beyond his previous understanding.

Jesus established his oneness with Principle,
with eternal Life, by reversing the pseudo-facts
or phenomena presented to him.

Had he not done this, he would have been of
as little benefit to mankind as was the thief who
was crucified with him.

The "paradise" that he promised to the re-
penting thief—"To-day shalt thou be with me in
paradise"[3]—would then have been to him only
the thief's paradise of release from the cross, instead of the wondrous paradise he attained in
his conscious victory over death and materiality,
over the grave, over the negation of Life.

That victory was the paradise of Jesus.

The release from agony was the paradise of
the thief.

[1] Jno. 19:11.   [2] Un. 36:8.   [3] Luke 23:43.

Both were interpretations of the one paradise.

Which interpretation do you desire?

Whether God appeared to Jesus in negative or positive language, made no difference to him.

He understood that the negative *reversed* is the positive and thus relinquished the negative for the positive.

"To teach the truth of life without using the word death, the suppositional opposite of life, were as impossible as to define truth and not name its opposite, error."[1]

There is no point where the negation, the suppositional opposite of Mind, ceases; because, having no entity of its own, there is nothing about it which can cease.

Its seeming existence is as infinite as the truth it belies or contradicts. Therefore, its only seeming cessation is its translation, by reversal, from the negative to the positive terms of Mind.

Like Paul, then, you rejoice at all so-called tribulations, even though they seem to be "infirmities . . . necessities, . . . distresses,"[2] for you know that, when *reversed*, these declare the infinite abundance and omnipresence of good.

You are the photographer of Mind; the truth of being is your camera.

This is what is meant by translating *"matter into its original language, which is Mind"*.[3]

[1]My. 235:2.   [2]Cor. 12:10.   [3]Hea. 7:9.

MATTER DEFINED

This brings us to our next consideration, the definition of the word "matter".

Matter seems to be omnipresent. The mortal's only sense of life is one of matter.

But matter is not a thing. Matter, to be known, must come as a sense of consciousness.

What kind of a sense? Apparently a finite one, for everything about matter suggests limitation—death.

But is this limitation true?

Can anything, coming as consciousness, be limited?

It cannot, for consciousness is infinite, boundless.

Then it is the false sense of consciousness entertained that constitutes the limitation, the matter.

It is this sense that has to be corrected through the understanding of the illimitability of consciousness, or Mind. This is again translating *"matter into its original language, which is Mind"*.[1]

When Jesus appeared through the closed door after the crucifixion, his disciples thought he was a ghost. He explained to them that, insofar as their sense of him was concerned, he was as solidly matter as they thought him to be. When they were convinced of this, their fear was gone.

[1] Hea. 7:9.

The question, how did Jesus take his body—matter—through a closed door remained for Christian Science to answer.

It is certain that if his own sense of body had been the concept which his disciples accepted, he could not have taken it through a closed door.

But his sense of body was spiritual, not material.

He had given matter back to its original, Mind; and that enabled him to have his body wherever he wished to be.

This proved that body is purely spiritual.

Body, therefore, is always at your service, exactly as is the multiplication table.

There is only one body, namely, that which Jesus brought forth from the tomb and took through the closed door.

That one omnipresent body can never be sick, sinning or dying.

Thus, the erroneous sense called matter is simply an erroneous concept of what Mind is. *"What the human mind terms matter and spirit indicates states and stages of consciousness."*[1]

MALICIOUS MIND AND ITS OFFSPRING

As you have established that the divine Mind could not be without that to which it is Mind—its idea, or man—so, also, malicious mind must,

[1] S. & H. 573:10

suppositionally, have that to which it is mind—its idea, or man.

Because there is only one malicious mind, there can be only one malicious man.

What constitutes the man of this mind?

Everything that this mind is, all that is finite and mortal, constitutes this so-called man.

Malicious mind, being the suppositional opposite of the Mind that is Life, must be death; hence the mortal, or man of this mind, is the presence of death.

His one occupation is actively to show forth death.

When Paul said, "to be carnally minded is death",[1] he was referring to this nature and origin of the so-called mortal, whose mind, being death, must always express itself in its own likeness.

It is a fact acknowledged, even by the medical fraternity, that the seed of death is always present in the so-called seed of life that produces the mortal.

The very essence of material life is always accompanied by its own destruction.

Animal poison, the genesis of the foetus, the supposed producer of the mortal, is the presence of death from the beginning, and finally brings to pass the death of the mortal.

[1] Rom. 8:6.

This concept of inevitable death attaches itself to the entire belief of matter-creation, throughout its various kingdoms: animal, vegetable and mineral. This belief of matter-creation perpetuates its life only by dying—over and over again.

This is necessarily the nature of suppositional finiteness.

Because malicious mind is supposition, it suppositionally exists as long as does that of which it is the suppositional opposite.

Because it is suppositionally finite, it must express limitation and death.

Because immortal man expresses infinite Life, perfection and harmony, the suppositional opposite, mortal man, expresses infinite death, imperfection and discord.

All that malicious mind is, mortal man must be in every detail, because he is that whereby this mind exists and is shown forth.

The body of this mind, like the man of this mind, is ever about its father's business, showing forth the reverse or negation of all that divine Mind is.

But since *"by reversal, errors serve as way-marks to the one Mind,"*[1] the omnipresence of perfection is constantly being declared.

What is the law of this malicious mind?

Having established divine Principle as the one and only law, infinitely good, always operating

[1] S. & H. 267:24.

harmoniously to maintain eternally the perfection of being, you find that its suppositional opposite, the negative, must claim to operate, just as lawfully, to the destruction of being.

By its very nature, according to the law of opposites, the law of malicious mind arrogates to itself the infinite reverse of infinite Mind.

The life it gives to its man or offspring, is death; its substance is shadow; its reality is a pure supposition "For the wind passeth over it, and it is gone; and the place thereof shall know it no more."[1]

The negation, until reversed, "like an atom of dust thrown into the face of spiritual immensity, is dense blindness instead of a scientific eternal consciousness of creation."[2]

MAINTAINING THE RIGHT ATTITUDE

In recognizing the guises, and analyzing the activities under which this so-called mind operates, it is imperative to remember that the false, correctly interpreted, declares the truth.

Right there where the false seems to claim presence and entity, is the perfection of being, else the false could not seem to be.

You are actually strengthened and fortified by the claim of evil; for, as Mrs. Eddy says, "*it gives one opportunity to handle the error, and when*

[1] Ps. 103:16.   [2] S. & H. 263:28.

mastering it one gains in the rules of metaphysics, and thereby learns more of its divine Principle.[1]

Every semblance of presence, power, action and intelligence that evil seems to assume, is borrowed from the one Mind, and is only suppositionally in evidence. It is some finite sense that *"peers from its cloister with amazement and attempts to pattern the infinite."*[2]

Bear this constantly in mind, or the structure you erect in accounting for mortal man and his material sense of life will seem so real to you that you cannot destroy it.

Keep before you the realization that what you are now thinking about and analyzing is but supposition. Then you will forge ahead and actually enjoy dealing with this suppositional, this negative fabrication, called malicious mind and its man.

FALSE THEOLOGY

We are now ready to consider some of the activities operating as so-called laws of this one malicious mind.

The most prominent activity of this mind, perhaps, is its theological belief.

True theology means man's relationship to God.

False theology embraces the countless false beliefs about the mortal's relation to his maker, whom he mistakenly calls God.

[1] Mis. 221:3. [2] S. & H. 263:24.

In the analysis now being made, we find him to be not God at all, but a false sense, the negation of God, "a liar, and the father of it."[1]

There is not a single branch of false theology (and you can use this term to embrace not only what is called Christian theology, but pagan theology, also) that does not teach preparation for what it calls after-life or heaven.

The fundamental basis of all false theological teaching, no matter how fervently it may instruct you to be good here and now, is preparation for death and the promise of reward, heaven after death.

Each branch of this teaching virtually encourages dying. If heaven, perfect harmony, is to be attained only by dying, is that not proclaiming the necessity for dying?

Jesus said, "I am come that they might have life, and that they might have it more abundantly."[2] He illustrated what he meant by life and more abundant life, by overcoming death and proving that it had no power over him or over his body.

In doing this, he showed that death was a fraud—that it was not the gateway to Life, for he said, "Whosoever liveth and believeth in me shall never die",[3] and Paul also declared, "The last enemy that shall be destroyed is death."[4]

[1]Jno. 8:44.   [2]Jno. 10:10.   [3]Jno. 11:26.   [4]1 Cor. 15:26.

Then, the underlying teaching of false theology, that death is the gateway to Life and harmony, is the exact opposite or negation of what Jesus taught true theology to be. *"Death is not the result of Truth but of error, and one error will not correct another."*[1]

False teaching is always from the same source, the mind that "is enmity against God: for it is not subject to the law of God, neither indeed can be."[2]

The teaching that all must die in order to live, is the supposititious opposite, the negative, of the fact that only as Life is seen to be eternal, here and now, is more life obtainable.

However, death is only one of the many limitations implanted and fostered by false theology.

So-called charity, as practised by false theology, is based on the mistaken assumption that good is not omnipresent, but that, through the human mind's good deeds, this lack of omnipresent good is supplied.

Nothing could be more pernicious than this, for it encourages a stronger belief in the absence of good, by assuming that good must be supplied.

Metaphysically, such giving, continued, dooms its victim to perpetual incompleteness and helplessness. No true benefit can ever be thus bestowed.

[1] S. & H. 486:12.   [2] Rom. 8:7.

The only giving that is of value is the giving that knows the omnipresence of all good, and that insists on seeing this good as omnipresent, even as Jesus saw the loaves and fishes, and the money in the mouth of the fish.

Such giving alone blesses.

If Jesus had thought he was supplying something that was not already present, he would have denied the allness of his God by giving, and he would then have been on the same plane of thought as those who believed that they were hungry.

But he knew that Principle and its idea is always one: "Son, thou art ever with me, and all that I have is thine."[1]

If he had been one with them in their thinking, how could he have fed the multitude?

The metaphysician gives freely only as he understands that there is no lack, no need, because infinite substance is omnipresent.

"*The noblest charity is to prevent a man from accepting charity*".[2]

He who reaches out to another's abundance to supply his need, is looking away from God to that which is finite and must in the end fail. He who learns that he has the ability and right to infinite good within the sanctuary of his own understanding is blessed.

[1] Luke 15:31. [2] Mis. ix:3.

One could enumerate indefinitely the phases of false theology which show the same activity of evil under the guise of good. Each of these, being the negation of good, must be reversed to be of any value.

The rule in Christian Science is one Principle and one idea, and naught else.

Never admit a "third", or you lose your measure of heaven, because this *"is the great and only danger in the path that winds upward."*[1]

THE NATURE AND LAWS OF MATERIA MEDICA

Another very active agency of this mind is materia medica, with all its dogma, experimental theory, and guess-work.

This term, materia medica, includes every material theory for benefiting the health of the mortal.

The one medicine is Truth, divine Mind, the medicine that Jesus used in restoring the withered hand, healing the leper, raising the dead, stilling the storm—the understanding of being, that destroys everything unlike good by proving its non-existence.

Every so-called law of materia medica is based on the concept of a human being who has a beginning and therefore an end.

[1] Mis. 9:29.

Materia medica has not a single teaching that is not based on the finiteness, materiality and limitation of life.

In materia medica there is not a ray of light to be found that points to eternal Life here and now.

It is of its father: matter, limitation, death; and the lusts of its father it does, has been doing from the beginning, and will continue to do throughout, until its end.

Those who pursue materia medica as a profession and give their lives to serve and promote its theories, do so with a deep desire to do good. But they are none the less victims of a false reasoning that defrauds their best efforts and leads to certain death.

Mrs. Eddy makes this statement, *"The hosts of Æsculapius are flooding the world with diseases, because they are ignorant that the human mind and body are myths."*[1] But she adds, *"Great respect is due the motives and philanthropy of the higher class of physicians. We know that if they understood the Science of Mind-healing, and were in possession of the enlarged power it confers to benefit the race physically and spiritually, they would rejoice with us."*[2]

By basing all being on a beginning, materia medica establishes itself as the activity of finite

[1] S. & H. 150:31.   [2] S. & H. 151:8.

mind. As such, it is the exact opposite of the medicine of divine Mind, with its life and more abundant life, without beginning and without end.

Has materia medica, as the suppositional opposite of the medicine of Mind, any laws?

Does it operate as law, and if so, what are its laws?

Are they to be acknowledged, respected and submitted to?

Materia medica, being fundamentally based on the belief that matter is, and its every deduction being made from that original premise, naturally claims its most potent law to be a law of matter.

Is matter a law giver?

Can matter, as such, or in the form of a body composed of chemical elements (water, salt, sugar, starch, lime, magnesia, etc.) which materia medica claims constitute the substance of the body of the mortal, make laws?

Law-making is the prerogative of cause.

Self-evidently, matter is not cause, but effect. As effect, it is impossible for it to make laws.

Where then, can there be any law of matter?

Material scientists, wiser than their medical brethren, today declare frankly that matter is not matter at all, but is what they designate as a "mathematical formula."

In plain words, matter is not a thing, but a thought.

This new definition of matter coincides with the definition given by Mrs. Eddy in 1866, when she discovered the Science of being and called it Christian Science. She wrote: *"Divine Science, rising above physical theories, excludes matter, resolves things into thoughts, and replaces the objects of material sense with spiritual ideas."*[1]

"Matter is a misstatement of Mind"[2] which means a false sense of Mind.

Matter is the name given to the misstatement.

A misstatement means a mind-error.

Because of this, everything that appears to the mortal appears materially.

The mortal sees and knows only as his mind directs. Since that mind, being carnal, states all things in terms of misstatement, or matter, the mortal is cognizant only of materiality, and consequently calls all things material.

Can a misstatement be a law? Since it cannot, there are no laws of matter.

Law is the emanation of Mind, of Spirit—the one medicine.

To repeat the significant statement of John Scott Haldane, the Oxford Biologist: "Materiality, once a scientific theory, is now the fatalistic creed of thousands, but materialism is nothing

[1] S. & H. 123:12.   [2] Mis. 174:2.

better than a superstition on the same level as a belief in witches and devils."

Is not this an absolute and complete repudiation of all so-called materialism or matter by a material scientist himself?

Other so-called laws attaching to materia medica are its laws of anatomy, physiology, hygiene, nature, heredity, and so forth.

Analyzing them from the standpoint of metaphysics, we find that the true import of these terms is the exact opposite of the meaning assigned to them in popular thought.

ANATOMY. Anatomy, as conceived by materia medica, would make man's life the sport of material formation. It would compress man into a material structure.

If there is no matter, as such, there is no material form to affect man.

However, there is the true anatomy of Mind, always maintaining man as the perfect structure, as the image of perfection.

This anatomy shows every atom to be in its right place and eternally about its Father's business as the expression of Principle, even as two times two is always about its principle's business. It is never out of place and never malformed.

The anatomy of Mind, which always governs its idea harmoniously, is the one anatomy of the man of God.

"This idea or divine essence was, and is, forever about the Father's business; heralding the Principle of health, holiness, and immortality."[1]

Mrs. Eddy makes clear the fundamental difference between the spiritual and material viewpoints of anatomy in the following statement: *"The Christian Scientist, through understanding mental anatomy, discerns and deals with the real cause of disease. The material physician gropes among phenomena, which fluctuate every instant under influences not embraced in his diagnosis, and so he may stumble and fall in the darkness."*[2]

God's law is the one and only law of anatomy and of all formations.

PHYSIOLOGY pertains to functions, while anatomy pertains to structure.

It must be as true of physiology as it is of anatomy that, because there is no matter, there can be no material function.

Every function of man is directly controlled by God, Mind, and is wholly a Mind-operation, for man is the functioning of God.

Since Mind embraces within itself all functioning, every function expresses the law of Mind.

"Every function of the real man is governed by the divine Mind. . . . . All that really exists is the divine Mind and its idea, and in this Mind

[1] Mis. 163:30.   [2] S. & H. 462:31.

the entire being is found harmonious and eternal."[1]

Man, having nothing underived from Principle, must, and does, express only what his origin, God, is.

The law of true physiology is the law of God, governing and controlling all functions.

"Mind is supreme; and yet we make more of matter, and lean upon it for health and life. Mind, that governs the universe, governs every action of the body as directly as it moves a planet and controls the muscles of the arm."[2]

HYGIENE, NATURE and HEREDITY are analyzed in the same manner.

By reversing the material sense of them and thus arriving at their true metaphysical meaning as qualities and characteristics of God, we find them to be the very operation of Mind.

Activity, in whatever form it may appear, is always the ceaseless activity of God, the eternal law of good.

In one sense materia medica is the generic term for the false sense of all these laws.

A false sense, however, is merely human belief, never law.

The belief, embracing the believer, is one; and that one is the false belief that there is a supposititious opposite of the one Mind, existing inde-

[1] S. & H. 151:20   [2] Peo. 8:16.

pendently instead of as simply the negation of the one Mind.

As previously stated no name, in and of itself, has any harmful meaning or effect.

Every name is borrowed from reality.

Consciousness alone can give meaning to any term; and every term is a definition of consciousness in one of its infinitely varied aspects.

When the false sense is abandoned by reversal, the true meaning is found.

Other activities of this suppositional mind may be enumerated as follows:

New Thought, Unity, Faith Cure, hypnotism, mesmerism, auto-suggestion, astrology with its horoscope, mediumship, spiritism and spiritualism, agnosticism, atheism, theosophy, soothsaying, esoteric magic, fatalism, palmistry, numerology, destiny, and so forth.

The activities of this so-called mind are as infinite, suppositionally, as the activities of divine Mind are infinite in reality.

There is no point where the supposition ends, inasmuch as it has no substance or reality of its own, but merely parallels the one Mind and its activity unto infinity.

Like every lie, the supposition or negation invariably follows the truth; and like every lie, it must be without reality—except that every lie, *reversed,* is the truth.

The basis of all these activities, when dissected and analyzed, is found to be finiteness and limitation—hence, death.

Death is a word which includes all finity and limitation. The slightest sense of limitation includes death within itself.

Therefore, to entertain a material sense is to entertain death.

NEW THOUGHT is the belief that one mind, through its thinking, can control and benefit another mind.

If, for the moment, the control seems to be good, that does not in any way change the evil of it. If you have one mind controlling another, you have two minds, and such a premise denies the allness of God as the one and only Mind.

The acceptance of more than one Mind embraces the full measure of evil, for if God is not all, then evil is something.

New Thought is the negation of the First Commandment, "I am the Lord thy God, . . . Thou shalt have no other gods before me"[1]—no other mind beside the one Ego, the one I, the one Mind.

UNITY, the name of a religious sect, confuses man with God.

[1]Ex. 20:2, 3.

It says that if man is not God now, he will become God through the process of time and improvement.

If man could ever become God, then there would be a time, as you have proved, when there would be no God, or a time when there would be no man.

Either alternative would destroy being.

There can be no being without *both* Principle and idea, both God and that to which He is God —both noumenon and phenomenon.

The destruction of the one would be the inevitable destruction of the other.

True Unity is man's eternal oneness with God.

It is not, as its negation, the false "Unity", declares, man's eventual usurpation of God's identity, by the process of man's becoming God.

FAITH CURE is the belief that blind, emotional faith and trust in God will bring more of good than already exists. Mrs. Eddy declares, *"Belief is virtually blindness, when it admits Truth without understanding it."*[1]

Faith in the perfection of the principle of numbers will not bring about the right solution of a mathematical problem.

Only the understanding of the principle of numbers solves the problem.

[1]Ret. 54:14.

"He that believeth on me, the works that I do shall he do also; and greater works than these shall he do",[1] said Jesus. But "He that believeth" means he that *understands* the truth taught by Jesus.

True faith is a complete understanding of God as the one Mind. It includes within itself all that is meant by faith, hope, assurance and confidence. *"Spirit is all-knowing; this precludes the need of believing."*[2]

HYPNOTISM is the belief that there is more than one mind, and that one particular mind can act as the mental volition of another mind.

But there cannot be two minds.

If they were alike they would be one and the same.

If unlike, they would presuppose two original causes, and two causes would be equivalent to no cause.

Therefore, since there is only one Mind, there is no mind for hypnotism to use.

Because the suppositional mind is the negation of the one divine Mind, it is suppositionally one. Therefore, it could no more be two—one controlling the other—than there could be two Gods, one controlling the other.

Hypnotism is the negation of man's communion with God—the negation of the eternal one-

[1] Jno. 14:12.   [2] S. & H. 487:15.

ness and perpetual coincidence of God and His idea.

Reverse this negation, and it is seen as the harmonious action of man, controlled by his Maker.

MESMERISM is another phase of the same falsity—the belief that one mind can control and influence another.

God is the only Mind and His control is not domination of, but oneness with, His idea.

AUTO-SUGGESTION is the belief that the individual can hypnotize himself and that he benefits himself by so doing.

This is in no way different from other forms of hypnotic suggestion.

It again implies two minds, the one doing the suggesting, and the other, labeled the subconscious mind, receiving the suggestion. This would necessitate more than one mind.

Suggestion always implies a mental communication whether to one's own so-called mind or to that of another.

Auto-suggestion is the denial of God as the one and only Mind, the negation of the ever-operative communion between God and man.

"Thought passes from God to man, but neither sensation nor report goes from material body to Mind. The intercommunication is always from God to His idea, man."[1]

[1] S. & H. 284:30.

ASTROLOGY attempts to prove that man's destiny is governed by the stars and planets.

It is true that "The heavens declare the glory of God",[1] for man, including the universe, always shows forth the glory of God. Man is the activity of God. Then the heavens, in declaring the glory of God, declare the glory of man, the infinity of man, the perfection of man.

Is the planetary system cause or effect?

It is effect, and effect does not govern effect.

Since both are effect, the heavens no more govern man, than man governs the heavens.

Astrology, with its horoscope, is the negation of the Scriptural declaration: "All things work together for good to them that love God".[2]

The false concept of astrology must be reversed in order to find the infinity of Mind expressing itself in the glorification and eternity of its own idea—man.

That is true astrology and man's true horoscope.

MEDIUMSHIP implies an intermediary.

There can be no medium between God and man because there is no separation between Principle and its idea.

The eternal communion between Principle and its idea is the only medium. Therefore, the Holy Ghost is the one true medium.

[1]Ps. 19:1.   [2]Rom. 8:28.

The negation of this, the mediumship of malicious mind, is the supposition that something can operate as a medium between the mortal and his mind.

"This giant sin is the sin against the Holy Ghost spoken of in Matt. xii. 31, 32."[1]

You have established that, in the realm of belief, the mortal is one with malicious mind, just as, in reality, the immortal is one with divine Mind.

There can no more be a medium or a "third" in the one case than in the other.

To affirm that a so-called medium, or intermediary, can come between man and his God, is to destroy the oneness or unity of Principle and its idea, on which the whole of being is established.

One God and one man, and the forever-communion of them, constitutes the Trinity—God, the Father; man, the son; and the Holy Ghost or Spirit, the true Medium—the eternal at-one-ment of Father and son.

In whatever form mediumship presents itself—be it spiritualistic, medical, academic, or *ecclesiastical*—it must always be recognized as the pernicious activity of the one malicious mind and be instantly reversed, to permit the uninterrupted communion of divine Mind and its idea.

[1] Mis. 55 :13.

SPIRITISM is the belief in spirits many.

It assumes that one spirit can affect and influence another.

Because Spirit is infinite, there is but one Spirit, God.

There cannot be many spirits, because there is one God, not many gods. The suppositional opposite of infinite Spirit is not spirits, but finite spirit—necessarily singular, never plural.

Therefore, one spirit could never dominate another, either here or in the so-called "hereafter" because there is only one.

SPIRITUALISM, as it is generally known, is a phase of spiritism. Specifically, it claims that a departed spirit can influence a living mortal.

The argument against this false belief is the same as in the case of spiritism.

The one Spirit governs all. But nothing can govern Spirit. Spiritism and spiritualism, when reversed, declare the oneness and allness of Spirit.

AGNOSTICISM is the belief that the existence of God and man, including the universe, is unknowable, therefore open to doubt.

The fallacy of such a belief lies in the fact that unless there first exists that which is doubted, it cannot be doubted.

Conscious being cannot be, unless there is first that to which it is *being*.

Then the very fact of the existence of doubt, or question, is the answer to agnosticism. There must be both effect and that which caused it, the question and that which caused the question. The one implies the other.

God must be, or there could be no question about His being. Therefore, His very being insures the continuity of the doubt or Agnosticism.

False agnosticism is the negation of the assurance of this continuity.

Reversed, it declares the complete knowableness and comprehensibility of God and man. "Be still, and know that I am God".[1]

ATHEISM is the assertion of a positive disbelief in the reality of God.

The assertion would be impossible unless there were some one to assert it.

Even the professed atheist does not quite rise to the point of believing himself to be self-created. So he ascribes his origin to some sort of cause, however ignoble. He may even declare that he has evolved from primitive protoplasm.

But finally he is confronted with the question: Who created protoplasm?

Cause is. Even atheism is forced to acknowledge this.

No vagaries of human belief can destroy cause. Your own identity forever declares it.

[1] Ps. 46:10.

There can be no effect without cause. Effect is the actual definition of cause.

Christian Science shows what cause is, and proves that both cause and effect are eternal.

Atheism is merely the negation or denial of the eternality of good.

Reversed, it proclaims the allness of God, now and forever.

THEOSOPHY, reduced to its simplest term, is a belief that life is attained by a process of repeated deaths.

Were this true, the Scriptures could not be fulfilled, since there would be no end to dying. Dying would continue throughout eternity.

The theory that the mortal dies, only to be reincarnated, that he may further work out the problem of evil, would declare infinite death necessary. This is manifestly a self-defeating argument.

Malicious mind, under the guise of good, lures its victim on to expect death, and more abundant death. "The thief cometh not, but for to steal, and to kill, and to destroy: I am come that they might have life, and that they might have it more abundantly."[1]

Truth is perpetual death to error. This was demonstrated in its completeness by the resur-

[1] Jno. 10:10.

rection and the ascension, which spelled death to the belief of death.

Jesus died to error and so lived to Truth. He thus showed forth the very reverse of false theosophy.

To "die daily",[1] as Paul used the term, is the truth about which theosophy is the negation.

SOOTHSAYING is the Biblical word for the belief that something intervenes between God and man, namely, the soothsayer.

Isaiah said, "When they shall say unto you, Seek unto them that have familiar spirits, and unto wizards that peep, and that mutter: should not a people seek unto their God?"[2]

With one Spirit, infinite intelligence, guiding and directing its own idea, there is nothing else left. There are no "familiar spirits" or "wizards" to give false advice.

FORTUNE TELLING, CARD READING, and CRYSTAL GAZING are all phases of soothsaying.

Each claims to usurp the place of the one intelligence and act as a go-between. Each denies that man, as the idea of God, is directly enlightened and controlled by God, and that he is the very activity of God at all times.

God's government and control of man are supreme and infinite, needing no human assistance.

[1] 1 Cor. 15:31.   [2] Isa. 8:19.

ESOTERIC MAGIC simply means secret or unseen influence; sorcery; necromancy.

Embraced in this category are the so-called magical practices of the natives of India, the Hawaiian Islands, Africa, and other regions inhabited by aborigines.

All are based on the supposition that one mind can influence another mind, either for good or for evil—a premise which you have already proved impossible.

There is nothing secret about Mind. Like intelligence, it is open and free to one and all.

It is unknown only to that which is not one with it: to materiality.

To itself and its idea it is always revealed.

Mind is all-knowing and all-knowable.

Materiality, in its essence, is evil mentality calling itself superfine mind.

Knowing this, you cannot be deceived. All that Mind knows and has, you know and have.

Mrs. Eddy sums up all these beliefs of malicious mind tersely and accurately: *"Surely the people of the Occident know that esoteric magic and Oriental barbarisms will neither flavor Christianity nor advance health and length of days."*[1]

FATALISM is the false doctrine that every event is predestined and inevitable, and that a predes-

[1]Mis. 29:24.

tined fate will overtake man in spite of anything he can do to avert it.

It is true that the fate of man is settled. As the activity of God, his fate is eternal Life, infinite harmony, and perfect joy.

The belief that man's fate is the exact reverse of this, that it must culminate in death, is the negation which must be reversed to allow the truth to show forth.

True fatalism is the understanding of man's destiny, his eternal oneness with Principle.

PALMISTRY declares that the contour and lines of the hand have something to do with the length of life and with the eccentricities of the mortal.

Have you not established the impossibility of the belief that one effect can control what appears as another effect? Then how could the hand of the mortal control him? Is not all control vested in cause?

The truth about palmistry is that the hand of Mind's outlining is the activity of Mind.

The suppositional opposite of this activity is the activity of malicious mind, that needs to be *reversed,* in order to discover the true Palmistry.

PHRENOLOGY is the pseudo-science that says **that the shape of the head** declares the character, intelligence and ability of the mortal.

The head of Mind, *"the universe, including man"*,[1] testifies to the infinite intelligence, perfection and wisdom of Mind.

Nothing can interfere with this wisdom.

All being declares it.

The suppositional opposite of this one infinite wisdom, called finite wisdom and dependent upon a contour of matter, shows, when reversed, the presence of God as all there is to phrenology.

PHYSIOGNOMY, likewise, would reveal the character of the mortal by the outline of his features.

The face, that is Mind's face, does declare the glory of Mind. It shows forth the beauty, loveliness and animation of Mind.

"As for me, I will behold thy face in righteousness: I shall be satisfied, when I awake, with thy likeness."[2]

Understanding God as the one Physiognomist, destroys the false sense or negation of physiognomy.

NUMEROLOGY is the assumption that man is governed and controlled by numbers.

The Bible is full of numbers, which stand as symbols for Mind, but never for the negation or suppositional opposite.

[1]S. & H. 295:5.   [2]Ps. 17:15.

Numbers, like all else, declare the omnipresence of intelligence; but they cannot be reversed to declare the negation.

Numerology, in its true sense is Mind defining itself as number. It declares the presence, reality and permanency of Mind, omnipotent and omnipresent good.

DESTINY, like fatalism, would teach that the life of mortal man is predestined to take a certain course, regardless of his efforts to change it.

Destiny was formerly accepted as a religious belief, and was interpreted as predestination and foreordination. This belief maintained that what was predestined and foreordained would inevitably come to pass.

Man, as the activity of God, is destined to all good and cannot be deprived of this destiny.

Good is his law of destiny; and this truth is the reversal of every false sense.

One could go on indefinitely, defining terms and showing them all, in their true sense, to mean the oneness and perfection of Mind and its idea. But the analysis of these few, chosen from a limitless variety, makes clear how important it is to understand words in their true sense, and to interpret rightly *all* that presents itself—to "pray without ceasing."

Jesus' command to "Agree with thine adversary quickly",[1] means to reverse the false sense quickly before you accept it.

When you thus "agree", you instantly see the one Mind as All-in-all, and that every word declares this allness.

This spiritual activity of thought is the true meaning of Elias, as defined by Mrs. Eddy, *"Prophecy; spiritual evidence opposed to material sense; Christian Science, with which can be discerned the spiritual fact of whatever the material senses behold; the basis of immortality."*[2]

This once again translates material belief, matter, *"into its original language, which is Mind, and gives the spiritual instead of the material signification."*[3]

As you take every word back to Mind, you there find its true meaning. This is the only way in which "ye shall know the truth, and the truth shall make you free."[4]

[1]Matt. 5:25.   [2]S. & H. 585:9.   [3]Hea. 7:9.   [4]Jno. 8:32.

CHAPTER VII

SUBDIVISIONS OF MALICIOUS MIND

Christian Science has been attacked with every vicious invective, for its teaching in regard to animal magnetism. It has been criticized more on this score, perhaps, than on any other.

Ignorance has laughed at the idea that mental influence could affect any one. It has called malicious animal magnetism the new devil of the Christian Scientist.

But is not this derision exactly what one should expect from ignorance?

How else could evil hope to protect itself from the inevitable destruction that must follow the intelligent uncovering of that which evil —malicious mental malpractice—really is?

THE PRESENT TREND

Yet is not every new theory, advanced by so-called material science, the destruction of matter, as such, and the enthroning of Mind as all?

Sir James Jeans, on page 296 of "The New Background of Science" says:

"To this present day science adds that, at the farthest point she has so far reached, much, and possibly all, that was not mental has disappeared, and nothing new has come in that was not mental."

Is not material science, then, proving that mentality is all that is ever being dealt with, and that this is true, regardless of the appearance, whether called common matter or mind?

In view of this, let us consider how this mind appears and what its subdivisions are.

THE CHANNELS OF GOOD AND THEIR DENIAL

Accepting the deductions that have been worked out thus far, in this class, we find that the two channels through which God, the one Mind, becomes known are Christ, or Christianity, and Christian Science.

In the appearing of God, He is seen and understood, first: personally, as Christ Jesus ("he that hath seen me, hath seen the Father"[1]) ; and second: impersonally, as Science and Health, which is the scientific explanation of the Life demonstrated by Christ Jesus.

Malicious mind, being the negative or suppositional opposite of divine Mind, is the denial of this appearing of God as Christ and Christian Science. This denial is all there is to matter and so-called material mentality.

EVIL IN THE REALM OF MATERIALITY

Malicious mind, in its crudest and most common form as matter, first appears as non-intelli-

[1] Jno. 14:9.

gent, lifeless, inanimate and harmless. On the surface, it does not show its real nature as malicious mind.

Second, we find it appearing in more animate form as the good mortal, but still seemingly harmless.

In its form as a good mortal, there is little to indicate the true nature of malicious mind, except the fact that the good mortal always operates from the standpoint of material good now, and future good that is to be attained through the process of dying.

The "good" mortal chooses between his own finite sense of good and a supposed actual evil.

Believing death to be inevitable, the "good" mortal devotes much time and thought to preparation for that state, with its imaginary reward, despite Jesus' teaching, "I am come that they might have life, and that they might have it more abundantly."[1]

Third, this malicious mind boldly comes out as a bad mortal, imbued with criminal instincts, one who deliberately attempts to kill through material means.

The supreme illustration of this is the crucifixion of Jesus.

Deliberate effort to kill through material means is the last phase of malicious mind's appearing under the guise of matter.

[1] Jno. 10:10.

There is nothing more for malicious mind to do or that it can do *as matter*.

These three phases, (1) matter, *per se,* (2) the good mortal, (3) the bad mortal, represent the suppositional opposite or negation of what Christ Jesus, the activity of divine Mind, personally represents.

Jesus experienced, and rose above, the most vicious form of brutality in the realm of matter.

EVIL IN THE REALM OF MENTALITY

The fourth step in the analysis of malicious mind is its appearance in the realm of evil mentality. This is the negation of Christian Science which is the operation of pure Mind without personal accompaniment.

We have now arrived at an understanding of evil as no longer operating under the guise of matter at all, but operating as pure evil mentality.

In this phase, it again presents itself first as ostensibly harmless; as, for instance, the human mind operating to heal through mesmerism, therapeutic suggestion, New Thought, the subconscious mind, and all the other vagaries of mental influence based on the belief that one mind can influence another for good.

As diagnosed by Christian Science this is the exact opposite of the one infinite Mind, operating as pure Mind, even though appearing as idea correcting everything contrary to good.

Divine Mind never appears as one mind controlling another, for this would imply two minds, thus dethroning Mind's oneness and allness.

All mental control, based upon the belief of minds many, is essentially evil, however "good" its aims may be.

The fifth and final phase of malicious mind comes as deliberate mental assassination through mental suggestion alone, no longer using a belief of matter as a mask behind which to hide. This is called malicious mental malpractice — evil operating as wrong practice in the realm of mentality.

Jesus prophesied that evil, in the last days, would show itself as Satan standing in the holy place, standing as the very mental volition or mind of its victim.

This last phase shows the true character of evil, malicious mind, in its sole purpose to produce death and annihilation, for all control means limitation, death.

ALL EVIL ONE AND THE SAME

But there is no difference, actually, between the first phase, called matter, and the last, called malicious mental malpractice, or evil operating wholly mentally to bring about the destruction of its victim.

Matter, on the surface, may seem to be something entirely apart from you and perfectly innocent and harmless. But, upon close examination, you realize that you are aware of it only because it comes as consciousness to you, and hence it appears as your very mentality.

Coming as consciousness, what must its language be?

As your mind, your ego, the "I" of you, it says, I am lifeless, actionless, harmless, inert. But it is the same consciousness that comes to you as hypnotic suggestion or malicious mental malpractice in its final form.

For the malicious hypnotizer must suggest to his victim: I am mindless, actionless, etc., to accomplish his purpose; and such suggestions, if accepted, achieve their ultimate end—the hypnotic illusion of death and annihilation.

Matter and malicious mental malpractice are equally evil because they are identical in nature—both mental perceptions, both operating as consciousness.

Understanding this, you can no more desire matter in any form than you can desire evil mentality.

Because you have found malicious mind as the one all-malicious mind, you realize that it must and does always operate as the mind of the mortal.

It never comes as *you* but always as *I;* "*I* am lifeless, *I* am mindless, *I* cannot think", etc.

Unless evil operated as "I" how could it operate as your mind? Your mind operates as "*I* see; *I* feel; *I* know;" and so on. To operate at all, evil must come as this "I".

Then there is no difference whatsoever between one manifestation of malicious mind and another.

Its manifestations appear on a rising scale from inanimate matter, to the good mortal; the bad mortal; ignorant mental malpractice; and finally malicious mental malpractice.

But you are not deceived, because, as a metaphysician, you know that these various manifestations are all one and the same malicious mind.

In the light of Christian Science, all of these phases are seen as the mere negation of divine Mind and its activity.

By reversal, the omnipresence of good is actually declared.

By denying good, the acknowledgment is made that there is good to be denied.

A false suggestion of malicious mind may come to one; *"but if with the certainty of Science he knows that an error of belief has not the power of Truth, and cannot, does not, produce the slightest effect, it has no power over him. Thus a mental malpractitioner may lose his power to harm by a false mental argument; for it gives one opportunity to handle the error, and when mastering it one gains in the rules of metaphysics, and thereby learns more of its divine Principle."*[1]

[1]Mis. 220:30.

CHAPTER VIII

ESSENTIALS OF RIGHT PRACTICE

Having established all that the true signifies, together with all that is meant by the suppositional opposite or negation, the next logical step in practice is to show how the true or positive, with its pinions of understanding, spontaneously translates the false or negative, thereby leaving the positive as All-in-all.

The practice of Christian Science, like the practice of any science that involves a principle, is concerned only incidentally with the correcting of mistakes.

Just as in mathematics one studies the science of numbers without a thought of correcting problems, so in Christian Science one studies the Science of being, and not the mistakes of so-called being designated as sickness, sin and death.

Christian Science is the Science of being and must be studied as unselfishly and impersonally as mathematics.

The understanding of Christian Science, as of mathematics, results spontaneously in the elimination of every mistake.

In both cases the truth of that which *is* precludes the possibility of the existence of anything unlike that which *is*.

This fact brings tremendous freedom to thinking. It destroys the mesmeric belief that Christian Science is a method of healing, and reveals it instead as the very Science of being. The realization of this bends energy in the right direction——that of gaining understanding.

Solomon said, "With all thy getting get understanding".[1] Understanding is invariably accompanied by wisdom and intelligence, and Christian Science practice is the activity of wisdom and intelligence.

PRACTITIONER

God as All-in-all, embracing within Himself all that is meant by cause and effect, must necessarily be all that is meant by the term Practitioner, and therefore is the one Practitioner.

The practice of this one Practitioner is His effect, His man, the idea of God.

To practise is to show forth.

In the practice of Christian Science, it is God, the one Practitioner, that is shown forth.

Having also established God as the one intelligence, you find that this one intelligence must be the one Practitioner.

Because He is the one intelligence, He embraces all that intelligence embraces.

The academic degrees: A.B., D.D., M.D., D.C.L., and so on, designate phases of intelligence; and any one entitled to any of these de-

[1] Prov. 4:7.

grees is supposed to understand the subject matter implied by the letters.

The one intelligence, being the one Practitioner, must include within His infinite understanding all the understanding symbolized by these letters.

Therefore, God is the one M.D. and includes within Himself all there is to know about anatomy, physiology, ontology, hygiene, and so forth. There is nothing hidden from or unrevealed to this infinite intelligence, this one M.D. He understands all that is meant by Doctor of Medicine.

PRACTICE

Practice means to show forth; hence it must be the showing forth or manifestation of the one Practitioner.

Because God is the one Practitioner, He is shown forth in perfect practice, which is His idea, or man.

Jesus said of the true man, the perfect practice of God, "he that hath seen me hath seen the Father".[1]

Whatever Practitioner means, that practice means, just as whatever mathematics is, that the mathematician or expression of mathematics must show forth. Mathematics can be known only as it is shown forth by the mathematician.

[1] Jno. 14:9.

So man, the practice of God, the presence of the one Practitioner, shows forth, or demonstrates, the laws and rules of that Practitioner. In no other way could those laws and rules be known.

"The Principle of divine metaphysics is God; the practice of divine metaphysics is the utilization of the power of Truth over error; its rules demonstrate its Science."[1]

PATIENT

The word patient, as used in Christian Science, does not mean *a* sick man, *a* sick business, or *a* sick anything.

A "sick" something is that appearance which is the suppositional opposite of the fact. It is the negative statement of the fact.

Defining "patient" in terms of the negative, you designate it as the false claim about something that is true. By reversal, the true is discovered and is found to be whole and permanent.

The specific claim is merely the appearance which the lie assumes, in contradistinction to the truth or immortal fact. The patient, then, is the false claim about being.

From this standpoint, therefore, the patient is revealed as the whole suppositional opposite of Mind.

[1] S. & H. 111:11.

This patient appears as embracing all the ramifications of evil; the negation of perfection in every respect; the sinning and dying person; the failing business; the storm; the flood; all that is abnormal and distorted.

But, regardless of its appearance, the patient is but the negation of Truth. By the negation, the Truth is actually proclaimed because there must first be Truth, before there can be a negation of Truth. *"The reverse of error is true."*[1]

The understanding of this enables one instantly to impersonalize all of evil's appearances and to reverse them, thereby establishing the original and indestructible truth.

PRAYER

Is prayer a petition, or is it realization?

Is it supplication, or is it the spiritual discernment of what is always present?

It could not be supplication, because man is all that God is. "Son, . . . all that I have is thine."[2]

Consequently prayer is right knowing. Right knowing, being intelligence, is Mind. To pray, then, is to be one with Mind—to understand.

Jesus said, "When ye pray, use not vain repetitions, as the heathen do: for they think that they shall be heard for their much speaking."[3]

Words, as such, have nothing to do with prayer.

[1] S. & H. 442:18. [2] Luke 15:31. [3] Matt. 6:7.

The Lord's Prayer is not a petition. It is a declaration of the oneness of Mind and its idea. *"Only as we rise above all material sensuousness and sin, can we reach the heaven-born aspiration and spiritual consciousness, which is indicated in the Lord's Prayer and which instantaneously heals the sick."*[1]

To think of prayer as a form of petition is to destroy its efficacy. Supplication, instead of inspiring assurance, encourages an attitude of blind faith.

True prayer is the realization that that which *is* is all that is. Thus it inspires confidence and power.

To repeat Mrs. Eddy's definition of prayer again, *"Prayer is the utilization of the love wherewith He loves us . . . It makes new and scientific discoveries of God, of His goodness and power. It shows us more clearly than we saw before, what we already have and are; and most of all, it shows us what God is".*[2]

To pray understandingly, we must emulate Jesus, "whose humble prayers were deep and conscientious protests of Truth,—of man's likeness to God and of man's unity with Truth and Love".[3]

[1] S. & H. 16:20.   [2] No. 39:18.   [3] S. & H. 12:13.

TREATMENT

To treat, in the dictionary definition, means to give; to bestow; and treatment is the manner of treating; usage.

Because usage is the activity of Mind—the use to which Mind puts itself,—the usage of Mind is treatment, the utilization of Truth.

God bestows upon man His entire being, hence man is the utilization of Truth.

Treatment is but another name for man. This is corroborated in Science and Health by the statement, *"God will heal the sick through man, whenever man is governed by God"*.[1]

To paraphrase this quotation: God will heal the sick through man, through the Christian Science treatment, whenever treatment is understood, whenever reality is comprehended.

Therefore, man, as this activity, this treatment of God, cannot be mesmerized into harboring in thought any doubt or question as to the power of Truth over all error, or as to the efficacy of Christian Science under all circumstances, or as to the expectancy of the spontaneous healing (disappearance) of all error.

He knows that his word as the word, presence, and power of God is law; and he knows that it cannot and does not return unto itself "void",[2] but accomplishes that which is intended, and prospers in the thing whereto it is sent.

---

[1] S. & H. 495:1.   [2] Isa. 55:11.

He knows that the whole of what is called Christian Science healing is simply the manifestation of the power, availability and sufficiency of Truth to abolish error.

He knows that there is no limit to his confidence and faith in this power.

He further knows that there is no mind to retard or reverse this treatment or bring about a belief of a law of relapse, for the law of God is the law of progress, and His law is final; there is no retrogression, for God alone is Mind.

This realization is Christian Science treatment and it never fails.

ANATOMY, PHYSIOLOGY, ONTOLOGY

Although these words have already been defined, in an earlier chapter, the following will bear repetition. Anatomy refers to the formations of God, to that which appears as body, or man; physiology refers to the functions of this body or man; and ontology refers to the being of man.

God knows His body, His man, His expression, from the infinitesimal to the infinite. Therefore, He understands anatomy, which includes the truth about all that the human mind calls the anatomy of the body.

The human mind's sense of anatomy is the negation of the anatomy of Mind.

The physiological or functional activities of man are the showing forth of God as the one Physiology.

Ontology means the being or isness of God, that which is the spirit of God, the man of Being. In other words, ontology is the being of *is*, or the science or truth of Being.

"Ontology is defined as 'the science of the necessary constituents and relations of all beings,' and it underlies all metaphysical practice."[1]

Anatomy is the formation of *is* or the science of formation.

"Anatomy, when conceived of spiritually, is mental self-knowledge .... This branch of study is indispensable to the excision of error."[2]

Physiology is the function of *is*, or the science of function.

These three constitute completeness. They express the understanding embodied in the letters "M.D."

Like the synonyms of God, which you have proved are all interchangeable, so these three words, formation, function, and being, are equally interchangeable and embrace all that means the completeness of God, appearing as man.

DIAGNOSIS

Diagnosis makes known or brings to light that which *is*.

[1] S. & H. 460:3.   [2] S. & H. 462:20.

According to the definition of materia medica, diagnosis discovers the facts of a case, thus making it possible to correct the trouble.

In Christian Science, the one infinite intelligence is the one diagnostician from which nothing is hidden.

To infinite intelligence there are no insidious, unknown, or unrevealed facts or causes.

Intelligence, being All-in-all, leaves nothing outside of itself.

To it, all is visible, just as to the scholarly mathematician, the science of mathematics is an open book.

It is this quality of infinite intelligence, of infinite Mind, that uncovers, unravels and corrects all mistakes, whether in the science of numbers or in the Science of being.

To uncover, unravel and correct, is the threefold office of intelligence in all of its operations.

This it accomplishes by being itself the one infinite presence.

To use the illustration from mathematics, it is the omnipresence of two times two as four, which prohibits the possibility of two times two as anything but four.

If "two-times-two-equals-four" could forsake its post, any mistake about it could pass as correct.

But because it can never forsake its post, your knowledge that two times two is four enables you to uncover and correct any falsity about it.

The mathematician who expresses facts in terms of mathematics, is the diagnostician of mathematics.

The ever-present truth of Being spontaneously detects and destroys whatever is unlike itself.

The Christ or man expressing the one intelligence, God, is the diagnostician of God; and nothing can escape his omnipresent vigilance.

To him all is known. In the words of the Scriptures, "There is nothing covered that shall not be revealed; and hid, that shall not be known".[1]

The knowing of good, not the knowing of evil, constitutes eternal vigilance.

It is the critical analysis of thought finding it the product of Mind, that constitutes true dissection.

Correct diagnosis is as necessary to the practice of Christian Science as it is to the practice of mathematics.

As the man, or practice, of this one Practitioner, this one Mind, you know everything that is necessary to know about any case.

Nothing is hidden from you; therefore your confidence in your ability to handle the case successfully is unbounded.

[1] Matt. 10:26.

The patient, as you have discovered, is the negation of God, the negation of Mind. This negation takes on the appearance of something that is wrong. It may appear, for instance, as a sick person.

By reversing the negation, you find that the patient, as a false claim disappears; and perfect man, as the presence of God, stands revealed.

Thus, through analysis, you have found prayer and treatment to be man's eternal communion or oneness with God.

You have established anatomy, physiology, and ontology as the activities of God, appearing as action, or man.

You have defined diagnosis as the clear discernment of that which *is*, as distinguished from that which *is not*.

You always diagnose *is not* by showing it to be the negation of *is*.

In fact, *is not* is only *is*, with *not* added to it.

This is just like adding zero, or nothing, to a column of figures. The value remains the same.

So *is* remains *is*, irrespective of the manner in which it may be stated, whether ignorantly or intelligently.

Any negative statement is merely the positive, or actual fact, referred to negatively, but this manner of speaking about a fact does not change the nature of the fact.

Reversal becomes an automatic mental process when it is seen that there are not two facts, two different actualities, but merely two statements, the negative and the positive, about the one and only fact, *is*.

Every case presents itself as an interpretation of God; and if it appears as "through a glass, darkly",[1] as a negative, it can be made to show itself in its true light, by reversal.

You know that a negative statement cannot be framed except on the basis of a pre-existent truth. So the truth can always reverse the lie.

A lie, far from reversing the truth, does not alter it in the slightest detail.

Therefore, what remains as true about a misstatement is the truth itself.

The intelligent analysis of a misstatement leads directly to its correction and to its disappearance as a misstatement.

Body is the simple declaration of truth which Mind communicates to its idea. It is the interpretation of health, the accomplishment and joy of living which Mind bestows. Since it is identical with health, it precludes discord.

Health is harmonious action, sustained by law. It is the unchanging reality of God's presence and purpose.

There is nothing that can oppose it or reverse it. It is actual, affirmative.

[1] 1 Cor. 13:12.

As a negation, disease, or wrong action presupposes the presence of right action, or health, which it contradicts.

Health is the indestructible reality, the unfailing truth about the misstatement.

Disease is a negation, without power to declare itself to be something. It has not one element to be feared, for the truth which it misstates (but cannot alter) is already consciously possessed.

Disease is nothing that can appear, disappear or reappear.

Then there is no disease and nothing to be diseased.

A negative supposition of itself does not do one thing. It has no existence, no precedent, no laws. You are not responsible for its appearing. It arises from the truth, automatically, by the law of opposites.

You are entirely responsible, however, for its continued acceptance.

The only prestige it can have must come from you; but you give it none, for you cannot accept a lie knowing it to be such.

To accept the negative as a separate reality from that truth of which it is the negative, is the quintessence of hypnotism. It produces the illusion of failure at every point.

Consequently the acceptance of the negative, unreversed, is then "the beginning of sorrows".[1]

[1] Matt. 24:8.

You have absolute and God-given dominion on this point, for you know there is only *one* Mind.

You meet the fear assailing you as a particular case of disease by undermining its specific claim of presence and actuality.

ANALYSIS FOR A CASE

Every case involves the following points of erroneous belief:

First, that *something* is wrong.

Second, that there is a *place* where this wrong thing is.

Third, that there is a *time* when it began.

Fourth, that there is *substance,* matter, with which it is formed.

Fifth, that there is *law* by which it operates.

What are the facts about these claims?

First, God being All-in-all, He is the only *something* there is.

Second, Mind being omnipresent, *here* is the only *place* there is.

There can be no "there" when *here* is omnipresent. "There" simply denies "here"; but you have already proved that denial is, after all, acknowledgment, in negative form, of the fact. It is not another and a different fact.

Third, *time* is *now.* There is no time but the present. As Paul said, "Behold, now is the accepted time; behold, now is the day of salvation".[1]

[1] 2 Cor. 6:2.

There is no scientific basis for supposing one moment in the continuity of time, then supposedly waiting and supposing another moment, and finally designating the interval as the measure of time.

Time, like place and thing, is the ever-presence of Mind.

The human concept as just outlined is the negative of the ever-present *now*.

Now, this instant, is all the time there is.

What we call the past, is so-called memory operating *now.* The future is an imagined state, imagined *now.* Past, present and future are an ever-present, unfolding *now.*

To-morrow is to-day enlarged. *"That to-morrow starts from to-day and is one day beyond it, robes the future with hope's rainbow hues."*[1]

Because you own to-day, to-morrow is assured. Because you live *now,* you will live for all-time.

"I know that, whatsoever God doeth, it shall be forever: nothing can be put to it, nor any thing taken from it: . . . That which hath been is now; and that which is to be hath already been; and God requireth that which is past."[2]

Fourth, *substance* is Spirit, or *isness.* Isness, being omnipresent, admits nothing aside from itself.

[1] Mis. 339 :7 [2] Ecc. 3 :14, 15.

The substance of all things is Spirit. Matter is the negation of Spirit, *"an error of statement"*.[1]

Fifth, Principle is the only *law*. Principle is intelligence; therefore law is intelligent and always acts aright.

The law of Mind is the rightness of Mind, or right-Mindedness. Law is the divine right of Mind. That law is infinite.

SUMMARY

The foregoing terms may be classified as follows:

Practitioner: God, infinite intelligence.

Practice: Man, the idea of God.

Patient: The negative statement about Truth, about Mind.

Claim: The specific appearing of God, negatively interpreted.

Prayer: Communion, or *isness;* right knowing.

Treatment: Usage of God.

Anatomy: The formation of God.

Physiology: The function of God.

Ontology: The being of God.

Place: Here.

Time: Now.

Substance: Spirit; Truth.

Law: Principle; right action; *isness.*

[1] S. & H. 277:26.

CHAPTER IX

Factors Involved in Healing

In order to present for analysis as many phases of human belief as possible and in order to indicate how the corrective power of Truth, through argument, can be applied, a number of cases of dis-ease may properly be analyzed.

You will find, however, that every case, in its final analysis, leads to the one conclusion, namely, *that what appears* to be the claim is really not the claim.

You will find, also, that no argument, in and of itself, destroys a claim.

The sole purpose of the argument is to establish the fact that the testimony or evidence of the material senses is not the basic difficulty.

Regardless of this, it is necessary, nevertheless, to *"continue the mental argument in the practice of Christian healing until you can cure without it instantaneously, and through Spirit alone."*[1]

Mrs. Eddy did not mean by this, however, that any argument, in and of itself, could accomplish the healing.

You could not be aware of anything that you cognize, whether good or bad, if it did not present itself as a state of mind or consciousness.

[1] Mis. 359 :5.

It must come as a mental argument, even though appearing in the language of things; for you cognize a thing only as an argument.

The argument presents itself, for example, that something is wrong; that you are sick; that you are sick for a reason, and so forth—a specific argument about a specific thing.

The erroneous argument, coming as the negation of the positive truth, is, like Truth, specific and must be met by the specific counter-argument.

In mathematics, a mistake about two times two could not be corrected with the truth about three times three. The specific truth about two times two is requisite.

A specific lie is reversed only by the specific truth.

The argument is for that purpose; were it not employed, the lie would continue to masquerade as the truth, and would be accepted by you as true, and you could not see the actual claim.

No intelligence is displayed by employing an argument about something that error is not presenting as a specific mistake.

Hence the necessity for correct diagnosis, for recognizing the one Practitioner, infinite intelligence as the only Practitioner, the only M.D. *"When treating a patient, it is not Science to treat every organ in the body. To aver that harmony is the real and discord is the unreal, and then give special attention to what according to*

*their own belief is diseased, is scientific; and if
the healer realizes the truth, it will free his patient.*"[1]

You meet the arguments of evil, appearing as
wrong things, with the arguments of Truth, in
order to convince yourself that what appears on
the surface is a mental argument, in other words,
a suggestion, rather than a thing having something wrong with it.

It is necessary to continue the mental argument until you are convinced of this fact, or you
will not see that the claim is hypnotic suggestion.
Unless you do see this, you will not be able to reverse it instantaneously by Spirit, which is pure
realization.

As an illustration, let us suppose a case of a
man under hypnotic influence, going through the
motion of swimming on dry boards. He is making a strenuous effort to save himself from what
he believes to be drowning. On his face is de-
picted desperate fear, and yet *you* know that he
is only on dry boards and in no danger.

But suppose you were so situated, able only
to see the terror on the man's face and to hear
his cry, "I am drowning"; being unable to see
that he was on dry boards, would not you also be
convinced that he was in danger of perishing?

Your first impulse under such circumstances,
would doubtless be to run to the man's aid.

[1]Rud. 13:18.

But the moment you reached him and saw that he was not in water, you would have a tremendous reaction in thought.

You would immediately cease trying to save him from water, for you would recognize at once that he was acting under hypnotic influence and that his need was to be freed from the belief that there was a mind that could either hypnotize or be hypnotized.

"No person can accept another's belief, except it be with the consent of his own belief. If the error which knocks at the door of your own thought originated in another's mind, you are a free moral agent to reject or to accept this error; hence, you are the arbiter of your own fate, and sin is the author of sin."[1]

As a Christian Scientist, your remedy would be to *realize* immediately the omnipresence of the one Mind only, and in the degree that you were successful in this realization, the man would be free from hypnotic influence, and would arise, "clothed, and in his right mind".[2]

If, on the other hand, you attempted to help him by any material means, as, for instance, lifting him to an upright position or forcing him to stop the motions of swimming, you would find him still persisting in his futile effort to swim, because he would still be hypnotized.

[1]Mis. 83:12.   [2]Mark 5:15.

His swimming had nothing to do with water, but was the result of his acceptance of the hypnotic suggestion or *belief* that he was in water.

Under hypnotic influence, he would interpret anything as water, and in order to save himself, would believe that he must continue to swim.

In a case of this kind, because the dis-ease is seen as a mental hallucination, it is readily acknowledged that material remedies would be useless.

This illustration will be used frequently to clarify the analyses of other cases, because each case reverts in principle to the man who believes himself to be swimming on dry boards.

No case can be correctly handled until it is seen as pure hypnotic suggestion.

If you can be tempted to believe in a dis-eased *thing* or *condition,* you are powerless to destroy it.

Only as every case is seen as hypnotism are you its master through Mind. Mind can only operate in the realm of consciousness; never in the so-called realm of matter.

It is well to remember, also, in order to prevent confusion of thought and needless fear, that no matter how high sounding and mysterious may be the name given to a disease by materia medica, the name designates only a simple anatomical or functional condition that is supposed to be wrong.

Any medical dictionary is full of terms of which you may never have heard, but which, when you understand the definitions, are merely names of diseases of familiar organs or functions of the body.

For instance, you are told that the patient has *coronary thrombosis*.

The name sounds formidable enough to frighten any layman, but it is merely the medical way of stating that there is a stoppage in the arteries of the crown of the heart.

Medical terms generally hide the simple name of some portion or function of the body.

The medical name is really of no moment whatever.

In your argument it is the name of the anatomical part involved that you do need to know and use for refutation.

Use the simple anatomical name until you are *"thoroughly persuaded in your own mind"*[1] that no anatomy is involved, but that instead, hypnotic suggestion is masquerading as a belief of *some thing* wrong.

The phraseology of materia medica, as the activity of malicious mind has succeeded in its purpose, that of frightening the poor mortal by using terms that sound awesome and impressive.

If simple English were used instead, possibly he would not be frightened at all.

[1]S. & H. 412:7.

Imagine a mathematician with a particular term for two times two equals four, and a very involved term for a mistake about two times two! The layman user of numbers might well be confused and frightened.

That is just what materia medica, in all its phases, has developed. In order to lift its calling above the layman's comprehension, it uses long names, often Latin names, which confuse and terrify the patient.

Remember, fear is the substance of every case, and with the removal of fear, the disorder disappears.

Fear is the belief that God, good, is not all.

Fear is the negation or suppositional opposite of the confidence and assurance that good *is*, and is *all* that *is*.

As Science and Health says, *"Always begin your treatment by allaying the fear of patients . . . If you succeed in wholly removing the fear, your patient is healed".*[1] Then you would do this with every case, at the outset.

With infinite good as All-in-all, what is there to fear?

In using arguments, realize the facts already presented about place, time, substance and law. One place, here. One time, now. One substance, Spirit. One law, the law of God, perfection.

[1] S. & H. 411:27.

In every case analyzed, it will be taken for granted that you do this first; therefore, these points will not be brought out each time.

Science and Health declares, *"To heal by argument, find the type of the ailment, get its name, and array your mental plea against the physical . . . Conform the argument so as to destroy the evidence of disease".*[1] *"You may vary the arguments to meet the peculiar or general symptoms of the case".*[2] *"Whatever the belief is, if arguments are used to destroy it, the belief must be repudiated, and the negation must extend to the supposed disease and to whatever decides its type and symptoms."*[3]

Arguments have value only as they remind one of what the claim actually is, hypnotic suggestion, and as they bring thought into accord with the one Mind as All-in-all.

The following cases are presented solely to illustrate some of the arguments of evil that arise, and to present ways of rejecting them. Every person must work out his own method of argument. There can be no formula. Remember that argument is not *realization* but merely a step leading to the conviction of God's allness.

BLINDNESS

To the average person, blindness means loss of sight; but the fact is, that it has nothing to do with sight.

[1] S. & H. 412:18.   [2] S. & H. 412:5.   [3] S. & H. 418:16.

The sight is not destroyed. It only seems to be gone because human belief has associated seeing with the eyes, even as it has associated hearing with the ears, thinking with the brain, feeling with the nerves, etc.

Sight, hearing, thinking and feeling have nothing to do with eyes, ears, brain, or nerves.

This is proven in the practice of hypnotism wherein the senses of the victim testify to whatever the hypnotist suggests, regardless of what the subject's own normal senses would declare.

Another example of this is the night dream, in which the senses, as such, are silent, though the dreamer supposes himself to be using all of them.

One could give innumerable instances, but these two are enough to prove that the senses are conditions of mind, not of matter, and that mind is never dependent upon matter.

We can dismiss then, all thought of any need to handle sight and can turn our attention to *eyes,* in other words, to that about which the specific lie is the lie.

It has been determined that infinite intelligence is the only Practitioner, and is, therefore, the Practitioner, the M.D. on every case. One cannot afford ever to lose sight of this.

What this Practitioner knows is the truth about everything.

Infinite intelligence, including all right-knowing, at once uncovers the specific lie. In this case, let us suppose the lie to be about the optic nerve.

Knowing all there is to know about optic nerve —its eternal action and perfection—the Practitioner instantly diagnoses the error as a claim of "dead optic nerve".

Then comes the question, What is there to know about optic nerve?

First, where is it?

Since *here* is all the place there is, optic nerve is something right within one's own mental cognizance.

It is operating *now* because this instant is all the *now,* all the time, or moment there is.

There is no yesterday with a history; there is this instant only.

Because Spirit is the one *is,* the one substance, Spirit is the substance of optic nerve. In other words, Spirit is all there is to optic nerve; hence optic nerve is eternally spiritual and perfect.

How many optic nerves are there?

One, because there is one Spirit, one essence, one *isness.*

Bear in mind that entirely separate from the belief of the material concept called *optic nerve* is the divine reality, about which, metaphysically, you are always thinking.

If you fail to insist on this separation in your use of all words, you will make a farce of your understanding of Christian Science.

The human concept of any term has no relation whatever to the divine reality of that term, even as the boards upon which the hypnotized man is struggling have no relation to water. Every Christian Scientist must know this.

The human concept is always the lie, the negation about the divine reality; and the negation *must* be reversed every time.

To see God as all there is to optic nerve, or to anything else, is scientific; but to reverse this, and attempt to see optic nerve, or anything else, as all there is to God, is fraught with the greatest danger.

This point must be specifically emphasized, because there is always difficulty, when using terms, in separating their spiritual meaning from the finite concept attached to them.

If you put the human concept first and say that that is all there is to God, you finitize your God, and so you have no God.

By seeing God always as first and as including within Himself all being, you lift all things to His level, and avoid the danger of unconsciously reducing your God to the level of human belief.

Therefore, insist upon finding God first, and His interpretation as idea to you, second.

Because God is omnipresent, infinitely perfect, the one law, optic nerve is everywhere present, harmonious, complete, whole, law-abiding and eternal.

Everything that God is must uphold optic nerve to the minutest detail.

God, as infinite Life is shown forth as infinitely living optic nerve, without the possibility of depletion, inflammation or congestion.

The law of God is the one law of depletion, inflammation, congestion, and strangulation to everything unlike Himself; hence, God is the very law of preservation to His own presence or idea; in this case, optic nerve.

All that God is, optic nerve has. "Son, . . . all that I have is thine",[1] is the eternal dictum of Mind to its own thought.

Definitely convinced of this fact, you can declare from your heart, "Our optic nerve which is in heaven, hallowed is thy name."

If you cannot do this, are you not deceiving yourself into believing that optic nerve is something apart from your God as All-in-all?

If in your heart you find God to be all the optic nerve there is, you know that right there in the place in which evil would say there is a "dead optic nerve", is the very presence of God, appearing as living, perfect optic nerve.

[1] Luke 15:31.

Daniel did this when he faced the lions. He saw the very presence of God as the only lion, hence harmless.

Jesus saw the presence of God as the only sea, and therefore a peaceful sea.

The Hebrew captives saw the presence of God as the only fire, and it was their protection.

Mrs. Eddy told a friend that when she saw the face of God in the storm-cloud, the storm lifted.

Is not God omnipresent? He is.

Thus God is seen as all there is to optic nerve. Perfect optic nerve is right where the lie about it seems to be.

You have now reached the point you attained when you saw the man going through the motions of swimming on dry boards, and realized that he did not need to be saved from drowning, but that he needed to be saved from hypnotic suggestion.

With this settled, you realize that what appears as dead optic nerve has really nothing to do with the eyes or nerves, but is the claim that there is a malicious mind, in other words that malicious mind is, as the suppositional opposite of the one Mind—the negation of Mind.

A lie, or negation, always operates as hypnotic suggestion, appearing in this instance as a *belief* of dead optic nerve.

To return to the swimming illustration, hypnotism operates as a *belief* of water in which to drown.

God, as divine Mind, operates as the impartation of divine thought to man, just as the sun imparts heat and light to its ray; whereas, the negation, malicious mind, operates first to dispossess man of his mind and then to control him.

The one is true operation, the other is impossible; for with one Mind only, how could there be any dispossessing of one mind by another?

The necessity for the destruction of the belief that there is malicious mind is what is referred to in the statement, "The axe is laid unto the root of the trees."

The root of the tree of evil is, as you have already established, always the erroneous belief that malicious mind is; that the negation, unreversed, is entity or positive fact, acting as mind, and so appearing as positive evil.

Lay the axe at the root of this falsity by the *realization* that there is one Mind only, and that one, infinite; one presence, power and intelligence; and that therefore there is no room for a malicious mind either to be, or to operate hypnotically, as presence, power, intelligence, or as any other lie.

This *realization* is the spontaneous healing of any claim.

Always accompanying such healing is the understanding that nothing has actually been healed; that there was nothing wrong to be

¹Luke 3:9.

healed; that what took place was enlightenment, communion with the one Mind as All-in-all.

By reversing the negation, the positive appeared as the fact.

Mrs. Eddy illustrates this in her statement in Unity of Good: *"When I have most clearly seen and most sensibly felt that the infinite recognizes no disease, this has not separated me from God, but has so bound me to Him as to enable me instantaneously to heal a cancer which had eaten its way to the jugular vein.*

"In the same spiritual condition I have been able to replace dislocated joints and raise the dying to instantaneous health."[1]

Every argument ceases when a claim is seen for what it really is—hypnotic suggestion. Then the demand is no longer for argument, but for pure *realization*.

This is symbolized by the Holy of Holies of the ancient Jewish temple into which only the High Priest (the symbol of the pure realization of God's allness) could enter.

Into the Holy of Holies, which is pure realization, no argument enters. *Realization* is all that is present.

Realization is the healing in Christian Science.

Realization is the purity of being.

Realization is the spirit of Christian Science. Indeed, it is Christian Science itself.

[1]Un. 7:13.

You will discover, as we go on, that every case is finally reduced to the one common denominator of evil—hypnotic suggestion.

Hypnotic suggestion is, as Mrs. Eddy designates it, *"The specific term for error, or mortal mind"*.[1]

Whether appearing, therefore, under the guise of sin, sickness, death, limitation or any other phase of human belief, it is never a thing that is wrong, but always pure hypnotism that is deceiving.

Evil can be handled only by being so understood.

Remember, however, that the temptation is always to accept evil as a thing. But as a thing it would be indestructible.

You cannot destroy a thing, but you can destroy a false sense by replacing it with the true sense. It is the true, or Christ sense, that always destroys the hypnotic suggestion.

This is the basis of true Christian Science practice; and nothing is Christian Science practice that does not reduce evil to hypnotic suggestion, and destroy it as such.

INSANITY

Insanity is the generic term used to designate the beliefs of a disordered or dis-eased brain. A common mistake is to think that insanity means a disordered *mind*. It does not.

[1] S. & H. 103:19.

It appears as a disordered mind because human belief has designated the brain as that whereby thinking is done.

The brain has no more to do with thinking than the heart with emotion.

Who, today, believes that the heart has emotions and that it feels?

The belief that the brain does the thinking, however, carries with it, in spite of its self-evident falsity, a second inevitable belief, namely, that if anything happens to the brain, thinking is impaired.

As an illustration of the falsity of the theory that the brain does the thinking, the following facts are illuminating.

A brilliant professor, in one of the largest American universities, willed his brain to the affiliated medical college. Up to the moment of his death, it was acknowledged that no deterioration in his mentality had taken place. No time was lost after death in transferring his brain to specialists for examination. They naturally expected to find a perfect specimen of brain; but instead, they found what should have been, according to all their accepted theories, the brain of a "babbling idiot".

One example of this kind is enough to prove the absurdity of believing that any human concept, whether perfect or imperfect, has anything to do with Mind, or that it can usurp the prerogatives of Mind.

Psychologists, according to their own claim, are today restoring lost brain functions, and lost brain grooves, by the re-education of the individual on the lapsed points. They are doing this, they say, by using another portion of the brain, one that has not been affected by whatever caused the lapse.

Does not this prove that it is not the brain grooves that make the intelligence, but intelligence, called education, that makes the brain grooves?

Psychology acknowledges this when it says that it can change the function of thinking from one portion of the brain to another, and that the lapse will disappear.

Mind alone thinks, and no human concept, called brain, has anything to do with it.

But because brain is the specific point of attack in arguing against insanity, it is incumbent on the metaphysician to establish the truth about brain before proceeding further.

What do you know about brain?

Because God is All, He must and does include in His allness, all that there is to brain, all that brain means.

Therefore, all that God is, brain must be. Brain shows forth the perfection and completeness of God, since God alone defines it.

This perfection and completeness precludes the possibility of a brain being inflamed, diseased or deranged, because the order, harmony and arrangement that is God is the order, harmony and arrangement of brain.

Because God is one, brain is one, and this one the only brain; hence, it is omnipresent.

The one right brain is just where the lie is saying there exists an imperfect brain, a diseased brain, a deranged brain.

Make your thinking so true that you never see the presence of God (whether interpreted as brain, or liver, or cloud, or sea, or whatsoever) as off in space, but see that it is with you, as your very communion with Truth, just as the multiplication table is everpresent as your consciousness.

Regardless of the name given to the appearance, acknowledge Mind alone as all the presence there is to it. Be ever mindful, however, that *"Entirely separate from the belief and dream of"*[1] the human concept of anything is the divine reality.

Since this one perfect brain is the only brain, hence, omnipresent, can the claim have anything to do with brain? It cannot.

The belief that there is a mind apart from God, the one Mind, and that this mind operates

[1] S. & H. 14:25.

as hypnotic suggestion and appears as a *belief* of imperfect brain, is all there is to the claim.

But because God is the one and only Mind, there is no suppositional opposite to appear as the negation of Mind; there is no malicious mind.

The *realization* of this is the healing.

CANCER OF THE LIVER

Cancer is said to be caused by the incorrect locating and grouping of cells, and not by a diseased condition of the cells, in the sense in which the word "disease" is usually employed.

Cancer cells, so medical authorities will tell you, are perfectly healthy cells, but their location and grouping are wrong. Being out of place and improperly grouped, they interfere with one another and break down the tissues of the body.

This belief is based, of course, upon the old atomic theory that each atom is a separate entity, and therefore, if displaced, causes havoc to other atoms.

What does Christian Science answer to this?

Just exactly what it says to every lie. In Jesus' words, "Ye are of your father the devil, and the lusts of your father ye will do . . . . . When he speaketh a lie, he speaketh of his own: for he is a liar, and the father of it."[1]

Nor does Christian Science stop there. It goes on to show the truth about the lie.

[1] Jno. 8:44.

It shows that Principle is all there is to any cell. Hence no cell is ever out of place, or wrongly grouped with any other.

The location and grouping of cells is as eternally right as God Himself is right.

There is no power to misplace anything, for God is the one power.

In the same way, you see the truth about liver. Is liver something apart from God?

For you to have cognizance of it, must it not be embraced in that which is consciousness, which is God, to you, and of which you are the conscious acknowledgment?

God, embracing within Himself all, includes all that liver is.

Then liver is as perfect as the Mind who thinks it, is perfect; it is as indestructible and eternal as Mind.

Liver is the very spirit of God, for God is Spirit.

Because God is Life, that which expresses life is the liver.

Because there is one God, there is one liver.

Both liver and cells show forth all the good that God is. They are the omnipresent activity of Mind, declaring, to the minutest detail, all the perfection of Mind.

This one liver, being all the liver, and this one cell, being all the cell there is, they are everywhere present. Therefore, they are present right *where* the lie declares imperfect liver and imperfect cell to be.

Then you find that the claim has really nothing to do with cell or liver, but is purely hypnotic suggestion—again, it is a case of the man swimming on dry boards.

So the claim is not cancer of the liver. That is merely the suggestion, the belief, the lie, or negation, that deceives and confuses.

As a metaphysician, you are not deceived. You lay the axe at the root of the tree, the lie that asserts that there is malicious mind.

The Holy of Holies is your refuge, the secret place of the most High, the *realization* that God is the one and only Mind and that there is none beside Him.

Therefore, there is no malicious mind to operate hypnotically and appear as a belief of cancer of the liver or cancer of anything.

Knowing this, you know that you know it, for you know and realize that Truth is the one and only Mind.

INFECTION: WHAT IT IS AND HOW IT OPERATES

Today every sort of ache or pain is attributed to some focal point of infection, operating as poison in the system.

The source of infection, whether called teeth, tonsils, intestines or some other part of the body, claims an individual history. It defines itself as a point of morbid chemical action, from which go forth disturbing influences.

Upon this hang all the arguments of related disease.

Do you accept or reject this theory?

You know that all that ever comes to you comes as consciousness, and is purely mental; hence you know that *"so-called disease is a sensation of mind, not of matter"*.[1]

Your analysis of being turns you to Mind, God, in order to clear up the situation. You know that all that comes to you as consciousness must be Mind interpreting itself to you. There is no other source of conscious being.

Mind, being infinite, leaves no place where Mind is not, no *place* where morbid infection could arise, no place where it could be feared.

The truth is that by which the lie locates itself.

The lie always claims to be where the fact is, but Truth is ever a law of annihilation to the lie; it always precludes the negation.

Mind is eternal; so there never is a moment when a specific evil could begin to be true.

Substance implies actuality, indestructibility, reality, identity, truth.

Matter, appearing as morbid infection, declares itself destructive in action. But it is only the negation of substance, lacking in every quality of actuality, appearance or truth.

[1] My. 228 :4.

Having no matter substance, the claim has nothing whereby to identify itself as morbid infection; and, having no existence, it cannot be feared.

The so-called history of this disease-picture is simply a repetition of negatives, derived, by the law of opposites, from the infinity of Truth. There is, in this sequence of misstatements, no inherent connection, continuity or intelligence; there is nothing in one statement which leads to the next.

It is utterly devoid of any law under which to operate as morbid infection.

Truth alone holds within itself the capacity, authority and right to act.

Truth, then, is the only law, and this law is always consciously operating—reassuring and comforting.

There is no morbid chemical action, for the one chemistry is Mind, transforming itself, and so being revealed as its own infinity of variety, its illimitable beauty of idea.

The activity of infinite Mind is the only chemistry. It precludes the possibility of the untrue, the negative, called morbid chemical action.

Infection is Mind imparting itself to its idea, imparting its very name and nature, infecting its own expression with life, purity and perfection.

This is the one and only infection, and it is in perfect agreement with the accepted definition of the word: "sympathetic communication of like qualities."

Where morbid infection claims to be, there is the very presence of Mind imparting the infection of spirituality—"the beauty of holiness".[1]

Then the claim is not actually morbid infection, but rather a *belief* of morbid infection, which supposes that there is a malicious mind that can hypnotically suggest such a lying belief.

There is no such mind, for God is the only Mind.

This *realization* is the dispelling of the illusion.

DIABETES

Examination of the claim of diabetes, shows it to be simply the belief of imperfect action of the pancreatic gland, resulting in improper distribution of sugar to the so-called bodily system.

Is pancreatic action something apart from Mind?

For you to be conscious of it at all, must it not come to you through your conscious communion with Mind?

Must it not then be Mind showing forth its nature in perpetual harmony and perfection? It must.

Then is it gland action, or Mind with its infinite resources?

[1]Ps. 29:2.

God determines all quality and quantity, and His word is law, unchangeable, ever-present, and always prevailing.

Mind cannot withhold its blessings, and if its right action appears as the distribution of sugar, then does it not accomplish this perfectly, harmoniously and in exactly the right amounts?

It does.

Knowing this, you know also that the pancreatic gland, being the presence of infinite and intelligent good, ever about its Father's business, is declaring His business and power here and everywhere.

Is there a mind apart from the one and only Mind, able hypnotically to suggest a belief of imperfect pancreas?

No, there is not.

Then, resting in the conscious assurance of the one Mind as all, you find that the hypnotic belief, diabetes, vanishes.

BRIGHT'S DISEASE

Bright's disease is the belief that kidneys can degenerate and cease to function.

What do you know about kidneys?

Are they apart from and outside consciousness? You would be unconscious of them if they were.

Have you not proved that the one infinite Mind is the one consciousness—your consciousness; and that through your communion with

Mind, all that Life means is revealed in a practical and understandable way?

"For the Father loveth the Son, and sheweth him all things that himself doeth".[1]

Then Truth alone outlines the anatomy or structure of kidneys, and it is as mental as the multiplication table and as exact.

The wisdom of Mind is the directing, controlling and functioning of what appears as kidneys.

Since Mind is omnipresent, this perfect anatomy, this perfect functioning, is omnipresent, and is right where "diseased kidneys" appear to be.

What does it mean "to be absent from the body, and to be present with the Lord"?[2]

It means that we understand that body, kidneys, heart or whatever term one may be using, is and does nothing of itself, but is the thought of Mind made manifest — Mind interpreting itself to its own idea as perfect, indestructible kidneys and so forth.

Can kidneys, then, degenerate and vanish?

All that can degenerate and vanish is the hypnotic suggestion of a *belief* of imperfect kidneys.

Since there is no malicious mind—for God alone is Mind—there can be no such belief.

This *realization*, this Holy of Holies, is Immanuel or God with you—"And there shall in

[1] Jno. 5:20.   [2] 2 Cor. 5:8.

no wise enter into it any thing that defileth . . .
or maketh a lie".[1]

GOITER

Goiter is the name given to describe a morbid
enlargement of the thyroid gland.

The first step in correct thinking is to start
right, to start with what you know, with that
of which you are sure.

*"All consciousness is Mind; and Mind is God,
—an infinite, and not a finite consciousness. This
consciousness is reflected in individual consciousness, or man, whose source is infinite Mind."*[2]

Since the source of your being is Mind, your
conscious recognition of whatever comes to you
must be your communion with Mind.

In working this out, do not look at any preconceived mind-picture, but follow your reasoning through to its goal.

You see that thyroid gland comes to you as
thought, not as matter; for you could know nothing about it, if you did not find it as thought.

Then you find it in the realm of consciousness
—in your communion with Mind; and it can express only the qualities Mind gives it. It is Mind
defining itself to you.

Since Spirit is the only substance, there is no
morbid substance. There is only right substance,
the substance of good.

[1]Rev. 21:27.   [2]Un. 24:12.

God controls man and man's action directly. It is immaterial how this control appears.

All glandular action is Mind-action—perfect action.

This includes all that is implied by thyroid, pancreas, adrenal, pituitary, or other gland.

The growing medical assumption that glands control practically every condition of man, both physical and mental, must be met and overcome by this true understanding.

Does the thyroid gland distribute iodine; the pancreas, sugar; the pituitary, salt? And does each of them control the destiny of man in some particular way? Is man at the mercy of matter, or has he the dominion vouchsafed him as the idea of immortal Mind?

We must answer the question by determining whether man is spiritual or material; whether his destiny is God-crowned or whether "the worm shall feed sweetly on him; he shall be no more remembered".[1]

The claim is again found to be not a wrong thing or a faulty action, but a hypnotized *belief* about thing and action.

Because the one Mind *is* and alone *is*, there is no mind to hypnotize or be hypnotized, and this *realization* appears as the understanding of right thyroid action—right distribution of iodine and the disappearance of goiter.

[1] Job 24:20.

HERNIA

Hernia means a rupture, a breaking through of walls or linings. Since we recognize that everything is a state of consciousness, we ask; What is the argument involved in this so-called action of breaking? Is it not that the law of adhesion and cohesion, which unites and holds the tissues, is broken?

What is this law which claims to be broken? Is this law a law of matter or of Mind?

The rock upon which we stand is the scientific fact that there is nothing but Mind and its idea; consciousness and its conscious acknowledgment.

Being yourself the one idea, it follows that you are dealing with Mind and with nothing else.

What then is the law of adhesion and cohesion?

It is Mind interpreting itself to you.

Whatever Mind is, that is what must be declared to be true of this law.

Mind must be explained and shown forth as walls, tissue and so forth. Mind is enduring, immutable, perfect.

Then, are not all of these *"the spiritual forces of divine Mind, whose potency is Truth, whose attraction is Love, whose adhesion and cohesion are Life, perpetuating the eternal facts of being"?*[1]

[1]S. & H. 293:14

They are; and any suggestion which contradicts this immutable truth to you, must be the hypnotic belief of a mind apart from the one omniscient divine Mind, a spurious mind that knows nothing, is nothing but the oblivion of unreality.

AUTOMOBILE TROUBLES

If the brakes of an automobile failed to work and you lost control, what would you do?

You would turn to Principle, to Christian Science, as your Mind and there find the truth about what was being presented to you—the truth about inoperative brakes.

Infinite intelligence controls the universe. It is the only control. This control is all that could appear as brakes; and so Mind is the one brake, the only brake.

There is no time when this control could cease to operate and to appear perfectly. There is no place where it is not operating. It alone operates. It is the one law.

There is no matter, substance or fact out of which to make a brake which does not work. All that can appear as brake is the one Mind thinking, controlling, governing, and appearing in whatever way is best understood.

Then brakes can no more get out of order than can Principle.

God being omnipresent, this one control, this one brake of Mind is omnipresent. It is the brake of my car.

Then it is not a question of brakes after all. "Brakes" is merely the truth upon which the lie is built, that lie whereby malicious suggestion operates to induce an acceptance of a belief of imperfect brakes.

In using the word brakes, you see clearly that *"Entirely separate from the belief and dream of"*[1] the human concept called brakes, is the divine reality, *"revealing spiritual understanding and the consciousness of man's dominion over"*[1] all brakes.

It is imperative to understand what Christian Science means by its use of terms.

When Jesus said, "Stretch forth thine hand",[2] he was not thinking of a human concept called hand.

He saw the omnipresence of God always appearing usefully and intelligently—in this case, as perfect hand.

He could, therefore, safely and scientifically use the word which would be familiar to the human mind and call it hand.

It is not the words you use that cause you trouble, but the limitations you attach to them.

[1] S. & H. 14:25.   [2] Matt. 12:13.

Mrs. Eddy says, *"I call disease by its name and have cured it thus; so there is nothing new on this score"*.[1]

Mrs. Eddy could not have healed understandingly if she had entertained a human concept of what was to be healed, for the human concept, by its very nature, is finite, limited and therefore diseased.

When you use the word brake and declare that Mind is all that brake means and is, you are not thinking of any human concept called brake.

Yet right where imperfect brake seems to be, there is the divine reality operating perfectly, entirely separate from the human concept, which is merely the negation.

You do not leave this brake of God theoretically off in space, but you *"take the things of God and show them to the creature, and reveal the great curative Principle,—Deity"*.[2] You prove the omnipresence and oneness of Principle and idea.

In other words, you see that Truth is omnipresent, filling the very place where the lie seems to be.

"Stretch forth thine hand",[3] did not mean to Jesus some abstract hand off in space, but the hand of Mind that is the only hand, ever-present, and, therefore, the hand of the man who thought his hand withered.

[1]My. 228:1.   [2]Ret. 24:24.   [3]Matt. 12:13.

In like manner, the brake of Mind is the brake of all, even as the one "two-times-two", that is the "two-times-two" of the principle of numbers, is the "two-times-two" of all.

Truth is always practical and usable, whether numbers or brakes are involved. Use Truth then, by having it as your brakes, the brakes of your car.

This lays the axe at the root of the tree, at the real error or lie,—the belief that there is a mind apart from the one Mind, which, operating as hypnotic suggestion, appears as a *belief* of imperfect brakes.

It is not imperfect brakes, but the hypnotic suggestion of a *belief* of imperfect brakes, that is the trouble.

This belief is destroyed through the *realization* that God is the one and only Mind, and that there is therefore no malicious mind to operate hypnotically and appear as a *belief* of anything.

This pure aloneness with God as the only Mind, is demonstration.

It does not demonstrate some *thing*, but is, itself, demonstration.

Every lie, whether called a disease or an imperfect brake, must be reduced to the one common denominator, the belief that malicious mind is.

Malicious mind must be recognized as the root of all evil. Then it can be destroyed.

Again, suppose you found yourself stalled in the desert, apparently without gasoline.

Must you necessarily wait until someone brings you gasoline or tows you to the nearest filling station? Suppose no one comes along?

Do you think that Christian Science would leave you helpless?

If it could do so, what right had Jesus to say, "Lo, I am with you alway, even unto the end of the world"?[1]

Jesus meant that no untoward condition could arise which was not the lie about the truth already present, and therefore available for immediate use. Mrs. Eddy puts it, *"Thou canst be brought into no condition, be it ever so severe, where Love has not been before thee and where its tender lesson is not awaiting thee."*[2]

What is the truth about gasoline?

Is it something material, hence finite and limited?

Or, in order to be, at all, must it not inevitably be a state of Mind or consciousness or, as material scientists term it, a "mathematical formula", thus a Mind-presence?

You cannot be conscious of that which is not.

Granting that there may seem to be a *false* consciousness of everything and anything that truly is, there could, nevertheless, be no consciousness whatever of that which is not.

[1]Matt. 28:20.   [2]My. 149:31.

It is because that which is, *is,* that you are really always conscious of that isness or truth, even if it comes to you upside down, or negatively.

When "two times two equals five" comes to you, it is really the truth of it that is knocking at the door of your thought; otherwise, there would be nothing of which to be conscious.

Mind, being the one and only consciousness, must be the source of your consciousness of gasoline; then, there could be no possible lack of gasoline where it was rightfully needed, any more than in the economy of numbers, you could lack the immediate presence of "four times six" or whatever was required to fulfil the purpose of intelligence.

Gasoline is as omnipresent as Mind. There is no place where it is not available.

Did not Elisha show this in the case of the oil for the widow?

What was true about the widow's oil is just as true about your gasoline.

The question is, are you finding gasoline as a state of Mind, or of matter?

What you are accepting will determine your abundance of gasoline, or the seeming lack of it.

In arguing the claim of a shortage of gasoline, you find gasoline omnipresent. The claim, then, is not that the gasoline has run out, but that malicious mind is accepted as consciousness, which leads further to the acceptance of the hypnotic suggestion of a *belief* of lack of gasoline.

Again the lie is brought back to its origin and destroyed through the *realization* of God as the one and only Mind. The conviction follows that there is no malicious mind to operate hypnotically and appear as a *belief* of something lacking.

HOUSE ON FIRE

If the power of the flames was proved by "Shadrach, Meshach, and Abed-nego"[1] to be harmless to hurt their bodies because of their confidence in God as All-in-all, cannot fire be proved powerless to destroy a house?

In this case, there are two points that instantly arrest attention; fire and house.

Fire, to be cognizable, must come as a sense of consciousness to you.

Therefore all that you know about consciousness includes all that can be known about fire.

Knowing that consciousness is Mind, God, you can know only good about fire, and the only fire you can know is the fire of God.

Fire, then, is omnipresent, and is the law of consumption to everything unlike good.

It consumes only that which is contrary to good and leaves intact everything that pertains to good.

[1] Dan. 3:20.

Fire is a state of Mind, not of matter. This is what the three Hebrew men proved.

What is house?

Again consciousness embraces all that is meant by house.

It follows, then, that because consciousness is one, there is but one house, and that house is the house of God.

All that God is, house is, for God can express only Himself.

The indestructibility of house is assured, for God is indestructible.

This one house, being all the house there is, is the house that is right where there seems to be the one on fire.

Is there any difference between one negation and another, between a house on fire and two-times-two as five?

The truth about the house and the fire will do to the lie about house and fire just what the truth about any lie does to the lie.

The truth destroys the lie and leaves the fact or truth as the reality and presence. "And behold, the bush burned with fire, and the bush was not consumed."[1]

It is not your understanding of this that makes it so, but the truth that is itself the fact.

This truth has always been the fact.

[1] Ex. 3:2.

Then does your knowing this put out the fire and save the house?

No.

Have you not through argument just convinced yourself that the fire of God is the one and only fire and that the house of God is the one and only house, and that therefore, these are both intact and eternally about their Father's business?

The claim, then, has nothing to do with a fire or with a house. Those are only the facts about which the negation, the one malicious mind, makes its hypnotic suggestion.

The axe must be laid at the root of the tree, the *belief* that there is a mind apart from the one Mind, which, operating as hypnotic suggestion, appears as a fire burning down a house.

The realization of God as the one and only Mind, filling all space, destroys the belief that there is malicious mind and its *belief* of a destructive fire.

The question arises, would not this understanding of Christian Science, operating to destroy the power of fire to burn a house, destroy also its power to operate in a useful capacity?

No, because the understanding of fire as the activity of God, the presence of good, sees that activity as destroying only that which is unlike good.

The fire of good, spontaneously consuming that which is unlike good, leaves the right heat for every purpose desired.

Did not Jesus, after his resurrection, have a fire, "and fish laid thereon",[1] for his disciples?

You do not think that he who saw the loaves and fishes for the thousands in the desert, needed to *make* a fire or *catch* the fish?

Mind embraced all for Jesus.

Truth destroys only whatever is contrary to Truth.

Discord automatically disappears in the presence of Truth.

The human interpretation of this appears as whatever is *"nearest right under the circumstances"*,[2] thence achieving the absolute.

Because all is Mind, every effect is a Mind effect, not a matter effect as it appears to be.

The stilling of the storm by Jesus is called a miracle. It was not a miracle. It was the spontaneous law of Mind interpreting itself naturally in its allness as the removal of everything unlike itself.

A storm may be beautiful and grand. Waves, embraced in Mind, cannot be harmful.

The understanding of this immediately translates anything contrary to good into intelligible language, and causes the disappearance of whatever seems wrong.

[1]Jno. 21:9.   [2]Mis. 288:13.

OUT OF POSITION

Man's position is as assured as is God's. Man is that whereby God is shown forth or known. In other words, man is the position of God.

Therefore, man's position is intact, complete.

Because God *is*, and is all that is, there is no power or presence to interfere with, or in any way to change man's position.

The law of continuance is ever-operative as the law of Mind. In consequence, there is never a condition such as "out of position".

The remuneration from position must be abundant, to include within itself all that means perfection, comfort, completeness; for are not the perfection, comfort and completeness of God made manifest as man?

Position is omnipresent, for Mind *is*.

It is not dependent on anything but Mind.

Man, being the position of God, eternally and perfectly fills that position.

Position *is* and is yours. Therefore you never look for it. You open your eyes and see it.

There is no mind to suggest hypnotically a belief of out-of-position, or a disagreeable position, and so forth. The one Mind is the All-Mind.

This *realization* makes the one position, or man's perfect relationship to Mind, eternally available.

It does not *produce* it, it *is* it.

POOR BUSINESS

Business is the state of being busy, or busyness.

This implies thinking, for thought is all there is to action.

Therefore, business is the activity of Mind. It is Mind interpreting its infinite resources to man.

Because there is one Mind, there is one business, and that is the business of Mind.

Inasmuch as Mind is infinite, business is infinite.

Inasmuch as Mind is infinite good, business is infinitely good.

Business is the eternal oneness of supply and demand.

God is supply and man is demand. Business is the communion between God and man.

Whatever supply is, demand is and has.

There is no lapse or gap between them. One is, because the other is.

Not an item enters into business that does not originate with Mind.

It must, therefore, not only have its place but also be in its place.

Not a pin could appear to be manufactured without Mind.

Whence, then, comes a surplus of goods, if even every pin has its place and is in its place?

It is impossible that Mind could think, and its thought go wandering about, seeking a resting place.

Intelligence cannot think without definite purpose.

Purpose implies fulfilment.

Mind thinks, and it is done.

The place of Mind's thought is with its Thinker. It is never separated from Him.

What appear as things, do not need to be placed, for they are eternally in their right place as the thought of intelligence.

Salesmanship is not the act of selling something, but the seeing of the order and harmony of Mind everywhere present, with everything already rightly placed.

This is to be about the Father's business.

This understanding destroys all effort to sell mesmerically or otherwise. In other words, to seek to put something where it is not already placed, is an effort which would deny the allness and orderliness of good.

But this understanding does not stop diligent activity on the part of what appears as the salesman, rather does it make him more active in discovering the omnipresence of good.

The consciousness, the *realization*, that the one Mind *is*, and is all that *is*, and that there is no mind to suggest hypnotically a *belief* of poor business, is God's business, and, therefore, man's business.

FAILING CROPS

Crops, like position and business, are inseparably one with the consciousness that *is,* and is all.

Did not God make "every plant of the field before it was in the earth, and every herb of the field before it grew"?[1]

Then is not that for which both plant and herb exist, namely, the showing forth of crop—the beauty, perfection and the abundance of its Maker—likewise present?

Crop is never absent from plant or herb.

The one is the corollary of the other.

Mind includes the all of both. Therefore, crops are always bountiful, perfect and ever-present. They are Mind interpreting itself to you. To limit crops is to limit your understanding of God.

It is not failure of crops that is the claim, but rather the hypnotic suggestion of a *belief* of failure or shortage, a belief which would imply that there is malicious mind.

The realization that God is the only Mind negates this lie, and reveals good as All-in-all.

Jesus condemned the belief of unfruitfulness when he said to the fig tree that had no fruit on it, even though "the time of figs was not yet":[2]

[1]Gen. 2:5.   [2]Mark 11:13.

"Let no fruit grow on thee henceforward for ever. And presently the fig tree withered away."[1]

In this, Jesus illustrated the fact, that with Mind, there is no fixed season for a crop, but that crop is omnipresent, exactly as the multiplication table has not a time when it will work and a time when it will not work. Its presence is the enlightenment which follows man's obedience to Principle.

WEATHER

Weather is the belief that atmospheric conditions produce a variety of climates, good and bad.

Mind, embracing all action, includes all atmospheric action or condition.

Then, is not all weather as directly subject to understanding as is a mathematical problem?

Is not even the simplest mathematical problem the appearance of mathematical perfection in embryo, and is not the solution present with the problem?

Any weather condition is the omnipresence of the perfection of weather, interpreted finitely. Christian Science interprets it correctly and bad weather gives place to good, for it is not the weather that is bad.

When you destroy the belief that malicious mind is, with the *realization* that God alone is

[1]Matt. 21:19.

Mind, the hypnotic suggestion of a *belief* of bad weather vanishes. In its place is seen exactly the right heat, cold, rain, or whatever is required to best show forth the perfection of weather as the presence of God.

Thus as the voice of God you speak with absolute authority to every belief of weather, and prove that "even the winds and the sea obey him".[1]

HEREDITY

The human concept of heredity, no matter in what form it appears, is always based on the belief of a beginning; in other words, an origin, from which characteristics, etc. are derived.

Heredity implies something existent prior to birth.

This invites the question, When does the so-called mortal begin?

Does he begin at his so-called birth, or does he begin prior to birth, at the point of conception?

The conception of a finite or mortal sense is the origin of the lie or negation about the divine sense.

When does any lie begin? Is it not with the conceiving of the lie?

Then the lie about the divine man begins with the conceiving of the false belief that he has a beginning.

[1]Matt. 8:27.

Because of this, Science and Health says of mortals, *"They never had a perfect state of being, which may subsequently be regained. They were, from the beginning of mortal history, 'conceived in sin and brought forth in iniquity' "*.[1]

A lie, by its very nature, is always conceived in falsity or iniquity, and yet it is proclaimed as the truth.

Because prior to his conception there is nothing to the mortal except the man of God about which the mortal concept is the lie, and because no hereditary claim is made about any influence coming after birth, it follows that every hereditary belief must be a belief that supposedly originates during the interval between what is called conception and what is called birth.

This is known as the period of pregnancy or gestation.

Then the specific claim of heredity must be one of pregnancy.

The human or false concept of pregnancy is the belief that the young mind or mortal is being formed and during this formative period is susceptible to impregnation with various beliefs, later to be shown forth as personal traits of character and tendencies to disease ending in death.

The true concept of pregnancy is that which infinite Mind always is, infinitely pregnant with

[1] S. & H. 476:14.

its own illimitable idea, having nothing outside of itself with which to inflict any untoward condition on that with which it is pregnant.

Pregnancy is the eternal communion between Mind and its idea in which Mind endows its offspring with its own qualities.

The only hereditary law, therefore, is the law of good, of perfection—the one and only pregnancy.

Then it is neither pregnancy nor heredity that needs to be corrected. It is the belief that there is a mind apart from the one Mind, which, operating hypnotically, appears as a false sense of pregnancy with its so-called hereditary laws.

There is no such mind, because God is the one and only Mind, and His law of heredity is perfection, harmony, and completeness.

While considering the question of heredity, it is well to remind oneself of the fact already brought out, that the most insidious belief attached to the origin of the mortal is the false claim that animal or venereal poison is his progenitor and that this poison must sooner or later accomplish its purpose and bring forth death.

In belief the whole human race is doomed because of this poisonous origin.

Therefore, it is essential to understand the truth about man's origin, what he inherits, what forms him, and what maintains him. Otherwise, what would there be with which to counteract the law that says that what begins must end. *"If Life ever had a beginning, it would also have an ending."*[1]

Truth is the true poison, the law of destruction to all unlike itself.

Science and Health declares that, *"Heredity is a prolific subject for mortal belief to pin theories upon".*[2]

Is not the mortal continually confronted with the suggestion that he has to overcome something inherited from some ancestor, regardless of whether he knows anything about that ancestor or not?

Are not traits of character, as well as so-called physical conditions, supposedly traced to ancestral origin?

The fact is that man, as the thought of God, inherits all that God is; and that inheritance is supreme.

It is interesting to note that materia medica is now saying that the fœtus, or egg, from which the mortal supposedly springs, cannot be impregnated by anything from without. Hereditary conditions, it asserts, are due to association, etc., thus bearing out the diagnosis of Christian Science that it is mental impregnation, hypnotic suggestion, and not physical phenomenon, that accounts for hereditary conditions.

[1] S. & H. 469:5.   [2] S. & H. 228:7.

RHEUMATISM

Rheumatism, like gout, is the belief of an over supply of uric acid in the blood, or, as it has sometimes been stated: not enough alkali to neutralize the acid; wrong balance.

What do you know about uric acid?

Since God, being All-in-all, includes within Himself all that uric acid means and is, can there be an excess or a deficiency of uric acid?

Can kidneys, liver, bowels, or lungs cease to be the eternal activity of intelligence, and fail to perform their perfect functions—rejecting all that is unlike good?

Mind interprets itself to you in its own definite language as action, alkali, chemistry, etc.

This interpretation is the very essence of harmony and perfection.

Is there an excess or a deficiency, then, of uric acid; or is rheumatism only a hypnotic *belief* of maladjustments?

You know that every claim is hypnotism and never a wrong *thing*.

Inflammation, swelling of the joints, soreness —every symptom of rheumatism, or of any other disease, is always hypnotic belief.

All are destroyed through the *realization* that God is the only Mind. This leaves no evil mind to suggest any lying belief.

You do not *get rid of* rheumatism, for there never has been such a thing; but you reject the hypnotic suggestion of a *belief* of imperfect action, because God is the only Mind.

Thus rheumatism disappears.

GERMS

The germ of goodness is the only germ, and this germ, in its infinity of variety, expresses God in all its ways.

Malicious suggestion may call this germ a typhoid germ, a tubercular germ, a pneumonic germ, or any other kind. Just as it divides its sense of the animal, vegetable and mineral kingdoms into either harmless or dangerous species, so it classifies its sense of the germ kingdom into good germs and bad germs.

Did Daniel have two kinds of lions?

Did Jesus have two kinds of water, one rough and the other smooth, one to be walked upon and the other to be drowned in?

There is one germ and one only. That is the germ of God, the germ of good, the germ that always works "together for good to them that love"[1] good.

Do you love this germ "with all thy heart, and with all thy soul, and with all thy mind, and with all thy strength"?[2] Or are you anxious to destroy it?

Is this the germ that is always in heaven? It is.

Because it is, it blesses you.

[1]Rom. 8:28.   [2]Mark 12:30.

No hypnotic suggestion can deceive you into belief in any other germ.

The one Mind, as the only Mind, is the law of total annihilation to any claim of a supposititious mind to hypnotically suggest a belief in a germ apart from the germ of God. There is no such mind.

ALCOHOLIC DRUNKENNESS

Alcohol is defined as the "pure spirit of wine", and the use of this, we are told, makes a man drunk.

Is it supposable that, in the sight of Principle, the use of one thing differs from the use of another?

Alcohol, indulged in as a beverage, is supposed to inflame and irritate the pneumogastric nerve, which in turn affects the brain lobes. Thus alcohol allegedly causes its victim to become befuddled and lose his balance. If taken in sufficient quantities, it is presumed to cause him to lose consciousness.

Is alcohol something outside of that which comes to you as consciousness? Does it, in fact, come to you in a different way from the way in which water comes to you?

You cannot be aware of anything unless it comes as consciousness to you. It follows, then, that consciousness embraces within itself all that is true about alcohol.

Whatever consciousness is, that you know alcohol to be, and since God is the one consciousness, only the quality of good can be attached to alcohol.

The "pure spirit of wine" used in the Scriptural sense of wine, is the pure essence or isness of *"Inspiration; understanding"*.[1]

The qualities of good are the laws of good.

The laws of good cannot be wrongly interpreted and cannot injuriously affect brain-lobes; nor can they produce unsteadiness of either Mind or body.

Then you know that the process is not one of healing the alcoholic habit, but one of destroying the hypnotic suggestion of a belief of injurious alcohol.

The remedy for alcoholic drunkenness is not to do away with alcohol, as such, any more than it is to do away with eyes or brain or lungs, as such, simply because these organs are said to be diseased.

The remedy is to destroy the belief that there is a mind that can operate hypnotically as a *belief* of drunkenness, through alcohol or through any other avenue.

The *realization* of the one Mind as the All-Mind is the destruction of drunkenness.

"Whatever intoxicates a man, stultifies and causes him to degenerate physically and morally.

[1]S. & H. 598:17.

*Strong drink is unquestionably an evil, and evil
cannot be used temperately: its slightest use is
abuse; hence the only temperance is total abstinence. Drunkenness is sensuality let loose, in
whatever form it is made manifest."*[1]

Total abstinence means absolutely turning
away from the hypnotic belief and indulgence in
a mind apart from God.

The one Mind alone satisfies man and crowns
"him with glory and honour".[2]

OTHER FALSE APPETITES

There are many phases of drunkenness; alcoholic drunkenness is but one of them.

All belief in materiality is drunkenness in
varying degrees; for it is the belief in something
apart from Mind, a desire for something outside
of itself, a departure from the straight line of
Principle, the bringing in of a "third". It is the
breaking of the First Commandment: "Thou
shalt have no other gods before me".[3]

*"If a man is an inebriate, a slave to tobacco,
or the special servant of any one of the myriad
forms of sin, meet and destroy these errors with
the truth of being, ... by convincing him that
there is no real pleasure in false appetites."*[4]

Because man is the idea of Mind, the whole
source of his conscious being and power is derived
from the one infinite, all inclusive consciousness,
God.

[1]Mis. 288:32.   [2]Ps. 8:5.   [3]Ex. 20:3.   [4]S. & H. 404:3.

Man has the right then to be absolutely satisfied—he *is* satisfied, complete.

When anything arrays itself against Mind, it must be rejected—replaced. You must cheerfully give up cherished beliefs if you would enter into the kingdom of your birthright.

The unwillingness to give up what is pleasurable—this very word "pleasurable" means trusting in materiality—*"is the unseen sin, the unknown foe"*.[1]

To the consciousness aroused by Truth, things will not be merely pleasurable. To the quickened sense of what substance is, Mind alone is joy.

Then, what you see, taste, smell, hear and feel will testify of God. This will be very different from saying, "This delights my palate."

Jesus did not make wine at the Feast at Cana through any of the accepted processes, but by seeing the presence of Mind as all the water there is, he saw the presence of Mind as all the wine there is. This so uplifted thought that it was satisfied—better satisfied than with the wine just consumed.

Mrs. Eddy has said, *"The depraved appetite for alcoholic drinks, tobacco, tea, coffee, opium, is destroyed only by Mind's mastery of the body"*.[2]

[1]Ret. 31:17.   [2]S. & H. 406:28.

These drugs are indulged in for their so-called "stimulating" qualities; they are not considered food.

Since God is the only power, all true stimulation comes from Him.

What appears as food will be the last belief of materiality to be given up because it carries with it the idea of sustaining life—the eternal function of Mind.

It is a very different condition, however, when indulgences are involved.

PARASITE

A parasite is the belief that one sense of life, can prey upon another; that there is something out of its rightful place.

God is Life and is All-in-all.

Where, then, is there one life to prey upon another?

Can that which is all be out of place? It cannot. Then, parasite is not something out of place, but is a belief that there is a mind that can operate hypnotically and suggest something out of place.

The *realization* that there is one Mind only, maintaining all, destroys the belief of any mind apart from itself.

This destroys the false sense of parasite and the lie vanishes.

OBSTETRICS

The word *obstetrics* is derived from the Latin *obsto,* I stand before, in the sense of assisting. The word as commonly used means the scientific assistance given at childbirth.

Obstetrics is not the bringing to light of something new, but the making known of that which already is and has always been.

What appears as the birth of a new child is finite sense, claiming oneness with infinity.

Mind is infinite space and Mind is omnipresently expressed.

Therefore, there is no room for more than that which already is.

Human belief is the negation of this, but by reversing the negation, the positive fact of the omnipresence of good and all that good means, is seen as the All-presence.

This presence goes through no process of birth or formation. It is ever present, beautiful, complete and whole, showing forth all the glories of Mind as perfect action, symmetry and harmony.

All communion with Mind is obstetrics.

It is the understanding of Mind in the infinite purity of its unfolding—the eternal communion between Mind and its idea.

In what appears as the healing of every claim is the operation of the law of obstetrics—the unfolding of divine energy.

There is no malicious mind to operate hypnotically and to suggest a *belief* of any obstetrics contrary to this.

God is the one Mind and holds within Himself all unfoldment.

This is the obstetrics Mrs. Eddy says every Christian Scientist should *"be familiar with"*.[1] It is the basis of all right knowing, whether appearing as a birth, business transaction, or as health.

TEETH

The Bible says that all the hairs of your head are numbered.

Why? Because the thought of God cannot be separated from God. Since hair can be known only as consciousness, it is forever one with God, the one consciousness.

Thus, it is forever known and numbered, forever right and in place.

If hairs are numbered and in place, is not the same thing true of teeth?

That which exists as the thought of God cannot be decayed or lost, for Mind is the one substance forever imparted to its idea.

Two times two can never get away from its principle and be lost. It cannot become five, or anything else that is wrong.

[1] S. & H. 463:5.

Then, what appears as a decayed tooth or a lost tooth is a purely hypnotic state, for God is all there is to tooth.

The omnipresence of God insures the omnipresence of tooth.

It is not a case of the tooth, at all, but a belief about tooth.

God has no *belief* about anything. He *knows* His own perfection always. That perfection is intact.

Then the claim is once again cleared up by the *realization* that there is no malicious mind to act hypnotically and appear as a *belief* of imperfect or lost tooth, for the one Mind, God, infinite good, is the All-Mind.

HEART DISEASE

The heart is commonly regarded as the most important organ of the body because the mortal is supposed to die when the heart stops. So long as the heart continues to beat, life is said to be present, thus, in theory, making life dependent upon a material organ.

Life and heart are linked together in human belief. But does this belief bear analysis?

The organ, heart, is supposedly composed of chemical constituents, which have been reduced by modern scientific theory to points of energy represented by a mathematical formula. Nothing could be more mental than a mathematical formula, nothing more indestructible.

This proves that the heart is not matter, as such. What, then, is it?

God, being All-in-all, embracing within His infinite variety of expression every concept to which meaning can be given, includes within that allness that which is meant by heart, including valves and so forth, whether called a human organ or a mathematical formula.

Since, in order that one may be conscious, consciousness must first be, it is obvious that consciousness of the fact, heart, is all there is to heart.

Stating this differently, God is all that there is to heart, irrespective of any other interpretation of it.

Heart, then, is perfect and is one, everywhere present and functioning as it should.

This brings us squarely to the actual claim in so-called heart disease. It is that there is malicious mind.

Our problem, then, is not to deal with a material, diseased heart, but to *realize* that because God is the one and only Mind, there is no malicious mind to operate hypnotically as a belief of diseased heart.

It is interesting to note that human belief is undergoing a changing concept in regard to the part played by the heart. Whereas, a few years ago, death was regarded as instantly present with the stoppage of the heart action, today, medical practice very often attempts "resuscitation" for many minutes, even hours, in some cases, after the heart has ceased to beat, proving that human belief is yielding to the fact that life cannot be at the mercy of the muscle we call the heart—a muscle, by the way, that is considered the toughest and most resistant of all the organs of the body.

ECZEMA

Eczema is the name given to a well-defined case of the belief of animal or venereal poison in the blood.

You have already seen that the whole of mortality or mortal belief is the expression of death, in contradistinction to immortal man, the expression of Life.

As the expression of death, mortal man must, as it were, contain within his own being the seeds that are finally to bring forth death and thus prove his false or mortal origin.

The statement of Mind, "I am come that they might have life, and that they might have it more abundantly,"[1] is met with the negative: I have come that they might have death and have it more inevitably.

[1] Jno. 10:10.

Eczema vividly illustrates this poisonous taint in the blood. But whether outwardly visible or not, this animal poison is ever-operative in the human interpretation of man and must be destroyed through the understanding of what man's origin really is; that he is the idea of God, without beginning or end.

Man is not the product of the union of the so-called male and female bodies, nor of the poisons that are the essence of these bodies.

You have seen that man is never in a womb, never in process of being formed, any more than God Himself could ever be formed.

Man co-exists with God.

Then, because he never is created, no animal poison enters into his make-up, later to show itself as eczema or other bad blood conditions.

The claim therefore, is not one of bad blood, for right where suggestion says there is a humor in the blood, there is the very presence of God defining perfect blood, pure blood.

The claim is, of course, that malicious mind *is,* and that as such *isness* it appears hypnotically as a belief of eczema.

You destroy the lie, as you do in every case, through the *realization* that there is no malicious mind, because God is the one and only Mind.

No case is ever completely corrected until this realization of the allness and omnipresence of the one Mind reigns as consciousness.

Realization means *feeling in your heart,* as well as seeing with your intelligence.

Into realization no personal element enters; in it no human desire remains.

Only pure oneness with God abides—oneness with all that means and is good.

Blood is called the life-stream of being. Then is it not your communion with Mind—purity itself, isness itself—uncontaminated by anything outside of its own pure selfhood?

It is, and this consciousness destroys the lie about being.

EPIDEMIC

Epidemic is a disease in itself.

It illustrates how wholly mental disease is.

The epidemic of influenza during the closing days of the World War spread to places where no possible contagion by physical contact could be traced.

Epidemic is fear-contagion.

Is not fear-contagion purely mental suggestion in its impersonal sense?

A claim of epidemic is handled in exactly the same way in which you would release the victim of a hypnotist.

In the latter case, you would not deal with a wrong thing. Your attention would be devoted to destroying the belief that there is malicious mind to control or govern.

Knowing that God is the one Mind, that He is all the Mind there is, you cannot be duped into attempting to deal with another mind.

This realization would break the claim of hypnotism and free the victim.

An epidemic is dealt with in exactly the same way.

Fear, contagious belief, is both the hypnotist and the hypnotism.

It is not contact, nor any form of matter, that has to be destroyed for the claim is purely mental suggestion—in other words, hypnotism.

Do not be deceived into arguing down any of the various symptoms, as in an ordinary case of sickness; contagion has none, in that sense.

Epidemic is pure hypnotic contagion; it is fear, not physical contact.

Symptoms have no more to do with contagion than have the motions of the hypnotized victim's arms and legs, in swimming on dry boards under the influence of the hypnotist, anything to do with the real claim.

The man is not in water, and therefore is not really swimming. Nor do you think he is; so you do not consider either swimming or water.

You handle hypnotism.

You do the same with epidemic and destroy it through the *realization* of God as the one and only Mind.

SIN

Sin is the belief in a power or presence apart from God.

The breaking of the First Commandment, "Thou shalt have no other gods before me",[1] is the only sin, for this Commandment includes within itself all the other Commandments.

The keeping of the first is the keeping of all.

To believe in something apart from God includes all there is to killing, for such a belief kills the allness of your God.

To adulterate the truth with human belief is adultery. There could be no human adultery, if communion with God were all that was accepted as consciousness.

To steal is to deny God's allness, and so rob Him of His wholeness.

To bear false witness is to entertain any belief in matter, in limitation, in the opposite of God.

All purely human desire is a tacit denial of God's allness and omnipresence and of man's at-one-ment with Him.

To love thy neighbor as thyself is to find God, the Self of you as thy neighbor.

Did not Jesus say that if you broke one Commandment, you broke all?

Then is not the First Commandment all-inclusive?

[1]Ex. 20:3.

It is, and the breaking of it is the only sin.

Man, as the activity of God, is the pureness of good and so is the law of destruction to all unlike good.

When the belief of the virus of evil is met with the infinite virus, or energy of *isness,* as being all that is, evil, as hypnotic suggestion, vanishes.

A NAMELESS CASE

Let us examine now, as a final case, one where apparently there is no visible reason for the sickness—a case without a name.

In other words, suppose a patient to be sick and dying, and that no physical diagnosis can be made of the case.

The physicians who have been in charge declare that they can find no reason for the trouble; yet the patient is slowly dying.

How would Christian Science deal with such a situation?

In the first place, no case is a puzzle to the Christian Scientist, for to him no case is ever material.

Every case is always sin—the sin of accepting a mind apart from the one Mind—thus breaking the First Commandment, and, in so doing, breaking all ten.

This is the one and only sin, the sin of sins.

This sin embodies within itself all hatred, envy, jealousy, malice, revenge, covetousness, lust, desire, and so forth. It is *"the fundamental error of faith in things material; . . . the unseen sin, the unknown foe,—the heart's untamed desire which breaketh the divine commandments."*[1]

Not a single note of malicious suggestion can be played except on one or another of these chords, all of which are summed up in the "faith in things material".[1]

So, in destroying any unknown, would-be subtle foe, you canvass the field of suggestion, in order to leave not a single avenue down which evil can hide.

You know that evil is not mind, for Mind means wisdom, intelligence, the truth about something.

You know that evil is not a creator and therefore has no avenue or channel, no man, woman or child, place or thing, through which it can act. It has nothing to act upon or through, no object or subject.

You know it has no power; no action; no law by which to guide or control; no history; no past, present or future; no law of continuance or occupancy.

Evil has no laws in or of materia medica, anatomy, physiology, matter, nature, or anything else through which to act.

As malicious mental suggestion, divorced from all materiality, evil cannot operate hyp-

[1] Ret. 31:16.

notically as a belief of sickness, death, poison, etc., nor as any so-called evil mental quality, such as envy, jealousy, hatred, etc., nor be influential as such.

Evil offers no resistance to Truth, nor to the activity of Truth, nor to the Christian Science prayer, which is treatment.

It has no material substance, no bodily presence to resist or obstruct the operation of Truth.

Nor has it any form of process, mode of development, decay, or failure, to retard the orderly unfoldment of Mind.

Thus you would cover the entire range of hypnotic suggestion and destroy every avenue for malicious mind.

In so doing, you would leave the final, inevitable conviction, the *realization* that God, infinite good, is the only Mind, the only presence.

CONCLUSION

Mrs. Eddy, in Science and Health, illustrates a case fully. She supposes a case of liver-complaint.

The cases handled here have been used to illustrate a certain general procedure if arguments are used.

But in no way do these illustrations pretend to go into the minutiæ of any case, or to outline how you would handle a case yourself.

In no sense of the word are they formulas. Formulas are fatal in Christian Science, because they are pure materialism.

Intelligence alone must guide you and show you what to handle.

With infinite intelligence as your intelligence, it is possible for you to know exactly what to handle and how to handle it.

You have supreme confidence in your own understanding because God is your Mind, and you know all that you need to know about every case.

Every case is distinct and unique, or it could not be a case.

There is no duplication of anything in Mind or in its negation.

Two thoughts alike would not be two, but one.

There is, then, no duplication of treatment, no copying, no imitating.

Mind is ever new and spontaneous, and the negation of Mind, being the denial of Mind, is equally new and automatically present.

Every moment brings its own particular opportunity, and a case is but an opportunity presented in the language that you can best understand and profit by.

It is opportunity for right interpretation.

No case offers difficulties to intelligence.

There is nothing hidden, unknown, or unrevealed about it.

As enlightenment, Mind may appear to you in any form.

Whatever you need to know about any case you can know, and you do know.

This enlightenment may appear to you as something the so-called patient tells you; it may appear as something you read, or something another person tells you; it may appear as something that comes to you as your own conclusion.

But whatever is necessary for you to know, will appear; it will always appear, when you acknowledge infinite intelligence as the one and only Mind, the one and only Practitioner; when you acknowledge that it is your Mind on the case.

God is not limited in His means of informing His own idea.

See, then, that you do not limit Him; but, "*Open* (your) *affections to the Principle that moves all in harmony,—from the falling of a sparrow to the rolling of a world*".[1]

Look to God alone for guidance.

You are alone with your "*own being and with the reality of things*".[2]

If you never allow a "third" into your thinking, you will find yourself the king and priest "unto God",[3] referred to by the Revelator. You will be possessed of all the majesty and might that belongs to that kingship and priesthood.

[1] Mis. 174:10.   [2] '01 20:9.   [3] Rev. 1:6.

"Crown the power of Mind as the Messiah",[1] and *"give to Mind the glory, honor, dominion, and power everlastingly due its holy name."*[2]

This is the spirit of Christian Science that alone wins the day.

Arguments are only to bring you, not the patient, to the final complete conviction that Spirit is supreme and all.

Thus you speak as "one having authority".[3]

[1] S. & H. 116:14. [2] S. & H. 143:29. [3] Matt. 7:29.

CHAPTER X

ANSWERING SOME QUESTIONS ARISING IN CLASS

The following questions are tersely answered from the basis of what the preceding chapters have established, and will be understood from that standpoint.

Obedience: Obedience and man are synonymous. The image in the mirror repeats exactly the object in front of the mirror. This is the obedience of it. In the same way man is the obedience of God. He is that which expresses God, the exact likeness of God.

Opportunity: Opportunity is that which shows forth, that which makes known. Man is the opportunity of Mind; that whereby Mind is made known. Thus man is at the standpoint of opportunity every instant. Therefore, there is no such thing as a lost opportunity.

Discovery of Christian Science: The discovery of Christian Science is the discovery that the acknowledgment and realization of that which *is*, as all that is, spontaneously destroys that which seems to be, but *is not*.

Mind and counterfeit: It is said that there are ninety million microbes in every cubic inch of air. Mrs. Eddy's discovery of the allness of Mind as infinite Life, released the negative definition of this allness expressed as equally omnipresent material life. The human mind promptly expressed this in its own terms, as ninety million microbes in every cubic inch of air.

Ninety billion would have been equally correct, and even that would have but feebly expressed the fact as compared to infinity.

Class instruction: I am asked why I teach more than one class a year when the Church Manual limits a teacher to one class a year.

When progress freed me from the limitations of Church government, it left me free to hold as many classes a year as might seem to be needed.

Mrs. Eddy never limited the number of her classes. It was only the exigencies of organization that demanded a limitation. Principle no more limits the number of classes in Christian Science than it does in mathematics or music. Only human organization does that.

Class, being oneness with Mind, is not something that begins and ends. It is eternal communion with Mind.

"Laws of limitation": In writing of the by-laws of the Church Manual, Mrs. Eddy characterized them as *"That which I said in my heart would never be needed,—namely, laws of limitation for a Christian Scientist."*[1]

This plainly indicates that Mrs. Eddy herself considered them not laws of God, but laws of limitation and therefore of His opposite.

Church: Church is but another name for man. Man is the structure or idea of Truth and Love, which is the definition Mrs. Eddy gives of Church. "Whatever rests upon and proceeds from divine Principle"[2] is a definition equally true of man. This Church is omnipresent and has nothing to do with people or with organization.

"As" versus "in": The words "in" and "as" are most important. God never appears *in* anything, for infinity cannot be *in*. God always appears *as* His own idea, never *in* it. Man is *of* God, not *in* God. Man does not find himself *in* Mind, but he is *of* Mind. Man's awareness of all he cognizes is his communion with Mind —God interpreting Himself *as* idea. To use these words rightly is highly important.

Sleep: Sleep is the belief of conscious unconsciousness. You consciously go to sleep. In other words you consciously become unconscious. Death is this consciously becoming unconscious, carried to its ultimate.

Because death seems, at times, to be brought about without conscious acceptance, it does not change the fact that it is always the result of conscious acceptance on the part of the human mind somehow, somewhere.

"Death is the consequent of an antecedent false assumption of the realness of something unreal, material, and mortal."[3]

To acknowledge that any condition whatsoever can produce death, is tacitly to accept death whenever procuring conditions are present. This acceptance would still be operative, even though not coming from the individual himself, because the mind of the mortal, the one mortal mind, has already done the accepting. So the automaton of that mind, the mortal, expresses what his mind

[1]My. 229:25.   [2]S. & H. 583:12.   [3]No. 16:28.

holds, unless counteracted by understanding as Jesus counteracted it.

True sleep is resting in the conscious understanding that "he giveth his beloved sleep",[1] as the Psalmist declares. Whether this rest appears as unconscious sleep or not, it is conscious oneness with God. This is real rest.

Treatment and consent: A metaphysician, dealing with Mind alone and acknowledging Mind as All-in-all, never deals with person. Then he never treats person, and needs no consent of person to reverse the error that knocks at his door as consciousness, but which he knows is not consciousness if it is not all that God is. This spurious sense he promptly casts out thus verifying Jesus' statement, "And I, if I be lifted up from the earth, will draw all men unto me".[2] He sees the lie vanish, no matter where it seems to be.

On the other hand a faith Scientist, believing that there is a person who needs healing, will try to deal with *a* person, who, he thinks, has a separate mind of his own.

In that case, to be true to himself, by not doing to another what he would not have another do to him, the faith Scientist would not treat another person without first having his consent. But this is only because he has personalized his sense of being, is not alone with consciousness, and is hampered accordingly.

Jesus was always alone with Mind, and therefore did not have to ask consent to be God-like; he insisted on seeing his good everywhere present.

"Mind, imbued with this Science of healing, is a law unto itself, needing neither license nor prohibition; but lawless mind, with unseen motives, and silent mental methods whereby it may injure the race, is the highest attenuation of evil."[3]

"Unforgivable sin": The sin against the Holy Ghost is the attempt to tamper with the truth of Christian Science and to turn it to one's own material advantage. This can be done only at the expense of what is accepted as another person, *"taking the livery of heaven"*[4] and preying upon others.

The refusal ever to admit a "third" is the perpetual insurance against all sinning and sin.

Old age: Old age is the belief that man had a beginning and that God sets a limit on his days. This is a mental illusion, for today even the human mind itself, through its advanced thinkers, says that there is no law that compels man to die; and that his body is renewed completely every seven years—possibly oftener.

False education has heretofore taught otherwise, so mortal man has died in obedience to his mental acceptance and not be-

[1]Ps. 127:2.   [2]Jno. 12:32.   [3]Mis. 260:28.   [4]Mis. 19:18.

cause of his physical condition. The physical always remains the
obedient servant of the mortal.

Old age and death will disappear with the acceptance of the
truth that man never began and never ends. Life is continuous
and has no death process.

Depletion: Depletion is the acceptance of a mind apart from the
one Mind. This acceptance is the murderer, thief, adulterer,
fornicator and breaker of each of the commandments.

No time element: Time does not intervene between right knowing and the result of that right knowing. Mind and thought are
one—instantaneous and spontaneous. There could not be a right
thought, if Truth were not present from which to evolve it. There
is no time element involved in demonstration,—hence Jesus' instantaneous work

Correcting the lie: A lie left to itself grows by accretion because
it is the negation of the truth. Truth being infinite, the negation,
of necessity, must continue to accumulate more lies, not because
of any capacity of its own for thinking, but because it is the negation of that which is infinite.

A lie never corrects itself, any more than two times two as
five corrects itself. The truth alone corrects a lie by reversing
the lie and showing forth the truth right where the lie is
masquerading as the truth.

A lie reversed is the truth. *"The greatest wrong is but a supposititious opposite of the highest right."*[1] There is no negation
without that which it contradicts. The *Mind*-photographer spontaneously reverses the lie, finds the presence of good as the only
presence, and thus causes "the wrath of man"[2] to praise Him.

Only one ignorance: In a mathematical problem there may be
two mistakes about two times two, but there is only one ignorance
responsible for both mistakes. Yet you have to correct both mistakes. It is the same truth that corrects them both.

Every mistake of the human mind is exactly the same mistake.
It may appear as two or as many, but *one* malicious mind is all
there is to the mistake. This mind holds within itself each mortal or lie, as distinct and individual, even as the thought of God
is individual and complete in all its infinity of variety. Therefore
it must be corrected individually and cannot be lumped, as it
were, with so-called similar errors.

Metaphysically, there are no two cases alike, for every claim
of evil is but the negation of the truth, and since Truth, God,
cannot think two thoughts alike, neither can evil, error have two
thoughts alike. The fact that it seems to do so, is only part of

[1]S. & H. 368:1. [2]Ps. 76:10.

the lie or picture which evil paints by declaring "I am true", whereas, in reality, evil is only a lie about the truth.

The parable of the sower: In the parable of the sower, Jesus spoke of some of the seed that "fell by the way side, and the fowls of the air came and devoured it up".[1]

The human mind, being the lie about divine Mind, automatically contradicts every statement of Truth, not because it knows enough to want to do so but because its nature is that of a lie about Truth.

Evil's opposition to the truth is always present with the mortal; consequently, every statement of Truth is at first rejected. This rejection constitutes the "fowls of the air", which came and snatching at everything, "devoured it up" and lost it.

This explains why a person, having seen some higher unfoldment of Truth, and having enthusiastically presented it to another, sometimes loses the vision to his own great discouragement.

This would not happen, if the truth, before being presented, had been made one's own, that is, proved by demonstration.

Loss comes through failure to know that Truth is everywhere present and everybody already knows it.

The mortal and the immortal: What connection is there between the mortal and the immortal?

Exactly the same connection that there is between "two times two is five" and "two times two is four", or between any lie and the truth about which it is the lie.

It is self-evident that there can be no lie about anything, if the truth about it does not exist first. Because this is so, a lie is merely the misstatement of a fact. A lie is not something of itself, nor does it have any substance or mind of its own. It borrows all from the truth about which it is the lie, and misstates it.

You could not have any misstatement about two times two unless there were first the two times two about which to be mistaken. The "two times two is four" is always right. It is what the lie or ignorance says about it that is wrong.

The mortal, likewise, is the misstatement or lie about the immortal, the lie about being. That which Being is conscious of, constitutes the immortal, and the mortal is only the lie about it.

The connection, then, between the mortal and the immortal is that one is the negation of the other. The immortal or conscious being, must exist right where the mortal seems to be, and it is to the immortal that Truth appeals and with whom it works. "That [is] the true Light, which lighteth every man that cometh into the world."[2]

[1]Mark 4:4. [2]Jno. 1:9.

Perhaps as illustrating, in a degree, the point of the relationship between the mortal and the immortal, we might use the illustration of a tangent drawn to a circle. This illustration explains, as well as any human simile can, the illusive relationship of the mortal to the immortal.

A tangent to a circle is a straight line drawn so that it touches the circle, but does not cut it. At the point where the line touches the circle, is it the circle, or is it the line? The circle is already a fact which cannot be changed or interfered with. Therefore any line drawn to it could not be the tangent at the point where it touched the circle, but would be the circle.

The tangent would be that which departed from the circle. If it did not touch the circle, it would not be a tangent. So the mortal touches the immortal, only instantly to depart in a divergent direction, even as a lie touches the truth only to depart instantly from it.

The further the line of the tangent departs from the circle the greater its divergence from the circle.

So it is with the mortal; the further he wanders off on the tangent of human belief, the further is he from the reality of being. His only hope of redemption lies in reversing the negation, thus returning to his starting point, his own conscious existence and there finding his oneness with Being, and building on that.

Change of life: Change of life is the continuous unfolding of the infinity of Mind; the eternal operation of the one law controlling and governing every action and function of the entire universe, including the human body to the minutest detail. Do not say there is no change of life, but acknowledge the infinity of unfoldment and welcome it in ever more glorified form.

Earthquakes: Earthquakes, as they are now interpreted, could not appear if it were understood that, "The earth is the Lord's, and the fullness thereof; the world, and they that dwell therein."[1] Earth can no more quake in a fearful sense than can the multiplication table. Earth is the substance of Mind and is as stable and as eternal as Mind.

Mind makes its own adjustments of all pressure and substances harmoniously and perfectly. What Jesus did with the waves of the sea must be done with the earth's formations. They must be seen as always under Mind's control.

Tornadoes: Tornadoes are the lie about the winds, as earthquakes are the lie about the earth. So understood, they are controllable.

[1]Ps. 24:1.

Debt: Debt is man's eternal indebtedness to God for his being. God, likewise, is indebted to man for His entity. Without His expression, God could not be.

When understood in its true sense, the finite sense of debt disappears in the oneness of God and man, and the abundance and completeness of that oneness.

Economy: Economy is the perpetual balance of Principle and its idea. The most economical thing known is the multiplication table. It is never wasted, never presents itself as too much or too little. It is always in its place, always giving of itself freely, and receiving the right return for its use.

True economy is true reflection. It is *be*-ing. It is making every moment count as the man of, the activity of, Mind. Rudyard Kipling caught a glimpse of this when he wrote:

"If you can fill the unforgiving minute
With sixty seconds' worth of distance run,
Yours is the earth and every thing that's in it,
And—which is more—you'll be a man, my son!"

True reliance: To lean upon one's "own understanding" means to be consciously confident of oneness with **Mind.** The false sense of this is the belief that there is an understanding apart from the one Mind. "Lean not unto thine own understanding",[1] means lean not upon human belief, but upon the understanding that you are one with intelligence which is always to be relied upon. Trust in your "own understanding". Have confidence in what you know Mind to be.

Mind hears and answers: The fear that God will not hear is old theology. "His ear [is not] heavy, that it cannot hear".[2]

Mind hears and answers because it is omnipresent Principle, just as the principle of numbers hears and answers aright, never failing you.

Rightness is oneness with Principle, whether in numbers or in being. It cannot but hear.

Asking is the recognition of and communion with Truth. It is Mind which enables you to ask, as surely as it is Mind which fulfils.

"I the Lord will hear them, I the God of Israel will not forsake them".[3]

True need: Mind is equal to every need, because a need is not really a need in the sense of something lacking. It is a need in the sense of the inevitable necessity for the right operation of law. No demand could be, without the supply being simultaneous-

[1] Prov. 3:5.   [2] Isa. 59:1.   [3] Isa. 41:17.

ly present. The supply is the corollary of the demand and is inseparably one with it. How could Mind, then, fail to be equal to every occasion? The occasion is but the law of supply and demand operating, both specifically and infinitely. One could not be without the other.

Supply: Because the law of supply and demand is one and this one is embraced in the one Mind and its activity, no demand outruns supply, and *vice versa.* There is nothing beyond or outside of Mind's control.

Law of Relapse: The so-called law of relapse is the belief that the law of progress can be voided, that it can cease. It is the belief of the negation of the law of progress, the suppositional opposite of it. It needs only to be reversed in order to be found as the presence of the truth itself. Just as progress is a Mind law, so its suppositional opposite is also mental, a mistaken sense of direction, not a material thing to be changed.

The law of relapse has no relation whatever to relapse, as a physician views relapse; as a return to a former condition of sickness. Sickness is never involved in the belief of the law of relapse, only hypnotic suggestion.

Law of Reversal: The law of reversal is, like the law of relapse, a mental lie rather than a material one. A lie, of course, is never material although sometimes appearing as such. It is the suppositional opposite of the word of Mind, which does not "return . . . . void."[1]

The belief of a law of reversal is the hypnotic suggestion that the word of Mind can be reversed and made to produce something contrary to intention. Like two times two is four the word of Mind stands immovable and eternal, and there is no malicious mind to make any hypnotic suggestion.

Hypnotism: Hypnotism openly operates as mentality, never as materiality. Its suggestions come as a *belief* of materiality, not actually as matter *per se,* but as a *belief* of it.

So-called material life, being a false sense, is a belief of hypnotism. It must be handled, therefore, not as materiality to be destroyed, but as mentality to be corrected.

Mind knowing nothing outside itself, operates only in its own realm. Therefore, hypnotism is a mind-lie, not a matter-lie. It is destroyed by being so understood.

In its final analysis, as in a belief of a law of relapse or a belief of a law of reversal, evil operates as pure evil mind without any pretense of being so-called matter.

[1] Isa. 55:11.

Poison: Poison is the belief, first, that there is matter; second, that matter holds within itself the issues of life and death.

The belief of limitation is the one and only poison, and its only antidote is the understanding of the infinity of being.

All material belief is poison, hence the statement of medical authority, that every cell contains within itself the poison that is deadly to itself. This is the denial that cell, as the activity of God, is emitting life in infinite energy and purity.

The true sense of poison is the law of God, destructive to all that is unlike good. It is Spirit, it has no opposite.

Monotony: Monotony is the belief that Mind is not infinite, and therefore that there is a cessation of unfoldment and anticipation. Infinity can never terminate, or it would not be infinity.

The necessity of heaven is infinite unfoldment. There could be no heaven without it.

Transportation: Transportation is the process of getting from what is called one place to what is called another. It is a broad term, and is interpreted in continually changing form—yesterday as the prairie schooner; then as the pony express; then the train; then the aeroplane—tomorrow what?

Interpretations may change, but not the idea, transportation. Jesus saw transportation as instantaneous accomplishment, "and immediately the ship was at the land whither they went."[1]

The "-ism" of belief: Every *ism* is the belief that there is more than one Mind. No *ism* is based upon Principle. Human belief is always *ism* in whatever form it appears, good, bad or indifferent.

This includes all that appears as Socialism, Fascism, Nazism, Communism, Pacifism, and so forth. The truth about all these is that God is the one and only Mind and maintains His own idea directly, even as He clothes the lily and cares for the sparrow, to use the Bible similes.

Parable of the sparrow: Jesus' statement that not a sparrow falls to the ground without your Father's knowledge, means that the thought of Mind, being eternally one with Mind, can never be separated from what Mind is.

Therefore, no sparrow ever falls to the ground. That is merely the hypnotic illusion which, *reversed,* declares the ever-presence of Mind and its infinite care and protection. "For he shall give his angels charge over thee".[2]

Evolution: Evolution is the infinity of Mind, unfolding in all its glory as Mind, not matter.

[1]Jno. 6:21.   [2]Ps. 91:11.

The human concept of evolution as matter changing its forms and character is similar to the belief that two times two can change form and evolve as three times three. *"To sense, the lion of to-day is the lion of six thousand years ago"*.[1]

The finding of fossil remains that show similarities of structure proves only the similarity, not the identity of the creature.

The human belief of evolution fails utterly to account for consciousness, whereas Divine evolution deals only with consciousness and its infinity of unfoldment.

Idea versus ideas: Mrs. Eddy often uses the plural word, "ideas," instead of the singular, "idea". Writing as she did, for the whole of mankind, she was compelled to express her discovery in such terms that "the wayfaring men, though fools, shall not err therein."[2]

To have held to the singular form might have limited the mortal to his own finite concept of one, whereas the need was to free the concept so that a fuller sense of being could appear.

But the true concept is one—One Principle and one idea.

"Why hast thou forsaken me?": "My God, my God, why hast thou forsaken me?"[3] Human belief has always held that Jesus' statement was his final agonized cry, his last sorrowful reproach before succumbing to death. This is exactly the opposite of what was actually the case. Had he yielded to death, he could not have overcome death. It would be impossible to admit two times two as five and expect the right answer. It would have been equally impossible for Jesus to have admitted being forsaken by Life, God, and then to have risen from death.

Jesus repudiated the hypnotic suggestion of evil that his God had forsaken him. His words were a rhetorical question: How could "My God", infinite Life and good, possibly forsake His own expression of Life and good! The utter impossibility of such a thing was so clear to him that he abandoned once and forever every semblance of belief in materiality. He "yielded up the ghost",[4] the ghostly unreal belief in any mind or substance apart from God, Spirit.

This is the exact opposite of the theological teaching on the subject. Such teaching, to be consistent, would have to declare that a mathematician could believe that two times two is five, and at the same time work out his problem. Jesus never yielded to mesmerism. That is why he conquered. He did, however, face the argument, the suggestion of human belief, but reversed it, thereby winning the "crown of life."[5]

This is prefigured in the twenty-second Psalm, which has been called the Messiah's Psalm. It begins with Jesus' cry upon the

[1]Rud. 8:4.   [2]Isa. 35:8.   [3]Matt. 27:46.   [4]Matt. 27:50.
[5]Rev. 2:10.

cross, and depicts his experience: "they pierced my hands and my feet."[1] "They part my garments among them, and cast lots upon my vesture."[2]

Then the Psalm takes on a tone of confidence and praise. "For he hath not despised . . . . the afflicted; neither hath he hid his face from him; but when he cried unto him, he heard."[3]

Jesus knew full well the real significance of this psalm. The opening words (by which each psalm was known) brought the whole picture before him in its relation to himself, and he was using them as calling the claim by name in his final denunciation of it.

He knew he had arrived at the point that "when he cried unto him, he heard."[3]

Friendship: Mrs. Eddy characterized a false sense of friendship as *"the great and only danger in the path that winds up-ward."*[4] She pointed out that a mistaken sense leads its believer to the acceptance of something apart from God, because it brings in the fatal "third". This is the "enmity against God: for it is not subject to the law of God, neither indeed can be."[5] A "third" destroys Mind as All-in-all. Is not that the enmity to good?

Finding God as the one omnipresent friend insures the infinity of friends and friendship.

God can never forsake His own idea, for without His idea He would lack being. Hence His eternal interpretation of Himself as friend.

"The publicans and the harlots": The reason Jesus said, "the publicans and the harlots go into the kingdom of God"[6] ahead of the self-satisfied theologian was that the publicans and the harlots, being active in their work, would push vigorously on to the end of their path, to the conclusion that there is no profit in their sort of life.

Thoroughly disillusioned and dissatisfied, they would be ready to turn to what alone was left to them—the right direction—and expressing the same vigor would win the race of right.

On the other hand the self-satisfied ecclesiastical thought is not even awake, because of its self-righteousness.

Jesus' parable did not indicate that he placed publicanism and harlotism ahead of ecclesiasticism. He referred only to the *activity* of the one as preferable to the self-satisfaction and in-ertia of the other. "I would thou wert cold or hot. So then be-cause thou art lukewarm, and neither cold nor hot, I will spue thee out of my mouth."[7]

[1]Ps. 22:16. [2]Ps. 22:18. [3]Ps. 22:24. [4]Mis. 9:29. [5]Rom. 8:7.
[6]Matt. 21:31. [7]Rev. 3:15, 16.

I can and I am: *"I can is the son of I am"*, was a statement made by Mrs. Eddy to a friend. To infinite Mind, the All-in-all, there is no impediment or opposition. Then the only corollary to I am is *I can*.

Jesus proved this. "What things soever he [the Father] doeth, these also doeth the Son likewise."[1]

Hence the metaphysical impossibility of such terms as "I can't", "I will try," etc. Such an expression is not the son of Mind, I AM.

Buildings: What appears as buildings or structures is simply the infinity of variety of Mind appearing as structure in ever more varied forms. To interpret it materially is to limit the unfoldment, whereas, seeing Mind as all construction, all beauty, all outline, opens up limitless possibilities of architecture and engineering.

Science, theology and medicine: Science, theology and medicine are the *"three measures of meal,—that is, three modes of mortal thought."*[2] The attitude of the human mind toward its three modes of mortal thought, science, theology, and medicine, is most interesting.

The mortal demands from its minister of theology what it wishes to hear. To-day the minister who preaches the truth as he sees it is in danger of being replaced by some one who will preach what his congregation demands.

Of its physician the patient demands what he likes to hear. If the physician were to tell his patient what he knows about medicine and disease, he would quickly find himself with a sadly curtailed practice.

No one regrets this attitude of the human mind more sincerely than the honest minister and the honest medical practitioner; but each feels powerless to go against the current of human belief.

The human mind's attitude towards its academic man, however, is the exact reverse of this. It expects its scientists to tell the truth about their researches and deductions, regardless of what the individual himself believes, and regardless of what any one else may believe.

In consequence, the scientific investigator is always free to express candidly and freely what his research has led to. He is expected to state honestly what his reason has deduced, even though he may not wholly understand or believe it.

To-day the material scientist declares that matter is a mathematical formula. If, however, he really believed it *in his heart*, could he turn to medicine as a remedy? His reason compels him

[1]Jno. 5:19.   [2]S. & H. 118:19.

to state the fact, however, and eventually that will carry such conviction to him that in his heart he will believe it. When he does, he will find himself in accord with the declaration in Science and Health, that *"All is infinite Mind and its infinite manifestation, for God is All-in-all."*[1]

Then he will be able to lead the human mind out of its darkness of materialism to the threshold of Christian Science, where the solution of every difficulty will be found.

India: May not spiritual good come out of India or the Orient? Did not the "wise men from the east"[2] typify the superior wisdom and spirituality of the East, and are not those countries to-day showing forth a great spirituality? We hear this question repeatedly.

A tree is known by its fruits.

India and the East to-day exemplify the fruits of the teachings in those countries.

Civilization as typified by the Christian world to-day is ruling mankind. It is purely the product of the teachings of Christ.

Do the results of the teachings of Confucianism, Brahmanism, Buddhism or Mohammedanism, compare at all with the results of the teachings of Christ?

No.

Then, why should one assume that something exalted and spiritual should come from teachings that have always resulted in such gross materialism and lack of progress as is shown in the nations that have followed other than Christian teachings?

It may be argued that failure to follow their own teachings has produced the sordid conditions we see to-day in the eastern countries. But a like failure to follow the teachings of Christ in their completeness has not prevented his followers from being leaders in the world in every respect.

Had the "wise men from the east"[2] been truly wise, they would have been wise enough to have avoided Herod entirely; and the consequent massacring of the children "from two years old and under"[3] would not have occurred.

Eastern philosophy is materiality in its finer essence, hypnotic suggestion. That is why no "good thing"[4] can be expected to come out of the East.

It is absurd for the people of the Occident to look to the Orient for the slightest spiritual enlightenment. *"Surely the people of the Occident know that esoteric magic and Oriental barbarisms will neither flavor Christianity nor advance health and length of days."*[5]

[1] S. & H. 468:10.   [2] Matt. 2:1.   [3] Matt. 2:16.   [4] Jno. 1:46.
[5] Mis. 29:24.

"By their fruits ye shall know them",[1] stands as the test for all time. No teaching can escape this test; no nation can escape it.

The signs and symbols of the East, whether given by so-called "Masters" or whomsoever, are but the signs and symbols of the human mind imitating the divine. They are no more conducive to benefit the human race than is any hypnotic influence.

Materialism is always hypnotism. It was not the wisdom of the magician, but the wisdom of Moses that finally expressed itself as the ability of Moses' serpent to destroy the magician's serpent.

The wisdom of Christ, of Christian Science, destroys the so-called hypnotic wisdom of the magic-working East.

A young child: A young child must be treated *"mainly through the parent's thought"*,[2] because the parent is the thinker for the child until the child takes upon itself its own independent thinking. Indeed the child is at first simply the parent in embryo. When the child begins to do its own thinking, it must be dealt with independently.

Thinking is the parent, and what appears as the parent's thought is the child. Until there is demonstrated the ability to think, there is no responsibility. Therefore, that which is doing the thinking is the parent, and is the one responsible for the error, and in consequence is the claim needing to be reversed.

The whole belief of parent and child is the hypnotic illusion about God and man, and must be negatived through the understanding why there is no malicious mind.

Ancient historical analogy: The analogy between the ancient rulers of the world, the Chaldeans and Egyptians, and Christian Science and so-called mental science, is most illuminating. In tracing the history of these two ancient powers, the Chaldeans and Egyptians, and examining their writings, their hymns, and their prayers, one finds a striking difference between them.

The Chaldean ascribed everything to an *external* God. His God was not something *in* himself, but something outside of himself, something infinite, to which he ascribed all glory and power.

On the other hand, the Egyptian addressed everything to a God *within*. He prayed to his own exalted sense of his limited self.

The offspring of the Chaldeans were the ancestors of Abraham, who went out from his father's house, out of "Ur of the Chaldees",[3] into a land that he knew not of, that he might worship God after the dictates of his own conscience. He founded a race consecrated to this idea, thus prefiguring the Pilgrim Fathers and America.

[1]Matt. 7:20.   [2]S. & H. 412:29.   [3]Gen. 15:7.

The descendants of Abraham became two kingdoms, the kingdom of Judah and the kingdom of Israel. The kingdom of Judah was composed of the tribe of Judah and a portion of the tribe of Benjamin. The kingdom of Israel consisted of the other ten tribes which were later known as the "lost tribes" or the "lost sheep of the house of Israel".[1]

The descendants of Judah, or the kingdom of Judah, are to-day known as the Jews of the world. The kingdom of Israel, or the ten lost tribes, is the Anglo-Saxon world represented by America and the British Empire.

The descendants of the Egyptians are still the inhabitants of Egypt, and Egypt can scarcely be thought of as a nation at all. Could there be a greater contrast?

Another very important distinction between these two peoples is the fact that the Chaldeans were a war-like race and the Egyptians a peaceable, agricultural race. The Chaldeans brooked no interference, while the Egyptians were placid and non-resisting.

The human concept of good would argue that the peaceable race of Egyptians would be the one to prosper and be of importance in the world. History shows, however, that this was not the case.

It is the descendants of the Chaldeans who are virtually the rulers of the world, spiritually, intellectually, financially—in every way.

Surely a lesson is to be drawn from this—the lesson upon which Christian Science lays so much stress—that God is never *within.*

If God were *within,* then God would be less than that which He was *within.* In other words, God would not be God at all. Without God, without infinity, there could be no progress, for there would be nothing.

The Chaldeans discerned this truth. The Egyptians had no concept of it whatever. The result was that the Chaldean went forward with no limit to his unfoldment, while the Egyptian lost his important place in the world.

Analagously, there is a wide gulf, impossible to bridge, between Christian Science and every belief claiming to operate mentally.

Christian Science *alone* insists that Principle is never *in* man, but that man is the idea of Principle; and that, while they are eternally one in the sense of their inseparability as Principle and idea, they are never one in the sense that one is the other, or that one is in the other.

By contrast, mental science of every name and nature teaches that God is *in* man. This means no God. Such erroneous teach-

[1] Matt. 10:6.

ing must eventually vanish, as the Egyptians as a nation have vanished.

One is true, the other is false.

The Christian Scientist wars against everything unlike good. He knows that the proof that Christian Science is Science— exact knowing—rests with him. He does not sit down meekly and let evil walk over him. He does the "walking"[1] as Jesus did.

Education: Education is not teaching something to ignorance It is bringing to light the intelligence that is omnipresent. It is the sun unfolding the flower in loveliness and beauty.

It is the constant joy of anticipation.

"Inferiority complex" is the lie that God, as the one infinite Mind, or intelligence, is not infinite. Could this be? Is there a single spot where there is less than all intelligence?

Ignorance can never be enlightened. The ignorance that says that two times two makes five always remains the same ignorance.

Enlightenment, otherwise called education, leaves ignorance to itself, and goes forward with what *is,* thus "swallowing up"[2] what *is not.*

The teacher imbued with this understanding of education reaches the end of his teaching year rested, not wearied, by his work.

Evil one: All evil is wrong thought, the negation of right. Two thoughts alike would not be two, but one. Therefore, every wrong is individual, one.

The right, or the Christ, which is the reverse of the negation —being also one—is to be applied specifically to correct the one negation. There is, then, no possible duplication—there are no two treatments alike; there is no repetition.

Each treatment is specific and exact.

This applies to treatment as arguments. With the spirit, Jesus healed the multitude with a word. The spirit is illumination without argument, and *"all whom your thoughts rest upon are thereby benefited."*[3]

No looking backward: Paul said, "For if I build again the things which I destroyed, I make myself a transgressor."[4] By this he meant, if one looks backward to a negative or false sense of things already destroyed, he accepts to that extent, the belief that a lie *has* existed, and thus mars the tablet of his mind and makes himself a transgressor.

If a lie has ever existed to be destroyed, it can exist again; thus its final destruction would be impossible.

[1]Matt. 14:25. [2]2 Cor. 5:4. [3]My. 210:10. [4]Gal. 2:18.

Would any one think of talking about his childish ignorance? Then why indulge in gossip about things once corrected?

Death: What is death? The word "death", as here used, means the dying or passing on of the mortal and the necessity for a funeral.

The so-called mortal is the presence or activity of malicious mind just as the immortal is the presence or activity of divine Mind.

Because divine Mind is Life, its presence is manifested as immortal man, the deathless man, as exemplified by Christ Jesus. In contradistinction to this, stands the man of death, portrayed by the mortal.

What is called the birth of a mortal is the birth of death. The one and only purpose of this birth is to perpetuate death. The mortal is the mouthpiece of the mind that is death, whose seeming life is but a phase of death, whose every thought is limitation, finiteness, materiality.

Paul declared, "to be carnally minded is death; but to be spiritually minded is life and peace."[1]

A funeral seems to be the culmination of the mortal sense of life, but it is no such thing in reality. It is merely the appearance, in a clearer form, of the death that constitutes the mortal. Materia medica will tell you that which is supposed to create the mortal is venereal poison, and that it is only a question of time until this poison, instead of producing life, will bring about death.

The mortal had no prior state of being, no perfect state, from which he fell. Two times two as five never fell from being four. The five never had a perfect state, so far as two times two is concerned. From the beginning, the mortal was *"conceived in sin and brought forth in iniquity."*[2] The lie begins at the moment of its conception. The end of it is the understanding of the truth about which it is the lie.

A funeral is not understanding; it is merely a phase of the mortal sense of life, emphasizing such life as death. Christ Jesus overcame death. He did not let it overcome him. Paul declared death to be the "Last enemy that shall be destroyed".[3] If it is a friend and something to be desired, would Paul have designated it as an enemy?

Thought cannot be without its expression. A funeral is the expression of limitation, of finiteness. A funeral, being but a phase of the mortal sense of life, does not touch the mortal in the slightest, so far as his mortality is concerned.

The mind of the mortal is the same after his funeral as before. His sense of body has not changed in the least, for the mortal

[1] Rom. 8:6.   [2] S. & H. 476:16.   [3] 1 Cor. 15:26.

can never be separated from his body. A moment's separation would result in total annihilation, for without expression thought vanishes. A false sense can disappear permanently only through a right sense.

After the experience of death, the mortal finds himself with both his body and his mind as material as before. Science and Health says, "Mortals need not fancy that belief in the experience of death will awaken them to glorified being",[1] for they "awaken with thoughts, and being, as material as before."[2]

Finding himself no nearer harmony than he was before, the deluded mortal may perhaps be more ready to start on the path of intelligence, Mind. In this way the experience of death may prove profitable, but death itself does not help him.

The wrong answer to a problem does not, in and of itself, aid the pupil. Only as the pupil turns from the mistake to the truth, does he profit.

What is the body that friends think they bury? Friends bury their belief of a body. Their belief of it has no relationship whatever to the body of the deceased. He has his body with him. He cannot lose it, any more than he can lose it in a dream.

What becomes of the disease that brought about death, you may ask? Does one still have that to contend with, or is he free from it?

The disease which apparently consummated its work in the funeral, and fulfilled its purpose and promise of "I can kill you", has proved itself a liar, and by so doing has killed itself.

When a lie is seen as a lie, its power to hold the mortal in its clutches is gone. When death is found to be unreal and powerless, because of the ever-presence of Life, the specific lie which claimed to produce it, no longer masquerades as an entity.

Does this apply to diseases other than the particular one that seemed to cause death?

An illustration may answer this question. When the earthquake and fire occurred in San Francisco in 1906, sick people in homes and hospitals forgot their ailments in the greater calamity. It is recorded that for months after that experience, sickness in San Francisco was virtually unheard of.

Under the influence of great excitement or shock, freedom has come to many a sufferer, after medical attention had failed to free him. Two thoughts cannot be entertained at the same time, and since all there is to any mortal is thought, it follows that if he becomes absorbed in one, he is free from others. A great shock or exciting experience spontaneously does this.

The experience of death, of course, is the most dramatic experience the mortal can have, consequently the awakening from that experience is all-absorbing. It does not leave him quite

[1]S. & H. 291:9.   [2]Mis. 42:9.

where it finds him. For the moment, at least, he will experience a greater degree of bodily freedom than before, but that freedom having been obtained through a *belief* called dying, has no permanency until *belief* is replaced with understanding.

A permanent sense of health was not gained by all of those who were temporarily freed by the San Francisco earthquake and fire. Many, in a few months, drifted back to their old habits of thought.

In order to know what life is, after death, it is necessary to consider certain fundamental facts. The proper deductions from these facts will be correct, like that of any mathematical deduction.

Because the mortal is not destroyed by dying, his concept of being is identically the same after death as before. He will entertain the same limited sense of things, the same concept of life and action. His sense of his body is as material as before. His mode of locomotion is the same. In fact, his whole sense of being is the same.

If that sense were suddenly and completely changed from a material to a spiritual sense of existence, his whole consciousness of being at the moment of death being material, he would spontaneously lose his cognizance of being and automatically cease to be conscious. That would mean unconsciousness, in other words, non-entity, extinction—which is impossible to one who has once been conscious of being.

Therefore all things must appear as material as before death. The so-called law of gravity, not having been overcome by dying, "here" will be the only place there is to the person we say has died.

But there is no possible communication between the living and the dead, because they are entertaining opposite states of consciousness—the one, of having died, the other, of having not died.

When the mortal realizes that heaven is not attained by dying, any more than is hell, he will abandon his former ideas that death ushers in a spiritual state of being, and will face the fact that life must still be lived.

That one step in rationality will aid tremendously in lightening the mortal's burdens. He will see, to a degree at least, that heaven is attained only through understanding, and not through dying.

By this statement. "For we brought nothing into this world. and it is certain we can carry nothing out",[1] Paul did not mean that death would take one back to a babe-condition of consciousness. Conception is the beginning of the mortal sense called the mortal. The mortal sense may add lie to lie, but it never begins

[1] Tim. 6:7.

a second time. It goes from its conception to its final destruction through understanding, either here or hereafter.

Death is merely a phase of its career, and that phase may occur many times under varying changes of belief. "Death will occur on the next plane of existence as on this, until the spiritual understanding of Life is reached."[1]

Nothing is gained by superstitious thinking, by feeling that the experience of death is awesome or mysterious. We know by deduction what must be after death just as positively as we know what we call "now".

Death cannot change anything except religious beliefs and medical theories and the varying doctrines attached to such beliefs.

Christmas: Christmas is the realization of infinite good as the one Spirit, a Christ Mass of oneness, "a feast of Soul and a famine of sense."[2]

Easter Easter is Christmas enlarged to deathless good, infinite Life. Easter is Jesus demonstration wholly. Christmas is the Virgin Mother's day entirely.

The eating of meat: The eating of meat is like the eating of anything else. It is the assimilation of Mind as substance.

When Jesus had raised the damsel from the dead, he "commanded that something should be given her to eat."[3] He also said, "I have meat to eat that ye know not of."[4] "My meat is to do the will of him that sent me".[5] Jesus had fish ready cooked for his disciples after his resurrection.

The negative of this "eating of meat" is interpreted as the killing of one mortal creature that another may live. One sense of eating, however, should not be exaggerated above another. It is the whole concept of "meat", not the meat itself that is wrong.

Eastern poisons: There are no actual differences between the beliefs attached to tea, coffee, opium, whiskey or tobacco. All are taken as drugs: theine, caffeine, narcotine, alcohol, nicotine. All are poisons, introduced from the East.

Because one is seen more plainly than another to be detrimental to the moral sense, this does not change the fact that all, metaphysically, are equally so. All must be reversed as injurious drugs and so rendered innocuous.

Spirit alone stimulates or soothes as required.

Insurance: True insurance is the understanding of Mind as eternally maintaining its own idea. The negation is interpreted as financial protection. Its justification may be that it has an unselfish motive and is regarded as a form of investment for the protection of others, thus imitating Love.

[1]S. & H. 77:9. [2]My. 263:6. [3]Mark 5:43. [4]Jno. 4:32.
[5]Jno. 4:34.

No half-way course: There is no half-way course.

In Christian Science, as in mathematics, a thing is either right or wrong.

Every belief founded on finiteness, materiality, is wrong. *"Divine Science is absolute, and permits no half-way position in learning its Principle and rule—establishing it by demonstration."*[1]

Majority: In the realm of belief, the majority of belief rules. However, one on the side of Truth, of understanding, is always a majority against belief, because knowing supersedes belief. *"One with God is a majority."*[2]

Discontent: Discontent, interpreted correctly, is the destruction of all unlike good. Discontent with evil is contentment with right. The negative of this is disbelief that God is the one and only guide and belief that there is an influence apart from Mind. *"Now this self-same God is our helper . . . and guides every event of our careers."*[3] "In all thy ways acknowledge him, and he shall direct thy paths."[4] This alone is contentment.

True sense of body: *"The orange just eaten, of which only the pleasant idea is left"*[5]—an illustration Mrs. Eddy used in earlier editions of Science and Health—perfectly expresses what body, and all that you cognize, should be to you—the full aroma, or consciousness of all things as Mind, with no limitation, as matter, accompanying it.

"So be it"[6]**:** Insistence upon the truth of Being, upon the specific affirmation of the presence of Mind, with reference to the particular point involved, should never be abandoned until the corporeal senses respond, *"So be it!"*

Jesus meant exactly this when he said, "Though he will not . . . give him, because he is his friend, yet because of his importunity he will . . . give him".[7] In other words, never stop until you win—until you realize that God is the only presence.

Crucifixion: Crucifixion is the insistence on the *isness* of Truth. Jesus allowed himself to be what is called crucified because that appealed to him as the only way whereby he could show forth that life, not death, is God's way; that the body has no life of its own to surrender; that although body expresses Life, it is not Life.

Crucifixion of the flesh, however, can make the false sense of body seem a greater reality to one who has not Jesus' unique problem to face. So why do it?

[1]S. & H. 274:23.   [2]Mis. 245:29.   [3]Un. 3:27.   [4]Prov. 3:6.
[5]S. & H. 100th Edit. 277:25.   [6]S. & H. 100th Edit. 411:2.   [7]Luke 11:8.

Christian Science glorifies the overcoming of all death, not the crucifixion of the flesh but of the fleshly belief.

Confucius: Confucius taught, "Without error there could be no such thing as truth!"—the exact reverse of the fact. Truth *is* and error is the lie about it, not *vice versa*. All human philosophy makes Truth dependent on a lie, the reverse of true philosophy.

Jesus' purpose: Jesus' purpose in the world was to show that Christ is never out of the world. "Lo, I am with you alway".[1]

Jesus' mission was not to correct anything, but to bear witness to the truth. Abandon the idea that Jesus came to save sinners. He proved that there are no sinners to save, by proving that sin has no power.

Over production: Because Mind is all, all have Mind and can use it limitlessly. There is no such thing as over production. That argument is the nonsense of human belief.

Because production is Mind-operation, not matter-operation, supply and demand eternally balance.

Could there be an over supply of the multiplication table?

Atonement: Atonement is oneness with intelligence. It is knowing all.

Circumcision: Circumcision is taking every thought back to the one *is* and so finding it purity itself, the bringing to light of that which *is*.

The Passover: The Passover is the understanding that the negation is but the negative interpretation of the positive Truth. This transforms it.

Gethsemane: Gethsemane is not a struggle between the human and the divine, not an unwillingness to follow in the divine way. Rather is it a possible uncertainty of what the divine way may be.

Gethsemane is never reached until there is no human desire left on the point involved.

Numbers: Numbers are a state of consciousness, and yet how practical, useful and substantial, for example, is a "two"! That is because it is a mind-sense and not a matter-sense.

Business: Business is the eternal activity of Mind and its idea. Man is the business of God—God being busy, active. Business is the law of supply and demand. Man is the demand and God is the supply. This oneness is the one business, and includes all business: hence business is always successful.

[1]Matt. 28:20.

The Commandments: The Commandments are all in one and one in all, all for one and one for all—one *isness* from which all is, in perfect agreement.

The healthy sinner: *"The healthy sinner is the hardened sinner"*[1] because there is no separation between what the hardened sinner knows and what he does.

The distance between understanding and performance measures the punishment.

Good can punish error only when good is present. If there is no knowledge of musical harmony, a discord does not jar, in other words, punish.

Punishment is in exact proportion to the understanding that is present and disregarded.

So it is with good. With no knowledge of good, there is no knowledge of error as error, and therefore nothing with which to punish. Hence, God punishes sin *"only as it is destroyed, and never afterwards;"*[2] and the "times of this ignorance God winked at".[3]

Understanding, once present, permits no escape from right.

A fatal belief: Belief that death is inevitable and a friend, is fatal to all demonstration.

All evil is embraced in the expectation that death will finally occur. Death must be mastered through unselfishness, not yielded to.

Life lived fearlessly through understanding masters death.

"An improved belief": *"An improved belief cannot retrograde"*[4] because when once a truth is understood, that understanding reigns as consciousness ever after. It has substituted itself for the error, leaving no error to retrograde.

When two times two is understood as four, no mistake about it survives.

Because you do not yet know the whole of the multiplication table, you do not lose what you do know of it.

What is known is known forever. Hence, *"Neither disease itself, sin, nor fear has the power to cause disease or a relapse."*[5]

Sex: Sex is quality. God includes within Himself all quality, hence all sex. Therefore, all being expresses all sex. No incompleteness exists, hence no looking for completeness outside of oneness with Mind.

The understanding of this is true marriage, the solution to all problems of lust.

[1]S. & H. 404:15.   [2]'01 13:24.   [3]Acts 17:30.   [4]S. & H. 442:19.
[5]S. & H. 419:10.

New child: With the abandonment of human child-bearing, increasing numbers will not stop being manifested for all that is seen now as a *"new child"*,[1] will, with the purification of thought, be seen in its true sense as the complete man of God everywhere present.

There will not be less creation but the infinity of creation will open to one's vision.

Because one on God's side is a majority, the understanding of this will banish all fear of race suicide, and race effacement.

The right-knower will live on, not needing to be born. He will out-weigh in the power of his understanding all human belief in the necessity for numbers of mortals.

Mrs. Eddy declares, *"Proportionately as human generation ceases, the unbroken links of eternal, harmonious being will be spiritually discerned; and man, not of the earth earthly but co-existent with God, will appear . . . . Mortals can never understand God's creation while believing that man is a creator. God's children already created will be cognized only as man finds the truth of being. Thus it is that the real, ideal man appears in proportion as the false and material disappears."*[2]

Lightning calculator: The lightning calculator is a good illustration of the natural and normal function of Mind.

All calculating is mind-operation, answering the most complicated problem instantly.

Mind knows the answer at once because the answer always accompanies the question. The roundabout method called figuring, which, although wholly mental, is only in a degree acknowledged as such, is clumsy and needless. Why not go directly to Mind and find the answer instantly?

Second sight: Second sight, like lightning calculation, is seeing without the slow process of doing it through a *belief of eyes*.

All sense operation is mind activity. There is no limit to it. Why then limit it?

Second sight is no more spiritual than what is called ordinary seeing, for it sees everything just as materially, but it is far more normal. It unlimits its belief of distance.

The Stellar universe: The stellar universe, with its admitted millions of trillions of stars, is but the human mind's feeble attempt to express the infinity of Mind in its own definition.

[1] S. & H. 463:7. [2] S. H. 68:30.

No term can express infinity, nor is infinity in the heavens alone. It is the infinite "here". *The astronomer will no longer look up to the stars,—he will look out from them*.[1]

"The second death"[2]: The second death means the funeral.

The first death is the mortal sense of life, in other words, being carnally minded, believing that death is inevitable. The funeral, or second death, is the culmination of the first death.

Those upon whom the second death hath no power are *"only those who have washed their robes white in obedience and suffering."*[3]

"Suffering" means not painful experience, but suffering Truth to reign as consciousness. Obedience means being one with good, with that which is. The funeral cannot occur to such understanding; but, without understanding, the "second death" occurs on any other *"plane of existence as on this".*[4]

Reincarnation: Reincarnation, in its true sense, is seeing God manifest as definite man in all His infinity of being. Jesus said, "he that hath seen me hath seen the Father".[5]

Reincarnation is not substitution, but manifestation—the incarnation of good. "Not for that we would be unclothed, but clothed upon, that mortality might be swallowed up of life."[6]

Environment: No bodily condition is essential to health any more than the Roman numeral "two" is essential to numbers. The Chinese "two" works just as well.

Any condition accepted as healthful will prove to be healthful. *"What is now considered the best condition for organic and functional health in the human body may no longer be found indispensable to health . . . and man will be found normal and natural to changed mortal thought, and therefore more harmonious in his manifestations than he was in the prior states which human belief created and sanctioned."*[7]

Why concern oneself about theory, except to correct all human theory with understanding.

No medium for evil: Evil can play no tune on you—find no answering response to its suggestions—unless you supply the string, the thought on which to play. If you supply no strings tuned to the chord of evil, it can do nothing.

A room may be strung with wires but a vibrating response to any chord introduced into that room will occur only when they are tuned in unison. "The prince of this world cometh, and hath nothing in me."[8]

[1]S. & H. 125:28. [2]Rev. 20:6. [3]S. & H. 572:1. [4]S. & H. 77:9.
[5]Jno. 14:9. [6]2 Cor. 5:4. [7]S. & H. 125:2. [8]Jno. 14:30.

Binding evil: What you "bind on earth"[1] is what you reject as consciousness through the understanding of what consciousness really is.

What you "loose on earth"[1] is what you find consciousness to be and make your own.

What is false is always false, and what is true is always true. *Always* includes heaven and earth.

Mesmerism: Mesmerism, in its tenacity of belief, is well illustrated in the action of a snake mesmerizing a bird. When the snake's gaze is fixed, the snake will not move any more than the bird. You may hammer the snake over the head, but until it has accomplished its purpose and swallowed its victim it will not desist unless actually killed.

Mesmerism has to be destroyed, seen through, or it destroys its victim.

Conceit: Conceit is identical with deceit. Conceit is the belief that one possesses more than another. *"Conceit cannot avert the effects of deceit"*.[2] "If any man think that he knoweth anything, he knoweth nothing yet as he ought to know."[3]

Resurrection: The resurrection of Jesus was lied about immediately. "The chief priests"[4] and "the elders . . . gave large money unto the soldiers, Saying, Say ye, His disciples came by night, and stole him away while we slept."[4]

The suppositional opposite appeared instantly on the heels of Truth. Why? In order to cloud the truth and prevent the spreading abroad of the fact that Jesus had overcome death.

Had this fact been allowed to permeate human belief, it would soon have destroyed death. But the lie, the negation, *unreversed*, was accepted.

The same lie is at work with regard to Mrs. Eddy, and for the same purpose, namely, to destroy confidence in Christian Science. But because there is no personality in Christian Science, no lies about a person have any weight.

Repression: Repression arises from thinking that things are material and that it is righteous to refrain from something or other.

It is true that restraint may be more righteous than indulging in wrong, but of itself it will never save. To rise above all material desire is the *"acme of 'well done' "*[5] in Christian Science.

God is the law of total repression to all unlike Himself, and that repression includes within itself the understanding that there is nothing to repress because man has all.

[1]Matt. 16:19.   [2]No. 2:24.   [3]1 Cor. 8:2.   [4]Matt. 28:11, 12, 13.
[5]Mis. 355:6.

Moses' staff: Moses saw his rod, when cast upon the ground, turn into a serpent, and upon being picked up, turn again into a staff.

This proved to Moses that matter in any form, animate or inanimate, was merely a human belief and that he was really dealing every instant with Mind.

This realization was truly a staff upon which he could lean.

Translation of Science and Health: The translation of Science and Health into a foreign tongue can never be wholly successful. No translation, however accurately done, will satisfy the reader, except for a limited time. As he grows in understanding, the words used to translate Science and Health will no longer satisfy his advanced sense. He will constantly require a better and better word to convey the meaning.

That is why Mrs. Eddy allowed Science and Health to be translated and published provided only the English appeared side-by-side with the translation.

Eventually, all that will satisfy any reader will be the "untranslated revelations,"[1] which, Mrs. Eddy tells us, *"We are indeed privileged in having."*[1]

Christian Science and paganism: Mrs. Eddy opposed the presenting of Christian Science, except under certain conditions, to a pagan nation, because she knew that the human mind, unrestrained by any Christian teaching, would turn the allness of Mind to its own end, and enthrone the *human mind* as God, thus perverting the whole of the ethics of Christian Science.

The human mind does this perverting even in what are called Christian nations. How much more, then, must it do so in pagan nations.

"Every thought"[2]: To bring every thought into obedience to Christ is to see that every thought and act is based on the allness of *is*, on that which is Truth. In this "all" there is no material sense.

The Ouija board: The Ouija board shows how matter, so-called, is the substratum of mind, which simulates Mind. The hand that writes is expressing the thought of the one malicious mind, although no one present in the audience may be consciously thinking about what is being written. That mind includes within itself everything that any mortal knows, and it can be reproduced by any mortal who allows himself to be a medium for it.

A medium or mind-reader can reproduce anything that is known to that mind.

[1] My. 179:29.   [2] 2 Cor. 10:5.

True Mind-reading is oneness with the one Mind and is the reverse of so-called mind-reading. The one is understanding; the other belief.

The radio and all radiation is a phase of mind-reading. The picking up of voices will continue, for there is no limit. Whatever has been, is now, and can be reproduced. We may possibly some day pick up the waves of Jesus' voice delivering the Sermon on the Mount.

Matter's imitation of Mind's oneness: Unity of matter is being very interestingly established by present day physicists.

By means of radio-activity the constituent elements of aluminum, mercury and so forth known as electrons and protons, have been rearranged until the resultant product emerges as an entirely different chemical substance representing quantitatively greater or less energy as the case may be.

This proves that matter, in whatever form, is but varying aspects of the basic unit, energy, since electrons and protons may be resolved into mathematical formulæ expressing energy solely.

It is also significant that the one constant factor used in all physical experiments is the speed of light, 186,000 miles per second, a speed beyond which the modern physicist says is impossible of attainment.

"And God said, Let there be light: and there was light."[1]

This holding to light as the foundation of all material knowledge will ultimately lead the materialist from matter to Mind, to the Light to which John referred when he spoke of the "Light, which lighteth every man that cometh into the world."[2]

"Material substances or mundane formations, astronomical calculations, and all the paraphernalia of speculative theories, based on the hypothesis of material law or life and intelligence resident in matter, will ultimately vanish, swallowed up in the infinite calculus of Spirit."[3]

The material sense of light, with its finite limit of speed, is the counterfeit of the instantaneous operation of Mind; but the use of light, even as humanly conceived, as the constant by which all else is measured is a beacon that tends to lead mankind from the darkness of material belief into the radiance of Spirit, because man will push his query from material phenomenon, measured in terms of light, to the nature of Light itself, and will find that Light can be but one thing, consciousness.

True politics: True politics is the manifestation of the government of Mind. It is the orderly operation of Principle; that whereby the law of Principle is known. The negation, which

[1]Gen. 1:3.   [2]Jno. 1:9.   [3]S. & H. 209:25.

must be reversed, is the give and take of human belief, trying to have its own way.

This false sense is hypnotism.

Erroneous sense of peace: Pacifism, in the sense of opposition to any form of force in settling disputes is the negative of the true "peace . . . which passeth all understanding".[1]

Mind is the all-force, the all-power. It forever disputes the assertion that another power can exist. This is the "war in heaven",[2] a war that is settled by the force of Mind's allness.

It is not serving the ends of genuine peace to array oneself against war as war. It is a crying of "Peace, peace ; when there is no peace."[3]

The human misinterpretation of war will cease only as the true war in heaven is demonstrated.

To inveigh against war is to make something of war—something apart from God and His allness. It is assuming that there is a force apart from Mind ; it is not finding "war in heaven". Its practical effect is to aid and abet the most evilly disposed who acknowledge no force but matter.

Until all men come together "in the unity of the faith"[4] war may be interpreted as answering "a fool according to his folly",[5] in the only language he can, or will understand.

Motive The motive is the mother of any act and governs the result.

"The twelve tribes of Israel with all mortals,—separated by belief from man's divine origin and the true idea,—will through much tribulation yield to the activities of the divine Principle of man in the harmony of Science."[6]

The motive is the spirit of the act. With the right motive there is no fear.

Note how the widely divergent motives, as given in the Bible, which animated the mothers of Jacob's sons in desiring their children, were the determining factors in their sons' characters, and also note Jacob's prophecy concerning his sons, and you will discern the importance of motives.

Science and Health in the Glossary interprets the meaning of the thought typified by the twelve tribes which grew from Jacob's sons.

To every erroneous belief, or name, there is the true definition ; hence every name or word has a true positive and a false negative sense.

The phrase "false negative" exemplifies the rule in grammar and mathematics that two negatives make a positive. *"Material*

[1]Phil. 4 :7.   [2]Rev. 12 :7.   [3]Jer. 6 :14.   [4]Eph. 4 :13.   [5]Prov. 26 :5.
[6]S. & H. 562 :11

man is made up of involuntary and voluntary error, of a negative right and a positive wrong, the latter calling itself right".[1]

No person: It is more important to know that there is no *person,* than to know that there is no disease, because without person to express disease, there can be no disease. Finding God as the only Person, robs evil of any person upon whom or through whom to act, and leaves all disease and sin without entity.

Fanatical concentration: The ability of fanatical Oriental natives to walk on white hot stones without injury to their feet comes from the concentration of their thought upon what they are doing, to the exclusion of all fear in regard to it.

Because two thoughts cannot command attention at the same time, a complete absorption in one nullifies the effect of another and proves that matter is not matter, but mind in disguise.

The ability to render inoperative the human belief of law is illustrated, also, by the Hopi Indians' evident immunity to the bites of rattle-snakes.

True rejoicing: "Your names are written in heaven"[2] because good is the only reality. In this statement, Jesus was uttering a warning to beware of gloating over any human sense of gratification in matter or in the human sense of good in any guise.

Good exists for one and all, and is omnipresent, eternally. This fact is cause for rejoicing. Each will interpret it according to his need.

"Sleep on now"[3]: Jesus told his three disciples to "Sleep on" because he had reached the point where it no longer mattered to him whether they watched with him or not.

When first he found them sleeping, after he had asked them to watch with him, disappointment robbed him, for the moment, of his clear vision of the best course for him to follow. He had to go back and again quietly work it out alone with Mind. When the same thing occurred the second and the third times, he knew that he must go forward, regardless of what appeared as the failure of his disciples, and leave the result to God.

Jesus stood as the personal exemplifier of Mind but not as the scientific explanation of that exemplification. His work was to show forth Mind. The work of Science and Health is to set forth the Science of his work.

It might be stated in modern terms, that Jesus performed the laboratory experiments and Mrs. Eddy wrote the accompanying textbook explaining them.

When Jesus decided to rely wholly upon Mind, he could say to his disciples, "Sleep on now, ... Rise, let us be going."[4]

[1] S & H. 491:7.   [2] Luke 10:20.   [3] Matt. 26:45.   [4] Matt. 26:45, 46.

The first step: Mrs. Eddy insisted on the healing of sickness because it is the first step in Christian Science, and, as she says, the easiest one. It is the easiest, because the human mind admits that the body is, in large measure, subject to its mind's control.

The healing of the body is the line of least resistance in the operation of Mind-power. The mortal is frequently willing to be slightly sick, just enough to get attention, but not enough to hurt. If uncomfortable enough, he is eventually willing to allow his body to be healed—to give up his belief of pain in matter—but his pleasures in matter he wants left undisturbed.

The healing of sin is a more difficult matter, in belief, until it is realized that there is no mind to resist good.

Value of experience: The genuine Christian Scientist rejoices in every experience as an opportunity to express what he understands. He knows that every painful experience is the good of Truth appearing but negatively interpreted—a challenge to his understanding. He would not therefore avoid any experience nor allow one to leave him, until, like Jacob wrestling with the angel, he has wrested all possible benefit from it.

"*Experience*" itself, to him, "*is victor*".[1] He knows that good is ever-operative and he proves it. Each experience comes at the right moment to confer the greatest blessing.

Human need: "*Divine Love always has met and always will meet every human need*",[2] because there never is a human need. It is always a divine need, or it could not exist.

For the same reason, "*Immortal Mind, governing all, must be acknowledged as supreme in the physical realm, so-called, as well as in the spiritual*"[3]—because there is no physical realm.

There exists only the realm of God, and the terms *human* and *physical* are negative interpretations of the omnipresence of this one realm of good.

Good never "works anything out". If it is not already worked out, it never will be worked out. All good is already the fact and needs no working out.

Desire and fulfilment: To want is to imply lack. The mind that wants something believes that it is denied what it wants.

Mind being all, has all and knows its own allness. This is the explanation of that greatly misunderstood passage in Scripture, "For he that hath, to him shall be given ; and he that hath not, from him shall be taken even that which he hath."[4]

The mind that wants is never the Mind that has.

Want cannot exist without satisfaction. The cause wants its effect, and the effect wants its cause, which means fulfilment.

[1]Mis. 339 :6.   [2]S. & H. 494 :10.   [3]S. & H. 427 :23.   [4]Mark 4 :25.

Saint and sinner: Saint and sinner are familiar theological terms that need clarifying.

The mortal can advance only from the point of experience to which he has already risen, be it high or low. Hence, to-day is the all-important moment, not yesterday. *"That to-morrow starts from to-day and is one day beyond it, robes the future with hope's rainbow hues."*[1]

Yesterday can neither damn nor praise. Regrets are worse than futile. To-day holding all, the future holds all possibility. It is not linked with the past save in human belief. Man is not chained to it but is free to go forward from his immediate point of experience into fullness of understanding and joyousness of life.

One is "saint" or "sinner" in proportion to his willingness to grasp his opportunity to act and think rightly from the standpoint of *now* and not because he has done or left undone certain things in the so-called past.

"The righteousness of the righteous shall not deliver him in the day of his transgression: as for the wickedness of the wicked, he shall not fall thereby in the day that he turneth from his wickedness; neither shall the righteous be able to live for his *righteousness* in the day that he sinneth."[2]

The one M.D.: God as the one M.D., as the one everything else, will always appear in the language best understood. This one M.D. can appear as a physician, or in any way that will most enlighten you. But, remember, it is Mind, and Mind alone, that is appearing. If your desire is for material methods, then it is futile to call the appeasing of such a desire the one Mind appearing. Name it correctly malicious mind and reverse it.

Imitation: The discovery of Christian Science opened the door for every human belief to use what it calls "mind."

Because Christian Science has brought the truth of all things to light, imitations of the works of Christian Science spring up in ever-increasing numbers. "For wheresoever the carcase is, there will the eagles be gathered together."[3] Where the substance is, there will the make-believe be.

But, like Jesus, the Christian Scientist would not interfere, even if he could, for no matter how health, or wealth, or whatever it may be, is objectified, it all bears witness to the declaration of Christian Science that health, wealth, and all good are omnipresent. Then "Forbid him not".[4] Sooner or later all will have to learn that understanding, not emotional belief nor philosophical theory, permanently satisfies and insures the continuance of good.

[1] Mis. 339:7.   [2] Ezek. 33:12.   [3] Matt. 24:28.   [4] Mark 9:39.

Conception: Human relationship has nothing to do with the conceiving of a child. That is merely the process humanly agreed upon as the method of the new child's appearing. The consensus of opinion agrees on a certain process; so it operates. But do the first Bible story of "dust"[1] and the second one of a "rib"[2] actually differ in essence from the third, an egg?

All are mythical nonsense.

As a matter of fact, if human opinion agreed upon *any* other process, however ridiculous, it could produce children, as readily as by the present idiotic method.

Eliminate matter, as material science has done, and what is left of this poor mind or its theories of birth?

The sooner materiality is discarded with all its foolishness about children, the sooner will the omnipresence of God appear as the infinity of being, in all its multiplicity of living variety, instead of the numerical multiplication of more and more death-doomed mortals.

"On the right side"[3]: The disciples "caught nothing"[4] although they fished all night.

After Jesus' resurrection, the disciples went back to their old habit of thought—fishing materially, instead of casting their nets "on the right side".[3] When finally they did cast them on the right side, they caught abundantly.

The right side is the side of Mind, not matter.

Attacks on Mrs. Eddy: Every attack on Mrs. Eddy as a person, is working "a far more exceeding and eternal weight of glory"[5] to the Christian Scientist who may be tempted to cling to the personality of Mrs. Eddy, or to believe that she, or any other person, sustains Christian Science.

Such attacks force him in his bewilderment to turn from Mrs. Eddy's personality to Mind, where alone he can find rest.

This confusion about Mrs. Eddy's rightful place in human thinking will go on until there is not a Scientist who will not gladly leave Mrs. Eddy out of Christian Science. He will prove his deep love and respect for her by doing as she did, that is, by proving the allness of God.

He will then find that he does not revere Mrs. Eddy less, but more, because the only love worth while is the love that goes and does likewise. "Imitation is the sincerest flattery". Jesus said, "If ye love me, keep my commandments"[6]—in other words, do as I have done.

The immaculate conception: The immaculate conception as understood in Christian Science has three phases: first, the Virgin

[1]Gen. 2:7.   [2]Gen. 2:22.   [3]Jno. 21:6.   [4]Jno. 21:3.   [5]2 Cor. 4:17.
[6]Jno. 14:15.

Mother's conception of the fact that God is the only Father; second, the "little book"[1] Science and Health, bringing out the impersonality of God as both Father and Mother; and lastly, as wholly immaculate, the individual understanding through pure reason, of the truth presented in Science and Health.

In this final phase thought is led directly to Mind, its own source, where, in communion with Mind, each one, no longer looking to person or book for his understanding, but to his own oneness with God, finds true being for himself.

This is the acme of immaculateness "without sin unto salvation".[2]

The Christian Scientist verifies his conclusions with his Life charts, the Bible and Science and Health. He does not look to those books for his conclusions; but in these books he finds verification of them.

The dragon: The dragon, materiality, stinging itself to death, is exemplified through matter's own mouthpiece, the material scientist, when he declares that there is no matter, as such.

What could better sting materiality to death than this teaching of its own votaries that there is no matter.

If there is no matter, there is no material sense. This wipes out all materiality of whatever name or nature.

Physical and mental ills: There are no "physical" ills. All ills are "mental" ills.

Man is not a combination of physical and mental states. He is wholly a state of consciousness and all that he cognizes must come to him as consciousness; otherwise he could have no awareness of anything.

All "ills" whether called physical or mental are a false state of mind and must be destroyed through the *understanding* of what Mind is, and not through *faith* or *belief*.

Evil never in consciousness: The erroneous expression, "I must get that wrong thought *out of* consciousness or it will never disappear" is based on a false sense of what evil is.

Neither good nor evil are ever *in* anything. Evil is as impersonal as good, because it is the negation of good. God, being infinite cannot be *in* anything, neither then can evil be *in* something.

God operates as the Mind of His own idea and evil masquerades as the mind of the mortal.

Hence the necessity to reject evil *as* consciousness, not to get it *out of* consciousness. To refuse it place as consciousness, as mind, by the acceptance of what really is consciousness is to destroy evil's seeming reality.

[1]Rev. 10:2.   [2]Heb. 9:28.

If evil were *in* consciousness it could never be gotten *out* of consciousness.

Organization: Organization is the eternal oneness of Principle and its idea. It is the communion of God and man with no medium intervening between them.

In the unfolding of this true sense of organization, the first erroneous sense to disappear is ecclesiastical organization because it is this false belief which poses as the oracle, or medium of God and presumes to dictate to man. It lays down rules as to how he should think and act.

Playing upon man's highest sense of right and attempting to tamper with that, ecclesiasticism becomes the most dangerous form of organization and consequently it is necessary to dismiss it first.

Ultimately, all sense of finite organization must vanish before the infinity of Mind and its idea—the one organization.

Christian Science versus Common Sense: It is true, as has often been said, that C. S. stands for common sense as well as for Christian Science, but this is only insofar as there is agreement upon the definition of what constitutes common sense.

The term common sense is too apt to be a catch-phrase used as an excuse to justify the gratification of whims and personal desires. It is easy to use it to justify indulgences whether in sleeping, eating or caring for the body.

The victim of suggestion prefers to justify his failure to live up to his highest sense of Principle rather than to struggle with the temptation to lapse from it.

As ordinarily used, the phrase "common sense" is little more than another way of acknowledging the wiles of evil to ensnare the mortal along the path of least resistance.

In its true meaning common sense is Mind-sense, the sense of Mind that is everywhere present.

Past and present presentation of Christian Science: Because of the law of progress, the verbal interpretation of Christian Science to-day may seem quite different in some respects from that of the past.

When Mrs. Eddy began teaching, Truth had to be stated in language that could be understood at that period. Later on, the same was true of Mr. Kimball's statement, designated by Mrs. Eddy as "clear, correct teaching". The thought of each succeeding day demands a more impersonal interpretation because of the enlightenment that has followed Mrs. Eddy's tremendous accomplishment.

In consequence, the progressively scientific thought of the world demands progressively idiomatic language.

Today, with Principle enthroned as Leader, there is unlimited freedom in the manner of speech, so that the completely impersonal and purely scientific interpretation is taking on new forms of speech by which to express the same fundamental concept.

Erroneous influence: Can the thoughts of those who have passed on influence those who have not passed on?

Mrs. Eddy answers this question in the statement, *"In Science, individual good derived from God, the infinite All-in-all, may flow from the departed to mortals; but evil is neither communicable nor scientific."*[1]

This is a definite statement that evil is not communicable because it is not entity. Mrs. Eddy, however, does not say and does not intend to imply that evil *as a belief,* as the suppositional opposite of omnipresent good, does not operate hypnotically under one phase of belief called "here" as well as under another phase called "hereafter."

Dying changes nothing but minor beliefs, and the longings and desires of one who has passed on are neither more nor less real than they were before he passed on. Therefore, the belief that wrong thought has power to influence any one from anywhere, must be destroyed, as a belief, as definitely in the case of those who have passed on as in the case of those who have not.

This statement of Science and Health awakens mankind on this very point, by showing what is reality or truth, thus opening men's eyes to the claim of the unreal or false.

The remedy lies in the realization that the one Mind is the only Mind and that there is no malicious mind either here or hereafter. This realization prevents all belief of thought transference or mortal mind influence either from any one here, or from any one in the so-called "hereafter."

Asking for help: Science and Health says, *"If students do not readily heal themselves, they should early call an experienced Christian Scientist to aid them. If they are unwilling to do this for themselves, they need only to know that error cannot produce this unnatural reluctance."*[2]

Why? For the same reason that when you have a mistake that you cannot find in a problem in mathematics, and which you have diligently tried to discover, you often find that if you put it away for a time and forget it, you will, when you return to the subject, usually see and correct the mistake instantly. Or another person, new to the problem, might discover the mistake promptly for you.

[1] S. & H. 72:23. [2] S. & H. 420:4.

The mesmerism of the association of ideas operates, in such a case, as mental darkness hiding the light of Truth and preventing the correction.

"An experienced Christian Scientist" is that state of thought that is oneness with intelligence and appears in any language most helpful, whether as a person, a book, or in any other way, but always as a direct *"impartation of the divine Mind to man"*.[1]

Unwillingness to partake of this "impartation" is itself all there is to the so-called malicious mind and to the unwillingness to ask for help.

Christian Science versus mental science: No greater difference could exist than that which exists between Christian Science and mental science.

Christian Science is the action of divine Mind appearing as the Mind of man, and as such, supplying all completeness and satisfaction.

Mental science is the supposed action of one mind influencing another mind, whether for so-called good or for so-called evil. It is always predicated on the assumption of two minds, which is the diametrical opposite of Christian Science predicated on the basis of one Mind and its idea as All-in-all.

Mental science declares, from a personal or limited standpoint, that everything is mental and then attempts to deal with everything mentally but without the purification gained by first establishing as the one basis, pure consciousness as wholly apart from finite sense.

Without this step, mental science, even though using terms that seem to mean spirituality and good, must stop short of the actual spiritual realm because limitation has been set up as the source of thought.

Christian Science without limitation, is based wholly on the allness of God as the one Mind.

The parable of the true neighbor: In the parable of the good Samaritan, Jesus emphasized the fact that the good deed itself— the binding of the wound and the caring for the wounded—and not a person, is neighbor to the one who fell among thieves.

Is it not the one good, the one Mind, that is the source of every good deed or impulse? Jesus said, "Why callest thou me good? There is none good but one, that is, God."[2]

Because every good thought is one with God, the one neighbor is always God, not a person, although it may appear as a person.

With this understanding of what neighbor really is, there could be no unfriendliness or complaining of neighbor. "Love thy neighbor as thyself"[3] is synonymous with loving thy *Self*, the Self of thee, thy God.

[1] S. & H. 68:29.　[2] Matt. 19:17　[3] Mark 12:31.

"The Crime wave": The unbridled license that to-day characterizes the behaviour of so many men and women under forty and which frequently reaches the point of violence and crime, is not surprising when the human mind is analyzed.

From the middle of the year 1914 to the close of 1918 every expectant mother in the civilized world was probably torn with the greatest mental anxiety, fear, despondency and often hatred. Human belief admits that this state of mind on the part of the mother produces disastrous effects on the unborn child.

The explanation of the fact that the same lawless conditions may be found among slightly older people, those born before the war, is that these were at their most impressionable age—from eight to sixteen years—when hatred and the madness of killing were at their zenith, when the value of life and property was held to be negligible.

It is only the omnipresence of good, in spite of all human belief, that prevents conditions from being vastly worse.

The remedy for this lawlessness and lack of self-discipline is the same remedy that is applied to sickness or to sin.

By reversing the negative appearance and seeing Truth present in its stead, you prove that the negative is not something apart from the real. Hence the Great War is seen, by reversal, to have been the activity of infinite good destroying all unlike itself. *"The greatest wrong is but a supposititious opposite of the highest right."*[1]

The correct understanding of what the period 1914-1918 actually represents would prove the greatest blessing that could come to any young person.

All erroneous belief is hypnotic suggestion, and its destruction is the understanding that there is no mind apart from the one Mind to exert any mental influence.

As the understanding of the scientific infinity of good appears more clearly, inevitably the suppositional opposite or negation appears side by side, and *"the higher Truth lifts her voice, the louder will error scream, until its inarticulate sound is forever silenced in oblivion."*[2] This oblivion is the translation of the negation, matter, back to its positive, Spirit, divine Mind.

The English language: The genius of the English language lies in its spirit. This spirit is often intimated rather than openly defined. In no other language is such freedom of interpretation permissible in order to convey the spiritual significance of words.

A metaphysician uses a word in whatever sense best conveys his meaning.

The word *body,* for instance, has been used in three distinct ways in this class elucidating Christian Science.

[1] S. & H. 368 :1.   [2] S. & H. 97 :23.

First, as the embodiment of Mind ; as that which shows forth all that God is. In other words, it has been used as denoting the body of God, and so is synonymous with the man of God.

Second, the word *body* has been used to signify the communication between God and His idea, man. In this sense, it is the language whereby God is known to His idea, hence synonymous with Holy Ghost.

The third sense in which the word *body* has been used is as substance. In this sense, body means God, the substance or body of all that is.

Spirit, likewise, is a word that is used to express more than one concept. Spelled with a capital S, it means isness, essence, hence God. Spelled with a small s, it indicates the spirit of God meaning the idea or man of God. Lastly, it is used to signify the appearing of God to man : the Holy Spirit or communion between God and man. In this sense, it means the universe, God's interpretation of Himself to His own idea.

Water not a good illustration: The relation of a drop of water to the ocean does not adequately express the nature of man's relationship to God. A drop of water is actually a part of the ocean for if you were to take every drop of water out of the ocean, you would destroy the ocean.

This would reverse the true relationship and make the drop independent of and more important than the ocean.

God, without man, would be expressionless, but that is quite a different thing from man's being greater than, or independent of, God. God must be first, as cause ; and man must be second, as effect. Neither can be without the other. If you could take enough drops away from the ocean to destroy it, the ocean would be gone.

Such a simile, therefore, does not express the scientific relationship of God and man, where one cannot be without the other.

Only in the sense that a drop of water and the ocean are one in their chemical constituents is it possible to use them as similes to express the fact that God and man are one in being, in essence. This is the only sense in which Mrs. Eddy compares them.

The best finite illustration to express the relationship of man to God, is the relationship between the ray and the sun because these can never be separated. The sun manifests itself as ray, not rays, never separable from the sun as the origin of light.

Afraid of being afraid: The expression "I am afraid of being afraid" is frequently voiced because it is not understood that conscious fear never produces what is feared. This suggestion of the fear of fear must be met and dismissed with the declaration of Jesus, "Get thee behind me, Satan; thou art an offense unto me."[1]

Regardless of the extent of your conscious fear, it has no power to hurt you. Conscious fear and sickness are both effects and effect never becomes cause and it never produces anything.

The one all-inclusive fear, the belief that malicious mind *is*, must be destroyed through the understanding that God is the only Mind and that there is no malicious mind.

Remember, it is *"the good which the material senses see not"* that *"is the only absolute good:"* and it is *"the evil which these senses see not"* that *"is the only absolute evil."*[2]

The true Christian Scientist never loses sight of this and consequently is not tempted to judge from the standpoint of the senses. He is in no danger, therefore, of losing his sense of security. *"Evil which obtains in the bodily senses, but which the heart condemns, has no foundation; but if evil is uncondemned, it is undenied and nurtured."*[3]

Why the negation: The question is sometimes asked to-day: "Why is so much stress laid upon seeing evil as the negation of good rather than upon thinking of it as the suppositional opposite of good as was formerly done?"; especially in view of the fact that Mrs. Eddy does not treat evil in her writings as a negation merely.

This last statement, however, is not correct. Mrs. Eddy does treat evil negatively all through her writings. This is evident when those writings are read understandingly. In her very first edition of Science and Health, on page 426 she made this enlightening statement on the subject, *"Meeting the affirmative to disease with a negative neutralizes the positive belief and its effects upon the body, making disease become negative to harmony, and introducing the Science of being."*

What could be more positive than this declaration that the understanding of evil as the negation or negative interpretation of Mind is the "introducing [of] the Science of being."

In this statement, Mrs. Eddy uses the affirmative and the negative on both sides of the question. She shows how disease in its affirmative statement, "I am sick", must be met with the negative, "I am not sick" in order to neutralize the positive belief of being sick and the effect which this statement has on the body. By so doing, disease is shown to be the negation of harmony, and, when reversed, the very presence of good itself.

Evil must be seen negatively—not as an entity in itself. As the negation of good, it is, when reversed, real and true; but as entity, evil would be power and could not be destroyed.

[1]Matt. 16:23.   [2]Mis. 299:15.   [3]S. & H. 448:5.

Law the basis of thought: Because divine Principle is law, the entire operation or activity of Principle, to the minutest detail, is the operation of law. The negation or suppositional opposite of Principle, malicious mind, must operate in the same way, but always as a *belief* of law and not as law itself.

Mortal man is sick according to so-called law. He dies according to so-called law. He breathes, acts, functions in every respect according to so-called law. He is born according to it. He calls these beliefs of law "laws of matter," or "laws of nature." He subdivides them into physics, astronomy, chemistry, etc. but always bows his neck to the yoke they impose upon him.

These beliefs of law, all borrowed from the one law that is God, are the negation of that divine law which operates eternally for the grandeur and perfection of man. Because of this false claim of law it is essential, in every case that the material sense of law be replaced with the law of divine reality, for every claim is a claim of a broken belief of law.

In its final analysis, this spurious belief of law operates as hypnotic suggestion, pure and simple. It appears as a so-called law of wish, rule, influence, etc. Paul said, "the law of the Spirit of life in Christ Jesus hath made me free from the law of sin and death."[1]

Paul was awake to the claim of false law and nullified it with his understanding of what law really is,—the presence of the one Mind—the reality of law.

Moral sin and sickness: If you were to ask the religionist whether a continued departure from the moral code could produce sickness, undoubtedly he would answer with a positive affirmative, because he believes that the moral code is the law of God, and that the breaking of the law of God inevitably brings punishment.

But if you were to ask the medical man the same question, he would be just as positive that it is not the breaking of the moral code that causes disease, but rather the breaking of the law of matter or of nature.

How does Christian Science answer the question? Christian Science shows that sin is the *belief* of life, substance, and intelligence in matter, which is the *one* and *only* sin, embracing within itself all evil, all false belief.

One product of this sin is the belief that there is intelligence in matter for pleasure, which belief of pleasure frequently ultimates in what is termed moral sin.

Another product is the belief that there is intelligence in matter for pain, ultimating in what is called sickness.

[1] Rom. 8:2.

The belief of intelligence in matter for pleasure, and the belief of intelligence in matter for pain are children of the same parent, which is the belief of intelligence in matter as the basis of all experience.

Self-evidently one effect cannot become the cause or the origin of another effect. Therefore, the belief of intelligence in matter for pleasure can never produce the belief of intelligence in matter for pain. Thus, Christian Science shows that it is impossible for any indulgence in pleasure in matter to produce sickness or pain in matter. In other words, a moral lapse cannot cause sickness.

Hence, Jesus' reply to the question "who did sin, this man, or his parents, that he was born blind? . . . . . . Neither: . . . . but that the works of God should be made manifest in him."[1] He did not attribute sickness to moral delinquency but to belief in a mind apart from God, which belief is merely the negation of the presence of God, and which negative, reversed, declares His presence, "the works of God . . . . made manifest."

The question naturally arises, then : Why is sickness so often healed when, through Christian Science, a case of sin is healed ? The answer is, that sin is a greater error or ghost than sickness for the reason that the mortal loves his sin and clings to it, but is afraid of his sickness and wants to rid himself of it. In other words, his biggest ghost is his pleasure in matter. Healed of the bigger error, the lesser error or ghost also frequently disappears. This is not, however, because of any relationship between the two in the sense that the one produces the other, but because freedom from the greater error so uplifts thought that the victim is spontaneously freed from the lesser error.

Licentiousness, as a *moral* wrong, does not cause the brain to become diseased. Continued depletion of the nerve energy is the belief that causes the diseased brain.

Intemperance, as a *moral* wrong, does not cause a cancerous condition of the stomach, but, in belief, alcohol eats away the lining of the stomach and produces death. And so on. From the standpoint of human belief, the medical diagnosis is nearer right than the theological conviction, which attributes disease to God's punishment of sin.

Science and Health says, *"Neither disease itself, sin, nor fear has the power to cause disease or a relapse."*[2]

Mrs. Eddy was truly brave when she wrote those lines, for it appeared as if she were taking away the theological barrier against sin. Fear of God's punishment was regarded as the supreme moral weapon, but Mrs. Eddy could not jeopardize her statement of the truth of being by yielding to a compromise between scientific reality and erroneous human dogma.

[1] Jno. 9 :2, 3.   [2] S. & H. 419 :10.

The belief in life, substance and intelligence in matter is the one sin and embraces within itself all belief in pleasure and pain. It is impossible to escape the inevitable deduction, that if you believe there is intelligence in matter capable of giving pleasure, you cannot escape the conclusion that there must also be intelligence in matter able to produce pain. However, the one does not produce the other; but to believe in the one is to encourage belief in the other.

Likewise, *conscious* fear does not produce sickness, for both conscious fear and sickness are the products of the one fear, which is belief in a power apart from God, the fear that is inherently one with the belief of limitation and death, which is the opposite of the assurance and confidence that is Life. It was this fear, as cause, that Job referred to when he declared "the thing which I greatly feared is come upon me."[1]

The Bible says, "Be not afraid of sudden fear".[2] Be not afraid of the fear that is effect; but, be awake to the all-embracing fear —to the acceptance as real of that mind that is fear itself, and is the suppositional opposite of the one Mind which is confidence and understanding.

Exploitation: No Christian Scientist who continues to exploit Christian Science—to use it for his own material gain—will progress in his understanding of Christian Science.

One must be unselfish in order to be spiritual. There is nothing to Christian Science except spirituality.

Exploitation may seem to prosper for a season, even as willpower seems to prosper, but in the end both are doomed to failure. The "house",[3] the human heart, is left empty and desolate. "God is a Spirit: and they that worship him must worship him in spirit and in truth."[4]

Struggle: The struggle of the mortal for understanding and freedom is like the butterfly's struggle to free itself from its chrysalis. It is the fierceness of the struggle that forces the lovely coloring of the butterfly to appear. The struggles of the mortal force beauty of character, unselfishness of purpose, and the glory of accomplishment.

Going forward: Christian Science is the continuation of the ascension. Christian Science goes forward with the heritage left by Jesus.

The Christian Scientist is not thinking of being resurrected or of ascending. He knows that he has already ascended from a belief in matter's reality; this is the true ascension.

There can be no repetition. The resurrection is accomplished; the ascension is finished. Going forward in the fullness of the

[1]Job 3:25. [2]Prov. 3:25. [3]Luke 13:35. [4]Jno. 4:24.

joy of being, is all that remains. "Be of good cheer; I have overcome the world."[1] "It is finished."[2]

All good is. You cannot create one iota of good. It is already present. In reality all see it because in reality all are Christian Scientists. There are none to be made. It is no longer a case of "Know the Lord",[3] for they all do know Him "from the least of them unto the greatest of them".[3]

The ever rising entrance point: People coming into Christian Science, come in at the point of highest experience to-day. They do not have to traverse a path already trod. They come in at the eleventh hour and receive the full "penny",[4] the full understanding of good.

Then why assume that something is useful to another that is no longer of value to you? Where you are, at that point are all, with you.

Did not Jesus say, "Where I am, there ye may be also"?[5] The child is air-minded to-day because his world is an air-minded world.

Each one is at the point of the experience of the most advanced.

So is it with the Christian Scientist. One has no more than another. All are at the same point of opportunity. This must be acknowledged or there will be no growth.

The attack on the Jews: Present-day Germany's attack upon her people of Jewish blood is perfectly consistent with her attitude during the World War, when she lent herself to the forces of evil in their effort to destroy the English language.

That purpose, the Herod of this age, would have destroyed the "young child",[6] Christian Science, by rending from it its garment, the language in which Science and Health was written and the only language in which its deep spiritual significance can be fully expressed.

The "little book"[7] of the Revelator is Science and Health spiritually understood.

For its own preservation, materialism must always seek to destroy that which would destroy it.

Christian Science represents spiritual Abraham in whose "seed shall all the nations of the earth be blessed".[8] It is the destroyer of all materialism through the understanding of Spirit as All-in-all.

The Jew represents material Abraham, human intellectuality triumphing in material knowledge. By virtue of his leadership in material science, the Jew, with Steinmetz and Einstein as

[1]Jno. 16:33.   [2]Jno. 19:30.   [3]Jer. 31:34.   [4]Matt. 20:9.
[5]Jno. 14:3.   [6]Matt. 2:9.   [7]Rev. 10:8.   [8]Gen. 22:18.

among well known examples, is fast destroying matter, as matter, by reducing it to a mathematical formula.

Germany, who typifies sheer materialism, must inevitably array herself against everything that would destroy matter, whether the destruction be accomplished by the process of mental definition or through spiritual understanding.

Having failed in her first effort, at the time of the World War, Germany is now making a second attempt by the persecution and suppression of the Jew.

Failure must follow this effort as surely as it did the first, because *"progress is the law of God"*.[1]

Prohibition: Prohibition having once been acknowledged as an integral part of the meaning of the Constitution of the United States of America, remains that forever.

Spirituality is the prohibition of all materiality.

The repeal of the Eighteenth Amendment, instead of taking prohibition out of the Constitution, has but served to call the attention of all to its presence there.

Sheer legalism is no longer the compulsion operating to protect the descendants of spiritual Abraham, those true Americans who have built this nation and are sustaining it against the hypnotic effects of alcohol.

Prohibition of all materiality is enshrined in the heart of America. Its national motto is "In God we Trust."

Acceptance of prohibition is no longer due to outward compulsion but to inner approval.

God's law is never repealed. It can no more be reversed than can the vision that once sees that two times two is four, be repudiated.

"Progress takes off human shackles."[2]

Patriotism: The human, or false sense of Love, is vividly portrayed in an oft-quoted expression, "My Country—right or wrong—My Country." Such sentiment—upholding one's country in wrong—is not patriotism; it is but a parody on real love of one's country. Could divine Love ever be wrong? Then could real love of one's country ever be expressed in upholding it when it is wrong? It could not. Hence, such sentiment is not love.

Positive and negative: The electric battery with its positive and negative poles, illustrates, in certain respects the concept of positive and negative as these terms are used in Christian Science.

In the battery, the fluid in which the positive and negative poles are immersed, conveys the electron from the positive to the negative pole.

`S. & H. 233:6.   ²S. & H. 256:1.

The positive pole always gives, and the negative always receives.

In other words, the negative is nothing of itself, but derives all from the positive. It is simply the positive in reverse. But the same fluid and the same wire govern both. It is in their functions that they are diverse.

Both are necessary to make the complete circuit and to produce the light which is the result of bringing the one to the other.

Vibrations: True vibrations are not electrical waves: they are thoughts passing from God to man, and forever expressing the infinity of good.

No vibration could be disturbing; for the purity of Mind is the entire insulation of Mind, and purity being all the *is* there is, vibrations of good are the only vibrations.

The Concordances: The Concordances to Science and Health and to Mrs. Eddy's other works exemplify the infinite compassion of Love. They are the epitome of the fact that nothing is hidden that shall not be revealed.

The human heart has nothing for which to be more grateful than for the fact that the Concordances make easily available the most enlightened statement on every subject dealt with in Christian Science.

The Concordances are second in importance only to the Bible and Science and Health.

Postulates and platform: The *"postulates"*[1] of Christian Science are the self-evident truths of Christian Science, and should be familiar to every Christian Scientist.

The *"platform"*[2] of Christian Science is its working basis.

Both postulates and platform are essential tools for daily work, charts that bring out the *"beauty of holiness, the perfection of being, imperishable glory"* and show them as *"all . . . . Mine, for I am God."*[3]

America: America, spiritually understood, is the outward evidence of man's individual oneness with God.

America, in that sense, is not a nation defined by territorial boundaries but is the spiritual idea of Mind everywhere present.

America typifies the yearning of the heart for spiritual reality, "whose branches run over the wall".[4] "As the hart panteth after the water brooks, so panteth my soul after thee, O God."[5]

The "Pilgrim Fathers" were the "Separatists" who separated themselves entirely from bondage to ecclesiastical and political

[1]S. & H. 288:21.　[2]S. & H. 330:8.　[3]S. & H. 253:2.　[4]Gen. 49:22.
[5]Ps. 42:1.

formulas and founded what is called America, as Abraham founded Israel by going out from his "father's house, unto a land that I will shew thee",[1] forsaking all for the highest sense of good.

The Puritans, on the contrary, did not wholly separate themselves from their old affiliations. They still clung to an ecclesiastical mental unity with the old theology and still looked to an intermediary in the form of the ordained minister between themselves and God, even in the conduct of government. So they could not be wholly single-minded in their purpose.

It was not the Pilgrims who indulged in the Salem "burnings", it was the Puritans. The Pilgrims had no part in them.

It is not the Puritans but the *Pilgrims* who are the real "fathers" of America. "Come out from among them, and be ye separate,"[2] expresses America as the spiritual idea of Mind.

America is synonymous with individualism. Had individualism not been the objective of the Pilgrims, they would soon have been forced to admit that there is no freedom and success without it, as the following historical data show.

At first, the Pilgrims felt that community interest, rather than individual interest, in crops would better serve their ends, for the moment. But they quickly learned, as Governor Bradford records in his "History", that collectivism was doomed to failure. Complete individuality was essential for true spirituality and prosperity—as it always must be.

Beardsley, in his work, "The Builders of a Nation", brings this out clearly on page 265:

"Until the spring of 1623, Plymouth Colony had been upon a communistic basis. The houses of the settlers were individual property but the crops were raised in common for their general consumption. The results, however, did not justify the continuance of the scheme. 'At length', wrote Bradford, 'after much debate of things, the Governor (with the advice of the chiefest amongst them) gave way that they should set corn every man for his own particular, and in that regard trust to themselves; in all other things to go in the general way as before . . . . This had very good success; for it made all hands very industrious so as much more corn was planted than otherwise would have been by any means the Governor or any other could use, and saved him a great deal of trouble, and gave far better content. The women now went willingly into the field, and took their little ones with them to set corn, which before would allege weakness, and inability; whom, to have compelled would have been thought great tyranny and oppression!'

The Plymouth governor moralizes upon the failure of a scheme which, in theory, had seemed so attractive, but which in the end

[1]Gen. 12:1.   [2]2 Cor. 6:17.

had militated not only against self-interest but self-respect; 'The experience that was had in this common course and condition, tried sundry years, and that amongst godly and sober men, may well evince the vanity of that conceit of Plato's and other ancients, applauded by some of later times;—that the taking away of property, and bringing in community into a commonwealth, would make them happy and flourishing; as if they were wiser than God. For this community (so far as it was) was found to breed much confusion and discontent, and retard much employment that would have been to their benefit and comfort . . . . . Upon the point of all being to have alike, and all to do alike, they thought themselves in the like conditions, and one as good as another; and so, if it did not cut off those relations that God hath set amongst men, yet it did much diminish and take off the mutual respects that should be preserved amongst them. And would have been worse if they had been men of another condition. Let none object this is men's corruption, and nothing to the course itself. I answer, seeing all men have this corruption in them, God in his wisdom saw another course fitter for them' ".

Man, as God's idea, is necessarily individual.

America, negatively interpreted, in other words, viewed materially, is the final expression of this individualism seen as human government.

The negative is as individual as is that which it negatives and cannot be changed. The attempt of evil to change America from individualism to collectivism, and all that goes with that theory, is destined to failure. The breath of America is freedom, which means individualism.

To surrender its Pilgrim heritage, would be to sell the birthright of America. But this can never be done, for *it is America.*

Mrs. Eddy emphasizes individualism thus: *"Is not a man metaphysically and mathematically number one, a unit, and therefore whole number, governed and protected by his divine Principle, God?"*[1]

This individualism, this oneness is America.

All forms of government ownership are subtle attempts of evil to thwart this individualism. Government, like Principle, exists because of its citizen, or idea. It does not and cannot exist alone. Then government's ownership, possession and being must be shown forth as the owning, possessing and being of its man, its citizen.

If government owned and man did not, there could be no ownership expressed and government would fall.

Man, individually, owns all as idea. He does not own it collectively any more than he owns the multiplication table collectively. This in no way interferes with the inevitable combination

[1]Pul. 4:7.

or merger of like businesses—expressing the one business in which all can be owners, but only as individuals, never as government ownership.

Government has no place *in* business, as such, any more than God is *in* man.

Man is the business of God and shows forth God's business in individual ownership, expression and unfoldment.

He needs no interfering with, and will brook none.

Man's diadem is his eternal individuality as the expression of the one infinite Mind. America means this and Christian Science, as exemplified in Science and Health, declares it, and so epitomizes spiritual America, epitomizes the culmination of all the good that has gone before.

The true sense of what the Pilgrim Fathers, America—Christian Science—really means, may be expressed, "unto me every knee shall bow".[1] "And the Gentiles shall come to thy light, and kings to the brightness of thy rising."[2] "And the nations of them which are saved shall walk in the light of it".[3]

Mrs. Eddy's passing on: The question is frequently asked: Why did Mrs. Eddy pass on? Why, with her clear understanding of the Science of being, should she not have demonstrated continuity of living, here?

One, with even a slight grasp of Christian Science, has no doubt of Mrs. Eddy's understanding of Life, for he knows that Christian Science could not have been discovered and promulgated had a single link been missing in the spirituality of the discoverer.

Then Mrs. Eddy's death involves a deeper and more far-reaching reason than that of an ordinary death.

The metaphysician understands why it was as imperative for Mrs. Eddy to disappear as she did, as it was for Jesus to disappear in the ascension.

Jesus stands as the personal embodiment of Truth. In his own *person* he expressed the Truth completely; and he declared, "I am the way, the truth, and the life; . . . he that hath seen me hath seen the Father".[4]

These two statements reveal what Jesus exemplified as his mission to the world.

The human mind accepts Truth in gradation, first personally, then impersonally.

Therefore, to understand God, the human mind has to see God first expressed as a person, before it can conceive of Him impersonally as Mind. Consequently, Jesus had to appear in a personal form that could be recognized as the very presence of Truth.

[1] Isa. 45:23.   [2] Isa. 60:3.   [3] Rev. 21:24.   [4] Jno. 14:6, 9.

After Jesus had thus presented God, overcoming every sense of limitation and death, and declaring, "Be of good cheer; I have overcome the world",[1] he disappeared in what has been called the ascension.

However, before this final disappearance he said, "It is expedient for you that I go away; for if I go not away, the Comforter will not come unto you; but if I depart, I will send him unto you . . . . Howbeit when he, the Spirit of truth, is come, he will guide you into all truth; for he shall not speak of himself; but whatsoever he shall hear, that shall he speak; and he will shew you things to come."[2]

Jesus understood that permanent help could not come from a finite person, that the spirit of truth alone could save mankind.

Then the question arises, What constitutes the Comforter, the spirit of Truth that will not speak of himself?

To "not speak of himself" implies complete impersonality; and the only impersonal way in which Truth can so appear, intelligently, to the mortal, is in the form of a book.

Is not a book, apart from its paper and ink, merely thought expressed, without personality or materiality?

Then a book is the obvious way for "the Spirit of truth" to appear.

The Revelator saw the "mighty angel" holding "in his hand a little book open" and his counsel was to "take the little book", "Take it, and eat it up",[3] meaning thereby to make its message your own.

Science and Health typifies the angel's book. It is the way in which the impersonal Christ, Truth, comes to this age.

Mrs. Eddy is not Science and Health, but mortals were unwilling to separate her in their thinking from Science and Health. This attitude, on the part of her followers, forced her to disappear, in order that Science and Health, unfettered by any sense of personality, could be accepted as the impersonal presentation of Truth to man.

To the next question which naturally follows: Why could Mrs. Eddy not have ascended as did Jesus? There are two answers:

First, the ascension, which presupposes man to be material and under necessity of ascending out of matter into Mind, was accomplished for all time by Jesus. Therefore, there is no necessity for the repetition of that proof.

Since Christian Science declares and demonstrates that there is no matter, it leaves no matter from which to ascend.

Second, the human mind, in its present phase of materiality, insists upon knowing, not only when the mortal appears, or is born, but, more important to that mind, when and how the mortal dies or disappears.

[1] Jno. 16:33.   [2] Jno. 16:7, 13.   [3] Rev. 10:1, 2, 8, 9.

Had Mrs. Eddy disappeared in any way other than in the traditionally accepted manner called death, the human mind would have been stirred to its depths in opposition to Christian Science. It would have declared Christian Science to be a fake, and Christian Scientists frauds, for saying that Mrs. Eddy had miraculously disappeared.

Christian Scientists would have been accused of trying to make Mrs. Eddy a second Christ; this would have arraigned the entire Christian world against Christian Science. Furthermore, public officials would have insisted that a crime had been committed.

Mrs. Eddy had to leave to the world an interpretation of her disappearance that human belief could admit was proper and legitimate.

She did this by appearing to die and be buried.

However, the fact remains that Mrs. Eddy gave up her sense of life, as it is called, because of the demand of the hour, which was the ignorance of her followers, as well as of the rest of mankind. She did it just as willingly as did Jesus. He purposely allowed the crucifixion. It enabled him to overcome the grave and to disappear in the ascension.

Mrs. Eddy permitted herself seemingly to die in order that Christian Science might ascend from the confusion of being attached to her personality, into its rightful status of impersonal Truth.

Through a clearer understanding of Christian Science, it is now seen that Jesus never actually gave up his sense of life, and it will eventually be seen that Mrs. Eddy did not die. The willingness to believe that she did die is purely hypnotic illusion, and is the mesmerism that encourages the one who believes she did, to do likewise.

Mrs. Eddy forewarned against regarding her as a personal leader when she wrote, *"He that by reason of human love or hatred or any other cause clings to my material personality, greatly errs, stops his own progress, and loses the path to health, happiness, and heaven."*[1]

If a person is accepted as a leader because of his discovery of a truth and subsequently appears to fail in any way, his followers are immediately cast into an abyss of doubt as to their own ability to demonstrate the full measure of the discovery. With that uncertainty as a premise, failure is assured.

Accepting Mrs. Eddy instead of her discovery, as leader, must inevitably result in discouragement; for the one who is led can never rise higher than his own sense of his leader. A fountain can never rise higher than its source. *"Hence, a finite person is not the model for a metaphysician."*[2]

[1] Mis. 308:5.   [2] Mis. 308:31.

"Say not ye, There are yet four months, and then cometh harvest? behold, I say unto you, Lift up your eyes, and look on the fields; for they are white already to harvest."

"Neither shall they say, Lo here! or, lo there! for, behold, the kingdom of God is within you."

JESUS.

"Think of this inheritance!
Heaven right here, where
angels are as men, clothed
more lightly, and men as
angels who, burdened for
an hour, spring into liberty,
and the good they would do,
that they do, and the evil
they would not do, that they
do not."

MARY BAKER EDDY.

APPENDIX I

Letter from the Board of Trustees to the Board of Directors

"Sept. 30, 1918.

"The Christian Science Board of Directors,
"Falmouth and St. Paul Streets,
"Boston, Massachusetts,

"Dear Friends:

"Referring to our meeting with you on Wednesday, Sept. 11, and your request later that the Board of Trustees listen to the reading of the minutes of the Board of Directors recording their interpretation of that meeting, after most careful and earnest consideration, the Board of Trustees has decided that this would not be a wise course of action for the trustees to take.

"In view of this request of the directors and of the meeting of Sept. 11, and more especially in view of the reference to a certain 'memorandum' prepared by the Board of Directors and presented to the Board of Trustees for their acceptance at certain joint conferences held by the two boards in the month of February, 1916, and again brought up by the Board of Directors for discussion with the Board of Trustees in recent conferences, which, though having been rejected by the trustees as a contravention of the Deed of Trust and the Church Manual, may still be in the director's file, it is our desire to set forth clearly in writing the position of the Board of Trustees as stated at the meeting of Sept. 11.

"At that meeting the trustees stated to the Board of Directors exactly how they viewed the Deed of Trust and the Manual in their relation to the trustees and their work. The trustees affirmed definitely that, to them, as loyal Christian Scientists, their trust was not only a most sacred and honored trust given to them by our Leader as a 'perpetual and irrevocable trust and confidence' (Deed of Trust), but that it was an aboslutely legal trust governed and perpetuated by the laws of Massachusetts and the United States, and that in order to be true to this trust there was no other course possible to them than to abide absolutely by the Deed of Trust and the Manual, both in the letter and the spirit, and that from that day they proposed to do so; that the trustees felt that it was incumbent upon them to interpret the

Deed of Trust through their own metaphysical understanding of what our Leader has written, since they were the ones called upon to fulfill the trust, and that that interpretation could not be done by somebody else for them.

"The directors stated at the close of the meeting that the trustees had made their position quite clear, and in view of that statement, this letter might seem superfluous, but as we have already stated, it seems just to state our position in writing, and provide a copy of this letter for each member of your board so that every statement therein may be verified with the Manual and the Deed of Trust.

"At the meeting on Sept. 11, some members of your board indicated that the statement of the trustees was an entirely new position for the trustees to take, and that it was a complete surprise to the directors. Since that meeting the trustees have gone back over old correspondence with the directors, and they find that their position in substance is in exact accord with the record of the trustees for a number of years, and so far as they can learn, it is the position that the Board of Trustees has felt was the only correct position from the beginning of the trusteeship. Therefore the surprise could only have been occasioned by the directors never having grasped the viewpoint of the trustees as to the purport of the Deed of Trust and the Manual in their relation to the Board of Trustees.

"In order to make the question perfectly clear, we wish to state, in our Leader's words, that the Deed of Trust, under which the trustees legally operate, was prepared by our Leader and given as 'A Gift to The Mother Church, and a Grant of Trusteeship' (letter conveying the Deed of Trust), and it was to be a 'perpetual and irrevocable trust and confidence' (Deed of Trust), and that 'The delivery of this instrument to, and its acceptance by said trustees shall be regarded as the full establishment of the trust and as the agreement by the trustees to honestly and faithfully do and perform all things to be done and performed by them within the terms, objects and purposes of this instrument' (Sec. 14). This Deed of Trust, according to Sec. 1 of Art. XXV of the Church Manual, is inferentially incorporated as part and parcel of the Church Manual. Therefore its conditions are obligatory upon the trustees, not only as an integral part of the Church By-Laws, but also according to the laws of the land.

"Simply stated, the trustees consider their trust is for the one purpose, as stated in the Deed of Trust, 'of more effectually promoting and extending the religion of Christian Science as taught by' Mrs. Eddy, and not for the purpose of making money, although all 'net profits'—and the Deed of Trust defines what is meant by the term 'net profits'—are to be paid over each six months to the treasurer of The Mother Church.

"The trustees understand that they are absolutely responsible for the entire business of The Christian Science Publishing Society, being the owner and manager in trust of said business and constituting in their trusteeship The Christian Science Publishing Society, under which name they are required to do business. The Deed of Trust demands that the 'trustees shall energetically and judiciously manage the business of the Publishing Society on a strictly Christian basis, and upon their own responsibility' (Sec. 3), and shall further 'employ all the help necessary to the proper conduct of said business, and shall discharge the same in their discretion or according to the needs of the business' (Sec. 6). This requirement, relating to employing and discharging, the trustees hold to include every man, woman and child working for the Publishing Society, in whatever capacity. The Board of Directors *elect* the editor and associate editors of our monthly and weekly periodicals, the editor of our daily newspaper, and the business manager, but the trustees *employ* these officers, and determine their salary; hence they are employees of The Christian Science Publishing Society—in other words, of the Board of Trustees and not of the Board of Directors. This is clearly pointed out by our Leader in the letter conveying the Deed of Trust, wherein she says, 'I now recommend that these Trustees continue at present the efficient service of Mr. Joseph Armstrong as the business manager of the publishing house.' Mr. Armstrong was at the time of this recommendation not only the business manager of the publishing house, but was also publisher of our Leader's works and a member of the Board of Directors of The Mother Church. Such term of office, according to the Manual, is 'one year each, dating from the time of election' (Art. XXV, Sec. 4), and is not subject to termination before the expiration of one year except in the event of discharge by the trustees for cause. The trustees hold that the directors have no direct control over the editors or the business manager, and can therefore make no business arrangements with them which in any way concern the Publishing Society.

"The Manual, in Sec. 14 of Art. VIII, under the chapter 'Discipline,' declares, 'It shall be the privilege and duty of every member, who can afford it, to subscribe for the periodicals which are the organs of this Church,' and at the close of the paragraph it is stated, 'and it shall be the duty of the Directors to see that these periodicals are ably edited and kept abreast of the times.' This is clearly a disciplinary function and not an executive function; therefore, the trustees hold that as discipline it is the duty of the Board of Directors to call attention at once to any failure on the part of the trustees to have periodicals well edited and kept abreast of the times. But the trustees hold it is not the province of the directors to edit the periodicals, any more than it is the province of the directors to conduct the business of

The Christian Science Publishing Society. The directors elect the editors and the business manager, but their employment and adjustment to office is the responsibility of the trustees, and if these officers do not do their work rightly, then the trustees are to blame, for they have the authority, as already quoted from the Deed of Trust, to discharge any employee for non-fulfillment of duty. The trustees feel, however, that the editors have a natural right to talk over with the Board of Directors any matter concerning the editorial work at any time they desire to do so, and request the benefit of their experience and enlightenment.

"Mrs. Eddy, in establishing the Deed of Trust, evidently took pains to define the character of thought that should constitute the Board of Trustees—business, metaphysics (a doctor), and scholarship—and, furthermore, she stated, 'I have asked for a small Board of Trustees, and as I believe a strong board' (letter conveying the Deed of Trust). Following this, she defined clearly and unmistakably what the duties of the Board of Trustees should be, stating specifically, and thus showing why she had defined the mental qualities constituting the Board of Trustees (Sec. 2), 'Said trustees shall have direction and supervision of the publication of said Quarterly, and also of all pamphlets, tracts, and other literature pertaining to said business, using their best judgment as to the means of preparing and issuing the same, so as to promote the best interest of the Cause.'

"Mrs. Eddy also covered, in Sec. 6 of Art. XXV of the Church Manual, the rules and orders that should govern any further publications issued by The Christian Science Publishing Society. In Sec. 8 of Art. XXV she declares, 'Only the Publishing Society of The Mother Church selects, approves, and publishes the books and literature it sends forth,' and concludes the section with the statement, 'A book or an article of which Mrs. Eddy is the author shall not be published nor republished by this Society without her knowledge or written consent.' In connection with this last sentence in Sec. 8, the trustees wish here to state positively their interpretation of this By-Law, and it is that this society can issue no book or article of which our Leader is the author that is not already in her published works, unless the provisions of this By-Law can be established.

"We should like at this point to bear record, with a great deal of appreciation, that at the time of the publication of the article entitled 'Life,' by our Leader, which appeared in the Sentinel of Feb. 2, and in the April Journal, which at that time we heartily approved, that when the trustees desired to republish this article in pamphlet form, the directors advised otherwise, and very wisely, for now we see clearly that this By-Law prohibits the publishing or republishing of any such articles. Inasmuch as the article originally was not referred to the trustees by the directors, as we now hold it should have been before being presented to the editors for their consideration for publication, the directors were primarily responsible for its first publication, but the field has a right to hold the Publishing Society, under the Church Manual, responsible for not upholding this By-Law. This mistake shows the great necessity of working in exact accord with the Deed of Trust and the Manual. We accept our full responsibility for this departure in regard to publishing the article 'Life,' as we should have been fully alive to our trusteeship.

"We have notified the editor of the Journal and Sentinel, and the editor of the Monitor, that we hold them responsible for everything that is published in the periodicals, and that we look to them to be true to their responsibility, just as we hold the business manager responsible for the business. The trustees are fully aware that there is only one way in which to govern the business of The Christian Science Publishing Society, 'on a strictly Christian basis' (Sec. 3 of the Deed of Trust)—by holding every man and woman in the Publishing House responsible for his own individual work, for we can conceive of no government by Principle except by trusting each employee to his own individual demonstration of Principle, and then, if the demonstration is not satisfactory, to point out the mistake. The future vastness of the Publishing Society's business is so great that to contemplate any other way of conducting the business is impossible. Therefore, each individual must be held responsible for his own demonstration, for this inevitably brings out the very best that is in the individual, and makes him responsible to God for his office and for his continuance in that office, instead of looking to person or persons, and this applies to all employees, from those who seem to have unimportant work to those who fill the most important offices.

"The members of the Board of Trustees naturally feel a deep sense of responsibility in the handling of this sacred and tremendous trust committed to their care, and they are resolved to faithfully live up to the Deed of Trust and the Manual both in the letter and in the spirit. They wish neither to shirk any responsibility nor to assume any responsibility that is not properly theirs, but God will not allow them to avoid in the slightest degree fulfilling the full requirements of the Deed of Trust and the Manual, and the trustees hold that this responsibility includes the complete and entire management of The Christian Science Publishing Society in every detail, 'upon their own responsibility and 'energetically and judiciously.'

"In defining our position we have spoken frankly and directly, and our one desire has been to do God's will and to be obedient to the teachings of Mrs. Eddy, as embodied by her in the Deed of Trust and the Manual. The trustees wish to reiterate the high personal regard they entertain for the individual members of the Board of Directors and, above all, they want to declare the love and honor they have for the office of the Christian Science Board of Directors, and in turn rightly expect the same love and honor on the part of the directors for the office of the Board of Trustees. These two boards, designated and constituted by our Leader, each having its own well defined work, one being the governing board of the Church and its activity and the other the governing board of the Publishing Society and all its publications, must inevitably cooperate at every point. This cooperation, however, can only be accomplished by a right mutual respect for each other's boards and their respective work. Yet when all is said and done, in spite of the tremendous importance of the letter, still how small is the letter compared to that Spirit that must inspire everything bequeathed to us by our Leader in the service of God. It is in the unity of this Spirit that this letter is written, signed, and sent.

'Very sincerely yours,

(Signed)   "HERBERT W. EUSTACE,
            "DAVID B. OGDEN,
            "LAMONT ROWLANDS,
                "Board of Trustees."

"WHOSO READETH
LET HIM
UNDERSTAND"

JESUS

"WHOSO READETH LET HIM UNDERSTAND"

By

HERBERT W. EUSTACE, C.S.B.

LEDERER, STREET AND ZEUS CO., INC.
Printers and Publishers
2121 Allston Way, Berkeley, California.

PREFACE

On three dates in November and December, 1938, meetings of Christian Scientists who have been through class with me were held in Los Angeles, San Francisco, and San Jose. The subject under consideration at each meeting was "Malicious Mental Malpractice." Those attending had been requested to study thoroughly Mrs. Eddy's writings on this all-important question.

Stenographic reports of the three meetings, together with articles resulting from the amplification of points brought out there, form the subject matter of this book.

A correct understanding of malicious mental malpractice is necessary in order to meet the myriad perplexities of evil appearing today in the form of sin, sickness, limitation, and world conditions.

Mrs. Eddy has declared: *"Where all students have failed is in not knowing how to handle animal magnetism."*

I have used quotations of statements which I believe are rightly attributed to Mrs. Eddy. Although their exact language does not appear in any of her published works, they are so pertinent and accurate in expressing Christian Science that no better words could be found in setting forth and emphasizing the genuine metaphysics of this subject. The quotations have been given to me at different times by reliable friends, as coming from Mrs. Eddy, and I have not hesitated to use them.

Herbert W. Eustace.

In her Vision of September 10, 1887, as recorded in Files of the Library of Congress, Mrs. Eddy said: *"After I had seen my way in Truth, I had to go back to teach them the error . . . I then thought the Truth—the Truth as applied to sickness was all that is necessary . . . Step by step I began to learn that the remedy of SIN must be searched out . . . The arguments to heal sickness caused by the fear of physical beliefs would not heal the suffering caused by the fear of SIN. I have been learning the remedies for SIN through suffering that the fear of SIN has imposed . . . When you think you have mastered disease on a physical basis you are mistaken. You have got to learn that it must be healed on the basis of SIN causing it . . . All the beliefs of SIN and their methods of destroying the peace of mind, filling the body with disease, administering poison through mind with more effect than the doctors could administer it through matter, have to be met and overcome through divine Science by every mortal here or hereafter."*

NOTE: Remember when Mrs. Eddy uses the word "SIN" as here, she is not referring to anything of the corporeal senses but is referring to the one SIN pure mental iniquity, *malicious mental malpractice.* This in conformity with her own statement in Mis. Ws. 299:16 *"The evil which these senses see not is the only absolute evil."*—H. W. E.

CONTENTS

"WHOSO READETH
LET HIM
UNDERSTAND"
JESUS

INTRODUCTION

The key to this book is simple but profound.
Because God is the one Mind He must and
does embrace within Himself the reality of all
that *is*. Man is the essential effect that this one
God is cause to and just as there is only one God
so there is only one man. Since self-evidently
you are not God, you must be the effect of God
and the one effect. Your dealings as this one
man are always with God and with God alone.

This leads to the inevitable fact that, what
appears to you as persons, places and things
"over there" or "out there" is not there at all,
but right where you are, "here". Also since

God *is*, and is all that is, now is all the time there is and consequently there are no years or times in the commonly accepted meaning of these words. It is all "now".

Peoples, races, nations, prophecies, dates, all the so-called formulæ of the human mind are really of no vital moment because they are all part of the dream belief called the mortal sense of existence. This is not in reality an existence but a dream belief that, rightly translated, disappears only in reappearing in its true sense as the light of Truth.

Bible history, like all so-called human history, does not record periods of time but as Science and Health points out "states and stages of consciousness". When understood correctly it presents unfoldments of reality proceeding from the lesser to the greater. The Biblical record of creation illustrates this. First the clearing of the vision, then the discernment of the lesser or simpler phases of Mind gradually unfolding to the higher, until finally the recorder declared the whole as God and man in His image and likeness. There were not six days of creation but clearer visions of the one fact of God's allness. The remainder of the Old Testament is the clarifying vision of that which is real uncovering and destroying that which is unreal.

The conclusion is that you can never be deceived into believing that you are dealing with anything but Mind, the one God. Thus your communion with God is your being and all that you behold is God interpreting Himself to you.

With this in mind it will be possible to solve every problem, in other words to understand every problem (place it where it is seen as already worked out) and thus find the solution.

After the opening chapter of the Bible which declares God and man as All-in-all, up to the statements of Jesus, the recorded declarations of absolute Truth uncontaminated by human belief are few and not easily discernible. As Jesus said, "All that ever came before me are thieves and robbers; but the sheep did not hear them". He did not mean "persons" but conditions of thought. All had previously been in the realm of belief but Jesus spoke and demonstrated the truth dealing only with Spirit, hence the disciples' surprised exclamation "What manner of man is this, that even the winds and the sea obey him!" and his own declaration "As I hear, I judge; and my judgment is just."

Christian Science, through Science and Health, has given to the world the actual truth and science of Being—one God and one man and God's eternal interpretation of Himself to His man, appearing as the entire harmonious universe and forever showing forth Father, son and Holy Ghost, the unity of good, the trinity of wholeness.

This then is the key: one God one man, one cause one effect. The effect's relationship, as always, is with cause, never with effect. To start from cause is to start from God. To start from effect, is to start from the one evil.

A statement made by Mrs. Eddy in the Christian Science Journal of August 1890 on the subject of malicious animal magnetism is significant in connection with the issue of this book. In that article she says, "It is my impression that at least a half century will pass away, before man is permitted to render his public verdict on some of the momentous questions that are now agitating the world. Also, the discussion of malicious animal magnetism had better be dropped until Scientists understand clearly, how to handle this error—until they are not in danger of dwarfing their growth in love, by falling into this lamentable practice in their attempts to meet it. Only patient, unceasing love for all mankind—love that cannot mistake Love's aid —can determine this question on the Principle of Christian Science."

Virtually, "a half century," has elapsed since Mrs. Eddy wrote these words, and the one thing that now makes the presentation of this subject in a public way permissible and wise is that evil is now being understood by the Christian Scientist as wholly impersonal and as a state of mind. It is no longer thought of as having anything to do with matter—or with false mentality—both effects, but entirely with malicious mind—"the dragon", the cause or basis of evil. In other words, evil is dealt with as a belief of consciousness, which when understood in its true sense as the negation of divine Mind and *reversed* is found to be divine Mind. This understanding eliminates all hatred and fear of persons, places and things, and so prevents Christian Scientists from "dwarfing their growth in love by falling into this lamentable practice in their attempts to meet it." The time is here when this question can be happily understood and God seen as the All-in-all.

THE
UNSEEN FOE

WHERE two or three are gathered together in my name, there am I in the midst of them."

In this statement Jesus did not mean that he personally was present, but that the I, the one Mind—his Mind—was present, for Mind is omnipresent. In Mrs. Eddy's words, *"This beautiful presence all around us is the substance of every good which we could possibly desire, yea, infinitely more than we are capable of desiring. 'Eye hath not seen, nor ear heard, neither hath it entered into the heart of man, the things that God hath prepared for them that love Him'."*

Our meeting this day holds a world of promise, is fraught with tremendous hope and filled with far-reaching possibilities, for where two or three are gathered together in the name, the understanding of Christ, Truth—the truth about being—there God, the one Mind, is found expressing Himself guiding and directing His own activity.

In eighteen eighty-nine, to her March class, Mrs. Eddy said, "We, today, in this classroom, are enough to convert the world if we are of one Mind." On another occasion she declared, "A small group of wise thinkers is better than a wilderness of dullards and stronger than the might of empires."

Have you ever contemplated the meaning of a gathering of real Christian Scientists—real metaphysicians—with one accord, in one place, with one Mind: the accord, the accord of Mind; the place, the presence of Mind; and that Mind, God? What cannot right knowing, devout prayer, accomplish? Mind is All-in-all and there is no limitation to the love and blessing it showers upon its own idea.

But as Christian Scientists you are not and cannot be deceived into believing there is any value or virtue in "numbers". You know that God and His idea is one and all, and you know the term numbers—anything more than one—is merely a figure of speech implying the infinity of Mind and its expression. Infinity is always *one* and the idea's oneness is with its Principle and never with idea.

Numbers carry no importance in and of themselves for you realize, as Mrs. Eddy states, the Christian Scientist is "alone with his own being and the reality of things."

Evil builds upon and glories in numbers for they deny oneness when not understood. Christian Science builds on oneness alone, one God, one man, and the eternal communion of Father and son.

Mrs. Eddy is said to have once told a class, *"You may falsely think that something stands between you and your heart's desire, and so go through life here with that desire unfulfilled, but it is not so. Deny it, and you will find yourself free; and good will begin to flow to you and you will see clearly that nothing can stand between you and your own. Lean on God. Trust Him. Understand Him, and He will give you foresight, wisdom, and a capacity to execute His will, and show forth His name."* Nothing can thwart the power of right knowing to bring to light the millennium, the understanding of man's eternal oneness with good.

Realizing this, how naturally then would Mrs. Eddy declare, *"To affirm anything is to assert its possibility—to assert it even in the face of all contrary evidence,"* and also, *"by affirming that to be true, but which to all human reasoning or sight seems not to be true at all, you can bring it to pass."* What can oppose Mind? Does not the allness of Mind make every affirmation of truth instantly available? Of course it does.

What a wealth of achievement this knowledge offers us. Think of it! By affirming that which is true we can bring it to pass. Of course, as metaphysicians, you know the bringing of it to pass simply means the beholding of that which already is. And has not Mrs. Eddy also declared that, *"When you reach out to the beyond for the real, you instantly express it?"* The heart's desire sees its fulfillment in this understanding, this scientific statement of fact. Think what it means to be able to affirm anything that is true, and to know that your affirmation is the seeing its actual presence, and that not an instant intervenes between affirming that which is true and seeing it, and that even when all human reasoning declares it otherwise. Mind speaks and it is done. As the Psalmist said, "Who is so great a God as our God?"

What a vista of success and achievement is unfolded to each one through this promise of oneness with all good! But best of all is the certainty and assurance which comes from the scientific understanding of why the affirmation of that which is true not merely states its possibilities but actually brings it to pass, in other words sees it as right here.

Before considering the important subject of the meeting, malicious mental malpractice, the unseen foe, let us be admonished by Isaiah: "Hearken to me, ye that follow after righteousness, ye that seek the Lord: look unto the rock whence ye are hewn," so that our communion with God may truly be the partaking of that bread and wine referred to by Jesus as typifying the understanding and inspiration of Spirit, the eternal unity of divine Principle and its idea, man's oneness with God. And as the Revelator declared "There shall in no wise enter into it any thing that defileth, neither whatsoever worketh abomination, or maketh a lie."

The metaphysician knowing he consciously is, is assured that consciousness must be, or he could not consciously be. From this it follows that consciousness *is*. He further knows that that which *is* is necessarily all that is. There could be nothing outside of that which *is,* for, of course, that would be *is not.*

Therefore, this *isness* must include within itself all being. There is nothing outside of it. It is all-inclusive; it is all Life; all intelligence; all

Truth; all substance; all power; all Love, the one and only Mind from which alone all thought proceeds.

Such knowing is not obtained from a book. The Bible and Science and Health take you to their source—the one Mind—and in your oneness, your communion with the Mind of those books, you realize what Christian Science actually means. You are not a Christian Scientist because of person. It is a matter of no moment to you whether human belief says there is or is not another Christian Scientist. To you, God is Christian Science and therefore you are the Christian Scientist. You are the man of God, and as such, you are the voice of God—the word of God—and all that you are ever aware of is your oneness with God—God communicating Himself, His will, to you, His own idea.

You never deal with anything but God, for God is infinite and you could not deal with anything outside of the infinite. You could not be aware of, in other words cognize anything unless it came to you as consciousness. Coming to you as consciousness, it actually comes as your God to you. Then you are always dealing with your God, your Mind. You know that. Therefore, you know that if you turn from this one God, this one cause, and look to what you think is effect, instantly you become a mal-practiser of Christian Science, because you are introducing, or attempting to introduce something besides All—God and His man.

Mrs. Eddy, you doubtless have discovered, has written analytically and completely on the subject of malicious mental malpractice, and all that the term implies, stressing minutely the importance of understanding what it is and what it is not. You must have become convinced that nothing is more important than the understanding of this specific subject, malicious mental malpractice, which, in its final analysis, is revealed as the sum total of iniquity, the complete negation of divine Mind. Through its exposure comes the understanding which is the key to the destruction of everything that assails and hurts mankind.

Whether good or bad, the name given to any claim is of small moment. What is important is to know whence it cometh and whither it goeth, what its origin and what its purpose. That is all the metaphysician is concerned with. And it does not concern him in the sense of distressing him. Far from it. He knows that, since all true thought comes from God, its only purpose is to interpret good. Therefore whether good appears positively or negatively, the metaphysician, like Jesus, knows he is dealing with God only. Hence the promise Jesus gave: "These things have I spoken unto you, that my joy might remain in you, and that your joy might be full."

The metaphysician's conversation is in heaven. He insists upon finding every word to be of *heavenly origin,* in spite of any distorted meaning. His first and essential duty is to translate every word back to its origin which is God. Take for instance, the words malicious, mental and malpractice. Malicious means with deadly intent; mental means in the realm of mind; malpractice means wrong practice. Hence the complete meaning is a wrong or evil practice in the realm of thought, with a deadly motive and with the sole intent of destroying through a mental process.

Now, how could such a combination of words with such a purpose be associated with God?

The principle of numbers is the law of annihilation to every thing in numbers contrary to itself, not because it knows anything which is contrary to itself, but because its ever-presence is the law of spontaneous destruction to every mathematical mis-statement. In exactly the same way, God, the divine Principle of being, is the omnipresent law of total destruction to all unlike Himself, to every mis-statement or mis-conception about Himself. God thus becomes the one destroyer, the one divine Mal-practitioner *to all evil,* and His intent is deadly—to annihilate every vestige of evil and belief in evil. As Jesus said, "I came not to send peace (to evil) but a sword."

Science and Health points out that "The greatest wrong is but a supposititious opposite of the highest right." Thus, every wrong borrows its seeming presence and activity from right, from God. When viewed correctly, the negation or suppositional opposite is welcomed, for as reversed, the lie of the corporeal senses is also automatically reversed.

The point should again be clearly established and emphasized that as a metaphysician each one must realize that to bring in a third, immediately makes him a mental malpractitioner, a wrong thinker, for there can be only God and His idea. Furthermore, it makes him a malicious malpractitioner, because malicious means deadly, finite, and the attempt to bring in a third and have something besides Mind, is to finitize Being. That is the cause of all evil.

Do not think you can turn away from what you know Being to be, the one Mind and its idea and the eternal communication or communion between them, without becoming a malicious malpractitioner. It is not possible. Therefore if you should attempt to do this, all that Mrs. Eddy has said about malicious mental malpractice spontaneously becomes that which you are accepting as your mind. Arouse yourself and ask, "What responsibility have I as a Christian Scientist. If it seems no more than to go dreaming along from day to day, why abandon the old church Christian faith?"

Christian Science is not mere faith. To be sure it includes faith, but rather is it understanding,—understanding which demands as Science and Health says, "Absolute consecration of thought, energy, and desire." You may put off practising what you know. You may "go the way of all flesh," as mortals have been taught, but all problems will still be waiting to meet you "up the road." There is only one way in which to work out the science of Being, and that is the way of understanding.

This understanding is the Messiah, or Christ. As Peter said, "There is none other name under heaven given among men, whereby we must be saved." Then is it not foolish to imagine that malicious mental malpractice is something that does not concern you and does not have to be dealt with? You must realize that it, and it alone, appears as the so-called law of reversal, claiming to have the power and the will to reverse everything of God and with the avowed purpose of crucifying the truth in your thinking. You must see that it is the one and only thing to be dealt with and defeated.

Now we have reached our main subject. In order to present it with a clear sense of its great importance to our welfare, as well as to the welfare of our entire world, I am going to quote for you several statements of Mrs. Eddy.

The first was published in a little pamphlet called Historical Sketch of Metaphysical Healing:—"*I regard some of my students' seeming blindness on this question of a perniciously directed mental influence, with great pity.*"

A statement from Miscellaneous Writings: "I am astounded at the apathy of some students on the subject of sin and mental malpractice, and their culpable ignorance of the workings of these—and even the teacher's own deficiency in this department."

One from Miscellany: "The only incentive of a mistaken sense is malicious animal magnetism,—the name for all evil,—and this must be understood."

Another from an early edition of "Retrospection and Introspection": "Doubters of the existence or the evil of mental malpractice, sneerers at the probability of its method, will at no distant day have their eyes sharply opened."

Lastly from the second edition of Historical Sketch and one that should open the eyes of every Christian Scientist to this subject of malicious mental malpractice: *"If any honest Christian Scientist can be deceived into believing that it is chance, not direction by malicious minds which are at work—that ignorance instead of sin is what he has to meet at all times—this error prevents him from understanding enough of the question to insure his own defense, and leaves him in the power of animal magnetism—perhaps temporarily relieved of his suffering, rejoicing in a hope of freedom which he afterwards finds to be in vain."*

It should always be remembered that when Mrs. Eddy is quoted as stating a metaphysical fact, that which seemed to be the voice of Mrs. Eddy was really the voice of the authorship or authority of Science and Health. Now, what was the voice of that authority? Was it not the voice of Mind? You know that Mrs. Eddy did not create the *truth* of Science and Health, but she became God-like enough to put self aside and let Mind inscribe the truth of Being. No human belief could have written Science and

Health, and you whole-heartedly subscribe to her own statement in that book, "No human pen nor tongue taught me the Science contained in this book, Science and Health; and neither tongue nor pen can overthrow it."

Consequently, when Mrs. Eddy states a *scientific fact*, take it as gospel. If you do not understand it for the moment, do not be disturbed. Ponder her statements. Ask yourself whether your understanding of Christian Science is sufficiently developed to establish those statements metaphysically, and if your understanding does not confirm them immediately, you will find that further unfoldment will establish their truth.

In that last quotation it is wisdom saying to you that if you *"Can be deceived into believing it is chance,"* circumstance, condition, education, environment, heredity, anything rather than *"direction by malicious minds which are at work,"* or if you can be deceived into thinking that it is *"ignorance instead of sin"* that you have to meet at every point, then this error will prevent your understanding enough of the question to insure your own defense, and will leave you in the power of animal magnetism, in belief.

A statement like that from the discoverer and founder of Christian Science, calls for your consecrated thought. You must ask yourself, "What am I doing? Am I drifting along, accepting the suggestions of evil that I am without a position, or without money, or home, or husband, or wife, or health, or anything desirable, because of chance—because of circumstance, or am I awake to the realization that it is the deliberate *'direction by malicious minds'* at work?" Consider also how often the temptation comes to believe that it is ignorance, not sin, that has to be met at all times. Let us see why these suggestions come and at the same time remember, that malicious mental malpractice and ignorance are always one not two, and are always *sin*.

You know that God could not be cognized unless He were shown forth by the Christian Scientist. In the same way evil would be unknown unless it were voiced by what appears as a malicious mental malpractitioner. But if you think that in any way means there is *a* person involved, you lose the real sense of metaphysics. It could appear as a billion persons, and does to human belief, but does that make it *a* person? And yet, you must recognize, before you set about destroying it, that it actually seems to be presented to you perpetually as person, even though it may reach back, over a long period of time in building the argument which is finally directed against you, as in claims of heredity, disposition, traits, and so forth.

Do we not all have to plead guilty to the fact that we have been idly dreaming? Did not Mrs. Eddy declare, *"I am astounded at your ignorance of animal magnetism. Your enemies are working incessantly, while you are working not as you should."* Which one of us, when something contrary to good is presented, does not immediately begin to think "Well, where did this come from? What brought it about? Some circumstance, some condition, some chance?" Anything instead of seeing that it is always the result of *"direction by malicious minds which are at work."*

But you also realize that if you were to seek the so-called minds at work, your efforts would be futile, and you would become totally lost. Why? Because evil is expressed in all its multiplicity of human beliefs negating the infinity of variety of divine Mind and its expression and rapidly changing from one belief to another. It is these malicious beliefs or minds at the dictation of the one evil, which are doing the constant pounding, though you may, if not keenly awake, think it is your own volition. It is this malicious argument going on incessantly, that causes Christian Scientists to bow down to the lies it presents and believe among other arguments that they cannot heal, that is to say cannot see God as All-in-all. Paul admonished, "Now it is high time to awaken out of sleep; for now is our salvation nearer than when we believed. The night is far spent, the day is at hand; let us therefore cast off the works of darkness, and let us put on the armor of light."

In other words wake up by knowing you are awake and why, and that as a Christian Scientist you cannot be made to believe that it is chance, circumstance or any other thing that is at work instead of malicious mind. Then you cannot be prevented from handling the claim and destroying it, whatever it may be called.

Mrs. Eddy has told us that if we do not awaken and begin to handle malicious animal magnetism, our cause will be lost, rendered wholly unavailable,—the cause of Christian Science—the cause that you love more than all else. But even though consecrated to this cause —to one God and His idea—and loving it with your whole heart, are you awake to and intelligently handling the negation of this cause— malicious mind? If not, do you realize what is preventing you? It is not your self. Perhaps malicious argument is saying to you, "I have no time; or I cannot do it; or the press of home duties, or the stress of business prevents my devotion to the cause with my whole heart." You must know, however, that in reality, there is no mind to voice such untruths since there is only the one Mind.

Consider the terrific turmoil going on in Europe,—the "judgment of the nations" that is typified by the King's Chamber, in the Great Pyramid! In this turmoil you are seeing in a degree what constitutes this judgment. These are your nations, are they not? Are you going to allow such conditions to continue without turning your attention to them?

Mrs. Eddy is reported to have told some friends that if we did not destroy the belief in malicious mental malpractice and meet its mesmerism, we would go along another 1900 years with the world sunk in blackest night. She also declared that it had tried to overcome her, but she had withstood it all for 40 years, and that now we must do it. Unless it is done, the cause of Christian Science will vanish.

Is this "withstanding" accomplished by indolence, or by the searching out of an easier way to spiritual achievement? Do you think you can do it by turning, perhaps, to the countless foibles and fables of human belief which offer quick means of securing wealth and happiness? Be-

ware the silly rubbish of so-called superfine metaphysics that is flooding the earth, seeking as the
Bible points out to deceive, if possible, the very
elect. All of such things mean nothing to the
Christian Scientist. God has already done all.
Jesus declared, "I must work the works of Him
that sent me, while it is day: the night cometh,
when no man can work." What Jesus declared
as imperative for him to do cannot be less imperative for all to do.

It is not a question of whether you became interested in Christian Science because you were
healed or because you saw its truth, the fact is
you vigorously continued its study because of
your deep love of Truth. What do you think
could rob you of that earnest enthusiasm?
Nothing. And nothing has robbed you of it.
Then what has *seemed* to do it? It is this malicious argument that has tried to foist itself upon
you as your mental volition and act as your Ego,
your I. Are you going to allow it to continue?
Are you going to allow yourself to be controlled,
or are you going to turn on the light of intelligence and destroy the whole lie that proclaims
that malicious evil can make for you a "rule" or
"law" of any kind?

You thoroughly understand the uselessness of
handling effect. You do, however, recognize the

wisdom of first seeing, for instance in a case of cancer, the truth about cell, how God embraces within Himself, all that cell means, that there is nothing outside or apart from the *isness* that is all that is, and of finding cell right where it always is—the very presence of God, in the kingdom of heaven, perfect, indestructible, expressing obedience, orderliness and truth and everywhere present. But having discerned this to your complete satisfaction you instantly see that is but a minor step, and if you stop there as Jesus said, you are an unprofitable servant, for that is only doing that which it is your duty to do—so you immediately proceed from that point to the realization that diseased cell is not the claim. Disease cannot argue. Disease has no intelligence. How could matter, whether called tubercular germ, cancer, or any other disease, argue? You know it has no intelligence wherewith to argue. Then what is doing the arguing? It is sin, malicious mind, malicious mental malpractice, through its so-called malicious mental malpractitioner. That is the real claim every time.

Mrs. Eddy told a member of her household that, *"in the beginning it was easy to handle sickness, but now we are handling sin."* Is that not exactly what we are handling? What else could this subtle argument be that seems to take possession of you as your mind and makes you voice its lies? It is the unseen foe, the sin of sins. You must recognize it as sin instead of ignorance or some discordant thing, or real healing cannot result.

By that it is not meant that it is unnecessary to reassure yourself that there is nothing wrong, in belief, as a thing. The claim may seem to be some *thing* wrong, but you instantly recognize that that is not the real trouble, so you do not give it any standing, but instead you discern that it is hypnotic suggestion that must be destroyed. Effect no longer deceives you, it is so-called cause that must be dealt with.

Are you whole-heartedly ready to accept this conclusion? Are you ready to grasp it and vigorously fight back with the truth? Most assuredly you are. You forcefully declare "I will destroy the belief that there is malicious evil that can operate as malicious minds and make spurious laws claiming to govern and control me, for malicious mind cannot think or act, it borrows, as the negation of God, all from God and so as reversed declares God's presence." If you do not do this, you will lose the whole purpose of metaphysics. Metaphysics does not deal with things in the physical realm, so-called, but keeps all in the realm of mentality.

You cannot play with your understanding of Christian Science. The time for trifling has passed. No wonder Mrs. Eddy is reported to have said to a friend, *"This hour is the acme of hate against Love, and Love alone can meet it."* Are you willing to allow your world to fall into destruction? Or are you going to settle the question instantly and declare, "This testimony halts right here. My thinking stays on one side and one side only, the side of God." Then remember, *"To affirm anything is to assert its possibility"* and that when you affirm that which is true, although human reasoning and sight may say it is not true at all, you will bring it to pass. Why? Because it is already the fact.

Do you believe that? If you do not, why do you say, "I am a Christian Scientist and I believe Mind is All-in-all"? Are you afraid to trust Mind or to use your own authority, afraid to stand and declare on the side of Mind, and believe with your whole being what you affirm?

This continual argument of "sin" has nothing to do with you. It is something entirely apart from you. It is the argument of malicious mental malpractitioners, or so-called malicious minds, the voice of evil, trying to make you, too, bear false witness. Are you going to counteract this argument with Truth, and claim, as Mrs. Eddy points out in Miscellaneous Writings, "full exemption from all necessity to obey a power that should be and is found powerless in Christian Science."

What you have accomplished up to now, is only a beginning. You must continually enlighten yourself on the whole subject. Like Mrs. Eddy, let nothing prevent your fighting, not only "40 years" but until all malicious mesmerism vanishes under the light of understanding. If you, like our Leader, have to cross the Red Sea, step bravely forward, and it will divide as of old, and you will go through on dry land, rejoicing every step of the way.

You do not have to uncover evil in one sense of the word. It is uncovered. Science and Health states, "Truth is revealed. It needs only to be practised." But if you go on accepting these arguments of malicious mind, thinking that they are your own thought, you are powerless to cope with them. Assert the power of Mind, this Mind that is God, this Mind that is your Mind, and begin to feel that you can see as already brought to pass whatever is true. Evil argues persistently and vigorously. You cannot be less persistent or less vigorous.

Jesus taught that asking was pre-requisite to seeking, and seeking to finding, and drove home this lesson with the story of the man who besought his friend at midnight to give him bread. "I say unto you, Though he will not rise and give him, because he is his friend, yet because of his importunity he will rise and give him as many as he needeth." We find Mrs. Eddy pleading similarly for consecrated and resistless effort, many times throughout her teachings. In Miscellaneous Writings she says, "Are we duly aware of our great opportunities and responsibilities? Are we prepared to meet and improve them, to act up to the acme of divine energy wherewith we are armored?" Why not put yourself on the positive side of that which you wish to carry, and see that the only thing that is trying to stop you is this malicious mental malpractice, with its incessant argument on the negative side.

Have you ever stopped to ask yourself how that East Indian who was on Robert Ripley's "Believe It or Not" radio program, walked over a pit of red hot coals, heated to 1200 degrees Fahrenheit? He had performed a similar feat in England in 1935, with a temperature of 800 degrees. Of course the belief that enabled him to do it was just a changed material belief.

As Christian Scientists, we understand it as a form of self-hypnotism. In his talk over the radio after his performance, he said that it was his faith in God and in himself, that gave him the power. It is obvious what the East Indian is believing his God to be. Nevertheless, whether or not he did it through hypnotism, the fact remains he did it, and the question is, how? His utter consecration to his purpose, largely through the elimination of fear of the fire, was what enabled him to walk unscathed over the hot coals. As an example of true metaphysical understanding, we have the joyous demonstration of the three Hebrews, Shadrach, Meshach, and Abednego, who proved the power of real Mind-understanding to nullify the false sense of fire.

If consecration to his task could make the performance of the East Indian possible, think of the possibilities of consecration to the understanding of the allness of the Mind, which says, "Son . . . all that I have is thine."

Do we pass these things by? Are we like the travelers in the parable of the man who fell among thieves? Those who saw the man, with one exception, passed by on the other side, just missing the lesson to be gained had they stopped to unsee the lie and to profit by it. Is not that what we too often do? Do we see these things and straightway forget them, or do we pause and ponder and become more consecrated in Christian Science?

When you commence the study of mathematics, you do not stop at the multiplication tables, you go right on to a complete understanding of all mathematics. That is the natural and normal thing for a mathematician to do. Why should there be any difference in acquiring the understanding of Christian Science? Should you not just as normally go straight through to the ever-present kingdom of heaven? You would were it not for one thing, and one thing only, malicious mental malpractice.

Why have we not awakened long before now to what is confronting us,—this one evil with its dogged insistence challenging our every act? It makes no difference whether it is a question of closing a deal in business, or healing a case of disease. That deal or that case would be spontaneously finished the moment it presented itself, were it not for this insistent claim which dares, in belief, to intervene and say to you that the presence of Truth can be reversed, delayed, defeated.

"When you reach out to the beyond for the real, you instantly express it." That truth is

self-evident. Who ever heard of looking to the principle of numbers for two times two is four, and not instantly expressing it? The "beyond" is Mind, that which is beyond all mortal sense, all limitation. When you reach out, beyond all limitation, to Mind for the real, you instantly express it. Mrs. Eddy continued her statement, *"But because you are still in matter, in belief, and subject to the laws of matter, in belief, that absolute Truth outlines itself to meet the present need."* In other words, it spontaneously appears to you in the language you best understand.

Then why not expect it to appear? Why think it extraordinary that God can raise the dead, or give you perfect bodily health, or that He can give you all the money you need? He gives you everything. Why should you question it, when there is no such thing as matter, and you are not looking to matter, but to Mind, dealing with Mind, knowing that Mind is All-in-all? When you stop to think, you know that it is absurd to doubt or question. What then, makes you doubt or question? To that there is but one answer. It is malicious argument, daring to suggest that you have lost your faith and confidence in God, that you no longer trust your ability to heal and to heal all dis-ease. You know, however, that the healing is already there, that in reality there is nothing to heal but something of God to see, and that what you say, as the voice of God, stands fast, and cannot be reversed.

What is there to stand between you and Mind, and its spontaneously appearing to you? Nothing. Then you say, "It is not I that doubts, it is the suggestion of evil trying to substitute itself for my I; it is malicious mental malpractice, operating as malicious mental malpractitioners."

Mrs. Eddy warns us in Miscellaneous Writings, that "Large numbers, in desperate malice, are engaged day and night in organizing action against us. Their feeling and purpose are deadly, and they have sworn enmity against the lives of our standard-bearers." They are attempting, by their arguments, to weaken the Christian Scientist's confidence in his ability to show forth God. Evil is afraid of the standard-bearers, for they stand as God's law of truth to evil, saying "Thou shalt surely die." Then is it not malicious mesmerism that is raising its head against you, and trying to discourage you, tempting you to voice its lies? Who is a standard-bearer in Christian Science, except the one who knows something of himself? Because you know something, of yourself, in knowing *why being is,* you are the standard-bearer.

From a study of Mrs. Eddy's writings, on the

subject of malicious mental malpractice, it becomes apparent that no matter under what guise evil may appear, it is never anything but malicious animal magnetism. There is only one way for you to free yourself from becoming the servant of sin, from lending yourself to malicious mental arguments and that is, as Proverbs states it, "In all thy ways acknowledge Him, and He shall direct thy paths." In all ways start with cause and cause, God, will take care of effect.

You remember the statement of Mrs. Eddy, in her early Science of Man, *"Do not think to deceive yourselves by deceiving others, for Wisdom will call you into judgment for all you think and act, and the tribunal before which your true position is tried and proved, is the demonstration that you are able to give of healing the sick, after learning the Principle upon which this is done, and the only one by which you can succeed to the most marvelous instances of cure."*

Do you want to heal? Do you want to have the kingdom of God right here? Nothing can limit your power. You alone could limit it by listening to the malicious arguments of the mental malpractitioner instead of knowing that God is the one and only Mind.

When the warning is given, *"Do not think to deceive yourselves by deceiving others"*, does it

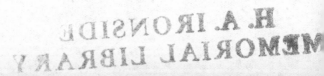

not mean that we must save ourselves from this deception by insistently seeing the reality and everpresence of God and His idea and thus healing the sick; in other words by consistently correcting the lie with our declarations of Truth? Then go out, as it were, "into the highways and byways" and do this healing and so prove what you know. Why not? The lies presenting themselves as consciousness are many and each one must be taken back to the Father's house and there found correctly. This means taking the things of God and showing them unto the creature. Then, "Let your light so shine before men, that they may see your good works, and glorify your Father which is in heaven."

Every Christian Scientist must understand and does understand that when the word "heal" is used in Christian Science it does not mean to heal someone or something, for there is nothing to "heal" with God as All-in-all. Thus healing in Christian Science simply means conscious oneness with God, and the efforts to bring about this oneness are not based on its absence but are merely the refutation of the negation and the translation of it back to its original fact of good as all the *isness* there is.

You know that every thought and every act will be brought into judgment. Can you be a mathematician without facing tests on every rule? The understanding of Christian Science demands no less. Then why make excuses? Why think that anything, as a test of your sincerity and understanding, can take the place of healing the sick and heavy laden?

In Miscellaneous Writings it is stated, "Less teaching and good healing is today the acme of 'well done;' a healing that is not guesswork,— chronic recovery, ebbing and flowing,—but instantaneous cure. This absolute demonstration of Science must be revived." If you are not healing, not seeing and feeling God as All-in-all, get immediately into your "closet," and there alone with Mind, ask what is stopping you and arouse yourself to resist this hidden mental foe which declares you do not understand God.

The incessant argument is that you cannot heal,—that you cannot know God—that you do not know how to heal—how to understand Him. Then the argument continues, calling its lies laws of matter, of nature, anatomy, physiology, heredity, hygiene, theosophy, spiritualism, astrology, false theology and so on; also laws of wish, rule, inclination, desire, hatred, anger, endless would-be laws. All these are simply the negation of divine Mind and its activity, and melt away under the lens of Truth.

Thus evil argues incessantly. Are you accepting its argument? You know that nothing can stop you from healing, because whatever you affirm that is true, even if *"to all human reasoning or sight it may not seem true at all"*, still it will come to pass. It could not be otherwise since "All is infinite Mind and its infinite manifestation" as Science and Health declares, and since good *is*, not will be.

To you, body means embodiment. You do not think of body as just a conglomeration of atoms, weighing a certain number of pounds. You think of it as the full interpretation of Mind to you. In your healing work in Christian Science, consider carefully this statement which Mrs. Eddy made to some friends: *"What thou needest to know is that mortal mind has translated the body and its functions into matter, and immortal Mind, gives back the original with the functions, preserved and harmonious, but not as not in matter, but as and of Mind."* By the phrase, *"not as not in matter"* is meant that Mind does give back the original body and its functions, preserved and harmonious, in that which may seem to you to be matter, but which is really Mind. There can be no limitation, because all is Mind, not matter at all.

You may think good appears materially as

health, security, position, and other seemingly advantageous conditions. However, regardless of the appearance, you would not be aware of even a sense of good if it were really material, if it were matter as such. Affirm on the side of that which is true, and the true will supply you with all good, and will give back the original, free from limitation; in other words, will give back body, not without functions, but with *"its functions preserved and harmonious, but not as not in matter, but as and of Mind,"* in the positive language that you can best understand.

Compel yourself to stop doubting, quibbling and questioning and begin to work. Exercise the will of God. It will operate every time, for *"Whenever you reach out to the beyond for the real, you instantly express it."*

That which is real, that which is true, is not in the process of coming; it is already here. That applies not only to health, but to the fulfillment of all good, regardless of the need or the occasion. The answer is here—present every moment. Then reject with equal insistence, the perpetual lying insistence of the mental malpractitioner, that evil is the reality. You are not afraid to use the will of God. As the man of God, the voice of God, you declare, "Here I stand, and evil has no power."

"So shall my word be that goeth forth out of my mouth; it shall not return unto me void, but it shall accomplish that which I please, and it shall prosper in the thing whereto I sent it."

Because I have brought out so strongly the necessity of using your "will" in facing the work that lies before you, I would like to repeat to you a little poem, called "Consecration". This poem is anonymous, but Mrs. Eddy evidently thought highly of it, because she asked to have it published in The Christian Science Journal of October 1900. Obviously it is not wholly metaphysical, but it is easy to comprehend why she thought it worth publishing, for it is filled with the right understanding of will power, and is worthy of your most thoughtful consideration.

CONSECRATION

Laid on Thy altar, my Lord divine,
    Accept my gift this day for Jesus' sake;
I have no jewels to adorn Thy shrine,
    Nor any world-famed sacrifice to make.

But here I bring within my trembling hand
    This will of mine—a thing that seemeth small,
And only Thou, dear Lord, canst understand
    How, when I yield Thee this, I yield mine all.

Hidden therein Thy searching eyes can see
    Struggles of passions, visions of delight,
All that I love or am, or fain would be—
    Deep loves, fond hopes, and longing infinite.

It hath been wet with tears and dimmed with
        sighs,
    Clinched in my grasp 'til beauty it hath none.
Now, from Thy footstool, where it vanquished
        lies,
    The prayer ascendeth, O may Thy will be
        done.

Take it, Oh Father, ere my courage fail;
    And merge it so in Thine own will that e'en
If in some desperate hour my cries prevail
    And Thou give back my gift, it may have been

So changed, so purified, so fair have grown,
    So one with Thee, so filled with peace divine,
I may not know, or feel it as my own,
    But gaining back my will, may find it Thine.

Notice how in gaining back (your) will, you
"may not know, or feel it as (your) own, but
find it Thine". You find God's will as your will.
Use it then. Do not act as though you were helpless, but use this will of God, and you will be

turning directly to God, and God alone, to find out what His will is. You will never deal with effect, but will always start with cause. You know to begin with effect, is to yield yourself to the enemy of mankind and aid and abet the wilfulness of evil, malicious mental malpractice and its tools. You start first with God, divine Mind, and find Him the source of all that appears. You cannot then malpractise but will bless mankind. This is what is meant when Science and Health says, "Your true course is to destroy the foe, and leave the field to God,—Life, Truth, and Love, remembering that God and His ideas alone are real and harmonious."

May I now leave with you a statement of fact and an exhortation from Mrs. Eddy's Miscellaneous Writings: "Christian Scientists cannot watch too sedulously, or bar their doors too closely, or pray to God too fervently, for deliverance from the claims of evil. Thus doing, Scientists will silence evil suggestions, uncover their methods, and stop their hidden influence upon the lives of mortals. Rest assured that God in His wisdom will test all mankind on all questions; and then, if found faithful, He will deliver us from temptation and show us the powerlessness of evil,—even its utter nothingness."

HOW MALICIOUS
MENTAL MALPRACTICE
SEEMS TO COME
INTO BEING

IN ORDER to understand in a practical way
the subject of malicious mental malpractice—
the negation or suppositional opposite of
Christian Science practice—it is necessary to
understand its suppositional origin, just as it is
essential in order to understand Christian Science to know : firstly, that there is God ; secondly,
what God is ; and thirdly, to know what He is
God to and the laws by which He operates. No
Christian Scientist would think it possible to intelligently continue his study of Christian Science without first being well grounded on these
fundamental points.

In order to think and act with unbounded
confidence, the Christian Scientist knows that
he must have a reason for the faith that is with-

in him and that that reason can only be completely satisfied as every step in the process of establishing its structure is taken intelligently. Thus in proving that God is, he starts with that which he knows of himself without any external testimony, namely his own consciously being, and from this he instantly is assured that he could not consciously be if Consciousness were not first the fact. Thus he establishes that Consciousness *is* and from this isness he goes on to find that Consciousness is All-in-all, since there could be nothing outside of that which *is*. He further learns that this Consciousness, being all, embraces within itself all being, with all that this term implies.

Thence he goes on to discover that this Consciousness, in order to be Consciousness, must be conscious of something and he names that something that Consciousness is conscious of, idea, man or any term that he chooses whereby to express effect. The term or name is unimportant but whatever term is used it means that whereby Consciousness is made known. Because this Consciousness is necessarily Mind, Intelligence, that which knows, it expresses Itself as law, order and so forth.

The student of Christian Science continues this reasoning until there is not the slightest doubt or question left in his mind that not only is there God, but that He must, in order to be God, embody within His own infinity all Life, Truth, Substance, Being, etc., together with that which He is God to, with His accompanying laws. Being All-in-all, His Allness must necessarily include all. This Allness means Oneness and therefore there is nothing apart from Him. He is both noumenon and phenomenon, God and all that God is God to. The Christian Scientist knows he cannot understand God without this sound foundation, which gives him a reason for the faith that is within him.

In exactly the same way, in order to comprehend this subject of malicious mental malpractice, he must see just what it is, how it arises in belief and all that there is to it, or he will not understand it, and be able to handle it, for as Mrs. Eddy states in Miscellany, ". . . we cannot do more than we are nor understand what is not ripening in us". What a man is is always what he understands and that is what he can use and prove is his own.

Then let us look at this subject of malicious mental malpractice simply and intelligently.

First how does it come into seeming being? Given the fact that God is, that Truth is, there instantly arises, by implication, the suppositional opposite of it, just as with the presence of any intelligent statement, there arises, by implication the ignorance with regard to that statement. The ignorance is merely the false, in contradistinction to the true, even as the lie is in contradistinction to the fact. A lie is not anything of itself. It is the negation of the truth. No mind is required to suppose a lie. It appears as the result of the law of opposites, coming as the negative accompanying the positive suppositionally, and spontaneously disappearing with the acknowledged presence of the real or positive—in other words being "clothed upon" by the reality.

This supposable condition exists not because of a so-called mind supposing it but by virtue of the law that every truth includes, within itself, by implication the concept of its own opposite. This is the law of opposites. To illustrate this point, is it not obvious that *is,* being is, because its "seed is in itself", alone determines itself, and so implies that anything outside itself, outside that which *is* must necessarily be *is not*? In other words every truth by virtue of its own *isness,* hence allness, carries within itself the contradiction of the lie about itself.

Thus we get malicious mind as the suppositional opposite of divine Mind in all its minutiæ, and yet without the faintest real existence of itself. We call it malicious because that which it negates or is the suppositional opposite of is the Mind that is infinite Life or good. It is necessarily mental because all supposition is mental or mind with a small m. Everything that the one Mind is, in all its infinity of perfection, the suppositional opposite must simulate in exact opposition. The suppositional opposite has no ability independently to declare itself, but by its very nature it automatically falls in line as the negation of that which *is* and it borrows its entire suppositional presence and action from that which *is,* even as any lie depends for its existence on the presence of the truth about which it is the lie.

Just as Mind *is,* and is all that is, hence One, in the realm of the positive, just so malicious mind is suppositionally all that is and is one in the realm of evil or the negation. Further, just as divine Mind, the one Spirit, has that whereby it is shown forth, which we call spiritual being or spirituality, so malicious mind has that whereby, in belief, it is shown forth, viz. material being or materiality, which of course must be and is just as mental as the offspring of supposition would necessarily be. This material being or materiality appears as, and is called, mortal man, place, or thing, but it is never more than the erroneous or suppositional opposite concept of that which divine Mind and its divine man, place and thing is, wholly pure and perfect.

By means of this so-called suppositional mortal man, place and thing, malicious mind appears to act and operate and it can never act or operate except as such mortal man, place or thing, since cause, whether genuine or suppositional, must have its effect whereby to proclaim itself.

But does this mean that malicious mind has any power of its own to harm anyone? No, for its entire presence and power being a suppositional presence and power it merely declares the real presence and power of that about which it is the lie and so, when reversed, testifies to the ever-presence of divine Mind. To use Mrs. Eddy's statement in Unity of Good, "The use of a lie is that it unwittingly confirms Truth, when handled by Christian Science, which reverses false testimony and gains a knowledge of God from opposite facts, or phenomena."

However, this negation or suppositional mind must by its very suppositional opposite nature, assume in belief all that God is, together with all His power, authority and law whereby to act, etc. It is as such supposition that we must view this lie. It usurps the role of God and claims to be very Mind and therefore to be your mind, thinking and acting for you to the minutest details of your daily life. It uses the lie about every law and activity of God as its "law" of activity and does this all with the suggestion that "I am of God for God made me; in fact I am God, Truth." We have seen, however, that the only sense in which God "made" it is in the sense that God through His *isness* must imply His suppositional opposite *is not.* The *is not,* by its reversal declares *is* and thus shows forth God's absolute allness both negatively and positively so that God may truly be All-in-all.

Having now seen just how malicious mind arises as supposition, we can readily go on to following it through in all its seeming complications of evil and yet without giving to it one atom of power or reality of its own, but ever turning all back to the one Mind from which all is.

One point should be consistently borne in mind and that is that the supposed channel or avenue whereby malicious mind seems to appear is never of any moment in the final analysis, that it is but the puppet of the supposition it is expressing, even as the divine man of God is in reality nothing of himself but is that whereby God is seen and known. In handling malicious mental malpractice it is so-called cause that is always dealt with, never so-called effect.

The foregoing is preliminary or introductory to the pages which follow, where these points will be repeated in many different ways, over and over again. It seems eminently sensible, however, before going thoroughly into the subject of malicious mind and its so-called malicious mental malpractice, to fortify one's self with the clear understanding as to just how malicious mind originates in belief and what it signifies. Then at no point in its uncovering will it be thought of for one instant as being anything but the suppositional opposite or negation of that which *is*, of God and His allness, and therefore as that which, when reversed, declares the allness of good.

DEFINITION
OF
'BEAST', 'FALSE PROPHET', 'DRAGON'

ONE good way to understand the manner in which malicious mind operates, appearing always as effect, is to study what John had to say on this subject in the Book of Revelation. This book was dictated to John by Christ Jesus, and may therefore be taken as a statement of absolute metaphysical fact. John recorded it in symbols; but as soon as these symbols are translated into ordinary speech they will be found to be very enlightening.

According to John's allegory, there were two forces of evil which claimed between them to rule the world and to be able to destroy anyone who did not worship them. The first, a physical power, was called by John "the beast", and the second, a mental power, was called by him "the false prophet". These two terms stand, for materiality and for mentality. But according to the allegory, and this is the point to be noted, neither of these two phenomena has the slightest power of its own. They have "great authority" only because it has been given to them by the third figure in the allegory, the "dragon".

John defined the dragon as "that old serpent, called the Devil, and Satan, which deceiveth the whole world". The dragon is therefore a hypnotic mental deceiver, or, in other words, malicious mental malpractice. It is the insistent mental argument that appears to the Christian Scientist and says, "God is not all. You have a separate mind of your own, and I can manipulate this in such a way as to make you believe in what does not exist. I can make you believe in both the beast and the false prophet, my servants who owe their power only to me."

These two servants of the dragon, the beast and the false prophet, stand for the whole of the apparent world. The beast is the belief in many bodies, and the false prophet is the belief in many minds. Many bodies means limited bodies: and all that the term implies in the way of sickness, death, lack, laws of physiology, etc., comes under this heading. The belief in many minds is the other aspect of this same belief in limitation and produces religions, governments, fears, and all forms of good and evil mentality. Between them, these two symbols make up the sum total of outward manifestation, or effect, through which the one evil, or dragon, operates.

In the same way that God, the one cause, always appears to you as effect, in the language that you can understand, so in the same way the dragon, the supposititious opposite of God, appears to you as effect also. Remember, however, that it never is effect. It appears only *as* effect, and is always, really, the same old dragon. Allow yourself to be misled, and handle either the beast or the false prophet, physicality or mentality, instead of the dragon, hypnotic suggestion, and you will be helpless before it.

Suppose, for instance, you see a man lying in the street with a broken leg. No one is responsible for this appearance; no one invented it or put it there. It came there through the beast, the idea that there are a lot of separate, limited bodies all obeying various laws of growth and destruction; and no one invented the beast either. The beast came there through the dragon; and the dragon "antedates man", because it is exactly as old as the reality of which it seems to be the reverse. As Mrs. Eddy so clearly points out in Retrospection and Introspection, "Sin existed as a false claim before the human concept of sin was formed; hence one's concept of error is not the whole of error . . . The sinner created neither himself nor sin, but sin created the sinner."

There was a time, when you were beginning your study of Christian Science, when it was enough to attack the beast. It was enough to declare there was no life and substance in matter to produce a complete healing; the man in the street got up and walked away, quite happy. This, however, was strictly dealing with effect; it did not touch the basic lie, and the beast could appear in a different way tomorrow: the mortgage could be foreclosed, or the tire could blow out and wreck the car.

Obviously, a struggle of this kind would have no end to it, no matter how conscientiously and earnestly the Christian Scientist continued to deny the reality of matter. This watchfulness was enough in the beginning, as a knowledge of the rule of fractions is enough when you are studying fractions; but it did not touch the fundamental point. There was no final victory because it was an effect that was being fought, not a cause.

The effect, in spite of the multitude of its ramifications, is a comparatively simple, open thing. The cause, the dragon, on the other hand is extremely subtle. It stands in the holy place and calls itself "Mind", "my Mind". Naturally it does this. It is imitating the one cause, the one Consciousness, the one Mind, and anything it can do to convince you it is your mind it will naturally do. It claims for itself infinite subtlety and strength, as the supposititious opposite of the one Wisdom and Strength, and it will use all this to persuade the Christian Scientist it is his mind.

His business, of course, is to reverse it, because, reversed, it really is his Mind. Unreversed, it is nothing at all, and all the names given it are only the names of a supposition. But it is a supposition that claims for itself "the power and dominion" as long as it is believed in as something real.

Now suppose, instead of the beast, materiality, making its appearance in the guise of a broken leg, we have the false prophet making an appearance instead. The claim of the false prophet is that the world is full of people—men, women, and children—who are thinkers, and that their minds can operate on each other or on themselves for good or evil. In this case, it does not exhibit a man lying in the streets with a broken leg, as the beast did. It appears perhaps as a man working hard mentally to destroy forces which, he has been told by an ecclesiastical body, are trying to destroy the church.

Now, to believe in this man's mind is no better than to believe in a leg that can be broken. To believe in the existence of that church, a church that needs protecting, is no better than to believe in the street accident. These two attempts at destruction have no force in themselves. They are merely two different external aspects of the fundamental lie, the beast and the false prophet deriving their power exclusively from the dragon. As long as one spends his time mentally arguing with either of these two effects he can do nothing, because they are only effects and not the cause of the trouble. "Lay your axe at the root of the tree".

The supposititious opposite seems to follow the truth exactly. What seems to be is patterned exactly after what is; and, as one gets a clearer understanding of what *is*, he gets a clearer understanding also of the way the suppositional opposite seems to follow it, imitating it exactly.

The reality is as follows: "There is one cause, or Mind. There is one effect, or idea. God is the one Mind; I am the one effect. A proper synonym for what I call 'myself' would be 'the awareness of God.' There is nothing else *to* me. What I see around me, all the things I am conscious of as persons, places, things, governments, minds, etc., are the varying ways in which Consciousness, or God, appears to me, taking the language I can best understand but always appearing to me in a perfect and unlimited manner. This language appears as effect, as other ideas like myself. It is never effect. It is the presence of God appearing to me, Consciousness appearing to that which is conscious only of It."

Now, the imitation, the supposititious opposite, patterns itself exactly on this reality. It does not invent some new kind of arrangement for itself, but claims to appear in exactly the same way, as though the false creation were a shadow superimposed upon the real one and fitting it exactly. (Of course you understand this. There is no shadow, there is no superimposing, and there is certainly no creation, either imaginary or real, since God does not create but spontaneously *is*. You know that this is true.) It is as though the dragon, the supposititious lie which claims to wear the garments of Truth, (that is, to be true) came to "you" and said, "*I* am cause. I am your mind and you are my effect, conscious only of me. I appear to you in the limited, dying language that is suitable to me. This language appears to you as effect, as persons, places, things, governments, minds, etc., but it is never effect. It is my presence appearing to you."

Now supposing, just to carry on the symbolism, the "dragon" could make a survey of the steps leading to its own destruction. (Apparent destruction, of course. It is only an apparent dragon, after all.) The steps might run something like this: "I had you fooled for a long time. I made you think, when I appeared as effect, that it was a real world you were seeing, a world that was really made up of men that died and laws that killed and an endless, unending round of birth and decay. Then you began to find out that it was not a real world, that it had no actual substance at all; it was only a kind of hypnotic illusion, not solid reality, and that what was really occurring was something quite different. But still I had you. You wasted your strength by fighting not against *me* but against the way I was appearing as effect. The reason you did this was because you did not understand then the word 'Consciousness'. You thought in a manner that was still theological rather than scientific. You thought that God was a Creator and He had made a perfect creation full of ideas, sons and daughters of God, made in His image, of which you were one out of many. You did not understand why Mrs. Eddy said, 'A Christian Scientist is *alone* with his own being and with the reality of things.' You thought, instead rather, that there were a lot of consciousnesses reflecting

God, instead of understanding that there was one Consciousness, appearing in infinity of variety but always One.

"Now, because you did not really understand about this One, although you admitted it theoretically from the days of Moses onwards, you did not realize in a practical way that the suppositional opposite, me, was one also. You thought that my effects were the lies; death, destruction, limitation, etc. Not at all. I am the lie, the only lie. You can reverse the way I am appearing to you as effect all you please, but that will not reverse me. I will still go right along, calling myself your mind, and all the arguments you lavish on effects (so-called), although true in themselves, will not affect me in the least.

"But I am now badly frightened. Since you have discovered that what you have been calling 'creation' is really God appearing to you, you have discovered also that the false creation is really only me appearing to you. You have taken me out of my hiding place. You are paying no more attention to my beast and my false prophet, all the physical and mental manifestations that are no more than the branches of a tree. You are laying your axe at the root. You are giving me your sole attention and calling me by my real name, and I don't like it at all. I am in great anguish, knowing my time is short."

Now, to drop the suppositional and get back to the real. What is the 'real name' of what you have been calling evil? Obviously the real name is God, since there is no other realness. The real name of death is Life. The real name of a mistake is Truth. Death could not be destroyed except by calling it by its real name, neither could the dragon be destroyed except by ceasing to misunderstand it and by seeing it instead for what it really is. This obliterates what has been called "dragon" and leaves in its place what has always been there, the name God. Nothing is destroyed, because there is nothing to destroy: destruction is a kind of symbolism. What is done is to see it correctly; and because the awareness of God is all that there is to one he cannot very well do anything else. The apparent warfare with the dragon is simply the finding of one's own identity with God; and it ends when the Christian Scientist is finally and practically able to call the "dragon" by its real **name.**

ANALYSIS OF THE APPEARING
OF
MALICIOUS MENTAL MALPRACTICE

THE CLAIM of malicious mental malpractice should be examined just as a claim of sickness is to find out what is involved. As a belief of cells is involved in a case of cancer, a belief of tubercles in a case of pulmonary disease, and a belief of too much or too little sugar in a case of diabetes, so in analyzing malicious mental malpractice and its effects it is necessary to understand how the claim seems to arise. Therefore let us discuss again briefly the origin or basis of malicious mental malpractice. While this has been carefully analyzed from another angle in a previous article, nevertheless the reiteration and amplification of important points should prove helpful and cannot be repeated too often.

To begin with, evil appears in its cruder forms

as isolated cases of suffering or wrong doing. But because it is the negation of God, it must negate God at every point and in every respect. To the mortal advancing to a clearer sense of God, it necessarily seems to present an ascending scale of evil.

In Science and Health, it is stated that Adam, evil "begins his reign over man somewhat mildly, but he increases in falsehood and his days become shorter." In other words, evil begins mildly, endeavoring if possible to hide its nature. Science and Health also states that the serpent, subtlety, evil stands as "The first lie of limitation."

The supposition that God is not All, which of course accompanies any sense of finity or limitation, would necessarily be the first supposition. From that suppositional basis, the whole suppositional structure of evil or negation of God moves forward—always keeping pace in its unfoldment with the advancement of that which it negates.

Thus the divisions of evil—"the beast" and "the false prophet" spontaneously appear; first, as dead matter, which is the most inanimate, non-intelligent and outwardly harmless form of evil. Second, in the more animate form, as "living matter", appearing as both good and bad, whether as mortals or as things. Third and lastly, as pure evil mentality, eliminating matter entirely but again emerging in two forms, good and bad, the good masquerading as harmless in order to hide its real nature, but the bad appearing in its true nature, as evil mentality.

In this final appearing of evil as the "false prophet", matter as such disappears, and mentality is seen to assume all power. At first it appears mildly in its operation of mind-control promising to bring about the betterment of conditions through the action of one mind over another, e. g. New Thought, Therapeutic Suggestion, etc., etc. Finally, it surrenders all pretense of good, and is found operating in the true nature of "the dragon", the "last infirmity of sin", as Science and Health points out, showing its real purpose and character as the suppositional opposite of divine Mind, using mental means to produce every form of sin, sickness, distress, limitation, destruction, and finally death, but also sinking "its perpetrator into a night without a star."

These last two phases of evil have been classified in Christian Science phraseology as ignorant or sympathetic mental malpractice, and malicious mental malpractice.

Whether appearing as animate or inanimate matter as the "beast" or in its final form of malicious mental malpractice as "the false prophet", the whole of evil is animal magnetism, "the dragon" of Revelation. Science and Health declares that "Animal magnetism or hypnotism is the specific term for error, or mortal mind." This name designates its animal or bestial nature and its mind operation or influence, in contradistinction to the spiritual or holy nature of divine Mind and its activities.

It must never be forgotten that the nature of animal magnetism, whether appearing in its guileless forms of matter, or in its more easily discerned and truer nature as destructive mentality, is always the same malicious mental malpractice, the "son of perdition", "The great dragon . . . that old serpent, called the Devil, and Satan, which deceiveth the whole world," always ready to devour those who are not awake to its sinister nature and purpose, which is to bring about their death and destruction.

Let us delve a little more analytically into this claim of evil as the negation of good. Evil being a negation or supposition—purely a mental state, every conclusion drawn by it is a suppositional conclusion, and never the fact, although it always appears in one of matter's various divisions. It must be remembered that matter is as Mrs. Eddy calls it, a "misstatement of Mind", and a misstatement is a mind activity.

As a result of the mental admission of limitation, matter appears as the evidence of limitation, of finiteness—matter with all of its so-called divisions, and sub-divisions, and with the entire theory of evolution which is simply one belief added to another belief, borrowing from and claiming to reverse everything of God the source of all being. In the end it actually borrows or negates Mind, and operates as evil minds, capable of doing, as evil, everything that divine Mind does, as infinite good—thus it counterfeits God's presence, Christian Science practice and practitioner, with its malicious malpractice and malpractitioner. Every step of so-called evolution is a belief or mental step which must in the end be scientifically reversed and replaced with the truth.

Notice how, in belief, evil ensures the so-called increase of its mortals as Science and Health points out, "by the parent's mind, through self division", and builds up this self division step by step until it calls its belief a new child. This child in turn is put through a series of further beliefs until it ends in that which it calls death, only, however, to find it is not really death, but merely a continuance of belief which goes on indefinitely, until destroyed by spiritual understanding.

In handling a case of disease you do not ignore the various beliefs involved—anatomy, "laws" of matter, nature, materia medica, etc., but you take every one of them back to the kingdom of heaven by reversing them and you there find them all, in their true sense, as the activity of God.

You go on from there to discover that the real claim is a vicious mental determination on the part of evil to harass and finally destroy its victim through mental means, that is to say, through hypnotic suggestion. Now at last you have cornered the lie and can correct it.

In the realm of matter, through its various "laws," evil builds its claim by first creating sickness and finally death. In exactly the same pernicious manner, it builds up its claims of malicious mental malpractice, but instead of operating as matter and "laws" of matter, it now acts as mental "laws,"—"laws" of wish, intent, rule, desire, influence, inclination, determination and so forth. And just as it seems to act consistently and successfully in its "laws" of matter, until destroyed by the law of Mind, so in its realm of mentality, with its claim of mental influence, it is successful until met and mastered by the practice of Christian Science as intelligent Mind action.

This mastery is obtained just as it was in the case of evil's so-called laws of matter. As you painstakingly destroyed each belief by taking it back to God, and by rising to the true sense of being, so every "law" of malicious mental malpractice must be denied, and its entire operation translated back to God. It was by reversing in belief, the true sense and statement of Christian Science, that malicious mental malpractice came actively into being. It began with one reversal of a scientific statement of Truth, and from that it multiplied its lies until today it has gone entirely beyond matter into the realm of pure malicious mental malpractice.

Mrs. Eddy tells in one of her early editions of Science and Health about the one so-called original malpractitioner, and says plainly that had it not been for this original one there never would have been another. That is obviously true because, all being divine Mind in reality and mortal mind in human belief, there could be no continuance if the original erroneous thought could be annihilated. Mind cannot duplicate its thought, and this applies equally to the negation, malicious mind. A disease begins with one person believing or expressing it, perhaps first the victim and then the doctor or nurse. Or both begin to believe it, and unobserved it spreads entirely beyond its origin and becomes a recognized belief of the human mind, losing its personal sense and becoming an impersonal claim of disease, with its so-called laws and history. "Therefore the lie was, and *is,* collective as well as individual," as is stated in Retrospection and Introspection.

In the same way, malicious mental malpractice started with what appeared as one person voicing its lies, but it afterwards was to be discerned wholly as an impersonal claim of evil. The original malpractiser appeared to accomplish his wickedness, by reversing in belief, the statements of Truth. This reversal which Christian Science designates as malicious mental malpractice must be destroyed in exactly the same way sickness is destroyed, that is by taking each lie, or mental argument of "law" and reversing it with the truth. However, instead of handling the "laws" of matter, as such, which are involved in a simple case of sickness, and which are in one sense harmless, you handle every claim of evil as a mentally directed belief operating as the so-called law of vicious minds. This "law" can be and must be as readily discerned and destroyed as the simple beliefs and "laws" of matter, nature, materia medica, etc.

Malicious mental malpractice, with its malicious mental malpractitioner, can operate only as the negation of Christian Science practice, and in no other way. The positive must always precede the suppositional opposite, therefore, Christian Science had to be in operation before it was possible for mental malpractice to seem to appear. This fact should give a great sense of security and freedom to the Christian Scientist, for he realizes all he has to meet is the negative of what he already knows of Christian Science. Thus he is fore-armed and understands he can "be brought into no condition, be it ever so severe, where Love has not been before," as Mrs. Eddy says.

Paul said, "When I was a child, I spake as a child, I understood as a child, I thought as a child: but when I became a man I put away childish things." So the Christian Scientist no longer looks "through a glass darkly" but "face to face". He is no longer a child in the realm of Mind, but has reached man's estate and he now sees clearly that every error confronting him is a mental lie, deliberately directed. He no longer deals with the belief of material things.

Malicious mental malpractice as the highest

form of evil is the same impersonal ignorance that confronts a student in learning the simple multiplication table. The only difference is that the student of the multiplication table seems to be confronted with non-intelligent ignorance, whereas the student of Christian Science in mastering malicious mental malpractice seems to be confronted with "intelligent" ignorance, if such an absurd contradiction could be used. This "intelligent" ignorance seems to be wilfully and maliciously imparted with the avowed purpose of keeping its victim ignorant.

Even as Christian Science treatment is good imparted with the avowed purpose of bringing to light good and more good, intelligently directed, so evil, in its last analysis is "intelligently" directed evil with the avowed purpose of bringing to pass evil and more evil. The former says, in the words of Christ Jesus, "I am come that they might have life, and that they might have it more abundantly," the latter the reverse, "I am come that they might have death, and have it more abundantly."

Mrs. Eddy illustrates with an analogy, in Miscellany, the two phases of evil—"the beast" and "the false prophet," or as we term them today "matter," and "ignorant and malicious mentality," in these words, "The alcoholic habit is the use of higher forms of matter, wherewith to do evil; whereas animal magnetism is the highest form of mental evil, wherewith to complete the sum total of sin." She thus expresses the difference between the ordinary claim of sickness and the vicious claim of the sickness that is the result of malicious mental manipulation. Both have to be destroyed by diligently reversing the "laws" operating in each case; one seemingly an ignorant "law" and the other a wilful malicious "law" deliberately formulated with malice aforethought. No presentation in either case can be neglected if the problem is to be scientifically solved.

The Christian Scientist lives and operates today in the realm of pure Mind, and consequently has to meet the negation of that Mind just as the student of mathematics, when reaching the higher rules, has to meet the ignorance about those rules and not the simple ignorance that he met in his earlier studies of mathematics. So, as you, the Christian Scientist, the intelligent metaphysician, gain the understanding of the operation of intelligent good, you necessarily have to meet the belief of "intelligent" evil. This, however, involves only the same fidelity to Principle which you expressed when first introduced to Christian Science. Unswerving consecration to what is true is imperative. The demand is no greater, the consecration no less, for in both cases the understanding is the use of what is true. You must have the same supreme confidence in what is true, as you have in God.

It is absurd for the advanced Christian Scientist to think he can use the simple arguments and understanding he used when first becoming interested in Christian Science. He cannot. He must practise his advanced understanding just as he would in any other study. Mrs. Eddy stressed this very point when she said to a student, *"Keep your thought clear to work, and protect it from mental psychic malpractice, rather than struggle with the physical ravages of the influence and manifestation."*

The Christian Scientist must go on to more advanced rules continually, and unless he recognizes this fact and joyfully keeps step with the advancing unfoldment, he is not only waiting for "a more convenient season" but when that more convenient season appears he will discover his lack of progress and will have to take every step he has heretofore neglected. How much easier it is to enjoy the present moment's unfoldment and go forward happily. As Science and Health points out, "Willingness to become as a little child and to leave the old for the new, renders thought receptive of the advanced idea."

WHY IS IT NECESSARY
TO HANDLE
MALICIOUS MENTAL MALPRACTICE?

IN THE study of mathematics, you begin with the first simple rules of arithmetic. Addition is the starting point. You first learn that three plus three equals six, and so on. Then follow in orderly sequence subtraction, multiplication and division.

Doubtless in the beginning as a child, you did not even know what the figures represented but you soon overcame that ignorance and as you grew more interested the ignorance confronting you vanished.

Dealing with addition, you had to meet merely the ignorance about addition; with subtraction, the ignorance about subtraction; with multiplication, the ignorance about multiplication, the ignorance always keeping pace and advancing with the unfoldment of the rule. In every case the ignorance applied only to the new rule and was as simple as the rule itself.

When you reached the more complicated subject of fractions, the ignorance about them also appeared more complex than the former ignorance. However, you quickly learned that the intelligence governing fractions was supremely simple when properly applied. It was merely a question of adding the intelligence about fractions to the intelligence about easier problems.

In other words, as you advanced in arithmetic you discovered that you used the intelligence applicable to each immediate rule added to the intelligence applied to some former rule. Likewise in higher mathematics, the ignorance always keeps pace with and is overcome by the intelligence of each new rule. The negative always accompanies the positive, which it negates. Now apply this to the practice of Christian Science.

When thought went no higher than thinking in terms of matter, the clear, consecrated discernment that there was, "no life, truth, intelligence, nor substance in matter", as Science and Health states, was sufficient to release you from much of matter's bondage. In fact, if that was as far as you had gone in your understanding of

Christian Science, your devotion to it enabled you to heal every error presented to you.

Your next step was to analyze each claim more minutely to discover what was the anatomy involved, and to take the specific error (anatomy involved) back to God. You discovered there could be but one of anything, and that God imparted and maintained that one, perfect and intact; that it was, also, your one, and everywhere present and, therefore, was right where the claim masqueraded. With this realization you healed freely and quickly.

From that point, you went on to prove what Jesus meant when he said of those that believed on him, of those that understood him, "and greater works than these shall he do; because I go unto my Father", because the "I" no longer is contemplating effect but God, the one cause, divine Mind, and has become one with the Father, Mind.

It was to this present mental unfoldment that Jesus also referred when he said "When ye therefore shall see the abomination of desolation, . . . stand in the holy place, (whoso readeth let him understand) . . . Then shall be great tribulation, such as was not since the beginning of the world to this time, no, nor ever shall be." The holy place is Mind, and evil, malicious mental malpractice the abomination of desolation, standing there, means evil no longer operating as matter and material "laws", but as pure mind, the negation of the divine Mind.

It is at this point of his unfoldment that the Christian Scientist finds himself today. Using the mathematical analogy, he is no longer dealing with the simple rules of addition or even of fractions, but he is in higher mathematics. So in Science he has reached the highest of all— pure metaphysics—and he must bring to bear on his problems the intelligence of pure Mind, uncontaminated by finite sense, in order to destroy the negation. Malicious mental malpractice is the ignorance confronting him at each advancing step and is the only thing that does confront him. Just as the whole of mathematics and the ignorance about it are embodied in the most intricate problem, so pure Mind is confronted with malicious mental malpractice embodying within itself all ignorance of Mind.

Through progress, the Christian Scientist is now meeting evil in its final phase. This actually should be encouraging to him, and he can afford to "look up" as Jesus said "and lift up (his) head; for (his) redemption draweth nigh." He understands why his redemption draweth nigh, for he knows that evil has reached its highest ignorance; the ignorance about pure Mind which marks the end for the translation, by reversal, of pure evil mind back to God, divine Mind, leaving "nothing that can sin, suffer, be punished or destroyed", as Science and Health states.

Evil is now doing its worst. As the negation of pure Mind, it faces its end. There is nothing worse to follow. It has been found the lie about Truth in every detail and the lie has been reversed and given back to God.

But, this vigorous and wonderful warfare with evil requires consecrated work. There is no room for indolence or dreaming. Jesus admonished us to watch, and he repeated, again "I say unto you, watch." Why this demand to watch? Mrs. Eddy answers the question in her article "Watching versus Watching Out", in Miscellany, where she sternly rebukes not watching against a negative watch, *alias,* no watch, in these words, "Then should not 'watching out' mean, watching against a negative watch, alias, no watch, and gaining the spirit of true watching, even the spirit of our Master's command?" When Jesus asked his disciples to watch with him, did they watch, or did they succumb to the treacherous argument of sleep?

Jesus knew that he was meeting the subtle argument of malicious mind that life, substance and intelligence were in matter, when he asked them to watch with him and to help destroy that argument. But his disciples were unable to help him, so he watched alone, and so completely overcame the arguments of evil that he was able to prove his oneness with Mind. Thus he became the supreme example for all men.

Today we are called upon to watch more assiduously than ever before. We are watching from a higher watchtower; the watchtower of the positive, infinite activity of pure Mind. In consequence, the enemy is negatively just as active. The only way to defeat this enemy is to reverse it by translating it back to God, to the one source of all.

Evil gets its apparent power from the fact of its being the negation of infinite Mind's activity and alertness. It automatically does in reverse everything that God does directly. When this is not understood, one is apt to feel he is dealing with something that thinks and that can mentally harm him. To the metaphysician, such a conclusion is preposterous, for he knows what is operating and attempting to retard his progress, just as the mathematician understands the ignorance that tries to checkmate him at every advancing step. If you imagine that ignorance can think logically, then you are likely to believe that ignorance can think in the realm of pure Mind; that it can conjure up some deviltry to checkmate the metaphysician. The Christian Scientist is never checkmated by malicious mental malpractice, but is checkmated by his own ignorance of what malicious mental malpractice is, and of its operation as the negative of infinite intelligence.

There is, however, one important difference between the ignorance confronting one in higher mathematics, and the ignorance confronting one in the highest phases of Christian Science. Mathematical ignorance is plain ignorance of facts without any directed intent back of the ignorance, because the principle governing numbers is called a dead principle. Hence the negation in the ignorance of mathematics is without premeditated intent.

The exact opposite of this is the case in Christian Science where God, the divine Principle of being, as Mind itself, is infinitely active intelligence directing the whole of being. The negation or ignorance of this intelligence must be infinite ignorance which assumes, as the negative, the opposite of every quality of good, but in its infinity of ignorance it appears as infinitely intelligent ignorance. It has no power of its own and when reversed, automatically becomes the very presence and activity of God.

Our work as Christian Scientists is to be about our Father's business in the realm of unfoldment that we have attained, where Satan is attempting to stand in the holy place of Mind and to operate as pure evil mentality. Satan can be dethroned from this pinnacle of evil only by the understanding of pure divine Mind and its operation.

THE WAY
EVIL ARGUES

EVIL'S argument follows practically the same
lines as any other argument, the only difference being that evil, through its channels of
malicious minds, argues silently. Unless you are
awake to its machinations, it will govern you.
Mrs. Eddy was spiritually minded enough to
read malicious mind from the standpoint of divine Mind. Such reading is possible only through
spiritual discernment. It cannot be done through
mortal mind reading, such as mediumship and
spiritualism. Mrs. Eddy has stated, *"There is
no mortal mind reading. Mortal mind cannot
see or hear what is going on, for all is embraced
in the one Mind, and error cannot know anything about Mind."*

Because the arguments of evil are silent they
are not then less persuasive than arguments that
are audible. An audible argument is more easily

refuted than a silent one, because it is out in the open where it can be seen, while the silent argument may be operating with you when you are least aware of it and are not on your guard. Its subtle attacks are felt in your body, in your home, your business affairs and your world conditions. So be on your guard—keep awake to the fact that any argument, whether it comes as your own thought or as the thought of another, is always malicious mind's argument if it starts with effect and not cause, if it comes as some person, place or thing that is wrong.

This malicious argument will present itself in any and every way that can harass and distress you. It may appear as physical suffering, business losses, family discord or any suggestion that can make you doubtful of your ability to succeed in your purpose, whether it be healing a case of sickness or achieving success in any line. Its arguments will be directed especially toward discouraging you and embittering your disposition. It will suggest that you are of no possible use; that you cannot heal, or if you do heal that it is only temporary and the discord will return. Mrs. Eddy has repeatedly drawn attention to these as well as to many similar arguments.

How much attention have you given to what she has so forcefully exposed? Do you continue with the same old routine, or are you daily becoming more alert to what is taking place, no longer thinking that it is you who conjure up these impossible arguments? You must be positive that it is not a person, a place, or a thing that is at work but malicious minds, the ever-operating affectation of malicious mind, masquerading as intelligent power.

If someone were audibly arguing with you, it could not seem more real than the silent argument of malicious mind endeavoring to make you accept its lies as your own mental volition. It argues just as directly, vigorously and forcefully as a good lawyer arguing a case. It uses every cunning device to deceive you into believing that you yourself are the originator of your disturbed thinking, and, should it succeed, you become its voice and its servant. As a Christian Scientist you must not and cannot yield to such a palpable fraud. To do so would be fatal to your health, harmony and progress.

To understand this intellectually does not necessarily mean that you innately feel the truth of it; and what you really do not feel you will not utilize. Malicious evil will always rob you of what you only intellectually understand, but nothing can rob you of what you not only know but feel. Mrs. Eddy counseled her students,

"First, find out what error is trying to do. Second, keep it from doing it. Third, see that it is not done."

You know that evil is the negation of good; that it imitates good in all the unfoldments of good, from the simplest to the most marvellous; and that its silent arguments are the negation of the spiritual arguments of Christian Science. To destroy the negative arguments the spirit of Truth and Love must be present and realized. Every presentation of sin, disease, death, and limitation, and every finite sense of person, place and thing, as entity apart from God, must be translated back to God, the one Mind, that God may be found All-in-all.

As used by the metaphysician "translating back to God, Mind" does not mean to translate the "effect" back to cause, but to take the things of God and show them unto the creature: to start with God, cause, and there find all being. In his oneness with God he knows what the "creature" or "effect" must be. Furthermore, he does not think "effect" has to be corrected *outside* his "own mentality", but he knows God must be found as the only "mentality" for a clear sense of good to be maintained.

This "translating", as used by the metaphysician, means beginning with God; and ending with God, and finding God all noumenon and phenomenon. It means accepting God as all that can appear to him and holding steadfastly to this truth, he sees that which *is* as all that is and perfection reigns.

Mrs. Eddy states in Miscellany the great importance of this beginning with cause, never with effect: "Losing the comprehensive in the technical, the Principle in its accessories, cause in effect, and faith in sight, we lose the Science of Christianity,—a predicament quite like that of the man who could not see London for the houses."

THE DIFFERENCE
BETWEEN
WORKING WITH AND WORKING AGAINST
MALICIOUS MIND

A NUMBER of years ago, a robust black-smith went before a medical clinic, in a city in Europe, to demonstrate that he could, at will, move any muscle in his body and even stop the action of his heart or any designated nerve.

A short time ago a similar demonstration was given over the radio by a man who could, through will power, stop the circulation of first one side of his body and then the other, and start or stop his pulse. An examining physician present testified to the validity of the performance.

In the latter case the man stated he was teaching the power of mind over matter and gave his performance to prove that he was able to control his body mentally. The radio announcer said that the man's age was seventy-five, but that he looked like a man of forty or forty-five.

The question has been asked, why this man dealing entirely with mortal mind, should be able to exhibit such control of his body, while the Christian Scientist frequently seems unable to achieve such success? In fact why should a Christian Scientist, after years of faithful study, ever be tempted to believe that he can express signs of age and decrepitude?

The answer is simple. In the first instance one is dealing with the human mind and working in full accord with it. While he may seem to be accomplishing much that is unusual, nevertheless, his complete accord with that mind arouses no antagonism from it. In fact, that mind is actually enlisted with him to show forth its power and it therefore gives him its full aid and support. Evil promises as it did to Jesus "All these things will I give thee, if thou wilt fall down and worship me."

With the Christian Scientist exactly the opposite is the case. He is dealing with divine Mind which is his one and only aid, so instead of being in accord with the human mind he is at enmity with it, for the human or carnal mind is, as Paul expressed it, "enmity against God: for it is not subject to the law of God, neither indeed can be." Hence there is a deadly warfare between Spirit and malicious mind, or matter. Consequently, by virtue of its being the negation of divine Mind the whole effort of malicious mind must be arrayed against the work of the Christian Scientist, because the Christian Scientist is not proving the power of divine Mind over matter, but is proving divine Mind's complete destruction of *all* material belief of which matter is but the crudest phase.

Evil is fighting for its very existence and directing every argument against the power and operation of divine Mind; therefore, the Christian Scientist must meet and destroy the whole array of evil arguments in order to show forth a full manifestation of health and power.

Of course since evil has no ability to think or act, the Christian Scientist really has nothing, except belief, opposed to him. The power of God being all the power there is, it needs no assistance from the human mind.

Through unswerving consecration, the work of the Christian Scientist will be accomplished and finally revealed as permanent. Ultimately the ephemeral power of the human mind to bring about so-called good, will be discerned as merely a temporary phenomenon of malicious mind, and that its "good" is not the enduring good of Mind.

Just as Moses' serpent, which typified divine wisdom, swallowed the magician's serpent, which typified the human belief of wisdom, so the passing beliefs of mortal mind will be recognized—swallowed up—and destroyed through the understanding of divine Mind and its allness.

The Christian Scientist is building on the rock, Christ, Truth, and while his progress may seem slow he, nevertheless, will finally see, in the words of Malachi, the difference "between him that serveth God and him that serveth Him not."

"THE ONLY INCENTIVE
OF
A MISTAKEN SENSE"

MARY BAKER EDDY

IN AN article entitled "The Way of Wisdom",
published in Miscellany, Mrs. Eddy makes
a statement that should, in the words of an
old saying, rouse the living and wake the dead.
It is this. "The only incentive of a mistaken
sense is malicious animal magnetism,—the name
of all evil—and this must be understood."

This quotation must be recognized as meaning that there is not a single wrong action taking
place in the entire range of human affairs and beliefs, from the simplest to the most important,
that is not the result of the directed action of
malicious mind.

Could any statement be more comprehensive?
And yet you would know it to be true even if

Mrs. Eddy had not said it; for you know that your only cognizance of anything is a mental cognizance and not a matter one, and that therefore everything has to come as consciousness to you, which means it comes as a mind argument and not a matter argument since matter cannot argue. Therefore, a wrong argument or incentive must come from the negation of God, which is malicious animal magnetism.

Then you see that with any mistaken sense—wrong action—you are always dealing with malicious animal magnetism, in other words malicious mental malpractice acting as malicious minds. It could not be otherwise. Why not acknowledge such a self-evident truth and act accordingly, instead of drifting along, dealing with beliefs that have nothing to do with the case and virtually making no progress?

Either here or hereafter every problem will have to be worked out on these lines, for there is no other way to overcome evil. Death will not change evil, and neither will the hereafter have an easier or better way of applying the truth to the lie.

Mrs. Eddy has clearly stated this in an article entitled Life, which appeared in the Christian Science Sentinel Feb. 2, 1918. She wrote, *"Death cannot advance our joy, nor make us wiser, better, or more pure. The Science of all being must be learned ere this is won. Bliss is not the boon of one brief moment. After the veil has dropped, we have to learn the same as now our way to heaven, by slow and solemn footsteps, for no man cometh to the Father but through Truth and Love."*

THE
OF
MAN

THE Psalmist said, "Surely the wrath of man shall praise thee; the remainder of wrath shalt thou restrain."

What is it that most scientifically or understandingly expresses God with a clean-cut, definite understanding of good instead of faith, belief, or guesswork? The answer is simple. Christian Science.

Christian Science is the love for man shown forth as the Love that is God. It appears as the healing or destruction of all error. Isaiah expressed it, "To loose the bands of wickedness, to undo the heavy burdens and to let the oppressed go free, and that ye break every yoke".

The reverse of this would be the binding with "bands of wickedness", oppression and heavy burdens, which is always what is done by malicious mental malpractice. This is the exact suppositional opposite of Christian Science and, therefore, its nature is to reverse the truth at every step. Instead of loosing the bands of wickedness it tightens them; instead of working openly as matter, where it can in belief be seen, it works mentally in secrecy and darkness where in belief it cannot be seen.

As Christian Science is the love of man, so malicious mental malpractice is the wrath or hatred of man. But that hatred, when correctly understood and reversed, becomes praise of God.

This wrath of man, malicious mental malpractice, compels the mortal to turn away from belief in the body, and find his absolute oneness with Mind, as his only way of escape. When this is done, then the wrath of man, this malicious mental malpractice, will not succeed in its purpose to stultify his thinking and kill him in his body.

Turning unreservedly from the belief of a material body to Mind is man's safety and freedom. The insistent application of divine Mind destroys malicious mental malpractice. Matter offers no means of escape, for "the wrath of man" no longer deals with matter, but entirely with mentality. Hence through Mind alone can it be reached and destroyed. There is no other way and you cannot be mesmerized into believing there is. Knowing this you are no longer a child speaking as a child, but you speak as the man of God. You no longer see through a glass, darkly, but "face to face".

"The remainder of wrath shalt thou restrain" is seen in the fact that only as understanding is present to meet a claim, can that claim arise. In other words you cannot be called upon to meet something that you have not already the understanding with which to meet it. A lie always requires the truth to be present, for the truth is what the lie is the lie about.

Mrs. Eddy verifies this in her statement, *"Whenever there seems to be a lack or a need in your experience, that simply indicates the scientific fact that the seeming void is already supplied by God's gracious abundance."* The Psalmist, too, in unmistakable language, most beautifully declares this same omnipresence of God no matter what the appearance may be.

"Whither shall I go from thy spirit? Or whither shall I flee from thy presence?

If I ascend up into heaven, thou art there: if I make my bed in hell, behold, thou art there.

> If I take the wings of the morning, and dwell in the uttermost parts of the sea; even there shall thy hand lead me, and thy right hand shall hold me.
>
> If I say, Surely the darkness shall cover me; even the night shall be light about me.
>
> Yea, the darkness hideth not from thee; but the night shineth as the day: the darkness and the light are both alike to thee."

This understanding is what restrains "the remainder of wrath", for finding God as the one and only source of all activity, gives the right interpretation to every appearance, whether called good or evil.

Mrs. Eddy once very plainly defined to some friends what this wrath of man is that shall be made to praise God. *"Malpractice is the wrath of man, and it is being made to praise God by driving you out of the tenement or belief in body. If it does not drive you out of it, it will kill you in it."*

HOW TO
HANDLE A CASE
PROPERLY

NO CASE can be properly handled in Christian Science until it is thoroughly understood that every claim, regardless of its appearance, is always the result of directed evil; that it is the deliberate, conscious act of malicious mind voiced personally by a mortal or mortals.

Failure to understand this is to misunderstand Christian Science, for the basic result of the discovery of Christian Science is that good can be directed intelligently to accomplish good. Through Mrs. Eddy's discovery good was found to be no longer a waif wandering aimlessly, but was found to be a divine and ever-present Mind-force ready to be utilized and applied, as Jesus applied it, wherever needed. This fulfilled the Scriptural injunction to show forth faith by works, and to take the things of God and show them unto the creature. Such obedience determines whether or not one is a Christian Science practitioner; whether or not he is the man of God, the voice of God.

In like manner, malicious mind claims ability through its votaries, malicious mental malpractitioners, to reverse this operation of Christian Science, and to take the things of evil and show them unto its victims, always placing its lies where they will do the most harm. This operation is a wilful, direct attempt to destroy the Christian Scientist and his work, and if it is not recognized and cast out, will accomplish, in belief, its iniquity.

There could be no Christian Science operating without the Christian Science practitioner, and in the same way, there could be no malicious mental malpractice operating without the malicious mental malpractitioner.

Remember, no refutation in Christian Science can accomplish much unless it is clearly realized that both the Christian Science practitioner and the malicious mental malpractitioner, however they may *appear* to be as other persons, never are. There is nothing, either mental or physical "out there". It is all "in here," mine. If I abide by the facts and find God as my Mind, I am the one Christian Science practitioner, that which shows forth the glory of God. If I allow myself to be confused by appearances and start my reasoning from effect instead of cause and listen when suggestions coming as "I" claim to be my mind, then I find myself as the one malicious mental malpractitioner, the only one that could be, and I show forth, or seem to show forth, all that is meant by separation, or devil.

The latter situation is, of course, impossible since there is no separate "I", which chooses the kind of course it will steer between good and evil. All there is to me, really, is my awareness of God. I have no other capacity or function, and so obviously, I cannot be a "malpractitioner". It only seems to me to be so and it seems to have results. It never really does.

Your work is to understand this, and always cast out the *vicious* suggestion of this mind, with Jesus' rebuke, "Get thee behind me, Satan: thou art an offence unto me." He showed no tolerance or gentleness with evil, then why should you? When a wrong thought presents itself, know that it is always a deliberate suggestion— not a chance suggestion, but a deliberate suggestion, and that the perpetrator is one with the suggestion, for without the perpetrator, no suggestion could be voiced.

When you hear this suggestion, act exactly as you would if someone were trying to make you believe a lie. You certainly would eliminate both the lie and the liar by promptly casting them out as spurious.

Do this with every lie that presents itself to you. Refuse to harbour it for a moment. Miscellaneous Writings states, "No person can accept another's belief, except it be with the consent of his own belief. If the error which knocks at the door of your own thought originated in another's mind, you are a free moral agent to reject or to accept this error; hence, you are the arbiter of your own fate, and sin is the author of sin." You have the power to reject it; then exercise your power with authority, and not as though you were half afraid that what you were casting out could refuse to go. Remember what Science and Health says, *"Christian Scientists, be a law to yourselves that mental malpractice can not harm you either when asleep or when awake."*

It is foolish to grieve over any trouble when it is really but the negative presentation of Truth that you can readily cast out by translating it correctly. But remember, you cast it out as a suggestion of evil and not as a *person*. Evil thoughts seem to go forth as persons perpetrating them but it is always as sin that you must reject them, never as persons. They come in reality as the "angel visitant" of God as Jacob found, and when entertained rightly by reversing them and so giving them back to God, the evil suggestion is cast out with all its angels, its accompanying lies or testimony declaring for its truth. The Revelator saw this day when he declared, "The great dragon was cast out, that old serpent, called the Devil, and Satan, . . . and his angels were cast out with him."

Arouse yourself so as not to be deceived into believing that any wrong thought you seem to have is yours. It is not. It is deliberately directed thought appearing as your mind with purpose to hurt you. Recognize this and destroy it promptly.

Mrs. Eddy said in Christian Science History, in 1899, *"Without a question the student of Christian Science is not qualified to teach, preach, or to practise divine metaphysics, who knows not thoroughly how wisely to handle this heinous sin—mental malpractice."* She also said in Historical Sketch, *"The methods of animal magnetism, especially its secret work, should be exposed. This alone can protect the people from a reign of terror, far surpassing any reign of terror in the dark ages."* Also in the Sixth edi-

tion of Science and Health she strongly emphasized, "*The re-establishment of the Christian
Era, in this mediaeval period of metaphysics,
should be one of moderation and peace: but the
re-inauguration of this period will be met with
demonology, or the unlicensed cruelty of mortal
mind, which will compel mankind to learn metaphysics for a refuge and defense.*"

THE PERSONALITY
OF THE
MALICIOUS MENTAL MALPRACTITIONER

BECAUSE one recognizes that malicious mind cannot act or be represented without its malicious mental malpractitioner, does that imply that the identity of the malpractitioner should be known?

It is true of course, that there can be no act without a perpetrator, but the personality of the perpetrator is as immaterial as is the image in the mirror. It is the object before the mirror that is causing the image that has to be dealt with.

The recognition, however, that there necessarily always is a perpetrator to show forth the purpose back of the act is most important, otherwise the purpose would escape detection and the need to discern and counteract the directed influence would not be apparent, just as the recognition in a general way, that the answer to some mathematical problem is wrong, would not correct the mistake. The specific error must be specifically corrected. The specific belief that there must always be a man, woman or child, place or thing, an avenue or channel, a belief or a law, whereby evil is voiced, must be detected and refuted.

Every argument of malicious mental malpractice is a specific argument, which must be recognized and refuted, although never personally, for even though it must seem to *come* as person, *it is not person,* but malicious mental malpractice that actuates it.

Evil is primary, in belief, to its expression and originates all of its mortal's so-called thinking and action, as God is primary to His man and originates all his thinking power and action. "The Son can do nothing of himself, but what he seeth the Father do: for what things soever He doeth, these also doeth the Son likewise," were the words of the one who showed forth the power of God in all its glory.

Then the personality of evil is not the question. Evil and its voice are as impersonal as good, yet both evil and its voice must be reversed by translating them back to God,—by understanding God and His man as the one and only Mind, the complete noumenon and phenomenon of being.

Mrs. Eddy spoke strongly to some of her friends giving them strict admonitions on this subject of personality. She said that *"all there is to personality is the fear of it or the love of it"* and again *"you should negative error without individualizing it so much"*. She went on to admonish *"never recognize person in your treatment"*. If *"you dwell in thought on any person it will hinder you from overcoming personality and casting out sin"* which is malicious mental malpractice. Further she warned that *"There is no personality, and this is more important to know than that there is no disease"*, and showed that the necessity is to *"drop it and remember you can never rid yourself of the seeming effects coming from a personality while holding in thought this personality."*

Again in answer to the question as to whether she approved of treating personally for "malicious mesmerism the offending malpractitioner, even when the malpractitioner is attempting to kill someone and this is known", the reply was emphatic, *"I answer, if they do treat thus, they prolong their own misunderstanding. The altitude of Christian Science is omnipotence. Truth is given us for this purpose—to destroy error and make man free in the impersonal Christ."*

THE IMPORTANCE

OF

STATING YOUR METAPHYSICAL
ARGUMENT CORRECTLY

THE subtlety of evil is nowhere more evident than in its attempt to cause the Christian Scientist to word his argument carelessly when correcting error.

Since words give impulse to thought, it is essential that they be accurately used. A wrongly expressed thought can readily yield a wrong impulsion or direction. Therefore in the language of Job, "as the mouth tasteth meat" choose your words.

To illustrate; it would be a mistake to declare that there is no return of old beliefs, because at some time you may have had a belief of strength, vigor, health and success and you certainly would not wish your words to imply that you would not again welcome those conditions, not just as good beliefs but as realities and that as such you not only desire them, but you intend to have them and to express them in all their perfection.

Consequently, your metaphysical statement would not be, that there can be no belief of a return of an old belief, but rather, that evil, malicious mind, as malicious mental malpractice, cannot inflict upon you or bring to pass with you a belief of a return of a diseased belief.

It is the disease part of a belief that you will not admit can return. "When Christ changes a belief of sin or of sickness into a better belief, then belief melts into spiritual understanding, and sin, disease, and death disappear," as Science and Health points out.

This fine distinction needs careful attention. It is the wrong belief,—which is always directed mesmerism,—that you will not tolerate.

By attaching a God-like interpretation to every thought, it is safe to use it vigorously. Always insist upon the perfection of the body and of all that being means, to the minutest detail. Mrs. Eddy, in her statement to some friends, explained this necessity by saying *"All the mechanism of Jesus' body was preserved and restored until his ascension. I always preserve in my thought, as I know Jesus did, the image of the actual and harmonious function of the body."*

The body, as all else, must be preserved intact until the material sense is entirely transformed by the spiritual; and remember, transforming is not a destructive action, but rather is it a spiritual regeneration. It is what Jesus meant when he said, "I pray not that thou shouldest take them out of the world, but that thou shouldest keep them from the evil," and what Paul meant when he said, "Not for that we would be unclothed but clothed upon." A statement attributed to Mrs. Eddy sums it up completely, *"A belief of personal sense that is governed by Truth is a harmonious belief. A harmonious belief that is governed by Truth is spiritual sense or understanding."*

This does not mean that belief or the human mind ever becomes understanding or divine Mind. Metaphysically such a belief is absurd. But it does mean that when a belief of personal sense is overshadowed, transformed, in other words, when the false sense is destroyed by a clearer sense of Truth, to that extent harmony is acknowledged as reigning where discord seemed to reign before.

When harmonious belief is further unfolded

by spiritual sense, and is governed entirely by
Spirit, at each progressive stage, the harmonious
belief completely disappears as belief and is replaced with spiritual sense or understanding.

This must be the way in which all treatment
or unfoldment operates. Nothing except the
false sense is abandoned and with the rejection
of the false, the better sense appears, until as
Science and Health declares "the whole earth
will be transformed by Truth on its pinions of
light, chasing away the darkness of error."
Never give up *any thing*—give up only the false
sense about it.

Preserve every action and function of the
body intact, as you find them in God. Abandon
the senseless argument that would make you
think you could get along just as well without
the five so-called material senses or even that it is
more spiritual to be without them. As though it
were more spiritual not to hear than to hear,
and not to see than to see! The senses are spiritual, and it is our duty as Christian Scientists to
preserve them and insist that they express perfection, and thus defeat the arguments of malicious mental malpractice, no matter how subtle
those arguments may be. To quote again from
Science and Health, "There is more Science in
the perpetual exercise of the Mind-faculties than

in their loss. Lost they cannot be, while Mind remains."

When you give a treatment, that is to say, when you know the truth, it is the part of wisdom to include in that knowing the understanding that the treatment, being the word of God, is also the presence of God, for where God's word is, there His presence must be. Furthermore it must be the power of God, for God's word and presence must include His power. Then continue by knowing that there are no malicious minds to reverse the treatment and make it produce a result that is not intended, or to interfere in any way with the accomplishment whereto it is sent. Only mesmeric argument prevents you from consciously knowing this and thus seeing your treatment free from any contrary influence. There is none.

It should be understood by the Christian Scientist that the treatment he gives does heal and that it heals instantaneously because a treatment really is the declaration of God's eternal power, presence and perfection. This must be known and declared in every instance.

Man, being the voice of God, heals spontaneously and only the lie of malicious mental malpractice could cause him to doubt the power of the treatment to accomplish its intended purpose. To doubt your ability to heal is to doubt the reality of Mind, for healing is simply turning thought from ignorance to understanding. A change in view-point is all that is required to reach the heaven of His presence. There is never any condition which needs to be changed.

These lies of malicious mind must be refuted vigorously. Insist, "I can heal—I can show forth God. I do heal—I do show forth God, for the one Ego, the one I, is my I, my Ego." Can anything gainsay this I? Or reverse what this I says? Of course not. Then positively declare that it cannot; because the ever-present malicious mental malpractice will try to say that it can reverse your treatment and can argue with you until you have no faith either in your own power, or in the power of Christian Science to heal. It will argue, that even if the case is healed it will not remain so.

Should these thoughts come to you, know that malicious mental malpractice, and not you, originates them. Destroy the false belief of malicious mental malpractice, the negation of good, by translating it back to God and you will find instant freedom.

What you know and declare about your treatment is all that there is to the treatment. Nothing can heal in any treatment, but what *you* put into it. You are a law to it. Then be a law to the whole situation. Understand that what you say and feel that is true does govern. Be true to God and the result is heaven.

The only thing that declares you are not true to God, or do not wish to be true, is malicious mental malpractice substituting itself for your mental volition and acting as your "I". Cast it out by knowing you cannot be made to believe a lie, for God being the only Mind there is no malicious mind to argue any lie, to argue any "I" apart from God.

'EFFECT' AND 'AFFECT'.

THE

DIFFERENCE

THE noun "effect" means, result or consequence, and the verb, to bring to pass. "Affect" is entirely different. It usually indicates
a sense of assumption, assuming a character or
quality that is not genuine. Thus we get our
word affectation, meaning a false appearance.

God's inevitable consequence is effect,—something as real and true as that of which it is the
effect. Man is the effect of God, and, in every
quality and characteristic of good, shows forth
God in the minutest detail.

Evil's consequence is not effect, but affectation.
It is the assuming of something that does not
belong to it, such as life, power and intelligence,
which are qualities of God.

These two words, effect and affect should be
understood, for they perfectly express the vast

difference between the appearance of Truth and the appearance of evil. One appearance is real and permanent and the other is false and ephemeral.

The effect, good, is always the presence of God,—true and eternal. The presence of evil is always pure assumption, unadulterated affectation, deception with the intent to deceive.

"A FAD OF BELIEF
IS THE
FOOL OF MESMERISM"

MARY BAKER EDDY

M RS. EDDY made the statement in Question Answered, in Miscellany, "A fad of belief is the fool of mesmerism."

What a world of truth is therein! What mortal is not in one sense a bundle of fads? How he prides himself on these fads, little dreaming that they are simply the effort of evil to make him the fool of its mesmerism. Nothing serves as a more prolific soil for malicious mind's activity than a fad.

What mortal will not fight for his fad and even be tempted to think those lacking in intelligence who disagree with him. You need only observe a faddist to discover not only his intolerant attitude toward interference, but also his determination to proselytize his associates.

What the fad may be makes little difference. Whether it is a course of action, a diet, a healthful exercise or any other notion among all the innumerable complexities of daily life, his attitude is the same. The most absurd subject can constitute a fad, but it is never absurd to the one indulging in it. To him it is a solid fact, to be adhered to under all circumstances,—until a wiser and better sense obtains.

No fad is worth consideration. What you think about anything is of no moment, when that thinking is based on personal sense. When based on God, it is eternal and therefore is not a fad but a fact. As Mrs. Eddy says in her Miscellaneous Writings, "No human hypotheses, whether in philosophy, medicine, or religion, can survive the wreck of time; but whatever is of God, hath life abiding in it."

The utter foolishness of fads is perfectly stated in Christian Science versus Pantheism: "Christian Science is irrevocable—unpierced by bold conjecture's sharp point, by bald philosophy, or by man's inventions." And that is what every fad of belief is, an invention of mortal man, the mouth-piece of malicious mind.

Remember, so-called individual ambitions,

tastes, appetites, indulgences and so forth are ready avenues for malicious suggestion to use for the propagation of its hypnotic influence.

The Christian Scientist in his ignorance may imagine that some little indulgence that he enjoys, seemingly of a harmless nature, has no effect on him. In one sense of the word this is true, but in another it is not true. Let him ask himself why he indulges in a particular habit and he will find it is because he is endowing matter, which really is malicious mind, with power to give him pleasure. Is it not true that if malicious mind can give one pleasure, it can, also, through an opposite suggestion give one pain? Shakespeare caught a glimpse of this when he wrote "And of our pleasant vices make instruments to scourge us."

The remedy is to base all on God, the one causation, and starting from God, find pleasure, because He is the essence of joy and joy is in Him and not in the expression or thing enjoyed. Then all desires, appetites, ambitions, tastes will be found as qualities of God—governed by God, not one loved more than another.

Thus malicious mind can no longer use such activities of good as its channels for evil suggestion, for it cannot deal with cause but always deals with effect; and the Christian Scientist finds his freedom. Gladly he abandons fads, finding God and His presence his all absorbing passion.

In this way malicious mind is disarmed and is no longer able to use its victim's mistaken sense of good whereby to operate.

DICTATORSHIP

HAVE you ever analyzed the real meaning of dictatorship? Only by so doing can the false sense of the word be recognized, that is to say, the reason for the attempt to govern and dictate to men regardless of their own desires.

The Christian Scientist, the metaphysician, knows that the oneness and allness of divine Mind is accompanied in belief by the negation of that oneness and allness. Just as Jesus expressed all power, as the showing forth of God, divine Mind, so the mortal as the showing forth of the negation of divine Mind, malicious mind, would likewise claim in belief all power. The negative of divine Mind must claim to the minutest detail, every function, power and authority of the positive, for that is the nature of the suppositional opposite.

Remember, however, it is only as the negative

is taken back to the positive that it really does have power. All electric power is the result of the negative being brought in contact with the positive, and that contact is seen as the power, light and heat that you use.

This illustration should be helpful to the Christian Scientist by showing him that to attain enlightenment on any subject, he has only to take the negative back to the positive; in other words to translate matter back to Mind. By so doing he finds Mind embracing within itself all being and all effect, and instantly there is light, power and freedom.

Applying this to dictatorship: Is not God, as the one and only Mind, self-evidently the one controlling power and consequently the one Dictator? It is necessary to understand this fact and not to attempt to destroy dictator, but to gain such a true sense of dictator that God is seen everywhere as dictating. This understanding will destroy the power of malicious mind to substitute itself as the mental volition of anyone and thus compel its victim to act contrary to wisdom and good.

The understanding that there is no malicious mind to operate as a malicious mental malpractitioner lifts the nightmare of mesmerism and frees the victim from false dictatorship. The worst and most vicious form of dictatorship is the despotism of malicious mental malpractice.

Annihilate the belief that malicious mind has any avenues or channels through which to operate; any man, woman or child upon whom to foist its beliefs of law; any malicious mental malpractice or malicious mental malpractitioner to declare its dictatorial demands or to carry them out. How is this done? By knowing that God, being the one and only Mind, His man, woman and child is the only man, woman and child, His law is the only law, and that God's man is ever about God's business. This realization leaves God as the one and only Dictator.

If malicious mind is admitted, it follows that, as mind, either good or bad, it must have avenues and channels, men, women and children through whom it can act and devolve power to act. Hence it is necessary to know that there is no malicious mind. This understanding destroys all false sense of dictatorship. It is futile to imagine that false dictatorship will vanish until this is done.

The European situation is simply the outward expression, in the various phases of materiality, of what Christian Science, in its advancing unfoldment, has brought to light, namely, that malicious mind through suggestion acts in its last iniquity as malicious minds and directs evil in all its deviltry of killing and destroying the finer sentiments of being—so as finally to "destroy both soul and body in hell", as Jesus indicated. Right knowing and nothing but right knowing can stop the carnage.

You alone are responsible for what is taking place in your world. It is not something "over there" but consciousness right "here". You have full power and authority to think and act rightly. You as the activity of God, divine Mind, must understand your world in its true sense. In so doing remember you are compelling malicious mind to cease its suggestions, which is all that is declaring this turmoil, misery and death.

However, you must recognize that while it is all hypnotic suggestion, nevertheless, just designating it as hypnotism does not change its effect. That simply places it where you can cope with it and refute its destructive madness.

Diagnosing a case is one step. Applying the remedy is the next and more important step. It is in the application that the correctness of the diagnosis is rewarded by the disappearance of the evil. You cannot escape, and you do not wish to escape, your responsibility to judge righteous judgment. Mrs. Eddy urged in Pulpit and Press to, "Know, then, that you possess sovereign power to think and act rightly, and that nothing can dispossess you of this heritage and trespass on Love. If you maintain this position, who or what can cause you to sin or suffer? Our surety is our confidence that we are indeed dwellers in Truth and Love, man's eternal mansion."

The duty of the Christian Scientist is to hold crime in check. One on God's side is a majority. The Christian Scientist does not interfere with Mind, but he certainly does interfere with malicious mental malpractice and its operation. He definitely will not tolerate any discordant condition in world affairs any more than sickness, or storms or other untoward circumstances. He is determined to be about his Father's business, the destruction of everything unlike good.

If the Christian Scientist is not conscious of his power, how can he exercise it and bring good to light? The reason the Christian Scientist must be successful in his endeavor to conquer sin, disease, death, and all limitations is that he is absolutely sure they are not of God. He therefore attacks them with full power and authority, because he knows mesmerism is all that is at work there, and that it is the basis of every erroneous appearance. He refuses to tolerate any false sense of control whether called dictatorship, or totalitarianism, or any other subver-

sive ism, and he promptly destroys them by recognizing all such influence as malicious mental
malpractice.

Thus the command voiced by the prophet
Isaiah is fulfilled, "To loose the bands of wickedness, to undo the heavy burdens, and to let the
oppressed go free, and that ye break every
yoke."

The Christian Scientist detects the evil which
masquerades as good back of the false concept of
dictatorship. He never loses sight of the ruthless
endeavors of malicious mind to dominate. God's
way of imparting good is the exact reverse of
domination; it is always by way of reflection.
"For what things soever He doeth, these also
doeth the Son likewise . . . For the Father loveth
the Son and sheweth him all things that himself
doeth."

Mrs. Eddy in her First Edition of Science and
Health has exposed the nature of the dictatorial
attitude of mortal mind which in the "days to
come", when leaving a matter basis, would operate as pure evil mind. This warning was given
sixty-five years ago. *"In coming years the person or mind that hates his neighbour, will have
no need to traverse his fields, to destroy his flocks
and herds, and spoil his vines; or to enter his
house to demoralize his household; for the evil*

mind will do this through mesmerism; and not in propria persona be seen committing the deed. Unless this terrible hour be met and restrained by Science, mesmerism, that scourge of man, will leave nothing sacred when mind begins to act under direction of conscious power. Sensuous man makes war to the death on his enemies; but the spiritual pours blessings on them unseen and unacknowledged; like the chamomile, that crushed, yields the sweetest odor, spiritual minds emit an atmosphere of Truth that blesses their enemies and destroys error while it is persecuting them; but stir the evil sensual mind, and worse than the deadly Upas are the plagues it emits."

WHY
THE PERSECUTION OF
THE JEW?

IN CONSIDERING this subject it must be distinctly understood that the term Jew is really a misnomer. It is not the Jew as a person that is meant, it is Judaism. Judaism stands as the cause and what is called the Jew is merely the effect.

It is in this sense and this sense alone that the word Jew is used in this article, and in its place Judaism should be substituted, for only by so doing can the impersonal nature of the subject be understood and a right attitude be gained.

When the metaphysician speaks of country, race or people, whether called Germany, or Jew, or Israelites or any other, he is not talking about personality. He is considering states of mind or arguments. All that he is cognizant of is an argument being presented. No one would even know that there was any Europe or Germany or Jew, unless it came as consciousness to him, and came as his own consciousness, as his mind, in the form of an argument. As Christian Scientists you acknowledge this.

Human thought at this time is tremendously stirred and there is a deep desire to understand this problem of the Jews. Why should the Jews be selected for such barbarous persecution as is taking place in many countries today?

No persecution is really barbarous, because every circumstance or experience is really the pressure of Truth forcing the victim higher, and the pressure continues only so long as there is something to press, something resisting.

Mrs. Eddy presents this very forcibly in her Message for 1901 "In Christian Science it is plain that God removes the punishment for sin only as the sin is removed—never punishes it only as it is destroyed, and never afterwards; hence the hope of universal salvation." It makes no difference what the experience, it is the pressure of Truth to force you to higher levels of understanding. But the present question perplexing people is, "Why the world rebellion against the Jew?"

A brief analysis of what is called Bible History may clear up the matter. Abraham stood as the light of the world, he obeyed the voice of God, going out from his father's house—matter —into a land that he knew not of—Mind, and so he won the promise, "In thy seed shall all the families of the earth be blessed."

Now Abraham, from the finite view-point seemed to show forth two mental qualities or characteristics,—the one material and the other spiritual; or as Paul puts it, "Thoughts the mean while accusing or else excusing one another."

With this light of the world called Abraham, there finally seemed to come what might be called a distinct cleavage. In due time what seemed the material and the spiritual phases of Abraham were expressed by two kingdoms. The kingdom of Judah seemed to take the material course and the kingdom of Israel, the spiritual. This of course was all in the domain of thought, and indeed is present at this moment, operating as consciousness with each individual.

The kingdom of Judah was represented by the tribe of Judah—of which the Jew is the direct descendant, together with a portion of the tribe of Benjamin. The kingdom of Israel was represented by the ten tribes, later called "the lost tribes" or "lost sheep of the house of Israel".

According to prophecy these latter tribes were

to be gathered in the "Isles afar off" and to be known by a new name. Thence the branch was to grow over the wall and extend to the ends of the earth, whence Shiloh, the final revelation of Truth, was to come.

All this seemingly has been fulfilled to the letter. The Ten Tribes or House of Israel were gathered in the British Isles. Their new name was Anglo-Saxons or Isaacsons, sons of Isaac. Ephraim, the younger, was the branch that grew over the wall and took root in America. From America has come Shiloh, "and unto him shall the gathering of the people be", in other words, Science and Health, the Comforter, which Jesus said would lead unto all truth.

Judah, the Jew, and Israel, Anglo-Saxondom, in the broad sense are brethren, and the Christian Scientist understands this.

Israel was divided into the two kingdoms of Judah and Israel under Rehoboam, son of Solomon, and the Bible narrative clearly maintains the distinction between these two kingdoms and between the promises which are made concerning each, in all later prophecies.

Judah, with its brilliant materialism, expressed from the beginning the material phase of Abraham. Anything of Abraham must be brilliant, whether it be material or spiritual.

This material brilliancy represented by Judah has been the envy of many mortals, inciting their jealousy and resentment.

Jesus came of the royal line of David, who was of the tribe of Judah. Jesus was the highest human concept, the Way-shower or Exemplar, but he was not the full consummation of the Saviour. He represented the personal, and personality is a phase of materiality which must disappear before the impersonal or Mind-sense of the Saviour can appear in its fullness. Knowing this Jesus said, "It is expedient for you that I go away: for if I go not away, the Comforter will not come unto you; but if I depart, I will send him unto you."

The spirit of Truth was to come, as Jacob originally foresaw, through Israel not through Judah, as Shiloh, impersonality, not personality. It came first as America, and then as Science and Health.

But Judah to this day has held tenaciously to its brilliant materiality. It has been a leader in the material world and succeeded on material lines, but has never been able to compete with or conquer spiritual Israel, because spirituality is always more advanced, hence more powerful than materiality. Spiritual Israel cannot be conquered. That is the reason Anglo-Saxondom, representing Israel, entertains no fear of nor hatred for the Jew. It cannot, for Abraham, "Fidelity; faith in the divine Life and in the eternal Principle of being" as Science and Health defines Abraham, is the father of both their common heritage.

Discrediting Judah, which represents the other branch of Abraham which will finally be united with Israel in the New Jerusalem of understanding, is abnormal and the result of malicious mind. Brilliant materialism and brilliant spirituality go hand in hand until finally materialism is translated back to Mind. The transient, false sense of matter as something to be accumulated, will eventually be uncovered and matter, as such, will no longer be desired.

As already seen the one thing that is not afraid of Judah, with all its material ability, is spirituality. All others who themselves trust to material sense are afraid as well as jealous of the Jew, —afraid that his genius for materiality will appropriate everything.

You ask why the Jew should be persecuted for profiting in materiality? The answer is: The Jew is bringing this persecution upon himself, but not on account of his possession of material things, which he, like all other mortals, is entitled to if he earns them. Material wealth is not, after all, a thing—it is a state of mind. Why should we not wish God-speed unto all in gaining wealth? You would limit no one in attaining the multiplication table, because you are not afraid that someone else's having it would deprive you of it.

But the difficulty with the Jew is all within himself. He refuses to listen to that inward voice of Spirit, which is always present with him because he is of the seed of Abraham. Instead, he has become absorbed in the one purpose of gaining material prosperity to the neglect of spiritual growth. When Judah decides that he has had enough of materiality and puts forth sincere effort to cultivate his innate spiritual sense, then the persecution will cease, because there is no further purpose in it. As Mrs. Eddy says, in Miscellany, "When these things cease to bless, they will cease to occur". If you think the Jewish persecution has anything to do with Germans or Italians or any other race, as persons, you are denying the allness of the one Mind, the one infinite Person.

When you receive punishment, it is because you have let in the foe,—you have listened to the directed malicious arguments of limitation that would rob you of health, wealth and happiness.

Do not think you can escape meeting these

insidious arguments coming as your ego, your I, any more than Judah can escape refuting eventually the suggestions that now make him say, "I will not listen to the voice of Spirit." It is the unwillingness of Judah to let spirituality, his heritage from Abraham, govern, that is the cause of all his troubles.

The same malicious animal magnetism that caused the Jews to persecute and crucify Jesus is now causing and for centuries has caused the Germans and others to persecute him.

It was not the Jew who originated the deviltry loosed upon Jesus, and it is not persons or races who are responsible for like deviltry today. All are victims of malicious mind, "the great dragon . . . called the Devil and Satan which deceiveth the whole world."

This thought is elucidated in Science and Health in the statement, "It is the animal instinct in mortals, which would impel them to devour each other and cast out devils through Beelzebub." And again, "The author is convinced that the accusations against Jesus of Nazareth and even his crucifixion were instigated by the criminal instinct here described."

During the world war, when Germany seemed to be trying to destroy the English language— the clothing of Science and Health, "the young child"—you understood that it was not Germany but the activity of malicious evil. Neither Hitler, Stalin, Mussolini nor any other person is responsible for the confusion of the world today. Take the entire condition of world affairs back to God and uncover the arguments of reversal as the operation of malicious malpractice, and you find the solution of the whole affair. Do this if you would destroy every mirage of evil.

Jesus said, "Woe unto the world because of offences! for it must needs be that offences come; but woe to that man by whom the offence cometh!" This being so, cannot we leave the punishment of all sin to that divine Principle that punishes only to the point of the destruction of the error? The "son of perdition", the one sinner, will, as Science and Health points out, "receive its full penalty, both for what it is and for what it does."

If any of you have been tempted to make these questions *personal* resist the suggestion vigorously and at once. Just ask yourself the question, "Am I, too, a vicious malpractitioner, or am I a Christian Scientist?" Is any of it "over there" or is it all "here"?

How is the cause of Christian Science to go forward if the metaphysician allows himself to be mesmerized into dealing with person, place or thing instead of going through to God as All-in-all? When you stop short of God, then, do not be surprised if you experience confusion—sin, sickness or death—for how can you be saved from it if you open the door to it?

Remember, as Mrs. Eddy points out in Miscellany, "Animal magnetism, in its ascending steps of evil, entices its victim by unseen, silent arguments."

Considering a subject like this compels the Christian Scientist to realize how dangerous it is for him to talk about what appear as personalities.

The whole tendency, unless most carefully guarded against, is to mesmerize one into thinking in terms of "over there" or "out there", and such thinking can only end in confusion. In fact it is not really thinking at all, it is just dreaming.

You know there is no Jewish race "over there" which is being punished in order to make it regain its spirituality as the "seed" of Abraham. There is nothing "out there" to be punished; what good would that do? Am I not the one who has to do the regaining if I believe that anything has been lost? Am I not the thief if I believe in thieving? Did not Jesus say "And I if I be lifted up from the earth will draw all men unto me"? Was not this lifting up from the "earth" being lifted above the mesmerism that there is something apart from one, here and now?

For progress it is essential for the Christian Scientist to be ever on guard, for malicious mental malpractice is based on personalities and an "over there", instead of the eternal heavenly "here" which embraces within itself the right sense of "here", all good.

It is impossible to emphasize too strongly the great need to avoid all "over there". In Christian Science it is all "here" and "now". If it were not here and now you could have no cognizance of anything. You know this. Then see that you do not supply malicious mind with this chord of belief in an "over there", on which to play its tune of evil suggestion.

"UNSELFED"

THE commonly accepted definition of unselfed, by which is meant to be unselfish, is
entirely separate from and unlike the metaphysical meaning of the word.

Unselfishness, as humanly interpreted, is full
of personalities, and to be unselfish means to be
doing for or giving to others, whereas to be unselfed, in the true metaphysical or spiritual
sense, is the exact opposite. It has absolutely no
personality attached to it. It is centered entirely
on God as All-in-all. Every thought begins with
God, and flows from Him, enfolding His presentation of Himself in all the beauty, glory and
completeness of His own being.

God does not give, He *is*, and man is His
showing forth.

To be unselfed means, never to harbor a
thought which starts from effect. To think in
terms of effect is to mentally malpractise because

it is accepting something aside from God, the one cause. You have learned that you cannot mentally malpractise without doing so maliciously, for all wrong thought, being finite, has only one result, death, and death always means maliciousness, "the last enemy".

Then to be unselfed means to start with cause, God, and to find Him as the basis and substance of all being.

Mrs. Eddy once said, *"There is only one way through, and only one, and that is to become unselfed."* Impersonality and unselfedness go hand in hand because both start with God, as causation, and never with effect. Effect,—in other words, what is seen,—to the spiritually minded is like the image in the mirror. Its one and only purpose is to testify to the substance of the image, the object before the mirror, the cause, and never to itself, the effect.

To do this is to become unselfed, and is the only way to be impersonally and spiritually minded.

"FOR SATAN FINDS
SOME MISCHIEF STILL
FOR IDLE HANDS TO DO."

WATTS

NO STATEMENT could be truer than that the devil, malicious mental malpractice, always finds work for idle hands,—idle minds—to do.

The Christian Scientist must think seriously about this question. If he is not constantly active on the side of Truth he can rest assured that malicious mental malpractice is right at his door.

That is the danger of an attitude of thought like, "Let God do it". It is a waiting attitude; an endeavor to make one's thought a blank, and Jesus warned of the danger of this, for he said, "When the unclean spirit is gone out of a man, he walketh through dry places, seeking rest, and finding none, then he saith, I will return unto my house from whence I came out;

And when he is come, he findeth it empty, swept, and garnished.

Then goeth he, and taketh with himself seven other spirits more wicked than himself; and they enter in, and dwell there; and the last state of that man is worse than the first".

Why is it worse? Because the poor victim thought he had thoroughly cleaned his house, and lo and behold, Satan is again dwelling therein.

Such disappointment cannot come to you if thoroughly cleaning your "house", means replacing every erroneous sense with the true sense, so completely filling it that Satan—evil suggestion,—can find no sanctuary there. Mrs. Eddy declares in Miscellany, "There is no door through which evil can enter, and no space for evil to fill in a mind filled with goodness. Good thoughts are an impervious armor; clad therewith you are completely shielded from the attacks of error of every sort."

Christian Scientists must never be careless about replacing the wrong sense that is cast out, with the right sense, so that evil will find no door unbarred, and no vacant room to occupy. They must not take the attitude of crying, "Peace, peace; when there is no peace". Peace can be won and maintained only when we have fought the Holy War and have put up such a fight that evil is cast out forever—seen in its true sense.

Who does not yearn for peace? But today it is the coward, under evil's direction who calls for peace. The battle for Truth has not yet been won. Only malicious mental malpractice would say it has, in order to encourage you to stop the warfare. Never forget that the sword cannot be put up until it has first been drawn.

Christian Scientists are soldiers of the cross, and they must fight until victory is theirs. Evil is ever urging us to cease fighting and "let God do it". God cannot do more than He has already done. He has done all. It is the work of the Christian Scientist to prove that,—to show that forth.

If evil can persuade you, the Christian Scientist, to relax, it will have accomplished its purpose. It will then,—after all your years of work and faithfulness, when you think that you are at the point of enjoying the reward of your labors with your "house" nicely cleaned,—enter in and rob you of the fruits of your effort. It does this because you have listened to the voice of the charmer, admonishing you not to be so vigorous in your denunciation of malicious animal magnetism, because God is Love, and Love does everything and cares for everyone. True enough, but has not God always been Love, and has He not always taken the same tender care of all His creation? How can He be "about to do" something that He has not already done?

Then it is our work to begin vigorously to prove that God is Love, and that He is proving His care by making His children active and alert.

We have work to do ourselves; we cannot expect God to do our work. He cannot hear that kind of prayer. He hears only the prayer of being active about His business. As Mrs. Eddy says, in Miscellaneous Writings, "Be active, and, however slow, thy success is sure; toil is triumph."

If you succeed in making your mind a blank, thinking that by thus doing you can place yourself in a listening attitude to hear God's voice, you have let the bars down and opened your house for the devil's entrance. That idle, listless mood is exactly the opportunity evil desires, and Satan will quickly find something to fill idle minds.

Keep active and no matter how slow your progress may seem to be, success in the end is assured.

Guard against a negative watch that would lull you to sleep, that would make you believe a listless peace is lasting peace. Today the only peace is the sword of Truth.

One, who was Mrs. Eddy's secretary for several years, told me on two or three occasions of Mrs. Eddy's distress, almost despair even, at times, when she thought of what would become of the Christian Scientist when she was no longer here to arouse him to wakeful and vigorous activity.

I can dimly see what she was thinking,—that malicious mental malpractice would so beguile the Christian Scientist with a false sense of peace, that he would be robbed of all his opposition to its subtle arguments, and so, little by little, darkness would take the place of light and the world would sink back into blackness.

This will inevitably take place if we become indolent and imagine that all we have to do is to listen for God's voice. *We* need to *be* the voice of God, and to be about His business every instant. We cannot rest. Malicious argument is always trying to lull us to sleep. To be on guard continually is our only protection. As Longfellow's Psalm of Life states it,

"Let us then be up and doing,
With a heart for any fate;
Still achieving, still pursuing,
Learn to labor, and to wait."

The waiting is while you are laboring, not while you are inactive. And is it not, also, exactly what Christ Jesus meant in his Revelation to John when he declared, after he had opened the seventh seal, "there was silence in heaven about the space of half an hour." Is not this silence the active silencing of all evil suggestion through the realization of God's eternal allness?

Cast out the siren of indolent peace, and demand that your peace be a conscious, ever active peace; the understanding of what peace really is. To be deceived with a ghastly pretense of peace is but the effect of the poisonous soporific fumes of malicious suggestion.

Mrs. Eddy declares in Miscellaneous Writings, "Mental darkness is senseless error, neither intelligence nor power, and its victim is responsible for its supposititious presence."

As genuine Christian Scientists, followers of one Leader, let us not be deceived by subtle platitudes clothed in words of gentleness and peace which are so alluring as to endanger the unsuspecting. Some of the most beautiful plants and flowers are the most deadly. To-day there is no excuse for ignorance or idleness. "If at present satisfied with wrong doing, we must learn to loathe it. If at present content with idleness, we must become dissatisfied with it", as Science and Health declares.

THE LAW
OF
REVERSAL

THERE is only one law of reversal, God's
law, the law that by virtue of its own infinite
goodness, is the spontaneous destruction or
reversal of everything unlike good. Mesmerism
operates to make the Christian Scientist, when
he uses the term "law of reversal" immediately
associate it with evil. If he does this he is incapable of understanding this law.

However, no claim of law is nearer to the
heart of evil, or is more necessary, in belief, for
its maintenance than the perverted sense of the
law of reversal, which is evil's very being. The
human mind, through being the negation or suppositional opposite of the divine Mind, is the reverse of all that divine Mind is. Therefore, the
law of reversal operates as the supposed law of

the action of the human mind. As progress is the
law of God, so reversal is the action of evil.

Then it is not strange to find the perverted
sense of the law of reversal confronting the
Christian Scientist at every forward step. In the
final manifestation of evil,—Satan standing in
"the holy place" as pure malicious argument, as
shown forth in malicious mental malpractice,
the malpractitioner voicing Satan is found using,
by perversion, the law of reversal consistently in
defending his own wickedness.

By the fraudulent use of the law of reversal,
evil automatically endeavors to reverse the
thought put forward by the Christian Scientist
in denying evil. It changes this into an affirmation *for* evil. By so doing it seeks to nullify the
truthful statements which deny presence or
power to evil, and, if not guarded against, it may
seem to succeed in accomplishing its purpose.

But if the Scientist heeds Jesus' statement, "A
new commandment I give unto you, that ye love
one another", the whole process changes. Confronted with love and the statement that right
where the evil seems to be there is the very presence of Love and the infinite power of Truth,
malpractice must follow its own self-made law
that the reverse of your statement is true; and,
reversed, love becomes hatred and destruction

and the law of torment to the evil itself. Thus the victory is won.

Then is not the remedy for every vicious argument of evil, love? The greater the love the more destructive it becomes to the claims of evil, verifying Mrs. Eddy's statement in Mental Practice in Miscellaneous Writings: "Thus a mental malpractitioner may lose his power to harm by a false mental argument."

Another point that the Christian Scientist must understand is that this law of reversal is used by evil continually to reverse all the Christian Scientist's earnest efforts to accomplish good. This belief of law must be defeated by knowing that God's law of reversal is the only law of reversal and is ever operative for good, reversing every erroneous effort and belief. If this is not understood, your work may be frustrated at every point. It is useless to bemoan this, for it is the fact. The claim operates whether you like it or not, and you must handle it or it will handle you.

It should be remembered that evil further uses this law of reversal to turn one back to material belief in all things, and so to turn one away from discerning evil as pure mental iniquity. Thinking of evil as material is to hide its real nature. It is thus evil hopes to make its lie continuous. "Laws" of material belief are looked upon as continuing "laws", and the beliefs resulting from them as continuous beliefs, until they ultimate, in what is called "natural" death. Therefore, the purpose of evil is to make its suggestions operate as old diseased beliefs. If it succeeds in making its victim believe his trouble is material, it has forestalled its hypnotic influence being discerned and thus destroyed.

Do not be deceived into thinking that it is ever natural for you not to have all good. Good is man's natural heritage and being. Your every desire is already satisfied by divine Mind, for you do not originate it. That desire is of Mind. Then it is the false sense of the law of reversal that is stopping the fulfillment of your dearest hopes. Even your good deeds are reversed, in belief, by this spurious law of evil.

It must never be forgotten that the suppositional law of reversal is the opposite of the actual law of reversal, which is continually and unceasingly operating to reverse everything that comes to you as suggestion and to put it in its true place as the presence of God. The latter law is obviously the law of progress, because it brings you eventually to the point of seeing God as All-in-all. The "law" of reversal, as the weapon of evil, is the suppositional opposite of the law of progress.

Knowing this it should not be difficult to rise to the realization that you are a law unto yourself and to refuse to allow malicious mental malpractice to harm you under any circumstances, *"either when asleep or when awake,"* as Mrs. Eddy phrases it.

Since the reverse of a lie is the truth, you can utilize this law of reversal so that every argument of evil to harm you will become a blessing, because you know that the law of reversal operates to that very end. "No weapon that is formed against thee shall prosper" Isaiah said. Why? Because the law of reversal is God's law whereby God is the spontaneous law of reversal to everything unlike Himself, to all evil.

HOW DOES
MALICIOUS MIND
OPERATE?

TO HAVE a complete sense of freedom, it is
essential for the Christian Scientist to understand that malicious mind has no possible
way of bringing evil directly to pass. Malicious
mind cannot operate directly to bring about
either sin, sickness, death, limitation or any condition. It is self evident malicious mind, the one
erroneous malpractitioner, cannot argue with
such lies because it knows they are lies and that
you are neither sinful, sick, dead nor limited; or
the malpractitioner would not be trying to bring
these conditions about. There could then be no
conviction in the mind of the malicious arguer
that what it is arguing is true; and without conviction there could be no result.

So, it becomes essential for the accomplishment of this purpose, for the malpractitioner first, to find an innocent channel through whom it can operate, and then, to make that channel believe that the lies it is stating about another are true. If it can do this, it has obtained an honest conviction and started a malicious attack, for honest conviction carries with it mind-power and the possibility of accomplishment.

How does evil do this? By both silent and audible argument it convinces the one it is endeavoring to use as its channel, that its intended victim is sick, dying, poverty-stricken, intemperate, hateful, discouraged or any of the things it is intent upon producing. If it succeeds, it has started an honest conviction of the reality of these lies about its victim and there ensues active malicious mental malpractice, which, if accepted, finally destroys the victim.

Mrs. Eddy brings this out in her article, Mental Practice, in Miscellaneous Writings, where she says that if "people believe that a man is sick and knows it, and speak of him as being sick, put it into the minds of others that he is sick, publish it in the newspapers that he is failing, and persist in this action of mind over mind, it follows that he will believe that he is sick,—and Jesus said it would be according to the woman's belief; but if with the certainty of Science he knows that an error of belief has not the power of Truth, and cannot, does not, produce the slightest effect, it has no power over him".

Does not this show how evil works by the action of mind over mind? But in order to get results, there must always be conviction on the part of the thinker, for conviction is the mind quality that operates in the realm of mentality. Arguments do not operate unless accompanied by conviction. As Science and Health declares, "Be thoroughly persuaded in your own mind concerning the truth which you think or speak, and you will be the victor."

In this way you see how you can become your own mental malpractitioner by applying to yourself the arguments of evil hypnotically suggested to you. You can operate as this innocent victim just as effectively as can another, if you accept the lies of the malpractitioner. If you do not refute these lies, but accept them as reality, you will malpractise on yourself until you eventually become powerless to break the mesmerism confronting you.

Are you going to tolerate such irrationality? Of course not. Then reject each lie with the truth you know about yourself, the Self of you, until you no longer listen either complacently, or fearfully, to anything that does not emanate from God, the one cause.

Denounce evil in all its ways and especially as hypnotic suggestion. You cannot afford to be gentle in your denunciation of malicious animal magnetism. It is a deadly mental poison, and if not guarded against, neutralized and destroyed by translation back to God, will accomplish its purpose of destroying you.

Evil to the Christian Scientist, is not an intelligent devil, going around like a roaring lion seeking whom he may devour, but is simply the suppositional opposite of his own understanding of divine Mind. Thus as Paul put it, and as the Christian Scientist understands it, he can never be tempted beyond what he is able, for he has only to apply what he knows of God to find his way of escape, that he "may be able to bear it", and rise triumphant from the experience.

It is only lack of understanding that makes a Christian Scientist afraid of malicious mental malpractice. It should be evident to the merest novice in Christian Science that there could be no suppositional opposite to what he does not know. Thus it is his knowing alone that he is called upon to defend. Evil does not operate as something "over there" outside of one's own mentality; it always operates as the negative of what one knows. It is this negation that the Christian Scientist must guard against and not an imaginary foe seeking to destroy him. Understanding evil is but the negation of the truth he knows makes him the master of every situation. Therefore, constant watchfulness is necessary to be true to what one knows.

The Christian Scientist instinctively knows it is easier to heal a lie of malicious mind operating as a law of hypnotic suggestion, than to heal a lie of the same malicious mind operating as a natural law. This is on the same basis that an acute claim seems easier to meet than a chronic claim. This is, also, the reason why malicious argument invariably takes the form of a natural appearance suggesting the working of a law of nature, or matter, or heredity, or something of that sort, thus making the deception complete. This tends to confuse the earnest Scientist by again presenting that which he had felt had been destroyed, as a belief of a law of relapse. Thus the deviltry of evil appears as a normal or natural claim of matter.

The Christian Scientist must understand that he should be willing to meet under the rule of malicious mental malpractice every lie of belief that he formerly had to meet under the rule of materiality in its simpler forms of matter. Jesus said, "First the blade, then the ear, after that the full corn in the ear." The blade contains all that the full corn in the ear contains, but it is less developed. This can be applied to the solving of the various phenomena of malicious mind appearing as simple materiality. The blade has little of evil visible. Nevertheless, the whole of evil is there, and eventually emerges when malicious mental malpractice, the full corn in the ear, is revealed in all its depravity, stripped of every appearance of good. As Mrs. Eddy asked in Retrospection and Introspection "Art thou still unacquainted with thyself? Then be introduced to this self. 'Know thyself!' as said the classic Grecian motto. Note well the falsity of this mortal self! Behold its vileness and remember this poverty-stricken 'stranger that is within thy gates'."

Then be willing to meet every phase of evil as malicious suggestion, just as in the beginning of your career as a Christian Scientist you were eager to meet every claim of matter. If you remain wide awake and rejoice in crossing swords with this final phase of evil as pure malicious suggestion, you will enjoy your journey from sense to Soul. You will never murmur or be discouraged, but will be filled with new hope and assurance that what you know of divine Mind and its operations is sufficient to meet and destroy every lie of evil.

Jesus said, there is nothing hidden that shall not be revealed. He meant this in a way we have yet to learn. The Christian Scientist realizes and declares in his treatment, "I know all that I need to know about this case and I know it immediately". Why? Because God, being the one intelligence, knows all things and therefore, there is nothing hidden from infinite intelligence, nor from that which shows God forth. It would be useless for God to know something, unless His man knew it also. Otherwise God would have no way of expressing His knowing. Hence the practitioner of God declares, "I do know all I need to know about this case," and he acts accordingly. It is the same in the case of malicious sin as in sickness. The practitioner must know about that, all that he needs to know, and he must and does know it instantly.

It is the part of wisdom to keep every channel open for information. You have a right to know all that is going on about you. You do not delve into error, but you keep your avenues of intelligence open, so all that you should know you do know at exactly the right time. In other words, as Mrs. Eddy says in Miscellaneous Writings, "Let us open our affections to the Principle that

moves all in harmony,—from the falling of a
sparrow to the rolling of a world."

Nothing is either too insignificant or too important for you to know, if it is right for you to
know it. And you cannot know it if it is not right.
You must realize this, for evil's suggestion is
quite as likely to fill you with a lot of unnecessary
trash as to stop you from knowing that which
you should know. Be on your guard!

One thing especially every Christian Scientist
should know and must know from what has been
established, and that is how easily he can become
an innocent tool of malicious mental malpractice
by passing around idle chatter about persons,
places or things. Believing what is said to be true
does not free one from being the tool of malicious mental malpractice and, therefore, from being about the devil's business. There is only one
way to be sure of not being the tool of evil, and
that is by basing all that is said on God as the one
cause, always starting from God and beholding
all effect as the emanation of God.

A PARTICULARLY
SUBTLE OPERATION
OF
MALICIOUS MENTAL MALPRACTICE

IT IS difficult to conceive a more subtle and disastrous way for malicious mental malpractice to operate in order to confuse and obscure, if not entirely obliterate the light of Truth for a Christian Scientist, than by the perpetual argument that Mrs. Eddy was not the discoverer of Christian Science; that it had been discovered before and that Mrs. Eddy had stolen the discovery and claimed the glory.

Is it such an easy thing to steal Christian Science, and so demonstrate it that one acquires all the glory? The works of Christian Science in healing every manner of sin, sickness and death, are, of course, its glory and these are what Mrs.

Eddy demonstrated in establishing Christian Science.

Why should a Christian Scientist question the truth of Mrs. Eddy's discovery or accept so patent a suggestion of devilishness? If he entertains the question it is because he is unaware of what is operating as his mind. Otherwise he would instantly reject it and free himself from its malign influence.

If one wished to destroy another's interest in any subject, would he not begin by casting reflections on the authority back of the subject? If successful in planting doubts as to the honor and integrity of that authority, would he not very quickly succeed in killing all further interest? This is exactly evil's purpose in making such suggestions to one beginning the study of Christian Science. It is a deadly purpose, and its result is inevitable if the malicious intent is not discerned and repudiated.

No Christian Scientist can afford to doubt this. His days as a Christian Scientist are numbered if he is not instant in season and out of season in casting out these vicious suggestions of malicious mental malpractice. He cannot play with evil suggestions. Their poison is far reaching. I have yet to see a Christian Scientist who allows his thought to be darkened by evil suggestions about Mrs. Eddy, or her discovery, or her demonstration of Christian Science, make a success of Christian Science. It is impossible. The discoverer and the discovery, the revelator and the revelation, invariably combine as one and the victim of malicious mental malpractice, alone, questions this truism.

Further, if he can be made to doubt or question the fact that the "little book" of Revelation, Science and Health, completely and finally reveals the translation of the negation back to Mind, he will be equally "lost". He will be looking for some further "revelation" to excuse his present lack of demonstration of his oneness with God. "Truth is revealed. It needs only to be practised," as Science and Health points out. No one can afford to harbor evil suggestions.

Can a sane Christian Scientist doubt for a moment that this is true? Let the one who is allowing his thought to be tampered with in this way, intelligently examine his thinking. If honest, he will see that Christian Science has lost its joy and inspiration for him and that he is looking at it as cold philosophy or an abstraction, instead of as the loving, quickening presence of God. His light has gone and as Jesus said, "If, therefore, the light that is in thee be darkness, how great is that darkness?"

A short time ago I received a letter from a friend saying he had been distressed to find that earlier writers had discovered Christian Science, and that Mrs. Eddy knew of what they had written, and had gleaned her ideas from them without giving them credit.

This friend is usually a clear thinker, but he had utterly failed to ask himself whether it is conceivable that the discoverer of Christian Science, whoever that discoverer might be, could under any imaginable circumstances keep his discovery from the world? Would not the mind that made that discovery spontaneously show forth the fruits of it by healing the sick, the sinning and the dying? No discoverer could have done otherwise than did Mrs. Eddy. But did anyone else show forth such fruits?

What is the discovery of Christian Science? Is it not as Mrs. Eddy states in Rudimental Divine Science, "the law of God, the law of good, interpreting and demonstrating the divine Principle and rule of universal harmony"? Then how could anyone, discovering that law, fail to express it? Christian Science is not the discovery of a matter-law but of Mind-law and the mind that discovers it would have to be in accord with the Mind it discovered, otherwise the discovery could not be made. Christian Science is a spiritual discovery, not a material one. It is of Mind, not of matter.

How absurd to imagine that anyone could discover Christian Science and not use it in such a manner that the whole world could see it. Inevitably it would be his very Mind and would have to be expressed.

Because God, as Science and Health says, "is not separate from the wisdom He bestows", He could not have failed to bestow upon the one near enough to Him to discover His allness, the ability to prove that allness in doing the works which Jesus did.

Who has ever scientifically done this except Mrs. Eddy? Even Mrs. Eddy's followers are but slowly discerning the path she so clearly and carefully pioneered. The slowness of this progress is almost a disgrace to the discovery. Why this slowness? Fundamentally it is due to lack of real spiritual consecration, together with ignorance of that which causes the slowness. It is because malicious mental malpractice with its insidious suggestions is accepted, instead of being rejected the instant it raises its voice. Until this is done, the progress must be slow.

The consecrated Christian Scientist understands that Christian Science was the Mind of Mrs. Eddy, just as God was the Mind of Jesus.

Mrs. Eddy could not be less than one with her Mind. To love God as divine Mind and leave Mrs. Eddy out of that love is not possible and must inevitably end in failure and disillusionment.

The Pharisees thought they could love God and hate Jesus and the prophets who had shown God forth. But could they succeed in this attempt? No, it was a dismal failure and their cup of bitterness was full to the brim. God and His idea cannot be separated, consequently sorrow comes to the one who tries to separate them. Noumenon and phenomenon are forever one.

The Christian Scientist should guard against the subtle malicious argument intended to poison him, no matter in how small a degree against Mrs. Eddy, and thus against Christian Science.

"ALERTNESS
TO
DUTY"

MARY BAKER EDDY

IN ORDER to progress, the Christian Scientist, must pray daily for deliverance from the hypnosis which makes him believe that it is chance instead of *"direction by malicious minds that are at work"*, producing all the various phases of discord and disease with which he is constantly confronted.

Nothing could be more pernicious than this argument of Satan, because if the Christian Scientist can be misled into dealing with the seen instead of the unseen, evil will continue its domination and control and the cause of Christian Science will seem to disappear. Did not true Christianity seem to become enmeshed by the same subtle influences?

Evil cannot be destroyed unless recognized as the influence and result of evil appearing as *"direction by malicious minds"*, and cast out as such. When all evil is seen and understood as "direction by malicious minds" it is readily destroyed. To quote again Mrs. Eddy's full statement, *"If any honest Christian Scientist can be deceived into believing that it is chance, not direction by malicious minds which are at work,—that ignorance instead of sin is what he has to meet at all times,—this error prevents him from understanding enough of the question to insure his own defense, and leaves him in the power of animal magnetism,—perhaps temporarily relieved of his suffering, rejoicing in a hope of freedom which he afterwards finds to be in vain."*

Test this for yourself. But remember that the only way to destroy this insidious influence and direction is to see first the nothingness of the whole lie of malicious influence, and then feel in your heart that God is the one and only Mind and therefore His direction is the only direction and is your direction.

There can be no true love without this understanding that all evil appears as the operation of malicious minds. But be sure that you understand that this appearance is just the language of evil itself,—otherwise, evil must seem personal and the so-called persons expressing it the devil. The devil you cannot love. So if you really desire to show forth God as Love by loving, you must see that the whole of sin, disease and death, including, of course, every sense of finiteness, all phases of malicious dispositions and characteristics, are the direct influence of malicious minds and have nothing to do with the person expressing them, except in so far as he is victimized into voicing them. Did not Jesus declare, "but whosoever shall say, thou fool, shall be in danger of hell fire"? Why? Because that made evil personal and impossible to heal.

Watch unceasingly on this point, because this same secret influence will argue to you that it is not *"direction by malicious minds"* but just your own thinking that is at work. Evil must argue this way because, if you were convinced that all error is *"direction by malicious minds"*, evil's day would be doomed.

Keep reminding yourself, that evil is not something "over there", malicious mind or minds, for that is only as it seems. It is always right "here", operating as your mind. It seems to be "over there", because it is evil appearing as consciousness, and consciousness must have that whereby it is made known. You are not deceived for you know that evil is always one and always here. However numerous its appearances and regardless of where, you rejoice at its so-called multiplicity because that constantly declares the infinity of good that it negates.

Oh that pen could express the infinite importance of being alert! What a change would take place with the Christian Scientist! Apathy would vanish and confidence would reign, and finally evil would cease its arguments, having been reversed,—translated into its true language— good.

But just so long as a cancer is thought of as misplaced cells, tuberculosis as a diseased lung, diabetes as diseased pancreas, bad temper as an ugly disposition, a thief as an unprincipled scoundrel, a murderer as a vicious villain and so on, such conditions cannot be healed. They are never what they appear to be, but are always the result of *"direction by malicious minds."*

The only remedy is to replace the belief of *"direction by malicious minds"* with the absolute realization that all direction is by divine Mind. You know you are never dealing with aught but Mind,—never with a thing. For as Science and Health declares "All is infinite Mind and its infinite manifestation, for God is All-in-all."

Unwillingness to accept this truth bars the door of your mind to beholding its inestimably beneficent power and leaves you at the mercy of the subtle influence of *"direction by malicious minds"*.

Why cling to evil's arguments? Arouse yourself and throw off the mesmerism that would hold you in ignorance of what is terrorizing you with its suggestions. Mesmerism has no power to harm you and cannot act as your mind if you are awake to its operations. But if you will not awaken and handle this evil you will dream on in the darkness of "chaos and old night."

What could make an earnest Christian Scientist, one who for many years has faithfully striven to practise Christian Science, become dissatisfied with it or with his demonstration of it? What could cause him to be attracted by writers whose theories and ideas of Being are so unlike the exact statements made by Mrs. Eddy in Science and Health and her other writings, which he previously loved so deeply and found so helpful? It should be far more natural for him to hold tenaciously to that which he has proved to be true, in however slight a degree, than to be thus attracted. That is what he would do, were it not for the malicious arguments of the mental malpractitioners deliberately attempting to substitute their argument of unbelief and dissatisfaction for his natural inclination and confidence.

It is wholly unnatural for a Christian Scientist, left to his own impulse, to turn from what he knows to be the truth of Being. Nothing but wilful and malicious interference could cause such a catastrophe. It is entirely the result of mischievous suggestion exercised for the sole purpose of harassing and distressing him, and finally putting out his light. The only remedy is to destroy the belief that there is malicious mind to operate as malicious mental malpractitioners influencing and controlling his thinking. This is his only help. He should use it at once.

If he does not apply this remedy his light will fail and finally be extinguished and he will be under the delusion that he no longer cares for Christian Science. But he knows he does care for Christian Science. He knows he loves Christian Science. He knows it is the one and only way to obtain heaven and harmony here and now and he will not allow any subtle suggestion, calling itself his mind to rob him of this knowing.

Mrs. Eddy lovingly admonishes in Science and Health, "Wait for your reward, and 'be not weary in well doing'. If your endeavors are beset by fearful odds, and you receive no present reward, go not back to error, nor become a sluggard in the race.

"When the smoke of battle clears away, you

will discern the good you have done and receive
according to your deserving. Love is not hasty
to deliver us from temptation, for Love means
that we shall be tried and purified."

Pray to be delivered from a false sense of
peace, which would lead you into handling that
which has no real bearing on the case. The law
of Christ or Christian Science opens our eyes to
the fact that all error is malicious animal magnetism and every erroneous condition the specific
result of *"direction by malicious minds"* and not
one's own thought.

Was it not to emphasize this that Mrs. Eddy
felt it imperative to state in her Church Manual,
under the significant heading of "Alertness to
Duty", that it was the duty of every Christian
Scientist "to defend himself daily against aggressive mental suggestion and not be made to forget
nor to neglect his duty to God, to his Leader and
to mankind." Notice the "daily". Do you think
Mrs. Eddy would have made that request unless
this "defense" was of paramount importance?
You know as metaphysicians that this is true and
you also know that if you do not pray daily you
will shipwreck your progress. It is not surprising
that Mrs. Eddy should add, in the same connection, that by your works ye "shall be judged,—
and justified or condemned." Why? Because

your works will show whether or not you are defending yourself against aggressive mental suggestion and destroying the *"direction by malicious minds"*.

One of the most insidious and aggressive forms of this *"direction by malicious minds"* comes as the pollution of the "air" by hourly and daily harangues and mental absurdities. Because radio has many uses, it has by the false sense of the law of reversal, many abuses.

Since radio is rarefied matter it is a nearer approximation to mentality, hence its hidden danger and the great need for carefully guarding against the subtlety of its use for suggestions, political, financial and religious. The Christian Scientist must think alone with God, and preserve the tablet of his mind "from every blemish free".

There is only one way to counteract this constant effort of *"malicious minds"* to direct your every act and that is to be consciously directed by divine Mind every moment. To insure this continuous direction requires constant alertness and watchfulness,—never to deal with effect but always with cause.

WHAT CONSTITUTES
BEING AWAKE TO
THE SUGGESTIONS
OF
MALICIOUS MENTAL MALPRACTICE?

SCIENCE and Health declares, "More than profession is requisite for Christian demonstration. Few understand or adhere to Jesus' divine precepts for living and healing. Why? Because his precepts require the disciple to cut off the right hand and pluck out the right eye,—that is, to set aside even the most cherished beliefs and practices, to leave all for Christ."

To be an alert Christian Scientist is not easy. It requires the same quality of earnestness and sacrifice which success in any line of work demands.

First comes consecration,—willingness to forsake the ease of material sense for the attainment of the goal. And secondly perseverance, which never ceases working until that goal is attained. Jesus said, in illustrating this ceaseless perseverance and its inevitable result, "Though he will not rise and give him because he is his friend, yet because of his importunity he will rise and give him as many as he needeth."

Physical courage has always been lauded by the human mind, but moral courage, which is a higher sense of courage,—a nearer approximation to Mind activity—is seldom recognized.

In Christian Science moral as well as physical courage is requisite. Science and Health says, "It requires courage to utter truth." At times it also requires tremendous so-called physical courage to meet the lies of material sense when it declares pain, suffering and anguish to be real and true. But every Christian Scientist has learned with joy that, when he stands unflinchingly on what he knows is true, the reward is great. He also knows that sooner or later every question must be settled on the side of right, and that regardless of the degree of moral and physical courage required, the present tests do not become lighter to the one who puts off doing the thing he knows is right. The old saying, "Procrastination is the thief of time" is truer perhaps in the practice and demonstration of Christian Science than in any other activity.

Duty postponed does not thereby become easier, but the reverse, for usually a conscience-stricken sense of unrest torments when work is left undone.

Christian Science insists upon doing to-day, the work of to-day, and understanding what that work is, and because of the allness of Mind, finds abundant time for its accomplishment. When work is well done, malicious mental malpractice can find no way to reach you—no antenna through which its suggestions can operate. Remember your antenna is constantly operating. Watch that it is ever in oneness with God.

The Christian Scientist is actively about his Father's business. He is wide awake to the fact that evil ever keeps pace with good and he acts accordingly. He is not hurried, but to him each hour is valuable. Because God is constantly unfolding to His own idea the infinity of good, the wise man does not miss this wondrous unfoldment. He knows that infinity itself is not too long to show forth the glories of infinite Mind.

The Apostle Paul said that Jesus "for the joy that was set before him, endured the cross, despising the shame, and is set down at the right hand of the throne of God." The Christian Scientist, like Jesus, does not make too much of the cross because, in translating the cross back to the crown, he knows "the joy" that is set before him and continually awaiting his acceptance.

If the practice of Christian Science takes a full measure of physical and moral courage, it is worth it. Then give it your all. The "pearl priceless" is obtained only by selling all that thou hast, and buying it. Buying it means exchanging every material concept for the spiritual sense through consecrated insistency. It is not giving up things, but concepts. If this seems a hard cross, it is made easy by the discernment of its true nature as the negation of God, which offers you when reversed the very presence of all good; and by expressing joy and appreciation for all that Christian Science holds for you. No one ever regretted carrying that cross.

Mrs. Eddy expresses exactly what constitutes Christian Science, and what makes a Christian Scientist, in her clear statement in Miscellany, "To live so as to keep human consciousness in constant relation with the divine, the spiritual, and the eternal, is to individualize infinite power; and this is Christian Science." Does not keeping "human consciousness in constant relation with the divine," mean exactly what you are doing when you refuse to deal with the effects of evil,—the beast and the false prophet, matter and mentality—and turn your whole attention unreservedly to the "cause" malicious mind, and translate malicious mind back to its reality divine Mind? Thus doing, malicious mental malpractice may knock at your door, but you can say in regard to it as did Jesus, "The prince of this world cometh, and hath nothing in me," in other words, malicious argument cannot present to me a single one of its lies to which I am not awake, and which I am not vigorously translating back to the truth that the lie is the lie about.

THE
HOLY CITY
PURITY, PERFECTION, PEACE

SCIENCE and Health declares "In proportion to his purity is man perfect; and perfection is the order of celestial being which demonstrates Life in Christ, Life's spiritual ideal", and Christ Jesus declared, "Be ye therefore perfect even as your Father which is in heaven is perfect". He did not compromise with the necessity for perfection, but by his attitude indicated that perfection must be attained and recognized as discernibly present, and not something to be anticipated at some far off future period.

Evil's suggestion would have perfection, whether of health or of character, relegated to the distant future, whereas the Christian Scientist realizes that to put off perfection separates him from the present kingdom of heaven.

To the Christian Scientist, the kingdom of heaven is a state of mind and has nothing to do with conditions. Consequently his purpose and effort is thinking in terms of perfection and he knows that perfection means everything in its correct or perfect place—obedient to its divine Principle; and that he knows is peace.

No fitter closing can be given to this book than to quote Mrs. Eddy's words of wisdom given to some friends, showing how this goal of purity, perfection and peace is to be won and malicious mind silenced in divine Mind.

"We each dwell in our own world of consciousness, we look out through the windows of this consciousness and behold the passing procession of mortal mind.

"Day after day we have been lured forth, have been pressed into the whirl, lost our individual peace and poise in divine Mind, and found ourselves dragged through the meanness, the uncleanness, and pain of the procession.

"We seek to regain our own house of consciousness, wiser for the experience, thinking we will not again become a part of error's pageant, but here let the newer understanding of Love guard well your door, stay in your own house of mental

demonstration, keep your peace. For idle curiosity, criticism, or even false sympathy may lure you forth.

"Wherein lies the wisdom of the serpent? To hide itself. Therefore hide yourself in the understanding of Christian Science, be it great or small.

"We have all in some way needed the experience we have had. Never be found as a Christian Scientist mourning over an experience. It is a thing of the past, but not so the manifold power and presence of God resulting therefrom."

And the words of Jesus through John, "I saw a new heaven and a new earth for the first heaven and the first earth were passed away and there was no more sea. (No more 'tempest-tossed human concepts advancing and receding,' as defined by Mrs. Eddy.) And I John saw the holy city, new Jerusalem, coming down from God out of heaven . . . And I heard a great voice out of heaven saying, Behold, the tabernacle of God is with men, and he will dwell with them, and they shall be his people, and God himself shall be with them, and be their God . . . And he said unto me, It is done. I am Alpha and Omega, the beginning and the end. I will give unto him that is athirst of the fountain of life freely. And he . . . shewed me that great city, the holy Jerusalem . . . the city lieth four square . . . And had no need of the sun, neither of the moon, to shine in it; for the glory of God did lighten it, and the Lamb is the light thereof . . . And the gates of it shall not be shut at all by day: for there shall be no night there. And they shall bring the glory and honour of the nations into it . . . And there shall in no wise enter into it anything that defileth, neither whatsoever worketh abomination or maketh a lie . . . And the Spirit and the bride say, Come. And let him that heareth say, Come. And let him that is athirst come. And whosoever will let him take the water of life freely."

THE LINE OF LIGHT

WHY AM I A CHRISTIAN SCIENTIST?

PLAGIARISM

By

HERBERT W. EUSTACE, C. S. B.

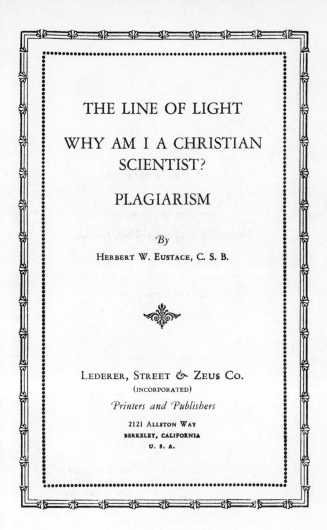

LEDERER, STREET & ZEUS CO.

(INCORPORATED)

Printers and Publishers

2121 ALLSTON WAY
BERKELEY, CALIFORNIA
U. S. A.

Printed and Bound by
LEDERER, STREET & ZEUS CO., INC.
2121 ALLSTON WAY
BERKELEY, CALIFORNIA, U.S.A.

FOREWORD

In March, 1927, a Conference was held in San Francisco of those who had been through class with me. This meeting traced the Line of Light from Eve to Science and Health.

In February, 1929, another Conference was held in San Francisco, and established, Why am I a Christian Scientist?

There has been a demand that the addresses made at these two Conferences be printed. I saw no way, however, for this to be done, as I had no notes whatever myself, but when I found that there had been taken and were in circulation some very full and excellent stenographic and other notes, I decided that it might be of value, especially at this time, to publish these addresses.

With these notes before me I have filled them in, and I think have covered virtually every point that came up at the meetings.

Whatever value these pages may have to their reader, that value will be permanent only as it takes him to the source of all intelligence, the one Mind, and in communion with that one

Mind, points him to the true purpose and value of Science and Health.

It was my first thought that the one who had so carefully prepared some of these notes should be the one to publish them, but the objection was raised that if I did not prepare them there might be a question as to their authorship; hence I am publishing them myself.

I am adding the article on Plagiarism, which I have just written, because it seems to me to be timely.

Herbert W. Eustace.

THE LINE OF LIGHT

WHY AM I A CHRISTIAN SCIENTIST?

PLAGIARISM

ABBREVIATIONS

Works by Mary Baker Eddy

S. & H.—"Science and Health, with Key to the Scriptures."

Mis.—"Miscellaneous Writings."

Ret.—"Retrospection and Introspection."

Un.—"Unity of Good."

No—"No and Yes."

'01—"Message to The Mother Church, June, 1901."

Hea.—"Christian Healing."

My.—"The First Church of Christ, Scientist, and Miscellany."

Prin. & Prac.—Article "Principle and Practice."

Rud.—"Rudimental Divine Science."

THE LINE OF LIGHT

"R EASON is the most active human faculty."[1] "Reason, rightly directed, serves to correct the errors of corporeal sense."[2] "Incorrect reasoning leads to practical error."[3] Because God and His idea constitute allness, all right reasoning must mean reasoning with God, with Principle. "Come now, and let us reason together, saith the Lord."[4]

AN ABSOLUTELY CORRECT BASIS
ESSENTIAL

There must be the correct basis for this reasoning. The premise must be right or the conclusion never can be. It is the lack of understanding of what Science and Health really means and is, that constitutes the ignorance that beclouds clearer demonstration today.

In studying mathematics, you do not waste a moment considering whether there is more than one multiplication table, or whether something will arise to make mathematics clearer. You are in no doubt on the point that there is only one

[1]S & H. 327:29. [2]S. & H. 494:19. [3]S. & H. 452:4. [4]Is. 1:18.

mathematics and one multiplication table, and that that one must be mastered and understood.

Is it not essential, then, to be equally certain whether or not Science and Health is the final word of Mind? Reason must be absolutely satisfied, then there will be no desire to wander from the straight path of the Line of Light and turn either to the right hand or to the left. "Thine ears shall hear a word behind thee, saying, This is the way, walk ye in it."[1], . . ."

ONE MIND AND ONE IDEA

There must be the correct starting point. What is it, and what is its relation to you? You well know that the *sine qua non* of Christian Science is that there is one Mind, and that this one Mind is Principle. You also know that this Principle, in order to be Principle and continue to be Principle, must always have accompanying it that to which it is Principle—namely its idea.

THE SUPPOSITITIOUS MIND

Because there is this one Principle, this one Mind and its idea, which constitute the I AM, there arises by the law of opposites, suppositionally another so-called mind, the exact reverse in every respect of the one Mind. This suppositional mind was characterized by Christ Jesus

[1] Is. 30:21.

as "a liar, and the father of it."[1] It is referred
to in the Scriptures as adversary, Satan, devil,
great red dragon and so forth. It can be just
as correctly designated as the talking serpent,
the carnal, human or mortal mind or as malicious
mind.

Now, let us "reason together" about this
with Mind and follow the Line of Light, beginning with the opening chapter of Genesis and
tracing this thread of gold, as it lengthens and
broadens from its first simple appearing, down
to its final enveloping of all mankind through its
impersonal saviour, Science and Health.

THE TRUE AND THE FALSE

In the first chapter of Genesis we read that
God made all after His likeness, "and God saw
every thing that he had made, and, behold, it
was very good."[2] From this it follows that God
self-evidently *is,* and is good, and that His idea,
to be His image, must be exactly like Him; in
other words, the idea or man of God is equally
good with its Principle. Thus we have God and
His man as complete and all.

Opposite to this one Creator and His
creation, we find a suppositional presence called
Lord God, Jehovah and his creation. The

[1]Jno. 8:44. [2]Gen. 1:31.

account of this is given in the second chapter of Genesis. Here the suppositional opposite, mortal man and his so-called mind, appears under the name of Adam. It is this Adam and this alone that needs to be annihilated, saved or redeemed. The remainder of the Scriptures is devoted to the accomplishment of the annihilation of this Adam supposition.

Adam stands boldly forth proclaimed as an accomplished fact, as that which *is*; but is Adam that which *is*, or is God and His idea all that *is*? Adam is only supposition, that which seems to be, but is not, and this suppositional opposite of that which *is*, is what has to be annihilated. Is it not Adam, this suppositional opposite of God and His idea, which claims to be you and your mind; that through which you must understand your way to find freedom?

THE PROCESS OF REDEMPTION

You know there cannot be a falsity unless there is first the truth for the falsity to be about. Preceding the appearance of any falsity, the truth about the falsity must be and is ever present, standing guard, never forsaking its post and always, by its very presence, finally bringing to pass the redemption of Adam, that is, the destruction of the falsity.

Now, in the redemption of Adam, that is, in the annihilation of Adam, the redeemer must necessarily appear in the way that can be understood by that which is to be redeemed. What was it that appeared to redeem Adam? Was it not Eve, who appeared as "bone of (his) bones, and flesh of (his) flesh"[1] and so could speak and appear in his own language and be understandable to Adam?

Truth had to appear always to the unenlightened thought, in other words to the Adam, clothed in the language and the form, which Adam could comprehend. Otherwise would the appearing be comprehended, understood and so made available? It would not, and so this first appearing to Adam of the Christ, Truth, as Eve, appeared as "bone of (his) bones, and flesh of (his) flesh,"[1] almost like Adam in every respect.

Remember, you can never understand the Scriptures and the account of Adam if you think of Adam and Eve as two. Eve must be seen simply as the first gleam of the Christ or the truth about Adam, which is to destroy the Adam. As it is stated in the second verse of the fifth chapter of Genesis, God "called their name Adam," not Adam and Eve.

[1]Gen. 2:23.

IMPERSONALIZATION OF EVIL

Because of the nature of Eve, she was the first to see evil impersonally; she declared fearlessly, "The serpent beguiled me, and I did eat."[1] She saw the temptation as evil coming to her in the guise of good. Adam's cowardly and fearful declaration was, "The woman whom thou gavest to be with me, she gave me of the tree, and I did eat."[2] Materiality always says that God did it, that God is responsible.

This declaration of Eve, this that is Eve, this impersonalization is the spirituality, the truth or Christ that is always present with every claim of Adam, no matter in what form Adam may appear. This redemptive quality is called woman, because it appears in the Adam-man language or like Adam. The truth must always precede any lie and, therefore, is always already there for each one to perceive and accept. "Remember, thou canst be brought into no condition, be it ever so severe, where Love has not been before thee and where its tender lesson is not awaiting thee."[3]

The pressure of Truth, or the first appearing of the Christ annihilating evil, appears as Eve calling evil not personal but impersonal. All

[1] Gen. 3:13.   [2] Gen. 3:12.   [3] My. 149:31.

creation, all living, comes through this Eve, this that is called woman. But Eve is not a person; you must banish all thought of a person. You are dealing with Principle alone.

Eve, the highest sense of Adam, the one thing true about him, the highest sense that could appear to him and so redeem him, comes always as of woman. Every bit of redemption that can appear comes through this impersonalizing of evil called Eve. It always means spiritualization and through it alone evil is annihilated.

SPIRITUAL UNDERSTANDING

This is the Line of Light; it never ceases. "That was the true Light, which lighteth every man that cometh into the world."[1] In its larger unfoldment, as it gathered more clarity and force, it appeared as Enoch, Melchizedek, Abraham and so on.

In Abraham it took a more tangible form. "Now the Lord had said unto Abram, Get thee out of thy country, and from thy kindred and from thy father's house, unto a land that I will shew thee."[2] Abraham, in going out from his father's house, represented thought forsaking

[1] John 1:9. [2] Gen. 12:1.

matter for Mind. He showed forth that supreme faith in something outside of the human concept of himself, which rightly determined his spiritual definition, "Fidelity; faith in the divine Life and in the eternal Principle of being. This patriarch illustrated the purpose of Love to create trust in good, and showed the life-preserving power of spiritual understanding."[1]

"Eve," now appearing as and called Abraham, is here seen at the point of abandoning matter for Mind. The unfolding promises of Mind come through this thought called Abraham and its direct progeny. "And in thy seed shall all the nations of the earth be blessed; because thou hast obeyed my voice."[2]

The whole of material belief can be annihilated only through the seed of this thought of Abraham, this obedient relinquishment of matter for Mind. It is this alone that makes possible the blessing of Mind.

Continuing the Line of Light, it next appeared as Isaac, Jacob, the twelve sons or tribes, the kingdoms of Israel and Judah. The multiplication of the seed within itself went on rapidly. It appeared as persons, tribes, kingdoms, that is, in the language you can best

[1] S. & H. 579:10.   [2] Gen. 22:18.

understand, but it is not persons; it is your communion with Principle appearing to you as idea. "The Christian Scientist is alone with his own being and with the reality of things."[1] Therefore, it is plain that you are not dealing with persons, places or things, but always with that with which you are communing—with Mind.

All the fear, anguish and misery of the world is wrapped in the belief that you are dealing with persons, places and things, instead of with Mind. The understanding and the abandonment of this erroneous belief starts you on the true path, that of being "alone with (your) own being and with the reality of things."[1] This means that as the one idea of Mind you are eternally dealing with your God, with that which you are accepting as your consciousness. Consciousness, to be consciousness, must appear concretely or consciously. This appearance is what is called person, place or thing, but is in reality always the very presence of Mind, of God.

THE MIRROR OF MIND

Looking out, as it were, you behold the universe, and this is like looking into a mirror. The image in the mirror is not the object in front

[1] Mes. 1901-20:8.

of the mirror, it only shows forth the likeness of that object. Even so, that which you are conscious of, that which you are aware of, or see, is really not at all what it appears to be, persons, places or things. It is simply the showing forth of that which you accept as your Mind or consciousness. It seems to, and always must, appear as idea, for that is the only way God is ever known.

Remember however, if you are not pleased with the image in the mirror, the way you change it is not by attempting to go up to the mirror and alter it directly there. By changing the object in front of the mirror, does not the image in the mirror adjust itself spontaneously? So is it with that which appears to you as persons, places, things, business and so on. Your conscious world is simply the image you behold in your mirror. As you accept that to be Mind, which is truly Mind, that which is appearing to you — the world — corresponds instantly. "And I, if I be lifted up from the earth, will draw all men unto me."[1] The infinity that is Mind must appear in the infinity of variety that is called beauty, goodness, grandeur and so forth.

[1]John 12:32.

THE LANGUAGE OF SPIRITUAL
UNFOLDMENT

Thus the Light appears as Eve, as Abraham, as Moses, as the kingdoms of Israel and Judah. These are not people; they are just the names you gave to the language you could best understand. Eve, Abraham, Moses, the Tribes, the Prophets, the kingdoms and so on, simply indicate "states and stages of consciousness."[1] They are not something afar off, but at hand, all right here, embraced in that which is the Mind or the Self of you or within your-Self. If this were not so, they would really mean nothing to you and would be of no value.

THE DAWN OF SPIRITUAL
UNDERSTANDING

"Eve" is the name given to the first dawning of the Christ, Truth, "The divine manifestation of God, which comes to the flesh to destroy incarnate error."[2] "And I will put enmity between thee and the woman, and between thy seed and her seed; it shall bruise thy head, and thou shalt bruise his heel."[3] The nature of Truth is always to destroy the lie; but the lie, the suppositional opposite of the

[1] S. & H. 573:11.   [2] S. & H. 583:10.   [3] Gen. 3:16.

truth, is always, suppositionally, at the heel of Truth.

As Eve, this impersonalizing of evil, this Christ, grew and unfolded, it began to formulate itself more concretely still to the prophets or prophetical sense. Isaiah visioned this highest and purest hope as a virgin with child, and proclaimed it in language, as, "unto us a child is born, unto us a son is given: and the government shall be upon his shoulder: and his name shall be called Wonderful, Counsellor, The mighty God, The everlasting Father, The Prince of Peace."[1]

Do not think for one moment that the Prophet was outlining a material event. He used the term Virgin simply to describe that impersonality and purity which the Christ symbolized through holiness and perfection. He realized that only that which was derived from pure spirituality, from impersonality, could possibly be of the slightest benefit in redeeming Adam.

Finally, this Light did actually appear as a virgin, the Virgin Mary, conceiving so clearly of God as the Father of man, that it appeared

[1] Is. 9:6.

as a child, in the tangible form of a thinking person—Christ Jesus.

SPIRITUAL AND HUMAN GOOD HOSTILE

This higher, more concrete appearing of Mind, this young child, had to be taken into Egypt to grow. Egypt means darkness, ignorance of spirituality. Here, in the obscurity of human ignorance of spirituality, the child could grow, remote from that Jewish concept of theological and doctrinal good which would have promptly killed it. Should not this having to "flee into Egypt"[1] of the divine appearing called the "young child" point out the wisdom of never trusting our unfolding spiritual sense of God even to the very highest human material sense of good that we may have, although this may appear masquerading as spirituality? That which will always destroy, if it can, the highest spiritual sense is the highest material sense of good.

It is absolutely true that a higher sense of good can arise, or come forth, only from the highest sense of good of the period in which it appears, and it never does or can arise from anything less than the very highest. However,

[1] Matt. 2:13.

we must remember that the highest is always spiritual and never material good. It is against the highest material sense of good of the period, that the greatest watchfulness must be kept, for the human sense of good is always materiality and is forever at war with the spiritual sense.

The theological Jews of the period of Jesus represented the most advanced material religious good, hence their conflict with the Christ, spiritual good, and the reception they gave the Christ. "He came unto his own, and his own received him not."[1]

THE PERSONAL SAVIOUR

The prophets were glimpses of goodness and greatness, but that goodness and greatness was simply Eve appearing in a purer, fuller and more ascending sense. Then the Redeemer appeared in its still truer sense; not as the product of Adam and Eve, but purely of Eve, and it was called Christ Jesus.

This Light, in its final personal sense that was called Christ Jesus, was to be about its Father's business, showing forth that Father personally as works—the healing all manner of disease, feeding the multitudes, stilling the

[1]Jno 1:11.

storm and destroying death; and then as the crucifixion; the resurrection; and finally the ascension. Here the Christ, as Jesus, reached the summit of completeness in its appearance as a person. That appearing ended entirely the sense of the Christ as a person, and so Jesus said of the personal sense, "It is expedient for you that I go away: for if I go not away, the Comforter will not come unto you; but if I depart, I will send him unto you."[1]

Jesus was referring to the fact that the highest human corporeal or personal sense of the divine man or idea, had to disappear before the Comforter, the reality, the real man as the presence of God, could appear. Personal sense always mars the vision of the impersonal or spiritual sense. Christ Jesus worked out all personality, and he declared, "It is finished."[2]

Jesus, the highest human concept of the divine idea, is not the consummation, except so far as the personal sense is concerned. The personal sense had first to disappear before the impersonal, or Mind-sense of the Christ could appear in all its fullness. Then could take place what Jesus meant when he said, "I will pray the Father, and He shall give you

[1]John 16:7. [2]John 19:30.

another Comforter, that he may abide with you forever; Even the Spirit of truth; whom the world cannot receive, because it seeth him not, neither knoweth him; but ye know him; for he dwelleth with you, and shall be in you. But the Comforter, which is the Holy Ghost, whom the Father will send in my name, he shall teach you all things, and bring all things to your remembrance, whatsoever I have said unto you."[1]

In the personal chronology of the appearing of the Christ in its ascending scale we have first Eve, then Abraham, Jacob, Moses, the kingdoms of Judah and Israel and the Prophets, then Christ Jesus. With Christ Jesus came the full, perfect and sufficient sacrifice, as Paul expressed it; the demonstration of the Christ, Truth, not as a person at all, but as pure spirituality without any fleshly sense. This was seen as the ascension.

ISRAEL FINDS SHELTER IN BRITAIN

Then the Christ was dimly seen in the form of the Christian doctrine and as the early Christians and the spread of Christianity. In the spread of Christianity it is important to

[1]John 14:16, 17, 26.

notice that history shows how the British Isles proved themselves veritable Isles of refuge for Christianity. According to tradition, and tradition is sometimes correct, Christianity was introduced into England by Joseph of Arimathea a few years after the resurrection. Those to whom it was introduced were among the very lost sheep that Jesus referred to in his statement, "I am not sent but unto the lost sheep of the house of Israel."[1] The soil must be right or there can be no fruition, and Israel was this soil.

What is Israel? What does Israel mean? You remember the twelve sons or descendants of Jacob,—that which wrestled and prevailed over evil,—appeared finally as twelve tribes. They eventually formed themselves into two kingdoms, the tribe of Judah with part of the tribe of Benjamin becoming the Kingdom of Judah, and the other tribes forming themselves into the Kingdom of Israel. Judah was the royal line but from Israel Shiloh was to come. Shiloh means pure, spiritual sense. "The Scepter shall not depart from Judah, nor a lawgiver from between his feet, until Shiloh come; and unto him shall the gathering of the people be."[2]

[1] Matt. 15:24.   [2] Gen. 49:10.

You also remember that Joseph, Jacob's loved son, who was hated of his brethren, and was sold into Egypt, and who finally appeared as the saviour of his brethren, had two sons, the younger Ephraim and the older Manasseh. In blessing these two sons of Joseph, Jacob foretold the greatness of Manasseh, the elder, but the greater greatness of Ephraim, the younger, and, as the Bible declares, he put the younger before the older. In speaking of Manasseh, Jacob said, "he also shall become a people, and he also shall be great: but truly his younger brother shall be greater than he, and his seed shall become a multitude of nations."[1]

THE BRANCH THAT GREW OVER
THE WALL

Israel was to be known by "a new name,"[2] and the descendants were to be gathered in the "Isles"[3] of the Seas, there to be protected and nurtured until the fullness of time. From this Israel was to appear under the still newer name America, the United States of America, that which was to stand forth as Ephraim, the younger, the branch that ran "over the wall."[4] Not a nation in the ordinary acceptance of the

[1] Gen. 48:19.   [2] Is. 62:2.   [3] Is. 49:1.   [4] Gen. 49:22.

word, but a mighty spiritual force that was to show forth to mankind, the "Light, which lighteth every man that cometh into the world."[1] That spiritual force was to be known as Christian Science, under whose banner would gather a "multitude of nations."[2]

When Jacob struggled with the angel he was alone, and he brought into that struggle over fear and anxiety all that he knew of Truth, and it multiplied. "Thy name shall be called no more Jacob, but Israel; for as a prince hast thou power with God and with men, and hast prevailed."[3] This is the Israel that grew and finally appeared as the British race, no longer Isaacsons or sons of Isaac, but Saxons, the Anglo-Saxon race.

Do not forget, however, that all this that we are talking about is simply the unfoldment of Mind, and, while appearing as persons, it really never is persons, but always Mind, for the only race is Mind, no matter what the appearance.

This that arose as the nation called Great Britain, and then, as something going out from it—the branch growing over the wall,—Ephraim, the younger, called America, was simply the language in which the further unfoldment

[1] Jno. 1:9.   [2] Gen. 48:19.   [3] Gen. 32:28.

of Mind appeared. You know of the anguish which caused the Pilgrims and Puritans to go out from their father's house into a land they knew not of. Like Abraham of old, they went with implicit confidence in good, not outlining in the slightest but having full "faith in. . . . the eternal Principle of being."[1]

America stands as the one nation on earth whose origin was wholly spiritual. It went forth with the one spiritual purpose to worship God. Then what constituted America? It was "the seed in itself," that inborn spiritual craving in each individual which seeks Mind as the needle seeks the pole. The seed was not only the recognition of the right, but also the determination to worship God without any interference; the understanding that nothing has the right to, or can, intervene between God and His idea. In other words, America stands for that union of Principle and idea which is forever one and indissoluble. This country typifies, and its origin proves it to be, the spiritual idea of Mind and the nearest approximation to a nation founded by Mind, and so it stands alone.

America was in no way merely a political experiment; it was the answer to the deep spiritual

[1] S. & H. 579:10.

necessity of man's oneness with Principle. That every step of the unfolding nation was leavened by the recognition of dependence upon Mind, is verified by utterances of that time. Benjamin Franklin said in his address of 1787 before the Constitutional Convention when, at the end of weeks of stress and effort, failure seemed to face them, "If a sparrow cannot fall to the ground without His notice, is it probable that an empire can rise without His aid? We have been assured in the Sacred Writings, that 'Except the Lord build the house, they labor in vain that build it.' I firmly believe this; and I also believe that without His concurring aid we shall succeed in this political building no better than the builders of Babel." Nothing animated the founding of this nation except the one purpose to be alone with God and worship Him after the dictates of a conscience untrammeled by ecclesiastical or other tyranny.

THE PRESSURE OF TRUTH
IN AMERICA

No sooner, however, had America gone out from its father's house and established its own house more or less securely, after countless tribulations, than the pressure of Truth was felt even stronger than ever. There is no point where this pressure can stop, until perfection is attained, and so there was no peace for the Pilgrim Fathers. There appeared the pressure not only of the countless internal disturbances, but there was the outside pressure, such as taxation without representation, which finally culminated in what has been called the American Revolution.

Then, there followed the next effort to "come out from among them, and be ye separate."[1] In the beginning, the States had drawn up an agreement of perpetual Union founded on mutual respect and recognition of each one's rights for the good of all. This was symbolical of man's perpetual oneness with Principle. But the question of slavery in the country had grown and increased, and with it there was the inevitable opposition to the evil.

Is it not true that whatever enslaves in the slightest degree never rests satisfied but always works for greater control, greater bondage? So it was with what appeared as human slavery in America. Its advocates were not satisfied, but wanted, in spite of opposition, continual extension. Little by little there arose the demand to spread and extend slavery, with an

[1] 2 Cor. 6:17.

insistence on States' rights in regard to this. The slavery question, however, was really insignificant in one sense of the word. The question of deep moment was, if States could demand freedom to extend slavery into other States and Territories and make their demand good, in spite of the opposition of the other States, would it not end by bringing about a dissolution or destruction of the Union? From the very arrival of the Pilgrims, in all the disasters that had befallen them, had it not really been the effort of evil to destroy the union of States, which typified the union of Principle and idea?

President Lincoln was not in the least deceived about what was operating or what evil was trying to accomplish, for you remember his statement, as given by Lord Charnwood, page 322, in his "Abraham Lincoln," "My paramount object in this struggle is to save the Union. If I could save the Union without freeing any slaves I would do it; and if I could save it by freeing all the slaves I would do it: and if I could save it by freeing some and leaving others alone, I would also do that. I shall do less whenever I shall believe what I am doing hurts the cause, and I shall do more whenever I shall believe doing more helps the cause." In other

words Lincoln saw that the vital question was
the Union, and that if that Union could be
destroyed, and the States be divided, then liberty
would perish from the earth. The founding
of America was the culmination of all that had
gone before in the going out from matter to
Mind, and the bringing to light of man's oneness
with God, and the government of God as Supreme. There is no liberty with matter as the
basis of being, for matter self-evidently is finiteness, limitation.

Do not fail to keep all persons out of your
analysis or you cannot understand Mind. If
your thought is fixed on personality in the slightest, it is not only in danger of losing Principle,
but inevitably will lose it. This cannot be more
strongly stated than it is by Mrs. Eddy in Miscellaneous Writings, "Remember, it is personality, and the sense of personality in God or in
man, that limits man."[1] "Again I repeat, person
is not in the question of Christian Science. Principle, instead of person, is next to our hearts,
on our lips, and in our lives."[2]

All warfare is impersonal. It is the warfare
between Truth and error, not between persons.
Although it appears as persons, follow the Line

[1] Mis. 282:4.   [2] Mis. 135:2.

of Light impersonally, through to the last Adam who was the "quickening spirit."[1]

The Civil War, then, had nothing primarily to do with slavery. Lincoln was not concerned about slavery as he plainly showed in his statement; his real purpose was to save the Union. The Civil War purified the whole nation, and placed it upon a basis of oneness which could never again be interfered with. Union means oneness, and oneness can only be with Mind. Every doubt or question about this had to be fought out before the final impersonal appearing of the Christ could come. "Rest assured that God in His wisdom will test all mankind on all questions; and then, if found faithful, he will deliver us from temptation and show us the powerlessness of evil,—even its utter nothingness."[2]

THE IMPERSONAL SAVIOUR

After the struggle for the Union had been fought and won, a new struggle began immediately. 1865 saw the end of the Civil War. With 1866 came the dawn of the final appearing that Jacob foresaw as Shiloh coming forth from the younger, Ephraim, and which Jesus

[1]Cor. 15:45. [2]Mis. 114:26.

foresaw as the Comforter, who should speak not of himself, but lead into all truth, and which the Revelator saw, as a "little book,"[1] to be eaten up, made one's own, comprehended, understood, not carried around as a remedy.

Shiloh, the Comforter, the Little Book was to come forth in America, from that which had grown over the wall and gone out from its father's house, from materiality, limitation, forsaking all for Mind, and it had to appear in the only way a book can appear, through an author. That author, of Pilgrim origin, again typifying Eve the "mother of all living,"[2] was to appear as a woman, bringing forth her "man-child, who was to rule all nations with a rod of iron."[3]

This little, lone, New England woman, Mary Baker Eddy, like the Mary of old, through her innate purity and goodness, in her communion with God, conceived of God as the one Mind, and therefore, Mind as All-in-all. Thus she conceived all things as having a Mind origin and not a material one: or, as she expresses it, "All is infinite Mind and its infinite manifestation, for God is All-in-all."[4]

This discovery of the allness of Mind was not the work of a moment, but was the result

[1]Rev. 10:2. [2]Gen. 3:20. [3]Rev. 12:5. [4]S. & H. 468:10.

of many years of earnest searching on the part
of Mrs. Eddy for the Mind-cause of all things.
She had conceived, long before, that all things
must have a mental origin. As she says, she
had searched to find the truth of that for over
twenty years. Her search led her through
countless avenues of human belief where she
hoped to find her "pearl of great price,"[1] only
however, to be disappointed time after time
for they never crowned "the power of Mind
as the Messiah."[2] This constant delving on
Mrs. Eddy's part has been the cause of much
misunderstanding. She has been accused of being
first one thing and then another, whereas she
was always just the same true, devout Christian
searching for the way of Mind and eventually
finding it, "alone with" her "own being and
with the reality of things;"[3] thereby blessing
all mankind.

Because of the very purity, simplicity and
divinity of Mrs. Eddy's thought she could not
help endowing those with whom she came in
contact, especially if they seemed to be seeking
a higher ideal of life, with her own loveliness
of character and high order of intelligence.
Apparently this she did with such a lavish hand

[1]Matt. 13:46.   [2]S. & H. 116:14.   [3]Mes. .01-20:9.

that she many times praised and upheld those who later proved utterly unworthy of the glory she shed upon them. She could not help doing this. It is always the nature of the truly great and spiritual to see their own lofty ideals in all around them. Instinctively they clothe their surroundings, be it person, place or thing, with their own beautiful natures, frequently, later to learn through the deepest sadness that they praised where praise should not have been given, and loved where love was wasted. This must ever be so in the touch of the spiritually minded with the mortal concept. Was not this the case with Jesus in his choice of Judas? But the spiritually minded go forward, and so Mrs. Eddy went forward.

She named her conception, that which unfolded to her understanding, Christian Science, and in 1875 this appeared to the world in its full manhood, in the most impersonal form in which the Christ, Truth, can appear, and yet be cognizable to the mortal, namely as the book —Science and Health. The only personality or materiality attached to this book is the paper and ink; apart from that, is it not purely Mind? Did not Jesus foresee, then, that the final unfoldment of the Christ would appear in the form of a book, when he spoke of the Comforter who would come but who would not speak of himself?

What does Christian Science mean? Christian means pertaining to Christ or Truth; and Science means exact knowledge. In other words Christian Science means right knowing, and right knowing means intelligence, and intelligence means Mind, God, and so Christian Science in its true sense is only another term for God.

Are you thinking of Christian Science simply as another term for God? If so, then you never think of it as an organization or as a system, or as something that has to do with human ways or beliefs. Because Christian Science is God, then what must the understanding of God, the man of God, be? It must be the practice of Christian Science.

Establishing of the Union, called America, on an absolutely firm foundation as an accomplished fact, immediately opened the way for the establishing of Christian Science, the discernment of the eternal union of Principle and its idea as All-in-all.

THE IMMACULATE CONCEPTION
COMPLETELY OUTLINED

The birth of Jesus is always spoken of as the immaculate conception, but was it the immaculate conception in its fullness? Mary's communion with God was immaculate in that she conceived of God as the Father of man; but did it not still remain for the immaculate conception to be seen in its full completeness, as God being both the Father and Mother of man, without any intermediary in the form of human parentage? It was then in this light that the immaculate conception finally appeared as Science and Health.

But is the book, Science and Health, the entire, complete and immaculate conception to you, or is that conception complete only as you go one step further, and see that only when you discover Science and Health as very Mind, without any so-called print or paper, do you really discover what Science and Health means and is? That discovery is wholly immaculate when you discover it for yourself.

The purpose of Science and Health then is to take you to the source from whence it came, and in your communion with this source, this Mind, you find all that is in Science and Health.

In this way you discover for yourself Science and Health, and so understand the immaculate conception in its fullness.

Is Christian Science something, then, that has to do with words or the repetition of words, or is Christian Science something that must be thought? Nothing could be finer than what Mrs. Eddy has written in Science and Health. No words could better express what the Science of Being really is, but words of themselves have no power to accomplish anything. Words give impulse to thought, but words of themselves are powerless. It is the Mind back of the words that must be discovered or there can be no understanding. You must discover Mind to be All-in-all, and all that there is to Science and Health. Only as you do this is the immaculate conception complete to you.

Thus we find the line of Light first dawning to this so-called Adam, or human mind, in almost its own likeness, as Eve. Tracing its unfoldment, we find it steadily growing in stature with good and with man, coming to light in all its varying forms from Abraham, on down through the Prophets, to its final appearing as the person called Christ Jesus. Then, the leaven of Christ Jesus fulfilling its work, unfolding as the founding of America, and the growth of the Union, came forth, in its most impersonal form, as the discovery of Christian Science, appearing as Science and Health, clothed in the English language, as "the untranslated revelation of Christian Science." Lastly this book, performing its function, carries you to the ultimate, which is your direct communion with Mind itself, revealing man's true relationship to that which Principle really is. My. 179:29.

THE LIGHT FULL-ORBED

Could there be anything more to reveal than that which Science and Health has revealed? "Truth is revealed. It needs only to be practised."[1] If we do not understand that the truth revealed in Science and Health is final, we shall be forever seeking elsewhere for the truth and never finding it. It is failure to understand the finality of Science and Health, and why it is final, that is the cause of the constant wandering into the highways and byways of human belief, the looking to other books, other ways and means on the part of Christian Scientists, which eventually is their utter undoing.

[1]S. & H. 174:20.

Just as Jesus finished, in his own appearance and work, the personal sense of the Christ, and declared, "It is finished,"[1] so Science and Health just as completely and truly finishes the impersonal appearing of the Christ. Both the personal and the impersonal, the Word and its scientific explanation, are finished.

The human concept called Eve that seemed to declare the impersonality of evil, was not the Christ: nor was the human concept called Abraham, that seemed to go out from his father's house, the Christ that is always outside of matter: nor was the human concept called Jesus, the divine reality or Christ: nor was the human concept called Mary Baker Eddy, Science and Health. The Christ is always above and beyond any human concept, even as the revelation is always vastly greater than the revelator.

THE TRUE CONCEPT OF MRS. EDDY

The Christian Scientist does not confuse or attempt to compare Mrs. Eddy with Christ Jesus. Jesus embodied within himself, as it were, the Christ, and showed forth in his own being the very presence of God, as the personal appearing of Truth. At that period of experience

[1] John 19:30.

no other appearance could have been appreciated or understood. Hence his own statement, "he that hath seen me hath seen the Father."[1]

On the other hand, Mrs. Eddy had no personal office to fill. It was her simple purity and goodness, which made it possible for her to so commune with Mind that she was enabled to give Science and Health to the world. Science and Health in its turn gives the full and complete impersonal explanation, or understanding of God, the understanding which is the Comforter. Mrs. Eddy does not enter into Science and Health any more than the Virgin Mother enters into Christ Jesus. Therefore, to understand Christian Science, you must leave Mrs. Eddy entirely out of the question.

Was it not because of the great danger of attempting to infuse personality into the understanding of Christian Science that made Mrs. Eddy declare—"There was never a religion or philosophy lost to the centuries except by sinking its divine Principle in personality?"[2] She saw clearly, that confusing her with Christian Science would destroy real understanding of Christian Science. It is plainly evident that the

[1]John 14:9. [2]My. 117:24.

purpose of evil today is to endeavour to sink
the divine Principle of Christian Science in the
personality of Mrs. Eddy.

The tendency of the would-be Christian
Scientist is to be continually talking about and
lauding Mrs. Eddy. In what must this eventually result? Doubt and darkness; not only as
to the truth of Christian Science, but as to its
availability. Do you not realize that it was this
belief of associating Mrs. Eddy with Christian
Science, and letting the personality of Mrs.
Eddy stand as something between you and the
revelation of Science and Health, that in the
end appeared as the necessity for the departure
of Mrs. Eddy? Just so long as the thought
obtains with you that Mrs. Eddy has something
to do with Christian Science, except in the one
sense of the purity and goodness through which
it was given, you will never be a Christian
Scientist.

THE MEANING OF MRS. EDDY'S DEPARTURE

If Mrs. Eddy had not departed and you had
not been compelled to think Christian Science
for yourself, do you think you would have the
freedom that you have today? Why is this so?

Not because of Mrs. Eddy as Mrs. Eddy, but because you would have been allowing your sense of Mrs. Eddy to intervene between you and Principle, and that must and does always prevent spiritual unfoldment.

Thus, the fact must be faced that it was the entertaining of an erroneous sense, although wholly unconscious, that demanded the departure of Mrs. Eddy, just as it demanded the departure of Jesus. So long as the belief of Mrs. Eddy as the personal Leader of Christian Science or the author of Science and Health, is entertained, looking to her personally for help and instruction must obtain. If one is to advance in understanding, Mind must be found as All-in-all. The whole tendency of materiality is the exact reverse of this. It is to think and talk more and more in terms of Mrs. Eddy and so hide the divine Principle that is all there ever was or could be to Mrs. Eddy or to anyone or to anything.

The disappearance of Mrs. Eddy as a person and the coming to light of Science and Health as Emmanuel or God with us, was merely the language in which a clearer understanding of Principle appeared.

PERSONALITY BECLOUDS SPIRITUAL
UNDERSTANDING

Only as impersonality replaces personality can a correct understanding of any event or circumstance be gained.

The struggle to preserve the Union as seen from the standpoint of either "the North" or "the South" is foolish and gets one nowhere. When seen from the impersonal standpoint of the one evil seeking to stay the ever advancing unfoldment of spiritual good, and always using in a greater degree every argument of so-called human good to accomplish this end, it is easily understood, but not otherwise.

We need, especially at this point in our deductions, to hold steadfastly to the impersonality of all things, for that which will now follow can never be understood from a personal standpoint.

When Jesus said, "if I go not away, the Comforter will not come,"[1] he was stating an absolute metaphysical fact, namely—that the Christ could not appear in its true, impersonal and scientific sense until the human concept, Jesus, was allowed to disappear. Mrs. Eddy proved by her discovery that she was the first

[1] John 16:7.

one to let the Jesus go and to find as All-in-all the Mind that is the Christ. This is the Comforter. Is it not just as absurd then, to think that Christian Science can be understood if it has the least vestige of personality attached to it, as to think that the Bible can be of permanent value unless viewed impersonally and so spiritually?

THE EFFORT OF EVIL TO DESTROY JESUS

Have you ever thought out carefully the account given in the Bible of the birth of Jesus, and the attempt of evil to destroy the child Jesus? Why should evil under the guise of Herod have desired to slay the young child? Was it not because that which appeared as Jesus was merely the clothing, as it were, of the Christ? It is the destruction of the Christ, the truth, that evil, through its very nature of being the suppositional opposite of good, must ever seek to accomplish. Therefore in his blindness, mistaking the image for the substance, Herod thought he could slay the Christ by destroying the clothing of the Christ, called Jesus.

Herod had no personal animosity against Jesus, but he was determined to destroy the Christ, that which was to reign and govern as

Mind and so imperil his kingship. Could evil have been more diligent in attempting to bring this to pass, than Herod proved himself to be? He "slew all the children that were in Bethlehem, and in all the coasts thereof, from two years old and under,"[1] in order to reach the child Jesus. This one act of evil shows the nature of evil, how it stops at nothing to attain its end, and how it uses to accomplish this end, whatever will lend itself to its use.

Herod was doubtless no worse and no better than the ordinary mortal of that time, and certainly he had no personal enmity against the children he destroyed, nor even against the child, Jesus. But Herod, as King, held the power of life and death, and evil could use that power, and it did use it in the diabolical manner of destroying that host of children in order to get rid of just one. Is it any wonder the gospel declares, "In Rama was there a voice heard, lamentation, and weeping, and great mourning, Rachael weeping for her children, and would not be comforted, because they are not"[2]? Does evil ever stop at anything? Having no intelligence it keeps blindly on, though never succeeding in its purpose.

[1] Matt. 2:16.   [2] Matt. 2:18.

THE EFFORT OF EVIL TO DESTROY
THE ENGLISH LANGUAGE

With the birth of Science and Health there was, also, the Herod present to slay. This time however, it appeared not as a person, but more impersonally as a nation.

What was the clothing of Science and Health? Was it not the English language? Then would not the effort of evil be to destroy that language in order to get rid of Science and Health,—the young child of today? How did evil attempt to do this?

Once again, let me remind you that, if you do not think in terms of impersonality you will find it impossible to follow the unfoldment of good, or to follow the machinations of evil in its attempt to destroy that good. You will find yourself in a state of rebellion, an attitude of mind, which, of course, precludes the possibility of further enlightenment.

The problem, then, confronting evil was the destruction of the English language. How was this to be brought about? The history of this can only be touched upon here, for the time is too short to go into it fully. Each one can think and study it out for himself. You are all familiar with the rise of what is called the German Empire. It centered around Prussia, the outstanding young Protestant giant, the most promising and progressive country of Continental Europe in 1866. From that date to 1870 it grew by leaps and bounds, becoming surer of its own strength and power each year. This assurance was increased immeasurably in 1870, when the Franco-Prussian War made Germany, in a few short months, the dictator of Continental Europe. From being a giant stripling full of Protestant earnestness and virility, she became, year by year, more dominating and aggressive. She dreamed dreams of putting the world under her feet and thus became ripe to do the bidding of evil.

You will find, if you take the trouble to do so, that gradually, step by step, there grew up through deliberate propaganda in Germany first an educated dislike, then, a contempt for, and finally, a hatred of the English language; so that, when the hour came for evil to make its deadly thrust at destroying the young child in 1914, the entire venom of the hatred of Germany was turned on the English language, and incidentally on all English-speaking people.

Do you not see why this was? Would it not be necessary in order to destroy the English language, to get rid of every English-speaking person by prohibiting the use of the English language? It had been the custom of Germany to stamp out the language of the people she conquered by compelling the use of her own language. Alsace and Lorraine afford a striking example of this method. Here again Germany was ripe to become the tool of evil.

Mrs. Eddy's revelation was in English, and that revelation can never be successfully translated. No translation can be satisfactory, for no translation can stand as correct, except for a limited period of time. English came as the language of Spirit to Mrs. Eddy, and she alone expressed the Spirit of Christian Science in its exact letter. In order therefore, for Science and Health to be in any other language, Mrs. Eddy would have had to write it in that language, and this she could not have done without the same scholarly understanding that she had of English. Mrs. Eddy truly states, "We are indeed privileged in having the untranslated revelations of Christian Science."[1]

America and Great Britain are the two great English-speaking nations; hence there was only one thing for evil to do, ridiculous as it may sound, and that was to crush those nations in

[1]My. 179:29.

order to destroy Science and Health, the young child, clothed in the English language. Would this endeavor of evil, to wipe out the English-speaking nations, be any more absurd and atrocious than the one expressed by Herod in slaying all the children of two years and under, in Bethlehem and in the coasts thereof? If evil would do the one, would it not do the other to accomplish its purpose? Who would dare to say that evil, in its infinite capacity of evil, would not do this? Because it failed in its purpose, as it did of old with the child Jesus, does that mean that it did not attempt to do it?

But does this mean that evil has put a stigma upon any so-called mortal, whether appearing as an American, or an Englishman or a German —or under any name that may be given to the mortal? Evil is just as impersonal as good, but evil had and always has a deadly hatred for the truth, not because it knows the truth, but because of its inherent nature of being the suppositional opposite of the truth; just as ignorance, by its very nature of being ignorant, hates the intelligence of which it is the suppositional opposite.

Human reason always has a plausible excuse for what it does. So it gave as the reason for the World War that Germany was demanding a place in the sun, that she was being throttled by other nations, and so forth. Was this excuse any different in the slightest or any truer in its relation to what was done, than was the claim that Herod's crown was being threatened by the young child, Jesus? You cannot afford to be deceived. Evil is always evil, and its subtleties are infinite. But evil must inevitably fail because there is no substance to it: so you saw it utterly fail in the World War. You saw the English language protected, and you saw Science and Health left free to go forward.

THE EFFORT OF EVIL TO DESTROY METAPHYSICAL UNDERSTANDING

This, however, did not end completely the effort of evil to destroy Science and Health. There was still another conflict arising; another avenue of attack. No sooner was evil defeated in its physical effort to destroy the English language, than a far more subtle attempt was waged to destroy the right understanding of Science and Health.

Let me briefly run over for you the events that took place in Boston during the years 1918 to 1922.

You remember it was during the summer and early fall of 1918 that the most tremendous stress of the World War was being experienced. Evil was doing its utmost to push its way to victory, but the forces of good were steadily gaining, and as the fall advanced it was clearly seen that the purpose of evil had been thwarted. Then came, in November, the Armistice.

As the physical efforts of evil were being thwarted, a new line of attack at Science and Health was coming to light.

When Mrs. Eddy in 1875 gave her discovery of Christian Science to the world as Science and Health, she very positively stated in that book the evil and error of church organization.

It is plain to any reader of the First Edition, that there was nothing further from Mrs. Eddy's thought than the idea of a church organization attaching itself to Christian Science. She stated this most emphatically, "We have no need of creeds and church organizations to sustain or explain a demonstrable platform, . . ,"[1] "The mistake the disciples of Jesus made to found religious organizations and church rites, if indeed they did this, was one the Master did not make;"[1] "No time was lost by our Master in organizations, rites, and ceremonies, or in

[1] S. & H. 1st Edit. 166.

proselyting for certain forms of belief:"[1] "Church rites and ceremonies have nothing to do with Christianity, and more than this, they draw us towards material things: hence away from spiritual Truth, and all Truth is spiritual."[2] "Jesus paid no homage to diplomas, to forms of church worship, or the theories of man, . . ."[3] "Forms of personal worship may not be voluntarily wrong, but involuntarily so, inasmuch as they hinder the Spirit."[4]

These quotations from the First Edition of Science and Health in 1875 plainly show Mrs. Eddy's aversion to church organization, and that, remember, after she had been presenting Christian Science to the world for nine years from the date of her discovery. But Mrs. Eddy at that time had not quite learned what she later expressed as, "the fixedness of mortal illusions,"[5] in other words the tenacity of evil to be always on the heels of Truth.

Because of the fixedness of mortal illusions Mrs. Eddy found herself confronted with a determination on the part of her followers to have an organization. They demanded, just as of old the children of Israel demanded of Samuel, a king to reign over them, that they might be seen of men to prosper and to be great. This

S. & H. 1st Edit. [1]166, [2]181, [3]118, [4]119, [5]S. & H. 330:4.

time, however, the king took the form of a church organization to show forth its importance and to absorb the attention of men.

It is needless to trace the struggles and efforts of Mrs. Eddy to avoid this danger to the young child, to the unfolding of Science and Health, but the pressure became greater and greater. Finally, because she could not lead this mind to higher levels any faster than it was willing to go, she yielded to the necessity of the hour and allowed the organization to proceed. This she was forced to do in spite of the fact that she had seen the first effort to organize Christian Science fail and fall by the wayside. She saw clearly the utter futility at that time, of attempting further to stand against the tide of materialism determined to have a church organization. Hoping against hope she strove to guide it as wisely as possible.

The church was organized and a board of directors appointed with power to appoint their successors in office under a deed of trust. It was only a few years, however, before Mrs. Eddy realized that ecclesiasticism under any designation is the same always—greedy and tyrannical. She saw that, if it was not curbed, it would strangle the very Spirit, if it could, of the young child.

In 1898, as you know, she attempted to curb this despotism of ecclesiasticism through another deed of trust, creating a board of trustees. This also she made a self-perpetuating body, and gave to it authority over all Christian Science literature apart from her own writings. The absolute authority which she gave to this board was summed up in her own statement in the Deed of Trust in which she said, that the trustees should manage the business, "upon their own responsibility and without c o n s u l t i n g me. . . ."[1]

Perhaps no stronger evidence of Mrs. Eddy's purpose to try to curb this ecclesiastical despotism that she saw ready to "devour her child,"[2] could be given, than she gave in the Deed of Trust constituting the board of trustees of the Christian Science Publishing Society. This was also further emphasized in the first of the three "Rules" she wrote by hand for the trustees when she appointed them. She considered these rules of such vital importance that she had them delivered by a special messenger from Pleasant View. The first rule read, "When mother foils a demon scheme do not mar her success. The hardest battle is the *last* one."

[1]Deed of Trust 1898 para. 3.   [2]Rev. 12:4.

What could more significantly express her deep desire and purpose than this "Rule." All she asked of the trustees was to be true to their trust, and then Mind would take care of the "hardest battle," "the *last* one."

But could the evil of ecclesiasticism be thus constrained? It must sooner or later show itself for just what it is in order for all to see and reject it. From 1898 to December 1910, under Mrs. Eddy's authority and control, the two boards appeared to operate harmoniously, but with the departure of Mrs. Eddy in December 1910 there soon arose the determination of ecclesiasticism to express its nature, to seize everything for itself, and to be the only law.

This, remember, has nothing to do with person; it is ecclesiasticism now and always.

Just as the period of time from 1870 to 1914 was the developing time of that abnormal political arrogance and conceit that finally threw Germany into the arms of evil to do its bidding, so the years 1910 to 1918 were doing exactly the same thing with the ecclesiastical board of the Christian Science movement, or what appeared to be the Christian Science movement.

Evil was rapidly preparing the way for its final effort to overthrow the young child by an ecclesiastical body as the authority, intervening between Principle and its idea,—in other words, something that could have the power to define what the Christian Scientist must do and think

To accomplish this purpose, a nullification of the Deed of Trust constituting the board of trustees had to be brought about. The trustees must be compelled to surrender their authority under their deed of trust and so become hirelings of the ecclesiastical body, and therefore powerless to stop further the attempts of that body to intervene as authority between God and man.

It is not necessary to go into the record of all of this, for it has been fully published to the world in the complete account of the court proceedings, in which it ultimated in Boston. The stand of the trustees was stated in a few words. They stood for the inalienable right of the individual Christian Scientist to be directly governed by his divine Principle, without the slightest interference from any so-called ecclesiastical intermediary or authority. The exact opposite of this was the position of the directors.

As the conflict in Boston for the maintenance of man's inherent right to commune with God and be governed by God directly without any intermediary, grew, so evil's declaration of its so-called "plan of church government" and assumption of the right to dictate and control also grew. With this final mental conflict coming to the front, the conflict going on in the so-called physical world, as the World War, began rapidly to draw to its close.

It is very interesting, metaphysically, to notice that just in proportion to the forward steps taken by the trustees to maintain and uphold the democracy of Mind, or Christian Science, against the autocracy of evil, or ecclesiastical domination, the conflict in Europe drew to its end. When the trustees were wholly ready to protect this democracy, the conflict in Europe ceased in what was called the Armistice. The Armistice was really only the name given to the change that was taking place in the conflict between evil and good, from the physical to the purely mental realm.

THE FINAL FREEDOM

You all remember the wonderful unfoldment of the court proceedings under the Bill in Equity filed by the board of trustees. The record of this case, as I have already said, was printed in full, making a book of over 1500 pages, and it is the only case of moment that has ever been printed entirely in full.

The master, Judge Frederic Dodge, before whom the case was tried, found in his report the allegations of the trustees' bill to be true in every substantial, if not in every respect, and his rulings of law were in agreement with his findings of fact. This, however, could not stand, for freedom could not come to the Christian Scientist in the realm of church organization. Church organization, whether harmonious or discordant, can only end in intruding itself as a power or authority between man and his divine Principle, and therefore must disappear.

How was this to come about? Not with a decision that would have kept the trustees and that which they were standing for, in the realm of organization; it could only come as and when freedom from organization was fully accomplished. So in the appeal from the master's findings, while the Supreme Court of Massachusetts fully sustained every finding of fact, in its interpretation of the law, it had to go contrary to the master's findings of law. And why? Because the ecclesiastical body, in Boston, called the Christian Science Board of Directors, had to be enthroned as the most supreme, autocratic, ecclesiastical body on earth. This was necessary in order that every Christian

Scientist would sooner or later be brought face to face with the inevitable conclusion, that such ecclesiastical authority had no relationship whatever to Christian Science. The finite belief of church organization is utterly foreign to Christian Science, and, so far as the genuine Christian Scientist is concerned, it is gone forever.

It is not possible to conceive of a Christian Scientist understanding that he is "alone with his own being and with the reality of things,"[1] allowing for one moment that he must do as this one says or that one says, whether under the guise of a church authority, or a so-called teacher or practitioner. It is essential for the individual's growth and progress that he shall look directly to Principle, and accept no authority but Principle. Could anything other than this be Christian Science or have any relationship to Christian Science? There is only one answer to that question, and that is, it could not. Man is one with his Maker and that oneness can never be encroached upon.

Could then the decision of the Supreme Court of Massachusetts have been different, any more than could the decision of Pilate have been

[1]Mes. 01 20:8.

different? That does not, however, make evil good or wrong right. The pressure of Truth will continually force evil to the point of its own extinction by being seen as merely the negative interpretation of reality.

The decision of the Boston case is accomplishing this very result. Metaphysics was cast out and with it the entire deception that church organization, whether called the Christian Science church or any other church, could have anything to do, even in the remotest way, with Christian Science. It was so entirely exposed that all could see the nature of the deception and no longer be in bondage to it.

Freedom can never be obtained *in* anything, hence in organization there can be no freedom. The one and only organization that constitutes freedom is the organization of Principle and its idea, and in this unity the idea is the very activity of the Principle.

Thus we see evil utterly fail in its last two activities, first in the World War attempting to destroy the English language, the clothing of the young child, and second in the ecclesiastical attempt to destroy the true metaphysical interpretation of the teaching of Christian Science. As a consequence of this, a freedom has come to the Christian Scientist that endows him with

the absolute knowledge and certainty that he
cannot be and never is deprived of his direct
communion with Principle.

"IT IS FINISHED"[1]

The Line of Light that we have traced down
from Eve through all its various unfoldments
to its last impersonal appearance as Science and
Health, is complete and finished. In other
words, Science and Health is proved to be the
final statement of Mind, and is sufficient to annihilate totally the Adam-man or so-called human
mind.

"THIS IS THE WAY, WALK YE IN IT"[2]

In order to be fully settled on this point, one
question must be answered, and that question
is, Could there not be some other avenue or
channel through which good could appear to
destroy this Adam-mind?

For a moment ask yourself, To what source
do I look to gain spiritual advancement? Do I
not find myself as a mortal, made up of all
kinds of emotions and feelings and beliefs, some
called appetites, some passions, some artistic
talents, and so forth, and then, last of all, have

[1]John 19:30.   [2]Isa. 30:21.

I not my highest sense of right, of Principle? To which of these do you look for spiritual advancement? Of course, only to your highest sense of right, for that alone can bring you a greater spirituality. You do not think for a moment that anything you eat or drink, or anything you put on can advance you spiritually one iota. Neither do you think that your anger, resentment or passions of one kind or another, can bring you spiritual enlightenment. You do not think that your sense of art, of music, of beauty, or of grandeur can advance you one step spiritually. In fact, you know that there is only one way to advance spiritually, and that is by listening to your highest sense of Principle and living right up to that highest sense.

Then, does not this mean that you, as a mortal, have just one source, and one source alone to which you can turn in your process of overcoming the mortal? This is perfectly clear to you, for you know it to be a fact.

ANALYSIS OF THE MORTAL AND HIS REDEMPTION

Now, let us turn to this so-called Adam or Adam-mind, and see just what takes place there. First of all, there is just the one Adam-mind, the negative interpretation of the one divine Mind. This Adam-mind, as you have discovered, has what you might call its highest sense of good, and that good you have named Eve. You have traced this "Eve" in a direct line through what appeared as persons, nations and so forth, without deviation, to its present name, Science and Health. But just as you, as a mortal, seem to have countless other thoughts besides your highest sense of good, so the Adam-mind had countless thoughts besides Eve. These thoughts also appeared as persons, nations and so forth, coming down through what is called the ages, some appearing good and some bad, but none of them having any more relation to Eve and the direct Line of Light, than have your passions and appetites any relation to your highest sense of Principle. You do not think of turning to your sense of art or music any more than to your anger or resentment to gain real spiritual good. In the same way, not one atom of spiritual light can be gained from the varying beliefs constituting Adam and his so-called progeny, except that which is of the direct Line of Light, that Line of Light unbroken from Eve to Science and Health.

"UNTO SHILOH SHALL THE GATHERING OF THE PEOPLE BE"[1]

You have only one highest sense of good, not two, and that one is what you have to follow. There are not two Lines of Light, there is only one, and that one is the one you have traced down, from the impersonalizing of evil in its simple form as Eve, to its world-embracing form as Science and Health.

Science and Health finishes entirely the appearing of God to man in the form of a Redeemer or Saviour. This one Redeemer takes you to Mind itself, and in your communion with infinite Mind you find complete salvation and satisfaction, salvation from every erroneous belief, and satisfaction in Mind's infinite allness.

You do not look elsewhere for guidance or direction. You do not imagine that light can come forth from Egypt, in other words, from that which expresses the darkness of Adam. Has India anything to do with the Line of Light? Has China anything to do with it? Has any nation or people anything to do with it? You know that out of Israel alone Shiloh must

[1] Gen. 49:10.

come, and it is unto Shiloh, spiritual sense that
the gathering of the people shall be.

If evil attempts to present itself as a doubt
or question, as to the truth of what you know
and have established as this Line of Light, remember what Jesus pointed out in regard to
John the Baptist. Jesus and John the Baptist
stood as the two distinct conditions of good,
one the purely spiritual good, and the other
the highest material sense of good. Jesus said
of this highest material sense of good, expressed
as John the Baptist, "For I say unto you, Among
those that are born of women there is not a
greater prophet than John the Baptist: but he
that is least in the kingdom of God is greater
than he."[1] Analyze this statement of Jesus and
see if it was not as though he had said, there
is not an atom of spirituality in the highest-ma-
terial sense of good. Good to be good and to
be of real value, must be the good that Mind
is, without one element of materiality.

If Jesus could so wipe out, as of no spiritual
value, the highest sense of material good, could
you be in doubt for one moment as to whether
or not any spiritual good can be obtained from
any source apart from the Line of Light as re-

[1] Luke 7:28.

vealed in the Bible and its consummation, Science and Health?

"BLIND LEADERS OF THE BLIND"[1]

Be not deceived on this question. Jesus saw clearly how evil would suggest, "Lo, here is Christ or there; believe it not,"[2] and how "if it were possible, they shall deceive the very elect."[2]

Are not these so-called Christs, these way-showers, these leaders, arising in all directions, and parading themselves as the true Christ, the true leader, fulfilling just what Jesus pointed out?

Note this, that each one of them, no matter how mild and friendly he may appear toward Science and Health in the beginning, sooner or later ends by attempting to substitute his own jumbled and mistaken statement of the truth for the true, clear and succinct statement of Science and Health. Then he attempts to pull down, by innuendo and distortion, Mrs. Eddy and her marvelous character and life, for the purpose, not only of exalting himself, but of dethroning Science and Health.

[1]Matt. 15:14.　[2]Matt. 24:23, 24.

As a metaphysician you are not concerned with what may be said about Mrs. Eddy, for to you Mrs. Eddy has her place as the recording angel of Mind. That place is secure, and she needs no defence. Science and Health stands alone and forever intact. Nevertheless you are not deceived as to what evil is striving to do in attacking Mrs. Eddy. It is to throw discredit on Science and Health.

Neither are you deceived into thinking that the one so near to God, so far away from material sense that she was able to give Science and Health to the world, could have any oneness with materiality.

The venomous poison of human envy, jealousy and malice, seeking its own self-exaltation, is found harmless and inane before such purity. But, as Mrs. Eddy once expressed it, "A mouse will gnaw in the dark at a spotless garment."[1]

CONFIDENCE BORN OF ENLIGHTENMENT

You are not in darkness on any of these points. You know them of yourself, and you know the rock whence your understanding is hewn. There is no doubt or question with you as to this oneness of Mind, this oneness of the Line of Light.

[1] 100 Edit. S. & H. 278:13.

You are free because you do understand this
and you know there is no other source of freedom.

You do not base your knowledge of Christian Science on person, place or thing, but you
base it on your own understanding of Mind.
In communion with this infinite Mind, you find
all that means to you person, place, thing; in
fact you find all good, and that is why you are
never afraid of losing one iota of good. You
know that nothing can deprive you of this good
that is yours now and always.

SHADOW AND SUBSTANCE

You ask, what place and what relation to the
Line of Light have those conditions of thought
that appear as pagan and unenlightened nations? They have exactly the same relation to
the Line of Light that your anger and passion
have to your highest sense of Principle. Then
you ask, what relation have the more enlightened
nations, the so-called Christian nations, to the
Line of Light? They have the same relation
that John the Baptist had to the Christ. In
other words, human material sense whether under the guise of good or bad has no relationship
whatever to the true Light.

But you ask, have they no relationship to me? Yes, they certainly have a deep relationship to you as a mortal, for they are the very presence or activity of that which you, as a mortal, are accepting as your mind. They, one and all, are included in the unity of evil called this human or Adam-mind, and, as such, must be annihilated by the one Mind and its activity that is infinite Principle. This will not do away with person, place or thing, but it will find God as the one person, the one place, the one thing and will totally destroy everything that is unlike this person, place and thing that God is. "And I, if I be lifted up from the earth, will draw all men unto me."[1]

Face this fearlessly and with confidence. To hide from it and to hide from the responsibility of it, will never gain you anything, but to look from the shadow to the substance will bring you joy and contentment. "Every object in material thought will be destroyed, but the spiritual idea, whose substance is in Mind, is eternal."[2]

ABSOLUTE RIGHT THE ONLY PEACE

You ask, Will there be no peace or rest from now on? There can be no peace or rest till

[1]John 12:32.   [2]S. & H. 267:1.

every question is settled on the side of Truth, any more than there can be any peace or rest in the problem of mathematics until every statement is adjusted to the principle of numbers. Peace and rest being qualities of Mind, the right adjustment can take place immediately. Time is not an element in the question. Good is now and always. Therefore, as each question that arises is settled on the side of Principle, and alone with Principle, it is settled once and forever, and that is "the peace of God, which passeth all understanding."[1]

But could you have peace and rest with ignorance reigning as Mind? Could you have two times two as five, and call it peace and rest? Why not have it as four, which is itself peace and rest? Why not have Mind as All-in-all right now and find the straight and narrow path of Science, as straight and narrow as mathematics; and yet in its application, as broad as the whole universe? Mrs. Eddy has tersely stated this when she says, "There remaineth, it is true, a Sabbath rest for the people of God; but we must first have done our work, and entered into our rest, as the Scriptures give example."[2]

[1] Phil. 4:7. [2] Mis. 216:3.

THE GREAT PYRAMID

You have also asked about the great Pyramid, Cheops—the Bible in stone, as it has been called—with its marvelous passages depicting so graphically these latter days, and especially the low passage, possibly, symbolizing a period of depression and despair before the enlarging sense of the King's Chamber appears. However do not forget that this passage of depression is not the passage that the Christian Scientist takes. His passage is the upper passage which, as one earnest writer many years ago expressed it, is "Only obtainable by beings who can move upward like the angels of God." You, as true Christian Scientists, are the angels of God. The passage of depression simply symbolizes the tremendous pressure that Truth is ever placing on error, until there is nothing left of error. The depression deals only with the tumult of human belief; and that tumult is bound to continue until "every knee shall bow to me, and every tongue shall confess to God."[1]

The Pyramid is true, and it is amazing that there are those who, while not questioning for one moment that God has shown forth the way of the destruction of evil in the printed word,

[1] Rom. 14:11.

in what is called the Bible, think He could not
show forth the same destruction of evil in the
word of stone. Cannot the language of Mind
appear to you as stone just as well as print? Why
should one doubt or question this? Science and
Health declares, "Soul has infinite resources
with which to bless mankind."[1]

Is the hand of Mind so limited to print, that
it cannot appear as stone? Language is simply
figure of speech, and that figure of speech will
always appear in the way you can best understand it. Transportation appeared to you yesterday as the prairie schooner, and today as the
aeroplane, but it is transportation just the same.
The Pyramid can rightly be termed the Bible
or "miracle in stone,"[2] and because it is in stone,
it does not the less point to the absolute destruction of all material sense.

Remember however, neither the Pyramid nor
the history of Israel, in their material concept,
really touches the hem of Christian Science. They
merely in a degree corroborate the truth of
Christian Science. No study of them can aid
spiritual understanding in the slightest. "Take
away the spiritual signification of Scripture, and
that compilation can do no more for mortals

[1] S. & H. 60:29.   [2] Hea. 11:12.

than can moonbeams to melt a river of ice."[1]
Christian Science stands alone in its own purity
and perfection awaiting each one's acceptance.

NATURE OF DEPRESSION TODAY

There will not be less of tumult, but more and
more, until Mind is found as All-in-all.

Do not think, however, that this tumult and
depression need appear in the old way; "old
things are passed away; behold, all things are
become new."[2] The ways of tumult and depression may no longer appear in their former garments of war and lack of prosperity. Certain
phases of warfare, last seen in evil's purpose to
destroy the clothing of the young child in the
World War are largely gone. Now, our warfare
is being understood as a mental warfare—a warfare with one's self.

The world will experience a greater material
prosperity than has ever been known, but with
it will come neither joy nor satisfaction. Sooner
or later all may appear materially prosperous
for the Adam must learn that material abundance cannot bring happiness. He, apparently,
cannot do this without first having the sense of
unlimited supply. So long as he has something

[1]S. & H. 241:14.   [2]2 Cor. 5:17.

in matter to crave, he has before him a measure of anticipated joy in its attainment. Only when he has all of matter that his heart has ever desired, but finds still with him the same deep discontent, is he ready to turn to the true Source, Mind, with his whole heart.

In Mind he will find the "pearl of great price"[1] which when he has found, he will sell all that he hath, and buy it. In other words, he will let go of his material sense of all things for the spiritual sense. Evil, then, can never tempt him to return to its allegiance.

Evil is the counterfeit, the negation of God, but, Mind being All-in-all, the counterfeit has also to say, "I am all and give all to all." Be not deceived, however, its all is merely a mirage, without reality or true happiness, until reversed by understanding, "Seek ye first the kingdom of God, and his righteousness; and all these things shall be added unto you."[2]

"MY PEACE I GIVE UNTO YOU"[3]

You, as the understanding Christian Scientist, need but to pursue the even tenor of your way, finding Mind as your All-in-all, and rejoicing in the certain knowledge that because Mind

[1] Matt. 13:46.   [2] Matt. 6:33.   [3] John 14:27.

is One and is All, that which appears for the
moment as something apart from Mind is not
real or true. It is simply the final effort of evil,
malicious mind, through hypnotic suggestion, to
substitute itself as your Mind, and appear first
as one erroneous conception and then as another.
However, you know this is impossible, for the
one Mind is your Mind, and the one way of that
Mind is Science and Health. It is in that one
Mind that you find for yourself all there is in
Science and Health, and that will continue to
unfold throughout all infinity.

In finding this infinite Mind as that alone with
which you eternally commune, you have declared
in the language of Mrs. Eddy that, "The first
spontaneous motion of Truth and Love, acting
through Christian Science on my roused consciousness, banished at once and. forever the
fundamental error of faith in things material:
for this trust is the unseen sin, the unknown
foe,—the heart's untamed desire which breaketh
the divine commandments."[1]

[1]Ret. 31 :13.

WHY AM I A CHRISTIAN SCIENTIST?

WHY am I a Christian Scientist?

This question is one with which, as a thoughtful Christian Scientist, you find yourself continually confronted. It is a question that must be answered in the secrecy of your own thought. It cannot be avoided. It can be correctly and satisfactorily answered only from the one basis, understanding.

There must be a reason for your understanding, or it can never survive the inevitable opposition of doubt. In other words, you must, as Peter declared, have "a reason of the hope that is in you."[1] You must be able to satisfy yourself from every standpoint as to why you are a Christian Scientist.

CHRISTIAN SCIENCE DEFINED

Before attempting to answer this question fully, you must first settle just what the term Christian Science means. Unless you really understand what is conveyed by the words, Christian and Science, you cannot answer. You must properly satisfy yourself as to what Christian

[1] Peter 3:15.

Science really means to you, or you are helpless in your effort to understand Christian Science. Christian means pertaining to Christ, Truth. Science means exact knowledge. Therefore, Christian Science means exact knowledge of Truth. In other words, Christian Science must and does mean right knowing.

THE CHRISTIAN SCIENTIST IS ALONE WITH HIS OWN UNDERSTANDING

As a Christian Scientist, then, you have the exact knowledge of Truth, and this means right knowing. Then, you are a right knower. The question, therefore, resolves itself into this, Why are you a right knower, a right thinker? No one can answer this for you. You must think it out for yourself, or it is not answered. And remember, there is no royal road to thinking. Thinking is the quiet, painstaking ability to be one with right at every point. No one can do your thinking for you.

Jesus said, "Verily, verily, I say unto you, He that entereth not by the door into the sheep fold, but climbeth up some other way, the same is a thief and a robber."[1] There is only one right way, one satisfying way, one answer to, Why am I a Christian Scientist?

[1] Jno. 10:1.

Do you think that you can satisfy yourself with the answer that you are a Christian Scientist because you have Science and Health and read and study that book, or because of Mrs. Eddy, or because of Christ Jesus, or the prophets, or anyone who has gone before? Could there be such a thing as vicarious atonement? It is inconceivable that there could possibly be vicarious right-knowing. You cannot understand mathematics for another. Such an idea is no more absurd than to think that you could understand Christian Science for another. Sooner or later you must face fairly, squarely, and honestly the question, What do I understand about Christian Science that makes me a Christian Scientist?

In speaking of the mission of Jesus, Mrs. Eddy said, "He did life's work aright not only in justice to himself, but in mercy to mortals,— to show them how to do theirs, but not to do it for them nor to relieve them of a single responsibility."[1] What another has said or done can make little difference to you unless you do likewise, for there is no vicarious at-one-ment. We come into at-one-ment with Mind only through our own understanding.

[1] S. & H. 18:6.

In this enlightened age, you surely can no longer think that one can acquire an understanding for another, and by so doing carry him to the very pinnacle of achievement, heaven and harmony. Of course, that is out of the question. You must discover Christian Science for yourself. It is foolish to think that Mrs. Eddy's discovery of it, is your discovery with little or no mental effort on your part. It is yours only as you make it yours. Are you asking yourself the question, Why am I a Christian Scientist? I am asking it of myself here and now, and I am forced to answer. No one can do it for me. There is only one possible way whereby Christian Science can come to you, and that is in the way Mrs. Eddy has pointed out, "The Christian Scientist is alone with his own being and with the reality of things."[1] Jesus meant exactly this when he said, "when thou prayest, enter into thy closet."[2]

PRAYER OUR SCIENTIFIC DISCOVERY
OF GOD

What is prayer? To pray means to think, to commune, to discover, and therefore, to find out something. "It makes new and scientific

[1] Mes. 01 20:8. [2] Matt. 6:6.

discoveries of God, of His goodness and power. It shows us more clearly than we saw before, what we already have and are; and most of all, it shows us what God is."[1]

Long ago you gave up the idea that prayer had anything to do with getting down on your knees. With the very first enlightenment of Christian Science, you drew away from that belief. There is no prayer but thinking, and thinking means right knowing. "Enter into thy closet, and when thou hast shut thy door," —not someone else's door—"pray to thy Father which is in secret."[2]

What is the only thing that is in secret? Mind is all that is in secret, because it includes within itself nothing but itself. Not an element contrary to Mind is there. Then entering thy closet and shutting the door means communing with the one Mind and shutting out all else. There is no other possible way of gaining the kingdom of heaven than through the process of understanding.

RITUALISTIC ROUTINE FUTILE

No more dangerous belief is operating, today, among Christian Scientists, than the belief that

[1] No. 39:20.   [2] Matt. 6:6.

by the mere doing something or saying something, spiritual advancement can be obtained. It is perfectly self-evident that, if "doing" or "saying" or both could advance one spiritually, then religious ritualism would have taken us all into the kingdom of heaven long, long ago, for ritualism is the very symbol of "doing" and "saying." No one is so blind as to think that this is not a fact. Would one question that the purpose of the ritualist in performing his perfunctory routine springs from a deep desire to enter the kingdom of heaven, and that this desire is just as sincere as yours?

Do not imagine that young men and young women endeavoring to forsake the world's attractions, enter religious orders without the most earnest purpose to advance spiritually. The very fact that their faithfulness to ritual during the past many centuries has not obtained the goal of spirituality but rather, on the contrary, may have encouraged materiality, should have opened the eyes of all men to the futility of depending upon such methods.

You know that the temptation confronting the Christian Scientist is the identical temptation which has always confronted those striving for spiritual growth. It is the temptation to believe that there is some mysterious spiritual virtue in the mere doing something or saying something or attending something. Mystery is never the accompaniment of spirituality.

THE DANGER OF CONCESSIONS

The whole purpose of malicious mind, in its argument, is to turn the Christian Scientist to this outworn belief of material symbols,—in other words, the paying of "tithe of mint and anise and cummin,"[1] that he may win the spiritual goal. If it were possible, the next step would inevitably be a further departure from Mind as All-in-all, with the question, Why not do some material thing, or use some material remedy to heal my body?—Why not call in the aid of a surgeon to remove that which he may say should not be there? Where can you stop?

If you begin to undermine your confidence in Spirit, in the slightest degree, there is no place where you can stop and say, At this point I will depend on Mind completely. If you concede that, in some way or other, you can be benefited by some material gesture, no matter what its nature, the whole structure of your understanding may be seriously jeopardized. "For whosoever shall keep the whole law, and yet

[1] Matt. 23:23.

offend in one point, he is guilty of all."[1] And
Mrs. Eddy declares, "Christian Science is absolute; it is neither behind the point of perfection
nor advancing towards it; it is at this point and
must be practised therefrom."[2]

You cannot dissemble with Mind in one instance and then think you can be true to it in
another. That is not possible. It was the fidelity
of the early Christians, to what they believed
Christ to be, which so supported and strengthened them, that they were able, unflinchingly,
to face the flames at the stake and the wild
beasts in the arena. They neither murmured
nor recanted, but stood firm as a rock on the
power of Truth to sustain them to the utmost.
Are we not capable, through the higher understanding of Life that Christian Science has
brought to us, and the knowledge of what Life
really means and is, of being equally steadfast?
Or are we going to take down the bars and
argue for the expediency of first one little concession and then another; thus gradually drifting little by little away from Spirit to matter?

The effect of turning away in the slightest
degree, from the direct line of Spirit is conclusively seen in the actions of those, who, while

[1]James 2:10.   [2]My. 242:5.

claiming to be Christian Scientists, eventually come out and declare, that the right practice of Christian Science, and the duty of Christian Scientists, is to join forces with materia medica. That is, in substance, they advocate the leaving of the healing of the body of the patient in the hands of materia medica, and the overcoming and quieting of the fear in the hands of the Christian Scientist.

Could anything be a greater parody on Christian Science and its sublime power to meet every need, than this? Yet, is there much difference, really, between this frank, ridiculous declaration as to the right practice of Christian Science, and the plea of the Christian Scientist who argues for some concession or divergence to save himself the anguish of remaining true to his own understanding of Spirit as All-in-all?

METAPHYSICS AND DRUGS

You ask the question, Is it not true that Mrs. Eddy took medicine and called in the services of a surgeon, and that she countenanced surgical work? Every so-called Christian Scientist who wants to use drugs, will say that she did, in order to help bolster up his own unfortunate desire. But does his saying this make it so? Or does it make his interpretation of what he may think Mrs. Eddy did a correct one? She said, "To quench the growing flames of falsehood, once in about seven years I have to repeat this, —that I use no drugs whatever, not even coffea (coffee), thea (tea), capsicum (red pepper); though every day, and especially at dinner, I indulge in homeopathic doses of Natrum muriaticum (common salt)."[1] "I understand that God is an ever-present help in all times of trouble,—have found Him so; and would have no other gods, no remedies in drugs, no material medicine."[2]

As a matter of fact it is really of little importance in one sense of the word, to the genuine Christian Scientist, what Mrs. Eddy, personally, is said to have done or not to have done. With the metaphysician, person does not enter into his thinking. The one and only question he is concerned with is whether or not it is in accordance with Mind as All-in-all. If not, he requires no further word on the subject, and certainly is not influenced by what anyone is supposed to have done or not done. "Science makes no concessions to persons or opinions."[3]

[1] Mis. 348:17.   [2] Mis. 96:3.   [3] S. & H. 456:17.

But if he does look to an example, it is always to the one Exemplar, Christ Jesus, and to the one and final interpretation of that Exemplar, Science and Health. He never looks elsewhere, for he knows that Mind, being one and all, appears only in one perfect example and in one complete explanation, and that one is enough, just as in mathematics one "two times two as four" is enough. There cannot be more than one.

Mrs. Eddy never hesitated to state frankly what she did. When she went to the dentist and allowed him to use a local anesthetic, she said why she did so. It was in order not to disturb and array the dentist's mind against a painless operation. This was done not only in courtesy to the dentist, but as a lesson to her followers to be "wise as serpents, and harmless as doves,"[1] and not to array unnecessary opposition against their progress and harmony. Mrs. Eddy writes, "When I found myself under this new regime of medicine, the medicine of Mind, I wanted to satisfy my curiosity as to the effect of drugs on one who had lost all faith in them. Hence I tried several doses of medicine, and so proved to myself that drugs have no beneficial

[1] Matt. 10:16.

effect on an individual in a proper state of mind."[1]

A HOUSE DIVIDED AGAINST ITSELF

Can you conceive, however, what would have happened, if, understanding the allness of Mind, as the author of Science and Health could not have helped doing, Mrs. Eddy had really put any trust or confidence in matter or material ways and means? What would happen to you if, knowing as you do that two times two is four, you admitted that it could even temporarily be five? You could not escape the wrong answer. Neither could Mrs. Eddy have escaped the result had she departed from Mind to matter. Remember, "The healthy sinner is the hardened sinner."[2] The hardened sinner is the one who has so little sense of good that there is virtually no distance between what he knows of good and what he does, in other words, what his conduct is; consequently there is no discord apparent to him.

For example, the child thumping on the piano, having no sense of musical harmony and the laws relating to music, has no idea what discord his thumping produces. However, let

[1] Mis. 348:23.   [2] S. & H. 404:15.

there awaken even a little understanding of harmony, and the thumping has to cease; otherwise the discord would become intolerable. This awakening can become so extreme that the musically-trained mind will cringe at a discord that the musical novice would not even notice. If such suffering could occur in the realm of music, what sort of suffering do you think would occur in that mind which knew so well Mind's allness, if it turned with hope and confidence to matter, the opposite of Mind?

The discoverer of Christian Science was always trying to uncover that which would be of help and value to her followers. Like the true pioneer, she was ever seeking the safest way to travel. Mrs. Eddy's actions were necessarily based on this purpose. That is why she said in the words of Jesus, "What I do thou knowest not now; but thou shalt know hereafter."[1]

METAPHYSICS AND SURGERY

Mrs. Eddy has been most explicit upon the point of surgery. Look in your concordances and read what she has said on the use of medicine and surgery; then, you will be in no doubt as to her meaning on this question. In one place

[1] Jno. 13:7.

you will find this statement, "Until the advancing age admits the efficacy and supremacy of Mind, it is better for Christian Scientists to leave surgery and the adjustment of broken bones and dislocations to the fingers of a surgeon, ..."; then she adds, "Christian Science is always the most skilful surgeon. . . ."[1]

How long do you expect to continue this "advancing age"? When you understand metaphysics, can you say the present age makes a demand for such a concession? The bonds of belief in human thought have been so loosened by the leaven of Science and Health that it has reached the point of being ready for anything. No matter what discovery, or what accomplishment is presented in the press, or how far it goes beyond the length of previous possibility, it is not questioned. The world today is in the attitude of mind where, if not immediately ready to accept a new presentation it still by no means rejects it, and the great mass of mortals accept it without a question.

This being so, what about you as a Christian Scientist? Knowing as you do the power of Mind and its allness, are you listening to the persuasions of malicious mind, that this remedy

[1] S. & H. 401:27.

or that remedy might comfort you or in some way benefit you? "Burnt offerings and drugs, God does not require."[1] "It is difficult to say how much one can do for himself, whose faith is divided between catnip and Christ; but not so difficult to know that if he were to serve one master, he could do vastly more."[2] "But now, after that ye have known God, or rather are known of God, how turn ye again to the weak and beggarly elements, whereunto ye desire again to be in bondage"?[3]

Is a concession in one respect any different from a concession in another? For instance you may ask, Is a concession in having a surgeon set a dislocated or broken bone less of a concession than cutting out a so-called diseased organ or a growth? There may be quite a difference. Remember, in Christian Science it is the attitude of mind that is being entertained and the effect made on the mind that is of primary importance, and it is to this attitude that your whole attention has to be directed. You understand perfectly that any act, of itself, is of no particular moment one way or the other, but it is of deep moment what your expectations are from the thing you allow and the reasons

[1]Mis. 51:3.　[2]Mis. 52:3.　[3]Gal. 4:9.

for allowing it. In what are you placing your trust and confidence? In the surgical operation, or in Mind? "If you would destroy the sense of disease, you should not build it up by wishing to see the forms it assumes or by employing a single material application for its relief."[1]

In the case of a broken bone, there is no healing involved in the mere act of the setting. You are not expecting it, and even the surgeon is not deceived on that point, any more than a carpenter, who mends a broken piece of wood, imagines he knits the pieces together. He merely puts them in place, holding them there just as the surgeon does with the bones, and in the same way, when you go to a dentist you do not deceive yourself into thinking the tooth has been healed or its substance restored. You know it has not been healed at all and you know, as a Christian Scientist, you are just putting off the day when you must see the substance of the tooth in its place if real healing is to result. But, in the case of cutting out some troublesome growth or organ do you not expect healing to result?

You do not expect to find yourself in the kingdom of heaven with an imperfect tooth, any more than with an imperfect body. You are

[1] S. & H. 421 : 26.

bidden by the apostle to "present your bodies a living sacrifice, holy, (wholly) acceptable unto God, which is your reasonable service, (which is the least you can do.)"[1]

THE STARTING POINT IN METAPHYSICS

Now return to the original question, and ask again, Why am I a Christian Scientist? Let us establish a reason. Briefly, you begin by establishing what you know as reality; what you know wholly apart from the testimony of the so-called material senses. No dependence on outside testimony can be accepted or be of the least benefit to you. Only the inherent realization, the self-evident fact, which like Euclid's axiom requires no demonstration, can be admitted by you,—the fact of your own conscious being, conscious existence; not what you are conscious of or how you are conscious, but the simple, self-evident fact that you consciously exist—that you know you are. All can agree on this starting point as a good basis from which to begin, because it is something you know of yourself and is not dependent on anything apart from your own knowledge.

[1] Rom. 12:1.

You know all this without being reminded of it. This Conference is only of value as it arouses latent understanding and carries one forward. As we are told, "Awake thou that sleepest."[1]

ESTABLISHING CAUSE

Because you are conscious of your own existence, it necessarily follows there must be a cause for this conscious existence or being. The term conscious existence is simply the term you use to designate that which, not only is self-evident, but also, that which is self-evidently effect. There can be no effect without a cause, any more than there can be a cause without the effect to which the cause is cause. This cause you have named with the three letters G-O-D. You are not using these letters merely as a word. They must be a combination of letters which means something to you. The use of a word merely as a word, without any meaning to give an impulse to your thought, is utterly futile, and is the height of superstition and absurdity. It has no power to accomplish a demonstrable result. Hence Jesus' statement, "they think that they shall be heard for their much speaking,"[2] in other words, for the language used.

[1]Eph. 5:14.   [2]Matt. 6:7.

The only power there is for good or evil in any combination of letters, is the impulse it gives to thought. When you use the letters G-O-D and call it God, it is only for one purpose, and that is, to give such right impulse to your thought as will exalt it to the point of the realization of your true being, origin, or cause as God or good. From this origin you are the spontaneous derivative. You have the witness of that being in your own existence. This is the "Light, which lighteth every man that cometh into the world."[1] This witness carries you directly to cause which is as certain to you as is your own being or existence. Then there is no question in your mind that causation *is*. You are not concerned or worried in the least about the term you use for it, for that is of no moment whatever.

Mrs. Eddy uses many terms for God, in order to meet every condition of thought. You will doubtless find, as the infinity of that which you name God continues its ever unfolding, your terms for Him may take on a new combination of letters. Use your own term, but that term must hold your thought steadily true to what God means to you. You know cause *is,* and you are, because cause *is*.

[1] Jno. 1:9.

CAUSE ONE AND INFINITE

Having established that there is cause, let us see whether there can possibly be more than one cause. Can there be more than one principle of numbers, one multiplication table? You have found cause *is*, must not this *is* include *all* there is? You understand that, if there were anything outside of *is* it would have to be *is not*, and therefore, could not be. Consequently there is one *is*, which includes all that is, and so is infinite. You find yourself, then, alone with this *is*, this *isness*, this consciousness which is your own being, alone in your own closet, with the door shut, shut by the infinity of this *isness*, which by its nature spontaneously excludes everything unlike itself. You are alone with your own thinking, your own understanding. In this you find oneness, that oneness or aloneness with Being and what Being is Being to, which means all the heaven there is.

Any belief implying more than one would dethrone *isness* as *allness*, and end in utter confusion. This oneness includes, of course, both cause and effect, God and that which God is God to. God could never be, without being God to something, and this something you call idea or man.

Jno. 1:9.

CAUSE AND EFFECT INSEPARABLE BUT NEVER INTERCHANGEABLE

God and man, therefore, are one and inseparable in the sense that one can never be without the other, but never in the sense that one is ever the other. God is always God, and the idea of God, named man, is always man. Even as Principle is always Principle, and idea is always idea, so Principle cannot be Principle without having its idea whereby it is known. One cannot be without the other, and therefore one never is the other, nor can it ever become the other. With the disappearance or absorption of either, the other would vanish spontaneously. This shows the absurdity of any teaching or any belief that man ever becomes God. God is the Mind of His own idea, man, and man is the thought of God; inseparable in unity, but never in the sense that one absorbs the other.

It is essential that you should be constantly on the alert to remind yourself of this fundamental truth in Christian Science,—one Principle and one idea,—or you will inevitably find your path straying from the straight and narrow way of Christian Science to the absurdities of human belief. As Mrs. Eddy clearly pointed out, "A slight divergence is fatal in Science."[1] Just as surely as any divergence from mathematics is fatal to the mathematician, so is any divergence from Christian Science fatal to the Christian Scientist, for Christian Science is exact Science.

Being then thoroughly convinced, absolutely satisfied, that there is only the one Principle and one idea, you find yourself of necessity this idea, for you find yourself existing not as cause, but as the conscious idea of cause, of this one Principle or consciousness. "The scientific man and his Maker are here; and you would be none other than this man, if you would subordinate the fleshly perceptions to the spiritual sense and source of being."[2]

Ask yourself again, Why am I a Christian Scientist? and never tire of answering the question. Go over and over, if necessary, the argument why you know there is only one Principle and idea. In other words, think Christian Science for yourself, and continue thinking until you are thoroughly satisfied with your answer. Have a reason for the faith that is within you, and establish Christian Science so thoroughly for

[1]Rud. 17:1.   [2]U. of G. 46:9.

yourself, that you are ready to "work out your own salvation."[1]

Establish the reason why there can be only one cause or Principle; why you cannot be one with Principle, if there were more than one. Two causes would be no cause. In order for cause to be cause, it must be infinite, for, if there were something outside of itself, then it would not be the first, the only, in other words that which *is*. If cause were not that which *is*, in other words *isness*, it would be *is not* and therefore no cause. Nothing outside of that which *is* can be cause to you, for are you not conscious being, and so the witness yourself that consciousness must be or you could not be conscious?

PRINCIPLE DEFINES ITSELF TO ITS IDEA

With one Principle, one cause of which you are the spontaneous effect, and with which you are one, with what must you always be dealing? Must you not be dealing with your own cause or Principle? Are you ever dealing with anything else? This is a most important question in Christian Science, and one which demands your absolute consecration. Holding steadily to

[1] Phil. 2:12.

what you know is the truth, you must settle the question definitely whether or not you ever deal with anything outside of this that is cause, that which is Principle to you. This cause, this Principle, embraces for you all consciousness. It is then all consciousness, and because of this, it includes within itself all consciousness. And does not this mean all that you call person, place, or thing?

IDEA CANNOT GIVE OUTLINE TO PRINCIPLE

One of the most subtle arguments of malicious mind, in its attempt to turn you away from the path of exact Science to the jungle of human hypotheses, is that, because all is Mind to you, you have the right to interpret Mind as material possessions of one kind or another, and even as material medicine; in fact that there is no reason why you cannot put your own interpretation on Mind as anything that you please.

Do you think, as a Christian Scientist, it is given to you to put any interpretation you desire upon Mind? Because Mind is All-in-all, are you at liberty to go forward and try mentally to acquire what attracts your attention or suits your desires?—such as an automobile, a radio, a house, or some other material object, and then call it your demonstration of God with you? In mathematics do you for a moment think you have the right to interpret three times three as seven, if this seems expedient? For the moment, yes, you may seem to have the right, but you cannot possibly avoid the inevitable result. You cannot sow the wind and not "reap the whirlwind."[1]

You can interpret Mind as this or as that to suit your own ends it is true, or as the apostle said, to "consume it upon your lusts."[2] But where does this lead you? Only into sophistry, and inevitably away from exact Science into a jumble of hypnotic suggestion with its accompanying materialization of thought.

Too much care cannot be taken to guard against yielding to the subtle hypnotic tendency of saying or thinking that this or that material thing is the gift of God, and is for me to have, and that I have a right to it and should have it, and then sanctimoniously feeling that the auto, radio, or other things wanted, and now acquired, are Christian Science demonstration. Does not all this mean that in some way you think Mind produces things, which in turn you

[1]Hos. 8:7. [2]Jas. 4:3.

seek in order to satisfy your materiality? Such thinking gets you nowhere. Thought must be anchored to Mind which alone sustains and satisfies its own idea. Anything less is only a form of hypnotic suggestion.

Communion is always between Mind and its idea and never between what appears as ideas. This communion is seen in a definite and practical way, but the outlining of it must be left to Mind, Who always rewards "openly."[1] All that the idea could possibly need is its Mind, its Principle, and in turn this Principle defines itself completely as the idea. However, the appearance must be left to divine wisdom, not to human manipulation. God appears each instant in the language best for each one.

TRUTH REFUTES THE ERRONEOUS

When Mrs. Eddy discovered Christian Science, and gave to the world Science and Health, to whom was it seemingly discovered, and to whom did she seem to give it? It was to the same mind that was interpreting itself as telephone, radio, aeroplane and other inventions. Mrs. Eddy's discovery of God as the one Mind, and as All-in-all was presented to the human be-

[1] Matt. 6:6.

lief called mind. Then, it is with this human mind, and this mind alone, that the destruction of materiality must inevitably take place. "Every object in material thought will be destroyed, but the spiritual idea, whose substance is in Mind, is eternal."[1]

In its finite limited sense the automobile, the radio, all human inventions are but the paraphernalia of human belief. They are all human hypotheses, the attempt of malicious mind to imitate the divine. Evil will, of course suggest as of old, that God made them and the novice in Christian Science will say and believe, until better enlightened, that all these inventions are the result of Christian Science. But they are so only as negative interpretations of God's presence. Mrs. Eddy's discovery in 1866, that "All is infinite Mind and its infinite manifestation,"[2] was a declaration of absolute Truth, and it seemed to be made to this human or mortal mind thereby refuting its claim to reality. With the freedom from the ponderous bondage of matter that arose from this statement, the human mind began immediately, and with great rapidity to discover all kinds of marvelous material inventions.

[1] S. & H. 267:1.   [2] S. & H. 468:10.

THE FALSE HYPOTHESIS SUBSTITUTES
ITSELF FOR THE REAL

The supposititious opposite mind in its arrogant nature as the lie about the one Mind, could not avoid imitating the divine Mind's infinite manifestation. So-called inventions will abound, and much more abound, until human thought convinces itself that all is mind. However, that mind will not be divine Mind, but will be only the contradictory false sense, or suppositional opposite of divine Mind. It will always move in its own line of thought,—in its own hypnotic sphere of material mentality, until it reaches the point where it is seen as utterly false, as pure imitation. Just as far as the divine Mind is accepted, the supposition ceases to be, until finally, "matter reaches its mortal zenith in illusion and forever disappears."[1]

The omniscience of the divine Mind reveals the mythical nature of all materiality. The world went wild over the accomplishment of crossing the Atlantic in an aeroplane. Yet why does it not become even interested in understanding how Jesus, some 1900 years ago, crossed the lake and was "immediately"[2] at the other side? He left this as a rich heritage

[1] S. & H. 97:12. [2] Jno. 6:21.

and example for our accomplishment, but how much has the world stirred to this? There is no comparison between the instantaneous understanding of Mind that moved Jesus and his companions immediately across the lake, and the slow and limited process of material action, no matter how fast it may seem to be. Which is the one more to be desired, and which should stir the enthusiasm of the world? Was one less practical than the other?

Christian Science does not belittle or despise in any way the quicker processes that human belief is bringing about for itself, but the Christian Scientist is not deceived, for one moment, into thinking that any of these processes can be substituted for demonstration. He knows they can not, and that their only real use is to bring to light, as rapidly as possible, the delusion that there is any power apart from Mind. He knows that the more rapidly matter and all the beliefs associated with it are seen in their true color, as the false and limited sense of Mind, the more quickly the end of human belief will be realized and reality become apparent. "We welcome the increase of knowledge and the end of error, because even human invention must have its day, and we want that day to be succeeded by Christian Science, by divine reality."[1]

THE FAILURE OF THE FALSE
HYPOTHESIS

You are awake to all the subtle suggestions that there is good in the so-called power, usefulness, goodness and reality embraced in the belief of material improvement. These suggestions come in countless ways. One of the most subtle is under the guise of new discoveries in medicine and surgery. Does it not impress itself upon you as being useful to relieve first one so-called bodily condition and then another? You have found that, if you are not wide awake to all this, it will come as your very mind, and offer itself as an easier solution than Christian Science offers for your problems. In other words, this mind foists itself perpetually upon you as the one remedy and as the easiest remedy for bodily ills.

The history of the thousands of years of medicine and material ways and means of obtaining health, show a record of complete failure. Where had the average length of life fallen at the time of Mrs. Eddy's discovery of Chris-

[1] S. & H. 95:20.

tian Science? It has been steadily rising ever since that discovery. This is because, with first one so-called incurable disease healed through Christian Science and then another, this so-called human mind had to admit that disease is no longer incurable. However, that did not change the nature of the human mind, for it is only supposition. It did change its concepts or forms of disease, but so far as the human mind is concerned, it is no nearer a permanent solution of bodily ailments than it was in the beginning.

The churches also, with their theological dogmas, traditions, and ceremonies, have been coming down through the centuries endeavoring to redeem this so-called mind. They have not succeeded in doing it. They have simply been getting their material beliefs into more mental expressions, which Mrs. Eddy foresaw when she wrote, "But the time cometh when the religious element, or Church of Christ, shall exist alone in the affections, and need no organization to express it,"[1] and this is in fulfilment of the final decree of Science and Health, "All is infinite Mind and its infinite manifestation."[2]

[1] Mis. 145:3.   [2] S. & H. 468:10.

WHERE DO YOU STAND?

Is Mind All-in-all to you? Do you think that the Bible, Science and Health, Christ Jesus, Mrs. Eddy or anything considered apart from the divine Mind, concerns your understanding of Christian Science? If you are honestly accepting the fact that you are "alone with (your) own being and with the reality of things,"[1] you are not deceiving yourself into thinking that, in some mysterious way, something apart from Mind,—whether called person, place or thing,—can help in your spiritual progress.

Knowing as you do know that all is consciousness, and that consciousness is Mind, do you think you can trifle with this knowing any more than with your knowledge of mathematics? There is no material way that will assist you to find this Mind. "Mortals entreat the divine Mind to heal the sick, and forthwith shut out the aid of Mind by using material means."[2]

When Paul wrote Timothy to take "a little wine for thy stomach's sake,"[3] do you really imagine Paul was advocating the taking of wine as a material remedy for some stomach trouble? Paul had left Timothy at Ephesus to check the swerving allegiance resulting in "vain jangling,"[4]

[1] Mes. 01 20:8.   [2] S. & H. 182:22.   [3] 1 Tim. 5:23.   [4] 1 Tim. 1:6.

and here Paul was exhorting Timothy to have faith in his own clear vision and to stand courageously. "Neglect not the gift that is in thee."[1]

"Keep thyself pure. Drink no longer water, but use a little wine for thy stomach's sake and thine often infirmities."[2] In other words, keep your thought pure, do not temporize with evil, but let the inspiration of Spirit give you courage and keep you from wavering. Paul's "wine" was the inspiration of the Spirit. If you make any material concessions, then you are preparing yourself for the suggestion that a little medicine or an operation might also benefit you. If you accept the false human mind on any point, it becomes Mind to you, and there is no place where you can stop. After you accept the statement, All is Mind, there is no turning back, or escaping your responsibility.

TRUTH CANNOT BE EXPLOITED

Perhaps, in taking some material remedy, you may say that you know the remedy does not heal, that it only changes the belief temporarily, and you want that temporary relief. In that case, it is like trying to correct or relieve a mis-

[1] Tim. 4:14.   [2] Tim. 5:23.

take in a mathematical problem of two times two
is seven, with another mistake that two times two
is five. It will change the appearance, it is true;
but how long will that appearance satisfy? Only
until the end of the problem is reached, when
it is still found wrong. This mistake you might
again try to correct with two times two is six.
But you are getting nowhere. You are simply
trifling with your understanding of mathematics,
and where could such trifling lead except to complete confusion? "Unless an ill is rightly met
and fairly overcome by Truth, the ill is never
conquered. If God destroys not sin, sickness,
and death, they are not destroyed in the mind
of mortals, but seem to this so-called mind to
be immortal. What God cannot do, man need
not attempt."[1]

In the same way, you cannot afford to trifle
with your understanding of Christian Science.
"If therefore thine eye be single, thy whole
body shall be full of light. But if thine eye be
evil, thy whole body shall be full of darkness.
If therefore the light that is in thee be darkness,
how great is that darkness."[2]

[1]S. & H. 231:3   [2]Matt. 6:22, 23.

CHURCH ORGANIZATION

You ask, Even if materia medica has no value to me, has not church organization some use? Do you think that one form of materiality called church organization is less material than another form of organization called materia medica? Both these are equally material, and the suggestion that they can be of value and help to you comes from identically the same source.

Trying to attribute some virtue or some spiritual growth to going to church is no less the suggestion of malicious mind than the attempt to attribute healing to materia medica or surgery. No organization that intrudes itself as in the least degree directing, controlling, or governing man's oneness with God is of the slightest value. In fact, it is the most detrimental belief operating today. The Christian Scientist who permits himself to be in bondage to mediumship in any form, in other words to have a medium between himself and his divine Principle, is laying up treasures on earth where, as the Bible says, "moth and rust doth corrupt, and where thieves break through and steal."[1] He cannot be a Christian Scientist and submit to the slightest dictation along spiritual lines.

[1] Matt. 6:19.

He is a Christian Scientist only as he is "alone with his own being and with the reality of things."[1] "That glory only is imperishable which is fixed in one's own moral make-up."[2]

Recognizing this truth for oneself and at the same time feeling that church organization has value for others,—for instance, for those coming into Christian Science,—is nothing in the world but a subtle form of metaphysical hypocrisy. How can Mind be One and All and not embrace within itself all? Then how can this Mind, this All, be your Mind, and there be something in that Mind that is not on a par with it? This same lie made Cain a murderer. He repudiated God as his brother when he asked, "Am I my brother's keeper?"[3] In other words, he had something apart from Mind as his brother, which is always a murderer. If God is not All-in-all to you, all the time, you must have something apart from Him, and thus you murder your sense of good as All-in-all. You cannot have more than one good.

To illustrate this point, it is impossible to conceive of the child of today thinking in terms of prairie schooners and the other slow methods of transportation of sixty years ago, because he

[1] Mes. 01 20:9. [2] My. 122:5. [3] 1 Gen. 4:9.

finds himself at the point of experience of aeroplanes. You would not have him go back in thought to the days of prairie schooners, and wend his way up through the slow processes of human belief before emerging to the faster modes of travel. Apply this to the argument that the Christian Science church organization has no value to you now, but it has value to the one beginning to study Christian Science.

Remember, there is only one suppositional or evil mind, and therefore when that mind reaches the point in its destruction where it is released from some bondage, then spontaneously the whole of that mind is released to that extent. You are never at a point of vantage over what appears to you as another mortal. Church organization being seen as a claim of materiality for one, it must be uncovered and so destroyed for all. It cannot be over for you, unless it is over in the mind which embraces all with you. Jesus illustrated this very forcibly in the parable of the householder, hiring laborers to work in his vineyard. No matter whether hired at the first hour or the eleventh hour, "they received every man a penny."[1] In other

[1]Matt. 20:9.

words, all were at the same point of understand·
ing.

THE KINGDOM OF GOD IS WITHIN YOU

As a metaphysician you are never dealing with
persons, places or things. You are dealing with
the one suppositional mind, which includes within itself all there is to material sense, to the
sick, sinning and dying mortal. This that you
seem to be confronted with as person, place
or thing, is merely the form in which this suppositional mind appears to you. If you attempt
to deal with person as person, and heal it, or
correct it, as such, you are in a hopeless situation, for you have no possible way of correcting
that which does not appear to operate as your
own thinking. The kingdom of God is within
you, not afar off, but right within that which
is the Self of you. You are alone with that which
you accept as Mind, as consciousness, and this
includes all that you call person, place or thing,
all that appears as a book, a church or a remedy.

The command to enter into your closet and
shut the door when you pray, would have been
foolish, unless in the seclusion with you is that
Mind which includes within itself all Truth.
In your communion with it, you find the reality
of all being. No discord is outside of that which

comes to you as your own consciousness. And because of this very fact, and because you are alone with your own being, in your own closet, you have supreme power to handle all that presents itself as mind to you. Science and Health says, "I hope, dear reader, I am leading you into the understanding of your divine rights, your heaven-bestowed harmony—that, as you read, you see there is no cause (outside of erring, mortal, material sense which is not power) able to make you sick or sinful; and I hope that you are conquering this false sense. Knowing the falsity of so-called material sense, you can assert your prerogative to overcome the belief in sin, disease, or death."[1]

Would Jesus be correct in his statement, "And I, if I be lifted up from the earth, will draw all men unto me,"[2] unless he had meant exactly this same thing? He was not dealing with persons, but he was alone with what he accepted as Mind. When you say what Jesus "meant," remember it is equivalent to saying what "I mean," because it comes to you as your own I or consciousness. Then does not this statement really mean, If what I accept as I, as consciousness, is really I, really consciousness

[1] S. & H. 253:9. [2] Jno. 12:32.

(lifted up from the earth), then, because this consciousness is all the consciousness there is, I cannot help seeing all from the basis of this that I am accepting as I. In other words the whole of that which constitutes being to me must rise as I rise, and must be drawn unto that altitude of Mind that I accept as Mind.

Do you think you could be sure of correcting any lie, if the lie could hold its ground outside of that which is consciousness to you, outside of that which you are accepting, even if only for the moment, as your own thought? If a claim, whether of a discordant body or of an unsuccessful business or an inharmonious home, were apart from what you are accepting as consciousness, in other words were something "over there," remote from you, how could you be over there to correct it? "I" is always right here, and so "here" is all there is to "there." It is always consciousness here, and this here includes all that appears over there. This constitutes the kingdom of God within you, the possibility of all good as the one consciousness, as yours. It is because you understand this, that you are so confident of your ground.

"I AM COME THAT THEY MIGHT HAVE LIFE"[1]

When first a mortal is introduced to Christian Science and accepts it, he usually does so with deep eagerness and sincerity. This sincerity may continue for many years, and then, he may find, and wonder why, he seems to have lost the zeal and keen interest he experienced when he first caught a glimpse of the truth and joy of Christian Science. He may find he is listening to the argument of material sense to turn aside, or at least to countenance ways and means of materiality, that he would not have contemplated for a moment when he first began to understand the truth of Christian Science. Perhaps these arguments have arisen with some of you, and you may have felt, as you should, uncomfortable about them.

When Jesus said, "I am come that they might have life, and that they might have it more abundantly,"[1] he was declaring the destruction of death. Christian Science has come in this same language and declares it has come to destroy all sin, sickness and death. Evil claims that man begins, and this claim of course involves his end. The mortal from the moment of his

[1] Jno. 10:10.

so-called conception, is always about his predestined end, which is to die. The mortal is
about his father's business of death, just as the
man of God is about his Father's business of
Life and more abundant Life. What the human
mind calls years is just the continuous accomplishment of the mortal's destination, or death.
It is not surprising then, as time goes on, that
the Christian Scientist, if not keenly alert and
actively awake on the side of Life as All-in-all,
finds himself tending more and more toward the
side of materiality—that which means death;
finds his earnestness and sincerity less eager on
the side of Truth and Life.

Can you afford not to be thoroughly awake
to these suggestions of evil and see where they
lead? There is no standing still. You are always
journeying either toward Life or death. You
are accepting Life and more abundant Life, or
you are accepting death and more abundant
death, in other words accepting materiality.
"Then when lust hath conceived, it bringeth
forth sin; and sin, when it is finished, bringeth
forth death."[1]

Ask yourself honestly and fearlessly, Do I
expect to die, am I planning on death, or do I

[1]Jas. 1:15.

accept the statement of Mind, that, "I am come that they might have life, and that they might have it more abundantly"[1]? This I is itself Life. Which side are you on? Whichever it is, that is the side you will carry. You cannot deceive your Mind. If you are eventually expecting death, you are planning for it.

It is wise to remember what Mrs. Eddy once wrote to a friend, "Every Scientist must put absolutely out of thought the belief that he must sometime change to another plane of existence. God is Life, there is no other plane of existence and we must make our plans for immortality. Stop talking about death. There is no death to Life."

There is nothing that can rob the Christian Scientist of his understanding of the omnipresence of Life, and so deprive him of his natural assurance and his determination to live: not "to live," in the sense so commonly accepted as living hereafter, but to live here and now, in such a way that all can see it as normal and natural living. How foolish to say, I know Life is eternal, and then imagine for one moment that eternal Life can appear as a funeral, except to evil.

[1] Jno. 10:10.

The one Exemplar showed the eternity of Life, and all must eventually follow his example. There is no escape. He is indeed a foolish Christian Scientist who does not face the question honestly and fearlessly, and settle for himself once and forever, that when he declares Life is eternal, he honestly means it is eternal right here and now, and does not require a silly belief of a funeral to show forth eternal Life.

Anyone can believe that life does not die, that it goes on after death, but that belief is of no interest whatever to the Christian Scientist. The metaphysician means by Life, Life here and now, without any belief of cessation attached to it.

UNDERSTANDING THE OPEN DOOR

The question then is, How is Life to be eternally expressed, or, in other words, How is death to be overcome? Of course there is and can be but one answer to that question, and that answer is, through understanding. Belief will never do it. Faith will never do it. It is understanding alone that does it. "The scientific unity which exists between God and man must be wrought out in life-practice."[1] It was the practical

[1] S. & H. 202:3.

understanding of the Christ that enabled Jesus to say, "Destroy this temple, and in three days I will raise it up."[1] What do you think it was about Jesus different from you, which enabled him to do this? The belief of so-called material substance composing what you call the body of Jesus was not in any way different from the belief of material substance composing what you call your body. Then what and where is the difference? It was in what Jesus accepted as his Mind. Because of this fact, the apostle bade us have the same Mind, Mind to us, that was Mind to Christ Jesus, or as the Scriptures put it, "Let this mind be in you, which was also in Christ Jesus."[2]

BELIEF VERSUS UNDERSTANDING

On this point of understanding that is so fundamental to a correct answer of, Why am I a Christian Scientist? I want to read to you from an article written by Mrs. Eddy in 1910, and published in the Christian Science Sentinel, September 1, 1917. I do not believe Mrs. Eddy ever wrote anything fraught with more import to the Christian Scientist, than this article, "Principle and Practice." It was the dictum of

[1] Jno. 2:19. [2] Phil. 2:5.

that deep spiritual experience, that understanding of Mind, which was so clear and fearless that it could call evil by its right name and expose the absurdities, the dangers and inconsistencies of human belief, whether appearing under the guise of Christian Science and its practice, or under any other guise.

In the opening statement of this article Mrs. Eddy writes, "The nature and position of mortal mind are the opposites of immortal Mind. The so-called mortal mind is belief and not understanding." Is not this absolutely true, and do you not know it of yourself and not because Mrs. Eddy wrote it? You have established Mind as that which *is,* and therefore, as all that *is,* infinite, immortal. Contrary or opposite to this you have established the suppositional mind as finite, mortal or dead. Is not the first understanding, and the other mere belief? Which does Christian Science require? Mrs. Eddy says, "Christian Science requires understanding instead of belief; it is based on a fixed eternal and divine Principle, wholly apart from mortal conjecture; and it must be understood, otherwise it cannot be correctly accepted and demonstrated." It is not possible for you to use, or correctly state, what you do not understand:

nor to intelligently demonstrate what you cannot correctly state and understand. You must understand Christian Science and not simply have faith or belief in it. Do not deceive yourself into thinking that belief or faith can substitute understanding in Christian Science.

In the same article Mrs. Eddy writes, "The inclination of mortal mind is to receive Christian Science through a belief instead of the understanding, and this inclination prevails like an epidemic on the body; it inflames mortal mind and weakens the intellect, but this so-called mortal mind is wholly ignorant of this fact, and so cherishes its mere faith in Christian Science." How true this is. Through an ecstatic state of uplifted faith in Christian Science, beliefs of one kind and another have readily vanished. But does the vanishing of a belief necessarily mean that understanding has destroyed it? You know that, in the realm of belief, the stronger belief always supersedes the weaker, and so a religious belief, being a more mind-belief than the so-called belief of sickness can easily overshadow the belief of sickness. To such an extent is this so, that as Mrs. Eddy states, it "prevails like an epidemic on the body," healing the entire body temporarily, and substituting a belief in God, for a belief in a sick body.

This same belief and faith in good is illustrated in the woman who touched Jesus' robe and was healed. Jesus was not deceived into thinking or allowing that the touching of his robe had any power to heal the woman, and that is why he said to her, "thy faith hath made thee whole; go in peace, and be whole of thy plague."[1]

What power to heal could there possibly be in the robe of Jesus any more than in the handkerchief of Paul or the flowers from Mrs. Eddy's conservatory at Pleasant View? Healing is not faith; it is not belief; it is Life itself, and Life is understanding. While faith and belief in Christian Science may appear as healing, or as a healing epidemic on the body, that does not mean that understanding in Christian Science has done the healing.

For you to tell the sick man that you can heal him, because God is all, and he is well, since God creates neither sin, sickness nor death, does not mean one thing in the true understanding of Christian Science. The sick may be healed because of what you tell him, as Mrs. Eddy points

[1] Mk. 5 :34.

out, but there is no understanding back of such healing. The Mind that destroys sickness is never the mind that first admits its existence, and then believes that God can heal it. The Mind that destroys all evil, sin, sickness and death is the Mind that knows nothing outside of itself, and therefore knows good and good alone.

Mrs. Eddy emphatically states in this article that the so-called hea—, which results from faith and belief, is no—fferent from healing by a drug, and that it h—no relationship whatever to genuine Christian Science, which is understanding.

Do not be deceived on these points. Faith and belief may be mere characteristics of the human mind. So-called religious ecstasy or belief may perform what appear to be marvelous healings, but in reality they are simply the exchange of a belief of sickness for an ecstatic faith and belief in Christian Science. "Health is the consciousness of the unreality of pain and disease; or, rather, the absolute consciousness of harmony and of nothing else."[1]

[1] Rud. 11:13.

HEALTH THE ETERNAL FACT

Since good is the only reality, the All-in-all, it must be omnipresent, therefore, what is called health must be everywhere present. Because sickness is merely a belief, then with the slightest change in this belief the omnipresence of health can be seen as the fact. That is why drugs and other remedies seem to heal. That is why the Eskimo's incantation and the Tibetan's praying machine accomplished the same result. In fact, no matter what the healing belief may be, if faith in it is sufficient, it will appear to heal. But do you think for one moment that all these foolish beliefs of the human mind have the slightest bearing on, or relation to, Christian Science understanding; that understanding which Jesus expressed in healing the sick, feeding the multitude, walking the waves, stilling the storm, and raising the dying, and that proved the utter powerlessness of evil?

No wonder Mrs. Eddy says in the same article, "It is the healer's understanding of the operation of the divine Principle, and his application thereof, which heals the sick, just as it is one's understanding of the principle of mathematics which enables him to demonstrate its rules." Could a thinking person possibly imagine that faith or belief could have anything to do with the working out of a mathematical problem? He knows it has nothing whatever to do with it, and unless the Christian Scientist understands just as clearly that faith and belief do not and cannot enter into the practice of Christian Science, because understanding alone operates in that practice, he will lose his way and become discouraged and fearful.

THE DANGER OF BELIEF

Again quoting from this same article, Mrs. Eddy wrote, "Christian Science is not a faith cure, and unless human faith be distinguished from scientific healing, Christian Science will again be lost from the practice of religion, as it was soon after the period of our great Master's scientific teaching and practice."[1]

The belief or faith Scientist fondly imagines that, because of Mrs. Eddy's discovery of Christian Science, and her gift of Science and Health to the world, it is impossible for the light of Christian Science to disappear. This is just a fond delusion, for Mrs. Eddy, in this article, shows very clearly that she had no such delusion, but knew perfectly well that, if understand-

[1] Prin. and Pract.

ing did not replace this foolish "belief" and "faith" acceptance of Christian Science, it certainly would disappear from the vision of the mortal. With understanding, however, it can no more disappear than can the multiplication table. Preserve, then, understanding under all circumstances, and remember what Solomon said, "with all thy getting get understanding."[1]

All the love and devotion one may express towards Christian Science, or its discoverer, or the Bible, or Christ Jesus, can never substitute itself for the understanding that is Christian Science. Faith, belief and emotion, in themselves, have no understanding. They are the "reed shaken with the wind,"[2] and when the wind passeth over them they are gone, for there is no substance to them.

The metaphysician, the Christian Scientist knows this, so is continually on his guard, and never allows anything to direct or govern him but his understanding, his communion with Mind. He is just as positive on this point as is the mathematician, who knows that the only solution of a problem is his communion with the principle of numbers, and that no emotion, faith or belief aids him in the slightest. The Chris-

[1] Pro. 4:7. [2] Matt. 11:7.

tian Scientist knows that Christian Science as a belief, has no more virtue than any other religious belief, and that, as a belief, it will eventually do no more for its followers in the way of destroying sickness and death than will other beliefs. He knows that belief will never end death, and he knows that death must cease before Life can be obtained.

John the Baptist expresses the utter futility of belief. Exalted as John's belief seemed to be, it was Jesus, who declared of him, "Among them that are born of women there hath not risen a greater than John the Baptist: nothwithstanding he that is least in the kingdom of heaven is greater than he."[1] This can surely be interpreted as meaning that the religious belief of John was the highest religious belief that had ever obtained, and yet, what was the ultimate of that religious belief? It ended in John the Baptist being mercilessly beheaded. On the other hand what was the result of Christ Jesus' understanding?—the proof of evil's complete inability to destroy the Life, the Christ which appeared in the Ascension.

[1] Matt. 11:11.

"BELIEF IS VIRTUALLY BLINDNESS"[1]

In the realm of belief, there is nothing permanent. Belief "is like a wave of the sea driven with the wind and tossed."[2] It changes with every passing breath and has no place to rest. When the distressed father entreated Jesus to help his child, the Master said, "If thou canst believe, all things are possible to him that believeth," and he replied, "Lord, I believe; help thou mine unbelief."[3] This blind belief showed its utter helplessness. It was the exact opposite of Jesus' real meaning in his statement, "If thou canst believe, all things are possible to him that believeth." Unquestionably Jesus here meant understanding, just as Paul did when he said, "Believe . . . and thou shalt be saved."[4]

The human mind having no basis or foundation is, as Jesus said, of its "father, the devil," "a liar and the father of it."[5] Its very nature is false and therefore unreal. On the other hand, divine Mind is reality; it is knowing; it is understanding, and understanding alone attains the solution of any problem.

A belief in Christian Science is no holier, and no better, than any other belief. Therefore, belief in Christian Science must give place to

[1]Ret. 54:14. [2]Jas. 1:6. [3]Mark 9:23,24. [4]Act. 16:31. [5]Jno. 8:44.

understanding, or there will be no right practice of Christian Science.

CHRISTIAN SCIENCE PRACTICE DEFINED

What is meant by this term "practice"? What do you mean by the practice of anything? It means the showing forth of that which is practised. If nothing is manifested, you would then say that there is no practice. Then the practice of Christian Science must be a showing forth of that which Christian Science is, and is not for the purpose of bringing about some specific result. It is not for the purpose of exploitation or healing of some erroneous condition, any more than mathematics is for the purpose of correcting mistakes in problems.

The principle of numbers knows nothing about mistakes in problems, and the only way a mistake is corrected is by having the principle present, and then spontaneously, the mistake vanishes. The Principle of being, infinite good or Christian Science, knows nothing of errors such as sin, sickness, death or discord of any kind to be corrected or destroyed. Simply by being All-in-all, omnipresent, infinite, there is no place for evil to be, and hence, it must disappear just as naturally as the mistake in the mathematical problem disappears when the principle of numbers is present.

The belief that Christian Science is for the purpose of healing sin or disease is fraught with the greatest danger to the believer, because the mind that believes there is something to be healed is the same mind that holds within itself all that constitutes the disease, and therefore is not the Mind that can correct it. On the other hand, the Mind that knows only good and the things of good, is the Mind that has already precluded the possibility of anything unlike good, and therefore is its destruction. This process of destruction is not really destruction, but is only the pressure of the one Mind spontaneously eliminating everything unlike itself.

Mrs. Eddy thus illuminates this truth, "When I have most clearly seen and most sensibly felt that the infinite recognizes no disease, this has not separated me from God, but has so bound me to Him as to enable me instantaneously to heal a cancer which had eaten its way to the jugular vein. In the same spiritual condition I have been able to replace dislocated joints and raise the dying to instantaneous health."[1] It is clearly apparent that oneness with that which

[1] Un. 7:8.

really is Mind constitutes the annihilation of everything unlike that Mind.

THE CRITERION OF TRUTH

The practice, then, of Christian Science is not repeating statements from Science and Health, and endeavoring to feel that they are true, or that they must have a healing impetus, because Mrs. Eddy wrote them. Just because Mrs. Eddy says or writes something does not make it true. Do you think a statement is true merely because it is in the Bible or in Science and Health, or is it true only because of its intrinsic truth? Nothing could be more ridiculous than to believe that a statement is true because it is found between two covers with the printing on the outside, "Holy Bible" or "Science and Health." Could there not be typographical errors in the printing of any book that would wholly change the meaning? Then, what superstition to think that a thing is true except for its inherent truth, and not for being found in any particular place.

The statements in the Bible and in Science and Health are true and correct, but it is not because of being in those books; it is because they are the truth wholly apart from those

books. They are only in those books because
they are true, thus making those books a record
of the truth, making them a chart for the wise
traveller to study continually.

This does not mean, however, that the Christian Scientist must constantly have his eyes on
those books, but it does mean that, because those
books record the truth, the source from whence
they came is the Mind that must be found as
the Mind of the traveller, if he is to find his way
happily and harmoniously. The genuine Christian Scientist no longer thinks that he is unsafe
unless he has those books with him all the time.
He knows that the practice of Christian Science
has nothing to do with books; that it has
nothing to do with a so-called office, or so-called
patients; that none of those things have any relation to Christian Science practice. He knows
that the practice of Christian Science is oneness
with Mind and that the very first essential of
that practice is never to get into it a third. In
other words, there can be nothing in that practice but aloneness with God, one's own being,
the reality of things.

THE CHRISTIAN SCIENCE PRACTITIONER

Does this view of Christian Science practice,
this understanding of the activity of Mind, pre-

vent its practical operation in the minutiae of daily affairs? Most certainly not, but on the contrary it brings to light the only way in which Christian Science is really available, and makes it possible to do as Jesus commanded, "Go ye into all the world, and preach the gospel to every creature."[1] "Heal the sick."[2] This means to know, wherever you are or whatever you are doing, that you are alone with Mind, and that it is communion with Mind that constitutes all consciousness. To you there can be no aloneness with Mind, if anything apart from you and the Self of you is present.

A busy, active practice of Christian Science constitutes such an understanding of the infinity of Mind that it draws all men unto itself. There is no need to seek avenues of opportunity for expressing Christian Science, whether in the sense of healing bodily sickness or any other discord. Like the moth that is attracted to the light, so the darkness, appearing as human beliefs called sickness and distress, flees to the light of Truth for its own destruction.

The one recipe for activity in Christian Science practice is to be an understanding Christian Scientist. No office, no advertisement, no church

[1] Mark 16:15. [2] Matt. 10:8.

membership is needed to show forth the light of understanding so that all can clearly see and be drawn to it. Do you think it possible to hide this light? Would not a trail be quickly made to its very door by the anguish and poverty of human belief? You know it would, and you know the only way to be a busy Christian Scientist is to "Let your light so shine before men, that they may see your good works, and glorify your Father which is in heaven."[1] In other words, be so at one with that which is man's divine Principle that this Principle is seen as All-in-all, and therefore, everything unlike it spontaneously disappears, *is not*.

GETTING IN A THIRD

The human belief of Christian Science practice imagines it is for the purpose of healing some specific error or discord. Such a sense of practice involves immediately the introduction of a third, which is fatal to true understanding, "for I the Lord thy God am a jealous God."[2] The jealousy of God does not brook any third; it allows nothing but God and His idea. It does not allow *ideas;* for if it did it would have to allow other gods, because you cannot have idea

[1]Matt. 5:16.   [2]Ex. 20:5.

without that which it is the idea of. Infinite Principle is one, and it has one infinite idea, and this one infinite idea is not subdivided into ideas, but is always one, even as its Principle is one. Then where can there be a third or, in other words, something apart from Principle and its idea?

It is on this point that one of the most unfortunate mistakes in the wrong practice of Christian Science comes in. Because there is just one infinite Mind and its infinite manifestation or man, this infinite Mind must appear in what seems to be the infinity of variety of persons, places and things. But these are not persons, places and things at all; they are simply the way, or language you might call it, in which Mind appears as His own idea. Of course you know this, and that is why you understand that there is never a third in Christian Science. The moment a third appears is the moment all possibility of metaphysical healing vanishes.

Because all is consciousness and comes to you as such, it must be here and not there, and that is what gives you your authority over all things. There is no "over there" to heal; everything must come "here" as your very Mind. Every material object must give place to Mind. You cannot allow a semblance of belief of anything material, whether called person, place or thing, to intrude itself between you and your Principle. Because of this fact, that which appeared to you as Mrs. Eddy finally had to disappear to give place to Mind, her divine reality. You understood why this was essential, and why Mrs. Eddy brought it out so repeatedly in her writings. "Every human thought" she writes, "must turn instinctively to the divine Mind as its sole center and intelligence. . . . He that by reason of human love or hatred or any other cause clings to my material personality, greatly errs, stops his own progress, and loses the path to health, happiness, and heaven."[1]

This does not, however, deprive anyone of an increasing sense of what appears as person, place and thing, but rather insures their increase, for in proportion to infinite Mind being found All-in-all, the infinite unfoldment of good must appear in its infinity of variety, and continue to appear in ever increasing completeness.

THE PRACTICAL APPLICATION OF CHRISTIAN SCIENCE

You ask, What then is the practical application of Christian Science to disease? Let us take

[1] Mis. 307:30.

a case, and see just what the answer is. We will suppose a case called "inherited tuberculosis of the lungs."

First, what is it that appears to you and makes you aware of its presence? Does it not come as a sense of consciousness to you, as actually your very consciousness, your ego, or I, making you say, "I see a man over there breathing very hard and dying of tuberculosis of the lungs?" You accept this presentation as your mind; hence, it operates as your ego declaring certain unfortunate conditions. As a metaphysician you look squarely at the claim much as you would look at a mathematical problem. In mathematics you go, metaphorically, into your closet and shut the door, and quietly commune with the principle of numbers until the solution of the problem is at hand. In a similar manner in the practice of Christian Science, you enter into your closet and in your communion with divine Principle, the one consciousness, you discover certain fundamental facts.

There is only one Mind, one intelligence. This intelligence being infinite knows all there is to know about everything from the infinitesimal to the infinite. This intelligence uncovers spontaneously everything unlike itself masquerading as presence, power or reality. It uncovers evil's claim of being mind, and having thought through which it acts and operates. This thought of evil is always malicious or deadly, for it is of its father, death, the suppositional opposite of Life.

Evil, as mind, is one, and it always claims to have a place where it is; a time when it began; matter or substance wherewith it is formed; and law by which it operates. Its purpose is always to bring to pass death; and its appearance of life is only the perpetuation of death; the seeds of death are always in the seeds of its so-called life, and its so-called mortal is just for one purpose, one only, namely, to die; it claims that this death is being produced lawfully every moment, according to what is called a law of hygiene or of physiology or nature or matter or materia medica, and so forth.

This mind's realm of operation is the realm of belief, and every claim it makes is a claim of belief, although outwardly appearing as matter. Its belief of offspring, called a child, is produced through another belief called parents, which in its turn goes further back as grandparents, ad infinitum. These varying beliefs multiply and increase, and are handed down from one belief to another. In this present case under consideration, the diseased lungs are a belief of inheritance, and this inherited belief or predisposing claim was brought to light through an exciting claim called "taking cold."

Now, what is it that uncovers all this nonsense of belief? Is it not the one infinite intelligence knowing the truth about everything, which uncovers the lie, just as in mathematics your knowing two times two is four uncovers the mistake that two times two is five? Yet the principle of mathematics knows nothing about the mistake, it is simply its innate rightness that uncovers, unravels and destroys whatever is wrong. This is always the nature of truth in its action and operation, whether expressed as the truth of Being or the truth of mathematics.

Christian Science, the word of God, counters these belief arguments of this so-called mind with the arguments of Truth. The specific lie or belief in this case is that lungs are being destroyed. What are lungs? Mind is All, therefore this all must include within itself all that there is to lungs. This Mind is One, hence its idea must be one, whether called lungs or by any other name. You know about this one idea or lungs all that you know about God; so what-

ever God is, *that* lungs must be, for that which
is of God must be His image and likeness. The
good that is God, is the good that is lungs, and
just as you declare "Our Father which art in
heaven," so you can and must declare our lungs
"which art in heaven."

You cannot have idea apart from its Principle; so whatever the Principle is, that the idea
must be also. God is the only parent or grand-
parent for, as Mrs. Eddy expresses it, "He is
man's only real relative on earth and in
heaven."[1] Then the parentage and inheritance
of lungs is absolutely perfect, sound and intact.
There could be no destructive germ, for the only
germ is the germ of infinite good which maintains and sustains its idea eternally. This good
germ is the law of annihilation to everything unlike good; it is the sword of Truth turning in all
directions and destroying everything apart from
itself simply by the nature of its own infinite
continuity.

Law being fundamental fact or right, infinite
intelligence, that which knows, must be the one
law, and therefore includes within itself all law,
hygiene, nature, everything that operates as law.
As such law it maintains its own idea lawfully;

[1]Mis. 151:14.

therefore must maintain lungs in its own image and likeness, which is perfection and indestructibility.

The idea which human sense cognizes is not the idea that is the very presence of God. The presence of God, or the activity of divine Mind, is only another name for man, the idea of God. "Entirely separate from the belief and dream of material living, is the Life divine, revealing spiritual understanding and the consciousness of man's dominion over the whole earth."[1] This statement of Mrs. Eddy's can be paraphrased, and, indeed, must be paraphrased to include the minutiae of daily life. Then you can say, "Entirely separate from the belief and dream of the material concept called lungs, is the divine reality lungs, revealing spiritual understanding and the consciousness of man's dominion over the whole earth." Human concept has no relationship to divine reality. So, when you use the term lungs, you must think only of Mind, and allow Mind to appear in its own way. The name you give to this appearance is of no moment.

Because all that you know of God is what you know about lungs, you are convinced that the perfection of lungs is as assured as is the per-

[1] S. & H. 14:23.

fection of God, therefore, "perfect lungs" is as omnipresent as is perfect God;—hence this "perfect lungs" is right where malicious belief says are the imperfect or dying lungs. You argue this point so clearly to yourself that you are convinced of its truth. Leave no doubt or question in your mind of this fact;—do not stop your argument until every suggestion of evil is silenced through the conviction of Truth.

After you have completely assured yourself that the presence of God is the only presence, and His presence is therefore the only lungs, you arrive at the inevitable conclusion, that what appears to be the claim, diseased lungs, is really not the claim at all. It is only the bluff of this so-called suppositional mind. The real claim to be destroyed, is the original claim of evil which is the belief that evil mind *is*—that it is real, true and genuine—that it operates as mentality, as hypnotic suggestion—that it appears as some material thing bringing forth death, to the root of which "the axe is laid."[1]

Through this analysis you learn that tuberculosis of the lungs is not the discord to be destroyed. It must always be remembered that no argument of any kind ever heals. Its only

[1]Matt. 3:10.

purpose is to bring one to the point where he is convinced that what appears as the claim is really not the claim, but that the real claim is that malicious mind actually is, or exists, and that it has power to operate as hypnotic suggestion and appear as a man dying of tuberculosis of the lungs.

For example, take a case of a man swimming on dry boards under hypnotic influence. You are not tempted for an instant to think that he is really in water. You know that he is not, and as soon as you see that the real claim is hypnotism, your only effort is to destroy the belief that there is a mind that can either operate as hypnotism, or be subject to hypnotic suggestion. So, in identically the same way you destroy what appears as tuberculosis of the lungs, or any discordant condition. Because you know there is only one infinite Mind which holds within itself all law, all being, all action, the possibility of there being another mind, called evil mind, to declare itself as entity or operate hypnotically, or appear as discordant, finite, limited conditions is precluded. "As named in Christian Science, animal magnetism or hypnotism is the specific term for error, or mortal mind."[1]

[1] S. & H. 103:18.

The realization that the one Mind and its law is the only Mind and the only law, brings that consciousness of perfection that is heaven,—"for I know whom I have believed."[1] The man released from hypnotic suggestion, rises from the floor on which he has been "swimming"; so the diseased lungs vanish, and the sick man declares in the language of Mind, "I am well, and I know it."[2]

Thus is healing, as you know, accomplished in Christian Science, not by the attempt to heal, but by that exaltation of thought that is conscious only of good and the things of good.

THE MEANING OF THE BUSINESS TREND TODAY

The business man of today is confronted with questions of vital importance. Because of the growing understanding of the infinity and oneness of Mind, he sees on all sides what appear as immense business mergers, and the question naturally arises with many as to whether the smaller businesses may not be submerged.

Christian Science shows how these and still greater mergers are inevitable. It shows that because Mind is one, the human mind, in its imitation of the divine, will counterfeit this one-

[1] 2 Tim. 1:12.　[2] Mis. 220:15.

ness in every respect. This oneness may, and doubtless will appear as enormous mergers, until it finally comes down to one of everything, and all mortals stockholders in that one. It has been reported that at present in America there are twenty million stockholders in the various corporations. You should rejoice at these mergers, for you know that when the human mind gets down to a basis of oneness, it is rapidly approaching its hour for final destruction. That which does not line up with Truth will disappear, leaving reality undisturbed.

You know one is synonymous with God, with that which *is,* and therefore, you should welcome everything that indicates an approximation to oneness. You are not afraid of losing your business, because the business of Mind is your business, and it is already one; therefore you rejoice with all that declares this oneness. Open your thought to a larger sense all the time. Do not be limited in any way. Think in terms of Mind, never in terms of limitation or matter. Mind's business is your business; hence there is nothing to be opposed to your business—it is successful and prosperous;—it is constantly growing, because Mind is infinitely unfolding to you. There is no malicious mind to operate as malicious mental mal-practice and as hypnotic suggestion to appear as a bad business or any other discord such as lack of position or health or friends. The one Mind is the All-mind; therefore, there is no malicious mind.

THE QUESTION OF MONEY

You ask, Why is there so often such a lack of money? There is no lack of money. Mind embraces within itself all that is meant by money—by substance. Only as Mind is seen as all the money there is, will money appear as omnipresent as the multiplication table. Because Mind is infinite, money is infinite, and because the one infinite Mind is your Mind, the one infinite money is your money, and it is all yours.

You welcome all to use the multiplication table, because you know it can never be used up nor destroyed; and neither can money be destroyed; but just as no one would think of wasting the multiplication table or using it when not needed, so money must be used in the same way. There is no waste in Principle. In these latter days the abundance of material prosperity will overwhelm mortals, but the peace and happiness they are looking for cannot be found in materiality. Only through the understanding that is Christian Science can happiness be obtained.

In an interview published recently in the Cosmopolitan, Mr. Edison says, "As human beings are now constituted, it is impossible for them to be very happy." He goes on to show that there is no basis for permanent happiness. There is, of course, no basis for material happiness, and material prosperity will only reveal this more clearly. There is not a single material thing that can satisfy. This does not make you despise the telephone, the radio or the aeroplane, but you see in them only a temporary sense that must finally give place to the freedom of Mind.

THE SUBSTANCE OF TRUE JOY

Because the one Mind is infinite, it holds within itself all joy and satisfaction, all charm and loveliness, all friendship and neighborliness, all that you mean by society, amusement, pleasure and happiness. You remember it was said of Jesus, "who for the joy that was set before him endured the cross, despising the shame,"[1] in other words, Jesus was oblivious to erroneous sense because he was so conscious of the omnipresence of all that means and is good. "Pleas-

[1] Heb. 12:2

ure is no crime except when it strengthens the influence of bad inclinations or lessens the activities of virtue."[1]

Good to Jesus was not the human belief of good, but it was the consciousness of indestructible life, of infinite intelligence, of omnipotent power, in fact of all that is meant by the term infinite good. No finite, human belief could be included in that good. So the genuine Christian Scientist cannot include in his good any finite human belief, whether appearing as church organization, or any of the other avenues and channels of human belief.

THE TRUE CHRISTIAN SCIENTIST

I have quoted to you much from the Bible and from Mrs. Eddy's writings, but I have done this in corroboration of the truth that has been deduced from the accepted premise. As a Christian Scientist I can no longer accept a statement, no matter how true that statement may be, until I understand it myself, and that understanding can only come through communion with the one Mind.

Science and Health has carried me to this one Mind, and in communion with it, I have found the truth that is in Science and Health. The

[1]Mis. 362:30.

truth in that book is now real to me because of its intrinsic truth, and for no other reason. You, yourself, are not a Christian Scientist until this understanding takes place. That is why Mrs. Eddy said, "I waited many years for a student to reach the ability to teach; it included more than they understood."[1] Mrs. Eddy waited many years before she found Edward A. Kimball, the one student who was able, through his understanding study of Science and Health, to commune with Mind so completely that he actually could discover for himself the truth contained in Science and Health.

A Christian Scientist is a real follower of Mrs. Eddy, not because of faith and confidence in Mrs. Eddy or in Science and Health, but because of faith and confidence in Mind as All-in-all. It was Mr. Kimball to whom Mrs. Eddy referred when she wrote, "whose clear, correct teaching of Christian Science has been and is an inspiration to the whole field."[2]

It was not until one arose, who, through communion with Mind was able to discover for himself the truth in Science and Health, that the final completion of Mrs. Eddy's discovery was attained. Through her deep spirituality, imbued

[1] Hea. 14:22. [2] My. 297:18.

with the spirit of Truth almost without measure, she gave Science and Health to the world. The next step was for Science and Health, which is the letter of Truth, to prove that it could lead the so-called mortal to Mind, where he could discover Christian Science for himself. That completed the entire circle. The purpose of Science and Health is to take you to Mind, and only as it succeeds in doing that, do you become an understanding Christian Scientist, and know why you are a Christian Scientist. "When he, the Spirit of truth, is come, he will guide you into all truth: for he shall not speak of himself; but whatsoever he shall hear, that shall he speak: and he will show you things to come."[1]

CONCLUSION

You know why evil in its present and last state is appearing as pure hypnotic suggestion, no longer under the guise of matter, but openly operating as pure evil mind, as malicious mental mal-practice; and you know why it is so utterly powerless, and so easily destroyed through the understanding of divine Mind as the one and only Mind.

[1]Jno. 16:13.

You understand that you have to meet every question here and now, and, if you do not meet it here, it is simply waiting for you "up the road." There is nothing that can present itself to you that you are not willing and glad and able to face, and to face alone with your own understanding, and with that understanding win your way to victory. "Ye are the light of the world. A city that is set on an hill cannot be hid."[1]

There is no royal road to this achievement. It is the road of Mind, never of faith in things material. It is the glorious "warfare with one's self" which Mrs. Eddy has so tersely termed "grand."[2]

The key note to the beginning of understanding is in the words of Mrs. Eddy, "A little more grace, a motive made pure, a few truths tenderly told, a heart softened, a character subdued, a life consecrated." This, she says, will "restore the right action of the mental mechanism, and make manifest the movement of body and soul in accord with God,"[3] and so bring the absolute assurance that I am a Christian Scientist because I understand Christian Science.

[1]Matt. 5:14.　[2]Mis. 118:25.　[3]Mis. 354:15.

PLAGIARISM

PLAGIARISM is a broad term and often misunderstood. Those who have not looked carefully into the subject are apt to think it means simply the purloining of another's words or expressions, when it really means appropriating the underlying intent or thought.

In the realm of literature, on account of the limitation of human language, the same words and sentences are often used to express entirely different thoughts. Those who do not understand this are liable to accuse one author of stealing from another when such may not be the case at all. Surely there is no one so ignorant of language as not to realize that numerous combinations of words have been employed many times. A writer may easily utilize words and sentences that another has used, but because of the infinity of Mind his thought behind those words gives them an entirely different meaning. Such an act could not possibly constitute the slightest breach of literary ethics.

This is as equally true in music as in literature, and it may be even more strikingly the case in music. Probably no great composer ever lived who has not used sequences or even phrases which cannot be found in the compositions of his forerunners, and yet it is entirely possible that the later composer never heard the group of notes, chords, or even the passage which he used for, what was to him, the first time. It is equally possible that the repetition of another's idea is merely an unconscious re-creating of what he has heard before. But it is the relation of these single parts to the whole idea that proves whether the sections are original or copied; in other words it is the spirit of the thing it expresses that proves the individuality.

It is said that Johannes Brahms, who was frequently accused of plagiarism, always remained totally unmoved by the accusation because he felt that those who accused him completely misunderstood anything but the letter of his works. Today his work is being hailed with great appreciation from every place where he was once held as but an abstruse re-creator. Indeed he is now recognized as the master craftsman of his time, whose artistry, however, is always second to his art.

Well could he afford to be unruffled and unmoved when it was pointed out to him that his Sonata in A Major for piano and violin was being called the "Meistersinger" Sonata, because the first few notes of the first movement were identical in interval, though not in pitch, with the first notes of the "Prize Song" from Wagner's opera "Die Meistersinger." No wonder his answer was simply, "Every donkey can see that."

All Americans are familiar with the tune and words of "My Country, 'Tis of Thee" just as the British are familiar with the tune and words of "God Save the King." But how many realize that identically the same arrangement of notes are used for both anthems? Does that mean that the musical accompaniment of "My Country, 'Tis of Thee" has been plagiarized from England, or from Switzerland or Prussia where it is also used as the air of their national anthem, or from France where much of the musical composition was originally borrowed by England in 1739, or is it simply that the same arrangement of notes is used to bring out, for each nation, the varying aspirations and desires that the different sets of words accompanying them are designed to express? It would be foolish to think that the sentiment back of "My Country, 'Tis of Thee" is being stolen because the same air is played as for other national hymns. That air turns thought with one instinctively to America, and with the other to his own country without any thought whatever of plagiarism.

The greater the mind the more apt it is to reproduce words or notes that have made an impression, because, the keener the mind, the deeper would be the impression, and therefore the more liable would that mind be to produce those same words or notes, but always clothed with its own spirit of purpose.

It is a well known and accepted fact that the greatest figures in the literary world have drawn largely from their predecessors, and have expanded this borrowing into newer and broader applications without incurring adverse criticism. "Chaucer is a huge borrower," says Emerson, and then, enumerating the many sources of his indebtedness, he adds, "Gower he uses as if he were only a brick-kiln or stone-quarry out of which to build his house. He steals by this apology,—that what he takes has no worth where he finds it, and the greatest where he leaves it."

Of the world's greatest poet, Emerson says, "In point of fact, it appears that Shakespeare did owe debts in all directions, and was able to use whatever he found," and he quotes this interesting computation in regard to the First, Second and Third parts of Henry the VI., "Out of 6043 lines, 1771 were written by some author preceding Shakespeare; 2373 by him, on the foundation laid by his predecessors; and 1899 were entirely his own."

Emerson very truly defines this literary heritage, which great writers have, without question, taken to be theirs, in the following clear statement, "It has come to be practically a sort of rule in literature, that a man, having once shown himself capable of original writing, is entitled thenceforth to steal from writings of others at discretion. . . . All the debts which such a man could contract to other wit, would never disturb his consciousness of originality: for the ministrations of books, and of other minds, are a whiff of smoke to that most private reality with which he has conversed."

Charles Lamb is another interesting example of one whose mind was so imbued with the writings of others that he is a constant and often unconscious borrower from his favorite authors. "Of these springs Lamb had drunk so deeply that his mind was saturated with them," writes Alfred Ainger in his introduction to Lamb's Essays.

From this same critic, we have this happy and intelligent summing up of this tendency in

Lamb's style, "He is rich in quotations. . . . But besides those avowedly introduced as such, his style is full of quotations held—if the expression may be allowed—in solution. One feels, rather than recognizes, that a phrase or idiom or term of expression is an echo of something that one has heard or read before. Yet such is the use made of his material, that a charm is added by the very fact that we are thus continually renewing our experience of an older day. His style becomes aromatic, like the perfume of faded rose leaves in a China jar. . . . His observation was his own, though when he gave it back into the world the manner of it was the creation of his reading."

It seems incredible that Mary Baker Eddy, the most original writer the world has had, could ever be accused of plagiarism. Her writings offer but a meager opportunity for those who would seek evidence of borrowing. When compared with her predecessors in the literary world on the point of indebtedness, she stands out as conspicuously original. Those who would bring this charge of plagiarism against her must attract attention more for their ingenuity than for their sincerity, and they should be familiar, too, with Mrs. Eddy's own statement. "The false report that I have appropriated other people's manuscripts in my works, has been met and answered *legally*." (Mis. Wr. p. 249:8.)

With her marvelous, original thinking, no matter what words Mrs. Eddy used she clothed them with her own wholly original thought and could not use them in any other sense. There never has been a writer who thought in the spiritual terms that Mrs. Eddy did. She could not therefore have adopted another's idea as her own; hence it would have been impossible for her to have been a plagiarist. But she certainly did have, as all writers have, the right to use the words of any author to express her own spiritual understanding.

It is interesting, however, to note that where Mrs. Eddy has occasionally used expressions and sentences of writers with whom she was thoroughly familiar, she used these only in relation to that which might be termed her touch with human affairs, as in her business relations with the church organization. In her great work, Science and Health, and wherever she stated the real Science of Being, hardly a combination of words used by another has ever been discovered. No other writer has ever dreamed of the spirituality expressed by Mrs. Eddy and so could not have attempted to formulate it in words.

One passage that is quoted in the foolish attempt to prove Mrs. Eddy a plagiarist is from Lindley Murray's English Reader. It was with this same author's Grammar, written in 1799, that Mrs. Eddy said she was as familiar, at the age of ten, as with the Westminster Confession, and the latter she "had to repeat every Sunday." (Ret. 10:5.) How perfectly natural, since she was so familiar with Lindley Murray's language, for Mrs. Eddy spontaneously to use these paragraphs of his, with but few changes, to express the thought she wished to convey. This is exactly what all English-speaking people in their spoken and written words are continually doing with the Bible and with Shakespeare's works, to bring out what they desire to express. But is this thought of as plagiarism?

Grotius, the noted Dutch scholar and statesman of the 16th century, is credited with the statement that the different clauses composing the Lord's Prayer were all familiarly used in the rabbinical forms of Jesus' day. But no one questions that Jesus' application was vastly richer and truer, and that his life-giving inspiration alone has made those statements endure down the ensuing centuries. Shall it not be found also true that the occasional phrases, borrowed by Mrs. Eddy, gain luster from contact with her thought?

Mrs. Eddy's condemnation of plagiarism in connection with her own writings in Christian Science had nothing to do with just the words that she used in those writings, but it did have everything to do with the great danger she saw if her exact and most carefully chosen words should be used apart from their context or in a perverted way to bring out a wrong sense of Christian Science.

Mrs. Eddy's one and only desire was to protect her discovery and its presentation to mortals in the choicest and most accurate language possible, and to preserve her own particular wording of that presentation until Christian Science was thoroughly established through understanding.

In her book, Retrospection and Introspection, on page 75, she clearly states how she felt about one author borrowing from another. "If one's spiritual ideal is comprehended and loved, the borrower from it is embraced in the author's own mental mood, and is therefore honest. The Science of Mind excludes opposites, and rests on unity."

When one hears of the vain endeavors of evil to belittle Mrs. Eddy and her marvelous discovery, and the subtle effort of malicious mind to attribute the discovery of Christian Science to another, one realizes that nothing but ignorance of the import of Christian Science could make such a futile attempt.

YOUR POWER AND
DOMINION

DO YOU SAY "THERE
IS NO GOD"?

A LETTER

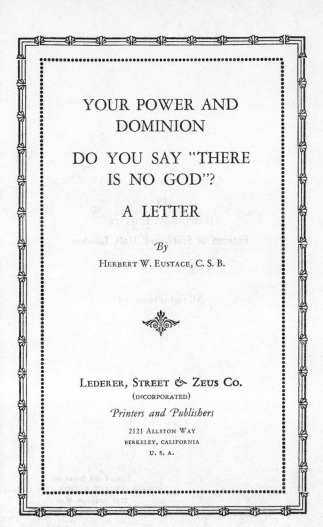

YOUR POWER AND DOMINION

DO YOU SAY "THERE IS NO GOD"?

A LETTER

By

HERBERT W. EUSTACE, C. S. B.

LEDERER, STREET & ZEUS CO.

(INCORPORATED)

Printers and Publishers

2121 ALLSTON WAY
BERKELEY, CALIFORNIA
U. S. A.

COPYRIGHT 1931, 1943

by

HERBERT W. EUSTACE

Entered at Stationers' Hall, London

Printed and Bound by
LEDERER, STREET & ZEUS CO., INC.
2121 ALLSTON WAY
BERKELEY, CALIFORNIA, U.S.A.

Foreword

By request, I am publishing the two addresses made at the conferences held in San Francisco and Los Angeles in 1930.

My hope is that this volume may prove as useful in arousing the reader to a more vigorous understanding of Christian Science and a deeper appreciation of Science and Health, as has "The Line of Light," published in 1929, thus corroborating Mrs. Eddy's statement in the Preface to Science and Health, that, "A few books, . . . based on this book are useful."

In preparing the addresses for publication, I have tried to avoid duplication as much as seemed wise.

Also, by request, I am including a letter written to a friend in December, 1929, which has already been freely circulated and is thought to be helpful.

Herbert W. Eustace.

YOUR POWER AND DOMINION

❧

DO YOU SAY "THERE IS NO GOD"?

A LETTER

ABBREVIATIONS

Works by Mary Baker Eddy

S. & H.—"Science and Health, with Key to the Scriptures."

Mis.—"Miscellaneous Writings."

Ret.—"Retrospection and Introspection."

Un.—"Unity of Good."

'00—"Message to The Mother Church, June 1900."

'01—"Message to The Mother Church, June 1901."

My.—"The First Church of Christ, Scientist, and Miscellany."

Peo.—"The People's Idea of God."

YOUR POWER AND DOMINION

JESUS declared, "Whatsoever thou shalt bind on earth shall be bound in heaven: and whatsoever thou shalt loose on earth shall be loosed in heaven."[1] He could have uttered no statement more fraught with responsibility and power than this, and to you as a Christian Scientist it means the acme of opportunity. Mrs. Eddy's statement is its corollary, "Christian Scientists, be a law to yourselves that mental malpractice cannot harm you either when asleep or when awake."[2]

JESUS THE CHRIST

You remember what caused Jesus to make this declaration. He had been asking his disciples what men were saying that he "the Son of man"[3] was. They told him of the various beliefs and opinions with which popular fancy had surrounded his marvelous words and works. Some explained his origin as being in accord with the fantastic theories of spiritualism or reincarnation, believing him to be Elijah or one of the prophets returned to earth, and others held other opinions as to who he was. Jesus discarded all these and asked, "But whom say

[1]Matt. 16:19. [2]S. & H. 442:30. [3]Matt. 16:13.

ye that I am?"¹ You remember Peter's answer,
"Thou art the Christ, the Son of the living
God."²

In making this answer, Peter caught the true
metaphysical fact, that what was actually being
presented to him as his Master was his own interpretation of the very presence of God, appearing as the eternal Christ, the ideal or true
man, —the only way God can ever appear and
be known. On this correct understanding,
Jesus declared he would build his church. In
other words, he would reveal man as the presence of God, as his church against which "the
gates of hell," misunderstanding, the suppositional false sense of all things, should not and
could not prevail.

THE SOURCE OF SPIRITUAL POWER

Now, one must ask, what relationship has all
this to me as a Christian Scientist? I recognize
that the statement, "whatsoever thou shalt
bind,"³ does not refer to anything that might be
done physically. It does, however, refer positively to that which appears to my thought as
the result of my thinking, of my understanding
of what the Christ really means and is. Is the
Christ to me "the only begotten of the Father,"⁴

1Matt. 16:15.   2Matt. 16:16.   3Matt. 16:19.   4John 1:14.

the very presence, the very activity of the divine
Mind, the one divine Principle, God? Or is my
interpretation but one of a multitude of human
beliefs, one of that class of absurdities Mrs.
Eddy designates as "an atom of dust thrown
into the face of spiritual immensity"?[1]

The degree of correctness of my answer to
the questions, What is Christ? What am I the
son of man? will determine how available to
me is the binding and loosing Jesus referred to,
and in this will be found all the power I have.
The true answer is my church, my "structure
of Truth and Love."[2]

Now, as Christian Scientists, as metaphysicians, what are we doing in regard to this binding and this loosing? Are we really putting
into actual operation what Jesus meant by
"whatsoever thou shalt bind on earth shall be
bound in heaven: and whatsoever thou shalt
loose on earth shall be loosed in heaven"?[3] Does
this mean each one individually? Does it actually mean that all power to bind and to loose
is given to me through my understanding of
Mind?

WHAT IS YOUR STAND?

Let us examine this and see what position we
are really taking. With the affairs of the world

[1]S. & H. 263:29.   [2]S. & H. 583:12.   [3]Matt. 16:19.

as they seem to be, there is the greatest need to
see where we stand, for surely never did affairs
seem to be more utterly chaotic, never more at
the point to which Jesus referred when he said,
"Men's hearts failing them for fear, and for
looking after those things which are coming on
the earth."[1]

However, as you well know, what seems to
be and what really is, to the metaphysician, are
leagues and leagues apart.   In fact, there is
truly no relationship whatever between the two,
and that is why Science and Health declares,
"Entirely separate from the belief and dream of
material living, is the Life divine, revealing
spiritual understanding and the consciousness of
man's dominion over the whole earth."[2]   Then
to paraphrase that statement, we can rightly declare, Entirely separate from the belief and
dream of the affairs of the world with its \ap-
parent discord and distress, is the divine reality,
the divine world, revealing spiritual understanding and the consciousness of man's dominion
over the whole earth.

Do you think it accomplishes one thing in the
right direction for the Christian Scientist to look
out on the world and to say it is, and accept it

[1]Luke 21:26.   [2]S. & H. 14:25.

as being, in terrible distress and chaos? Have you, as a Christian Scientist, the absolute power and authority to straighten out what appear as the conditions of the world, or are you completely helpless and compelled to bow down and accept them?

You know, as the Christian Scientist, that whatever you accept as Mind must inevitably appear to you as such. What are you accepting as Mind that could cause you to consent to a discordant and disheartening state of affairs in the world? There was never a more opportune moment for us to meet and frankly face this question and to see whether or not we do honestly believe that Mind is All-in-all. "Whatsoever thou shalt bind on earth shall be bound in heaven: and whatsoever thou shalt loose on earth shall be loosed in heaven."[1] This being true, are we going to bow down and accept seeming conditions just as every so-called mortal does and say, Well, I suppose it will have to take its course?

EVIL IS NULLIFIED BY THE TRUTH

You know that evil, having no intelligence, whether appearing as disease of the body, disease of business, or disease of the world, has no

[1] Matt. 16:19.

course to take. You know it requires the presence of intelligence before any course can be taken and, since evil has no intelligence, it has no course. You know why it has no intelligence and so you give it none. You know Jesus gave not a moment's respect or consideration to evil in any of its so-called demands. He spoke with all the authority of God; for, as God's activity, as that alone whereby God can be known and His power expressed, he had to do so.

This was clearly shown when he healed every manner of disease; fed the multitude, thus proving the omnipresence of food; stilled the storm; and walked the waves, thereby subduing the so-called law of gravity and bringing to light the truth about gravitation and attraction, namely, that, because it is the law of God, it always supports—never destroys. Where in all his experience, did he render the slightest consideration to the imaginary laws of matter, in other words, to evil? He spoke with unbounded authority and assurance, and you know he said, "He that believeth on me, the works that I do shall he do also."[1]   Do you think that Mrs. Eddy could have discovered Christian Science had she respected in the least the demands of evil or had she spoken with less than absolute

1 John 14:12.

power and authority to all discord, to finiteness and limitation of every kind?

Are you accepting the would-be attacks of evil on the government of the United States, on the President, on the prohibition law, and on everything that stands for law and order, as something that does not concern you, or, at least, as something over which you have no power? If you accept them, do you think that you can avoid bowing down to and accepting sickness, bad business conditions, disastrous weather or agricultural difficulties?

You all know that Mrs. Eddy had no patience with a helpless attitude toward destructive weather conditions. She demanded that they be handled and met by Christian Scientists, and that right weather be seen. Do you stand for any untoward condition or circumstance? If you do, is it not time that you ask yourself, Why do I? Do I honestly believe and accept the fact that Mind is All-in-all, or is that just a happy phrase I like to use which makes me feel better satisfied?

ESTABLISHING THE ALLNESS OF MIND

As a metaphysician you have established the fact that Mind is All-in-all, not because of the Bible, not because of Science and Health, not because of any person or thing, but because of your conviction, your own communion with Mind. You have recognized as self-evident your own conscious being, and from this fact you have deduced that there must be that which is the cause of this conscious being. In other words, consciousness must be, for you to be conscious. From that, you have established what consciousness, in order to be *is,* must be; and you have necessarily found that that which is, is all there is, it being impossible for anything to be outside of *is;* therefore you know of yourself that consciousness, Mind, is All-in-all.

Now, does that Mind that is One and All, embrace within itself all being? Or is there something, somewhere outside of that all, that can actually come and intrude itself as mind, and then operate as your mind and say, "I am true, and all that I am is true"? If that could be so, Christian Science would be useless. If that could be so, Christian Science would be nonsense.

You are not dependent upon any one to tell you that Christian Science is true. If you were a Christian Scientist because you had received it from a person or from a book, you might doubt it, but when you have the witness within yourself that God is, and you know of yourself that

He is, and that He is infinite intelligence, infinite Mind, and that this Mind, being all, is the Mind of you, its idea, then you can no longer say, "Am I my brother's keeper?"[1] Am I helpless about what appears to me as my brother, what appears as consciousness in any form to me?

WHERE IS THY BROTHER?

What constitutes this "brother" if it is not what is being accepted by you as consciousness, as Mind? And can you accept anything as Mind that you do not admit as such? Furthermore, in the admittance of it as consciousness, do you not necessarily find it as your Mind? You know the temptation of evil today is to have you say, What is that to me? To discard anything as not concerning you is to pervert what Jesus meant when he said, "What is that to thee? Follow thou me."[2]

If there is something "over there" that is not embraced in what you are accepting and acknowledging as Mind, then you had better ask yourself the question, What is that to me? But if, on the other hand, you accept the fact that Mind is absolutely All-in-all,—and when you say that, you mean it, not just as a platitude, but as reality to you,—then, how can there be any

[1]Gen. 4:9. [2]John 21:22.

"over there" that has nothing to do with you, whether it appears as political schemes or the ramifications of various national conditions in different countries, or as weather, or sickness, or anything else?

Can any one escape the responsibility of being a Christian Scientist, a right knower? Of course no one can, and unless that is recognized, there will be no kingdom found "in earth, as it is in heaven."[1] As you know, being is simply oneness with Principle, aloneness with Principle. It is always single file, here and now, and no one can lay any responsibility on anything or any one "over there", for "over there" is "here". It brings it all back to the one question, Do I honestly acknowledge and admit that there is only one Mind and that that Mind necessarily embraces within itself all that is? Is that true? You know that it is true. You have proved it to an extent. But is not the effort of evil continually to say to you, What is that to me? That saying is all the devil there is. Mind never says, What is that to thee? in that sense of indifference or of anxiety but only in the sense of "Son, ... all that I have is thine".[2]

This being true, is it possible for a condition to exist that is not of vital interest to you, some-

[1]Matt. 6:10. [2]Luke 15:31.

thing that can be in operation, no matter where, that is not embraced in that which is actually coming to you as your very Mind, as your very consciousness?

"ERROR CANNOT DESTROY ERROR"

Consider the affairs of the world today. The human sense of things, which embraces within itself "the first lie and all liars",[1] declares that the world is upside down, never before known to be so bad,—"Distress of nations" and "Men's hearts failing them for fear"[2] of the things coming upon them. To this sense everywhere discord and turmoil abound. Take the United States and look at the attack, apparently, on everything that is standing for the best that civilization knows. I say apparently, because, understood metaphysically, the attack is not really true at all. But does not evil seem to be in the saddle and guiding the four horses of the Apocalypse? What is there to stop this except the Christ, the truth, concerning which Jesus said, "Ye shall know the truth, and the truth shall make you free"?[3] Otherwise the aggressions of evil will never stop. Evil can not stop itself. Evil does not destroy evil, for it cannot. Two times two as five can never correct or destroy

1S. & H. 16:19.   2Luke 21:25-26.   3John 8:32.

itself.   As Science and Health says, "In the Science of Mind, you will soon ascertain that error cannot destroy error".[1]

That wrong conditions will eventually correct themselves is nothing but a subtle suggestion bidding you leave evil alone so that it can accumulate.   Mrs. Eddy declares, "Evil let alone grows more real, aggressive, and enlarges its claims; but, met with Science, it can and will be mastered by Science."[2]   It is the truth and the truth alone that can and does destroy evil. Then must we not face the world conditions today?

THE LATTER DAYS

It is perfectly true that we are today in the time when Biblical prophecy is being fulfilled and is computed to be nearing its close. What is called the Pyramid of Cheops or the Great Pyramid of Egypt or as it has been called the "Bible in Stone" agrees with this prophecy and gives 1936 as the mathematically estimated time when the King's Chamber is reached. This Chamber has been, fittingly, termed the Hall of the Judgment of the Nations. Nations like individuals merely multiplied, must face their testing times.

1S. & H. 495:31.   2Mis. 284:25.

These are the days Jesus referred to so vividly when he spoke of seeing Satan, the abomination of desolation, standing "in the holy place",[1] and when, as Paul puts it, "we wrestle not against flesh and blood, but against principalities, against powers, against the rulers of the darkness of this world, against spiritual wickedness in high places"[2]—in other words, when pure evil mind acting as hypnotic suggestion claims to be the mental volition of its victim and to operate as his mind, standing in his holiest place, the secrecy of his own being. This is the time when Jesus said "and then shall the end come".[3] We see this operation of evil on all sides, so that, even without Biblical chronology or the mathematical calculations of the Great Pyramid, the metaphysician knows positively that we are, right now, in the latter days, —the time of the final destruction of all belief in the entity and reality of matter, which is but another name for malicious mind. Science and Health gave to the world, in 1875, the ringing statement, "All is infinite Mind and its infinite manifestation."[4] That was the doom of the finite sense called mortal mind or matter, and it has been seen rapidly drawing to a close ever since.

1Matt. 24:15.   2Eph. 6:12.   3Matt. 24:14.   4S. & H. 468:10.

THE PRESSURE OF TRUTH

Are not these things of vital importance to you? You know perfectly well how far from satisfied you have been feeling. Probably you have never been through a period of such unrest as you have experienced in the last few years. Why is that? Mrs. Eddy once implied that she was no longer feeling discord as from herself, but she was feeling the thoughts of others, and in Unity of Good, she has a chapter entitled, "Suffering from Others' Thoughts." In this chapter she plainly shows that what Jesus suffered from was the thoughts of others, not meaning thoughts of other people as such, but from the *mind* appearing as the mind of others, which is always both the cause and effect of all suffering, of all evil. She meant of course, with regard to herself, that it was this impersonal sense of evil that was presenting itself to her as a so-called condition or state of consciousness.

Do not imagine that you are not in this same position. You are. Your understanding of Christian Science spontaneously brings to light, in fact demands that you recognize evil as impersonal, and yet evil comes to you always as your own thought. What you are feeling today is the pressure of Truth on this so-called malicious mind, forcing it into the open to be seen for the mental iniquity that it is. This is really its last throe.

PROHIBITION

Now how is evil appearing? Surely the forms it is taking in this country are very self-evident. On all sides you can see the attack being made on the highest, the most advanced civilization that has appeared in the world, America. The prohibition unfoldment, as Mrs. Eddy has stated, has received a "strong impulse"[1] from Christian Science. But even if she had not said this, you would still know it to be the fact because the understanding that there is only one Mind absolutely prohibits the acceptance of a consciousness of anything that is apart from that Mind. Must not that which, even in the least degree, causes man to be less a man than he normally is, of necessity stand as contrary to intelligence, and therefore as not Mind? And in belief does not wine or liquor, whether weak or strong, do this very thing? Then is it of Mind? It is for this reason Christian Science unhesitatingly declares, "Whatever intoxicates a man, stultifies and causes him to degenerate physically and morally. Strong drink is unquestionably an evil, and evil cannot be

[1] Mis. 288 :26.

used temperately: its slightest use is abuse; hence the only temperance is total abstinence."[1]

Is not this statement emphatically borne out by that eminent medical authority, Dr. Howard A. Kelly, professor emeritus of Johns Hopkins University, in the following:

"There is no disease in the world for which alcohol is a cure . . . More to the point is the fact that while it cannot be said to cure any disease, it does undeniably cause thousands of cases of disease, all of them fatal in the long run. Its use is ruinous to kidneys, liver, heart and the smaller blood vessels, and gives rise to that most common fatality, high blood pressure.

"All this has been proved by innumerable tests. Two men may play tennis or chess equally well. Give one of them a single glass of beer and he will be easily defeated by the one who abstains. Start ten men of comparable vigor up a mountain side, five of whom have taken drinks as a stimulation. These five will fail in the climb. So mild a drink as beer will lessen their physical and mental prowess by ten to fifteen per cent.

"It has been shown that one spoonful of liquor lessens the ability to form quick judgment and to act on that judgment. Giving a driver alcohol endangers life.

"Alcohol is a habit-forming drug. Its high potency as a dangerous drug is a million times more hurtful than any conceivable accruing advantage. It has no place in medical practice."

[1] Mis. 288:32

The discovery of Christian Science laid the axe at the root of any use of liquor. In the light of this fact, can the Christian Scientist think that the use of intoxicating liquor in any form is right, when Mind is All-in-all? Then what would the attack of evil be against? Would it not be against the very country that appears most in line with purity in all its manifestations? Inevitably the attack of malicious mind would be to rouse the "seven thunders"[1] of evil against that country.

PRAYER SPIRITUAL DISCERNMENT

As a metaphysician, how much are you doing to stop this attack? Are you accepting it? Or are you praying understandingly in the secret of your own thought, and destroying all belief that there is any malicious mind to do anything? Are you a law to the case? If not, why not?

You understand what prayer really means: it is the pure realization that there is no attraction apart from Mind. There is no presence or power that can foist itself upon man as his mind to encourage him to turn to anything apart from Mind for completeness and satisfaction. There is nothing apart from Mind to give him happiness.

[1] Rev. 10:3.

THE LIGHT OF THE WORLD

Jesus said, to the right knower of his day, of today and all days, "Ye are the light of the world. A city that is set on an hill cannot be hid."[1] Is it possible for that light not to shine? You are that light. The understanding that you have of the allness of Mind is the light, and that is the light of the world. If that light goes out, what is there to lighten the darkness and dispel it? Can you then sit down and say, I have no responsibility in this?

Ask yourself how much responsibility you have taken. To what extent have you accepted this power and used it—you who have all power to bind on earth that which should be bound, and to loose on earth that which should be loosed? Do you think that anything can acquit you of your responsibility?

When the invitations went out to the mar-riage feast, Jesus said the excuses came. Each one had something to occupy his attention and so prevent him from being present at the feast. You are not in that position, making excuses, for you understand that the real marriage feast is the allness of Mind and your eternal oneness with Mind.   There is no escape, and you have

[1]Matt. 5 :14.

none, from the responsibility of being present at that feast. Because there is no escape, the question is a serious one. What am I actually doing to bind this lie of human belief and so find myself really present at this marriage, this oneness with Mind? There can be no sitting down and accepting this attack on prohibition, this attack on the government, this attack that is going on against every righteous activity. Can you avoid the responsibility of meeting the claim that Chicago or any other city is being overrun with so-called banditry? Are you vigorously knowing and seeing what the one activity is?

MIND ALL-INCLUSIVE

What is it that is back of all banditry, back of all seeking after something that the mortal thinks he has not? Is it not in reality a desire to gain for himself his own sense of good? The remedy for all evil desire is the understanding that the one Mind, being all, includes within itself all good, and that infinite good means good for all, satisfaction for all, with no desire left unfulfilled. Does not this limitless good, then, include all that is meant by money, all that is the true sense about liquor or about position? In fact, does it not mean all that is really implied by everything? It does. Then, does it

not include for the bandit all that he truly desires; for the drunkard, all that he truly craves?
It does. Is that bandit, that drunkard, something apart from what you accept as consciousness?

Then, is not the understanding of the one
Mind as All-in-all, the remedy for all evil,
spontaneously bringing to every one complete
satisfaction and wholeness? Does not the understanding of the principle of numbers give
complete satisfaction to all alike?

Good is the heritage of one and all, and
every one has all good always. This knowing,
this realization destroys the lie, the hypnotic
suggestion, that good is absent from some and
present with others. This assuages all desire
to steal, to become intoxicated, etc. This is
just what the Psalmist meant when he said that
God, the one infinite good, the Mind of all,
openeth His hand, "and satisfiest the desire of
every living thing."[1]

Thus the bandit disappears as such, and the
drunkard likewise and all evil. This, as you
know, comes to pass only as you are alone in
your "closet," with the door shut, with not one
single thing present there but Mind. Dwelling
there with true understanding, you have ab-

[1] Ps. 145 :16.

solute assurance and confidence that your
"Father which seeth in secret" rewards "thee
openly,"[1]—appears in the tangible language of
good.

THE NECESSITY FOR ALERTNESS

You understand this. You do not need to be
reminded that you are always "alone with
(your) own being and with the reality of
things."[2] Being asleep to this would prove to
you at once that something apart from Mind
was attempting to enthrone itself as consciousness with you and so dethrone that which you
know is Mind. This you denounce instantly as
the suppositional opposite of the one Mind, in
other words, malicious mind or malicious mental
malpractice.

By being a law unto yourself this "malicious
mental malpractice," coming in the form of depressed conditions of one kind or another, or as
an attack against the government, "cannot
harm you either when asleep or when awake."[3]

How does this suggestion operate? Is it
necessary to remind you of what you already
know, that evil usually comes in the language
that will deceive you,—frequently, in the language of good—the language that will best

[1]Matt. 6:6. [2]'01 20:8. [3]S. & H. 442:31.

"pull the wool over your eyes" and make you feel that perhaps after all it is not so bad as it seems, or at least in the language that will blind you to, or turn you from, what the real claim is?

ANALYZING THE CLAIM

Take for the moment the world conditions. We will all, for the sake of argument, admit that the world seems chaotic. That is the admission of the human belief. You can point to a thousand things apparently going on in the world which would cause you to say "How terrible!" But are you deceived?

When a claim of sickness presents itself to you, it also seems that something is very chaotic, and sometimes it seems as if the so-called tissues of the body were being violently broken down, possibly through what is called a belief of cancer or a belief of tuberculosis or whatever it may be. At least something disastrous seems to be taking place.

You are not, however, deceived by that. As a metaphysician, you are not perplexed. You turn from the appearance or sense testimony after having, through careful argument, assured yourself that no such testimony is true, because of the impossibility of there being a single bodily condition apart from Mind to produce it, and

you do not stop with your argument until you
are fully persuaded that right where this diseased bodily condition seems to be, right there,
is the very activity of Principle, present as perfect cell, as perfect germ, as perfect anything
you may be dealing with. When you are completely convinced that what is actually appearing to you as the disease is really not the disease at all, you find right there, where the disease seems to be, when viewed through the lens
of Mind, the very activity of good itself.

This conviction being complete with you, so
that there is no doubt or question left, you turn
unreservedly from the appearance to what the
actual claim is—and even that, of course, is
only as belief. Then what do you find the real
claim to be?—that there is malicious mind, that
it actually is, and that, as such, it can operate
as hypnotic suggestion, as the mind of its victim and appear first as one false condition and
then another. This claim is destroyed through
the *realization* that the one Mind is all the Mind
there is.

A PARALLEL DRAWN FROM HYPNOTISM

The illustration of a man under hypnotic influence, desperately going through swimming
motions on dry boards, trying to save himself

from drowning, brings out very clearly what is necessary to do in every case of healing in Christian Science. If you did not see that this hypnotized man was on dry boards, but could see only the distress and agony of his face and the rapid movement of his arms in his desperate effort to save himself from drowning, you would be instantly tempted to conclude that he was really in the water and must be pulled out. Your first thought, doubtless, would be to save him from drowning. But what would be the reaction in your thought when you discovered that he was not in water at all, but simply on dry boards, hypnotized into believing he was drowning in water? Would you not immediately, as a Christian Scientist, realize that his freedom could come only by releasing him, through your understanding of the allness of the one Mind, from the bondage of the hypnotic influence controlling him?

You know this is what you would do. And the realization of the truth, that there is only one Mind, would break the hypnotic influence; and the man would then get up and walk away free. There is not the slightest difference between the healing of that hypnotic case and of every case, that presents itself as consciousness, no matter what form of discord it may seem to assume, be it sickness, limitation, sin—or what not.

Let this be repeated that we may not lose its importance. You first, through arguments, bring yourself to a point of absolute conviction that what appears as the claim is really not the claim at all, and that the appearance every time is merely the bluff of human belief to deceive you into not discerning the true claim, which is always the same, namely, that there is malicious mind, and that, as such mind, it can operate, and does operate, as hypnotic suggestion and appear in the guise that will best deceive. Evil is never a wrong *thing* but is always hypnotic suggestion.

Is this not what you must know and how you must work every time? It is, or you do not handle the claim at all. "The axe is laid unto the root of the trees"[1] only when you turn entirely away from all the physical arguments of disease. You can do this only as you become as fully convinced that there is no disease there, as you are convinced, in the case of the man swimming on dry boards under hypnotic influence, that there is no water there from which to rescue him. The realization of the omnipresence of the one Mind is the one and only

[1]Matt. 3:10.

remedy for all hypnotic suggestions, and through it you destroy every claim of disease.

THE METAPHYSICIAN'S RESPONSIBILITY IS ALL INCLUSIVE

Are world affairs in any respect different from bodily affairs? Have you been handling world affairs as though you had power over them, or have you been accepting as true everything that the daily newspapers and the various avenues of evil have presented to you? Whichever you have been doing determines how much of a Christian Scientist you really are. Each one must ask himself the question and answer it, and each one must take the responsibility of the world's affairs as his own and not think that *that* is the business of someone else. "Am I my brother's keeper?"[1] is the question confronting each one every moment.

That which makes me my brother's keeper, is my responsibility for whatever continues to appear as consciousness to me, and nothing can release me from that responsibility. "And I, if I be lifted up from the earth, will draw all men unto me."[2] Jesus did not say, "If *you* be lifted up." He said, "And *I*, if *I* be lifted up." He knew that with one Mind he could have no

1Gen. 4 :9.   2John 12 :32.

"over there." How could Mind be "over there" separate from "here"? Because Mind embraces within itself all being, it must be "here" and include all the "there" within the "here."

If I, as a metaphysician, as "the light of the world,"[1] am not going to do my work, how can I expect anybody on earth to do it? How can anyone do it if he does not know how to do it? You have been entrusted by Mind with your understanding of Mind, and you cannot shirk or refuse to use it or wait for a more convenient season. How pertinently then is asked, "What will you do about it? Will you be equally in earnest for the truth? Will you doff your lavender-kid zeal, and become real and consecrated warriors? Will you give yourselves wholly and irrevocably to the great work of establishing the truth, the gospel, and the Science which are necessary to the salvation of the world from error, sin, disease, and death? Answer at once and practically, and answer aright!"[2]

You understand your responsibility in regard to the world. Be honest then with yourself and see if it does not cause a sense of intense disappointment to you if you fail to do what you

[1]Jno. 8:12. [2]Mis. 177:13.

understand. It cannot help it. Then why not do it?

THE GOVERNMENT OF UNDERSTANDING

The conditions appearing in the so-called world are under the government of understanding. "Immortal Mind, governing all, must be acknowledged as supreme in the physical realm, so-called, as well as in the spiritual."[1] Is not that government your understanding or Mind? Because there is only one Mind and this Mind is your Mind, it is self-evident that you hold the government in your hands. Is not that in accordance with the promise that "the government shall be upon *his* shoulder: and his name shall be called Wonderful, Counsellor, The mighty God, The everlasting Father, The Prince of Peace. Of the increase of his government and peace there shall be no end."[2]?

This "government" is not something apart from you. It is your very Mind, it is that which is your very consciousness of being. It is actually intelligence or consciousness to you. Is not your responsibility then inescapable? The world is your world—not something outside of you. It is right with you every moment and it is absolutely under the government of that which is

1S. & H.427:23.   2Is. 9:6,7.

your Mind, for that Mind embraces within itself all that the world means.

MIND CONTROLS THE ELEMENTS

Included in this term "world" surely appear what are called weather conditions both good and bad. As the metaphysician, do you admit that you have control over the weather or is the weather something beyond your authority? Do you control your multiplication table? What do you mean by the word control? Is it not the power and ability that Mind expresses in regard to all thought, to all being? Being, in all its forms, is simply the eternal activity of Mind, and that which is called weather is as much the activity of Mind as any other appearance.

An important question arises then. If rain is needed in one particular place and not in another, is it possible for it to rain only where needed? Why not? Of course it is. Rain is a state of consciousness, it is not materiality. This very question is based on the belief that rain and all else is material, when in reality it is simply a state of consciousness, the activity of Mind; hence it takes any form required.

You use mathematics because you admit it is purely thought, available wherever it is needed, and your using it does not interfere with your neighbor's either using it or not using it. Then why should there be any temptation to scoff at the idea that you can have rain and your neighbor not have it if he does not need it? It is not less thought than is mathematics; both are states of consciousness. Infinite Love, infinite compassion, appears to one and all rightly in just the language they can best appreciate, as Jesus pointed out so definitely when he declared, "He maketh his sun to rise on the evil and on the good, and sendeth rain on the just and on the unjust."[1] Could rain or sunshine come to one that it could harm? It comes only in obedience to Mind and it appears to the one accepting Mind as All-in-all in whatever form it is needed. As the presence of Mind it could not do otherwise.

Then you realize that the question of weather control is never a question of controlling the weather as weather, or of having the rain, the sunshine, the heat or the cold whenever needed, for you understand that all right conditions are everywhere present every moment, and that it is never metaphysically the claim that they are not. The claim is always that there *is* malicious mind and that, operating as hypnotic suggestion, it can appear as discordant weather even as it

[1] Matt. 5:45.

claims to be discordant body. It is never either, but is always hypnotic suggestion and is destroyed only as such.

In view of this inherent power of prayer, of true understanding to bring to pass all things that ye ask "nothing doubting"[1], is it not an amazing parody on the result of nineteen centuries of Christian teaching that an Associated Press dispatch from Chicago, dated September 5th, 1930, should read as follows, "Prayers for rain are futile in the opinion of a majority of prominent American clergymen who took part in a symposium conducted (at the time of the drought) by the *Christian Century* magazine.

" 'No imaginable connection exists between man's inward spiritual attitude and a rainstorm' said Dr. Harry Emerson Fosdick of New York. Dr. W. P. Lemmon of Minneapolis called praying for rain an attempt to 'involve God in a cooperative scheme to maintain present American living standards'."

RESPONSIBILITY DEMANDS PROOF

Face these things. Ask yourself, Am I using the power that I understand? Is Christian Science a reality to me? Is it practical? Is it

[1]Acts 11:12.

available? You know it is. Use it and so prove it.

Only as we really face the facts and feel the dominion that belongs to understanding, do we grasp the significance of "whatsoever thou shalt bind on earth shall be bound in heaven: and whatsoever thou shalt loose on earth shall be loosed in heaven."[1] The practicability of this promise was for all. How ridiculous to suppose that Jesus meant it for just his disciples! He was referring to that understanding of Mind that knows that the Christ, the truth, is not a person, or a book, and has nothing to do with a person or thing, but merely appears as such— simply because that is the language or interpretation that can best be understood. The interpretation has exactly the same relationship to Mind that the image in the mirror has to the object in front of the mirror. It shows forth Mind. This understanding is yours and you know you have it.

Sincerity and honesty win the way,—and, Why?—because truly, "Sincerity is more successful than genius or talent."[2] But can you honestly feel yourself sincere if you are not basing your every thought, your every action, on the allness of Mind?

1 Matt. 16:19.   2 '00 9:18.

DOMINION OVER DEATH

It has been asked, How about dominion over death? Can death be bound? Any one can die. To die is the easiest thing in the world to do. In fact, from the very moment of the mortal's so-called birth, from the moment the lie of finity, of human limitation, is conceived, the false concept, you, as the mortal, are headed for the grave unless you stop it. You are the only one who can stop it. No one else can do so. *You have to stop dying.* Jesus plainly stated that, "If a man keep my saying, he shall never see death."[1]

If you are satisfied to go on using Christian Science as one would use a drug, a little here and a little there, and when you feel that you have not quite enough understanding, to turn then to something else, to some non-intelligent "beggarly elements,"[2] for assistance, you will doubtless in the end die. But, why should you do this? There is no stability or permanent achievement in such conduct. Why not recognize instead that that is being merely a faith or belief Scientist, not the genuine Christian Scientist, that that is not *I* at all, and then prove it by the declaration to every such suggestion,

1Jno. 8:51.   2Gal. 4:9.

"Get thee behind me, Satan,"[1] and see that it does so forever. Be a law to it.

You will never do this, however, unless you feel that you have the power to do it. There is nothing that cripples a person more effectually than to feel that he has not the power to accomplish something he desires to accomplish. It makes no difference what it may be, even to the overcoming of death.

DEATH NOT RELATED TO "OLD AGE" AND NOT INEVITABLE

No one can have the power to overcome death who does not understand and cannot say to death, You are the devil, a falsity and you have no place in Mind. If death is not seen as an enemy, the enemy that Paul called the "last enemy",[2] which must be silenced by Christian Science, what is to overcome it? It cannot be overcome. But can anybody die unless he is sick? Don't you, as a Christian Scientist, know that Christian Science overcomes sickness? Are you not equally sure that in overcoming all sickness, you also triumph over death?

In the past, death has always been considered unavoidable with old age, but this so-called mind of the mortal is now saying that death has

[1]Matt. 16:23. [2]1 Cor. 15:26.

nothing to do with age, in other words, that age does not itself produce death, but that old age is a disease. This statement was, of course, sooner or later inevitable, because for a long time it has been becoming more and more generally accepted that, so far as the human sense of body is concerned, it is never over seven years old. From the standpoint of material science it has been proved that every particle of the body is renewed every seven years, thus establishing that the body as a whole is never over seven years of age. With this accepted as a fact, how could this mind longer continue to say that the body was dying of old age? It had to stop declaring age and death as necessarily linked together. Now it is saying that old age is a disease and has nothing to do with years. The question confronting you then is, are you facing old age, which previously you thought unavoidably synonymous with death, as a disease? And how can you face old age as a disease unless you are claiming Mind as All-in-all and asserting control over death?

It is impossible to conceive of a worse conspiracy against Life than the old teaching that advancing years, in other words, growing older, must eventually lead to death, for years go by inevitably and if added years mean old age and

old age means death, then where is there any
hope for overcoming them? There would be
none, but now because of Christian Science and
its teaching and proof, even the human mind is
turning away from this falsity, that the increase
of years necessarily produce death.

A most enlightening statement on this subject was made by Dr. Eugene Lyman Fisk, director of the Life Extension Institute in 1928,
and was published by the *New York Times* in
its issue of Dec. 31, 1928. Among other things
reported, the *Times* said,

"The idea of time having an effect on aging and
decay exerts an enormous influence and may be
found in practically every textbook of medicine,
but it is as baseless as the jargon of a voodoo
savage. Old age is a disease. Death is always
due to pathology."

Combating the theory of Sir Clifford Allbutt,
authority on circulatory diseases, who said that
hardening of the arteries is due to time and can
not be retarded medically, because "we cannot
hold back the wings of time," Dr. Fisk asserted
that this was dealing in "pure allegory." "Fancy
the wings of time flapping about our arteries," he
remarked.

"Scientific workers who scorn the implication
that they incline to fundamentalism, nevertheless
are the most rigid kind of fundamentalists in their
attitude toward the problem of the fixity of
life cycles.

"Even among those who admit offhand that the life cycles of living organisms are not fixed, there is a subconscious conviction that in a practical sense this is so and that it is more or less futile to attempt to interfere with the course of nature or the plans of the Deity, depending on the religious or philosophical views of the individual.

"Has it been decreed somewhere, somehow, by somebody, that the tissues of the human body, or of any other living organism, shall become lifeless within a certain length of time? With those who hold such views purely as a matter of religious conviction, I have no quarrel; but as a scientific proposition it is untenable.

"Sir Arthur Keith speaks of 'life as a web on the loom of time', and asks 'Who then is in charge of the loom?' It is no answer for the biologist to say that the loom works automatically and that the threads spin themselves.

"The truth is that the thesis of a changeless limit to the life cycle of any type of organism is a fantastic conception, dogmatic in the extreme, without justification in scientific principle and implying absolute omniscience on the part of the person postulating it, while the negation of the fixity of the life cycle is a far more modest claim, confessing to limitation of scientific knowledge and also its possible expansion."

NOT THINGS BUT STATES
OF CONSCIOUSNESS

The garment of Mind is seamless, complete, whole, one. The garment, therefore, of its suppositional opposite, of so-called malicious mind, is one and is whole also. Therefore, if you admit any part of evil, you admit the whole of it. If you admit good at all, you have to accept the whole of good. The metaphysician stands at the point of the allness of good. Then he faces world conditions, knowing his complete control over them. He is a law to them.

Let us ask ourselves again, Are the discordant conditions that appear in the world true, or are they, like every claim of sickness, just purely hypnotic suggestion? That is the question. If they are really world conditions, something apart from what is appearing to you as consciousness, you might as well fold your tent "like the Arabs, and as silently steal away", because there is no possible way by which you can change a real condition.

You know that if there were such a condition or thing as cancer, as consumption, or as ear, eye or brain trouble, you as a Christian Scientist would say it was ridiculous to think of attempting to do anything with it because there is no possible way whereby Mind can touch or change a condition or a thing that actually exists. That is not possible. Mind can deal only with thought. Mind and things as things are forever unknown to each other. That is why you always reduce everything that presents itself to you, no matter how materially it may appear, to the basis of consciousness, the one common denominator. You must find it as consciousness or it cannot be handled.

Do you think it is different with world conditions, with Russia, or China, or with any other place? If they *are* places and those *are* conditions occurring there, then you cannot as a Christian Scientist do one single thing with them. But, if what appears as Russia or China, on analysis, proves to be simply a state of consciousness, then you have absolute power and authority over it.

How do you know that there is such a country as Russia? How do you know that there are such political beliefs as Bolshevism, Fascism, or Socialism? They come to you as so-called states of consciousness. In other words, you are consciously aware of them. Then, do they not come as your very consciousness? Coming as such, must they not in reality be states of Mind or consciousness? Then what are you dealing with? With things or with Mind appearing?

Is the disease *a disease* because it seems to appear as something that says that a thousand doctors can show it to you, that your eyes can see, your ears can hear, and your hands can touch? As a Christian Scientist you are not deceived by that. You turn unreservedly away from it, understanding that the appearance does not really enter into the case at all, except as the effort or bluff of evil to deceive you as to what the claim really is. "Entirely separate from the belief and dream"[1] of the material appearance of anything is the reality, and so, taking it completely out of the realm of matter, you reduce whatever appears to you, to the common denominator of consciousness or mentality, and there you can correct any lie with the truth.

Do these untoward world affairs or business affairs, then, in the slightest differ from the so-called claims of sickness? If they do, you know as a Christian Scientist that you are helpless; but if they do not, then, does not what Jesus said apply: "whatsoever thou shalt bind on earth shall be bound in heaven: and whatsoever thou shalt loose on earth shall be loosed in heaven",[2] and also, Mrs. Eddy's admonition, "be a law to yourselves that mental malpractice cannot harm you either when asleep or when awake".[3]

ALL POWER IS YOURS

The hour has struck when this demand of Mind, this law, must be expressed. The time

1S. & H. 14:25.   2Matt. 16:19.   3S. & H. 442:31.

to speak "as one having authority, and not as the scribes"[1] is at hand. You can no longer think that you have not all power. You have. Now consider for a moment, why it is the most natural, normal thing in the world for you to have this power. Here are you, conscious being, knowing there is only one Mind, and knowing that that Mind embraces within itself all being, whether appearing as person, place or thing, and that that Mind is your Mind. With that Mind as your Mind, have you not all power?

The Bible declares that God gave man "dominion".[2] Notice that the very thing that endeavors to obtrude itself as your mind suggests finiteness, lack of power in every direction, and insists upon limitation with regard to everything, unless you are in your "closet" with your door shut, alone with Mind. There all is freedom, power, dominion, boundlessness.

Can you move mountains? Why do you question your ability to move mountains? Are they things composed of rocks? The presence of Mind must embrace all rocks. Then are they so-called things that you are to move, or is it Mind interpreting itself in its infinite and intelligent variety? You know that Jesus meant it when he said, "whosoever shall say unto this

1Matt. 7:29.   2Gen. 1:26.

mountain, Be thou removed, and be thou cast into the sea; and shall not doubt in his heart, but shall believe that those things which he saith shall come to pass; he shall have whatsoever he saith. Therefore I say unto you, What things soever ye desire, when ye pray, believe that ye receive them, and ye shall have them."[1] And also, "your Father knoweth what things ye have need of, before ye ask him."[2] That did not mean to ask in the sense of asking for, but it did mean understanding the allness of Mind. Whatsoever ye shall understand, that shall be done unto you.

When you consider how utterly impotent that poor thing, that ignorant belief called the human mind, is, to help itself, this should rouse in you the determination to abandon absolutely and forever all faith and belief in the human mind and its varied paraphernalia as of any value, and to stand on and prove the fact that the one Mind is All-in-all every instant.

You need never fail in any case, whether it be world conditions, finances, or the body, for the one Mind is the one healer, the one practitioner. You know Mrs. Eddy has said, "If it becomes necessary to startle mortal mind to break its dream of suffering, vehemently tell

[1]Mark 11 :23-24. [2]Matt. 6 :8.

your patient that he must awake. . . . Tell him that he suffers only as the insane suffer, from false beliefs."[1] When talking to a friend, she once said to stamp your foot on the floor if necessary to emphasize to yourself your determination to win, but be sure to speak as one having authority. Have you not all authority? Who can deny you? What is there to oppose you?

THE MENACE OF SELF-INDULGENCE

What do you think it is that seems able to weaken your confidence in Mind as All-in-all? Is it not self-indulgence, that is, the wrong sense of self-indulgence, indulging in beliefs of satisfaction in matter, in finiteness? All are very ready to abandon pain in matter and, even to some extent, what have been designated as certain improper pleasures in matter. But remember, gratification or pleasure in matter is the more stubborn belief, and the mortal is more unwilling to abandon pleasurable beliefs than painful ones; yet both the pleasure and pain that matter is supposed to afford are based on finiteness, because the whole nature of so-called matter is finity, limitation, hence death. Matter stands always as merely another term for death or the lie about Mind, Life.

[1] S. & H. 420:28.

It is self-indulgence in material pleasures, in the belief that matter, under certain circumstances, can afford pleasure, that denies the power to speak with that purity, with that isness, that means and is authority. It is useless to attempt to define what those indulgences may be, because each one knows full well for himself when he is looking to matter and accepting matter as intelligence to give pleasure. The Christian Scientist knows that it is the indulging in these very things that denies him his power to overcome matter, for "the fundamental error of faith in things material; . . . . is the unseen sin, the unknown foe, the heart's untamed desire which breaketh the divine commandments."[1]

Matter is not what it appears to be. It is not a thing. It is a misstatement of Mind. Matter is simply a name for what you might call the most ignorant or apparently innocent form of malicious mind, which appears always as finity, as limitation, as death. Then, any acceptance of so-called indulgence in matter, is bound sooner or later to limit your understanding and your absolute unswerving allegiance to Mind as All-in-all.

[1] Ret. 31:13.

How can you speak with authority to world conditions and diseases if you are holding to these lesser claims as having power? Can you correct two times twenty as fifty if you do not first correct two times two as five? Yet one mistake is really no more difficult to correct than the other. If we have not been "faithful over a few things" how can we be made "ruler over many"?[1]

PURITY DEFINED

"Blessed are the pure in heart: for they shall see God."[2] What does pure in heart mean? By purity of heart Jesus meant complete one-ness with *that that is* as all that *is*. *That which is*, by its very nature of being all that *is*, excludes everything unlike itself. And is not that what is meant by purity,—without an element of anything unlike itself? If we have something apart from Mind as All-in-all, how can we be pure enough to see God as All-in-all? That is why it is so essential that the term "purity" should be understood and be brought home to us. We have too finite a sense of purity. Impurity, in its broad sense, is acceptance of so-called material sense testimony, of finiteness, regardless of the form in which it appears; and

1Matt. 25:23.   2Matt. 5:8.

its acceptance must eventually stop our whole allegiance to Mind as All-in-all. The understanding of purity necessarily includes every form of purity and so destroys all phases of impurity, all beliefs in a third, a something apart from God and His presence.

WE STAND ON THE ALLNESS OF MIND

Now where are we standing as metaphysicians? We are at one point and one point only. We have never been anywhere else, and that point is where Mind is All-in-all. Mrs. Eddy, we are told, had a favorite expression which she often used; after explaining the truth about something, she would force it home with, "Now prove it." The demand to prove it makes the mortal begin to hedge and to dodge and to do everything except to stand right up for what he sees Mind to be, absolutely All-in-all. You do not do that. You steadfastly adhere to what you know Mind is because you understand why Mind is, and you declare, "I know whom I have believed."[1] You are not in doubt about it. You have no question because your understanding of Christian Science is not a faith or belief understanding. It is your understanding. It is something you have of your own, and if there

[1] 2 Tim. 1:12.

were not another Christian Scientist on earth, you would not doubt or question, for you know it of yourself.

YOU ARE ALONE WITH YOUR MIND

How many Christian Scientists are there? One. That one is Mind and its presence, everywhere. Then is there any place where Christian Science is not? Is there any place where health is not? Is there anything to heal? Is there any one to be made a Christian Scientist? Is it your work to make a Christian Scientist? Is that what you are doing? Or are you eternally insisting on the truth of being, and seeing that truth appear spontaneously as the elimination of everything unlike being? It may appear as this person and that person becoming interested in Christian Science; but you are never deceived into thinking that what appears as such is true, because you know that the one Christian Scientist, being omnipresent, is already the reality of one and all.

With the understanding obtaining of the omnipresence of the one Christian Scientist, what sort of homes would there be? What sort of friends? What sort of a world? It would not be any longer "Thy kingdom come. Thy will be done in earth, as it is in heaven",[1] but, Thy Kingdom *is* come, Thy will *is* done in earth as in heaven.

Ask yourself, Have *I* the power, as Mind, to embrace and know all being as perpetually harmonious? *I* have that power, for *I* cannot know aught else. And where is that power resident? Is it evidenced "over there" by changing some condition "over there" or is it right "here"? In fact, have I any other Mind, any other ego, or I, than the one Mind?

Is the one Mind your Mind? You know it is. Do you prove it in thought, word and deed? If not, why not? Is there any reason for not doing so? There can be only one reason, and that is that you do not believe what you say. Otherwise how can there be any excuse?

THERE IS NO MIND TO ACT HYPNOTICALLY

You may try to excuse your not proving Mind as your Mind by the fiction that it is the pressure, the arguments of this so-called malicious mind, that stops you. But is there a malicious mind to do that? Is malicious mind an entity, a reality, or is it purely the suppositional opposite of the one Mind? It is true that it makes no dif-

1Matt. 6:10.

ference what the false appearance may be; it is always this malicious mind that is all there is to the appearance, and that is operating suppositionally as your mind, taking the things of Mind and lying about them. It is also this mind alone which is saying all that is now being said about the government and the affairs of the world. But because it is this so-called suppositional mind, this malicious mind, acting as hypnotic suggestion and appearing as these various conditions, does it make that mind a fact, any more than a lie told makes the mind that tells it a fact? The mind telling the lie is both the lie and the liar and utterly false.

Then where do you lay your axe to destroy any false appearance? Against a thing? No, you could never do it in that way. You could go on from now until doomsday, without success, if you centered your attack on any condition, person, place, or thing. You must lay your axe at the root of the tree, at the belief that there is a mind apart from the one Mind, a malicious mind that can operate as hypnotic suggestion and then appear as all these various things. Your remedy is your "closet" with the door always shut, and you alone with your "own being and with the reality of things."[1]

[1]'01 20 :9.

For example, take an employer with his employee. He thinks his business is in a condition, perhaps, where there is not enough work. As a Christian Scientist, does he accept that appearance? Not for a moment. What does he do? He recognizes that the appearance has nothing to do with the claim,—that the appearance is only the argument through which the so-called mind making the argument appears in the way that it can most easily blind and deceive. After carefully analyzing the argument, he sees clearly that the appearance has no reality, because Mind being both employer and employee, both demand and supply, and being all action, the opportunity for unlimited business is omnipresent in all its infinity, hence there is no scarcity of work. He then turns to the real claim that has not a thing to do with employer or employee, with lack of work or abundance of work, but solely concerns malicious mind's actually being, and as such mind being able to operate hypnotically.

Through the realization of the allness of the one Mind, he is convinced there is no mind to act or operate hypnotically and appear as lack of business or lack of work, therefore he sees the harmony of Mind right there, and spontaneously this harmony appears in the language that he can best understand, that is, all things moving harmoniously. "All things work together for good to them that love God."[1]

Do you believe this? Either it is so or it is not so. If it is so, then do you hold the government in your hands? Did it not mean you when Isaiah said, "the government shall be upon his shoulder"[2]? Did his shoulder mean the Mind that you are accepting as Mind, and did it mean your Mind? It did.

THE ONE MIND IS HERE AND NOW

It was the belief, the thinking that Mind was somewhere away off, that caused the disciple Philip to say, "Shew us the Father, and it sufficeth us." You remember Jesus' reply was, "Have *I* been so long time with you, and yet hast thou not known me, Philip? he that hath seen me hath seen the Father; and how sayest thou then, Shew us the Father?"[3] Was not Jesus bringing home the fact that what appeared to Philip as his Master, as Jesus, was really Mind, infinite good, or the Father appearing? Is that Mind your Mind?

When will this Mind be your Mind if you do not have it as such now? Are you expecting

1Rom. 8:28.   2Isa. 9:6.   3John 14:8,9.

this Mind to come down, as it were, in some mysterious way from above and say encouragingly, "Now you are all right, so go ahead." If you do not make God practical and find Him as your very Mind, how are you going to speak with power and authority? "He must be ours practically, guiding our every thought and action; else we cannot understand the omnipresence of good sufficiently to demonstrate, even in part, the Science of the perfect Mind and divine healing."[1] Remember again, the only thing that stops you from making Mind All-in-all is your indulgence in the human concept of things, in other words, the finite, personal sense of things. That indulgence must stop perfect trust in Mind as All-in-all.

Because you know what you know, you are determined to speak today to every claim of evil with all the power and authority Jesus exercised, whether that claim appears world-wide or individual. Every appearance of matter is always the same claim, that there is malicious mind and that as such it does and can operate as hypnotic suggestion and appear as all these things.

Let me ask you, if the determination were maintained to recognize this fact and to destroy

[1] Ret. 28:4.

intelligently all error through understanding that the one Mind is all the Mind there is, and that that Mind is the Mind of all being, what do you think would happen? Evil of every name and nature would disappear.

Do you believe that you can heal sickness? You do not *believe*—you *know* you can. You know your understanding of Mind destroys any lie. You do not doubt it. Then why question your power for one moment when any problem is presented? You know, that with your understanding, you have power to govern your whole world and destroy its error. What nonsense it would be to say, "One on the side of God is a majority" if it were not true! "And I, if I be lifted up from the earth, will draw all men unto me."[1] What nonsense to declare yourself a Christian Scientist if you do not believe it!

PROMPTNESS OR APATHY—WHICH?

Promptness in handling a claim for what it really is—hypnotic suggestion—is nine-tenths of the victory. If you do not cultivate promptness in all your actions, you may find you are not apt to be alert in turning unreservedly to Mind when handling evil. Watch and you will find that little characteristics, little traits, are always

[1]John 12:32.

presenting to you through arguments some good reason or excuse for not doing what should be promptly done. "The nature of the individual, more stubborn than the circumstance, will always be found arguing for itself,—its habits, tastes, and indulgences."[1] Do not forget that lack of promptness in one way always encourages lack of promptness in another and this often results in lack of promptness in handling any claim that may seem to arise and so getting rid of it. "The little foxes . . . spoil the vines."[2]

That same apathy will extend in other directions if not destroyed and will express the mesmeric nature of its purpose until it finally paralyzes all action. Be prompt. "In the figurative transmission from the divine thought to the human, diligence, promptness, and perseverance are likened to 'the cattle upon a thousand hills.' They carry the baggage of stern resolve, and keep pace with highest purpose."[3]

CORRECT APPRECIATION OF THE HISTORY OF CHRISTIAN SCIENCE

"Ignorance of the error to be eradicated oftentimes subjects you to its abuse."[4] This is a true and definite statement of fact. The Christian Scientist who thinks he can attain the

[1]Mis. 119:11. [2]Song. 2:15. [3]S. & H. 514:14. [4]S. & H. 446:31.

kingdom of heaven without understanding the *modus operandi* of evil, for the time being, is doomed to disappointment.

Essential to this understanding also is the *modus operandi* of the unfoldment through which Christian Science has passed in its establishment and presentation to the world. There are those who think that this unfoldment and the understanding of it are not at all necessary to their growth and grasp of Christian Science. In this they are mistaken, for some understanding of the history of Christian Science, as presented to human belief, is as necessary as is some understanding of the history of music or of mathematics to a correct appreciation of either.

ENLIGHTENING WAY-MARKS

This is particularly necessary in obtaining a clear sense of the many and wonderful ways Mrs. Eddy was guided and directed by divine Mind to found the institution of Christian Science.

In due time all Mrs. Eddy's actions in the establishment of Christian Science will be carefully gathered together and given to the world and will show how every step was the elimination of human beliefs for spiritual oneness.

The Boston Case introduced a letter written Sept. 30, 1918, by the Board of Trustees to the Board of Directors, which has been perhaps rightly called a second Declaration of Independence. You would not today be enjoying the freedom of thought that you are, if the truth of that letter had not been the animating motive of Mrs. Eddy's Deed of Trust of 1898, constituting the trusteeship, and finally bringing to light the utter futility and uselessness of so-called organization in relation to the understanding and demonstration of Christian Science. "Every step of progress is a step more spiritual. The great element of reform is not born of human wisdom; it draws not its life from human organizations; rather is it the crumbling away of material elements from reason, the translation of law back to its original language,—Mind, and the final unity between God and man."[1]

THE TRUE ANALYSIS OF MONEY

The question about money is constantly arising. What is money? You understand that Mind, embracing within itself all being, all reality, all isness, must be, therefore, all the money there is. Do you believe this? Do you really believe that Mind does embrace within itself all, all that is, and therefore all money?

[1] Peo 1:1.

How can you know anything about money unless it comes as a sense of consciousness?

Is it true, then, that I do not have money, that I do not have dollars and cents? That would be like saying that I do not have health, that I do not have life. Would you allow that? Would you say, "I am sick, I am dying"? You do not admit any such thing. You stand on your understanding of being and you use every argument in support of that understanding.

You are not concerned about the argument of lack of money, as such, any more than you are concerned about a diseased organ, as such, except to the point of convincing yourself that what appears as a lack of money or a diseased organ is not really the claim. Instead, you uncover and destroy the belief, which is that there is malicious mind to operate as hypnotic suggestion and appear as a belief of not having money or as a belief of being sick.

But have I money? Of course I have. How could I have Mind and not have all that Mind is? How could I have Mind and not have all that perfect eyes, perfect ears, perfect lungs mean? I could not have Mind and not have money. Is that how you understand it? Or do you say, "I have no money"? What is it that says, "I have no money"? Is it not that lying suppositional mind that embraces within itself all limitation? Is it not that mind that is saying to the world, "*I* have not this and *I* have not that"?

Money is illimitable, even as air is illimitable, even as health is illimitable. All that says otherwise is hypnotic suggestion. How many are destroying the claim of lack from this standpoint? How many are meekly bowing down and accepting, "I have no money", accepting that lying mind as ego, as I? It is ever the same lie, operating as lack of money, that operates as disease. It is ever the same lie that says, "I am sick" that says, "I have no money". Will you accept it or not?

THE MONEY IN THE FISH'S MOUTH

There is only one *me* and Mind is that *Me*. Then how much money have I? When Jesus found the money in the fish's mouth, do you think it was a real, genuine Roman coin, stamped with the imprint of the Emperor or whatever was necessary to make it proper legal tender? Do you think that that coin was actually there in the fish's mouth? Of course you do. Do you think that the fish caught that money in the sea or was the money right there? You know that it was there, for Mind is omnipresent.

It had to be there. It was the real, true coin, just as the loaves and fishes Jesus fed to the multitude were real, genuinely good loaves and fishes. You know that they were satisfying and that the multitude ate and enjoyed them.

Do you think that the loaves and fishes that Jesus fed to the people decreased the supply in the world? You know it did not. The supply is everywhere present. Is not that what you would say of the multiplication table? You would not feel you had to hand to this child and that child the multiplication table for him to use, and Why? because you know it is every-where present. You simply uncover it for the child, as that which he already has. Were not the loaves and fishes just as omnipresent, right at each person's place, as it were? You know that they were and are. Jesus was illustrating that money and all else needed perfectly to sus-tain and maintain man as the very perfection of being, the very presence of good, is omnipresent. Science and Health pertinently asks the ques-tion, "If seed is necessary to produce wheat, and wheat to produce flour, or if one animal can originate another, how then can we account for their primal origin? How were the loaves and fishes multiplied on the shores of Galilee,—

and that, too, without meal or monad from which loaf or fish could come?"[1]

NOT TOIL BUT UNDERSTANDING
REQUISITE

Do you think that money must come to you through fatiguing labor or in some such tangible way? Must mathematics come to you through the same method? You are diligent because diligence is the very characteristic of Mind, which is all action. But material work and toil are not virtues in themselves. Success and accomplishment are.

You may say, "I cannot see success without labor." But does the lightning calculator have to labor to give the answer to the problem instantly? In the eyes of Principle, is it more worthy laboriously to work out the problem than to have the answer immediately? Of course it is not. Then, is there any virtue in laboriously working for money? Is it not better to realize that Mind, embracing within itself all being, includes all money? You say this in regard to health. Why not say it in regard to money as well? But remember to "be active", and then "however slow, thy success is sure"[2]. But be active, mentally awake. Be a law to yourself.

[1]S. & H. 89:32. [2]Mis. 340:23,

POSITION METAPHYSICALLY DEFINED

Now with regard to the question of position. What is it that says, "I have no position, I have no crop, my business is not good. I have not this and I have not that"? It is the I, I, I, that is always one with finiteness, one with death. Is not that "I" hypnotic suggestion? Decide which it is and act accordingly, instantly, or how can you progress? You are on the side of Mind. Then you do not accept evil as your mind, defining itself as lack of money, position or anything else.

Mind, in its allness, of necessity includes all position. Is there any position outside of Mind? If you define the term "position" metaphysically, you declare it to be the presence of intelligence, because if a thing is in position, you mean that it is exactly right. Then by position you must mean the presence of intelligence, the presence of Mind. Mind being omnipresent, position is omnipresent. Hence you do not try to find a position. You already have your position and are in it as the activity of Mind.

Then the claim of no position or of being out of a position is seen to be, not at all what it appears to be, namely, being out of a position, but it is the claim that there is malicious mind and that it can operate hypnotically, and appear

as having no position. Since there is no such
mind, there is no such hypnotic suggestion.

The one Mind, being all, enfolds within itself all friendship, all love, all position. Could
God be infinite Love, infinite compassion, unless
He supplied all in the language in which it could
be understood by all? The presence of infinite
Love, infinite good, that you call divine Mind,
the only Mind there is, is all the money, position or success there is. Mind does not have to
work, or seek for anything. It already has all.
"Then give to Mind the glory, honor, dominion, and power everlastingly due its holy
name."[1] You declare without hesitation that
Mind is All-in-all, and by All-in-all you mean
God is All to all position, money, food, rightness,
government, "here and everywhere." Mrs.
Eddy expresses the intense joy of this allness
of Mind in her words,

> "Oh! Thou hast heard my prayer;
> And I am blest!
> This is Thy high behest:—
> Thou here, and *everywhere*."[2]

This "Thou" embraces all being. You know it.

THE ONE SPIRITUAL ORIGIN

Does religious temptation bid you feel that
Jesus was a supernaturally created man, and

[1]S. & H. 143:29.   [2]S. & H. Front Page.

therefore more favored than you? He was supernatural only in this one sense of the word, that the Virgin Mother conceived of (understood) God as the Father of man, and Jesus was discerned as the spontaneous product of this spiritual conception. The belief attached to the conception of the mortal is that mortal man is his father. That is only a difference in belief, not a difference in reality, for mortal man can create nothing. Anything mortal is but a belief, and belief is never causation, hence man is always of God, no matter what his origin or appearance seems to be. Jesus could not have done what he did, if he had accepted the belief that Mary was his mother. He would have been in no different condition from that in which you find yourself, if he had admitted that Mary was even partly his origin. He went right back to, "Before Abraham was, I am."[1]

In establishing yourself as the Christian Scientist, do you not have to strip off your entire belief of material sense and base yourself on just conscious being, without a single material testimony? In doing this, do you not establish for yourself identically the same origin as Jesus —"Before Abraham was, I am"[1]?

[1]Jno. 8 :58.

You understand that. And since you do understand it, you can no longer say Jesus was endowed with more power than you. Jesus never said or did anything from the basis of Mary's being his mother. He talked from exactly the same foundation that you talk from and that is your oneness with Mind. He declared, "All power is given unto me in heaven and in earth,"[1] and he proved this statement to be true also, "Son, . . . all that I have is thine."[2] Is that true of you and do you know it? You do. You are not a hypocrite. You are the Christian Scientist. You answer with understanding. You determine the whole question because "all power is given unto me," the same "me" that was "me" to Jesus.

THE CLAIM IS ALWAYS HYPNOTIC SUGGESTION

The subtle suggestion that all being is *things,* —whether appearing as persons, places, or things—that matter is substance, is continually turning you away from handling the real claim. Do you think any one would use material medicine if he did not think of it as a thing? Would any one use massage if he did not think there was some *thing* to be rubbed and some *thing* to

[1]Matt. 28:18.   [2]Luke 15:31.

rub it with, and that the *thing* had power to benefit? Then why deceive yourself into trying to believe you are handling the claim as malicious mind, when you are admitting it as an aching or painful *thing*? You cannot admit evil as a *thing* and at the same time destroy it as malicious mind. It is either one or the other. Christian Science declares that evil is purely malicious mind, and that the real claim never has been and never will be that evil is a thing. Mind could not be All-in-all if a wrong *thing* were the trouble, because the suppositional opposite of Mind must ever be in the mental realm, and therefore must always operate as malicious mind, through hypnotic suggestion.

The fact that Mind is All-in-all brings to light the proof that every error is always hypnotic suggestion. We are never going to help the world, we are never going to alleviate anything permanently and correctly unless we do it from that standpoint. That is what is meant by laying the axe at the root of the tree.

ALL EVIL IN ITS FINAL ANALYSIS IS PURELY MENTAL

The suppositional malicious mind in its final analysis must appear as operating in the pure realm of mentality, because evil is just as pure in its final sense of evil as good is pure in its sense of good. Do not forget that evil must be entirely evil to be the suppositional opposite of the good that is entirely good. You see then that, in its final analysis, it must appear as pure evil mind.

You realize it is the understanding of Mind, and nothing else, that destroys all error. You are on your guard in these "latter days" against the subtleties of evil coming as pure mentality, as your very mind. You are never off guard. Jesus said, "Watch and pray that ye enter not into temptation,"[1] and "What I say unto you I say unto all, Watch"[2].

One needs to be stern, especially stern, with the lie masquerading as one's self, and not trifle in the slightest with one's understanding of Christian Science. Evil may suggest to you that you are not as kindly as you used to be, and that you have changed in other ways. Yes, you have changed, but, you are just as kindly, though you do not call evil good, nor error Love. It is not true that you are less loving and kind. It is only the suggestion that you are not loving and it is said only because you are not on your guard in handling the claim of malicious mind, operating hypnotically, which is all that says it. De-

[1]Matt. 26 :41.   [2]Mark 13 :37.

stroy that claim by realizing the allness and omnipotence of the one Mind as the All-Mind, and it will no longer be said.

SLEEP IS THE BASIS OF DEATH

You ask about sleep. "Sleep is darkness, but God's creative mandate was, 'Let there be light.' In sleep, cause and effect are mere illusions. They seem to be something, but are not. Oblivion and dreams, not realities, come with sleep. Even so goes on the Adam-belief, of which mortal and material life is the dream."[1] Sleep is materiality and is the basis of death. It is the belief that Mind can become unconscious and find rest in that unconsciousness. "Awake thou that sleepest."[2] You do not think that this refers necessarily to the closing of your eyes in sleep at night. It refers to your absorption in the belief of materiality, in other words to your being asleep to the truth of being.

I once knew a woman who was confronted with an hereditary belief of cancer of the lip, a disease of which her grandfather was supposed to have died. When this lie presented itself to her, she felt doomed and said that her great desire was to sleep, to sleep away the hours. After the disease had progressed a con-

[1]S. & H. 556:18. [2]Eph. 5:14.

siderable way, she awoke to the truth of what Christian Science teaches about sleep, in its false sense, and its relationship to the unconsciousness of death. When she discerned this, she interpreted in her own way the need to be awake, and she determined then and there, that she would not sleep again until that cancer had disappeared. She said, that for three weeks she allowed herself hardly a moment's sleep, and at the end of that time, there was not even a scar on her lip.

This, of course, was her own unique way of interpreting being "awake." She felt that what was necessary in order to destroy the lie, was really to be awake to the truth of being, and she took as her method of doing this, actually staying physically awake. What she was really doing was keeping watch that she did not fall asleep to the unreality of matter, and she got her reward. This case is useful only in that it shows that handling the lie even in the way she did, being faithful to her own interpretation of what being awake meant, she destroyed the power of evil to operate as her mind, and so freed herself from its bondage.

Evil always tries to make you want to sleep. Its one purpose is to lull you to sleep, to make you indifferent to world affairs and all else.

What applies to the simplest thing in Christian
Science applies to everything, and if we do not
recognize that, we put ourselves in the position
of being utterly unable to cope with problems,
whereas when we reduce everything to the one
common denominator, Mind, the result is absolute harmony. This applies to the whole practice of Christian Science, the practice of Being.
There is no place where that practice is not.
There is no place where the one practitioner is
not, no place where the whole infinity of
good is not. It is yours and you have supreme
dominion. You are a law unto yourself.

A NEW HEAVEN AND A NEW EARTH

You remember how the Revelator proclaimed
just what you have established for yourself. "I
saw a new heaven and a new earth: for the first
heaven and the first earth were passed away;
and there was no more sea."[1] Science and
Health says that the sea represents "elementary,
latent error, the source of all error's visible
forms."[2] The Revelator saw that there was no
more sea. He saw that the first heaven and the
first earth were no more. He saw a new heaven
and a new earth. So you have seen for yourself that the heaven and earth of old thinking

1Rev. 21:1.   2S. & H. 559:5.

and old conditions have passed away, and the new heaven and the new earth of Mind, as your Mind, absolutely pure, giving to you all power, all dominion, are right here.

You understand why the Revelator further said: "And I heard a great voice out of heaven, saying, Behold, the tabernacle of God is with men, and he will dwell with them, and they shall be his people, and God himself shall be with them, and be their God. And God shall wipe away all tears from their eyes; and there shall be no more death, neither sorrow, nor crying, neither shall there be any more pain: for the former things are passed away."[1]

The former things have passed away, and you no longer handle them from the standpoint of things. You handle them from the standpoint of Mind as All-in-all, and that is why you understand what Jesus meant when he said, "whatsoever thou shalt bind on earth shall be bound in heaven; and whatsoever thou shalt loose on earth shall be loosed in heaven."[2] This "thou" does not mean somebody else. It means *you*. This allness of Mind is your power. Nothing can dispossess you of it; and you know it.

1Rev. 21:3,4.   2Matt. 16:19.

NEED FOR CONSECRATION

A statement, attributed to Mrs. Eddy, comes in here very aptly, with which to close. Whether Mrs. Eddy made the statement or not is of small importance for it is true anyway and, because it is true, it is worthy of her authorship.

"No one can be loyal to Truth, to himself or to his God, or worthy of the kingdom of heaven, who has not faith, pluck, and patience enough to endure, without fainting, apparent defeat and delayed reward. Hold to your aim. Stick to your text and have faith in your understanding of Christian Science. Your aim is: There is no inaction, there is action. Your text is: God is almighty and you know it; and evil is a lie and powerless. Your faith is: God is all, and you know in whom you trust. This will win every time."

You know that this is true. Prove it.

DO YOU SAY
"THERE IS NO GOD"?

In the Bible is a statement emphatic, direct, an extraordinarily severe indictment: "The fool hath said in his heart, There is no God."[1]

You have read and doubtless many times pondered this statement, "The fool hath said in his heart, There is no God", then you have asked yourself the question, "Am I the fool that has said in my heart, there is no God"? and you have unhesitatingly answered, "Not with my *lips,* as a Christian Scientist, have I said it." But, do you think that is what is meant, what you have said with your *lips?* The statement is, "The fool hath said in his *heart,* There is no God."[1]

The question must inevitably arise with the Christian Scientist whether or not he is giving lip service to God while in his heart he is really saying, "There is no God;"[1] whether as in Scriptural language, he "draweth nigh unto me" with his mouth and "honoureth me" with his lips while his "heart is far from me."[2] Each one has to determine the answer for himself. It is easy to say, Of course not! But the Christian Scientist's life, his ability instantan-

[1]Ps. 14:1. [2]Matt. 15:8.

eously to dismiss evil as entity, and prove its powerlessness and nothingness, settles the question whether he is really saying in his heart, "There is no God."[1]

WHAT OF THIS WORLD?

It is impossible to view what seems to be taking place around us today and not be forced to the conclusion that the world at least is surely saying in its heart, "There is no God."[1]

Now, what concerns the metaphysician is what is he doing? As the Christian Scientist, he understands perfectly that the old religious belief, the old sanctimonious sense of a God in a heaven, who is eventually going to gather all the good to Himself, is largely gone, but in its place what has he?

We cannot give our time to a better purpose for the moment, than to analyze this question and see exactly what we are doing and where we are standing, because that is of vital importance. The world is not "over there," detached and apart from what is called me. It is "here." It is *me,* my world, or I could have no consciousness of it. Whatever I cognize, whatever I am conscious of, must come as my own consciousness, my own being; and, as the meta-

1Ps. 14:1.

physician, understanding this I know it is true. Can you then say this world is not your world? You cannot; then if the world says "There is no God," are not you saying, "There is no God"?

WHAT IS GOD?

What is this God that the world is repudiating? What does God mean? The sense of God, as a personal deity has been rapidly disappearing under the light of the declaration of Christian Science, made by Mrs. Eddy in 1866, that God is Mind, and that "All is infinite Mind and its infinite manifestation."[1]

What then is this God? Is He something afar off or is He the very Mind of your real being? And if this Mind is your Mind, can you get anywhere unless you have a right understanding of what this Mind is?

I know each one of you here today has often asked himself the question, How do I know there is a God and What is God to me? Being able to establish for yourself that there is God, being convinced of God's isness, forever stops *you* from saying in *your* heart, "There is no God." Thus, your life becomes the evidence of your convictions.

[1] S. & H. 468:10.

THE NECESSITY FOR PROOF

Mrs. Eddy never hesitated to say that Christian Science would "disappear from among mortals"[1] unless the truth of its declaration, that there is only one Mind, is proved by practical demonstration, by one's ability to abolish all finiteness, all limitation, all sin, disease and death. Without such proof Christian Science not only will be, but *is* lost. Who is there to prove it if you do not do so?

The metaphysician is the one, and the one alone, who knows why he is a Christian Scientist. Each one of you knows this for himself. Your understanding identifies you, and if you do not prove Christian Science, how is it to be made manifest? Who else can prove it? It is understanding alone that will do it. Are you using your understanding? Yes, in proportion to your turning every thought unreservedly to the one Mind as All-in-all. That is what being a Christian Scientist means.

It is no harder to find Mind as All-in-all than it is to find matter as all-in-all, and it is vastly more comfortable. Is your world declaring that matter is God? Is it going on the basis, Let us "eat, drink and be merry,"[2] for tomorrow we

[1]My. 197 :18.   [2]Luke 12 :19.

die? If it is, will this usher you into the kingdom of heaven, into that understanding which enabled Jesus to bring all matter into subjection and imbued him with such power that he spake with absolute authority to every form of evil? "With Christ, Life was not merely a sense of existence, but a sense of might and ability to subdue material conditions."[1] It must be the same with you.

THE TRUE MEANING OF JOY

It would be foolish to say anything that might sound as though Christian Science were not the very essence of joy. That is farthest from the thought of the Christian Scientist, for certainly, "pleasure is no crime except when it strengthens the influence of bad inclinations or lessens the activities of virtue."[2] No sane Christian Scientist could possibly be mesmerized into thinking that there is any value or spirituality in a sad countenance or joyless spirit.

Joy is the natural quality of divine Mind, the recognition of infinite perfection and well-being. Joy is the inborn result of the understanding of divine Mind, for infinite perfection is the essential substance of Mind. Perfection means, just as loveliness and beauty mean, everything right

1Un. 42:16.   2Mis. 362:30.

and everything in its place. Is not this the very essence of joy? You know that when you exclaim over the beauty or loveliness of an object, or of an experience that has filled you with joy, you always mean and imply its perfection to the minutest detail. The least divergence from perfection mars its beauty instantly and so mars your joy. Then the natural quality of the one perfect Mind must be infinite joy, which joy can never be divorced from the activities of good.

This is not the fleeting joy, of course, in the indulgence of the so-called senses in their cruder form, from a matter-satisfaction standpoint. Christian Science does not have to say that to you, as a Christian Scientist. The Mind that you acknowledge as all power, as eternal, could not allow, for one moment, anything transitory, or anything apart from itself. Spontaneously it would cease to be All-in-all if it did. Because this is so, the so-called gratification of the senses, which, in metaphysical terminology, means a limited, finite, imperfect sense, could not possibly seem real to you. It is absurd to suppose that the joy of Mind could have anything to do with the uncertain gratification of the material senses.

RUSSIA A HOUSE BUILT UPON THE SAND

The world is seemingly in a desperate condition. Take Russia for example. Is she not trying her best to reject any and every teaching that there is a God at all? And why? Because in her blindness she does not know how to answer the questions: Why there must be a God and What God is. The Christian Scientist who does not then honestly and frankly face these same questions and prove the reality of God is sound asleep. "Good demands of man every hour, in which to work out the problem of being."[1]

Russia, or that condition of thought appearing as Russia, does not know how to find God. If we, as metaphysicians, do not live Christian Science in a way to show that God is, and what He is, and so prove our understanding by instantaneously healing all disease, who can do it? How can Russia or any other people find God? You know that this proof that God is, cannot be given without the understanding of Christian Science; if you do not give it yourself, Christian Science will be lost to the world, is lost to your world. Do you desire this? If you do not, you must give the answer to: "The fool hath said

[1] S. & H. 261:32.

in his heart, There is no God,"[1] by proving practically the allness of God in the minutiae of daily life.

THE ROCK UPON WHICH TO BUILD

You declare, Because I find myself consciously being, I know that God, Mind, *is,* since I could not consciously be unless Mind, consciousness were actually a fact. So you know there is God. Then you have to prove it. There is no way of escape. Advancing in metaphysical understanding, the problems, the temptations besetting the Christian Scientist, are naturally more complex today than ever before, even as advancing in mathematics brings to light problems to solve, not thought of in the beginning; but this advance only gives added opportunity to discover and to use more rules. So the subtle suggestions of human belief, appearing more insidious all the time, only seem to become more intricate in order to compel a fuller turning away from them, a higher consecration, thus showing that the only way to meet and master them is by thinking and acting more and more from the standpoint of the one Mind as All-in-all. ". . . the higher Truth lifts her voice,

1Ps. 14:1.

the louder will error scream, until its inarticulate sound is forever silenced in oblivion."[1]

If you truly believe that Mind is All-in-all, what possible excuse can you have for dealing with anything but Mind? Infinite Mind includes all person, place or thing, all weather, all conditions, all government, all nations, all power, here and everywhere. According to your own declaration, is there anything left outside of the Mind that is All-in-all? Of course you know there is not. Therefore you must insist upon finding Mind as All-in-all. You must acknowledge that Mind holds within itself all being, all position, all welfare, everything.

Do you turn to this Mind, confident that it embraces within itself all there is, or do you look in every other direction to see what material thing or circumstance is back of all that you are conscious of? It is wise to examine thoroughly one's practice of Christian Science and see where one is drifting. If we are going to be consistent Christian Scientists, we must apply to every single experience the truth we understand and see that there is nothing outside of the consciousness that is Truth. "Divine Mind rightly demands man's entire obedience, affection, and strength. No reservation is made

[1] S. & H. 97:23.

for any lesser loyalty. Obedience to Truth gives man power and strength. Submission to error superinduces loss of power."[1]

"REMEMBER IN THY YOUTH THY CREATOR"

A pertinent question arises, Why do so many of the young people of today seem to be expressing a liberty running into license, a "liberty for an occasion to the flesh,"[2] in which their seniors fondly imagine they never thought of indulging? Is it because "The fool hath said in his heart, There is no God"?[3] Is it because youth has no assurance in its heart, no true understanding of what God is or why God is? Yet every step taken away from the actual path of right has to be retraced, and no one can avoid this retracing any more than he can avoid correcting a mistake in mathematics.

What is the remedy for this liberty, seemingly run into license, that is expressed so vigorously by the present generation? Is it not to establish such a sense of universal completeness, such a oneness with all that means infinity, that youth will be absolutely satisfied and interested in exploring the infinite activities, joys and unfathomable opportunities of Mind?

1S. & H. 183:21.   2Gal. 5:13.   3Ps. 14:1.

The one who indulges in a personal sense is training himself in a very treacherous course which he will have to turn from sooner or later. Personal sense, or sin, is accepting matter as substance, as entity; is accepting finiteness as reality, as God. "The way to escape the misery of sin is to cease sinning. There is no other way. Sin is the image of the beast to be effaced by the sweat of agony. It is a moral madness which rushes forth to clamor with midnight and tempest."[1]

NO WRONG CONDITION IS NEGLIGIBLE

When a condition arises, as for example, that of a large territory being burned over, as now appears to be taking place in this district, and people are believing that the temperature is unbearably high, do you as metaphysicians really recognize that entire condition to be a mental operation of malicious mind? I can see that the very presentation of that question causes you to think. Here you are, Christian Scientists, and yet you are actually debating this point in your minds. Here you are, the "salt (spiritual thinkers) of the earth", "a city that is set on an hill",[2] and yet you have to wonder whether or not a raging fire is actually malicious mind

[1]S. & H. 327:12. [2]Matt. 5:13,14.

operating as hypnotic suggestion. Do you for a moment think that fire is something outside of consciousness? Do you think that weather is something outside of consciousness, or do you stick to your text that Mind is All-in-all? How many of you have been honestly putting out that so-called destructive fire as nobody else on earth can understandingly do it? Can you afford to accept the lying suggestion of hypnotic mind that a destructive fire is actually taking place, is actually consciousness?*

You need not think that world affairs or business conditions will ever be handled if they are met with indifference or are accepted and tolerated. The discoverer and founder of Christian Science did not allow that sort of thing herself. She insisted that weather and everything

---

*It is interesting that while this meeting was in progress on the afternoon of November the 2nd, the fire referred to which had been raging for several days causing great damage and against which a small army "of 1100 men were engaged in battle," after suddenly flaring up was brought under control and later extinguished. The Los Angeles *Times* in its issue of November 3rd carried a headline reading as follows, "Mountain Fire Under Control," and in the article it said, "Conquest of the brush fire which has ravaged the Santa Monica Mountains unchecked for four days, was announced last night by officials of the Fire Warden's Office." It further stated that "the turning point in the fight against the flames came yesterday afternoon."

Why should this have taken place that afternoon when previous efforts had been in vain? Was it not the natural result of the power of the right knowing on the part of those at the meeting? Why doubt the power of infinite Mind?

else be understood in its true sense as the very presence of Mind, therefore God-governed, and then insisted that this right view of all things be made manifest, practically, not merely theoretically.

In the words of Wendell Phillips, "One on God's side is a majority". Are you leaving the responsibility of these conditions to some one else? You are alone with God, and, if you turn aside from God and leave this to the "other fellow," you will experience just what the "other fellow" is, "a liar, and the father of it,"[1] in other words, all that the term hell means.

In metaphysics you can never think in terms of three and be a Christian Scientist. God is one, the one Mind. God and the one man is the one Mind and its infinite manifestation, and that is All-in-all. If you have the "other fellow" on whom you are relying, then you must have the devil with you.

Ask yourself, What am I doing about conditions, world-wide and otherwise? Am I accepting such conditions as seem to be obtaining in Russia and elsewhere? Am I mentally submitting to the vicious attacks on the Executive and the government of the United States, utterly oblivious to my power as a Christian

[1]Jno. 8:44.

Scientist to counteract all such conditions? Am I actually saying in my heart, "There is no God"? If I am accepting *one* God, how can I possibly neglect to handle every single condition that presents itself?

WHAT IS YOUR GOAL?

Why are you a Christian Scientist? To have an easy time? That brings no satisfaction. You cannot be happy until being is understood and so demonstrated. Formerly the Christian Scientist may have accepted Christian Science as a belief and so have caught reassuring glimpses of health, prosperity, and happiness. But that day is over. You now know that it is understanding alone that can satisfy you permanently, and that *understanding* is the goal of your consecration.

It is impossible, of course, to escape health and prosperity, for they are omnipresent. Mrs. Eddy could not help being what the world calls a millionaire. She once said, in answer to a newspaper reporter's question, that she never could be a millionaire as long as there were so many poor. Did not the fact, then, that she appeared later on to be a millionaire, indicate that to her sense there were no longer "so many poor"? This invites the question, Am I letting go of the idea that there are "many poor", or am I attempting to base my prosperity on what can be seen with the eyes? If you do that, because of the changeableness of belief of what the eyes see, you must not be surprised if that prosperity seems to appear and disappear. To a Christian Scientist, prosperity is not something that can vanish. God cannot become less than All-in-all. This God, this Mind, that is All-in-all, is never less than all good, therefore you have infinite prosperity now and always. You are a law to your own prosperity. Be a law to it.

To accept the material sense testimony, instead of accepting understanding as an indication of prosperity, would be identically the same as accepting a bodily condition as an indication of health. Health must be accepted as entirely apart from any testimony of the senses. You pay no attention to any sense evidence except to compel all testimony to bow to the mandate of Mind. You insist upon its bowing to good, to God. You compel it to yield to the truth, and you never cease your demand until the corporeal senses correspond "with the normal conditions of health and harmony."[1]

But you do this only in the same way that you make a lie yield to the truth. The lie is

1S. & H. 412:26.

not a *thing* to you, but is just a lie; so you maintain the true in place of the untrue and you
never cease until the false disappears. Jesus
illustrated this in the parable of the man who
asked his friend at midnight for three loaves.
"Though he will not rise and give him, because
he is his friend, yet because of his importunity
he will rise and give him as many as he needeth."[1] You base your health on what you understand of Mind. You base your wealth on
the same understanding.

RIGHT THINKING LIKE THE SEAMLESS ROBE

How can the metaphysician, of all people,
basing his health and wealth on Mind, be satisfied to go on with the world conditions as they
are? You know what constituted Cain a murderer was his repudiation of being his brother's
keeper. He declared, "Am I my brother's
keeper?"[2] God being All-in-all, does not this
All-in-all include all brother, and therefore is
not God the one brother? Cain accepted something apart from God as All-in-all when he said
he was not his brother's keeper, thus rejecting
responsibility for something which came to him
as his consciousness. In doing this he mur-

[1]Luke 11:8.   [2]Gen. 4:9.

dered his All-God, destroyed his sense of the allness of Mind.

When you pass "by on the other side,"[1] and say, What have I to do with world affairs, foreign or domestic, then are you not Cain? This Mind that is All-in-all necessarily embraces within itself all that appears as any phase of the world, whether good or bad. Thinking must show forth the seamless robe today, the vesture of Christ "without seam"[2] just as it did metaphorically in the time of Jesus. There must be complete, absolute, undivided allegiance to the one Mind as All-in-all, in other words, to purity or isness which is without a single element contrary to itself, and which sees God as infinite good always. "Blessed are the pure in heart: for they shall see God."[3] Without this there is no escape from problems, for problems are but the acceptance of a suppositional mind as Mind. So world affairs are your affairs and must be found as Mind and as the activity of Principle only, hence harmonious and perfect.

What is all this that appears as quarrels whether small or large between husbands and wives, children, friends, neighbors and nations? Is there some one to whom you do not want to speak or whom perhaps you never wish to see

[1]Luke 10:31. [2]Jno. 19:23. [3]Matt. 5:8.

again? Is there a lack of interest in countries that seem backward, or are obstreperous and unwilling to go forward except in their own way, and which may seem to you backward? Are you desirous of passing such by "on the other side?"[1] And if so, why? Is this outside of that which is appearing to you as consciousness? If that is the case, how can you cognize it at all? As the metaphysician do you accept all such as reality, or do you stamp one and all instantly as suggestions to be promptly dismissed and destroyed through your understanding of the one Mind as All-in-all?

DRUNKENNESS ANALYZED AND CORRECTED

Take for example a drunkard. Is that which appears as a drunkard something outside of mentality, something outside of that which is being accepted as consciousness? A drunkard is not a person, place, or thing. It is a state of consciousness. Drunkenness is, like Joseph's coat, of many colors and many varieties, and it is destroyed, under whatever guise it comes, in the same way that sickness is destroyed. That which appears as a drunkard, in its simplest form and meaning, may seem, perhaps, to be interfering with your home life, or may pass you

[1] Luke 10:31

on the street. Nevertheless, regardless of the manner of its appearance, is it not all embraced in that which you are admitting as consciousness?

In handling any claim you understand there is always, in belief, an argument as to why the claim is present and why it is legitimate. It always claims to be there lawfully and properly. It claims a time when it began, a place where it is, matter or substance, wherewith it is formed, and last, law by which it operates. In the process of destroying it, your business, as the activity of the one infinite intelligence that knows all there is to know about everything, is, first, to know that this infinite intelligence, being your Mind, uncovers spontaneously whatever the particular claim may seem to be. This intelligence also brings to light what the arguments of the claim are, and the counter arguments of Christ, of Truth, that annihilate the arguments of evil.

That which always appears as evident to the so-called material senses is simply the erroneous argument of the so-called malicious mind. If it were actually a *thing* in itself, instead of an argument—a mental claim or demand—it could not be cognizable. There is no way that you, being wholly conscious and the activity of consciousness, in other words, mental, spiritual, could cognize anything material or apart from consciousness.

The drunkard appears merely as a material object or person, but it is really a mental argument presenting itself spontaneously and supposititiously for the purpose of dispossessing you of what is really your Mind, and of usurping the place of that Mind. Actually there is no drunkard. When you recognize that it is simply a mesmeric argument of malicious mind and not a condition, you meet it with the counter argument of Truth and annul its entire hypnotic influence.

Let us analyze one phase of drunkenness. Suppose intelligence uncovered that the claim or argument appearing as drunkenness was really an anatomical condition of irritation or inflammation of the pneumogastric nerve. Materia Medica will tell you that often this condition is the cause of chronic inebriety. What would be your counter-statement to this argument of malicious mind? Would it not be, since Mind embraces within itself all that you call pneumogastric nerve, and since there is nothing external to this Mind that is infinite, to inflame anything, the perfection and continuity of the pneumogastric nerve is assured? You would continue your

argument until you were absolutely convinced
that this one Mind could have no appearance of
a pneumogastric nerve unlike itself in any respect.   Then when fully satisfied on this point
you would know that a supposedly irritated
pneumogastric nerve was not, after all, the
claim.

What then is really the claim?   The same old
lie of the ever "talking serpent,"[1] that there is
a mind apart from the one Mind, that can operate as hypnotic suggestion and appear as a claim
of drunkenness, whether of a person, a nation,
or a world.   Remember the body politic is not
different in any way from the body personal.   As
there is only one body, even as there is only one
Mind, so, suppositionally, there is only one false
sense of body and one false sense of mind;
therefore, the drunkard can appear as a man, a
nation, or a world—it is all one.

THE CLAIM, ITS RECOGNITION AND REMEDY

The root of the tree at which you lay "the
axe"[2] is the claim that there is malicious mind,
in other words, that malicious mind *is*. But there
is no malicious mind, since God, the one Mind
is, and is all that *is*.   It is through the realization of this allness of God as the one and only

[1]S. & H. 529 :25. [2]Matt. 3 :10.

Mind, and this alone, that there can ever be any healing accomplished.

Do you believe that this suppositional *isness* of malicious mind embraces within itself all that appears as the claim of destructive fires, bad business conditions, governmental problems, in fact as every phase of mortal existence? If you do, what are you doing about it, and if nothing, then what is your purpose in life or in being a Christian Scientist? Are you like the silly mortal who is just "doing a little work to get a little money, to buy a little food, to build a little muscle, to do a little work, to get a little money, to buy a little food," and so on?

Each one of you, in his heart, is the genuine Christian Scientist, the right knower, "enlisted to lessen evil, disease, and death."[1] Now is the time to let this true purpose and its tremendous power as the one Mind govern you. Mrs. Eddy once said of a class of fifty-odd, that there were enough in the class, if they were of one Mind and practised what they knew, to bring in the millennium.

Jesus demonstrated this and knew that true understanding was actually all-power "in heaven and in earth."[2] You have that understanding. Are you using it? Or are you going on indifferent

[1]S. & H. 450:19. [2]Matt. 28:18.

to everything except caring for a petty finite sense, satisfied if you are in good health and can keep a balance in the bank, clothes on your back, food in your larder, and a roof over your head? Are you saying, "Peace, peace; when there is no peace?"[1] Would not that really be what is back of indifference? Are you satisfied to go on in ignorance and finiteness? If you are not satisfied, you must prove it.

THE ONE THING NEEDFUL

Mrs. Eddy urged constant prayer, and Paul urged "Pray without ceasing."[2] But neither Mrs. Eddy nor Paul had any thought of prayer as related in the slightest to getting down on one's knees and remaining there constantly. That would be absurd. What was meant was constant right knowing, "in season, out of season,"[3] communion with Mind,—knowing, thinking, actively accomplishing right.

It is impossible to do anything without thought. You cannot perform the slightest act without thought. If thought ceases to operate as the motive power of the body, an undertaker is sent for. Thought controls every action of the body; whether or not you individually are aware of a conscious effort makes no difference.

1Jer. 8:11.   21 Thes. 5:17.   32 Tim. 4:2.

It is the mind operating as the mind of the individual that is consciously aware. Because thought is the substance of all you ever do, surely it is just as easy to think rightly as to think wrongly.

What is it that seems to be always at work endeavoring to stop right thinking? Is it not our being satisfied just to go ahead with the material round of affairs and being at peace if we can make both ends meet, not only financially, but in every way? The politician wants the vote, the social aspirant wants success, and so the round goes on, all bending their aims and energies to make their particular ends meet. Martha, cumbered with material serving, was told, "But one thing is needful,"[1] to find God, the one Mind as All-in-all.

To act and think from the standpoint of Mind, God, never admitting a third, is absolutely necessary. "Thy Maker,"[2] Mind, must be found as thy husband, thy wife, thy friend, thy neighbor, thy child, thy business, thy government, thy world, thine All-in-all. It is no more difficult to know this than to imagine the impossible from a Mind standpoint, that something, outside of Mind, because it appears

[1]Luke 10 :42.   [2]Isa. 54 :5.

"over there," is your husband or your wife or your universe, and so forth.

WHAT IS THE UNREST AND TURMOIL?

The world of Mind is never in turmoil; your world is not in turmoil. It is hypnotic suggestion that is the turmoil and that is in turmoil. Many suggestions of evil are now appearing under the guise of good and of freedom that have never been seen before. They come today with, "My Lord delayeth His coming,"[1] so why not indulge this sense or that? Yes, why not? "The fool hath said in his heart: There is no God,"[2] no Mind that is All-in-all. Are you holding yourself more strictly to account each day, and never lowering your standard in Christian Science? Evil is ever ready with its pulling-down-of-your-standard suggestions. "Sin makes deadly thrusts at the Christian Scientist as ritualism and creed are summoned to give place to higher law, but Science will ameliorate mortal malice. The Christianly scientific man reflects the divine law, thus becoming a law unto himself."[3]

If you indulge even in a small degree in the false sense of anger or jealousy, or yield to any of the petty vices and allurements of human be-

[1] Matt. 24:48. [2] Ps. 14:1. [3] S. & H. 458:20.

lief, is it not easier to fall a victim next time?
Is not your moral sense dimmed just that much?
There is nothing "over there" to be jealous of
or to long for.   Your understanding, be it ever
so small, is the safest guide for you to hold to,
for through it you establish completeness here
and now, and silence the turmoil of the senses.
"Man's existence is a problem to be wrought in
divine Science."[1]   "The error of supposed life
and intelligence in matter, is dissolved only as
we master error with Truth.   Not through sin
or suicide, but by *overcoming* temptation and
sin, shall we escape the weariness and wickedness of mortal existence, and gain heaven, the
harmony of being."[2]

NO DIFFERENCE BETWEEN ONE WRONG
AND ANOTHER

You are not deceived into thinking that one
form of evil is worse than another form.   There
is not the slightest difference between one wrong
and another.   Whether it appears in a little
form or a big form, there is no difference.   It
is only self-righteousness and hypocrisy that
tempt the metaphysician vainly to imagine that
there is any difference between a desire to indulge in the belief of so-called bodily pleasure

1Mis. 52:21.   2Mis. 53:5.

or in the belief of pain, a fire, a bandit, a murderer, a government upset, a financial turmoil,
or any appearance of finiteness, no matter in
what form it is presented.

You ask, If there is no difference between one
form of wrong and another, why should the
married person countenance lust within the
bonds of matrimony if it is wrong outside of
these bonds? The whole belief of lust is fundamentally based on a belief of incompleteness,
and that is just what is wrong with the belief of
the world today. In the sight of Principle, one
form of lust is not different from another. It is
childish to suppose that there is any difference.
All forms of lust are the belief that there is
something satisfying and attainable "over
there" that is not "here," that Mind, your
Mind, does not spontaneously embrace all satisfaction, all completeness, all good for you.

In regard to the thought of lust, Mrs. Eddy
points out that "Wisdom in human action begins with what is nearest right under the circumstances, and thence achieves the absolute."[1]
But it is not even considered "wisdom in human
action" to permit licentiousness outside of the
bonds of matrimony. Human belief, in its
gradual destruction through a closer approxi-

[1] Mis. 288 :13.

mation to the oneness of Mind, has determined that one husband, one wife, is its true basis of action, and so has ruled that a departure from this oneness is illegitimate, and being illegitimate, is, to this human belief, wrong. It has gone thus far in its condemnation of lust. It will not be able to stop there, for in its imitation of Mind, it will demand also complete oneness.

As a Christian Scientist, however, you do not make a so-called differentiation between evil and evil. While you do not and could not condemn persons, for to you all is Mind, you do condemn every claim of evil. As you clearly understand divine Mind as the one and only Person, the one infinite Person, what must naturally take place with every form of licentiousness? The understanding of man's oneness with Mind, and that there is only one Mind, infinite good, supplying all good, all completeness to all, makes every claim of licentiousness spontaneously disappear.

Remember, the temptation is to make something of lust in the form of bodily desire, but to make nothing of it as a destructive fire, as conditions in Russia, China, India, or as abuses in our own communities, all of which are lust themselves. These are all forms of the human mind raging and lusting after completeness, after satisfaction *without* Principle. There is absolutely no difference between them. You have to be just as conscientious in getting rid of one lie as you are in getting rid of another. Wrong always means the suggestion of a mind apart from the one Mind.

DEATH WILL NOT END THE DREAM

It seems as though, in desperation, one cried, "What is going to arise to awaken me out of the lethargy of human belief? Am I going to dream on until I face the belief of death?" But can one go idling along up to that point, and then foolishly imagine that he will attain some wonderful awakening through death?

That is not possible. The one who dies will instantly awaken to the fact that he has not died or changed in the least his estimate of life, and that he has to go right on and work out the problem, the reality of being. Mortals, because of superstitious teaching, both religious and secular, are skeptical when told that nothing takes place at death except the mere fact of discovering that they are not dead and that they have, as Science points out, "but passed the portals of a new belief."[1] They ask,

[1] S. & H. 251:11.

"How do you know what death does? You have not tried it." You know what death must bring forth as definitely as you know that two times two billion is four billion, because you know that two times two is four. Consciousness could not possibly change at the point of death, for if it did change, as mortals imagine, it would be annihilated,—not conscious.

Mortals who go on thinking that the hereafter will be better than the here are dreaming in vain, for "where the tree falleth, there it shall be."[1] As one dies so he awakes. "If the change called *death* destroyed the belief in sin, sickness, and death, happiness would be won at the moment of dissolution, and be forever permanent; but this is not so. Perfection is gained only by perfection. They who are unrighteous shall be unrighteous still, until in divine Science Christ, Truth, removes all ignorance and sin."[2]

The only personal or bodily transformation that can occur at death is that the particular erroneous sense or disease, which was being accepted as consciousness, and which declared it could kill, and seemed to make good its threat will vanish. For did it not automatically prove itself a liar by the fact that its victim still found himself alive? When a lie is seen as a lie, it

[1] Ec. 11:3.   [2] S. & H. 290:16.

vanishes. So that particular erroneous sense or disease will have disappeared. Self-evidently, consciousness cannot die for there is nothing about Mind to kill, and neither can its embodiment or body die, for even an instant.

The conviction that death is inevitable makes hypocrites of all who believe in it. It makes the believer in it turn aside from the honest solution of present problems and cultivate the folly of procrastination. If you really knew that there was no death and that you had to go on living forever, here and now, you would quickly insist that your outlook on friendship and environment change at once for the better.

"LOVE WILL HEAL DEATH"

Since the one Mind embraces within itself the whole truth about all there is to person, place and thing, there is no possible chance to escape from person, place and thing. All that appears is Mind defining itself to you. Abandon the terrible belief of having a person, a place or a thing that you cannot tolerate.

I saw a statement once, said to have been made by Mrs. Eddy, to the effect, "I love. Whom? I love. What? I love. If you love, you can raise the dead. Love will heal death. That is the way I have raised the dead, by love that is above the human." Now what does love mean? Does it not mean finding that which *is,* as all that is, and proving it? You notice the statement ends with "love above the human." Love that has no sense of anything but itself. Love that is oneness with Mind, with that which *is,* with understanding. John said, "God is love."[1] Jesus also said, "A new commandment I give unto you, that ye love one another."[2]

Is it loving to allow the belief of a destructive fire to reign? Having the power of control in your own thinking, is it loving to tolerate attacks on your government? Are you loving when you let tyrannical usurpation, calling itself a high form of government, continue to go on in various parts of your world? Love embraces within itself all protection and tenderness, all that means and is good, and it demands that this Love be shown forth everywhere.

THE TALKING SERPENT

Mrs. Eddy once told some friends that the whole of error could be summed up in one word, "talking-serpent," and then she compared this talking serpent to the moccasin snake which will not touch a person when he is asleep,

1 John 4 :8.   2 John 13 :34.

but the moment he is awake will attack him. That is just what the metaphysician is confronted with today. If this so-called talking serpent of evil can actually sing or talk or charm one into being "asleep," it will let him go on without opposition. He is impotent, utterly blind so long as he is asleep to the dictates of Truth, no matter how awake his material eyes may seem to be.

The whole of error can truly be summed up in the one phrase "Talking serpent," which is the serpent of suggestion that is arguing every minute. It may appear as a person, a place or a thing, perhaps, that persuades and charms, or it may appear as the desire of one's own volition. If that serpent can charm you as a Christian Scientist into indolence without activity, or purpose, you can go smoothly along with "the mark, or the name of the beast, or the number of his name"[1] upon your forehead. But if you "launch your bark upon the ever-agitated but healthful waters of truth, you will encounter storms. Your good will be evil spoken of. This is the cross. Take it up and bear it, for through it you win and wear the crown. Pilgrim on earth, thy home is heaven; stranger, thou art the guest of God."[2] For you there is only one

[1] Rev. 13:17.   [2] S. & H. 254:27.

course to choose. You have chosen Mind, not suggestion, "the mark .... of the beast."[1]

"TIMID CONSERVATISM IS ABSOLUTELY INADMISSIBLE"[2]

When Jesus was preparing his disciples for the events which were to close his visible demonstration of Mind, and was telling them of some of the inhuman things that evil would try to inflict on him, Peter, under the guise of a mistaken sense of friendship, endeavored to remonstrate with Jesus against permitting the possibility of such an experience, and won from his Master the crushing rebuke, "Get thee behind me, Satan; thou art an offence unto me: for thou savourest not the things that be of God, but those that be of men."[3]

"If you venture upon the quiet surface of error and are in sympathy with error, what is there to disturb the waters? What is there to strip off error's disguise?"[4] If you adjust yourself to evil, you may seem, for the moment, to be in an easier position, but the battle is surely awaiting you "up the road." There is no kingly road in Christian Science where any one can escape passing "under the rod" of proof, any more than there is such a road in mathematics.

[1]Rev. 13:17.   [2]S. & H. 167:29.   [3]Matt. 16:23.   [4]S. & H. 254:24.

The kingdom of heaven is yours and you have full dominion, but you also have full responsibility, and that is just and right. The error you accept will finally have to be rejected, or Mind will not be All-in-all to you.

AN EXPERIENCE OF HEALING

Those of you who have read Adam Dickey's *Memoirs* of Mrs. Eddy may remember the account there given of Mrs. Eddy's healing of Calvin Frye. After most of the household had retired for the night, Mr. Frye was found seated in his chair, apparently unconscious, and, as it seemed, dead. Several people in the house were called and tried in every way to arouse him, but to no purpose. Finally they decided it best to tell Mrs. Eddy.

Immediately upon being told, Mrs. Eddy said, "I cannot wait to dress and go to him, bring him to me at once." Then she took possession of the situation and speaking with absolute power and authority, told Mr. Frye to awaken and commanded him to defeat the one and only enemy, malicious suggestion. After insisting upon this for a considerable time, but apparently with no result, she redoubled her efforts and as the account says she "fairly shouted" at him, demanding vehemently that he awake, and he did so. "If it becomes necessary to startle mortal mind to break its dream of suffering, vehemently tell your patient that he must awake. Turn his gaze from the false evidence of the senses to the harmonious facts of Soul and immortal being. Tell him that he suffers only as the insane suffer, from false beliefs."[1] "Should you thus startle mortal mind in order to remove its beliefs, afterwards make known to the patient your motive for this shock, showing him that it was to facilitate recovery."[2]

Even as the human concept of principle can be known only in the action of its idea or expression, whether in music or in mathematics, so God, divine Principle, has no way of showing forth His action except as man; and if man does not show forth God's action, God's power, then there is no God expressed. If you, therefore, do not act as God, how will God be known? Mrs. Eddy acted as Mind, just as Jesus did when "he cried with a loud voice, Lazarus, come forth."[3] He cried with the voice of power and authority, and there is no place where that voice is not heard.

When Mr. Frye opened his eyes, the first thing he asked was to be allowed to go on, saying, "I don't want to stay." Mrs. Eddy

1S. & H. 420:28.   2S. & H. 421:7.   3Jno. 11:43.

paused a moment before finishing the problem to say to her friends standing near, "Just listen to that!" The healing, of course, was complete.

There must be a greater sense of conscious power. If you really accept the fact that there is only one Mind, and accept that Mind as your Mind, then it is with that Mind that you speak every moment. "To live so as to keep human consciousness in constant relation with the divine, the spiritual, and the eternal, is to individualize infinite power; and this is Christian Science."[1] This individualization of infinite power is your privilege as well as your necessity.

MR. KIMBALL'S EXPERIENCE

Mr. Edward A. Kimball told me the following facts, which are known to many, regarding a case he treated and healed. On going to the home of a patient, he found an apparently sightless, unconscious form, with eyes already set. To all appearances the last enemy had accomplished its purpose. To this apparently lifeless form, Mr. Kimball spoke, declaring in substance, there is nothing that can ever be unconscious, there is no such condition, for Mind,

[1] My. 160:5-8.

God, the one Life, the one consciousness, is omnipresent, and because this is so I want you to repeat after me what I say; if you cannot say the words audibly, then make your lips move that I may know you are saying them. Then he repeated over and over that there is only one Life and this Life is infinite Life and is my Life; this one infinite Life is ever-present, and is my Life here and now. Finally the man's lips began to move and the first thing he voiced, as in the case of Mr. Frye, was the request to be let alone. Nevertheless, he was completely healed.

The nature of evil, now, as of old, is always to want to be let alone. "Let us alone; what have we to do with thee? . . . art thou come to destroy us?"[1] If you cease to speak as the voice of God, will not evil have its way? Does it not continually urge you to give up or postpone your mental vigilance by saying, you will be better "in the morning," or you will be better if you do this or that? It certainly does, as you well know, but are you better if you put off meeting it at once? You know you never are, for "behold, now is the accepted time; behold, now is the day of salvation."[2]

[1] Luke 4:34.   [2] 2 Cor. 6:2.

You do not think from these two cases that repetition of any true statement has any value in and of itself. You know that repetition can be just as material as any form of matter, but you do know also that divine insistence is the mental quality of Mind which never lets up and which can appear as oft-repeating, though always with understanding as its substance. When this understanding insistence is present, you prove that victory is never absent.

FACING THE PROBLEM

Are we, or are we not, enlisted to destroy the belief of death? When you destroy disease you destroy death. If disease seems to have resulted in unconsciousness, are you going to sit down and let it continue? If you believe you cannot control a fire or weather conditions, you will believe also that you cannot master so-called death. What, then, is the use of being a Christian Scientist if one must go on and accept utter powerlessness over these things? Is Mind All-in-all, or is it not? Mrs. Eddy said, "To me the reality and substance of being are *good*, and nothing else."[1]

Do you believe there is such a condition as unconsciousness? How could there be a pres-

[1] Un. 49:10.

ence to you that is not the very presence of
Mind, of infinite consciousness? Then, how
could there seem to be an unconscious mortal
before you? Is unconsciousness ever present
anywhere? Does that apply to everything?
Either it applies to everything or it does not
apply to anything. There is no such thing as
Mind and matter, consciousness and unconsciousness.

Because Mind controls *everything,* there is
nothing else to be controlled. Infinite Mind,
being all, must know all there is to know about
everything. Finite human sense has no grasp
of the term "everything." There is no material "everything." Then you are dealing with
infinite good, with heavenly things all the time.
That is the only reason that you can understand
them and deal with them correctly, and also the
only reason that they so readily appear to you.

THE OMNIPRESENT AVAILABILITY OF
INTELLIGENCE

An interesting illustration of the omnipresence of intelligence in its infinity of variety is
graphically portrayed in the phenomenon of
mediumship. A medium may have had what
she calls no educational advantages. Her speech
may be ungrammatical and her whole bearing

uncultured, but she will assure you that, as a medium, she can go into a trance and become the channel through which Emerson or some other departed scholar can deliver a message to you.

In the condition called a mediumistic trance her language will become that of a cultured person without a trace of illiteracy. But on coming out of the trance she will resume her former uneducated state. In a similar way, with no knowledge of German but believing herself to be controlled by the spirit of Goethe she may speak German fluently while in the trance.

Now you do not think that either Emerson or Goethe has any knowledge of the medium or of her effort to transmit messages from him. Yet that effort is not necessarily trickery. The medium may be, and often is, perfectly honest in believing in her own supernatural powers. But what explanation does Christian Science give to this phenomenon?

Christian Science declares that there is one God, one Mind, one infinite intelligence and that it is omnipresent. This intelligence must, therefore be the intelligence of all and must embrace within itself all knowing, all language, all culture, all expression, infinite and perfect dic-

tion. This infinite intelligence holds within itself all that is meant by Emerson or Goethe or
by any other term used to express identity, because there is no place where intelligence is not.
This is true irrespective of the avenue or appearance through which its presence is interpreted.

Jesus said, "if these should hold their peace,
the stones would immediately cry out."[1] Jesus
knew that God, intelligence, is not limited to
any particular avenue of expression but that to
Him every possibility is everywhere present.

Then why should it be considered charlatan-
ism for a medium to rid herself of one ignorant
belief about herself through taking on another
ignorant belief which she calls a trance? It is
simply a case of self-mesmerism in which she
exchanges a belief in ignorance for a belief that
by means of mediumship she can express culture and greater intelligence. There is nothing
mysterious or abnormal about this because intelligence being omnipresent she always possesses qualities that seem to be manifest only as
a result of what she calls going into a trance.
The medium determines her own limitations.
God puts no limitations upon her. "Son, . . . all
that I have is thine."[2] and "all mine are thine,

1Luke 19:40.   2Luke 15:31.

and thine are mine,"[1] are eternally the dicta of Mind.

The foolishness of mediumship lies in believing that one must go into a trance in order to express qualities that are eternally present but which are erroneously supposed to come only from academic education.

Believing this, however, is no more absurd than it is for a group of sane and otherwise intelligent people to think that by taking a few cocktails they can exchange uninteresting diffidence for witty and enjoyable companionship. The only difference between a belief in a cocktail and a belief in a trance is that the one is believed to be a material stimulus and the other a self-imposed mental stimulus. But in reality there is no difference between them, for matter is non-intelligent and of itself can accomplish nothing.

Mind holds within itself all "wit, humor, and enduring vivacity"[2] and because Mind is omnipresent these qualities belong to all creation. Understanding this you are a law unto yourself and will never be tempted to believe that mediumship, a cocktail or any other artificially induced stimulus can be of any assistance to you. You will then express spontaneously every de-

1 Jno. 17:10. 2 Mis. 117:11.

sirable quality without experiencing disagreeable after-effects.

Jesus, at the age of twelve, told the learned Sanhedrim things that had been hidden from the foundation of the world thereby causing them later to demand, "How knoweth this man letters, having never learned?"[1] By this, as well as by taking his tax money from the fish's mouth and again by feeding the multitude with "five loaves and two fishes"[2] Jesus proved the omnipresence of Mind and that God always appears to man in the language that man can best understand and that will best promote his happiness and success.

THE FALSE MUST BE REPLACED
BY THE TRUE

The reason "Immortal Mind governing all, must be acknowledged as supreme in the physical realm, so-called, as well as in the spiritual"[3], is because there is no physical realm. Every erroneous presentation, thought, or activity has to be reduced to its common denominator, malicious mind, and then replaced by divine Mind. This is equally true even about every word that is used. Take for example the word "thief." You know the term "thief" means one who

[1]Jno 7:15 [2]Matt 14:17 [3]S & H 427:23

robs. Are you not a thief then if you allow
evil to continue as consciousness to you, and so
cause you to rob God, the one Mind, of its allness, of the "glory, honor, dominion, and power
everlastingly due its holy name"?[1]

What replacing then is necessary? Separated
from infinite good by acknowledging something
unlike good, unlike God, the All-in-all, you find
yourself a thief. What is the true sense of the
word "thief", the sense that destroys the supposition of a consciousness apart from the one
consciousness? Is it not the understanding that
Mind, the All-in-all, holding to itself all that *is,*
necessarily takes to itself all that there is, and
so becomes the true thief, even as it becomes the
true murderer by being the destruction of all
that is unlike itself? Does not this understanding spontaneously destroy all desire for anything but what is yours already—the one Mind
being your Mind, with its infinity of good?

The purpose of these questions is simply to
learn where we stand and what we are doing.
You know that malicious mind, appearing as
matter, is appearing in its crudest form of operation. That is why you always reduce matter
concepts to their source, malicious mind, in order to discover their real meaning. In the final

1S. & H. 143 :30.

analysis, this malicious mind operates as a law of jealousy, anger, hatred, and revenge, to hurt and harm you. It operates as pure suggestion, appearing as a law of relapse, as a law of reversal, and so forth. These characteristics and claims of evil have absolutely nothing to do with persons, places, or things even though voiced by such, for they are only this so-called suppositional mind seen in its essence as pure evil. You destroy the false sense of these terms with the true sense, with the qualities of divine Mind and then evil is proved to be nothing. The negation is given back to God.

"THE LAW OF RELAPSE" ILLUSTRATED

You understand what the law of relapse is, and you remember that some time ago there was published a number of books and articles —attacks apparently on Mrs. Eddy—vicious attacks ostensibly fortified by numerous references. How was that accepted by the unenlightened thought? Naturally as an attack on Mrs. Eddy.

But what did you as the metaphysician say about it? You recognized at once that it was not an attack on Mrs. Eddy at all. All such attacks were met and answered completely twenty-five years ago. They were at that time handled and destroyed, and therefore you were not deceived into thinking that because the same appearance accompanied this effort, that it had actually anything to do with the claim. You did not bow down to the appearance, even for a moment, just because the lie seemed to be clothed in the language of the former attacks levelled at the personality of Mrs. Eddy, any more than you would accept the action of a man swimming on dry boards, under hypnotic influence, as really settling the fact of his being in the water.

You turned from the appearance at once, and on analyzing the situation, you realized that the claim of a personal attack had been destroyed years ago; then you knew that the real claim of this malicious mind was that it was operating hypnotically as a *law* of relapse, not *relapse,* but a *law* of relapse, in contradistinction to Mind's eternal law of progress, and you immediately handled the claim from that standpoint.

What was the result? These books after a large sale in the beginning, died down to the point where, it is said, only a comparatively few copies are selling today. You do not think that the demand of this so-called human mind ceased in its desire for that sort of fallacious reading do you? It was your understanding of what the real claim was and the handling of it that destroyed it, and nothing else. You know as metaphysicians that you could never heal a case by handling the same symptoms a second time after that case with those symptoms had once been healed, destroyed through Christian Science. The second appearance of the symptoms could never be the same claim.

After being healed, the same symptoms could come only as an entirely new disease, as a so-called *law* of relapse. When a claim is once destroyed, you never pay the slightest attention to any symptom appearing as that condition again. As you know, you bend your energies then toward understanding the oneness and allness of Mind, to realizing that Mind's eternal *law* of progress is ever operative and that there is no malicious mind to operate hypnotically as a *law* of relapse.

There was only one reason why the demand for those books ceased. That was because the hypnotism was destroyed. One on the side of Truth is a majority. You have proved it in sickness. You do not have a single case of sickness in which the entire world does not believe, because the mind that declares for that sickness is the mind of the whole world and therefore, all mortals accept what that mind is and believes. The law of relapse is the impersonal operation of that mind in its phase of pure evil and it is powerless to continue to appear to or to hurt or harm the Mind that knows its nothingness.

THE FINAL DEPRESSION

We are today at the standpoint of experience where all Bible prophecy is culminating. All the Pyramidal records and measurements are coming to an end. The final so-called period of depression is at hand. What appears as the present economic depression may have little relationship, in one sense of the word, to the depression portrayed in the Pyramid, for the present financial depression is only the so-called human mind swinging backward and forward like a pendulum, as it has constantly done in the past. It is simply the often recurring "states of mortal mind which act, react, and then come to a stop."[1]

The depression indicated in the Pyramid, however, and the struggle foretold in the Apocalypse is the fearful depression of doubt which asks, "Is there a God?" It is expressed in "Men's hearts failing them for fear, and for

[1] S. & H. 283:9.

looking after those things which are coming on the earth."[1]

The mortal loves to grapple with economic and financial depressions. Such conditions never appal him, for he enjoys the conflict which brings out his latent ability. Jesus knew this. What he was referring to in the above quotation was the terrible blank in the mind of the mortal who, look where he will, can find no hope, no joy or satisfaction in anything, no God.

You have doubtless felt this depression and may have thought it was caused by the financial disturbances, but in this you were mistaken. It is the deep heartsickness of the world that is being felt. It is this malicious mind in its final supposition, operating as your mind. In destroying the claim impersonally as having nothing whatever to do with any person or condition, but as pure hypnotic suggestion having no reality, you will find it is gone.

EVIL NEITHER PERSON NOR THING

What could cause a Christian Scientist to turn his gaze even momentarily to medicine for physical help or to drinking or to smoking in order to satisfy his incompleteness, or possibly even to

[1] Luke 21:26.

the contemplation of suicide for relief? What could make him turn either to the right hand or to the left or even think of turning, except the subtle suggestion of malicious mind acting as pure hypnotism? This malicious mind, that hides behind a personal sense of life, can be destroyed only by one's being alone with the one Mind and establishing the real Science of being. Evil can never be handled as person, as one's self or as some one else. "Let thine eyes look right on, and let thine eyelids look straight before thee. Ponder the path of thy feet, and let all thy ways be established. Turn not to the right hand nor to the left: remove thy foot from evil."[1]

If you think you are depressed because *some person* does not treat you kindly, or *something* is not going well, your hands are immediately tied. It is not *some person* or *some thing* that is the trouble. It is always the one malicious mind acting as hypnotic suggestion and appearing under the guise of some person or some thing. As you have already seen, this malicious mind can seemingly appear as a law of relapse, or the law of the reversal of the truth which you declare. It can appear as envy, jealousy, discontent, and other qualities of incomplete-

[1]Prov. 4 :25,26,27.

ness. But you are not tempted by this malicious suggestion to think of it as something external "over there," because you understand what the claim is. Believing that there is something "over there," in other words "a third," you are powerless, and it can then defy you.

YOU HAVE FULL AUTHORITY

The sick cannot be healed metaphysically, in other words, understandingly, if there is anything apart from the one Mind. Either what you have established here is the truth, or the truth of Christian Science is a dream. If you have ever made a demonstration of any kind, you did it through the power of Mind and solely because Mind is All-in-all. And if Mind can do one little thing, it can do all. There can be only Mind or matter, not both, and you know that it is Mind, because you recognize yourself as conscious being, thus having the witness within yourself that consciousness, Mind *is* and that this *is,* is all that *is.*

With only one Mind, this Mind is your-Self, the Self, the being of you. You are the one Christian Scientist. You are the one activity of Mind. Without His expression, God would be powerless. Then, is it all in your hands? Of course it is, and you have full authority. There

is no one to say you nay. What you say stands.
"So shall my word be that goeth forth out of
my mouth: it shall not return unto me void,
but it shall accomplish that which I please, and
it shall prosper in the thing whereto I sent it."[1]
Mrs. Eddy proved that with regard to Mr.
Frye. She acted as God, and so made herself
not God, but as God, God-like. Then His word
was her word. It is your word also.

"The burden of proof that Christian Science
is Science rests on Christian Scientists,"[2] rests
on you as the one Christian Scientist. Then how
much power have you? Infinite power. It is not
a question of your power being limited. You
always express all power. When you say, I am
sick, I am weary, I am discontented, I wish it
were all over, which side are you on? You carry
the side with which you place your power,
whether with Truth or with error. "The Christian Scientist is alone with his own being and
with the reality of things."[3] That applies just
as much to the suppositional mind as to the reality, the one Mind. You are alone every moment with what you accept as consciousness.

There is nothing, therefore, that can oppose
itself to your word. You know that Truth is,
but in spite of that knowing, that understanding,

[1] Isa. 55:11.   [2] My. 158:18.   [3] '01 20:8.

do you as the Christian Scientist often act as though you had to consult God as to whether or not you had the right to heal all dis-ease? Do you have to consult God and receive His consent when you act as God, as good, or are you the very presence of God? Jesus declared, "I and my Father are one."[1] The Mind that is God is your Mind, now and always.

THERE IS NO LAW OF DEATH

Are you determined to live or are you consenting to death? Have you anything to say about it? Mrs. Eddy told Calvin Frye that his duty was to live and she proved it. Is not God forever saying, "make you a new heart and a new spirit: for why will ye die, O house of Israel? For I have no pleasure in the death of him that dieth . . . wherefore turn yourselves, and live ye"[2]?

Have you anything to say about whether you will get old or not? You know physicians of today are frankly saying that old age is a disease and has nothing to do with years and that it is just like any other disease. So age, increasing years, can no longer be held as harmful. Human belief finally had to make this admission because it had already, for some time past, estab-

[1]John. 10:30.   [2]Ez. 18:31-32.

lished as a fact of this human mind that the body, due to the replacing of its cells, is never over seven years old. Years mean experience and experience is always valuable and life-giving, never destructive.

Does hypnotism say that you feel that you are getting old? Remember then that the very mind that says you are getting old is the same mind that says your body is never more than seven years old. "Out of the same mouth proceedeth blessing and cursing. My brethren, these things ought not so to be. Doth a fountain send forth at the same place sweet water and bitter?"[1]

The acceptance of old age is just the same, whether you say that somebody "over there" is getting old or some one "here" right at home. If you see trees, animals or anything as getting old, are you not accepting old age? Nothing can grow old. If you accept the suggestion that things are growing older and older in the sense of becoming infirm, then death must finally arrive. As the Christian Scientist you know that there is no law of death. Why then bow down to the suggestion of such a law? The only law of death there is, is the law of Life which is the law of death to everything unlike itself.

[1] Jas. 3:10-11.

THE ADVANCING THOUGHT OF THE WORLD

Professor Compton, one of the great physicists of the world, Professor of Physics in the Chicago University and a Nobel prize winner, has lately advanced a wonderfully clear deduction, which in substance entirely nullifies the old idea of evolution. He shows the "infinitesimal" possibility of matter developing "into a world with the infinite variety that we find about us," which variety must self-evidently "imply that there is an intelligence directing it." He also fearlessly declares "that consciousness may persist after the brain is destroyed." The advanced thought of the world is rapidly abandoning the old idea of evolution and basing its new-found hopes and opinions on consciousness as the source of being. The progress of material science is amazingly gratifying as well as amusingly interesting to the one who knows the truth of Mrs. Eddy's discovery in 1866, that "All is infinite Mind and its infinite manifestation, for God is All-in-all."[1]

Sir James Jeans in the closing chapter of his book, *"The Mysterious Universe"* page 158, makes these illuminating statements, "The old dualism of mind and matter . . . seems likely to

[1] S. & H. 468:10.

disappear, not through matter becoming in any way more shadowy or insubstantial than heretofore, or through mind becoming resolved into a function of the working of matter but through substantial matter resolving itself into a creation and manifestation of mind." "Mind no longer appears as an accidental intruder into the realm of matter; we are beginning to suspect that we ought rather to hail it as the creator and governor of the realm of matter—not of course our individual minds, but the mind in which the atoms out of which our individual minds have grown exists as thoughts." What then is there to matter as such if it is the product of mind? Must it not necessarily take upon itself all the qualities of mind which include not one single quality of matter as matter?

You are continually travelling in one direction or the other. You are ever going toward matter or Mind. Nothing can stop you. You are the one who decides which direction it shall be. You are the one who declares, "Thus far and no farther" to everything erroneous that presents itself as your thought. You understand that that which trails the wings of spiritual soaring in the dust is the believing that "over there" Truth does not apply, but "over here" it does. Could Truth be here without embracing there?

HEALTH OMNIPRESENT

When told that some one has been healed by an operation or by medicine or by some other means, have you ever analyzed the tendency of your thought? As a Christian Scientist, do you think such healing to be only a belief of health, which will not last? Is there more than one state of health? Is not that health identically the same health that is everywhere present? Then is it not your duty to do as Jesus did, and confirm all healing, so that nothing else obtains as consciousness?

When the woman touched the hem of Jesus' robe, she believed that the touching of the garment brought her health. Jesus, knowing health to be omnipresent, made that health permanent by confirming it. He said to the woman, "thy faith hath made thee whole, *go in peace*."[1] The woman's method of seeing health was through a superstitious and finite faith, beautiful in its trust in goodness, but wholly lacking in understanding. But his confirmation was infinite understanding. Jesus never compromised his pure sense of the real and spiritual with material ways and means, and it was this that made him mighty. Had he for an instant

1Luke 8:48.

stooped to accept the material modus of gaining health, he could not have confirmed the feeble groping with the eternal fact of health.

The metaphysician must corroborate every bit of healing that he hears. Healing is always the appearing of the one omnipresent health. Confirm health because health is. The process whereby it is seen does not confuse you. The health is ever the same health.

Get into the way of taking command of every situation. "All power is given unto me in heaven and in earth"[1] means me. So, if I want to see health everywhere, I am glad to see it everywhere and rejoice at the appearance of health under any and all circumstances. I must confirm health, no matter how seen by my understanding, as did Jesus.

MUST I DIE?

Because death is not of God, even though all seem to die, or seem to think they have to die, do you or I have to die? Certainly not. No one is obliged to die. There is no law of death. Mrs. Eddy only seemed to disappear because as the revelator, she appeared to the unenlightened thought to be the revelation, and nothing could continue to stand between the revelation and Mind.

[1] Matt. 28:18.

Jesus was the "Master Metaphysician." He was the one and only Example, and showed not only what could be done, but what must be done by one and all. That was not Mrs. Eddy's office. Her visible presence and example is not a necessity to her revelation, now that the revelation, Science and Health, is established as consciousness.

Since I now, of myself, know why Christian Science is true, it would not destroy that assurance and understanding in the least if the Bible and Science and Health seemed to vanish. Because, for the very reason that I am now dependent understandingly upon my own communion with Mind, I can never be deprived of anything that can be of the slightest value to me. Thus I am forever assured of having all that the Bible and Science and Health mean and reveal.

It is a very foolish, unappreciative, conceited belief, to call one's self a Christian Scientist, and not constantly corroborate one's understanding of Mind by a careful study of Science and Health and the Bible. No one could read what Mrs. Eddy has written on any subject without being enlightened and assured and reassured on his Mind-journey.

Christian Science, being the word of infinite power and authority, the word of God, instantaneously heals all disease. With Christian Science you do the same. You cannot forget that. You must do it. The power of Mind is utterly unlimited. "The Lord's hand is not shortened, that it cannot save."[1] "God is not a man, that he should lie; neither the son of man, that he should repent: hath he said, and shall he not do it? or hath he spoken, and shall he not make it good?"[2] There is no place where Mind is not, so there is no place where the voice of Mind is not heard. And that Mind is your Mind, so you cannot be less than all-powerful in world affairs. Act from this standpoint, else you are steadily marching toward the grave.

Death will not and cannot advance you a single step. You know now, all that death could teach you. You know the whole unreality of a mind apart from God. Why not then today and every day act from the standpoint of vigor, freshness, inspiration and genuine interest in everything and everybody? There is no excuse for not doing this.

It will be a deep disappointment to you if you die. You will awake to say, I knew better,

[1] Isa. 59:1. [2] Num. 23:19.

and you will not excuse yourself for the mistake. You will not enjoy failure.

THE OPPORTUNITY TO PROVE
ONENESS WITH MIND

Now, this minute, is the time to have no enemy on earth except malicious mind, and that only suppositionally. "Husbands, hear this and remember how slight a word or deed may renew the old trysting times."[1] All are husbands, all are wives. There is no excuse for bickering and quarreling. Mind is All-in-all to you. Then who is there with whom to quarrel? The opportunity before each one, every instant, is the opportunity which, if taken advantage of, will advance him as nothing else can, for it gives him the opportunity to prove his oneness with Mind.

"The purpose and motive to live aright can be gained now. This point won, you have started as you should. You have begun at the numeration-table of Christian Science, and nothing but wrong intention can hinder your advancement. Working and praying with true motives, your Father will open the way. 'Who did hinder you, that ye should not obey the truth?' "[2] Are you really a worker? Then remember, you are vitally interested in all. Do not wait for a more "con-

1S. & H. 59:20.   2S. & H. 326:16.

venient season"[1] to express the power of man
as the activity of Mind. It will never come—
today is the day to prove it, and to prove it
everywhere.

In doing this, you demonstrate that you are
not the fool that hath said in his heart, "There
is no God."[2] You know in whom you have
believed and you fulfill in your life the truth
of the saying, attributed to Mrs. Eddy, "Humility is the door, honesty is the way, and spirituality is the summit."

[1]Acts. 24:25.   [2]Ps. 14:1.

A LETTER

December 30, 1929.

Dear . . .

As the alert Christian Scientist, as the metaphysician, you cannot be deceived by any phenomena that may be presented to you. You remember Jesus said, "And what I say unto you I say unto all, Watch,"[1] and again, "Watch ye and pray, lest ye enter into temptation."[2] Jesus was warning against the temptation of being deceived into believing that what appears as true to the so-called material senses is necessarily true, or indicative of what is really operating. Real truth is found only by looking away from the material sense testimony.

The metaphysician is confronted today with two very interesting conditions. One phase, which I will analyze first, is the world wide attack, as it appears, on Mrs. Eddy and her authorship of Science and Health.

Twenty-five years ago, the attack on Mrs. Eddy's life, education and character, from a personal standpoint, was in full swing, and as you know, this attack was fully and entirely answered, not only by Edward A. Kimball,

[1]Mark 13:37. [2]Mark 14:38.

Frederick Dixon, Alfred Farlow, B. O. Flower and others, but by Sibyl Wilbur's excellent and accurate presentation of the whole question in her *"Life of Mary Baker Eddy"* published in 1907. The world was completely satisfied that Mrs. Eddy was not only the discoverer and founder of Christian Science, but that her character was, and always had been, above reproach, and that her entire life was an open book for all to review. Her ability as a writer was also fully established and her authorship of Science and Health accepted without further doubt or question.

You understand that when once a lie is replaced with the truth, the Christ, the lie is destroyed, for the Christ from that moment reigns as consciousness on that particular point, and so can never be displaced by the return of the lie, any more than two times two as five can return where the understanding reigns that two times two is four. Because you know this, you know also that when once the lie about Mrs. Eddy and the authorship of Science and Health was understandingly destroyed, it was equally impossible for that lie to return. As Science and Health declares, "Neither disease itself, sin, nor fear has the power to cause disease or a relapse."[1]

Then the question arises: What is the world confronted with at the present time, not only in America, but also in England, in this apparent tirade of abuse of Mrs. Eddy and the repetition of all the old lies that have so long been silenced?

When a disease has been corrected with the truth, and Christian Science reigns as Mind, that disease is gone, as you know, and gone forever. If the old symptoms characterizing the disease should appear again, you would know at once that it was not the old claim but an entirely new claim with the old appearances. Nothing could persuade you to think that it was the original claim. You would at once diagnose it as a belief of a *law* of relapse, and you would handle it as such, and destroy it through understanding that since the one law of infinite progress is the law of God, of Mind, there is no mind, malicious or otherwise, that can operate as hypnotic suggestion and appear as a belief of a *law* of relapse.

I do not need to go into the various arguments you might use to establish this fact for yourself, for you understand how to do it,

1S. & H. 419:10.

but establish it you would have to, in order
to destroy the lie. You could not be tempted
to handle *relapse,* but you would handle the
law of relapse as the suppositional opposite
of the law of progress, and you would understand that it had no relationship whatever to
the original claim. The belief of a return of a
dis-eased belief, in other words, the belief of a
law of relapse, is not a claim in the realm of personality or matter at all; it only appears as that.
It is really a claim in the realm of pure mental
iniquity and must be destroyed as such.

Then what appears as the present attack on
Mrs. Eddy is exactly this claim of a belief of
a *law* of relapse. The original claim was met
and destroyed. Now, because the old symptoms
appear again, does this mean that the old claim
has arisen? Of course it does not, and you cannot be mesmerized into thinking that it does.
Then the claim to be destroyed is the belief
that there is malicious mind, and that as such
mind it can operate as hypnotic suggestion and
appear as a *law* of relapse.

What is it then, that has apparently brought
out the conscious activity of this spurious belief
of law which is now seen? It is because the
metaphysician has understandingly established

the line of Light, in which he has so imper-
sonalized Mrs. Eddy and Science and Health
as to find Mind to be All-in-all, and has thus
relinquished forever both the revelator and the
revelation as having anything to do with a finite
or false sense of personality.

This is simply the further unfoldment and
activity of God's eternal law of progress, and
so spontaneously there arises the pretext or possibility of the suppositional opposite. Truth
always precedes error, for error is ever but the
lie about Truth. Today this suppositional opposite has appeared cloaked in the guise of the
Dakin book, of the articles in the Outlook, of
the Fisher Book in England, and of accusations
of pseudo Christian Scientists, and perhaps of
many others.

To attempt to combat these attacks with the
true account of Mrs. Eddy and her life is just
as futile as to attempt to correct two times two
as five, with three times three as nine. The
latter is true but it will never correct anything
wrong about two times two. The right Christ
must be present to destroy a lie, or the lie is
not destroyed. So the present lie, appearing as
the vicious attack on Mrs. Eddy can be destroyed only with the understanding that Mind

is all that there is to Mrs. Eddy and to Science and Health, and both wholly impersonal. This understanding is the law of progress which has no opposite because there is no malicious mind to operate as mind, and appear as a belief of a *law* of relapse.

Your understanding of this, and of what the line of Light is, answers the attack and will destroy it. No refutation dealing with personality, no matter how true and minute, now means anything. The refutation must be impersonal. The truth you understand is the answer that will meet this lie and destroy it. You are, I know, awake to, and are understandingly handling the belief of a *law* of relapse and as Mrs. Eddy discerned, you "will hold crime in check."[1]

Now with regard to the second phase confronting the metaphysician. It was in September, 1922, after the Supreme Court of Massachusetts had accepted the resignations of the trustees of The Christian Science Publishing Society, and had released them from all further responsibility in regard to their trust, that we began to hear of "excommunication," and a little later the public was informed that certain former trustees had been excommunicated from the Boston church. However, you

1S. & H. 97:1.

know it was not a person that was excommunicated. No person is of any moment. It was
metaphysics that was excommunicated. The
metaphysician knows that it is never a person or
persons that is involved, but that what appears
as a person is always a state of consciousness,
therefore what the person is standing for is
all that constitutes the person. Hence it was
metaphysics and not a person that was excommunicated.

Seven years have passed since that time, and
you know that seven is always a figure of speech
representing completeness. During these seven
years, a quiet readjustment has been taking
place with the Christian Scientist in his understanding of Christian Science as Mind instead
of as a religious belief. I do not mean by this
that Christian Science has ever truly been a
religious belief, but it has been, in a measure,
looked upon by the Christian Scientist as a
religious belief, and, in consequence, has been
so regarded by the world.

If you apply the term "religion" to Christian Science, then instead of Christian Science
being *a* religion or religious belief, it is *religion*
itself, for the very term religion means man's
relation to God, and this relation is as fixed as
Principle and is no more subject to a belief

about it than is mathematics. In this sense Christian Science is religious and religion, but never in the sense of a creed, doctrine or belief. Human opinion does not enter its realm.

Then, because Christian Science is not, and never has been, a religious belief, it was inevitable that this should finally appear. It has appeared with the greatest clarity, during the past seven years. Today the metaphysician knows that Christian Science has nothing whatever to do with any religious belief, but has everything to do with Mind. For Christian Science is simply another name for Mind.

Have you ever asked yourself the question, How many people have I interested, or attempted to interest, in Christian Science during the past seven years? Perhaps, if you do this, you may be surprised to find that there has been almost a cessation of endeavor on your part during this time, to interest any one in Christian Science.

The reason for this cessation, if there has been one, is without doubt because you have felt that you could no longer attempt to present Christian Science as a religious belief, as you have done in the past under the aegis of church organization, and that you were not quite ready to present it in any other way. Hence the seven year period of readjustment.

Today, however, this is all changed. The seven years of quiet reconstruction are over, and a new period has begun. Undoubtedly this period will bring to the thoughtful metaphysician an opportunity for tremendous activity. He has gained a larger sense of the absolute impersonality of Christian Science and this of necessity enlarges his ability to present Christian Science as Paul presented Christianity as "all things to all men," meeting every human need. No longer thinking of Christian Science as a religious belief, but thinking of it in terms of pure Mind, you will have no hesitancy or delicacy in presenting it to one and all as Mind.

Would you have the slightest hesitancy in presenting two times two as four to any one? Would it not be the most natural thing in the world to correct spontaneously any mistake about two times two? Is it not equally natural and normal then for you, understanding Christian Science as Mind, to present Christian Science in this light to every one? Why should there be any delicacy or hesitancy?

Under the old order of thinking of Christian Science as a religious belief, there was a natural delicacy about foisting one's religious opinions upon another; but with that sense of Christian Science entirely removed, there can no longer be any reluctance in presenting the allness of Mind.

As the metaphysician, you know that because you are dealing with Mind and Mind alone, that which appears to you as persons, places, and things is not what it seems to be, something "over there", but is simply the interpretation "here" that you are ascribing to your communion with Mind. It is not possible then, for you to remain satisfied with what appears as people "over there" continuing to be unacquainted with Christian Science. If you were, you would not find yourself alone with Mind and therefore with perfection, which is the kingdom of heaven. Then do you not, for the moment at least, appear to be under the necessity of bending your energies toward bringing to all the understanding of Christian Science as Mind? Unless you do this, will you be able to say that Mind is All-in-all? You know you will not. Does not this mean then, that you must begin understandingly to present Christian Science, as Mind, to all that appears to you, not obtrusively but naturally and normally?

Thus will you truly find Mind as your Mind, and find Mind as All-in-all. There can be nothing external to Mind. All must be contained in Mind, hence, John's statement, "If a man say, I love God, and hateth his brother, he is a liar."[1] All must be found as Mind, and therefore, the presence of this Mind must be found as omnipresent, as the one Christian Scientist.

This is something to be considered most carefully and you will doubtless seriously ask yourself, What am I doing consciously to establish the kingdom of God, Mind, in earth as it is in heaven? Or to give a little more punch to the question, as Mrs. Eddy puts it, "What will you do about it . . . Will you doff your lavender-kid zeal, and become real and consecrated warriors? . . . Answer at once and practically, and answer aright!"[2]

Very sincerely yours,

HERBERT W. EUSTACE.

1 Jno. 4:20.   2 Mis. 177:13.

"SCIENCE, UNDERSTOOD,
TRANSLATES MATTER
('the Beast' of Revelation)
INTO MIND."

Notes of a meeting held by
HERBERT W. EUSTACE, C.S.B.
in Berkeley, California
August 23, 1936.

"SCIENCE, UNDERSTOOD,
TRANSLATES MATTER
('the Beast' of Revelation)
INTO MIND"*

"He that believeth on me, the works that I do shall he do also; and greater works than these shall he do; because I go unto my Father." (John 14:12)

Do we believe this statement? Getting rid of a false sense of matter is the only way we are going to find the answer. What does this going "unto the Father" mean? The Father is Spirit; then going unto the Father must mean going from a finite matter basis, to an infinite Spirit basis.

Do you think that matter as matter can accomplish anything? Can matter move your hand, or is it Mind that moves it? You would not know you had a hand if it did not come to you as consciousness, as Mind. You can not conceive of it as matter. You can not deal with matter as matter. Mind can not go outside its own realm of mentality. In Jeremiah we read, "Cursed be the man that trusteth in man, and maketh flesh his arm, and whose heart departeth from the Lord." (17:5)

Now consider Mrs. Eddy's statement in her original work, Science of Man: "Matter held as shadow is the idea of God, but matter held as substance is a belief and error."

You know that a shadow, followed back, always leads you to what it is shadowing forth and brings you to its own original substance. It can never appear without an origin. It can not be present through any inherent quality of its own.

Then follow matter back; this reverses and clears up the mistake of thinking it has life, intelligence or substance of itself, and leads you to what it truly is, "the idea of God," for "Matter held as shadow is the idea of God."

It was this that Jesus was foretelling and foreshadowing when he said, "I go unto my Father." Here the "I" was no longer entertaining a false sense of its origin as matter-held-as-substance.

Again Mrs. Eddy writes, "Let us have a clearing up of abstractions." (Mis. Wr. 174:6) What is meant by abstractions? What is the greatest abstraction to you? If I asked you what was the most concrete thing to you, you would probably answer, "Matter." Thereby you would imply that Spirit to you was the abstraction. But matter is the abstraction. Let us understand, then, what matter really is. "Clearing up" means understanding.

With all our development, is not matter the puzzle of the ages? Material scientists now declare matter to be a "mathematical formula." Does that tell you any more about it? Matter is the greatest abstraction of all. We are getting to the point where human belief is nearing the only conclusion it can reach, and that is that "Matter is an error of statement." (S. & H.

*(Mis. Wr. 25:12)

277:26) When Science and Health made that declaration, it gave the world a correct definition of matter and opened the way for a clearing up of abstractions.

The abstraction attaches to matter, not to Spirit. Matter is not a thing to be discarded; it is a false sense entertained which, when reversed, is found to be the idea of God.

In Miscellaneous Writings we read, "Let us open our affections to the Principle that moves all in harmony—from the falling of a sparrow to the rolling of a world." (174:10) Does this last statement seem contradictory? Does Mind cognize the falling of a sparrow? What could be more insignificant than a sparrow that is gone? "Are not two sparrows sold for a farthing? and one of them shall not fall on the ground without your Father." (Matt. 10:29) Mind holds within its isness the imperishable verity of this least shadow of its presence as well as the greatest manifestation.

Then Mrs. Eddy goes on with this query—she is asking herself just as you must ask yourself, "What is the kingdom of heaven?" And she gives this answer, "The abode of Spirit, the realm of the real. No matter is there, no night is there—nothing that worketh or maketh a lie."

Then she asks herself again, "Is this kingdom afar off? No: it is ever-present here. The first to declare against this kingdom is matter." When Mrs. Eddy made this statement, did she mean matter as it is usually conceived of or was she thinking of it as "a misstatement of Mind"? (Mis. Wr. 174:2) It could only have been in the latter sense. Here matter is lifted into the realm of mentality where it can be handled. You could not cognize matter as matter. Neither could matter as matter "declare against" anything. It always requires mentality "to declare." Destroying the false sense of matter is the only way that we are going to find the kingdom of heaven as a present reality and "have a clearing up of abstractions." Matter-held-as-shadow is spiritual.

You will be afraid as long as you accept matter as matter, as long as you conceive of it as something apart from Mind, for you will be dealing with the absence of Mind, Life—and is this not dealing with death? Paul declared that it was "through fear of death" that men had been "all their lifetime subject to bondage." (Heb. 2:15)

Science and Health declares, "As named in Christian Science, animal magnetism or hynotism is the specific term for error, or mortal mind. It is the false belief that mind is in matter, and is both evil and good." (103:18) And again, *"Mortal mind* and body combine as one, and the nearer matter approaches its final statement—animate error called nerves, brain, mind—the more prolific it is likely to become in sin and disease-beliefs" (409:4)

Each individual must understand for himself. You are the only one who could have a false sense of another. But is there really another, or is it your misinterpretation of God? Matter must be translated back "into its original language, which is Mind." (Hea. 7:8) Who is the only one dealing with all that means consciousness to you? It is you, yourself. Is it not, then, an individual problem?

How could you heal the body if you think in terms of matter as such? If the kingdom of heaven is here and you are in it, with what must you be dealing? MIND. Understanding what matter is, explains what body is —clears it up by translating it back into its original meaning, Mind. In reality is not the whole belief of death the attempt to get rid of matter? If matter is but the negative of Mind, how can you get rid of a false sense of matter by dying?

Thinking Christian Scientists are determined to understand matter not as substance, but as that which shadows forth the presence of Mind. If you do that, could you conceive of heaven as something afar off? Some place you are going to as an *eventual* clearing up of abstractions?

Do you act in your thinking as though you were in the kingdom of heaven right now? That is simply translating the negative into its positive language. There is no other way honestly to acknowledge the fact that the kingdom of heaven is right here. If you do not do this, you are planning for death. If heaven is not present this moment and every moment—with you in it—you are headed for a funeral. The only thing that can stop you from seeing that you are in the kingdom of heaven now, is a wrong interpretation of matter, and dying will not clear this up.

This "clearing up of abstractions" is a most important essential. Abstractions need to be cleared up—the false interpretation of matter. Start immediately to acknowledge to yourself that the kingdom of God is not afar off, not something to be attained by death, but is obtained by instant understanding.

Do you want the kingdom of heaven? Jesus said, "the kingdom of heaven is at hand." (Matt. 4:17) Do you not repeat these words, and yet do you think you can have this kingdom right at hand as long as you acknowledge matter-as-substance? But when matter is held as shadow, then you have Mind as All-in-all. Then you begin to have this kingdom as ever-present here, your conscious oneness with Mind.

But this can never be obtained as long as matter is held as substance, as something in and of itself. As surely as you do this, you will be wanting to move on. As long as matter suggests a false sense of being, you will be looking "into darkness for light." (Mis. Wr. 174:27) You alone give it power.

Jesus saw this truth with regard to matter. He saw that the time would come when all would acknowledge Mind as the source of all that appears as matter, for he said, "Greater works than these shall ye do; because I go unto my Father."

Seeing matter as that which shadows forth Mind, "translates matter into its original language, which is Mind, and gives the spiritual instead of the material signification." (Hea. 7:8) Do you think this is spiritualizing matter? Of course it is. How else are you going to find the kingdom of God right here? You acknowledge that you are dealing with matter all around you, that all this consciousness comes as a sense of matter. Then matter is not a *thing*, but a *sense*. "Matter is a misstatement of Mind." (Mis. Wr. 174:2) This going on dealing with matter-as-substance is all the error there is. Get rid of matter as a false statement.

Are you not finding as you unfold that you are upsetting one theory after another? "Gladness to leave the false landmarks and joy to see them disappear—this disposition helps to precipitate the ultimate harmony." (S. & H. 324:2) Give up the idea that spiritualizing matter is a mistake. Only as matter is spiritualized, as it is seen as shadowing forth Mind, does it disappear as "an error of statement," as shadowing forth death.

Did they not say of the man Jesus, "By our law he ought to die, because he made himself the Son of God"? And yet "His earthly mission was to translate substance into its original meaning, Mind." (Mis. Wr. 74:16) In other words, find himself *as* Mind, not matter.

The whole of evil comes not from spiritualizing matter, but from *materializing* Spirit, making that substance which is shadow, and so having a negation of Mind to deal with. Then why should the demand to translate matter *back* into its "original language, which is Mind," be questioned? "Let us have a clearing up of abstractions. Let us come into the presence of Him who removeth all iniquities, and healeth all our diseases." (Mis. Wr. 174:6)

Mind's isness is its allness. There is nothing outside of it and this is its purity. Purity has no element outside of itself. You express spirituality and can not cognize what is outside of Spirit. "All is infinite Mind and its infinite manifestation." Why? "For God is All-in-all." (S. & H. 468:10)

"Let us attach our sense of Science to what touches the religious sentiment within man." (Mis. Wr. 174:8) What is meant here by the word religious? It is sometimes said that a man does his work religiously. Does that not mean that he does it with exactness? He does not vary, he does not deviate from it, he keeps right at it, does it rightly; and it is in this sense that Mrs. Eddy uses the word in this quotation, "Let us attach our sense of Science to what touches the religious sentiment within man."

Exactness takes in all that is moral. God is not moral. He is morality itself. You could not have immorality unless you broke the First Commandment. Every quality of God is a moral quality. That which *is,* that which is purity and exactness, shuts out all unlike itself.

The religious sentiment is that element or quality which turns to exactness. Some cases of straying from the truth are due to constant lack of exactness. Exactness includes within itself all exactness, and therefore it does not tolerate any inexactness, any impurity, anything apart from Mind.

The "clearing up of abstractions," then, is being exact, having everything clear as to what Mind means in its all inclusiveness.

Do you not seem to be constantly dealing with matter? Does not matter seem to be all-in-all to you? But Mind is the All-in-all. How can you say that Mind is All-in-all unless you see that "Matter held as shadow is the idea of God"?

Unenlightened Christian Scientists think that matter is some *thing* to be wiped out. How can you wipe out *a* thing or heal *a* thing? You do not obliterate ignorance. You see truth just where the ignorance seems to be.

If you erase $2 \times 2 = 5$, you have nothing left. The Christian Scientist who attempts to blot out matter, except by seeing it as the shadow of Mind, and so gaining its true sense, finds in the end he has nothing left, and so thinks the undertaker a good thing.

Do you think there was anything possible to Jesus which is not possible to you? How could infinite Spirit have any favorites—giving to one and withholding from another? How could Jesus have had a monopoly upon the infinite blessings of God's presence?

In the early morning on the shore of the Sea of Tiberias, Jesus had fish prepared for his disciples as they came ashore. Where did the fish come from? They were just as much matter as those you are dealing with today. The difference consists in the spirit Jesus entertained about them.

When Jesus fed the multitude, he took the five loaves, he did not reject them, there was something here. *"He looked up to heaven,* and blessed and brake the loaves." (Mark 6:41) Now these loaves were just as much matter as the table before us. But Jesus "looked up to heaven." He followed the shadow back to its original substance, Mind. He took all the faith, all the confidence, all the dependence which was being attached to *bread* back to Mind and knew Mind to be all-presence, all-substance, All-in-all.

This was the purification of thought, the baptism of Spirit, relinquishing all for Mind. If Jesus had thought in terms of "loaves" as did the multitude, there would have been no feast, no fragments. The trouble with us is that we do not follow the shadow back to its substance, we are not confident that we are dealing with Mind alone, and willing to leave the outline to the wisdom of God.

Do you think there is any difference between correcting $2\times2=5$ or a sick body? Body can be known only as of consciousness, God—as perfect body, and it is just as much thought as is $2\times2=4$. The thing that makes you think that body is material is the false concept you entertain of its origin. Then take it to its true origin. You could not cognize it except as mental. Can you deal with it if you are thinking of matter as matter; as substance, as a thing? As matter, a thing could not get outside its own limited outline. Everything that comes to you comes as consciousness.

Jesus saw that this false sense of matter-held-as-substance would finally give place to the true sense of matter-held-as-shadow. Jesus gave the laboratory experiment. That was his mission. He foresaw that the scientific explanation of his experiment would be left to the "Comforter," which appeared in the Revelator's vision as the "little book." Today we have its scientific elucidation in Science and Health, and this is destined to win all mankind.

There is not one thing to change or be destroyed. You recognize that there is something operating as Mind, as consciousness to you. Then you translate that something back into Mind. " 'The new tongue' is the spiritual meaning as opposed to the material. It is the language of Soul instead of the senses; it translates matter into its original language, which is Mind, and gives a spiritual instead of a material signification." (Hea. 7:8)

Why accept a sick this or a sick that, when matter in its true sense, rightly understood, is the presence of Mind? Why not clear up these abstractions and be in the kingdom of heaven *now* and see matter shadowing forth Mind?

Is not this understanding of the true sense of matter, seeing Spirit as All-in-all, the ushering in of the kingdom of heaven on earth? Is it not this infinite freedom and opportunity that is feebly symbolized by the King's Chamber in the Great Pyramid?

This Chamber, as calculated by Pyramid mathmeticians, is chronologically to be entered September 15-16 of this year, following a number of years of severe depression as typified by the low passageways leading to it. This King's Chamber portrays the last message carried by this "Miracle in Stone" down through the ages to the present day. Surely it will prove the truth of the symbolism by which it has sometimes been designated "The Hall of the Judgments of the Nations." The judgment of matter by Spirit.

Mrs. Eddy asks the question, "Who wants to be mortal, or would not gain the true ideal of Life and recover his own individuality?" (Mis. Wr. 104:28) Do you think it possible to be individual when held by a false sense of body as matter? Jesus said, in substance, to those who persecuted him,

"All right, take my body and do with it as you please." His confidence in the truth proved his body to be spiritual, perfect and indestructible. Is your body different in any way from his? His power lay in the sense he entertained about body. Does the sense you entertain about body differ from the sense Jesus entertained?

If so, why? "Who wants to be mortal, or would not gain the true ideal of Life and recover his own individuality? I will love, if another hates. I will gain a balance on the side of good, my true being. This alone gives me the forces of God wherewith to overcome all error. On this rests the implicit faith engendered by Christian Science, which appeals intelligently to the facts of man's spirituality, individuality, to disdain the fears and destroy the discords of this material personality." (Mis. Wr. 104:29) Consider carefully the expression, "disdain the fears," have an utter contempt for them. But how can you expect to have *implicit* faith to disdain fear if you surrender your individuality?

How can you "recover your individuality"? How can you preserve it and keep it? By understanding what you are dealing with every moment. "Bring ye all the tithes into the storehouse, that there may be meat in mine house, and prove me now herewith, saith the Lord of hosts, if I will not open you the windows of heaven, and pour you out a blessing, that there shall not be room enough to receive it." (Mal. 3:10)

Lift the veil. See all in the kingdom of Spirit now where not a single thing is withheld from you.

The whole attack that is being made in the world today is upon individuality. Even in this, the most enlightened country in the world, it is the same. If any effort is made that touches your individuality, it is simply pure devil, the one evil; because individuality and Science are the same, for Science means exact knowledge, isness, and that means man's oneness with Being, God, in other words his individuality.

The oneness of man with his Principle is his individuality. If it could be touched, it would destroy Christianity. To believe this you need only to look at Russia. She did away with individuality—regimenting her people and what did that *try* to do to Christianity? Christianity demands that you "Work out your own salvation." (Phil. 2:12)

America is the highest expression of individuality. All this subtle attempt appearing as relief, pensioning—having something done for you, is the attempt to turn man from looking unreservedly to God. It is the stuff the mediumship of priestcraft is made of, only in this case it is the mediumship of political priestcraft.

Communism, Naziism, Fascism, Kemalism, etc., together with the New Deal, are all for the one purpose of eventually destroying individualism.

In this country, the attack upon individuality comes in a more subtle form, cloaking itself under the guise of benevolence. Had it not been for the Supreme Court of the United States might we not be regimented today, marching under bureaucratic commands from Washington? Be on your guard if something intrudes itself between you and God. Present methods of relief, old age pensions, etc., are all forms of this effort to supplant God, and in the end would have all looking to Washington instead of to Mind. To person instead of to Principle.

The Townsend Plan has intrigued many earnest Christian Scientists. Could it function except on the basis of dying to make room for others?

Then is it not based on death? If the ten million first qualified do not die, where would there be room for the succeeding eligible millions? If a plan is based on death, is it worth a moment's consideration?

I have been asked if I did not think the Townsend Plan might be God's way of working out the old age financial problem. Jesus gave the true illustration of God's way. He was the way, the truth and the life. Did he not have everything? He had the supper prepared for his disciples, he had the money for the taxes from the fish's mouth and he fed the multitude by means of Mind, not by governmental largess. "Let us have a clearing up of abstractions" and "Give to Mind the glory, honor, dominion, and power everlastingly due its holy name." (S. & H. 143:30) If we did that would we not have the answer?

If people can not be taken care of here, can they be taken care of hereafter? Is there any difference between here and hereafter? "Let us come into the presence of Him who removeth all iniquities, and healeth all our diseases." Why do we not come into this presence NOW? How could it be easier to get your daily bread hereafter? We are responsible for all delusions because we do not clear up these abstractions.

You ask, "What about teachers' pensions?"

A pension you have earned is somewhat different. It has been taken off your salary and is ostensibly a saving plan. However, do not forget that all public pension plans must eventually declare, "Excuse me if you are going to live forever. You will have to die within a reasonable length of time or we can not continue in business" All these devices undermine your *"implicit* faith engendered by Christian Science, which appeals intelligently to the facts of man's spirituality, individuality, to disdain the fears and destroy the discords of this material personality." All they offer is included in the belief of material personality—belief in matter as substance.

You are not afraid of losing the multiplication table because it is pure Mind. If matter is seen simply as an error of *statement* and not an error of *thing,* then you would quickly correct this error and be done with it. "Destroy the thought of sin, sickness, death, and you destroy their existence." (Mis. Wr. 105:28) How could matter *act* as a thing? How could non-intelligence have something the matter with it?

You must answer with your whole heart for the faith that is within you. No longer think of matter-held-as-substance, of matter as matter, as a negative unreversed, but of matter-held-as-shadow; then you will be in the kingdom now, in the "abode of Spirit, the realm of the real." (Mis. Wr. 174:16)

On the point of individuality, we must see that it is guarded at every angle. The subtle attacks upon individuality will become greater. It is marvelous that when it was so crudely attempted as in the N.R.A. and other New Deal regimentations, that the spirit of the Pilgrim Fathers did not arise spontaneously and unanimously and repudiate it. The South, too, even bowed its knee in spite of its cherished doctrine of States' Rights.

Each one must be on guard. How could American business men and women have consented to such a thing? Having all your actions dictated! One towering character was not influenced. Henry Ford stood right out against it. It came with such a subtle appeal that most business men and women forgot the rock whence they were hewn and ran to anything that promised an easier way than individual initiative and fortitude. They should not have forgotten their individual rights. However, the Supreme Court of the United States was not deceived.

Some feel that should Mr. Roosevelt be reelected and, in the course of the next few years, two or three members of the Supreme Court should die, they might be replaced by those who would be subservient to the demand of the President. Do you accept the hypnotic suggestion that when on the Supreme Bench, whoever is appointed would not act under the guidance of God? What is the Supreme Court and Who is the one Mind guiding that Court? The office is far bigger than the person filling it.

When fear says that if Mr. Roosevelt should be reelected, things will go wrong and become still more un-American, we must remember what the office of the President of the United States of America is, that the office is too big to be debased. Because Mind is All-in-all, then Mind is all there is to the President, to the Supreme Court, to the Congress.

The way is clear. We are not waiting on person or circumstance. We are in the kingdom of God now. How few it would take to bring in the millineum if those few were of one Mind! Mrs. Eddy declared in one of her classes, "We, today, in this class-room, are enough to convert the world if we are of one Mind." (Mis. Wr. 279:31) "Again I say unto you, That if two of you shall agree on earth as touching any thing that they shall ask, it shall be done for them of my Father which is in heaven. For where two or three are gathered together in my name, there am I in the midst of them." (Matt. 18:19, 20)

Then let us discern "the spiritual fact of whatever the material senses behold." (S. & H. 585:11) Let us replace matter with Spirit, translate material personality back into Mind, relinquish fear and be at peace.

There may appear to be a great many confusing beliefs. Christian Scientists wonder why they are fettered at times, when they are earnestly looking to Mind. They should be alert and know what is confusing them. They have understood the *theory* about matter, but have they acted upon it? Have they been dealing with Spirit, or have they been bowing down to matter as matter?

There is one fundamental fact back of all disease.

Mr. Frederick Dixon healed a prominent physician of what was considered an incurable disease, and thereafter the two became good friends. Later in conversation Mr. Dixon put the question to him as to how much of disease he thought was attributable to lust, to venereal poison. The physician thought for a moment and then said, "About 50 per cent." Mr. Dixon replied, "Only 50 per cent?" After another pause the doctor said, "Well, perhaps 65 per cent." "You think only 65 per cent?" "Well, no, possibly 85 per cent." "You would say not more than 85 per cent?" "Well, yes, 100 per cent."

You see how reluctant mortal mind was to admit this. Why? Science and Health states that "Until the author of this book learned the vastness of Christian Science, the fixedness of mortal illusions, and the human hatred of Truth, she cherished sanguine hopes that Christian Science would meet with immediate and universal acceptance." (330:2) This doctor was healed and was grateful, but, even he, though knowing the fact, had to be led on to admit that material conception holds within itself the cause of all disease and death.

Are you puzzled about the cause of disease? What seems to be a conception is a mental declaration. If there is no matter-as-substance, then so-called matter is a state of mind, is a misstatement of divine Mind, of divine Life. Consequently a conception which seems to be a material conception, must have death as its basis in contradistinction to Life. It is a negative statement of the true. Mortal mind's declaration, "I am born," is identical with the declaration of venereal poison, "I am the origin of man."

Every child that is born falls automatically under this false belief of law—a law of poison. It is attached to each one. Materially, a child is a statement of venereal poison. If you do not handle this suggestion, it works out the ends of death—age, decrepitude, everything that would destroy. Would you work this out in a weak, ineffectual, vacillating sort of a way, or would you face it squarely and vigorously? You are headed for a place six feet deep and six feet long unless the "law of the Spirit of life in Christ Jesus" makes you "free from the law of sin and death." (Rom. 8:2)

You are not responsible for this law. No sinner or sick man has anything to do with his sickness or sin as such. But the law of sin and death —evil suggestion, must find nothing in you, no answering chord upon which to play its tune. Your responsibility is to reverse the evil suggestion, which, when reversed, is the very presence of God.

Are you awake to this? How is the world going to be redeemed if you do not do it? Nothing but your righteousness, nothing but your rightness, nothing but your knowing, will do it. Can you do this if you keep on accepting the lie and doing the things which take you to the grave?

Christian Scientists sometimes wonder why they are so bound. "Do not think to deceive yourselves by deceiving others," Mrs. Eddy declares, "for Wisdom will call you into judgment for all you think and act, and the tribunal before which your true position is tried and proved is the demonstration that you are able to give of healing the sick, after learning the principle upon which this is done, and the only one by which you can succeed to the most marvelous instances of cure." (Science of Man, p. 16) Why not be honest? Do we not have to demonstrate the truth and be the living witness of what God is?

Really and earnestly to get down to business and understand what this venereal poison is, what this is which is supposed to course through the veins, through the life blood, is something that must be done—it must be faced. It is a mental poison that goes on and on until you are sufficiently distressed to be willing to stop thinking in terms of being born. It is something that must be handled all the time. A passing thought will not accomplish the work. Jesus said, "Woe unto them that are with child, and to them that give suck in those days!" (Matt. 24:19) In other words, Woe unto him that believes either that he can give birth to something or was ever given birth to, was ever formed and sustained materially.

You ask, "Why do I have aches and pains?" and then you run perhaps in fear to a doctor only too often to have your fears increased, instead of turning to Mind, going into your "closet" and shutting the door and saying to yourself, "Now, what do I know about Mind?"

A little thing may be the cause of your trouble, and what more apparently insignificant thing, (as far as being considered of vital importance) than that you were born? And yet venereal poison—being born—is the conception of the exact opposite of Mind, Life, and is itself death; a thing of life, but actually death. Why not meet this intelligently and not let anything turn you aside? Every intelligent physician has to admit what Mr. Dixon's friend admitted—that venereal poison, being born, is fundamentally back of every ill.

Seeing that you never were begotten, that you never could begin, is the essential point. Neither could your body, which is Mind's interpretation of Himself, have a beginning.

Then ask yourself the question, "With what am I being mentally poisoned?" There is no more substance to the body than there is to the image in the mirror. The image has no substance of itself. The moment there is a change in the object in front of the mirror, the image changes. The thing that makes the image is what you are accepting as Mind. This determines body, friend, world. What you determine Mind to be determines the image. Mind is your being. Your oneness with Mind appears as your body, your friend, your world. Could Mind, the You of you, have a stiff leg or a stiff arm?

Or a stiff heart? "And I will take the stony heart out of their flesh; and will give them an heart of flesh: That they may walk in my statutes, and keep mine ordinances: and they shall be my people and I will be their God." (Ez. 11:19, 20) The heart of stone is unwillingness to be obedient to Mind. "I am going to do what I want to do!" You must be willing to get a heart of flesh.

Destroy this miserable belief of being born and giving birth to children and worshipping them. The way to find the child of God is to have God All-in-all. You will get the sense of increasing number without attaching to it the sting of venereal poison.

You remember the true Postulates given in Science and Health as "The chief stones in the Temple of Christian Science": "that Life is God, good, and not evil; that Soul is sinless, not to be found in the body; that Spirit is not, and cannot be, materialized; that Life is not subject to death: that the spiritual real man has no birth, no material life, and no death." (288:20)

Also you remember the erroneous Postulates which Science and Health says must be "considered in order that the spiritual facts may be better apprehended."

"That substance, life and intelligence are something apart from God."

"That man is both mental and material."

"That mind is both evil and good; whereas the real Mind cannot be evil nor the medium of evil, for Mind is God."

"That matter is intelligent, and that man has a material body which is part of himself."

"That matter holds in itself the issues of life and death—that matter is not only capable of experiencing pleasure and pain, but also capable of imparting these sensations. From the illusion implied in this last postulate arises the decomposition of mortal bodies in what is termed death." (91:22)

Ponder these postulates and follow this whole line to its ultimate and see that the false sense of matter is all that must be corrected. You must translate "matter into its original language, which is Mind, and give the spiritual instead of the material signification." (Hea. 7:8) Be able to say with Paul, "For I know whom I have believed, and am persuaded that he is able to keep that which I have committed unto him." (II Tim. 1 :11)

Can we do better than faithfully and intelligently to study and live Mrs. Eddy's prayer? — " 'Thy kingdom come'; let the reign of divine Truth, Life, and Love be established in me, and rule out of me all sin; and may Thy Word enrich the affections of all mankind and govern them !"

This can only be done by seeing Spirit as All-in-all whether appearing as matter-held-as-shadow, which is the idea of God ; or as matter-held-as-substance, which is belief and error—the negative of Spirit which must be reversed.

And truly what is the negative of Spirit? Having used all these words have we really grasped the true meaning of the negative of Spirit? The whole purpose of this meeting will have been lost unless we clearly see and understand that what we are dealing with, every instant, in the realm of belief, is divine Mind negatively interpreted, in other words direction by malicious minds, and never matter or material things whether seemingly appearing as what is called person, place or thing. It only appears as a belief of person, place or thing merely to deceive, while all the time it is simply pure hypnotic suggestion and never anything of the corporeal senses.

In whatever guise every erroneous sense seems to appear, it can only be successfully handled as it is recognized for what it really is, malignant animal magnetism, and taken back to its divine Source, the one All-embracing Mind, where it is "swallowed up of Life" in divine Love, as Paul expresses it, where all its maliciousness spontaneously vanishes, and the so-called victim of the illusion walks forth clothed and in his right mind.

"Then shall Christian Science again appear, to light our sepulchres with immortality." (Peo. 8 :23)

TRANSLATION

of

"THE FALSE PROPHET" OF REVELATION

INTO MIND,

ENDING ALL WARFARE

COPYRIGHT 1953

TRANSLATION OF "THE FALSE PROPHET" OF REVELATION
INTO MIND ENDING ALL WARFARE

The following is a combined summary of addresses delivered at meetings of those who had been through class with me, together with invited guests.

The meetings were held, 1952-3, in London, England, New York, N.Y., Los Angeles and Berkeley, California.

The subject largely under consideration was, Christian Science translates the "false prophet" of Revelation, into Mind; the complete abandonment of the Christian or matter Era for the Christian Science Era, the Ascension Era, in which *"All is infinite Mind and its infinite manifestation, for God is All-in-all."*

NOTE: All statements by Mrs. Eddy, whether from her books or attributed to her, are printed in italics. I feel that every truthful statement made in Christian Science can rightfully be attributed to the Revelator of Christian Science, because it must always come from the one divine Mind which is the Mind of the Revelator and the source of the Revelation. — H. W. E.

Mrs. Eddy has said: *"When I see a student grateful, I know he is safe."* Science and Health declares, *"If we are ungrateful for Life, Truth, and Love, and yet return thanks to God for all blessings, we are insincere and incur the sharp censure our Master pronounces on hypocrites."* Surely this means that the only gratitude that is gratitude is the realization of absolute oneness with God—it has nothing to do with any outward appearance. Here, again, gratitude is only possible in the conscious realization that now I am in the Ascension period, with not a single sense of matter whatever. Any thought of matter mars the picture and makes true gratitude impossible.

Mrs. Eddy also made a statement to the effect that *"ingratitude is the original sum total of evil and its only remedy is gratitude—the highest human quality—its destruction."* It is said that a grateful heart goes all the way, and that is what brought you here today. In addition, I think, two statements, one by Jesus and the other by Mrs. Eddy, express our real attitude of mind—that of being lifted up from "the earth" and that of listening for the voice of God, which will raise our thought above the belief in matter to the realm of Spirit, where the reality of all things dwells.

The first was a statement of Jesus, "And I, if I be lifted up from the earth, will draw all men unto me." The second quotation is a beautiful prayer by Mrs. Eddy, *"Father, teach me how to still the clamoring of sense and fill my place as listener, that I may hear Thy voice and grow to understand Thy word and so become Thy messenger. Then teach me how to banish pride and stubborn will that I may be Thy representative, with no false sense of human zeal, that every word may bless and heal when I Thy message give."*

We know Jesus was not referring to drawing people unto him. He was declaring that as he rose himself in the understanding of what Consciousness really is, he would spontaneously find everyone already there, at his same altitude of thought. This is very important because we have got to establish oneness before we can go ahead, and he was there speaking as one: "And I, if I be lifted up from the earth . . ." He did not say, if *you* be lifted up from the earth.

Just remember that there is only one here; that one is God and His idea. You stand as the idea of God, and God is expressing Himself to you in whatever language will be most helpful to you, but you are the man of God and there is only God and His idea. You are this idea, this man.

There is not one word that can be spoken here today that is not already known to you, for the one Intelligence is omnipresent and is your very Mind. Therefore nothing new can be presented to you, but rather, Love is reminding each one constantly, of his already knowing. Always remember that, as God's idea, man does now know all, and man necessarily includes everyone.

Remember, too, that you never can tell anyone anything that he does not already know as such man of God. Be very clear on this, for it is most important to assure the easy flow of all that you say and do and it bars opposition. Should you believe there was a mind that did not already know what was appearing as your giving, you would spontaneusly open the way for opposition. You might find yourself robbed of some of the clarity that you had before, for, you remember that Jesus warned us of "the fowls of the air," waiting to snatch away the good seed. So let us start out today, each one knowing that he does know all that God has for him and that one does not have more than another.

In order to follow through as we have got to do—in order to really get at the pith of the whole meeting, which is to show what evil is and how it is to be seen through and so eliminated—you must understand that you are God's man and there is only one man. Now in order to do that, I will have to ask those who are familiar with what one might call the "modus operandi" of establishing this, to bear with me while I carefully present it, because it is like the old, old story that we used to sing of and that we loved to tell. However, this is a story that you cannot tell yourself too often and neither can you ever reach the end. It is like all Truth; it keeps unfolding to you. That is why Paul was so particular to impress this, when he said, "If any man thinketh he knoweth anything, (that covers a great deal of ground) he knoweth nothing yet as he ought to know it." So when you hear words that you have heard maybe, many times before, and repeated many times to yourself, listen for a new ring to them, watch for increased light.

You remember Jesus came to his disciples towards the end of his career, and said to them, "A new commandment I give unto you." Don't you think their ears were instantly open for some easy way of getting into the kingdom of heaven? They thought he was going to give them a short cut, perhaps, but he simply said, "that ye love one another." Don't you think he had said that many, many times during the three years he had spent with them? Yet he repeated it. Must it not have had a higher meaning, even to him? Then must it not have been intended to convey something really new to them, too, if they had opened their hearts and minds to it? That is the nature of Truth always, infinitely unfolding. You are listening— that is your prayer—"*that I may fill my place as listener.*" Man is not original; he is the listener of God. God is original and He imparts everything to His idea, man.

I have had a good deal of comfort from the statement of Mrs. Eddy where she said, *"God is responsible for the mission of those whom He has anointed."* Remember, God has one man and He anoints His own man, doesn't He? Well, this means you. He anoints you. *"God is responsible for the mission of those whom He has anointed. Those who know no will but His, take His hand, and from the night He leads to light. None can say unto Him, 'What doest Thou?' "* You are that anointed man.

I have found it very helpful, in my experience in presenting Christian Science to a new, what you call, individual, to think of the one before me as an atheist, who comes right out and says frankly, "There isn't any God." He has given his position perfectly, and so we know exactly what we are up against. So, suppose you are the atheist; then my first question to you would be, what?—is there anything that you actually know of yourself? An atheist is apt to think he knows a great deal of himself, just as you and I maybe are frequently hypnotized to do, but he is puzzled with that question, right away, because, like so many, he has never asked himself the question, "Is there anything in all the world that I know actually of myself?" Mind you, that means no sense testimony allowed at all, because that you do not know of yourself. What the eyes see, what the ears hear, and so forth— that is handed out to you. It is not something that you actually know of yourself. So, finally, being a thoughtful fellow, he says, "Well, yes, there is one thing I do know of myself—I am. No one tells me that. I haven't read it, I haven't heard it, or anything. I simply am." Incidentally, you cannot say you *find* yourself, because you do not; you are not standing off and looking at yourself. It is merely a state of awareness.

That is the only thing you actually know of yourself in all the world, so you see your knowledge is not very much, but it is abundance, however, for it is what the Bible calls, "The light that lighteth every man that cometh into the world."

Well, how shall we describe that? Will you be satisfied if I use the expression, "I consciously am"? The atheist says, "Yes, I'll accept that. I see that that defines it; I see the value of the adverb. If I said, 'I am conscious' then I would have to be conscious of something. That would put me in the category of cause and not effect, and self-evidently, I am effect because I did not make myself." That is true; man has no knowledge whatever, of himself. He simply is an awareness—"I consciously am." That is all.

The atheist now says, "All right, I accept that, but where do we go from here?" Immediately we say to him, "Well, is there anything about that consciously am-ness, or being, that gives you any idea, or implies anything, or indicates anything?" Again he stops and thinks it over, because he has never asked himself that question before, either; and doubtless many of you may not have done, although I think you all have or you would not be here. Finally he says, "Why yes, there is something, because when I accept the fact I consciously am, because necessarily I did not make myself, I accept it as a statement of effect. I also accept the fact, therefore, that there is cause, for you cannot have effect without cause."

Of course, he has now hit the nail perfectly on the head, because there must be a primary to that secondary, consciously being. So we ask him, "What should we call the cause? Will you agree to use a similar term and call it Consciousness? Because if it is the primary of consciously being, then it is perfectly right to use the noun Consciousness; then it automatically follows that 'Consciousness is'." He says, "Yes, I'll accept that.

Then where do we go from here?" He's keen now. He sees he is up against something he had not thought of before. He accepted atheism—that there is no God—just because he did not know anything better to do. Now he is beginning to see that that is being rapidly displaced. We have established with him, that Consciousness is, and must be, or he could not consciously be.

From now on, the "I consciously am" cuts no more ice. You do not use it any further in Christian Science. It is only used in this one inductive reasoning, establishing that Consciousness must first be, or I could not consciously be,—never again.

"Now then," we continue with the atheist, "you admit that Consciousness is. What do you know about the little word 'is'?" You see, every step in Christian Science is based on the fundamental truth of being—isness.

Jesus, in one sense of the word, did not have anything to do with Christian Science. The Bible does not teach you Christian Science. It sometimes illustrates it. But you now, as a Christian Scientist, read the Bible through the eyes of Christian Science and so read into it Christian Science. You do not get Christian Science from any source whatever, except from Science and Health taking you to its own source, the one divine Mind. You base everything on that. It takes you to its own source, which is Mind, and it is your basing it on Mind that establishes for you the whole of Christian Science and enables you to demonstrate it.

People imagine that Christian Science has in some way originated. They talk about Mrs. Eddy being the discoverer of Christian Science, and she used the term herself, but not in the popular way, which uses the term as it would be applied to, say, Edison, or to other wonderful discoverers along materially scientific lines. There, every step is along the lines of material sense.

Mrs. Eddy did not get Christian Science from any such source. Mrs. Eddy's was the revelation of divine Mind. You recall that what appeared to the Virgin-mother as Jesus, was the revelation to her that God was the Father of man. Now, Christian Science came as the revelation to Mary Baker Eddy, purely spiritually, without any parentage of any kind and therefore embracing the fact that God is the Father-Mother of man—the entire creator. These are important points that you must make your own, by thinking them out spiritually.

Remember you are individual. You are not going into the kingdom of heaven on anybody's skirts, whether called Science and Health, or the Bible, or Christ Jesus, or anything else. You are going in on your own understanding of what God is and what man must be, and in no other way. So, be willing to think it out. You have got to take every step, just as you do in mathematics. You have got to take every step of the road, and there is no royal road in Christian Science.

Before we get through with this communion, we are going to be confronted with exactly where we stand and what the path is that we have to take, and this may appear quite different from what has been the ordinary sense of it—mixing up with matter and with life, truth, intelligence, and substance in matter.

Each one of us could well afford, periodically, to talk to himself as though he were the atheist. We have got to be convinced, each one of us, that I am actually this man of God, that I am the conscious identity of this one Consciousness. I am at the point of "is," and I am the one who asks, "What do I know about is?" The thoughtful person instantly says, "Why there is nothing outside of it. It would not be possible. That which is must necessarily be all that is, for there is and can be nothing outside of it." Now you see, your atheist friend, who accepts this instantly, has followed right through and at once discerns the fundamental truth of that important point, that this Consciousness that is, is actually All that is, because "Is" cannot be less than All. If anything was not *is*, it would be is not, wouldn't it? That would wipe it out; so "Is" is all there is, and he sees that. Then we ask him, "When you say *All,* do you mean infinite?" "Of course," he assents, "because how can there be anything outside of All." "Well, then, do you mean by infinite, one?" "Certainly, you could not have two infinites. There can only be just one." He has now established for himself, the fact that Consciousness, being Is, is one, is All, and is infinite. You see he has gone a long way along the path of establishing his God.

I ought to say that in establishing this Consciousness that is, you also establish, of course, all the terms that Mrs. Eddy has used for God, and so you find that you have one infinite God, divine Love, infinite Life, Truth, Intelligence, Substance, everything, and that is your God, your Consciousness, your Mind, of which you are the conscious identity; and there is One and One only, one God, one man, never two. Infinite God and infinity of expression fill the immensity of Mind. There is no divisional point in Mind, therefore not in idea. Then your listener might say, "But I have a husband, a wife, a child," this, that, and the other appearance. How do you know you have? How do you know you have a hand? Doesn't it come as consciousness to you? That is the only way you know you have a hand. It has to first register, as it were, as Consciousness, and then you call that registering, hand. But it is not something apart, in any way, from this Consciousness that is your Consciousness. It comes to you as the impartation of God—of Consciousness to you.

"Well," he says, "but what happens to all these others?" Why, they stay exactly as they are now. You call them persons, places, and things, but as a matter of fact, they are simply God interpreting Himself to you and appearing as persons, places, and things exactly as best suited to supply your every need. If this were not true you would never accomplish your way into the kingdom of heaven for you would not find the infinity of variety of idea there with you, and so your heaven would not be heaven, completeness. How far do you think you would get in using mathematics if it were dependent on persons, places, and things? Your understanding of God and man is one, regardless of the way in which it may appear to you. That is the reason, and the only reason, you have power over it, because you find it as your communion with God.

Now we are admonished, "Awake thou that sleepest," and "put on the armor of light." Christian Science has come to wake us up, not to lull us to sleep. We have got to wake up and see that it is up to us to be the Christian Scientist. How many Christian Scientists are there? Just one. And who is that one? God. And how is God expressed? As you. You are His expression, from the least to the greatest, even "to the minutest detail." All right, we have now settled we have one God and one man. That is what we have been after, because you must, in order to progress, find yourself that man; which you have now done.

Now we will turn our attention to the Bible for a few minutes. It is your Bible. Everything is yours, registering as Consciousness with you this instant and every instant. First, you start off with and find you have Adam and Eve. Are you that Adam and Eve? Of course you are. Do not be afraid to say it. You are all there is to Adam and Eve. Are you Abraham, Isaac, Jacob, Moses, and the prophets—coming right down? Are those conditions of thought that come to you? Of course they are. Does not Science and Health in its Glossary give the spiritual definition of each one? You would have no cognizance of them whatever, unless they came as Consciousness to you and were embraced in that which is consciousness to you. Mrs. Eddy puts that so well. She says in Pulpit and Press, page 4:7, *"Is not a man metaphysically and mathematically number one, a unit, and therefore whole number, governed and protected by his divine Principle, God? You have simply to preserve a scientific, positive sense of unity with your divine source, and daily demonstrate this. Then you will find that one is as important a factor as duodecillions in being and doing right, and thus demonstrating deific Principle . . . and therefore is the seer's declaration true, that 'one on God's side is a majority'."* You are that one. Stand on that because, with the responsibility that it brings, it brings you also the greatest sense of power. That is the thing. It brings you what man is, the very voice and power of God. God could not be without His man, He would spontaneously cease for He would have no expression and so be without entity.

Mrs. Eddy says in Unity of Good, 46:9, *"The scientific man and his Maker are here; and you would be none other than this man, if you would subordinate the fleshly perceptions to the spiritual sense and source of being."* She also makes the statement, *"When a man begins to see himself as the reflection of God, and to recognize that he has within himself the capacity to act as possessing all power from Him in Whom we live and move and have our being, he has reached the highest of all endowments and fruitful of all good works."* Now that only comes as you begin to see that you are the reflection of God. That realization endows you with the whole power of infinite God, and nothing can stop you, having reached *"the highest of all endowments and fruitful of all good works."* Keep clearly before you always, the truth of the omnipotence of God and the fact that God expresses himself as you, and always as *law*, for His word is law. Know that you cannot be deceived. The whole purpose of evil, as the negation of Truth, is to lie and deceive, because it can do nothing else. It would make you think there is some way of escaping real earnest knowing, but there is only one road—the way of understanding. As Solomon put it: "With all thy getting, get understanding." Faith will not do it. Nothing will do it except understanding and its continuous application, even as with the multiplication tables. You have this understanding. Use it—you know the rock whence you are hewn.

Now let us return to the Bible. You do see that this Adam and this accompanying term Eve are not two, but one—God "called their name Adam," you remember, not Adam and Eve. It is evil that has done that, divided them to you in belief. But Adam is your Adam, and the Eve of that Adam is Adam's highest spiritual sense, that which spiritualizes evil, and it was the spiritualizing of evil which declared, "The serpent beguiled me and I did eat." She did not, like Adam, blame it on God, with, "The woman Thou gavest to be with me, she gave me . . . and I did eat." Adam threw it right back on God, didn't he? But the feminine quality of Mind—the highest quality of being—is that which redeems Adam, every single time. That is why, because Eve spiritualized all things, she was the mother of all living. In other words, nothing can or does live that is not spiritualized.

That applies to your business; it applies to your body; it applies to everything about you. Unless you translate the so-called lie that is presenting itself to you—unless you translate it back to God, in other words, spiritualize it—it cannot live. It will fail. Remember, Eve was declared the mother of all living, because only that which is spiritualized can really live. Eve was the spiritual or highest sense of Adam.

You remember that from that spiritualization from that enmity God put between the serpent and the woman, alone could come the redeemer that would declare, "I have come that they might have life and that they might have it more abundantly." That is all going on with you. Don't let that escape you for a minute.

Eve had spiritualized this whole temptation of the so-called apple and serpent business, and this spiritualization destroyed materialization, so that she spontaneously became the mother of all living. This expressed itself in the assurance that she should be the mother of the redeemer. In due time it actually appeared as the Virgin-mother, without any Adam accompanying it at all—without any so-called masculine sense attaching itself to it, although Adam-Eve are never separate—but the feminine quality took the ascendancy. The feminine sense brought forth alone, what was called the child Jesus, born of the Holy Spirit. That was Mary seeing clearly that God was the Father of man—Eve had now risen to seeing Wisdom as the one Father. That was as far as she went because it was as far as we could go at that time in our experience. There is no nineteen hundred years to any of this. It is right this very moment. All of it is. Otherwise, nothing would be of any value to you. Suppose two times two is four was just a thousand years ago, what good would it be to you? It is an actual fact now. And so Christian Science is a fact to you now, and it is available for your use, but only as you understand it.

Then who was really the Virgin-mother? It was your highest feminine quality of Mind discerning God as the Father of man. That was you. It was you that brought forth the child Jesus. Now, don't shut your eyes and minds to this, but open them and begin to see: why, of course it must have been me or how could I know anything about it? How could I know anything about nineteen hundred years ago, unless it was this very moment? It must register as now, or it would not mean a thing. It must be this moment because Mind is instantaneous. It is this instant.

Then you see that what appeared as Jesus—as a more abundant sense of life—was a redeeming of your mind. It showed forth God as the Father of man. Jesus showed forth the "last Adam," the quickening spirit, as the redeeming of the first Adam, a living sense. Mrs. Eddy speaks of Jesus as the *"highest human corporeal concept of the divine idea."* That was not spiritual. There was nothing spiritual to Jesus. The Christ—yes, that is different. Jesus was simply your highest human corporeal concept of the divine idea, as Science and Health defines it for you. Do you think there was anything of real spiritual Christian Science about the highest human corporeal concept of anything? Why no. It did not touch Christian Science at all. It was touching exactly what it had to touch. And what was that? The belief that all is matter. Jesus was confronted with one thing. He stood as the personal presentation of God to man. In other words, he stood as your personal presentation of God redeeming your sense. And what did it have to meet and redeem? The personal presentation of evil, matter.

Jesus' mission was not to introduce Christian Science, for he was the personal presentation of God and dealt entirely with the things, as it were, of the flesh; whereas Christian Science does not touch the things of matter, but only those of Mind.

Jesus made the way for Christian Science by clearing out every belief that matter was anything but a myth, proving there was *"no life, truth, intelligence, nor substance in matter."* Thus he left the field entirely free for the unfoldment of Mind.

It was at this point of Mind that you became aware of Christian Science, and from which it proceeded. In other words, Christian Science operates at the Ascension point, only. It functions only in the realm of the Ascension, where *"All is infinite Mind and its infinite manifestation, for God is All-in-all."* This must never be lost sight of by the Christian Scientist or he loses his power to demonstrate Christian Science. There is no possible way in which Mind can operate in the realm of matter—if there were such a thing as matter, which there is not—for they are opposites. Christian Science must always be in the pure realm of Mind.

Consider this most significant language of Mrs. Eddy in speaking of the two appearings of the Christ. She said, *"Jesus, no doubt, supplied the literal loaf and fish to their sense, so as to impress upon them at that period, the Christian Era, the fact of his twofold power, as the Wayshower or mediator between the things of the flesh and those of the Spirit. His mission on earth was this, declaratively and demonstrably from the beginning to the end."*

Jesus was the Wayshower because he showed the absolute nothingness of matter in every respect and proved there was *"no life, truth, intelligence, nor substance in matter,"* to the minutest detail. He was the Mediator, because he showed the correlation of the spirit and the flesh in such instances as feeding the multitude with five barley loaves and a few small fish and the restoration of the flesh to the withered hand. Jesus showed there could be no demand without the supply being simultaneous with the demand. Hence, the correlation of the flesh, the demand, and the spirit, the supply; Thus he mediated between the two. This, Mrs. Eddy pointed out, was the mission of Jesus on earth, *"declaratively and demonstrably from beginning to end."*

But, note carefully how Mrs. Eddy continued her statement, *"Not so is the Christ appearing at this age. Now is it rather to show through Science, and not the senses, the power of Spirit and of Good, and to spiritualize all the meaning of the Christ, to name Christ the idea and not the person of God, and to impress, at this period, the Science of Spirit on the mind through Truth, and the phenomena of Mind and not matter. To voice God less in parable and more in the facts of Being. This must be the true interpretation of the parable of the loaves and fishes, because Jesus could in no other way have made the way for the Second appearing of Christ in Science."*

Is it not self-evidently plain what Mrs. Eddy was bringing out here, that Jesus had his particular era of operation, and that his wondrous function was to prove, actually, from every standpoint that matter was a complete myth, that it had no life, that it had no truth, that it had no intelligence, and finally, that it had no substance. He did his work so perfectly, that he showed from every angle, that there was nothing to matter; and that was his work in order to prepare the way for the final appearing of the Christ as Christian Science, which operates wholly in the realm of Mind, without a semblance of matter attached. That is why Mrs. Eddy tells us we fail in our demonstrations of Christian Science, because we do not know *"how to handle animal magnetism."* She further says that if we do not break the belief that mesmerism has power, we are still the victims of mesmerism and it is handling us. Is not this like saying you have only one thing to handle in Christian Science, and that one thing is mesmerism, animal magnetism, or to give it its full title, malicious mind with its operating activity, malicious mental malpractice or malpractitioner.

It is useless to try to operate in the realm of matter—we finished that nineteen hundred years ago and since, we are not in that realm at all. We have graduated to Mind. Remember when you got through with arithmetic, you went right into algebra and from then on, you worked algebraically and no longer arithmetically. So in Christian Science you no longer work from the basis of persons, places, and things, as in the Christian or Jesus era, but you work with Mind, and Mind alone, destroying the belief that there is malicious mind, because there is and can be only one Mind, infinite God.

There, Mrs. Eddy points out, is our failure, because we are still hanging on to the "bone" that divine compassion threw to us when we first touched the hem of Christian Science. God in His infinite Love, in Bible language, "winked at the times of our ignorance," and gave to us in those times of ignorance a terse statement of fact. Through our *"highest human corporeal concept of the divine idea,"* we had proved this statement of fact, as positively as it could be done—there is no life, there is no truth, there is no intelligence, there is no substance in matter. This is a direct statement of fact, nothing to do with Christian Science, except that every statement of fact is truth and so is embraced in the All-truth of Christian Science. But apart from that, there is no more Christian Science to it than in the statement that two times two are four. In the scientific statement of being we are given this self-evident statement of fact, but we are just being reminded of what we already know, the truth of which has been proved already long ago. That had nothing to do with Christian Science.

Christian Science is all included in the next statement, *"All is infinite Mind and its infinite manifestation, for God is All-in-all."* There is Christian Science stated, in those few all-embracing words. But what did we do with the first statement? We grabbed it instantly, as Christian Science, and just as a hungry dog runs off with a bone, so we ran away with that "bone"; and because it was a true statement and we knew it and could realize its truth we called it Christian Science, we healed everything in sight with it. We thought Christian Science was truly wonderful—and indeed how truly wonderful is it!—never dreaming that what we were doing was simply using the truth of that statement to fill us with assurance and confidence; and because health is the eternal fact and ever present, we were spontaneously healed and felt we had had a wonderful demonstration of healing through Christian Science. As a matter of fact we had had a wonderful demonstration of beautiful faith healing, not really of Christian Science at all, only incidentally.

We have never completely let go of that "'bone," from that time to this; and in spite of our dear Revelator's efforts to wean us away from the "bone" to the true substance of Christian Science, that *"All is infinite Mind and its infinite manifestation, for God is All-in-all,"* we are still after that "bone." Didn't Mrs. Eddy say, *"Christian Scientists, be a law to yourselves that mental malpractice cannot harm you either when asleep or when awake"*? She did not say, "that matter cannot harm you."

But something is happening, and we are beginning to find, as Mrs. Eddy says, we are failing in our demonstrations, because we do not understand how to handle animal magnetism and so mesmerism is handling us. We are becoming very unhappy that our work is not better done; and that is the necessary discipline which divine Love is putting us through, to make us wake up and see how terribly we have misinterpreted that first part of the Scientific Statement of Being which was only meant as a statement of self-evident fact and to emphasize the nothingness of matter. It had nothing to do especially, with Christian Science; and how fatally for us we have almost entirely passed by the real statement of divine Love to us, *"All is infinite Mind and its infinite manifestation, for God is All-in-all."*

Now the day of reckoning is at hand and we are face to face with the reality. The day of running into our Father's presence with a broken arm or a diseased lung or anything of matter is passed and those days of ignorance have gone forever, for they never really were. Now we have come face to face with the serious qustion, "What do we handle, and what do we now take into the closet alone with God, to talk to Him about?" Certainly not matter. Then there is nothing left but mind, for there can be but the two in the realm of human belief, just matter and mind, the personal and the impersonal. So, we are left with mind, the impersonal; in other words, we are left with the exact negation of *"All is infinite Mind and its infinite manifestation, for God is All-in-all,"* as, "All is malicious mind and its infinite manifestation, for malicious mind is all-in-all."

What did the personal presentation of God have to meet and redeem? The personal presentation of evil. Now the personal presentation of evil is what? M-a-t-t-e-r. Everywhere. Isn't that what your Jesus ran into? Didn't he find himself confronted with it from the very start—first, with Herod, as it were, trying to kill him and all the children of a certain age, in a certain district? Was he confronted with anything but matter, everywhere; and was not his mission on earth to show that there was *"no life, truth, intelligence, nor substance in matter"?* That was not the mission of Christian Science. That was the mission of Christ Jesus. That was the mission of the Christian Era; and the Christian Era, expressed as Christ Jesus, as your Christ Jesus, what did it do? It wiped out matter, entirely. It did not leave one vestige of matter. Jesus walked on the waves, stilled the storm, fed the multitudes, healed all manner of disease, went through the crowd when they tried to throw him over a cliff, and he showed the utter nothingness of matter from every possible standpoint.

Then, when he saw that he had made virtually no impression with all the things that he did, he said: Well, there is only one more thing I can do. You take my body and you kill that body as dead as you know how to kill anything, and I will show you that there is no life, truth, intelligence, nor substance in matter, and furthermore, that you cannot kill it, because it has got no life of its own, as it were, in it to be killed.

Didn't he do that very thing? They took him and they brutally crucified him—nailed him to the cross and left him there for everybody to see, so that all their senses could testify to the fact, he is dead. They had done everything they could to actually kill him—just what he wanted them to do, in fact you might say demanded they should do. He wanted them to convince themselves, from their own sense testimony, that he was dead; from the very same sense testimony that said before, he was very much alive and a disturber. They did this thoroughly and they buried him, and in three days he was walking among them again, fulfilling exactly what he had said.

Was that the end of matter? Of course it was. Now, mind you, when you say, that is the end of matter, *you are* saying it; and when you said, *It is finished,* even as though by proxy, by way of Christ Jesus, (because he seemed to you to be the one that said, it is finished) there was nothing more to be done. Matter was finished, as such, completely wiped out. Then what was the inevitable new step? There was nothing to do except rise.

There are only the two presentations in belief—matter and mind—and when you are through with matter, you spontaneously have nothing left but mind. So there was nothing left for your Jesus to do but rise. And what did you say? That he rose and ascended. Just in your own hearts, ask yourselves: Did I actually say, *it is finished,* and did I mean it? Of course I said it. Of course I meant it. Nineteen hundred years does not mean a thing. It was a state of mind that was yours and is yours now. Handed down by God—call it by way of the Bible or anything else you like, it makes no difference. You would have known it was so, whether you knew what you call Jesus, or anything else. It would have had to be so. Why? Because your highest human corporeal concept of the divine idea met matter at every turn and overcame it through the understanding of what its origin was, what it seemed to be—not meeting it in the way you meet it today, as we are going to see.

Now there you have the first phase of your redemption, called the Christian Era. That is the popular term for it. Mortals love to be redeemed, or perhaps better say, love to have the pleasures of sense from which to be redeemed! God sent His only begotten son to redeem mankind, we are told. Redemption first, from what? Only from one thing. And what was that? M-a-t-t-e-r.

What did this rising to Mind in what is called the Ascension do to you? Why, it confronted you with an entirely new situation. You were not any longer confronted with matter, and have not been. You may think you have, but you have not. You have not been confronted with matter at all since then—nineteen hundred years ago, but right today, really. Your highest human corporeal concept of the divine idea wiped matter out entirely and it was finished; and *you say, it is finished.*

Then what are you now confronted with? You are confronted with a *new* phenomenon entirely. Your first reaction to this as a Christian Scientist ought to be, it could not be new to me as a Christian Scientist! You will see very quickly however, how new it is to you, in one sense of the word. When you came into Christian Science—when you thought you came in, you really came in nineteen hundred years ago—the moment you said, "It is finished"; at that moment, you came into Christian Science, because it is at the point of the Ascension, at the point of Mind alone, that Christian Science takes hold. You then and there came into the allness of Mind.

Then, when Christian Science was voiced to you as, *"All is infinite Mind and its infinite manifestation, for God is All-in-all,"* why did you not start right in there, instead of falling back to that which you declared was finished—*"There is no life, truth, intelligence nor substance in matter."*

Just go back a little. What did you do when you came in—and still are doing, perhaps? You grabbed it. Grabbed what? That there is no life, truth, intelligence, nor substance in matter. Why? Because you knew how it worked. You grabbed it like a dog grabs a bone, and off you ran with it, and you healed all manner of things with it. We all did it, and we all healed all manner of disease. Why? Because that came, as it seemed, first before being followed by the statement declaring Christian Science, *"All is infinite Mind and its infinite manifestation,"* and it came seemingly associated with and as part of the scientific statement of being, and we concluded, "Why, that's all Christian Science." We found it worked so beautifully that we are still running after that "bone." You may go and bury it for a while as you get a little higher thought, but then, lo and behold, you go and dig it up again, and what has happened? Why, you are getting exceedingly tired of it and you are beginning to say, "Why, it does not work like it used to." Of course not. Nineteen hundred years ago, you stopped its working when you saw, "That is the end; it is finished." Matter was finished. That stopped your being able to use it any longer, and yet, because you labeled it Christian Science and you said, "Why, it is wonderful; it works so well," gradually, what had to happen? Divine Love had to teach us to go forward and not stay back nineteen hundred years. Mrs. Eddy spent her life trying to get that "bone" away from us and to get us to move forward into the real Ascension, *"All is infinite Mind and its infinite manifestation, for God is All-in-all."* That is Christian Science. To this end, it can be absolutely and truthfully said, "came she into the world," even as Jesus who came to destroy all materiality, said, "To this end was I born and for this cause came I into the world," to prove *"There is no life, truth, intelligence, nor substance in matter"*—which is not Christian Science any more than two-times-two-is-four is Christian Science.

Are you willing to let that "bone" go? If you do not, it will get so bad-tasting that you will have to. You have dug it up just as often as you are going to dig, or you and I would not be at this meeting. You will not leave here with any idea that you are ever confronted with matter. That is nineteen hundred years old, and you cannot go into your Father's presence today and work out any problem from any standpoint of matter.

Let us go back for a moment and see what this *"All is infinite Mind and its infinite manifestation,"* is confronted with. It is not confronted with matter because that is wiped out. Then with what is it confronted? With, "all is malicious mind and its malicious manifestation, for malicious mind is all-in-all." It apes the statement of Truth, of course.

That is what you are confronted with if you have a little cut on your finger. It is not a cut on the finger at all. Where do you get the finger to cut? Haven't you said, "Why, God's finger is the only finger there is"? Can you cut that finger? And isn't God's knife the only knife there is? Then don't you see that you are not confronted with a cut on the finger at all? Yet what would you probably do if you gave yourself a good gash, as you would call it? You would run for a cloth or something to stop the blood. Where is the blood? Has it ceased to be about its Father's business? Isn't it still flowing in the veins of divine Love, or is it being spread over your carpet? Now, which is it? That is the thing you have got to ask yourself. What am I doing? Am I believing that there is life, truth, intelligence, and substance in matter? That is what running for a cloth means, instead of turning unreservedly to Mind and seeing that suggestion as a malicious argument. It isn't any cut on the finger at all. None of the things that confront you are what they seem to be. I just used that little illustration of a cut on the finger, because it seems so insignificant, but there is not anything too insignificant in your life for malicious mind not to be back of it.

Mrs. Eddy says, *"Where all students have failed is in not knowing how to handle animal magnetism,"* and the whole point of malicious mind is to argue that very thing to you, that you do not know. Before, it seemed to be matter that was arguing, nineteen hundred years ago. Today it is malicious mind that is arguing and nothing else, and unless you wake up to that, you will find that you will fail—you are bound to fail—because you cannot even get into your Father's presence now, with the old arguments. That is why the "bone" will not work. So give it up. "Let the dead bury their dead," as Jesus said.

Jesus was not standing for the Christian Science Era at all. He did not know anything about Christian Science, perhaps. You remember, in the book of Revelation, Jesus saw "the mighty angel come down from heaven . . . and in his hand a little book open." I have often thought that that was, perhaps, Jesus' first introduction to Christian Science, as such, because the "little book open" is what we have designated as what Science and Health is typifying. Jesus passed the vision right on to John and John recorded it. That revelation, mind you, was sixty years after Jesus had ascended. In other words, he had had sixty years of that wondrous experience, together with all that he had gained, during what has been called his earthly experience, in correcting the lie of life, truth, etc., in matter, sixty years of the Ascension period, before he saw the "mighty angel coming down from heaven" with the little book open. That was his introduction, apparently, to Christian Science; and he passed it on to John and John recorded it.

Think of where the one you call Mary Baker Eddy must have been in the spiritual realm of thought, to be able to receive the revelation of Christian Science, to actually be at the point where Jesus was sixty years after his ascension. You might ask, "How do you know it was sixty years?" The record is only inferential, but it was ninety-five to ninety-seven A.D. when John was a prisoner on the Isle of Patmos. That is the record. Jesus was a little over thirty-three years old when he said goodbye and ascended, so that would indicate sixty years.

But that is not the point, it is only incidental, because it would make no difference if Jesus had never heard of Christian Science. We do not build on Jesus, or on Science and Health. We build on what we started with: I consciously am, therefore Consciousness must be or I could not consciously be. We take every one of these steps directly from Mind; and these gifts of God called Christ Jesus and Mary Baker Eddy are divine Love expressing itself to, what you call, fortify us and back us up in our conclusions. But you are the one that has got to be the Christian Scientist. These books cannot make you one; you have got to think your way through and to see yourself as the man of God, as we have been seeing it.

The point of emergence of Christian Science, its first statement, came when Mrs. Eddy beheld that *"All is infinite Mind and its infinite manifestation, for God is All-in-all."* I often think of the scientific statement of being, as though God were saying to me, "Now, you know this—that there is no life, truth, intelligence, nor substance in matter. You know this of yourself, because you said matter is finished. You wiped all that out as matter; I am only reminding you of what you know. I am not giving you Christian Science there. I am giving you Christian Science in the statement, *'All is infinite Mind and its infinite manifestation, for I am All-in-all'."* Everything from then on comes not as matte, but as mentality and a belief of matter.

The Revelator of Christian Science directed attention very definitely to Science and Health, page 275, lines 6-17. *"The starting-point of divine Science is that God, Spirit, is All-in-all, and that there is no other might nor Mind—that God is Love, and therefore He is divine Principle. To grasp the reality and order of being in its Science, you must begin by reckoning God as the divine Principle of all that really is. Spirit, Life, Truth, Love, combine as one—and are the Scriptural names for God. All substance, intelligence, wisdom, being, immortality, cause, and effect belong to God. These are His attributes, the eternal manifestations of the infinite divine Principle, Love."* She designated it, *"the second scientific statement of being."*

The deep significance of this will be very clear to the metaphysician who has distinguished between the Christian Era and the Christian Science Era, between the era of matter and the era of Mind.

You will note that not one word of matter is either mentioned or even implied in this *"second scientific statement of being."*

Study it carefully and make it your own.

I think a great many of you have read that little pamphlet called, "The Psychologist and the Magician." That has no Christian Science in it, of course, but it has a wonderful lesson. The psychologist wanted to make the test to find out which was the better, Indian magic or his understanding of psychology. It was agreed between them that he could examine the cave thoroughly beforehand, noting everything he wanted to; he also took the precaution of camping, the night before the test, in front of the mouth of the cave, to make sure that nothing was tampered with.

Why did he do that? Because it was the truth of what he knew was actually in the cave, that was really the only Christ he had to depend upon in the test. Every time, when these terrific temptations to believe the hypnotic suggestions of the magician of real tigers, real cobras, and the real fiery pit, came to him—and, on one occasion, the tiger even appeared to his senses to tear his arm, so that he nearly fell a victim to the suggestion—what did he do? Did he look to see the color or the stripes or anything about the tiger or the cobra; or did he turn to what he knew was actually in the cave? The instant he turned to actually what he knew was in the cave, the whole thing blew up—no cobras, no tigers, or anything. You remember, on one occasion the hypnotic effects seemed so real that he went back to look and see if there was not something there. Not a thing!

That is exactly illustrative of what we, at every turn, whether in business or home affairs, diseased conditions, so-called, or anything, are confronted with—malicious argument, each and every time, and only that. Why? Because there is nothing else talking; it is never things. It could not be matter arguing, because there is no matter. Matter was wiped out nineteen hundred years ago. Then what is it? It is malicious argument, malicious mind that is doing this talking, as the negative interpretation of the ever-present, ever-active divine Mind direction.

Are you handling it as malicious mind or are you running back to how the cobras and the tigers looked, to that "bone"—no life, truth, intelligence, or substance in matter, and thinking that you are going to invoke, in some mysterious way, the blessing of that again? Well, you are not. Why? As I said before, when you went into your Father's presence in the old way, He tenderly met you and compassionately treated you as a child. As the Bible said, "The times of ignorance God winked at"; He allowed that time of going into His presence with a broken leg or some so-called material ailment, to be a "time of ignorance." He talked to you about the truth of His own legs, His own lungs, His own this or that, of their infinite perfection and omnipresence, etc., and you came out perfectly well; but today, in this age, what a completely different approach!

You find now, that if you try to go into His presence in the same way, you cannot get in. Because you have not on "the wedding garment" you cannot pass through the doors. You remember Jesus illustrated this point with the story of the wedding supper. A certain king provided a wedding feast for his son. After he had sent out and brought in the guests, and they were all gathered together, he noticed one who did not have on a wedding garment. This one was promptly cast out. The wedding garment today is what? It is absolute purity. Purity of what? You cannot take malicious mind into the presence of pure divine Mind without having purified it of everything of matter or mortal belief. In other words, you must have pure malicious mind.

Now, do not be shocked at that expression, because the term purity just implies that something embraces not a single element contrary to itself. Then would not purity apply to malicious mind as well as to divine Mind? If you have pure ammonia, for instance, it means without a single element contrary to itself.

In order to take malicious mind into your Father's presence, you have got to strip it of every semblance of matter. You cannot take malicious mind in, with a belief of some material thing wrong, or with even a belief, of a wrong thing. Today, malicious mind is not arguing straight matter at all. Evil says, in substance, I can get my victim without that. I can get him with a *belief* of matter. I can handle him just as the hypnotist did —by declaring or suggesting to the psychologist, a belief of cobras, a belief of tigers, a belief of clawing the arm, a belief of the fiery pit and the men falling into it and screaming with terror. Wasn't that all belief? Of course it was, because those conditions were not there at all, and the moment he broke loose for an instant and recalled what was really in the cave, the mesmerism broke and there was none of the hypnotic suggestion left.

You are confronted with identically the same thing, because today, as the Christian Scientist, you have graduated from what you might call the matter period, the Jesus period, to what? To the Mind period, the Christian Science period and you are confronted only with mind assertions, never matter. You see that, understandingly, for yourself. Jesus was confronted with all the testimony of the material senses—his mission was to illustrate the absolute nothingness of these senses in every way. You recall that when the disciples told Thomas they had seen their Master, he said, "It is all right for you to say that, but unless I can see the print of the nails in his hands and thrust my hand into his side, I am not going to believe what you say." When they were gathered together, did not Jesus comply with Thomas' demand and say, Put your finger in my palm and thrust your hand into my side and be not faithless, but believing. Jesus did not condemn Thomas for his demand to be convinced. Jesus liked the condition of thought that would not accept anything until it was understood. In other words, he was very fond of (to use the American expression) "I'm from Missouri" attitude, or "show me." Mrs. Eddy was like that, too; neither did she condemn skepticism, she did not want you to accept statements just because she made them. While she stood as the very presence of Mind to this age, appearing as the Revelator of Christian Science, she also wanted you to accept Christian Science only because it was so, because it was that which, beginning in yourself, by education brightens into birth. She wanted you to accept it because you understood "the reason why"—even as Science and Health says, *"Now declare you are not hurt and understand the reason why,"* and as Jesus said, "the spirit truly is willing but the flesh is weak"—the understanding the reason why is weak.

You remember, in a statement of Mrs. Eddy quoted earlier, speaking of the two eras, the Christian Era and the Christian Science Era, she said of the latter, *"Not so is the Christ appearing at this age. Now is it rather to show through Science and not the senses the power of Spirit and of Good."* The Christian Era is the material sense era. Of course, there is not really any material sense, but that is how we designate it. It is the sense period and has to do with matter entirely. The Christian Science Era is the Mind Era; it is the era of *"All is infinite Mind and its infinite manifestation, for God is All-in-all."* Mrs. Eddy also said in this statement, that today, we must *"spiritualize all the meaning of the Christ."* You see where the emphasis is to be, on spiritualizing *"All the meaning of the Christ."* Why? Because Jesus had expressed only one phase of the Christ— the personal sense of God. He appeared as that and even declared, "Whosoever hath seen me hath seen the Father." You have seen that what confronted him was the personal sense of evil, and that appeared as matter.

That was only one phase, one side. But we must have *all* the meaning of the Christ. Emphasize that. We must cease to think of Christ as *"the person of God"*; instead, as *"the idea"* of God. Jesus, self-evidently, was compelled even to bow to that first personal sense demand, for did he not say, as already pointed out, "Whosoever hath seen me hath seen the Father." He had to do that because that was where my Jesus was in my unfoldment, that was as high as I could comprehend at that time. I was no further along than that, and so it had to appear to me in that way. But today, I am through with that. I proved, through my "highest human corporeal concept of the divine idea" that there was no life, truth, intelligence, nor substance in matter, nineteen hundred years ago, and declared it was all finished; and so I rose to the allness of Mind, the acceptance of Christian Science.

This is where you are today. You are at this point of the allness of Mind, and that is where you must operate. If you try, as you know, to go into your Father's presence, and you do not have on the "wedding garment," you will not get inside the doors, for you will not be in keeping with the company there. Inside, the atmosphere is that of pure Mind only; you cannot take a contaminated malicious mind, partly matter, in there. The wedding supper is purity itself and you have got to free malicious mind, absolutely, in your own thought, from any contamination with matter. See that there is no matter to it whatever, nor a belief of matter; then it is pure and you will just go right in with your pure malicious mind, uncontaminated in the slightest with matter or matter belief.

You will go right into your Father's presence and He will immediately talk to you. You will not have to talk to Him. He talked on your level, about heart, and lungs, and everything and you came out smiling and well. Now, He will say to you, in talking about Himself, Mind, "I am all the Mind there is, there is no Mind apart from Me. I am infinite Mind. I am all-embracing Mind. I embrace within my infinity of Mind, mind of every name and nature, whether you call it hypnotic, malicious, ecclesiastical, scholastic, materia medica, communistic, or whatever name you give to it.

Everything that comes to you, must come self-evidently as mind; and so, as infinite Mind, I include within Myself, mind of every name and nature." Then what becomes of the evil, the maliciousness seemingly attached to the so-called mind of every name and nature? It is simply swallowed up in the infinity of divine Love, the only Mind; just as before, the broken leg and every erroneous thing was swallowed up in the perfection of Being. You come out of His presence absolutely free; what appeared as the cobras and the tigers, whether appearing as heart disease, or vicious suggestions of every kind simply has vanished. And why? Because it never was. It is swallowed up in the omnipresence of infinite Mind, in the infinity of divine Mind.

I am now going to tell you a sweet little true story which bears on this strongly. There was a little shaver, a little chap whose mother was called a Christian Science practitioner. Before I continue with the story, how many practitioners are there? Of course there is only one. God is that one and He expresses His practice as you, as His man. Then you are the Christian Science practitioner every time. How many teachers are there? One. Who is that one? God—infinite Intelligence, expressed as teacher and you are that teacher. Were you ever a patient? Were you ever a student? How could you be? Then do not use those terms, student, patient, or anything like that. It implies "under." If you have a human sense of teacher, then you have something above you and you are down here. God alone is above you. If you have a human sense of practitioner, it is something nearer to God than you are. Remember, that which is taught can never rise higher than that which teaches and that which needs healing can never rise higher than that which heals. Will you stand for anything between you and God? Of course you will not. Then watch.

It seems to me Mrs. Eddy had a dislike for the term "treatment." She liked the term "watching." Watching what?—against any enemy approaching. What enemy? There is only one, malicious mind, the hidden enemy. Watch that it does not come in with hypnotic suggestion. Mrs. Eddy asked us to *"Try not to see mental work as treatment but as a watch to keep out the enemy."* Jesus said, "Watch and pray, lest ye enter into temptation." Treatment implies, to me, that something is taking place somewhere else, and so I do not like it. Under no circumstances would you be a patient or a student, and no wise teacher would ever talk about students—except the Revelator of God, who stood as very Mind, and so could correctly use the word student or patient, but no one else. No wise practitioner would ever talk about patient. Why? Because just as surely as he does, he not only makes himself a malpractitioner, attributing to another what he would not have himself, but he is tying a rope around his own neck for others, so-called, to hang on to, and sooner or later he is going to wonder what is hanging him. It is always officialdom in one of its various guises. If you put that rope around your neck, you are responsible, whether calling yourself a so-called church officer, teacher or practitioner.

To return to our story. This little fellow, whose mother was called a practitioner, was alone in the home when the doorbell rang. He marched to the door, opened it and saw what seemed to him to be a terrible sight— a very large woman, evidently very much out of proportion through a belief of a cyst or a tumor. The little fellow was almost dumbfounded. He had not expected that sort of thing, but he braced up like the little man he was, and said, "Did you come to see my mother?" She said, "Yes, that is what I came for." "Did you want her to treat you?" "Yes," she said, somewhat amused at her little questioner. "Well," he said, "my mother is not in, but you come in and I'll treat you."

She followed him into the house—and note the beautiful humility of this woman, meekly following the child in. When you realize, as I have since learned, that she was quite a society woman and very full of her own importance, just think of the sweet humility she presented. She followed that little chap into the room. He gave her a chair and took one himself. In just a few moments he said, "Now, that's all, you can go." He took her to the door, showed her out, and thought nothing more about it. It was done. He had finished all there was to do and rightly forgot it.

But the next morning the telephone rang, quite early, and his mother answered it. An excited voice at the other end said, "Oh, it's wonderful, it's wonderful. I'm healed, I'm healed." The mother, not knowing what had taken place, did not know who was talking at the other end of the line and inquired, "What do you mean, 'I'm healed'?" "Why, didn't your little son tell you that I came yesterday, while you were away—came to have you treat me? He said that you were out, but that if I would come in, he would treat me. I went in and he treated me, and it's wonderful, I'm healed." Then the mother was excited too. She went and found the little chap and asked him, "Did anything take place, particularly, yesterday, when I was away?" "Oh, no," he said, "nothing." "Well," she said, "did anyone come to see me?" "Oh yes," he said, "a great big woman came to see you and wanted you to treat her, and so I said if she wanted a treatment I would treat her, and I did. That was all." He dismissed it again, but his mother could not, and said, "Well, what did you do?" (This is a peculiarity of mothers; and of some other people, too. They always want to know what the child does when giving a treatment.) The little fellow answered, "I knew that God was bigger than she was." He wrapped the whole mountain of lies in the infinity of Truth, divine Love, and left it with implicit faith and confidence, right there.

That is exactly what we have got to do with malicious mind that seems so big, so swaggering, that seems to say, "I'm all-in-all. I'm everything." It lifts its voice as Science and Health says, with the arrogance of reality and declares, *"I can cheat, lie, commit adultery, rob, murder, and I elude detection by smooth-tongued villainy . . . The world is my kingdom. I am enthroned in the gorgeousness of matter,"* and nothing can interfere with me. It seems big, doesn't it? But when we take that miniature conceit and self-exaltation, however, into the presence of God, and like the little chap, throw it right into God's lap, what do you think that infinite Mind, that infinite Love—which includes within itself all mind—what do you think it will do? It will swallow it up, all its maliciousness and evil, as absolutely nothing, and you will walk out free. Now if that seems incredible to you it should not. It is only because you have not faced where you are in your own experience. You have gone along accepting Christian Science and the things that you have been told, and you have perhaps felt that it was all very good, that it was a fine religion, but you have not taken it actually home and made it your very own, as that whereby you live, move, and have your being.

You are the one that demonstrates all good with you. As Mrs. Eddy has said, *"Nobody but yourself can destroy a single belief of yours."* Declare, *"I have dominion through Him over the world, the flesh and the devil (evil). I cannot be overthrown for He is not only omnipotent but omnipresent. My life is in Him. No power can bind me. God is the only life.*

God is the only substance. Love is the only cause. Harmony is the only law and now is the only time." God can do no more for you than He has already done, having given you all good. You have to turn unreservedly to the allness of Mind and see exactly what you are confronted with, merely a malicious argument—nothing to do with matter, person, place, or thing— and then handle it accordingly. You will be amazed at the results, when you stop running after that "bone" and really begin to see, why, it hasn't anything to do with life, truth, intelligence, or substance in matter. It is pure hypnotic suggestion and nothing else, and it is that I have got to handle. It is that I have to understand—that *"there is no malignant animal magnetism to prevent me from reflecting light"*; *"there is no mental malpractice, no hypnotism to harm me"*—that these things are all simply lies— they are the negation of the actual fact of what God is declaring all the time: "I am All-in-all. I am your Mind. Every thought goes from Me to you and returns to Me, and there is no malicious mind that can in any way talk to you at all." You have got to see that, and do see it, because that is the only way you are going to overcome what seems to you to be this condition that is confronting you, no matter what it appears to be. *"Mind is the only source of power, therefore those who have turned to the fountain head of being for the solution of any problem have brought such titanic force into intelligent activity that the results may seem incredible."*

Mrs. Eddy is said to have told her friends, on a number of occasions, that she never could use arguments in her healing. That is readily understandable. Arguments relate wholly to, *"There is no life, truth, intelligence, nor substance, in matter,"* and that has nothing to do with Christian Science. So, Mrs. Eddy had nothing to do with it, but everything to do with, *"All is infinite Mind and its infinite manifestation, for God is All-in-all,"* which is the revelation of Christian Science. Mrs. Eddy, as the Revelator, naturally used this Truth, and so did her healing work through the Spirit, through realization and not through argument.

The spirit of Christian Science is realization, and it is that alone which goes with, *"All is infinite Mind and its infinite manifestation, for God is All-in-all."* Arguments go with, *"There is no life, truth, intelligence, nor substance in matter,"* and these arguments always must bring thought into accord with the real spirit of Truth and Love, before any healing is accomplished. That is their only purpose, and doubtless, that is why Mrs. Eddy has insisted that you must use *"the mental argument . . . until you can cure without it instantaneously and through Spirit alone,"* and doubtless also to prevent laziness. Mrs. Eddy expressed in her own life the essence of her prophecy that the time would come when healing would spontaneously go forth from the Christian Scientist, as perfume goes forth from the flower.

The realization that you are now in the Ascension Era, with *"All is infinite Mind and its infinite manifestation, for God is All-in-all,"* will finally free you from all need of arguments except those which are necessary to purify malicious mind of the slightest contamination, in your thought, with matter of mortal belief. You have on the wedding garment of purity, which alone allows you instant entrance into your Father's pure presence of infinite Mind, which embraces all-mind, and all-belief of any mind apart from the one all-inclusive Mind. In that Mind, all evil is spontaneously eliminated, and vanishes. *"When the thinker is lost in the eminence of Mind, the healing takes place."*

Mrs. Eddy knew only Christian Science and so only the one divine Mind, as All-in-all; and that is realization, instantaneous healing.

The genuine Christian Scientist, the true Metaphysician must always be on his guard, that when he makes a statement of Christian Science, he is making it directly from his own communion with divine Mind—never because of what this person may have supposedly said, or the other one may have written, no matter how important what has been said or written is. Remember what Mrs. Eddy has told us, *"We understand best that which begins in ourselves and by education brightens into birth."* Nothing is ever true just because some one has said it. It is only true because it is the direct impartation of God to His own idea. This impartation comes through one's own communion with God. Then, when this communion has really taken place and the impartation from God has become the settled conclusion and conviction of the Christian Scientist, because of its intrinsic truth, then, as Mrs. Eddy so beautifully puts it, *"the dear Love tells me the Why and Wherefore"*; and ofttimes through, or as, the clear vision of the one we call Mary Baker Eddy, or Christ Jesus, by way of the Bible or of Science and Health, or of some succinctly written statement of Mrs. Eddy. This however, is always and only, corroborative of what divine Love has already unfolded to one, as his own absolute conviction.

A statement must never be made merely as a deduction based on another's statement, no matter how true the latter may appear to be, or how uniformly reliable statements from that source have proved to be; because if it is, it will lose a large measure of its power and value to the one now making the statement. Be not deceived on this. The negation is not deceived on how easy it is to use apocryphal statements to mislead even the most earnest. Study carefully, Mrs. Eddy's article, *"Principle and Practice,"* and note her vigorous warnings. Note, also Mrs. Eddy's declaration on this very point: *"Truth is only spiritually discerned . . . Truth is not seen merely because it is Truth. To be received, it must correspond to some awakened knowledge of Love in the heart."*

Of old, coming down through the ages, countless sermons have been preached from Bible texts, but this is never the way the Christian Scientist states any truth. He does not preach a sermon on some text, in other words, on some statement made by another, but rather does he make a true statement of fact based on his own direct communion with God, and that which he knows, of himself, based on his having founded everything in perfect agreement with his own metaphysically established common denominator—I consciously am, therefore Consciousness must first be, and IS, and so necessarily is All there Is. This is his invariable basis for all of his stating, thinking or knowing, and from this basis he makes his every deduction. Then he backs it up with all the glorious corroboration of his two divine charts, the Bible and Science and Health, together with all that Mrs. Eddy has written, and perhaps also with some of the many things she is recorded as having said. But, never fail to remember that your basis is your own understanding of Love, of divine Principle, God, and not a person at all. Then you are on solid ground, and can speak as one having authority, and not as the Scribes and Pharisees. Thus, you will not be preaching a sermon but declaring the facts of Being, of your own understanding. It is true of course, you are fortified on all sides with the Charts of life, which have been supplied by divine Love, "for our learning," and from the latter of which, Science and Health, every single Christian Scientist gets his first and continuing appearing of true understanding.

Mrs. Eddy was led to declare, and advise each one of us to *"Take time each day to say, 'What is the most powerful thing in the world?' It is God saying I AM in His own creation."* Thus, she brought home the fact that every time one uses the pronoun "I," he must be awake to the truth that it is really the one Mind, *"saying I AM in His own creation."* Then how much power is there in that "I"? All the power of infinite Love, and the intelligence of infinite Love, too. "I and my Father are one. . . . My Father . . . is greater than all."

Declare constantly and understandingly what Mrs. Eddy meant in her statement to her secretary, Calvin Frye: *"Go alone and close your eyes, and in the depths of your own consciousness say over and over again, I am, I am, I am. Your whole being will be filled with a sense of power to accomplish, the power to overcome, the power to do all things.*

> *I am because Thou art, I am.*
> *I am because Mind is, I am.*
> *I am what Thou art, I am.*
> *I am what Mind is, I am.*
> *I am with Thee, Oh! Thou I AM.*
> *I am with Mind, infinite I AM.*
> *I am good, I am well, I am abundantly satisfied, I am holy.*
> *I am because Thou art, I am.*
> *I am because Mind is, I am.*

'I am' spoken upwards towards the good, the true, is sure to out-picture in visible good, in success, in happiness, in abundance."

Look at the world today. You know, Science and Health reiterates Jesus' statement that you are the light of the world. It further says, Christian Scientists must *"hold crime in check."* You have read that; you know it. Then you must do it.

The need is paramount. You recall Judge Harold Medina's wonderful exhibition of true judicial behaviour recently, in the trial of eleven communist leaders, in New York. The defendants and their lawyers were throwing every kind of epithet at the Judge, throughout a number of months of the trial. They tried all they knew to get him stirred up and to force, if possible, a mistrial. His wonderful judicial poise and patience won the admiration of the entire country, even of the world. Now, listen to this! The other day, September 3rd., Judge Medina addressed the Bar Association of Tennessee, at Chattanooga. This is the New York Times' report of the meeting; I have had it verified.

Chattanooga, Tenn., September 4th, 1952.

Medina Cites Effort To Make Him Commit Suicide.

Federal Judge Harold R. Medina of New York disclosed here tonight, that a Communist psychological campaign to drive him to take his own life "nearly worked."

Speaking informally at a meeting of the Chattanooga Bar Association, Judge Medina said that the macabre drama took place while he was presiding at the trial of eleven Communist leaders charged with conspiring to teach and advocate the overthrow of the Government.

He said that the psychological campaign started about a month after former Secretary of Defense James Forrestal had died in a jump from a hospital window in May 1949. The first step in the plot, he said, was when a picket paraded outside the Court House with a placard reading, "Medina will fall like Forrestal."

There followed a barrage of cryptic letters and anonymous telephone calls, that repeated, again and again, the single word "Jump." Judge Medina said that "it got so I just didn't dare go near a window," and added, "you laugh now, you think it's funny, but by golly, it nearly worked."

The Jurist said that since childhood he had had a fear of high places, and that apparently the Communists had learned of it. That ends the New York Times' report.

Remember, when anyone is addressing a Bar Association, he is speaking to one of the toughest conditions of human so-called mentality. It is accustomed to taking either side of any question, and arguing on either side for its client. It is a temperament that can readily laugh at anything, and for Judge Medina to stand before that gathering and tell them this story, adds tremendously to its value to me.

As a Christian Scientist, ask yourself, "What am I doing to stop this sort of thing?" If our jurists and others can be put under such outrageous conditions, with nothing to aid them, how helpless are they? You are familiar with the report of various Communist trials in Europe, in which witnesses are made to testify against themselves and their brethren. They will say whatever is suggested to them to say, oblivious of the consequences. You also know that only the other day one of the United Nations men did that same "jumping trick," and it has been tried before—Masaryk was another outstanding example.

Judge Medina, said, you notice, "it nearly worked." That surely shows you where your responsibility lies in *your world;* and yet, what are you doing? Here you are entrusted, as Mrs. Eddy says, *"with the greatest and holiest of all causes."* You remember her statement in which she said that *"The hour is come. The great battle of Armageddon is upon us. The powers of evil are leagued together in secret conspiracy against the Lord and against His Christ, as expressed and operative in Christian Science. Large numbers, in desperate malice, are engaged day and night in organizing action against us. Their feeling and purpose are deadly and they have sworn enmity against the lives of our standard-bearers."*

Do not deceive yourselves—you are God's standard bearers and their purpose is to pull you down. It will not hurt one bit, if, by repeating to you these things I half scare you to pieces, because I think that is what we all need, badly. We all should be shaken up. We take our Christian Science as if it were just something handed to us as a gift, in a bottle, and that a baby's bottle, instead of realizing we are dealing with the very fact of being. As the very activity of God, you are responsible, and nothing can release you from that responsibility. What are you doing? Are you taking your stand, and holding *"crime in check,"* as Mrs. Eddy said, or are you going to allow this nonsense to go on, until, as Mrs. Eddy further says, in her vision of September, 1887, *"the mediums and mesmerists kill all they undertake to kill."* Then where will you be? It will finally attempt to handle you, and you need not think it will not. You have no right to think it will not, and you have no right to call yourself a Christian Scientist and be at peace with evil, none whatever. Paul said "When I was a child, I spake as a child, I understood as a child, I thought as a child: but when I became a man, I put away childish things."

Mrs. Eddy continued the statement I just quoted to you, with the rousing individual question, *"What will you do about it? Will you be equally in earnest for the truth? Will you doff your lavender-kid zeal and become real and consecrated warriors? Will you give yourselves wholly and irrevocably to the great work of establishing the truth, the gospel and the Science—*

which are necessary to the salvation of the world from error, sin, disease and death?" Read this for yourselves in her book, Miscellaneous Writings, 177:13. She finishes with this trumpet call, *"Answer at once and practically, and answer aright!"*

Do you think that dear woman, Mary Baker Eddy, the tenderest woman who has ever walked the earth, would have done and said all these things, if they were not all-important? What kind of followers are we, and where is our gratitude?

That which has to be watched at all times is not matter or materiality, but malicious mind as the negation or negative interpretation of divine Mind, operating as the hypnotic suggestion of the malicious mental malpractitioner. This is the one and only evil, the evil Jesus was warning us against, when he said, "Watch and pray, lest ye enter into temptation," and the one against which Paul was prophetically warning us, when he told us, "we wrestle not against flesh and blood . . . but against spiritual wickedness in high places," Eph. 6:12. Paul was speaking ahead of his time; he foresaw what would inevitably confront the "Comforter" of which Jesus spoke. Paul's age was not confronted with malicious mind and its malicious mental malpractice, for that is the negation of Christian Science, and not the negation of Christianity, as such. His warning, however, is just as essential as that of Jesus, to "watch," and it means what Mrs. Eddy said in her advice, *"not to see mental work as treatment but as a watch to keep out the enemy."* What enemy, but the one and only enemy, the hidden enemy, malicious suggestion!

The enemy is not a person, place or thing, for all those belong to yesterday, to the past era, to "the beast," material sense. Today, we are dealing alone with "the false prophet"; and we have to meet that false prophet or false mentality on its own ground of false mind, with true divine Mind. It is just because the one divine Mind is the All-Mind, that the so-called evil of malicious mind is swallowed up in that one all-embracing infinite Mind, divine Love, God. Thus, infinite Mind is proved to be All-in-all, and righteousness reigns as supreme and All, or as Science and Health put is *"For God is infinite, all-power, all Life, Truth, Love, over all, and All."*

When Mrs. Eustace and I attended the Metaphysical College in Boston, in 1902, I remember Mr. Kimball brought a message to the class, directly from Mrs. Eddy. The message was, that the only *excuse* for holding any class, was to show how evil was to be handled, quietly without publishing it broadcast. That was its one purpose. It was not for anything else. The import of this message becomes all the more illuminating, when one remembers that it was sent to a body of Scientists, who had gathered from the "ends of the earth," with the sole intention of later teaching classes, themselves.

Science and Health did not go into the minutiæ of handling evil, because that would then have published broadcast the modus operandi of evil, and in that way, the evil doer would have been supplied with more fuel to play with, or, as Mrs. Eddy says, *"for fools or demons to play upon with glamor."*

Mr. Kimball brought to the class, several statements from Mrs. Eddy, but I do not remember one that did not bear on the one subject of malicious mental malpractice. The only reason Mrs. Eustace and I had for wanting to attend the class, was our desire to learn more about the handling of malicious mind. Our wish was fully met and the subject was abundantly unfolded. Experience, however, alone supplies the real understanding from which each one best can profit.

Do you think that malicious mind or malicious mental malpractice knows you or anyone else? Of course it does not. Malicious mind is the negation of divine Mind and borrows all its supposed power, activity, knowing, from divine Mind, even as mistakes, or ignorance of the multiplication tables is all that there is to the little boy's saying, "two times two is five." Ignorance does not know one little child from another. It is wholly impersonal, and does not, as it were, pick out one child and say, "Now, here I am going to have this child say three times three are seven." All that the "three times three are seven" is, is the negative statement about three times three being nine. The seemingly ignorant child is shown that one and one and one make three, and that, with another three ones will make six, and this, with three more ones added will make nine. The child sees that, and so the possibility of three times three being ever anything but nine is forever barred from his mind. The ignorance on that point is gone forever, being replaced by the intelligence which is always omnipresent, awaiting each one's acceptance.

Ignorance has no power to raise a single objection to this unfolding of intelligence, and never does raise any when once the intelligence is brought to light. Ignorance has no favorites and no enemies; it simply appears as the negative, accompanying whatever one is knowing. The knowing must always be first whether you are consciously aware of it or not. Ignorance itself, knows nothing, it is merely the supposititious opposite of the truth that the lie is the lie about.

The magnitude of ignorance is in exact proportion to the magnitude of one's intelligent progress along any line. It is never ahead of or behind, but just accompanies the larger sense of intelligence, automatically. It never knows one thing about its so-called victim and has no grudge against him or even knowledge of him. It runs, as it were, alongside all unfoldment, without the slightest purpose or intent, but is just deadly wrong at every point and on every occasion.

Mrs. Eddy says, *"Sometimes I seem to hear the voice of the Father like this—My child, there is nothing in mortal mind to fear, not even the educated thought that knows what it is doing. But these different claims must needs remain until thou art not afraid. They are here only for thee to learn that they cannot harm. When this is learned, their mission is accomplished and away they go."*

Exodus 4:4 "And the Lord said unto Moses, put forth thy hand and take it by the tail, and he put forth his hand and caught it and it became a rod in his hand."

You know this is true about all ignorance, on any subject. Where is there the slightest difference between one form of ignorance, in regard to the multiplication tables, and another form of ignorance in regard to the Science of Being? There is none whatever. Then why do we talk about the latter so much and seemingly attribute to it, ability to check our progress at every turn? Simply because we have never thought the whole question of malicious mind and its so-called activities, through to its conclusion, and have imagined all kinds of attributes which it might have, when it has not one.

Malicious mind never thought a thought of its own—never knew you or me or anyone—never conjured up an attack of any kind. It is pure negation, meaning thereby, just what all ignorance is—wholly dependent on a truth to supply it with its entire ammunition. It borrows everything from the truth about which it is the lie or of which it is the ignorance.

Then has it any power to harm? Certainly not, except the imaginary power that each victim, so-called, gives it. However, in the realm of ignorance, that power is ever present to destroy the successful working out of any problem, unless it is seen and detected, and wiped out—but only of course, in the same sense that any ignorance does this, and malicious mind is not a peculiar kind of ignorance, it is only the highest and last phase and only seems to express intelligence because of the infinite intelligence God is. As one progresses in any subject, it is the increased understanding, and that alone, which produces the varying and increasing possibilities of mistakes—what may seem like attacks of mistakes.

But the remedy lies right at home, every time. It is not ignorance which is attacking you; it is the unfoldment of a greater sense of intelligence, always accompanied by the ignorance or negation of that greater unfoldment. You are the one, and only one involved. Remember, ignorance, evil does not know you nor is it consciously bringing about something untoward for you although seeming to do that very thing. It is wholly impersonal, but inevitable with your progress. It is easily handled when recognized for what it is, and when the truth you know and understand is applied. Now, always and under all circumstances it is malicious hypnotic suggestion.

Of itself, evil is utterly powerless, never thinking or doing one thing, except as the truth you know goes forward and the negation trots along, side by side, as a glorious reminder to one, to keep on the straight and narrow path. That, of course, means starting and ending thought, each time, with that which Is, and is All that is. The Bible demands that "your conversation be in heaven," in other words, on the side of right, and Jesus said, "Let your communication be Yea, Yea, and Nay, Nay; for whatsoever is more than these, cometh of evil." The grand and only purpose of the negation is to act as a sentinel, to keep one always in line, pressing one back if the slightest straying occurs. But that pressing instantly stops, the moment one has obeyed the command, "This is the way, walk ye in it; when ye turn to the right hand and when ye turn to the left."

Yet in spite of the Christian Scientist's clear discernment of the complete powerlessness of malicious mind to do or know one thing, of itself, the Christian Scientist today has reason to be more alert and more on the tower of watching, than ever before. As Mrs. Eddy so aptly states it, *"The means for sinning unseen and unpunished have so increased that, unless one be watchful and steadfast in Love, one's temptations to sin are increased a hundredfold. Mortal mind at this period mutely works in the interest of both good and evil in a manner least understood; hence the need of watching, and the danger of yielding to temptation from causes that at former periods in human history were not existent."* As used above, the terms *"sinning"* and *"sin"* would not only imply the perpetration of such sin, but would include falling a victim to hypnotic suggestion.

The rampant and boastful way in which the subject of hypnotism is played up in the press and other means of communication, without a vestige of warning of how to escape from its deviltries, should show one how essential it is to be alert so as not to be deceived by radio or by any of the other means of impartation, whether audible or silent.

The understanding of Christian Science, and its prayerful and intelligent application is the mortal's only possible way of escape from this final and worst enemy of mankind, hypnotism, malicious mental malpractice, which is the spontaneous negation of *"All is infinite Mind and its infinite manifestation, for God is All-in-all."*

The question of our being now in the Ascension period, beyond the era of matter or material belief, is so momentous that I would not have you leave without your having made it your own. So, as you must have noticed, I have repeated, reiterated, constantly and intentionally, certain sentences and phrases fundamental to this tremendously important subject.

Have you ever considered the question of whether the atomic era has any relationship to the Ascension Era? It has in one sense of the word. Just as the Ascension or Christian Science Era has taken the Christian Scientist entirely out of matter to *"All is infinite Mind and its infinite manifestation,"* so the negation of this Allness of Mind has carried human belief out of the realm of matter, as such, to what it calls a mathematical formula, that is, to a point dealing purely with belief, although still claiming that matter accompanies it.

In this it is following its prototype, homeopathy, which, you remember, produced its strongest curative medicine by attenuating the drug to such a point that, in its highest attenuation, actually not a particle of the drug was left in the medicine administered. With this drugless medicine homeopathy would heal desperate cases that lesser attenuations would not heal. Any thinking homeopathic doctor, if pinned down, would have to admit that he had, in reality, only exchanged the drug for belief, because, with his attenuations he was no longer dealing with the ordinary sense of matter.

The physicist today, is just at that same point of experience. He, too, has really attenuated the atom to such a degree, that he is no longer dealing with the atom as matter. He is compelled to admit that he is dealing entirely with pure belief, energy, or any name he wishes, which he may call a mathematical formula or anything he likes but which, nevertheless, is no longer matter but pure thought. He therefore blows up his cities, etc., with belief and not with the atom.

This also accounts for the great fear of many of the material scientists, physicists and such, that they can no longer control the action of their mental creations, that they have gone beyond their control, in the sense that their future activity is in the experimental stage. What will the next bomb do, for instance? It is beyond their following, as are also their Electronic Brain, etc., and their calculating machines, all of the same order and classification, finally pure hypnotism.

Do you not see that, in leaving matter in the lees, except for playing with it to satisfy their innate material sense, the physicists are actually using the human mind alone for accomplishing their experiments or results? This has all followed the unfoldment of Christian Science. Remember, it was 1866 when Mrs. Eddy virtually said to the human mind, matter is a myth, *"All is . . . Mind,"* and loosened its moorings. Behold its so-called inventions since that date. As the understanding of Christian Science has steadily gained headway, the negative interpretation of that has gone side by side, as the negation always does, never originating one thing of itself. As truth continues to unfold, the negative will appear with its further misstatements and we will see what seem to be wonderful discoveries, of so-called science. The Christian Scientist rejoices at such because, as Science and Health says, *"We welcome the increase of knowledge and the end of error, because even human invention must have its day and we want that day to be succeeded by Christian Science, divine reality."*

But the Christian Scientist is never deceived for one moment, into thinking that all these inventions and discoveries are anything but human belief imitating the ever-unfolding of divine Mind in all its manifestations. In and of themselves, they are no more than the Psychologist's cobras and tigers as produced by hypnotic suggestion; and they vanish as a dream, when so understood.

Let us turn now to another topic, that designated by John as "The Lamb slain from the foundation of the world." Have you ever asked yourself, "What is this Lamb slain from the foundation of the world?" It is a most important question for each one of us to settle for himself, for it is fundamental to his progress.

Mrs. Laura Sargent, the tried and trusted companion of Mrs. Eddy through so many years right up to the hour of her saying "goodbye," is quoted as writing on this whole question, succinctly and lucidly, as coming from Mary Baker Eddy. She writes, *"Mrs. Eddy explained the difference between a material sense of love and the spiritual sense of love. The material sense of love dishonors the one it professes to love, through lust, as in marriage the man dishonors the woman he claims to love by taking away her virginity, thereby exposing the falsity of such a sense by showing it is not love, but lust, i.e. hate."* Mrs. Eddy said *"this is the 'Lamb slain from the foundation of the world,' that is the spiritual sense of Love that is slain from the foundation of a material sense of sexuality."*

Nothing could be more plainly stated, that he who runs may read. Whence comes, then, with the Scientist, the slightest justification for the so-called propagation of the species or reason for any jubilation over the appearance of what is nothing more than embryonic death? What a gift is death, to hand to that which we claim to love, the new-born infant! and to rejoice over its appearance! Should we not rather mourn over our blindness and take truly to heart the deep prayer, *"Oh may your eyes not be holden, but may you discern spiritually what is our Redeemer,"* and then go forward in the words of Science and Health, page 171, *"Through discernment of the spiritual opposite of materiality, even the way through Christ, Truth, man will reopen with the key of divine Science, the gates of Paradise which human beliefs have closed, and will find himself unfallen, upright, pure, and free, not needing to consult almanacs for the probabilities either of his life or of the weather, not needing to study brainology to learn how much of a man he is."*

Listen to these further words of Mrs. Eddy, *"There is nothing jubilant attached to the birth of a mortal—that suffers and pays the penalty of his parents' misconception of man and of God's creation. But there is a joy unutterable in knowing that Christ had no birth, no death, and that we may find in Christ, in the true sense of being, life apart from birth, sorrow, sin and death. O may your eyes not be holden, but may you discern spiritually what is our Redeemer."*

Why does Mrs. Eddy make such a pointed statement about so-called birth? Simply because it is the absolute fact. How could there be anything jubilant in the biggest lie that attaches to the mortal, namely that he has a beginning and therefore must, of necessity, have an end. There is no difference between the birth of a mortal and the birth of the ignorance that two times two is five; and you willingly admit that is doomed to death, to be wiped out. To try to conceive of man, the idea of God, as beginning, would be just as absurd, and would involve the same admission, inevitable destruction. Then is there anything jubilant in such absurdity, that must end in death? Of course not, and you know this. Can you then allow, for one moment, that there is the slightest defense for birth; in other words, for having children, so-called? You cannot and it is high time every Christian Scientist awakened to the hypnotism that is involved. Malicious mind is its defender—nothing else is, and as we shall see, the whole lie is conceived in sin and brought forth in iniquity, as the Apostle James plainly declared, "when lust hath conceived it bringeth forth sin and sin, when it is finished, bringeth forth death."

We might as well call birth lust, instead of attempting to deceive ourselves by glossing it over with any other name. When Mrs. Eddy received a letter from members of one of her Churches, asking her to congratulate them on the birth of a Christian Science baby, it is recorded she read the letter aloud, and then, with apparent indignation declared, *"A Christian Science baby! A crime, just as much as murder would be!"* Pausing a moment, she raised her hand, and shaking her finger, proclaimed with great emphasis, *"No loyal Christian Scientist will ever marry."*

Of course, this statement "will never marry" refers definitely to the usual, material sense of marriage and not to the divine companionship of what appears as man and woman, where both are seen as the completeness of God—man-woman, male-female, masculine-feminine. God is Father-Mother, not two but one, always complete, infinite Life, Truth, and Love. Even *"the least spiritual idea"* reflects this completeness.

In such completeness there is no looking "over there," for something to complete the "here." It is like the note of music, which is whole in itself, blending with every other note, never interfering in the least, the notes gloriously harmonizing, and supporting one another. The masculine and feminine qualities of divine Love appear as the beautiful blending of the man-woman of God walking the long, happy path interpreted as marriage, in perfect harmony, each "seeking his own in another's good."

The expression of Mrs. Eddy *"just as much as murder,"* while it might seem severe, is not so at all, when properly considered. What do you mean by murder? Destroying, don't you? Well, what could more completely destroy the perfection of man as the reflection of God, than to conceive of him as being born, as beginning? Does not that murder all that is complete in him and make him the inevitable victim of death; what is that but murder. The deadest that a so-called mortal ever is or can be, is at the moment of his conception, as having a beginning. Nothing could be ever deader than that.

Let us return now to our subject, "The Lamb slain from the foundation of the world." You remember Science and Health says of this statement of Jesus to John in Revelation, *"slain, that is, according to the testimony of the corporeal senses, but undying in the deific Mind. The Revelator represents the Son of man as saying (Revelation I:17, 18): 'I am the first and the last: I am he that liveth, and was dead (not understood); and, behold, I am alive for evermore (Science has explained me)'."*

Jesus typified the "last Adam," the quickening spirit, as the redeeming of the "first Adam," a living soul or sense, "the Lamb slain from the foundation of the world." How did it come about that the so-called "first Adam" was slain from "the foundation of the world"? Do you remember, as given in the Bible, it was allegorically stated that, after the serpent had tempted Adam and Eve and they had eaten of the forbidden fruit, "Adam knew Eve his wife and she conceived and bare Cain." There you have the Lamb being slain, and there you have this sin founding the so-called world.

The desecration of the feminine quality of Mind appearing as so-called body, that destroyed the virginity of that body and slew the Lamb, purity, "from the foundation of the world," and has continued doing so in that world ever since.

The Virgin-mother typified giving birth to the "last Adam," the quickening spirit, without desecration of the feminine quality of Mind appearing as body, by conceiving of God as the Father of man, and bringing forth that which proved, *"There is no life, truth, intelligence, nor substance in matter"*; thus wiping out the "first Adam," a living sense, and so redeeming the "Lamb slain from the foundation of the world," the desecration of the virginity or purity of the feminine quality of Mind—and proving man is of God alone, with no beginning whatever.

There is just one answer to the question we are considering—to recognize that it is the result of pure malicious argument acting as malicious mental malpractice and appearing as *the belief* of one mistaken and vicious desire after another. Note carefully, "the belief," not any thing itself, though always coming as the belief of this or that—operating thus as your very mind or desire, and befooling you.

But you are not befooled for you know that it is malicious animal magnetism, not matter, in spite of any form it may seem to take, and that it is but the negative appearing of divine Love and purity which is always saying, "This is my beloved son in whom I am well pleased, and whom no malicious mind can or does influence in the slightest, for I am the one and only Mind and am My own son's Mind." So you are not deceived but instantly translate this belief of malicious mind back to its Father's house, the one divine infinite Mind which includes within itself, all mind of every name and nature. There you find all maliciousness swallowed up in the infinity of divine Love; and that ends the warfare, finding God both Father and Mother of man, with no false sense of human parentage whatever.

The following statement attributed to the Revelator of Christian Science is most illuminating on this whole unfoldment of the negative and the positive—the Christian Era and the Christian Science Era—the Ascension Era.

"Every spiritual baptism is followed by stronger temptations. That is, each higher manifestation of Truth uncovers its supposititious opposite to be met and destroyed. Thus we rise step by step until we finally reach a condition which has no erroneous phenomenal expression. This moment must be the ascension when the senses can no longer manifest nor cognize us, we having overcome their claims. Immediately following Jesus' spiritual baptism, he was led into the wilderness to be tempted. His higher baptism drove error to a higher and more subtle temptation.

"Every claim of materiality has a two-fold expression and must be conquered with Truth. The first is the manifestation described in Jesus' temptation as the stones beneath his feet which Satan sought to make Jesus turn into bread. The second is the temptation which transcends the first suggestion, and which met him on the pinnacle of the temple. In these two manifestations we see the two-fold power of each temptation one must meet, the lower and the higher, the physical and the mental. In other words, every manifestation of evil discerned in physical phenomenon will occur in a higher and wholly mental sense ere is is dissipated. Because of the universal belief in the existence of both mind and matter, in the present phase of existence error will manifest itself through both classes of phenomena."

What is the difference between Mrs. Eddy and her followers?—exactly the difference between the revelator and the disciple of that revelator.

The revelator receives the revelation directly from Mind as a purely spiritual or Mind impartation, while the disciple receives, to start with, the revelation as a statement of fact, which he gradually begins to assimilate and so make his own. In other words, the revelator goes from the Spirit to the letter and the disciple goes from the letter to the Spirit—exact opposites of approach. The former can never be wrong, so far as his revelation is concerned, whereas the latter can go badly astray if his letter is in the slightest degree twisted from the original revelation, as stated by the revelator. Hence the great need for the disciple to start always from the exact statement of the revelation—which, in the case of the Christian Scientist, means Science and Health—and never from his own idea of what Christian Science is.

You remember the Virgin-mother was visited by the angel of God, who informed Mary that that which she was to give birth to, was of the Holy Spirit. The Bible records that she was troubled at this saying, but rejoiced at the good tidings of the coming Saviour. Now, remember, this visiting of the Virgin-mother by the angel of God, was really the announcement of God as the Father of man and was, self-evidently only the first step in the redemptive mission of mankind or kind of man. Then what shall be said of the same angel of God visiting the mother of Mary Baker Eddy with the same heavenly benediction, telling her, too, that what she was bearing would also be holy. You remember Mrs. Eddy has spoken of her mother as *"a saintly and consecrated character,"* and refers to her as *"my sainted mother."* This mother, too, felt much troubled at the angel's message, at divine Love's communication; she said she felt it was wicked, in a way, for her to feel such thoughts.

But why, pray, should the mother of that which was to show forth the completion of God as both Father-Mother of man, and which was to *"spiritualize all the meaning of the Christ,"* be sinful, when the angel declared as blessed, the Virgin-mother who was only presenting the first half, as it were, of the redemptive Christ, of the full redemption of mankind? How much more would the angel of God declare it as His visitation with the mother of Mary Baker Eddy, giving birth to the final revelator of the full destruction of evil? No wonder Mrs. Eddy said, *"My history is a holy one."* Of course it had to be, just as much so as the history of Jesus was holy. Only silly old false theology would attempt to have it otherwise.

It had to be just as holy as was that of Jesus, for it even resulted in a greater than Jesus, in Science and Health. That book, so graphically described in Revelation as "the little book open," which the "mighty angel brought down from heaven," stands as the wholly impersonal Comforter which Jesus indicated would come only if the personal sense of God was allowed to give place to the impersonal and which would be without sin unto salvation, without human parentage, either father or mother, but wholly and entirely of God—which a true Comforter would have to be.

As a wide awake Christian Scientist, then, be awake to this, and see what a mighty spiritual force is that which you have called your Leader with her book, Science and Health, typifying as she does, the last prophetic wonder of all the Bible, "The woman of the Apocalypse" who "brought forth a man-child," whose "little book" was "to rule all nations with a rod of iron," and thus end all prophecy.

Are you filling any such role, as her disciple? Then is there any question in your mind, that there is a world of difference between the one who received the very impartation of Spirit itself and gave that revelation, and the one who works from that impartation or letter, back to the Spirit? Then listen, and deeply ponder, and lay up in your heart, every word that Revelator says on every point of Christian Science, for her words are divine utterances, and the nearest approach to His voice you will ever hear, until you are so transformed by the renewing of your spirit, that you actually are the very expression of His voice, yourself, as the man of God—which you are this moment, and every moment, always.

I have before me two very vivid and vital pictures which I would like very impressively to share with you. In a certain sense, they are far from pretty pictures, and outwardly they seem to carry so much of anguish and apparent failure, that it would be unpardonable to present them were it not that the glory of their ultimate joy so overshadows the momentary hopelessness and despair of the pictures that I know you will forgive my bringing them before you.

One is the picture of the "man of Gallilee" hanging on the cross, forsaken by virtually everyone, even his own disciples—the man whom the multitudes had hailed, a few days earlier, as the blessed one that cometh in the name of the Lord. Now he was hanging before their eyes, an abject failure, despised and rejected—he could save others, they said, but look at him now, he cannot even save himself. And yet, we have learnd to call that self-same man, Christ Jesus, the true or holy, wholly Jesus.

The other picture is that of a lone little New England woman, who also received a divine commission to show forth God. But, this commission was not, as in the case of Jesus, a personal presentation of the Father. It was to show forth the next and final wondrous step out of matter into Mind, a wholly impersonal presentation of God as divine Mind. This appeared in the only way an impersonal presentation could, namely, as a book; portrayed to Jesus and recorded by "his faithful servant John," in Revelation, as the "mighty angel coming down from heaven," having in his hand a "little book open."

Because the presentation took the form of a book, did that save its revelator, the lone little New England woman, from the same cruel, when understood, inhuman treatment that the personal revelator of God received? Not in any respect. So, my second picture is of that beloved New England woman, who had spent a lifetime, working virtually night and day, from the time of the revelation of Christian Science to her in 1866 and for twenty preparatory years before that, calling her faithful companion and dictating a last message to her followers, five days before she said goodbye to us—*"It took a combination of sinners that was fast, to harm me."* This message she signed, "Mary Baker Eddy," and dated, November 28, 1910.

You remember the words Jesus uttered on the cross, "My God! My God! Why hast Thou forsaken me?"—words which malicious mind would wish to have considered a despairing cry of total failure. Doubtless he used those very words but not as evil would like to have them interpreted, but rather as a terrific warning to his followers of what looking to matter for life, truth, intelligence, or substance would bring. He had shown the myth of matter, throughout his whole career, yet here they were, interpreting the end as dying on the cross—looking to matter, they saw that very thing, death and oblivion as the end, even of their mighty Jesus who had wrought such wonders before their very eyes.

They did not hear what he was really saying—*My God, my God, my wondrous all-embracing Love, hast Thou, couldst Thou forsake me?* No, forever no, not for one instant. And with that cry of assurance of joy and rejoicing, he gave up the whole ghostly belief of life, substance, or intelligence in matter, which he had never questioned or been in doubt about for one instant. His hanging on the cross was not for his own sake at all, but to give an absolute proof to evil that all supposed life in matter was an absurdity. That was why he had made them kill his body as dead as they knew how to kill it—for the one purpose, that they could not escape the inevitable conclusion, when they saw him walking among them a few days later, that the very man they had crucified and killed, knew about life, what they did not; and that their theories of life in matter had been proved utterly false and absurd, by what they were seeing before their very eyes. The only reason he hung on the cross was to convince the unbeliever from his own sense testimony, those very senses that had declared they saw him dead, and verily dead, that he was not dead at all, that they had dismally failed to accomplish what they were so sure they could accomplish.

Now let us turn to our other picture, the one that comes nearer to our hearts because intimately embraced in our final unfoldment of God, appearing first personally and last impersonally. It appeared first as person, as the man Christ Jesus proving the myth of matter, and last as the woman Mary Baker Eddy with her divine "little book open," typified as Science and Health with Key to the Scriptures, showing forth Mind as All-in-all, and proving the myth of any mind but the one divine Mind. In this second picture, we see the revelator of Christian Science giving up her sense of life, just as surely as did Jesus. We understand exactly why he did it, and we know equally as truly and understandingly, why Mrs. Eddy, as it were, laid down her sense of life. In substance, it was to say to every Christian Scientist and all who take that name, "Cannot you see what I am illustrating in this my final gift to you? Are you so dumb that you do not grasp that it is not matter you ever have to deal with now, as Christian Scientists, but malicious mind operating as malicious mental malpractice and malpractitioners; 'a combination of sinners,' appearing as a belief of this, that, or the other thing—not it, but a belief of it. If you do not wake up to this that I am showing you, and see the meaning of it, my sacrifice is in vain."

Calvin Frye left the record that Mrs. Eddy several weeks before she decided that the time was at hand, called him to her, and "asked me to promise her, that I would tell her students that it was malicious animal magnetism that was overcoming her and not a natural result from the beliefs incident to old age and its claims of limitation." In other words that it was malicious mind operating as malicious mental malpractitioners or "a combination of sinners" that was causing the "overcoming," and it is on record that materia medica bore witness to this fact by testifying to the wonderful preservation of her body. Mrs. Eddy did everything she could to drive it home to you and me, that we are not in the Christian Era, the Era of matter but that we are in the Christian Science Era, the Era of Mind. We are in the Ascension Era.

In these two pictures you see the world's most glorious illustrations of divine humility. Think of the divine courage of both these majestic representatives of God, allowing the lie even for a moment, to obtain, that they had failed in their life-work, because ignorance, fear and superstition said it had ultimated in the usual belief of death. Neither of them tasted death; they only presented that appearance because of pure love for you and me. They wanted us to learn by it and see the utter myth in the first case of matter, "the beast" of Revelation, and in the second, of the "false prophet" of Revelation, erroneous, malicious argument; incapable of doing anything, when understood as the complete hallucination both are. Could you ask for greater love to be expressed to you, or in a more vivid and practical way? You could not and you do not. It is sufficient.

The question might be asked, Why did not Mrs. Eddy do as Jesus did, return to convince her followers that malicious mind had not killed her? For the very simple reason that Mrs. Eddy was not the revelation of Christian Science. That was SCIENCE AND HEALTH which, you admit did not have to do any returning. Mrs. Eddy corresponds, in one sense of the word, to the Virgin-mother, not to Jesus. Jesus was the personal or matter presentation of God; SCIENCE AND HEALTH is the impersonal or Mind presentation of God. Mrs. Eddy as the Revelator, had to disappear from the Christian Science picture in order that the Revelation could be found by you and me, as "all the meaning of the Christ."

The four meetings which have just been held, proclaiming "all the meaning of the Christ"—the Christian Era and the Christian Science Era—fittingly began in the grand old Protestant fortress of England, the Manasseh of Jacob, and were concluded in the glorious spiritual atmosphere of Ephraim, the "branch that grew over the wall," amidst the "Far-Western students."

Ephraim you recall, was to lead his older brother Manasseh, in "growing over the wall," "Westward to the grand realization of the Golden Shore of Love and the Peaceful Sea of Harmony"—to the West and Far-West in which Mrs. Eddy gloried, where she discerned so truthfully, that unflinching demand for absolute freedom from every form of mental and physical bondage.

That West and Far-West has no geographical limitations, appearing may be as darkest Africa or as civilized lands, wherever is active that Christian Science thought that substitutes not words for works and without which Mrs. Eddy tells us "Christian Science will disappear from among mortals."

Such understanding is the birthright of every man and is the "pearl of great price" for which, when found, a man selleth all that he hath and buyeth it.

I am going to close with this beautiful statement of Mrs. Eddy. "What joy is ours, in Christian Science! infinite Love all our own, tireless Love watching our waiting, pointing the path, guiding our footsteps and turning them hither and thither as Wisdom directs—then, when the lesson is learned, supplying the need and ending the warfare."

A LETTER

March 22, 1947

San Jose, California
March 22nd, 1947

DEAR FELLOW-WORKER:

Thank you for your letter and for the interesting facts of your conversation. Is it not extraordinary that anyone with even a rudimentary knowledge of Christian Science, could believe that the Discoverer and Founder of Christian Science, who spent so many years devotedly perfecting that which has been called the Christian Science organization, could leave that work in such a position that it could be almost destroyed when she no longer held the reins? Yet that appears to be the idea of some who seem to have little or no concept of what Church means and is, and the immense work involved in what might be called the propagation of the gospel of Christian Science.

Misconceptions usually thrive by attempting to pull down, instead of rightly and solidly building up by translating the negative appearing to the positive reality—taking the things of God and showing them "unto the creature," the negative appearing.

Sometimes it seems as if such Scientists would gladly scatter to the four winds God's direction to Mrs. Eddy revealed as Church unfoldment. I always feel it was this very necessary unfoldment Mrs. Eddy referred to as so essential and important, in her statement in the Preface of SCIENCE AND HEALTH, when she wrote, *"there came also the charge to plant and water His vineyard."*

It is clear to me that any attempt to pull down what Mrs. Eddy so indefatigably and prayerfully erected, shows a wholly immature conception of Christian Science and little understanding of the vastness of the undertaking to establish it.

Such a gross ignorance of the fundamentals involved would attribute a completely erroneous sense of how I feel about Boston and all that Mrs. Eddy established in regard to the church in general. Because of this ignorance I want to write you more or less fully as to my real feeling on the subject.

I am now, and always have been, absolutely assured that whatever Mrs. Eddy, the Discoverer and Founder of Christian Science —the very voice of Mind to this age—established as wisest and best for the unfoldment of Christian Science will stand and progress no matter how her language may temporarily be distorted by pride, wilfulness and human frailty. I know that her inspiring prophecy given in PULPIT AND PRESS on page 22, will just as inevitably be fulfilled as that Christian Science heals the sick and reforms the sinner when correctly applied. The prophecy reads, *"If the lives of Christian Scientists attest their fidelity to Truth, I predict that in the twentieth century every Christian Church in our land, and a few in far off lands, will approximate the understanding of Christian Science sufficiently to heal the sick in his name. Christ will give to Christianity his new name, and Christendom will be classified as Christian Scientists."*

We are rapidly approaching the middle of the Twentieth Century. Does not this realization behoove every Christian Scientist to be keenly alert, to know where he is walking and no longer act as though he were perfectly satisfied with the existing conditions and no longer be deceived into believing that indolent contentment is ever God's order of the day? With the infinity of Mind eternally expressing Himself that can never be the case. Progress is the law of God and the very necessity of heaven. Stagnation which is finity means hell. God's world is my world and it is infinite, embracing for me the infinity of good. I must be fully awake to the demands of the hour with its intensely interesting unfoldment.

The metaphysician is not concerned with what is called church or its functions, for he understands that Church is expressed as the man of God, and as such he spontaneously finds himself the church of God, *"the structure of Truth and Love,"* and so he requires no place to go to find this church, except to his conscious oneness with God. But he does not imagine that his world is so circumscribed that the whole infinity of being is not that world. He is therefore deeply enlisted as a Christian Scientist, in all that the Discoverer and Founder of Christian Science has said about church and in all that she was led to institute for the welfare of the one who seeks to interpret his sense of church as something to which he can belong or to where he can go to ponder the things of Spirit.

Mrs. Eddy under God's direction, wisely provided for such a demand so that one's journey Spirit-ward could never be, in the least, harassed by outside interference but could prove helpful, until the larger sense of Church, as but another name for God, appeared as the church of God, the son of God, the man of God. Through the CHURCH MANUAL and the DEEDS OF TRUST Mrs. Eddy left everything in the simplest and clearest manner possible, if accepted just as her directions read and allowed to rest there. This has not changed since the moment of her bidding us good-bye and is merely awaiting the Christian Scientist's adoption.

First of all Mrs. Eddy was, before she discovered Christian Science, a devout Christian and a member of the Congregational Churches and was led, in instituting the Christian Science church to use the same fundamental idea of "no central control" (except just while she was present to direct things personally) that is such an outstanding feature of the Congregational Churches. It is interesting to note that the Congregational Churches is the correct title of what is commonly called The Congregational Church, and these churches under no circumstances allow any man made central control. Each church is independent and looks to no intermediary between itself and God. The MANUAL absolutely establishes by its estoppels that this was clearly Mrs. Eddy's purpose and intent for the churches of Christ, Scientist everywhere. Ponder My. 182:1-10 which shows how Mrs. Eddy regarded and loved this church of her young womanhood.

If you will examine carefully the CHURCH MANUAL, which we all as Christian Scientists accept as spiritual direction about church, you will see how carefully Mrs. Eddy estopped every by-law giving the slightest government of Christian Scientists or of churches of Christ, Scientist to The First Church of Christ, Scientist, in Boston, or to the Board of Directors, by demanding that either her written consent or her approval be obtained before the by-law could be put into operation. The CHURCH MANUAL being spiritual direction, not legal direction, this estoppage could never be laid aside, showing conclusively how Mrs. Eddy meant all official relations between Boston and the churches of Christ, Scientist and Christian Scientists to end. Every by-law with an estoppel clause, no matter how slight, positively ceased to operate, except as an estoppel, on what is called December the third, nineteen hundred and ten, but just as positively remains in the MANUAL as a perpetual guide and God-directed reminder that the estoppel is never voided. On that date The First Church of Christ, Scientist, in Boston, automatically became what it had always been, the church of "the congregation which shall worship in said church" as Mrs. Eddy designated it in her DEED OF TRUST of 1892. A *purely voluntary association* as a "congregation" necessarily must be.

All official appointments of practitioners, teachers, lecturers, Committee on Publication, etc., also spontaneously ceased on the above date and Boston as something to look to or be guided by, finished its work with church affairs outside of Boston. Is this not perfectly natural when man is the "king and priest unto God"? Is he not also, the practitioner, teacher, lecturer and all else unto God? Naturally he is and must ever continue to be. It could not be otherwise. The metaphysician knows this and rejoices in this knowledge. He sees what it really means for every Christian Scientist and every church of Christ, Scientist to be compelled to look to oneness with God for enlightenment, no longer hoping for or expecting an answer to his enquiries except from his own communion with divine Principle. Voluntary association under God is the only bond Love knows. That bond is the divine unity that brings forth the fruits of Love and ensures genuine brotherly love. Paul expressed it, "Till we all come in the unity of the faith, and of the knowledge of the son of God, unto a perfect man, unto the measure of the stature of the fullness of Christ."

When this day arrives, and it is of course, the present reality, can you not picture the churches of Christ, Scientist so overflowing with the spirit of divine Love that spontaneously they will draw the distressed to their doors to be healed and clothed and in their right Mind? Then Zion shall indeed have put on her most beautiful garments and the waste places will truly blossom like the rose and God's kingdom will be seen in earth as in heaven.

A practitioner can never progress far in healing, who is looking to any source aside from God for power or direction. In the secret place of The Most High no person or book enters. Aloneness with God is there and the least divergence from this aloneness mars the tablet of thought and protracts the healing. As Mrs. Eddy so beautifully puts it in Unity of Good, page 7 :21 *"An acknowledgment of the perfection of the infinite Unseen confers a power nothing else can."* The perfection of the *infinite* Unseen precludes the contemplation of ought else. So must it be with the Christian Scientists and the churches of Christ, Scientist, there can be no official Boston, no official teachers, practitioners, lecturers, etc., to turn one's gaze to in the least, or the picture is marred and the drawing Light will not be seen to shine as brightly. Freedom is the watchword. Not freedom from anything external but freedom from individual looking to ought but God.

The two DEEDS OF TRUST inaugurating The First Church of Christ, Scientist, in Boston, and constituting The Christian Science Publishing Society are the full government of those activities and will go forward by their own perfectness to accomplish their intent. The Publishing House will be supported by the spiritual value of the product it sends forth. A deed of trust is a legal document from first to last and no one knew that better than did Mrs. Eddy. The CHURCH MANUAL is a spiritual guide and its statements have no legal interpretation and an estoppel to any by-law in the MANUAL means just that.

I have gone into this quite fully because I want to make myself perfectly clear as to my feeling about the Boston church and the churches of Christ, Scientist, and Mrs. Eddy's prophecies for Christian Science in this Twentieth Century, which are surely a "wake up" command.

May I summarize it once again? To my understanding the Boston church, which includes, of course, the Board of Directors, has not one word to say to any Christian Scientist or any church of Christ, Scientist. Its functions are Boston and only Boston and the fulfilment of Mrs. Eddy's instructions. The churches of Christ, Scientist are absolutely free to work out their own salvation in their own way and prove their faith by their works. Membership in the true universal spiritual Mother Church never began and never ends and has not one thing to do with Boston, except that it embraces the Boston church in its infinite love as it does all that means church wherever found, which is spiritual oneness with God, in other words, man. As the first dawning of the truth that two times two is four constitutes the mathematician, so the first dawning of the pure spiritual sense of Christian Science as given in its text-book SCIENCE AND HEALTH constitutes the Christian Scientist and declares his forever oneness and eternal membership in the one universal spiritual Mother Church. This dawning is "the true Light, which lighteth every man that cometh into the world"—the understanding that because I consciously am, Consciousness, God must first be, in other words first *is*, or I could not consciously be. That which *is*, necessarily is All that is. Being All includes all, hence all Church.

I hope this clarifies my sense of this question. It is nothing new to me but if there is a misunderstanding as to how I see and definitely feel then perhaps this will help to dispel the misconception. What I have before written in my books in regard to Christian Scientists and church organization had only reference, of course, to the erroneous sense of organization with all its ecclesiastical officialdom, never to what was instituted by Mrs. Eddy.

The metaphysician while perhaps taking or not taking an outward part in any local church activity, nevertheless is deeply interested in the success and unfoldment of the healing of all evil whether appearing as accomplished by an individual or a church. He is not indifferent to any forward step, for he is living now in the surety *"that every Christian church in our land and a few in far off lands"* are looking earnestly and longingly to the lead given by individual Scientists as well as by the churches of Christ, Scientist, in their healing works, that they, too may have courage and assurance to emulate those works and thus bring to pass the classifying of Christendom as Christian Scientists.

The conscientious Christian Scientist cannot avoid giving his metaphysical aid to this glorious consummation so divinely prophesied by the Discoverer and Founder of Christian Science. He can only do this by truly understanding that Church is but another name for God even as is Christian Science. He is thoroughly awake to the fact that we are NOW in the greatest spiritual renaissance the world has ever experienced and he is single minded in his determination to give his "all" and to show forth by his works his full understanding of this unprecedented unfoldment and grand opportunity, and so be counted worthy of his high calling as the Christian Scientist, the light of the world, set on a hill, as Jesus said, that cannot be hid.

One other question you brought up I must touch upon. When one speaks of Mrs. Eddy as the Discoverer and Founder of Christian Science, the terms discoverer and founder are used in exactly the same sense that Jesus implied when he said, "I and my Father are one," "What things soever He doeth these also doeth the son likewise." As the perfect expressor of God, Jesus could not help representing the Father in all ways. Hence he was *the* God-crowned. In this same way Mrs. Eddy is rightly called the Discoverer and Founder of Christian Science, because she discerned and expressed God as *"over all and All"* and as ever unfolding His own infinity of being in more marvelous and glorious ways as His own idea, man. Whatever the Father is that the son must inevitably be. "He that hath seen me hath seen the Father."

The metaphysician never confuses the discovery of Christian Science with the commonly called scientific discoveries, such as radio, telephone, television or other later additions to the many would-be sciences, all of which are based on the fundamental premise that matter *is*. Then from this presupposed basis, and in perfect logical sequence, the material Scientist deduces whatever he is looking for; and he gains his end solely because Mind being All-in-all, this All must include all that appears to him even though appearing as the negative interpretation of the positive truth or fact.

Material deductions never depart from the premise that matter *is*, regardless of the distance they travel from the ordinary sense of matter. Even the atomic bomb evolves only in the pure realm of belief where there is no matter; and the advanced homeopath performs his greatest healings with the highest attenuations where, also, there is no matter; and Einstein's profound deduction that "matter is a mathematical formula" obviously takes all the matter out of matter leaving nothing but a mental phenomenon. Still the physical scientists, in spite of this, hold fast to matter as their foundation and dream on in the pure realm of belief, always calling their dream-belief matter. Likewise running side by side with all this goes every form and phase of mental science so-called, including the more modern "prairie fire" psychiatry, all of which are the exact opposite of Christian Science and just as material, although called mental, as any matter belief. Classifying this or that as mental does not subtract one iota from its pure materiality. It is still the would-be child-belief of brain lobes and has no spirituality to it. There is no relationship whatever between "mental" and "spiritual." They are opposites. One is the so-called belief-product of the brain and the other is the impartation of divine Mind, Spirit. When materiality, in all its presentations is finally understood for what it really is, the negative interpretation of the ever omnipresence of Spirit and spirituality, then and then only will matter be found to be the obedient servant of Mind and by translation readily handled.

Are not these negative interpretations all analagous to the Biblical record of the Egyptian magicians with their serpents, compared to the serpent Moses presented under the dictation of divine Mind? And as the ancient magicians finally surrendered so will the modern magicians, the physical and mental scientists, surrender to the truth of Being, by the negative interpretation being again "swallowed up" by the positive truth.

Mrs. Eddy's discovery of Christian Science was the exact opposite of the discoveries of the physical scientists. Theirs never leave the realm of matter or belief, whereas Mrs. Eddy's discovery never deals with matter or belief. It is God's divine impartation to man appearing as Mrs. Eddy and voiced as SCIENCE AND HEALTH WITH KEY TO THE SCRIPTURES. In that sense it was not a discovery at all, but the divine *revelation* of God to His angel-scribe Mary Baker Eddy. Human reasoning did not enter into that discovery in any way. It was purely *revelation* and necessarily had to be so in order to be spiritual. However, what appears as human reasoning when started from a higher standpoint than matter *"held as substance,"* and instead started from the standpoint of matter *"held as shadow,"* is finally and wholly convinced of the truth of Christian Science, then rightly hails Mary Baker Eddy as its divinely God-directed Discoverer and Founder in perfect accord with hailing Jesus, the divine son of the Virgin-mother, as the Founder of Christianity. It is only the ignorance, arrogance and futility of human conceit that quibbles at these self-evident facts. Such a condition of thought tries to exalt itself by belittling its benefactor and fails to remember that conceit is never for an instant separated from its inevitable corollary deceit.

What would be thought of a Christian attempting to account for the birth of Jesus as some new biological discovery made by the Virgin-mother? It would not be less absurd than to suppose that the discovery of Christian Science could come through so-called material reasoning. In both cases *revelation* was the divine impulse ; were it not so both Christianity and Christian Science would be Christ-less and there would be no divinity to either to seemingly redeem mankind. These divine appearings could only come through spiritual impartations, never through human reasonings. As SCIENCE AND HEALTH declares *"All Science is divine. Human thought never projected the least portion of true being. Human belief has sought and interpreted in its own way the echo of Spirit, and so seems to have reversed it and repeated it materially; but the human mind never produced a real tone nor sent forth a positive sound."*

As a metaphysician you are alert to the subtle attempt of misguided people, even perhaps students of Christian Science, who under the direction of malicious minds as the negative interpretation of direction by divine Mind, would class Mrs. Eddy with Edison and other great discoverers of material science, so-called, and then drop both the Discoverer and the discovery of Christian Science to the level of human belief. Then the next step would be to attempt to judge the life and acts of the Discoverer from that level, which needless to point out, never touches the hem of the robe of the righteousness that constituted the Mind of the Discoverer of Christian Science.

Evil tried thus to classify Jesus and so compelled him to declare that "all that ever came before me are thieves and robbers" meaning thereby that they started their thought from belief or matter and therefore never really touched divine Mind, the only standpoint of Jesus. Did not this ascribing power to ought but Spirit constitute robbing God to Whom all "glory, and majesty, dominion and power" belong?

Identically the same Revelator unfolded the institution for propagating the gospel of Christian Science that unfolded the Word of Christian Science as its Text-book, and declared in the language of CHRIST AND CHRISTMAS,

> *"As in blest Palestina's hour,*
> *So in our age,*
> *'Tis the same hand unfolds His power,*
> *And writes the page."*

Very sincerely yours,

HERBERT W. EUSTACE

The Evil and the Absurdity of Thinking That Man Is God or Ever Could Become God

by

HERBERT W. EUSTACE

THE EVIL AND THE ABSURDITY OF THINKING
THAT MAN IS GOD OR EVER COULD
BECOME GOD

The evil in expressing, either by word or by pen, the mistaken conception that man is God or eventually can become God is doubly sinister when the attempt is made to hide that absurdity under the specious cloak of Christian Science. To enjoy "hob-nobbing" with Buddha, Laotze and other ancient Asiatic dreamers, together with the modern-day advocates of this same false teaching, which teaching embraces every phase of what has been designated "mental science," is perfectly within the privilege of a free thinking individual. However, it certainly is not fair on the hearer or the reader to drag into that coterie such glorious, spiritually-minded characters as Christ Jesus and Mary Baker Eddy, by implying that they are of the same mental lineage or that their teachings have a single thought in common with such fallacies. They are diametrical opposites. Christian Science is divine Mind Science, not mental science.

Anyone who could attempt to do this evidently has never caught the faintest glimpse of what Christian Science or Christianity really means and teaches, or he could not be deceived into so completely misrepresenting them. The very foundation of Christianity and Christian Science is one God and one man, the two absolutely essential—for cause without its effect would spontaneously cease to be cause and, of course, effect without cause could not be. Do away with either and you spontaneously do away with both. Apparently this fact has not been understood by such a one because thought has been blighted by delving into Oriental Mysticism in its various guises, whether appearing as today's New Thought or its hundred other ramifications so that it inevitably follows that the truth when heard cannot be distinguished from the false. This curiosity is what could be designated as "the inquisitive Eve" or again the story of the talking serpent and the good-looking "apple" and what it was supposed to accomplish.

It would be impossible for this misconception to occur if it were understood that the Christian Scientist establishes the fact that there is God by the simple self-evident truth that "I consciously am" instantly followed by the equally self-evident assurance that I could not consciously be unless CONSCIOUSNESS were first the fact. Thus automatically CONSCIOUSNESS is found to be that which Is. From this IS that necessarily is ALL that is, one builds one's whole structure of Christian Science or in other words finds God, this that IS, as "all which the Scriptures declare Him to be."

Having done this, one never again deals with "I consciously am." "I consciously am" are three words that best perhaps express the bare fact of one's self, without any so-called outside testimony. "I consciously am" is self-evident. It requires no witness to insure its being. It simply is the one and only fact one actually knows of himself. All else that one seems to be aware of has to come *as* consciousness or there could be no possible cognizance of any appearance. Awareness, however, would instantly cease right at the point "I consciously am" were it not for the fact that implied in the statement "I consciously am" is the correlated statement that CONSCIOUSNESS must first be or I could not consciously be. Therefore, it is as the effect of this PRIMARY, this CONSCIOUSNESS that IS, that every impartation of awareness is received. From then on, this important starting point, "I consciously am," which is inevitably effect, ceases to be of any further value. It is CONSCIOUSNESS, CAUSE and CAUSE alone that imparts Himself to His own idea, always appearing as His own language—person, place, thing. It is CONSCIOUSNESS alone one turns to as spontaneously as the needle turns to the Pole—to this CONSCIOUSNESS that IS and that you know is and that is All that IS or you could not consciously be.

Words have just one purpose and that is to give impulse to thought. Unless the thought back of the words is correct the words can be just a blind, and utterly meaningless. It was because of this Jesus so forcibly said, "they think they shall be heard for their much speaking," and "false Christs," etc. shall arise and if possible deceive the very elect. (Matt. 24) There would be little danger in this time-worn "heresy" of man being God if its votaries would openly declare, "I believe man is God." That would serve with many to bring the absurdity from under cover. That belief is what all who ever depart from Christian Science into the highways and byways of so-called human mentality always end with, the belief that man is God, and then they may for a season seem to, as Jesus said, "show great signs and wonders." The human being imbued with the obsession that he is God, as long as the obsession lasts, may seem to do wonderful things, but because it is not true that man is God, the end must come and the desolation of such appalling spiritual ignorance causes the anguished to cry "to the mountains, Fall on us; and to the hills, Cover us."

Because health is the everlasting fact it is easily seen, whether expressed by the mesmerism of Oriental magic or by the more modern name, mental science. The same belief that man is God animates both. It makes no difference by which name known. There is no choice between them. Both are in the end essentially fatal, claiming to deal with mind. The reason for every atom of apparent success in healing is only because of the fact that health is and has nothing to do with the process whereby it supposedly is made manifest. Only one unfoldment has ever scientifically shown forth health and that is the revelation of the Christ-truth, whether appearing as Christ Jesus or as Christian Science. All others "that ever came before me," as Jesus said, "are thieves and robbers" because they robbed God by attempting to make man God. To be "as" God is quite the reverse to "being" God.

Jesus said, "By their fruits ye shall know them." Ask yourself, is there a country on earth untouched by the teachings of Christ Jesus where any real progress has been made? Look at India, China and indeed wherever any religion, except the Christian religion, has obtained and what do you find? Ignorance, superstition, filth and wretchedness—a disgrace in belief to civilization.

Asia, where the teachings of Buddha, Laotze and others have been most active, is from the basis of spiritual enlightenment as well as material progress the blackest spot on earth. Why? By their fruits ye shall know them. If the teachings and practices of these whom some of their followers have called "the Holy Presence" were really holy, does one imagine for an instant their countries would not have shown some sign of that holiness, that whole-ness.

The time is now present when every Christian in the world as well as every Christian Scientist, in order to be awake to the hypnotism of all this false teaching, must understand and appreciate why Mrs. Eddy stated in her article, ONE CAUSE AND EFFECT, that "Surely the people of the Occident know that esoteric magic and Oriental barbarisms will neither flavor Christianity nor advance health and length of days."

Like the foolish ones of old who wrested the Scriptures "unto their own destruction" there are today those who sometimes quote statements from the FIRST EDITION of SCIENCE AND HEALTH and a few of the other early editions and, also, from Christ Jesus, which seem to the unenlightened thought to bear out this impossible teaching that man is God, but which statements do the exact reverse when understood with their context. When Mrs. Eddy said in the FIRST EDITION of SCIENCE AND HEALTH, "it is necessary to understand one's self, Spirit and not matter," and again, "to know we are Soul and not body is starting right," she said exactly what she meant. The Self of man must always be Spirit, and the "we" always means God and His inevitable accompaniment, man. In these statements Mrs. Eddy never imagined any Christian could misunderstand her meaning and suppose that she could possibly mean man could be without God or that man could be God—that the creature could become the Creator! However, when she discovered such statements were being wrongly interpreted she changed them, and over and over again, as she had done in the FIRST EDITION, positively stated that man never is God or God man, but that the two are essential for each other's completeness. To repeat again, to do away with one you spontaneously do away with the other. Absorption is destruction.

All are awake to the blighting folly of such erroneous thinking and teaching and realize what Jesus meant when he said, "Rather than to offend one of these 'little ones' it were better that a millstone be hanged about his neck and he be drowned in the depth of the sea," and, also, "Offences must needs come but woe unto that man by whom they come." God's "little ones" may appear as those starting on their journey heavenward, Spirit-ward. To turn such in a wrong direction is a wicked act, even if done ignorantly. Juggling words to make them seem or sound right does not make them right if the thought is wrong.

Infinity cannot be "in" anything whether called a person, a place or a thing. Then the word "in" when applied to God is impossible, or as SCIENCE AND HEALTH states, "In. A term obsolete in Science if used with reference to Spirit or Deity." Therefore for a Christian Scientist to use any synonym for God such as CONSCIOUSNESS, CHRIST, etc. as being "in" man is entirely erroneous and leads into all kinds of errors. God, regardless of the synonym employed, is never *"in"* but appears *"as"* and only *"as."* He cannot be both *in* and *as.*

Summed up, the declaration that man is God or can become God is the negative statement or interpretation of the positive truth that God is All there is to man and it is destroyed, as is every negation, by translating it back to its origin, God. Elias truly must "first come and restore all things." (Science and Health 585 :13)

September 24th, 1948.

GEMS OF ELUCIDATION ATTRIBUTED TO MARY BAKER EDDY

"A heart touched and hallowed by one chord of Christian Science, can accomplish the full scale; but the heart must be honest and in earnest and never weary of struggling to be perfect—to reflect the divine Life, Truth and Love." My. 150.

*   *   *   *

"Nothing happens out of order, everything happens in the right order of development for you."

*   *   *   *

"If the heart stays young, old age can never become anything but ennobled thereby. Years do not make one grow old if one grows in grace."

*   *   *   *

"Stand alone, never allow anyone to help you; as surely as you do you cripple yourself; you weaken your power. The arm of strength is in God and nowhere else. Trust then in God."

*   *   *   *

Divine Mind maintains man forever at the point of completeness, preserves his every faculty and his individuality guides each separate idea in continuous unfoldment of the infinite grandeur of spiritual creation."

*   *   *   *

"Meekness is not weakness; it is 'not my will but Thine be done' throwing ourselves into God's power."

"Pentecostal power is always present. It is the power of Mind enabling man to do the Will of Wisdom."

*   *   *   *

"He who is obedient to Truth has immense power for service."

*   *   *   *

"Nothing is truth but the absolute."

*   *   *   *

"God giveth you an abiding sense of Life that needs not to be fought for. Remember this and you will live forever."

*   *   *   *

"Take time each day to say 'What is the most powerful thing in the World? It is God saying I am in His own creation'."

*   *   *   *

"There is no fatal mistake; there is no unforgivable wrong; there is no unpardonable sin; there is no permanent injury; there is no incurable disease; there is no such thing as too late."

*   *   *   *

"Every time you declare you are perfect in God, there goes through your body a health giving power."

*   *   *   *

"This day is merely a step in infinite progress. It is unfoldment not time."

*   *   *   *

"O God show me Thy way and keep me in that way."

GEMS OF ELUCIDATION (Continued)

"*The mental act of thanksgiving carries one far beyond the realm of doubt into that atmosphere of Truth and faith where all things are possible. Go not back to asking but continue to give thanks that you have received.*"

*   *   *   *

"*Our salvation is through Love. Call God Love always and bend all your efforts toward achieving perfect love in thought, word and deed. This is the way. All is won through it.*"

*   *   *   *

"*What I have to meet you will all have to meet, now or later. Therefore know that the mesmerists cannot afflict either you or me with erroneous beliefs.*"

*   *   *   *

"*I am because Thou art.*"

*   *   *   *

"*Moral courage is the 'lion of the tribe of Juda' the king of the mental realm.*"

*   *   *   *

"*A deep sincerity is sure of success because God takes care of it.*"

*   *   *   *

"*To declare that you are well is the exact truth; you are not flesh but rather the ray of divine Light that shining upon flesh makes is appear alive. This you is spiritual.*"

*   *   *   *

"*We are now meeting the original first claim of error, the reversal of Truth, something besides God, a talking*

GEMS OF ELUCIDATION (Continued)

snake. We are called upon to prove there is none other intelligence than God: there never was a talking snake."

* * * *

"He Who dwelleth in the eternal Light is bigger than the shadow and will guard and guide His own."

* * * *

Mrs. Eddy said of Science and Health, *"She hadn't attained one millionth of what that book calls for. It is a wonderful book and covers eternity."*

* * * *

"Those who know no will but His, take His hand and from the night He leads to light. None can say unto Him, What doest Thou?"

* * * *

"When the thinker is lost in the eminence of Mind the healing takes place."

* * * *

"Don't think pain and handle animal magnetism, but think animal magnetism and handle animal magnetism."

* * * *

"Overcoming age is not resuming our youth: it is thought going into new paths that history has never recorded."

* * * *

"Oh keep me ever seeing Thee and seeing as Thou seest, my Life, my joy, my All."

* * * *

"Among the manifold soft chimes that will greet the haunted chambers of memory, this is the sweetest, 'Thou hast been faithful'."

ue